THE JESUITS
IN HISTORY

The Society of Jesus
Through Four Centuries

The JESUITS IN HISTORY

The Society of Jesus Through Four Centuries

BY

MARTIN P. HARNEY, S.J., M.A.

PROFESSOR OF THE HISTORY
OF THE REFORMATION
BOSTON COLLEGE

THE AMERICA PRESS *New York*

1941

IMPRIMI POTEST

> James H. Dolan, S.J.
>
> Provincial, New England Province

June 21, 1941

NIHIL OBSTAT

> Arthur J. Scanlan, S.T.D.
>
> Censor Librorum

IMPRIMATUR

> ✠ Francis J. Spellman, D.D.
>
> Archbishop, New York

August 21, 1941

MANUFACTURED IN THE UNITED STATES OF AMERICA
BY THE VAIL-BALLOU PRESS, INC., BINGHAMTON, N. Y.

To my brother and fellow-Jesuit,

The Rev. James M. Harney, S.J.

In conformity with the decree of Urban VIII all expressions regarding the sanctity or holiness of persons not yet canonized or beatified are made without any anticipation of the decision of the ecclesiastical authorities.

PREFACE

The occurrence of the fourth centenary of the founding of the Society of Jesus offers a fitting occasion for the study of its history. Its friends proclaim and its enemies concede that the order's activities have constituted no small part of the world's history during these four hundred years. The Jesuits, as the members are commonly known, were in the forefront of the Counter-Reformation; they have wielded a wide influence in education with their *Ratio Studiorum* and their hundreds of colleges and universities; they have produced a whole system of asceticism in the *Spiritual Exercises* of their founder, Ignatius of Loyola, and in the innumerable books that have translated the spirit of the *Exercises* into devotional life; they have engaged in great and constant warfare with the opponents of Catholicism and have participated in many vital controversies within its ranks; they have planted the Cross in most of the foreign mission fields and in doing so have become explorers, linguists and ethnologists; finally, in their own ranks they have bred many saints and martyrs, scholars and scientists, writers and orators. Throughout the long period of its existence the Society of Jesus has been ardently loved by its friends and just as intensely hated by its enemies. It grew through two centuries and a quarter to be one of the most numerous of the religious orders of the Catholic Church; it was then suppressed by several rulers and eventually by one of the Popes; and by another Pope it was resurrected to become in this day numerically the largest religious order. A volume in popular treatment of this varied and striking history of four hundred years would seem to be appropriate at this time. To produce such a book has been the purpose of the author.

The authorities most used in compiling this history, and on which most reliance was placed were: the *Monumenta Historica Societatis Jesu;* the *Archivum Historicum Societatis Jesu;* the *Acta Sanctorum* of the Bollandists; Duhr, *Geschichte der Jesuiten in den Ländern deutscher Zunge;* Astrain, *Historia de la Compañia de Jesús en la ancien Asistencia de España;* Frias, *Historia de la Compañia de Jesús en su Asistencia Moderna de España;* Tacchi-Venturi, *Storia della Compagnia di Gesù in Italia;* Hogan, *Ibernia Ignatiana;* Poncelet, *Histoire de la Compagnie de Jésus dans les anciens Pays-Bas;* Fouqueray, *Histoire de la Compagnie de Jésus en France (1528–1762);* Burnichon, *La Compagnie de Jésus en France (1814–1914);* Zalenski, *Les Jésuites en la Russie*

Blanche; Foley, *Records of the English Province of the Society of Jesus;* Hughes, *History of the Society of Jesus in North America, Colonial and Federal;* Garraghan, *The Jesuits of the Middle United States;* the *Jesuit Relations; Acta Romana Societatis Jesu; Memorabilia Societatis Jesu;* the *Letters and Notices of the English Province;* the *Woodstock Letters;* and *Mid-America.*

The writer must acknowledge a special debt to Pastor's *History of the Popes,* Vols. XII to XXIX of the English edition and Vols. XIII to XVI of the German edition; the references in the footnotes give only a partial idea of the value of this monumental work in the organization and composition of the present volume. Of similar help has been Koch's *Jesuiten-Lexikon,* a veritable mine of information on the Jesuits and the Society of Jesus, and Heimbucher's *Orden und Kongregationen der katholischen Kirche.*

The author wishes to pay a special tribute to the Rev. Robert Schwickerath, S.J., who conceived the idea of this book and directed its production. The opening chapter was largely suggested by him, while the chapters on the *Spiritual Exercises* and the Constitutions were based almost entirely on his notes.

Gratitude must also be expressed to the Very Rev. James H. Dolan, S.J., Provincial of the New England province of the Society of Jesus, and to Rev. James T. McCormick, S.J., former Provincial, for their sympathetic encouragement, to the Rev. William J. Murphy, S.J., the President of Boston College, and the trustees of that institution for their financial help, and to the following fathers of the Society who have aided with their many valuable criticisms and suggestions: Rev. John F. X. Murphy, S.J., Rev. James L. Burke, S.J., Rev. Gilbert J. Garraghan, S.J., Rev. John S. Keating, S.J., and Rev. Edward A. Ryan, S.J.; to Rev. Francis X. Talbot, S.J., editor of *America,* Rev. Daniel M. O'Connell, S.J., and Rev. Charles G. McManus, S.J., who saw the work through the press.

Martin P. Harney, S.J.

Boston College
September 27, 1940.

TABLE OF CONTENTS

INTRODUCTION

Religious orders play an important part in the history of the Christian Church, both in the exercise and development of spiritual life and in the propagation and defense of the faith; they play too an important part in the history of general civilization. Their greatest accomplishments are part of the Western tradition, for religious orders strictly so-called are mostly a feature of Latin Christianity. In the monasticism of the Eastern Church, though monasteries were at times numerous, there has been no variety or differentiation; all followed more or less the rule of St. Basil, all were contemplative bodies and none were devoted in a special manner to the active life of teaching or of caring for the sick. The word "bodies" is used deliberately, as in the East there were no religious "orders" in the exact sense of the term. Compare with this the wonderful variety of religious orders and congregations in the Western Church! One has but to glance through Helyot's work,[1] more than two hundred years old, yet still valuable with its eight hundred and ten beautiful colored plates of the different religious and their various habits, some simple, others quite picturesque, some not only in the common black or white or brown but even in red, light blue, purple, or yellow, to be convinced of this variety. One is almost tempted to apply to the Church and her orders the words of the Psalmist "Regina . . . circumdata varietate," "A queen standing resplendent in a variety of adornments." [2] The religious orders are the special manifestation of the Church's wonderful religious vitality, her spiritual arms and, at the same time, her special ornaments.

More interesting and more important than the externals of religious societies, are their constitutions, their special manner of life, their particular work. The types of religious orders vary considerably. The history of the development of religious orders in the West is a fascinating study: the beginnings with the hermits of the deserts of Egypt; the cenobitical life of Pachomius and his followers; the marvelous achievement of St. Benedict and his numberless disciples; the emergence of the Canons Regular; the inception at the height of the Middle Ages, of the great orders of Friars, Dominicans, Franciscans, Augustinians and Carmelites; the appearance of the Clerks Regular, among them the Society of Jesus;

---

[1] Helyot, *Histoire des ordres monastiques, religieux et militaires et des congrégations* etc. Paris (1714–1719).

[2] *Psalms.* XLIV, 10.

and lastly the organization of the numerous congregations of men and women of more recent times.

Three phases in the development of religious life are especially noteworthy. The first is that of progressive organization and centralization. At the start ascetics lived alone; then the monks associated together under a superior in communities or monasteries, but with every house independent of all others. Later on monastic houses combined in so-called congregations; most famous among the Benedictines were the Congregations of Cluny and St. Maur, and in these later days, the Congregations of Montecassino, England, Switzerland, Bavaria, France among others. Far greater centralization was introduced by the various orders of Friars, who divided their particular organizations into provinces and placed these under one head superior, called Master General, Minister General, or some similar title. The centralization was even more pronounced among the later orders and congregations, above all, as will be seen, in the Society of Jesus.

A second phase is the progressive change in external work. The monks of old purposed to devote themselves primarily to their personal sanctification and to the worthy and solemn performance of the Opus Dei, the divine office, the liturgy in its widest sense.[3] This does not mean that external work was entirely neglected; on the contrary, monastic orders, particularly that of St. Benedict, did tremendous work for the propagation of the faith, the colonization of wild territories, the preservation of literature and the education of youth. Later orders made work for the spread of the faith, the defense of the Church, the salvation of souls much more a direct and explicit objective of their organization. This was done by the Friars of the Middle Ages, by the Society of Jesus and later Congregations. In some instances the very name chosen pointed to the special work an order intended to emphasize. The official name of the Dominicans, "Friars Preachers," aptly described their principal activity. The sons of the "Poor Little Man" of Assisi, the "Friars Minor," by the example of their simple, poor life wanted to proclaim to a world, absorbed in the pursuit of riches and luxury, the power and the saving value of the humility and poverty of Christ. When one hears the titles of such religious societies as "Sisters of Charity," "Sisters of Mercy," "Little Sisters of the Poor," "Brothers of the Christian Schools," there is no need to inquire what special work they have proposed to themselves. This procedure inevitably brought about an important change. Whereas the monastic orders observed, some even vowed, stability, i. e. the obligation of permanently remaining in the same monastery, the later orders were characterized by great mobility: the members not only moved about far

---

[3] The venerable rule of St. Benedict often speaks of the Opus Dei, and in chapter XLIII it is said: "Nihil operi Dei praeponatur," "Let nothing be put before the Work of God."

more in the pursuit of their apostolic or charitable occupations, but could also be transferred from one religious house or even province to others. There had been an interesting anticipation of this mobility and more direct apostolic activity among the monks of one part of Christendom, the monks of Ireland. Filled with an unquenchable desire of apostolic wandering afar, they went to Scotland, England, eastern Gaul, southern Germany, Switzerland, Austria, northern Italy, there to establish monasteries, and above all, to bring the light of the Gospel to nations still sunk in the darkness of paganism. But their action was rather exceptional. Mobility and the more direct apostolic activity was to become an essential feature only of later religious orders. It was to be a striking characteristic of the Society of Jesus.

The third phase is the increasing differentiation of the practices of the religious bodies from older ones. In consequence of greater devotion to external activities, certain features of the older orders were abandoned, e. g. among the Jesuits a special religious "habit," or vestment, and the choir, the singing or recitation of the Divine Office in common. Others were added: prolonged studies, a longer period of novitiate and general spiritual formation, the taking of the final vows only after a long period of testing and training. It cannot be a matter of surprise that when those changes appeared first, there was opposition from churchmen, even from members of older religious orders. The changes were frowned upon as "innovations," undesirable and even unlawful, for they abolished what to many appeared essential parts of religious life (especially the choir), or added what seemed to be incompatible with monastic spirit. When, in the thirteenth century, the Friars, especially the Dominicans and Franciscans, began their momentous work as teachers in the universities, there was violent opposition, particularly by a powerful party led by William of St. Amour. They contended that religious must be all like the monks of the earliest period, devoting themselves to prayer and manual labor, and that teaching was in absolute opposition to the monastic ideal. It was then that St. Thomas Aquinas wrote a magnificent vindication of the work of the new orders of Friars in a book which even today deserves to be studied for a deeper understanding of religious life and religious activity.[4] Strong objections were also made at that time to the general labor of the Friars in the sphere of preaching and of hearing confessions. These objections will be met again, as well as additional ones which were later raised against the Society. Even members of the Mendicant orders failed to understand the new features introduced by the Society in order to meet the new needs and the changed conditions of the times.

---

[4] *Contra Impugnantes Dei Cultum et Religionem.* (A.1257) "Against Those who attack the Worship of God and Religion" (i. e. the Religious State). There is an English Translation: *An Apology for the Religious Orders,* edited by John Proctor O.P., S.T.M. London, (1902).

As religious orders played so important a part in religion and for religion, Catholics will not be surprised when they hear that their foundation is, in some way, attributed to a special influence of Divine Providence. That, indeed, has been explicitly stated by numerous Popes in regard to the orders of St. Benedict, St. Francis, St. Dominic, and others; it has also been said by Popes in regard to the foundation of the Society of Jesus. But this is a point which the historian need not investigate. There are, however, other points which will interest him and his readers. It must be discovered what special elements, conditions of the period and current intellectual and social trends influenced the foundation of religious orders and determined their specific character. Again, and this is a very significant point, it must be shown whether there was any special reason for the foundation of a new order and what particular needs of the time it answered. Furthermore, it will be important to understand what influence the founder of a religious order exercised on his foundation; what special gifts, intellectual, moral and religious, he possessed which fitted him for this work. It should be seen too by whom he was assisted: who, and what manner of men, the first and foremost companions were. This naturally suggests the subject of the first two chapters: the first, the times, or the historical background of the foundation; the second, the men, or the personality of the founder and his first companions.

CHAPTER I

THE HISTORICAL BACKGROUND

The founder of the Jesuits, St. Ignatius of Loyola, who was born in 1491 on the eve of the discovery of America and died in 1556, lived in an interesting age, one of the most interesting in all history. His childhood and youth belong to what may be called the end of the Middle Ages, his manhood to that most important period, the Reformation, more correctly termed "the Protestant Revolution of the sixteenth century." The end of the Middle Ages, the fourteenth and fifteenth centuries, frequently has been spoken of as a period of decline. There is some truth in this, as there was a decline of certain prominent features of the Middle Ages: a decline (or rather disappearance) of feudalism, a considerable decline of scholasticism, also a decline of the political power of the Papacy. Such expressions, however, as "decline of the Middle Ages" are apt to be misleading, especially if implying that there was nothing but decline. There was much else: much activity, political, social, intellectual, artistic, literary and religious. The historian of the Papacy, Dr. Pastor, begins his great work with these words: "With the exception of the period which witnessed the transformation of the pagan into the Christian world, the history of mankind hardly offers one more striking than that of the transition from the Middle Ages to modern times." [1] It was a period of great personalities, of Ferdinand and Isabella in Spain, the Emperor Charles V and Francis I of France, of a Leonardo da Vinci, Michelangelo and Raphael; it was too the day of Columbus, Vasco da Gama and Magellan.

It was a time when many and important new things came into being. It was the period when the great art of printing was established which, more than can be imagined today, revolutionized the whole intellectual world. It was the era of the greatest geographical discoveries; the attainment of the sea route to India and, above all, the finding of the New World, the very name of which points to the unheard-of novelty of the event. It was the age when a Catholic cleric, Copernicus, revealed a new world in the sky, a discovery already anticipated more than half a century before by two other clergymen, the English Bishop Pecock and the German Cardinal Nicholas Cusanus. Thereby man's view of the universe was completely revolutionized. It was the period of the Renaissance. This

---

[1] Pastor, *History of the Popes*, St. Louis (1898–) Vol. I, p. 1.

famous "rebirth" of classical literature has often been misunderstood as if the classics had been unknown during the Middle Ages; what was new was an extraordinary enthusiasm for the ancient classics. It was during this time that the medieval schools were reformed and transformed by the "humanists," when the classical education was established which, until most recent times, was the very foundation of higher education. This classical, humanistic education, St. Ignatius and his early disciples were to make the basis of their famous schools. Archaeology developed along with the enthusiasm for the classics, and historical criticism received a powerful impetus from the eager search for authentic texts of the ancient authors.

In the higher or university education, there was a continuation of the zeal of the thirteenth and fourteenth centuries. In the fifteenth century, more than thirty universities were founded, not a few of which remained famous for centuries; some are even today great centers of learning. Suffice it to mention the following: Louvain, Leipsic, Tübingen, Freiburg, Alcalá, St. Andrews, Glasgow, Aberdeen, Copenhagen, Upsala. As regards the so-called Grammar schools, or Latin schools, an even greater zeal was manifested. Urged on by piety as well as by civic pride, individuals and groups devoted large sums for their foundations. In Germany these classical academies were numerous; in the forefront stood the schools taught or managed by the "Brothers of Common Life," to be found in many towns in the Netherlands and in the Lower Rhine Valley. Their school at Deventer had 2,200 scholars in attendance in 1500; two of its most famous students were Thomas à Kempis and Cardinal Nicholas Cusanus. Similarly grammar schools were numerous in France, Scotland and England.[2] Of course the term "numerous" is to be taken in a comparative sense; it is hardly correct to speak of a well defined and highly organized system of schools and studies. The remark of Father Pollen, S.J., in his life of St. Ignatius gives a good summary view of these pre-Reformation schools: ". . . Of course there had been schools, and very praiseworthy institutions they were, but their homely staffs and very restricted numbers made them unfit to meet the cry for improved and extended schooling, which the Renaissance evoked."[3]

In the history of art the period is most remarkable; in the history of painting it is unique. No other period can be compared to it. In the hundred years from 1450–1550 lived the following great painters: Fra Angelico, Fra Filippo Lippi and his son Filippino, Botticelli, Perugino, Pinturicchio, Francia, Mantegna, Bellini, Fra Bartolomeo, Luini, Del Sarto, Palma Vecchio, Correggio, Tintoretto, Veronese, and the three

[2] For the English Schools cf. Leach, *English Schools at the Reformation*, Westminster (1896).

[3] J. Hungerford Pollen, S.J., *St. Ignatius of Loyola*, N.Y. (1922), p. 126.

giants, Leonardo da Vinci, Michelangelo and Raphael. It is what may be called a staggering list, yet it is by no means complete for Italy alone, and the artists of other countries have not been mentioned.

In architecture there was also amazing activity. The Renaissance churches may not equal the greatest of the Gothic monuments of the past; still many of them are grand edifices. It is also well to remember that some of the most magnificent specimens of Gothic architecture were built or completed in the fifteenth century, as the wonderful town hall of Louvain, the glorious steeple of the Minster in Ulm and St. Stephen's tower in Vienna. Of the famous Renaissance churches the first above all is the great St. Peter's in Rome, planned to be a worthy central church of Christendom and to give outward expression to the greatness, the splendor and the power of the Catholic Church. The number of noble ecclesiastical edifices erected during this period is astonishing. Dr. Pastor gives a long list of such churches in Italy alone.[4] In other countries similar "sermons in stone," "prayers in stone," were built during the same period either in the still persisting Gothic, as the numerous beautiful buildings in the Tudor style in England, or in the new Renaissance style, in which many splendid churches were erected in various parts of Europe.

Much more fundamental is the condition of religion during that period. The construction of numerous churches which has just been mentioned, was one manifestation of religious fervor. What may strike some as unexpected is the great number of saints of the period, far greater than is commonly supposed. Dr. Pastor in his fifth volume is able to list eighty-eight "Saints and Blessed" in Italy alone. While it must be admitted there were evils and abuses in some religious houses, it can also be established that vigorous efforts were made during the period to restore primitive observance and discipline. New life was visible in the many religious orders, the Franciscan Observantines, Dominicans, Augustinians, Carmelites and Servites, as well as in the Benedictine Congregations of St. Justina in Italy, of Bursfeld in Germany, and in the famous Windesheim Congregation of the Canons Regular in the Netherlands. That there was spiritual fervor among religious orders is proved by the fact that numerous religious, especially Friars, followed at once the geographical discoveries and the conquistadores, and with burning zeal and by the greatest sacrifices and hardships spread the kingdom of God in the newly discovered pagan lands.

As regards the religious spirit of the people, great zeal was manifested in the performance of religious devotions. All life was permeated by an atmosphere of devotion and profound piety. In fact, it is interesting to know that three of the most popular devotions of modern time received

---

[4] Pastor, *History of the Popes*, Vol. V, pp. 69–76.

their special and final development in this period: the Stations of the Cross; the devotion to the Seven Dolors of the Blessed Mother (a great devotion to the Sorrowful Mother on Calvary was already prominent in the thirteenth century, but the devotion to the Seven Dolors belongs to this period); lastly, the Rosary (no matter what share St. Dominic may have had in the origin of the beautiful devotion, the present form with its fifteen mysteries appears for the first time in this age.) [5] Practical books of devotion, of instruction of the people for the reception of the Sacraments, etc., were among the earliest printed books.

Another, perhaps even deeper, evidence intimately connected with religion, is that of charity. "Never did the love which Christ kindled in the hearts of men burn more brightly than in this period," says Dr. Pastor who gives a list of charitable institutions, hospitals, orphanages, homes for old people, for incurables and other needs, which were founded during these times. [6] The large cities had numerous hospitals. Florence alone increased its number to thirty-five in this age. Rome, under the inspiration of the Popes, had many homes of mercy, and there was hardly a small town that did not support one hospital besides other charitable institutions. The care of the sick was well organized and the patients were carefully and skilfully attended. One of the most remarkable proofs for this was furnished by Martin Luther. On his journey to Italy he was not at all impressed by architecture and paintings, but he gave an almost enthusiastic description of Italian hospitals and the excellent care bestowed on the sick. [7]

What beautiful and touching forms this spirit of charity assumed may be seen from the institution founded by the great Cardinal Cusanus. In his native Kues, on the Moselle, he built a hospital with a beautiful chapel. This institution was to support thirty-three men (in honor of the thirty-three years of Our Lord's life); only such men were to be admitted who were advanced in age, good Catholics, and, for some reason or other, entirely destitute. What is most remarkable is the fact that in spite of the storms of the Protestant Reformation and of the French Revolution that broke over the country, this house has continued for nearly five hundred years to be the home of thirty-three poor people. And it is still doing its charitable work today.

The period, then, was not one of universal decline, least of all of general religious decay. Religion was not dead, nor was it dying. On the con-

---

[5] *Analecta Bollandiana*, Vol. XII, pp. 333–352. On the "Stations" see "Way of the Cross" in *Catholic Encyclopedia*, Vol. XV, p. 569. On the "Rosary," *Catholic Encyclopedia*, Vol. XIII, p. 186.

[6] Pastor, *History of the Popes*, Vol. V, pp. 36 ff.

[7] It is worth while to read Luther's account of Italian hospitals as given by Pastor, *History of the Popes*, Vol. V, pp. 66–67.

trary, there was much profound piety, even religious enthusiasm and exalted faith. At the same time it was an age of contradictions, of startling contrasts. There were dangerous tendencies abroad, and evils and abuses in Church, state and society. To give a correct picture of the age these defects too must be discussed, and even at greater length. It is not that the evil had been more prominent than the good features. But a clear knowledge of the dangerous conditions and tendencies of the time is absolutely necessary in order that one may understand correctly and fully first the rapid spread and immense expansion of Protestantism, secondly various important phases of the new order, the Society of Jesus.

To discover what and how great the evil conditions and tendencies were, one need not go for proof to the gossip of chroniclers or to the bitter sarcasm of satirists. There is ample and often appalling proof in the decrees of councils and synods, in the letters of the Popes, in the declarations of zealous cardinals, bishops and fervent religious.[8]

Instead of many sources it will be enough to quote one ecclesiastical document of unimpeachable and even official authority, the celebrated *Consilium delectorum Cardinalium et aliorum Praelatorum de Emendenda Ecclesia*, "Memorial of the appointed Cardinals and other Prelates of the Roman Church on Ecclesiastical Reform." [9] Pope Paul III in 1536 appointed a Reform Commission, consisting of nine eminent and most zealous prelates: four Cardinals (Contarini, Caraffa—later Paul IV —Sadoleto and Pole), two Archbishops, one Bishop, one Abbot and Father Badia, O.P., Master of the Sacred Palace. They were to prepare a memorial, pointing out the most serious ecclesiastical abuses and evils that needed reform. Learned, sincere men, eye-witnesses of what they told, they performed their task with amazing frankness and fearlessness. A Protestant editor of the document [10] remarked: "A new spirit evidenced itself in the Court of Rome with its publication." Cardinal Quirini rightly called it the "golden memorial." It is a landmark in Church history. It anticipated and prepared the gigantic work of reformation accomplished later by the Council of Trent. Of rather interesting coincidence is the fact that while these distinguished men were working out their great plan of reform, St. Ignatius and his first companions entered Italy on their way to Rome to offer their services to the Holy See. Their order, soon to be founded in the Eternal City, was to become one of the chief instruments in the carrying out of the reform decrees of the Council of Trent.

---

[8] Abundant material is found in the many volumes of Dr. Pastor's *History of the Popes;* in Dr. Janssen's *History of the German People;* in Father Tacchi-Venturi's first volume of the *Storia della Compagnia di Gesù in Italia.*

[9] Published in 1538. Text in Mansi, *Suppl.* V., 593 seq. Also in Kidd, *Documents of the Continental Reformation,* pp. 307 ff. Discussed in Pastor, Vol. XI, pp. 165-172.

[10] Kidd, *Op. cit.,* p. 305.

The "Memorial" marked twenty-eight abuses which called for reformation. Nor were these abuses which had crept into the Church through the Reformation; the time between 1517 and 1536 was all too short for such evils to have arisen. The authors themselves declared explicitly that the abuses had existed "for quite a while" and "under the present Pope's predecessors" (certainly during the time of St. Ignatius' youth). Lest the description of the evils in the Church, given in the following pages, be thought exaggerated, the text of the "Memorial" will be used as a guide, with historical facts adduced in proof of the opinions of the illustrious authors.

The greatest evil in the Church at the time was not, as is often said, clerical immorality, but the misuse of ecclesiastical wealth in various forms. The Church was wealthy, particularly in the German Empire where one-third of the landed property is said to have been in the possession of bishoprics, abbeys, churches, etc. One of the worst abuses in this regard was Pluralism, the simultaneous possession by one man of several benefices. The holder of the benefice enjoyed the revenue, often large, sometimes immense; a substitute, frequently poorly paid, performed the work of the office. Pluralism, despite many efforts to check it, had increased in the thirteenth and fourteenth centuries to reach appalling heights in the fifteenth. There were prelates who held two, three or more bishoprics, besides several rich abbeys and other benefices. Personal attention to the spiritual functions of all was an impossibility, hence auxiliaries, or vicars, had to be employed. The added evils of absenteeism, also vigorously denounced by the "Memorial," were but a natural consequence. Some of the Popes must share the blame because of their too freely dispensing from the numerous prohibitions of Pluralism. A few instances will show to what degrees the abuse had gone: Giuliano della Rovere (later Pope Julius II) had six bishoprics and many abbeys; Rodrigo Borgia (later Alexander VI) had at least thirty bishoprics, abbeys and other benefices; Cardinal Passerini, probably the worst case, held over fifty benefices.[11] Italians were unduly favored with bishoprics and benefices in other lands, to the great dissatisfaction of the people and the clergy of those countries.

Connected with Pluralism was another great evil, Nepotism, the favoritism shown to relatives, particularly by the showering of dignities and lucrative offices on them. It was a fault of several of the Popes. Clement V and John XXII each raised five kinsmen to the office of Cardinal; Calixtus III, despite the excellent virtues displayed in his tenure of the Papacy, failed sadly, especially in his favor to his nephew Rodrigo Borgia, who later as Alexander VI became one of the worst offenders in this regard.

---

[11] Pastor, *History of the Popes*, Vol. VII, p. 203.

The temptation to advance one's relatives was great; it was but "natural," only too natural. Still, it is an exaggeration to call Nepotism, as one historian did, "the original sin of the Papacy"; many, in fact the majority of the Popes, kept free of the fault.

The many material emoluments connected with ecclesiastical benefices caused princely houses to be most anxious to have their sons provided with them, often in their early youth. Thus Giovanni de' Medici and Alfonso, the son of the king of Portugal, each, before he was sixteen years old, was raised to the cardinalate. Other benefices were sometimes bestowed on boys seven years old after they had received the tonsure; the instance of Giovanni de' Medici is not the only one. An additional danger lurked in these great temporal emoluments of the benefices; it was the temptation to obtain them through simony. This vice too was condemned in the severest terms by the authors of the "Memorial"; indeed, they deplored the fact that "this pestilential vice is only too common in the Church."

Still another grave misuse of ecclesiastical wealth was the monopolization of the higher and richer positions in the Church by the nobility, particularly in countries like Germany where many bishoprics in addition to their wealth were also temporal sovereignties. What is more repulsive, princes had bishoprics bestowed on their illegitimate offspring; to give one instance of many, the wealthy see of Saragossa was occupied in succession by three illegitimate descendants of Ferdinand of Aragon. Bishoprics, abbeys and canonries became sinecures in the literal sense of the word for young nobles. Some cathedral chapters by special statutes admitted only sons of nobility; several, only sons of the highest aristocracy. In the German Empire, during the hundred years before the Reformation, of the two hundred and twenty-five bishops, all but twenty-five were nobles, and at the outbreak of the revolt seventeen of the thirty-three sees were occupied by scions of the highest princely families. Too often the aristocrats on the episcopal thrones acted as grand seigneurs in little contact with the people. The democratic character of the Church, of which much has been said, had largely disappeared in many places during the Middle Ages. Remembering that St. Gregory VII in the eleventh and Gregory IX in the thirteenth century had strongly objected to making birth and family the decisive reasons for elevation to ecclesiastical dignities, it is dissatisfying to find Aeneas Sylvius (later Pope Pius II) in the fifteenth century defending the practice. Possibly sometimes the appointment of one of princely estate may best serve the Church; but to defend such a course as a general principle would seem to prove that the spirit of worldliness had increased considerably in the Church.

It would be wrong to think that all these aristocrats were unworthy bishops. Yet not a few of them were without real vocations, having been destined by their families for ecclesiastical careers. They lived primarily as temporal lords, absorbed in material and political interests; and some did not possess even the necessary theological and spiritual training for their office. This, more than anything else, explains why hardly any German bishops made a vigorous stand against the rising Protestantism and why an immense portion of the flocks—"sheep without shepherds" —so easily followed the enticing voice of the innovators.

One of the princes who remained loyal to the Church, Duke George of Saxony, very appositely wrote: "It is as clear as daylight that the origins of all the heresy lie in the way in which prelates enter the Church. Now it is, alas, not the least scandal of Christendom that we laymen . . . when we appoint our own children, brothers and friends to bishoprics and other Church dignities, are not in the least concerned about the 'door' by which they enter, but think only how we can manage to push our own people in, whether under the threshold or in through the roof—we do not care. This is the custom with us princes. These gentlemen who get in by such ways behave as if they had purchased their benefices for their own possessions . . . Moreover, we laymen who by God's ordinances have been placed in power are so grasping . . . that when we have the property of monasteries and other religious foundations under our rule we are inflamed with covetousness and try to get these lands into our own possession." [12]

A striking example of what has been said is the case of Archbishop Albrecht of Mainz, a scion of the princely house of Brandenburg-Hohenzollern. Being a younger son, he was destined for an ecclesiastical career. At twenty-three he was made Archbishop of Magdeburg and Bishop of Halberstadt, yet in a short while he was coveting the vacant Electoral Archbishopric of Mainz. The steps taken by him to obtain this important post, have been labeled by some historians as simoniacal, by others as virtually or equivalently so. Whether simoniacal or not, his accession to the new dignity involved him heavily in debt; and to pay his debt he obtained from Leo X the commission to publish in many parts of Germany the indulgence granted by that Pontiff to all who should contribute to the building of the basilica of St. Peter in Rome. By the terms of the commission he was permitted to take from the proceeds of the indulgence the sums needed to repay his debt. It was the preaching of this indulgence, it will be remembered, that occasioned Luther's "Ninety-Five Theses," and thus precipitated the Reformation. Pastor called the whole Mainz affair a disgrace for all concerned and the catastrophe that followed almost like a judgment from Heaven.[13]

Now all this stands in close relation to the founder of the Society. St Ignatius in his *Spiritual Exercises*, in the most fundamental meditations

[12] Janssen, *History of the German People*, London (1896) Vol. V, p. 67.
[13] Pastor, *History of the Popes*, Vol. VII, p. 333.

on the "Kingdom of Christ" and on the "Two Standards," felt bound to emphasize the necessity of detachment from wealth, because, ever intensely practical, he saw the fearful harm done in his day by love of wealth within the Church. In his "Rules for making a good election" he advises the retreatant to meditate seriously "whether to accept or refuse a benefice." In the present time the significance of this advice may not be apparent at first. But in the light of the facts so far presented, what tremendous import it has! Father Rickaby makes the following comment: "In Catholic times and Catholic countries men took up the priesthood as a career. . . It is worth while looking at the list of Wolsey's preferments. All over the world there were Wolseys on a smaller scale." He then enumerates Wolsey's bishoprics and abbeys and continues: "Did he hold all these prelacies for the good of the people over whom he was set? Ought he ever to have been a bishop at all? These questions were too seldom asked at the time, and the neglect of them spelt ruin for the Church. Here was the evil which the Exercises went to remedy." [14] In another place he says, "To understand the cautions (given by St. Ignatius concerning the use of wealth) one should be versed in the history of Nepotism." Even more appropriate is his remark: "Had there been Clergy Retreats previous to the sixteenth century, the world would have seen no other 'blessed Reformation.' " [15] The paramount influence of the Spiritual Exercises on the true reform of the Church was to be part of the providential mission of St. Ignatius.

What has been noted concerning the claims of nobility and family interests in regard to bishoprics and cathedral chapters, can equally be applied to the monasteries and convents. Many of these, particularly the wealthy ones, were open only to the sons and daughters of nobles; the vocations of many such religious were often largely a matter of the parents' choice. It cannot be a matter of surprise that, when Luther made fearful onslaughts on religious vows and declared monastic life "unnatural," "anti-Christian" and "diabolical," many of those who had embraced this life without a true vocation gladly availed themselves of the proffered "evangelical liberty." In the fifteenth century numerous attempts were made to reform monastic institutions. Opposition to such reforms was particularly determined in aristocratic monasteries of men and convents of noble ladies, and the recalcitrant religious were supported in their rebellion by their noble relatives.

There were several other examples of the misuse of ecclesiastical wealth censured by the "Memorial." The methods and the lives of the alms-collectors were severely reprehended. Chaucer's picture of the

---

[14] Joseph Rickaby, S.J., *The Spiritual Exercises of St. Ignatius with a Continuous Commentary*, London (1923) p. 156.

[15] Joseph Rickaby, S.J., *Waters That Flow Softly*, New York (1907), no. 74, p. 91.

Pardoner, though probably overdrawn, is by no means fictitious. The "Memorial" complained that many of these collectors "deceived rustics and other simple people" and recommended that "they should be completely suppressed." Too frequent "Indulgences" were censured. At the time there were too many Indulgences preached, one condition of which was a money contribution for some hospital or for the building of a church. In itself the practice was perfectly legitimate, but at the end of the Middle Ages it was much overdone. Furthermore, not all indulgence-preachers observed the necessary prudence and ecclesiastical decorum. Tetzel, whose preaching furnished the outward occasion of Luther's attack, was personally a good man, yet his doctrine in regard to the indulgences for the dead is not the accepted one and his methods were highly sensational.[16]

Finally among the evils connected with the misuse of ecclesiastical wealth was the fact that whereas some prelates derived large revenues from accumulations of rich benefices, there were numerous priests who had hardly enough to live on. This was especially true of the "chantry priests" or "altarists," whose principal, often sole, occupation was the saying of masses for which foundations had been established. Their numbers were far too large for the resources of their support. In some places their numbers were almost incredible; at Breslau, a city of 19,000, there were 122 such priests attached to one church and 114 to another; Mainz with 6,000 had 500 clerics.[17] Even Catholic historians have spoken of an "ecclesiastical rabble" of the times. The situation was replete with danger. Lack of occupation often resulted in an idleness little conducive to priestly holiness. Far more serious evil lay in the necessarily insufficient support; very many were forced to eke out a living by side occupations little in keeping with their sacred character. Here was a most ominous source of discontent. Small wonder that a considerable number of such priests at once joined the religious revolt of 1517.

The condition was aggravated by the fact that a great number of these clerics were insufficiently educated. Defective clerical education is the first abuse mentioned in the "Memorial." It is stated that "in the ordination of clerics, particularly priests, there is not sufficient care and diligence; on the contrary, rather frequently men, often mere adolescents, without good morals and entirely untrained, are ordained." If the complaint contradicts those apologists who can see no serious defects in sacerdotal education in the Middle Ages, it by no means confirms the charges of wholesale and dense ignorance. The authors do not say that the clergy were "generally ignorant" but that "a good many were admitted to sacred

[16] Grisar, *Luther* (English translation), London (1916) Vol. I, p. 329.

[17] Janssen, *Geschichte des Deutschen Volkes*, Freiburg (1913) 19th. and 20th. ed., Vol. I, p. 742.

orders without sufficient knowledge." This was due to the fact that at least in the later Middle Ages there were no seminaries for priestly candidates; and herein was the greatest defect in medieval education. In the earlier ages the bishops directed the education of their priests; [18] gradually schools developed about the cathedrals, the so-called cathedral schools. In some monastic schools also, besides the younger religious, aspirants to the secular clergy were instructed. With the rise of the universities both types of schools declined, the best students and the most capable professors being irresistibly drawn to the more famous seats of learning. Several Popes tried to keep the cathedral schools going. The III Lateran Council (1179) decreed that "at every cathedral there should be a teacher to instruct gratis the clerics of that church and poor students. A benefice should be assigned to this teacher. The same should be re-introduced into other churches and monasteries if, in the past, something of this kind had been assigned for that purpose." [19] Because this decree was not carried out in many churches, the IV Lateran Council (1215) issued stronger legislation. [20] Even this precept was not universally observed, as St. Thomas Aquinas, a contemporary, has borne witness. [21] His testimony has been substantiated by the modern scholar Denifle. [22] Time and again up to the Council of Trent, attempts were made to revive the theological lectures at the cathedrals. The "Memorial" urged the Pope to insist that "the bishops should have at their cathedral a teacher to instruct the younger clergy in general knowledge and good morals." Instruction by one or two teachers was a poor substitute for a seminary staff; yet according to the "Memorial," even this meager instruction was not given everywhere.

It may be thought that a large proportion of the candidates went to the universities. Actually the number of clerics who were university-educated was small. It has been frequently stated that "only about one percent of the clergy were able to attend university courses;" [23] possibly this is too great a minimizing, still there is the testimony of a Dominican friar Fabri, writing in 1490, that when he was a youth there was not one in a thousand clerics who had seen a university town. [24] Furthermore university towns were by no means the best places for the education of priests, since there were no sufficient provisions for the spiritual and moral training of the candidates. Indeed there was much licentiousness among me-

---

[18] Viéban, "Seminary," *Catholic Encyclopedia*, Vol. XIII, p. 695.

[19] Canon XVIII, Mansi, XXII, p. 227.

[20] Mansi, XXII, p. 999.

[21] Cf. Appendix no. I.

[22] Denifle, *Die Universitäten des Mittelalters bis 1400*, Berlin (1895) Vol. I, p. 708.

[23] Viéban, "Seminary," *Catholic Encyclopedia*, Vol. XIII, p. 695.

[24] Janssen, *Geschichte des Deutschen Volkes*, Vol. I, p. 757.

dieval students. Jacques de Vitry's account of the immorality of students at Paris in the thirteenth century, has often been quoted.[25] Denifle, though he seeks to explain the unfavorable condition, does not deny the fundamental correctness of the statements.[26] The "colleges" in the universities improved the situation; but as the numbers of their inmates were small, the majority of the students did not have their protection. It has been conjectured that "a certain percentage of clerical students must have obtained their training in the 'scholae externae' of the larger monasteries." [27] As will be shown later, there were few scholae externae at any time, and extremely few at the end of the Middle Ages; the monastic schools therefore did not offer a possible substitute for the seminary.

The great majority of priests, up to the Council of Trent, received their education from some parish priest; a training in the elements of Latin, the most necessary knowledge of Christian doctrine and, particularly, the practical training in the ecclesiastical rites. It was a practice of great antiquity. The Council of Vaison (529) [28] laid down the following: "Parish priests should keep in their houses unmarried lectors (young clerics) to instruct them in psalmody, ecclesiastical learning, and the Law of the Lord, and thereby prepare capable successors." The council, it is interesting to note, declared that such was the custom all over Italy. This decree did not, as has been often stated erroneously, provide for the teaching of children; it dealt solely with sacerdotal education.[29] Such training must have been insufficient and elemental under the best circumstances, when the parish priests were both capable and zealous. The fact is, it was altogether too easy to become a priest; hence the excessive number and doubtful quality of many in the period under discussion. This defective education helps to explain why so many priests offered little vigorous opposition to the violent and frequently clever Protestant propaganda. Even the loyal and good priests were often helpless because of their lack of sufficient learning. They were to be pitied rather than condemned.

All this was remedied in the Council of Trent. In its first sessions in 1546 it had only urged the re-establishment of the lectureship at the cathedrals; but in one of its last sessions in 1563, it laid down the detailed plan of the modern seminary. This was the most salutary reform of the

---

[25] Rashdall, *Universities of the Middle Ages*, New ed., Oxford (1936) Vol. III, p. 439.

[26] Denifle, *Die Universitäten des Mittelalters*, Vol. I, p. 672.

[27] Mannhardt, "Notes on the Training of the Pre-Reformation Clergy," *The Historical Bulletin*, St. Louis, Vol. VII, p. 5.

[28] Mansi, VIII, 725.

[29] This is emphatically asserted by a leading Catholic historian, Dom Leclerq, O.S.B., who in Hefele-Leclerq, *Conciles*, Vol. II, 2, pp. 1112–1113 states: "ces écoles, on le voit, n'ont rien de commun avec l'enseignement public."

council; rightly could some of the members say: "If we had done nothing but this, it would be worth all the labors and sacrifices of this long council." [30]

But how is this great change from the moderate demand of 1546 to the positive and detailed injunction of 1563 to be explained? Something decisive had happened in between. It was the founding of the Collegium Germanicum in 1552 by St. Ignatius. The Saint was convinced that the most important reform for the Church lay in the better education and training of her priests; he believed also that one of the surest ways of preventing the threatened extinction of the Church in Germany was the establishment at Rome of a college for the training of German priests. In this new institution he provided for a thorough course in philosophy and theology, and even more important, a most solid moral and spiritual training. The Collegium Germanicum, Dr. Pastor calls the first modern seminary.[31] Cardinals and bishops observed its workings and in 1563 the Council of Trent based its seminary decree on the organization of this sacerdotal college of St. Ignatius. Other zealous men continued to develop and improve the seminary: St. Charles Borromeo (who personally investigated the operation of the Germanicum), St. Vincent de Paul, and especially the Sulpician Fathers.

The treatment of clerical education leads to the discussion of a wider topic, the general education of the times. The discussion is necessary for the removal of misconceptions which make it impossible to understand the general educational work begun by the Society soon after its establishment. It has already been pointed out that at the end of the Middle Ages there was considerable zeal for education. But some Catholic admirers of things medieval go beyond this to maintain that medieval education reached a height of perfection such as has not been attained since. Thus one excellent writer declares: "Christianity organized a system of schools, elementary, secondary and higher . . . , formed a public system of education in a sense which had never been realized before nor has been since." [32]

Certainly it could not be a complete system when the highest and most important part, the seminary for priests, was lacking. There was system in the philosophical and theological studies, especially in the order of St. Dominic. In what is now called secondary education, there was very little system; in the elementary education, there was none whatsoever. One great defect in medieval education, according to Denifle, was the failure

---

[30] Pallavicino, *Hist. Conc. Trid.* Liber XXI, c. 8, n. 3.

[31] Pastor, *History of the Popes*, Vol. XIII, pp. 219–230. See also *Lexikon für Theologie und Kirche*, Vol. IX, p. 458, and many other historians.

[32] Pierre J. Marique, *History of Education*, New York, Vol. I, p. 202.

to attempt correlating or coordinating the various types and grades of schools.[33]

Benedictine schools are often mentioned as a most numerous source of popular education. There are two flourishing periods in the history of the Benedictine schools: the first extended up to the twelfth century; the second began after the Council of Trent and continues up to the present day both in Europe and America. But from the twelfth to the sixteenth century there was a decline, as leading Benedictine historians admit.[34] One of the reasons for this decline has already been given; others are to be found in the fearful ravages of the Hundred Years' War and other such catastrophes. This idea of a very large contribution to popular education in the later Middle Ages, is based on the incorrect assumptions that there then existed an enormous number of Benedictine monasteries, some put it at 37,000,[35] and that extern schools were maintained by many of these monasteries. 37,000 at one time is an incredible figure, nor is it accepted by Benedictine scholars. Dom Uttenweiler estimates that the total number of Benedictine monasteries throughout the whole course of the order's history (1400 years) is between 20,000 and 37,000.[36] Dom Braunmüller sets the number of monasteries in the early part of the fifteenth century at 15,000.[37] The large number given by medieval chroniclers must be accepted only with the utmost caution. Critical historians have come to the conclusion after careful and detailed study that the enumerations of this period must be divided not only by two, or three, but sometimes by ten.

Very few of these monasteries maintained schools for any except their own monastic students in the late Middle Ages. The decline of such schools amid the terrible losses occasioned by the catastrophes of the time, has already been noted.[38] Furthermore not all branches of the Benedictines devoted themselves to this type of education. The numerous Cistercians were forbidden to have in their houses students other than their novices; and the Congregation of Cluny, to which for a long time numerous Benedictine monasteries belonged, so occupied itself with the solemn celebration of the liturgy as to preclude educational work. During the Middle Ages every reform in the Benedictine order involved the curtailment of teaching labors. The education of extern pupils was

---

[33] Denifle, *Die Universitäten des Mittelalters*, Vol. I, p. 798.

[34] E. g., Baeumer, Hilpisch, among others.

[35] Alston, O.S.B., "Benedictine," *Catholic Encyclopedia*, Vol. II, p. 446; Willman-Kirsch, *The Science of Education*, Beatty, Pa., Vol. I, p. 191; and in many popular writings, e. g., article in *Thought*, April 1933, and in the *Catholic Mind*, 1933.

[36] Uttenweiler, O.S.B., "Benedictiner," *Lexikon für Theologie und Kirche*, Vol. II, p. 157.

[37] Braunmüller, O.S.B., "Benedictinerorden," *Kirchen-Lexikon*, Vol. II, p. 351.

[38] Cf. also the writings of Dom Hilpisch, O.S.B.

considered a cause of the decline of religious discipline. Cluny has been instanced, another case would be that of the Bursfeld Congregation. In the reform decree of Benedict XII in the fourteenth century, the *Benedictina*, issued for the whole order, while the zealous pursuit of studies was urged upon the monks, the teaching of such as were not novices together with the religious was explicitly forbidden. A similar decree was issued for the then numerous Canons of St. Augustine.

May it not be said that henceforth outsiders were taught in the schola externa, which, according to a very common idea, the monasteries conducted besides the schola interna for their own religious? Some writers have stated that most, others, that many monasteries, at least the larger ones, had such a double school. Recent historical investigation has shown that such opinions are seriously exaggerated. Denifle declared that "it must be called a grave error to say that most monasteries had a school for externs." [39] After most extensive investigations he himself had not found half a dozen. Michael, S.J., a leading authority on medieval Germany, discovered for the thirteenth century in the Empire one institution that certainly, and two others that possibly had a double school.

The best schools of the time, as has been noted, were found in the Netherlands, the schools of the Brethren of Common Life. Not a few Benedictine monasteries sent their candidates to these institutions, or sought to obtain recruits from them. The Brethren themselves in some places taught; but in most of their schools they were content to give the moral and religious training, while they entrusted the literary education to secular priests and laymen. The whole period was characterized by an increasing "secularization" in many aspects. More and more schools came into the hands of the seculars; and with this appeared another "abuse" which the "Memorial" deplores. It speaks of "a grave and pernicious abuse in the public higher schools, particularly in Italy, in which many professors of philosophy teach impious doctrines [40] . . . and in the lower schools the boys now commonly read the *Colloquies* of Erasmus, in which many things are found that lead untrained minds to impiety; hence this work and others of a similar nature should be forbidden." The teaching of impiety was a result of what has been termed the "pagan humanism," of which more later.

The actual educational situation at the end of the Middle Ages has well been described in the words of Pollen, S.J., quoted above on page two of this chapter. It seems certain that there were not enough schools at the time, and that there was a real call for a new Catholic teaching

---

[39] Denifle, *Die Universitäten des Mittelalters*, Vol. I, p. 658.

[40] In 1513, the Fifth Lateran Council had to declare that there were two men at that time who followed a false philosophy and asserted that the rational soul was mortal. The Council strictly forbade teachers to propound such errors.

body fit to supply the needs and demands of the time. This is clearly proved by the fact that as soon as the Society began to teach youths, there was a clamor from all sides for Jesuit schools. Nor was this because so many schools had been destroyed by the Reformation. The demand for Jesuit schools came from Italy, Spain, Portugal, from countries in which the Reformation had not destroyed a single school.

The Renaissance and Humanism have been mentioned. They were not in themselves hostile to religion; rather they were indifferent, much depended on their use in a good or evil direction. Not a few manifestations were distinctly neo-pagan. A large part of Renaissance art was at variance with the Christian ideal of purity. Even a few very objectionable paintings can be attributed to such great artists as da Vinci, Michelangelo and Raphael. A considerable portion of the literary productions were thoroughly pagan and are among the most immoral ever written. It is humiliating to think that men, who later became Cardinals, as Bembo and Bibbiena, had written most objectionable poems, dramas, and romances. Some of the humanists, in their excessive enthusiasm for the ancient classics, imbibed from them the pagan spirit, with disastrous consequences in their moral lives. It is not necessary to say more here, as this subject has been discussed in detail by leading historians.[41] The evil influence of this neo-paganism on education was rightly deplored by the authors of the "Memorial." Was there not need of a teaching body that would take over the educational material and methods of the time; that would teach the classics, but do it in a wholly Christian spirit, "like bees," to use an expression of some early Fathers, "gathering the wholesome honey, but avoiding the poison"? This, indeed, was the guiding spirit of the education in the numerous Jesuit schools of later days.

In many treatments of the pre-Reformation period, the morals of the people, and particularly of priests and monks, and even of nuns, occupy a very prominent place, too prominent and altogether out of proportion. Clerical immorality is often put down as one of the chief causes, if not the foremost, of the Protestant Reformation. Yet such was not the case. Luther himself declared explicitly that he rebelled because of the erroneous doctrines of the Church and not on account of its moral corruption.[42] The corruption, which no one will deny, was not universal. There were many good cardinals, bishops, priests and religious. One of the most attractive figures in medieval literature is Chaucer's "Good Parson of the Town." Now Chaucer, no flatterer of the clergy, would scarcely have represented the "Good Parson" as a type, had there not been in his mind several instances of noble secular priests. There were undoubtedly many scandals among the clergy of the later Middle Ages. But need this be

[41] See especially Pastor, *History of the Popes*, Vol. I, pp. 1–56 and Vol. V, pp. 98–180.
[42] Cf. Appendix II for Luther's statements.

surprising when one considers what has already been said about the lack of seminaries with the consequent deficiencies in religious and moral training; the intrusion into ecclesiastical positions of many, especially of the nobility, for mere material considerations; the entrance into monastic life of large numbers of young men and women without true and sincere vocations. Such defects and abuses were most emphatically condemned by ecclesiastical authorities in pre-Reformation days. The authors of the "Memorial" were exceedingly outspoken in admitting the existence of grave moral abuses among certain religious men and women; and they suggested practical remedies, even radical ones, such as the suppression of certain lax communities.

Frankly and fearlessly the "Memorial" called attention to the abuses at the Roman Curia. Only a few years previous the zealous Pope Adrian VI sadly admitted grave defects in the Curia, deploring especially the too frequent dispensations (e. g., in regard to Pluralism) and the money accepted for them and various other benefits conferred.[43] For more than a century before in councils and in books the cry had been heard for "reformation in head and members," by "head" being meant the Pope and his Curia. The troubles were of long standing; they had been exaggerated by the Avignon Exile, and much more by the Western Schism, when two Papal courts, and at one time three, asked for the religious and financial support of Christendom. Sharp and constant complaints against the Papal financial policy for a long time were undermining loyalty to the Holy See, especially in Germany. How far these criticisms were justified is hard to say, but it is certain that they were widely believed in at that time. Dr. Pastor says: "Again and again was the complaint made that chancery dues, annates, medii fructus, and consecration fees were unduly raised or unlawfully extended . . . Even men devoted to the Church and the Holy See . . . shared in the dissatisfaction, and often declared that the German grievances raised against Rome were, from a financial point of view, for the most part only too well founded." [44] Soon enemies of the Church were to use these complaints, heightening them to a national and racial grievance, as a most formidable weapon in their revolt.

There was an undeniable decline as regards the character of the Popes of the times. Not as if there had not been striking individuals among them; Alexander VI was a very gifted man and a capable administrator; Julius II, a truly kingly character; Leo X, a great patron of art and literature. But what was needed at the time was not a mere administrator, nor a warrior Pope, nor a Maecenas, but a Pontiff like St. Gregory VII, a Pope burning with zeal for the true reform of the Church. Unfortunately during the half century before the outbreak of the Reformation,

---

[43] Kidd, *Documents of the Continental Reformation*, p. 109.
[44] Pastor, *History of the Popes*, Vol. VII, p. 327.

some Popes were elected whose earlier lives, before their priestly ordination, had not been free from moral irregularities. Such were Pius II,
Innocent VIII, Julius II, all of whom had grown up under the fatal spirit
of the pagan Renaissance. The worst case is that of Alexander VI. The
very fact that such men were elected to the Papacy proves also, to say the
least, a weakening of moral tone in the electors. These unedifying facts
were widely known; gossip, not satisfied with facts, added crimes to the
existing faults of individual Popes. The report of such faults, real or
fictitious, could not but greatly weaken respect for the Papacy itself.

Other causes contributed to the decline of the Papacy. Its external influence began to dwindle in the last third of the thirteenth century. The
attack on Boniface VIII by the mercenaries of Philip IV of France, "the
crime of Anagni," was a shocking instance. The greatest harm was done
by the Western Schism, which, in the words of a French historian, almost
pushed the Church off from its rock foundation. The forty years' dispute
between two, and towards the end, three claimants of Peter's throne, the
sharp division of nations, so many for the Roman Pope, so many for the
one of Avignon, the practical impossibility of a decision, with great men,
even saints, supporting either side, all bred a widespread confusion on
the most fundamental ideas concerning the Papal power. Some began to
wonder whether one supreme head of the Church was really necessary,
or whether the Pope's primacy was of divine or ecclesiastical institution.
The situation grew worse with the advocacy of the Conciliar Theory,
which maintained the superiority of a General Council to the Pope, by
many, even by such exemplary and learned men as Cardinal D'Ailly and
John Gerson.

One reason for the development of the anti-papal views was the fact
that medieval theology, with all its excellence, had no sufficient treatment
of the doctrine of the Papacy, particularly in what concerned the primacy.
The much used *Sentences* of Peter Lombard contained no specific treatise
on the Church, nor did the *Summa* of St. Thomas. All the elements concerning the Church, the primacy of the Pope and his infallibility are
found in the *Summa*, but only incidentally mentioned and not systematically developed. This insufficient emphasis on the Papacy and the primacy
explains in part the rise of the revolutionary theories concerning the Papal
power propounded in the writings of William Occam and in the *Defensor
Pacis* of Marsiglio of Padua and Jean of Jandun, works which anticipated
some of the most radical teachings of Protestantism. Later on, a few theologians, as the Dominican Torquemada, expounded the doctrine on the
Church and the Papacy correctly and thoroughly; but as their works were
not made part of the ordinary theological training, they had little influence. One instance will show how far the confusion on the nature of the
Pope's primacy had gone. St. Thomas More testified at his examination

before the King's Council that it was only after ten years of study that he was convinced that the primacy was not of ecclesiastical but of divine origin.[45] If for a time such was the mind of one so learned as St. Thomas More, what must have been the confusion in ideas of many lesser men? Certainly it is not surprising to find Luther's bold denial of the Papacy so readily accepted by hundreds of thousands. It was the very boldness of this denial that inspired Dominican theologians, such as Catharinus, Prierias and Cardinal Cajetan, to give adequate treatment to the doctrine of the primacy. As soon as the Society was established, its members were among the most zealous defenders of the Papacy, and it may be said that the most vigorous and most successful champion of the Pope's primacy was the Jesuit theologian and Cardinal, St. Robert Bellarmine.

Aside from dogmatic misunderstandings, the Church, and the Papacy particularly, suffered much during the Middle Ages from attacks and hyper-criticism of convinced Catholics. The harsh treatment of the Popes by German emperors, French kings and Italian princes is well known. Perhaps not so well known is the incredible irreverence of the Roman people, who during the medieval times drove twenty-six Popes out of Rome, most of them good men, the last of them, the saintly Eugene IV.[46] In these ages of faith, as one French writer put it, "indeed, the old demons were only chained and not destroyed." [47] One may add, they often broke loose.

There was entirely too much faultfinding that was exaggerated, unwise, passionately bitter, and often maliciously false. Nor were the only faultfinders poets and lay chroniclers, often they were ecclesiastics, monks and friars. To mention one of many: Matthew Paris, monk of St. Albans in the thirteenth century, the foremost medieval historian of England, betrayed so astonishing an antipathy to the Mendicant Friars and above all to the Roman Curia, that Bellarmine suspected "that his first editors, the heretics of Zurich, probably had added many things which created antipathy to the Roman Church." Yet the offensive passages are in the original manuscript. The most striking instance of an unfair critic of the Popes, is that of the great poet Dante. Thoroughly orthodox, passionately devoted to the Catholic Church, and burning with zeal for the reform of abuses in the Church, yet in his unbridled passion, he became very unjust to several Popes, most of all to Boniface VIII. With terrible invective, pitilessly and ferociously, he pilloried this good, unfortunate

---

[45] Cf. Bridgett, *Bl. Thomas More*, p. 347, London (1891) for the source of More's misunderstanding.

[46] On Pope Eugene, cf. Pastor, *History of the Popes*, Vol. I, pp. 294–295.

[47] *Apologétique*, published in Paris under the direction of M. Brilland and Abbé Nedoncelle, Paris (1937) p. 581. "Certes, les vieux démons n'étaient qu'enchaînés et non détruits."

Pope, even going the length of accusing falsely this "prince of the new pharisees" of having promised absolution for a sin not yet committed.[48] "Forgiveness of future sins," later in the Protestant revolt, became a common slander to hurl against Popes, preachers of indulgences and priests in the confessional. Another reckless critic, yet a good man, was Savonarola, who on the eve of the Reformation, fearfully denounced in the pulpit Pope Alexander VI. Whatever this unfortunate Pontiff's faults were, he was still Pope and the open pulpit was not the place to air them.[49]

It will not do to pass off these exaggerated criticisms and violent denunciations as nothing but medieval humor, above the understanding of dull witted moderns. If it was humor, then the humor was certainly carried altogether too far. In the case of Dante and many others, it was not humor but personal hatred. Neither can these attacks be excused as domestic disagreements which are not felt too keenly and, anyhow, accomplish little harm. The revilings of one's own wound the deepest.[50] As to their comparative harmlessness, these harsh judgments—often false —and these bitter reproaches were to prove a veritable mine of accusations for the Protestant polemics of the two centuries following the Reformation. Some of the most revolting slanders cast up to Catholics were not the lies of Protestants, but the old calumnies of Catholics. Medieval defamers of the Popes were paraded as "witnesses to the truth." On their assertions the Protestant polemicists charged: that several Popes, among them the great Sylvester II, John XXI and Boniface VIII, had made compacts with the evil spirit; that Hildebrand (St. Gregory VII, one of the best and greatest Popes in all history) was guilty of immoral relations with the noble Countess Matilda; that the Popess Joan was a reality. Harm was done to Catholics themselves. Bitter criticism of the Popes and malicious stories retailed about them, could not but chill the hearts of many and destroy their reverence for the Papacy. Minds were prepared for the cry: "Rome is Babylon; the Pope is anti-Christ," Luther's slogan.

So devotedly attached to the Holy Father are Catholics today, that it is hard for them to conceive how certain Catholics of the period discussed could so attack Peter's successor. What has brought about this change? There was first of all a reaction against the Reformers' ferocious attacks on the Papacy and their appalling hatred of the Popes. For no matter how the proponents of the new religion differed on numerous matters of theology, on one point they all agreed, hatred of the Papacy. Catholics were

---

[48] *Inferno* XXVII, 85–120, especially 100 ff.

[49] Rickaby, in commenting on the Tenth of the Rules for Thinking with the Church in the Spiritual Exercises, says: "Here it is difficult to believe that St. Ignatius was not thinking of Savonarola."

[50] Psalm CLIV: "If my enemy had reviled me, I could verily have borne with it, but thou my intimate friend."

repelled and disgusted; by natural reaction their respect increased and a deepening affection was engendered. Among other contributing causes may not this also be enlisted, the existence of a new, widespread and powerful order, which made the defense of the Papacy one of its foremost objectives and which—an entirely new thing in history—made its professed fathers take a fourth vow, one of special obedience to the Supreme Pontiff.

The general situation was further complicated by dangerous economic conditions which caused unrest and a rebellious mood, particularly among the rural populations. The Peasants' War of 1525, for which Luther's preaching cannot escape some blame, was not the first of such agrarian revolts. Within a quarter of a century before Luther's appearance, there had been a dozen similar insurrections, although not as widespread, nor as violent as that of 1525. These uprisings were by-products of the radical changes that had occurred in agriculture, industry and commerce. To these changes many factors contributed: the desolation and loss of population, especially of agricultural workers, owing to the Hundred Years' War, the War of the Roses and similar conflicts, and to the Black Death and other widespread pestilences; the disappearance of much of medieval feudalism, with the consequent emergence of new types of land tenure, new methods of husbandry and the enclosure of large farm-areas for sheep-raising; the amalgamation of the merchant guilds and the decay of the craft guilds resulting from onerous restrictions; the steady diminution of the gold and silver supply. Limitation of space does not permit a discussion of these economic changes and of their good and evil consequences; that may be found in the many works which treat of this period.[51]

More ominous than economic distress for the welfare of the Church was royal absolutism. For a century the power of the monarchs had been steadily increasing. The anarchical quarrels of great feudal barons had been crushed out in the establishment of strong, centralized national states; the fashioners of these new political entities, the kings, achieved in the process a tremendous enlargement of their prerogatives and the elimination of almost all restrictions on their personal rule. The revival of Roman Law, in the course of the Renaissance, helped much, for one of its basic principles, the absolutism of the ruler, offered a philosophy for the new exaltation of kingly power. Whatever may have been the external manifestations of government, the actual and sole rulers of England were the Tudors, of France Francis I and Henry II, of Spain Ferdinand and

---

[51] See e. g., Janssen, *History of the German People*, Vols. I, II and particularly Vol. IV, pp. 121–369, "The Social Revolution." It is of interest to note that Capitalism began to develop in the latter part of the Middle Ages, as is proven by the history of the Welsers and Fuggers in Germany and the Chigi, Altoviti and other merchant princes in Rome. On the Chigi cf. Pastor, *History of the Popes*, VIII, 116 ff.

Isabella and later their successor, Charles V. In Germany the situation varied a bit: the Emperors were unable to obtain a strong unification and sole rule in the Empire; but the numerous petty princes in their own states ruled with as much absolutism as the mightiest of the foreign monarchs. Only one restraint on kingly power was left, the Church. But the royal absolutists strove to master the Church by usurping its prerogatives, dominating its administration and controlling its finances. The Pragmatic Sanction of Bourges and the Statutes of Provisors and Praemunire [52] are instances of royal encroachments in the ecclesiastical domain. The evils resulting from such interference have already been described in the statement of Duke George of Saxony. The time was soon to come when only the complete, unshared dominance over all things religious, would appease certain royal absolutists, even though the cost were the apostasy of whole nations.

The authors of the "Memorial," as they viewed all these evil conditions, might well have been dismayed. One modern Catholic writer has said that the Church was suffering from "hardening of the arteries." Yet this figure is wrong, for that disease is fatal, whereas the Church was soon to renew her strength. Far more appropriate for this time would be the expression of the fourteenth century St. Catherine of Siena: "the Spouse of Christ, the Church, standing emaciated with pale face, but the features were still those of the Spouse of Christ." There were signs of a great revival, a real reform; new orders were springing up, the Theatines, Barnabites and Capuchins; the old orders were regaining their pristine fervor; and a rebirth of Scholasticism had taken place in Spain. All seemed to point to a most hopeful interior reform. But at that point came the dreadful catastrophe of religious revolution, the Reformation.

It will be unnecessary for the purpose of this work to trace the course of the Protestant Revolt: the various beginnings in Germany, Switzerland, France, Scandinavia and England; the constant extension of Luther's, Zwingli's and Calvin's teachings; the tyrannical enforcement of its acceptance by Henry VIII, Gustavus Vasa and German princes, such as the rulers of Saxony, Brandenburg and Hesse. The main facts are fairly familiar to all. Suffice it here briefly to review the situation at the time of the founding of the Society of Jesus.

The Catholic Church was suffering the worst disaster in its history. In whole sections of Europe its existence had been stamped out, while in many others its disappearance seemed a certainty. Northern Germany, large areas in Southern Germany and Switzerland, Scandinavia and England were definitely lost. Almost all the rest of Germany, even the Rhineland, was doubtful territory, as were France, the Low Countries, Hun-

---

[52] Cf. John Tracy Ellis, *Anti-papal Legislation in Medieval England*, Washington (1930).

gary and Poland. Italy itself could not be counted as too safe; Spain and Portugal alone seemed certainly Catholic. Within the Catholic ranks despair, confusion and divided counsel paralyzed resistance. Everywhere the forlorn defense of the old Faith appeared to crumble before the on-slaughts of the victorious innovators. On the very points where the enemy made their main attack, justification, the Papal power, a married clergy, Catholic theologians were often unable to present a united front. Derision greeted the Papal reform programs; openly expressed scepticism challenged Paul III's call for a General Council. These very steps towards reform and a council were checkmated by the intrigues of states and the ambitions of royal privilege. It seemed as if every news from the North would bring reports of new defections to a bewildered and disorganized Catholicism.

The general moral tone was decidedly lower twenty years after the Luther revolt. The heresiarch towards the end of his life had to lament in anguish: "I am tired of this hideous Sodom. All the good which I had hoped to effect has vanished away. There remains nought but a deluge of sin and unholiness, and nothing is left for me but to pray for my discharge." His lament was echoed by Melancthon, his chief assistant: "The morals of the people, all that they do and all that they neglect to do, are becoming every day worse. Gluttony, debauchery, licentiousness, wantonness, are gaining the upper hand more and more among the people, and in a word, every one does just as he pleases." [53] Of the territories still debatable much the same might have been said; and in the safely Catholic countries too grave evils cried aloud for remedy.

On the other hand in these certainly loyal countries a better day had begun to dawn. The Counter-Reformation, or more exactly the Catholic Reformation, was already a fact in Spain; while in Italy saintly men, bent on a thorough reform, were becoming prominent and more numerous in the Curia and in the Episcopacy. In both countries the older religious orders were reviving their best ideals, and newer religious orders were beginning their salutary labors. Among these newer orders was one, which, because of its numbers, methods of training and influence, was to be even more effective in resisting the Reformation and at the same time in achieving the work of Catholic reform; it was the Society of Jesus.

This new Society, however, was not being founded for the explicit purpose of counteracting the Protestant Revolt; its purpose was a far more general one. Yet its history could not but have been influenced by the Reformation. Protestantism was essentially a rebellion against author-

---

[53] For judgments on the low morals of the lands which had accepted the Reformation, uttered by Luther, Melancthon and other Reformers, consult Janssen, *History of the German People*, Vol. XVI, pp. 8–20; also Vol. VI, pp. 520–535, and Vol. VII, p. 141 ff.

ity, hence a remedy was found in the strict obedience of the Society; the Reformers' revolt was directed above all at the Papacy, a most effective answer was to be had in the Society's absolute obedience to the Popes and in the special vow of obedience to the Holy See. The very last addition to the book of the *Spiritual Exercises* by its author, St. Ignatius, was the "Rules for Thinking with the Church," intended by him as a powerful antidote to the propaganda of the innovators. The very bitter and many-sided attack against Church and Pope necessitated a strong reply, hence the efforts of early Jesuit theologians were in a large measure in the field of controversy; one of them, St. Robert Bellarmine, is honored as the prince of controversialists. The Popes turned especially to the Society of Jesus to halt the Protestant advance. In stopping its hitherto almost ir-resistible progress, the fathers of the order gained considerable success, nay more, they reconquered large sections that appeared certainly lost. If today in Central Europe, in Germany, Switzerland, Belgium, Holland, Austria, Hungary, Bohemia and Poland, some seventy-five million Cath-olics are found, to a great extent the fact is due to the labors of the Society of Jesus.

CHAPTER II

THE MEN

From the preceding chapter it might be thought that the sixteenth century was probably the most disastrous in the history of the Catholic Church. It was, however, not all disaster. The tendency is always present to look one-sidedly and exclusively at the dark features of certain ages. This was done for centuries in regard to the Middle Ages. It is done again today in what concerns the evils of our own age. Catholics are apt to do the same in regard to the sixteenth century, the time of the terrible apostasy from the Church. They fail to think of the wonderful Catholic revival, frequently styled the *Counter-Reformation,* which more appropriately should be called the *Catholic Reformation.* Of it is true what a modern Catholic writer has said: "History has shown over and over again that bad periods are followed by happy recoveries, recoveries so glorious that the time of stagnation seems to be a sort of transitional stage, preparatory to the wondrous thing that is to be, a kind of winter sleep wherein the powers are collected, before the awakening of spring." [1]

That recovery, too little known and appreciated by Catholics, was indeed a most glorious one; a wondrous one such as could hardly have been expected from the conditions preceding it. The recovery was manifested in every phase of ecclesiastical life. There were great Popes, particularly the three reform Popes, St. Pius V, Gregory XIII and Sixtus V. In that century was held the Council of Trent which, if not the greatest of all councils, was surely one of the greatest. Its result was a true reformation in all Catholic life, intellectual, moral, religious. It was an age in which new and powerful religious orders and congregations sprang into existence: Capuchins, Jesuits, Oratorians, Ursulines, and many others. It was a period of missionary activity to pagan lands which is without parallel in the annals of the Church. Above all it was a day of saints, great and famous saints. In Church history there are three periods which are especially distinguished for the number of famous saints. The first belongs to the age of the Fathers. From 350 to 450 flourished in the East, Athanasius, Basil, Gregory of Nazianzus, Gregory of Nyssa, John Chrysostom, Cyril of Alexandria, Cyril of Jerusalem, Ephrem the Syrian; in the

---

[1] Adam, "The Spirit of Catholicism" (Transl. by Dom Justin McCann, O.S.B.), London (1929) p. 224.

West, Hilary, Ambrose, Jerome, Augustine—the greatest of all the Fathers—and Leo the Great; thirteen out of the twenty-nine Doctors of the whole history of the Church. The second period is the thirteenth century which presents the Dominicans, Dominic, Albertus Magnus and Thomas Aquinas; the Franciscans, Francis of Assisi and Bonaventure and the sweetest woman saint of the Middle Ages, Elizabeth of Hungary. The third period is from about 1530 to 1630. Foremost among the saints of this epoch are: the holy Pope Pius V—the first canonized Pope in centuries—the saintly Bishops Charles Borromeo, Thomas of Villanova— the Augustinian—and Francis de Sales; the devoted priests, Cajetan of Thiene, John of the Cross, Peter of Alcantara, Philip Neri, Vincent de Paul, that wonderful apostle of charity; among the holy women the great Theresa of Spain. The newly founded Society of Jesus gave to the Church a number of saints in this same period: Ignatius of Loyola, Francis Xavier, Francis Borgia, Peter Canisius, Robert Bellarmine, the lay-brother Alphonsus Rodriguez, and the three youthful saints, Stanislaus Kostka, Aloysius Gonzaga, John Berchmans. Truly it was an age wonderful for sanctity, in which Ignatius of Loyola founded the new order of the Society of Jesus.

St. Ignatius [2] himself was born amidst events most stirring and significant. The armies of Ferdinand and Isabella were still battling before the walls of Granada; but a few short months and this last stronghold of the Moor would fall into their hands. Then would be brought to a close the crusading epoch of Spanish history, seven hundred years and more of warring to free Spain of the Crescent's shadow. A few months further on and Columbus, guiding his three frail caravels out of Palos harbor, would open up a new epoch, grander and more glorious still. From that courageous and adventuresome spirit which was Spain's, the Saint would forge a weapon that was to combat successfully the evils which oppressed the Church at the time of his birth.

In the mountain solitudes of the province of Guipuscoa, a little to the west of the small town of Azpeitia, amidst the Spanish Basques, stood the castle of Loyola. Within its rugged walls in the year 1491 [3] a son was born to Don Beltran Yañez de Oñaz y Loyola and his lady Donna Saenz de Licona y Balda. Both were of the lower Basque nobility and for the times fairly well-to-do. Their union was blessed with several children. The new son, the last one, was baptized with the name Iñigo after a local saint, a Benedictine abbot of Oña. Later on, especially after 1537, the bearer, probably wishing to honor the martyred Bishop of Antioch, himself changed it to Ignatius. He was evidently early destined for the

---

[2] For lives of St. Ignatius cf. Bibliography.

[3] Confer Dudon, S.J., *St. Ignace de Loyola*, Paris (1934), Appendix 5, p. 613, for the dispute as to the year of the Saint's birth.

clerical state, having received the tonsure when very young. As has been pointed out in the first chapter the younger sons of the nobility were often destined by their parents for the clerical state; this was true of a brother of Ignatius and also of Francis Xavier. But the idea in Ignatius' case must have been given up, for while still young he was released from the clerical obligations. After a childhood spent in the lonely castle under a stern, if a bit worldly-minded father, at the age of thirteen he became a page in the household of a family friend, Juan Velasquez de Cuellar, Lord Treasurer for Ferdinand and Isabella. In the retinue of this important functionary he often had occasion to visit the royal court, although he never became a royal page, as is sometimes stated. His education was provided for in the household of Don Juan and was what the lads of his social standing in the Spain of those days received. As far as literary attainments went, it gave hardly more than the ability to read and write.

On the master's death, in 1517, the young man definitely adopted the profession of arms as a career, taking service with the viceroy of Navarre, the Duke of Najera, Don Antonio Manrique de Lava. Iñigo developed into a typical Spanish warrior knight, keenly responsive to the ideals of his class, ever rejoicing in the chance of conflict. Early in his soldiering career he displayed qualities of leadership in a successful restoration of the discipline of a mutinous battalion. Except for his strong Spanish faith there was not an indication of future sanctity in the wild young warrior. Father Astrain, S.J.,[4] has drawn a good pen picture of the youthful Don: "During all this period of his youth there is not noticeable in Ignatius any striking quality to mark him out from among the noble knights of his time. He possessed indeed a robust faith handed down to him from his forefathers; but as a member of a court and a soldier, he had his share of that free spirit and quarrelsome boastfulness so common in those days." A less favorable statement of his faults is made by Father J. Hungerford Pollen, S.J.:[5] "While there is no sound basis for believing him to have been sunk in vice and shameless excesses, it would seem that in the heat of youth and amid the fires of temptation, he was sometimes carried into sins of lust, pride and passion." The last is confirmed by the statements of men who knew him most intimately: Gonzales, Laynez and Polanco, his personal secretary for years.

An active and honored career following the standard of his sovereign, Charles V, on European battlefields or extending that monarch's sway over far distant lands with the conquistadores, apparently was marked out for this younger son of Don Beltran. Whatever were the dreams of

---

[4] Astrain, *A Short Life of St. Ignatius Loyola*, (Eng. trans. by Hull), London (1928), p. 2.

[5] Pollen, *St. Ignatius Loyola*, New York (1922), p. 6.

his youthful fancy, they were soon rudely shattered. The celebrated revolt of the Communeros in Castile drained the old kingdom of Navarre
of all available troops. The weakened defenses offered Francis I the long-
sought opportunity of wresting all of Navarre from Spanish rule. Accordingly in 1521 a French force of 12,000 under André de Foix pushed forward towards the meagerly garrisoned Pamplona. Resistance was so
useless that the townspeople and many of the soldiers were for surrender;
indeed the magistrates opened the city gates to the French. The citadel
held out. There was no surrender there, for a hot-headed young knight,
Iñigo de Loyola, inspirited the reluctant garrison to resist to the last
extremity. Worldly-minded though the caballero was, yet in one incident
he manifested a deep faith, making his confession, in the absence of a
priest, to a lay companion, a practice not uncommon in the Middle Ages.
The French moved in assault against the fortress, but with no success. The
besieged soldiers put up a stubborn resistance, urged on by the sight of
Don Iñigo sword in hand ranging through their ranks, now encouraging
them by brave words, now leading them in person. But at length the
valiant young leader fell, brought low by a cannon ball that fractured
his left leg and slightly wounded his right. With Iñigo's fall, resistance
collapsed and Pamplona's citadel was in the hands of the French.

The victors in admiration of the bravery of the wounded don treated
him most courteously, even permitting his transportation to his brother's
castle, for recuperation from his wounds. The period of convalescence
was considerably prolonged by Iñigo's insistence on a resetting of his
injured left leg. The leg had been poorly set the first time. To remedy
the defect, the limb had to be rebroken and a piece of protruding bone
sawed away. The young soldier bore the excruciating agony without a
murmur or a sign, except a desperate clenching of his hands. Such was
the strain, that the fever resulting almost carried him off. After receiving
the Last Sacraments he rallied and the crisis was passed, but long weeks
of lying abed stretched out before him. He was to carry a limp to his
grave. To while away the endless hours, he asked for something to read,
some of the romances then so popular in Spain, such as *Amadis of Gaul*.
There were none to be had among the few books which the remote castle
of Loyola possessed. In fact only two books were available: a Spanish
translation of the *Life of Christ* by the Carthusian Ludolph of Saxony,
and another Spanish translation, that of the *Flos Sanctorum* of Jacopo
de Voragine, a popular medieval collection of lives and legends of the
saints. There was nothing else, so perforce Iñigo had to read them. After
a while they did not prove such bad entertainment and gradually his
interest was intrigued by the combats of God's warriors. The worldling,
however, was still strong in him, for he would lay aside his reading to
dream by the hour of deeds of valor performed by him for the honor of

a very noble lady. Whether the lady really existed or was a mere fictional creation of his thought, cannot be determined. But regularly he would come back to reality, and the emptiness of his day dreams would dawn upon him. Then Ludolph's work or the *Flos Sanctorum* would be perused more intently than before. Grace worked slowly but gradually; and as he came to recognize in St. Dominic and St. Francis forthright heroes, the convalescent soldier experienced an ever growing desire to imitate their achievements. His moods still varied on occasions, but at length his determination was sealed, he would devote himself completely to God's service. He was the veriest tyro in the things of the spirit. Nevertheless, slowly and in small ways, even at this stage, he was developing that spiritual discernment which later was to make him such a master of the interior life, the author of the golden "Rules for the Discernment of Spirits" in *The Spiritual Exercises*. The life of penance first appealed to him. It was the only one he knew, and he was keenly conscious of the need of reparation for his own misdeeds. So his thoughts were filled with designs for fasting, disciplines, abstinences, and above all a pilgrimage to Jerusalem. After that there was to be a Carthusian's cell at Seville.

Recovery completed, Iñigo set forth on what for him was his knightly, albeit spiritual quest. His first goal was the renowned Catalonian shrine of Our Lady of Montserrat, not far from Barcelona. Three days were spent there in seclusion, during which, with sentiments of deepest contrition, he made a minute general confession of his whole life to a prudent Benedictine, Dom Juan de Chanones. The heroes of the chivalrous romances usually spent the night before receiving the order of knighthood in prayerful vigil before the altar. This young knight of God would begin his service of his divine Master in a similar fashion. On the vigil of the Assumption, August 14, 1522, having divested himself of his worldly attire, he put on a long tunic of rough hemp with a rope girdle, the uniform of a beggar. Thus arrayed he betook himself to the shrine which held the time-honored picture of our Lady; then after hanging up his sword and jewelled dagger by the altar, he prayed through the whole night.

When the morning came, he fortified himself with Holy Communion and commenced the first steps of his new life. In the nearby town of Manresa, on its outskirts, were some caves where he planned to spend a while in penance and prayer. To the little town then he betook himself; in one of its hospitals, that of Santa Lucia, he found a dwelling-place. Part of his time he devoted to caring for the sick, part to begging, but the greatest share was given to his devotions in the caves. Possibly with little concept of it, St. Ignatius was entering into a novitiate of spirituality. He was to be led through all manner of spiritual experiences; only by the most agonizing mistakes was he to learn heavenly wisdom and moderation. In the beginning, his only notion of holiness seems to have been that of external penances. He practised appalling austerities and underwent great fasts and abstinences. The pious people of the town began to notice him, and they were not long in coming to the realization that beneath the beggar's apparel was hidden not only a noble but a saintly heart as well.

At first his soul overflowed with spiritual joys and consolations; whatever temptations assailed him he found no difficulty in overcoming. After a while he began to experience dryness, weariness, sadness and bitterness of soul. It all puzzled the neophyte, but he persevered. These initial trials were but preludes to the fierce spiritual storms which now assailed him and almost brought him to the very brink of despair. Agonies of doubts and scruples over his past confessions drove him frantic; try as he would, he could attain to no peace of soul. He frequently confessed to a learned and wise Dominican friar, but his repeated accusations brought no surcease to his terrible uncertainties. The Dominicans of the Manresa convent, moved by pity at his unfortunate state, took him in, offering him a cell in their house. But the end was not yet. In fact his worries so increased and despair so gripped him that at one time he was sorely tempted to self-destruction. In his inexperience he attempted to bring his trials to an end by continuous fasting and prayer, only to bring himself to death's door. His confessor intervened with drastic orders of obedience. At length by unswerving faithfulness to the orders of this director, he passed through his trials to peace of soul, a peace which never afterwards left him. After the storms had gone, Ignatius received gifts of contemplation in a high degree, spiritual illuminations, a deep knowledge of divine mysteries and of the science of souls. Later on he was to affirm confidently that "he thought to himself that even if no Holy Scriptures had been given us to teach us the truths of faith, he would nevertheless have determined to give up life itself for them, solely on account of what he had seen within the soul." Once he confided to Laynez, one of his companions and his successor in the generalate of the Society of Jesus, that at Manresa he had learned more in the course of an hour than all the ages of the world could have taught him. It was not in boasting that he thus spoke, for he was notably reticent about all his spiritual experiences.

Great fruits came from Manresa. The first was the book of the *Spiritual Exercises*. Ignatius from time to time wrote down his thoughts that they might be of profit to others; gradually out of these notes grew that remarkable book of asceticism, the *Spiritual Exercises*. In a later chapter more will be said about its nature and method. It will be sufficient here to note that it was the product of his experiences with temptations and of his enlightenments by mystical favors. Most of the book, the chief meditations at least, was composed in the last months at Manresa. Later on some complementary parts, such as "The Rules for Thinking with the Church," were added. The essence of the *Spiritual Exercises* was the immediate product of Manresa. The second great fruit was a personal one, intimately connected with the first, namely the asceticism of St. Ignatius. It was a spirituality capable of the highest mysticism, and yet perfectly adapted to the capacities of the ordinary soul. It was a sane asceticism; his own painful excesses had taught Ignatius an enduring moderation. One of its most characteristic qualities was an intense personal love for Jesus. Loyola so often and so vividly meditated on the life of the Saviour that in his prayer he practically lived again the scenes of Christ's sojourn on earth. There was nothing that he recommended more insistently to souls than the cultivation of this intimate knowledge and lively personal attachment to Christ our Lord.

The third great fruit of Manresa may be said to have been the Society of Jesus. It cannot be maintained, as a later incorrect tradition would have it, that in the cave of Manresa Ignatius knew clearly and certainly that he was to be the founder of the Jesuit Order. But it is true that in the midst of his visions and spiritual experiences the idea of a group working for God in some way presented itself to him. Many things were made known to him, the significance of which he did not then fully comprehend; later on when he was actually organizing his order, their complete meaning dawned upon him. Consequently when writing the Constitutions, his frequent answer to those who questioned him about what they thought were novelties, was that "he had seen it in Manresa." In that sense Manresa may be considered the cradle of the Society of Jesus.

In the last months at Manresa, his fears and worries banished, Ignatius progressed far in the spiritual life. With the return to health he began to think of the pilgrimage to Jerusalem, something he had longed for from the very first days of his conversion. His personality demanded activity; much as he admired the contemplatives, he came to realize that their life was simply not meant for him. A year passed and he was off for Palestine, garbed as the poorest peasant pilgrim, supporting himself on the way by the alms he begged. From Barcelona he took shipping for Italy, landing at Gaeta. From there he pushed on direct to Rome, where he arrived March 28, 1523. His two weeks' stay in the Eternal City with a round of visits to the various shrines, was climaxed by the blessing of the venerable Pope Adrian VI. One would like to fancy that the grand old reforming Pope by some intuitive recognition picked out from the midst of pilgrims the man who later on was to do so much to carry into effect his own baffled plans. Ignatius' plans took him to Venice where he hoped to obtain passage. His hopes were pretty well dashed when he arrived at the city of lagoons. Two months before, Rhodes had fallen, and now the Mohammedan fleets swept the whole Levant. Most of the pilgrims whom Ignatius accosted were returning or were abandoning their venture. Scarcely one could be met possessing hardihood enough to venture forth on a journey that had every prospect of ending on the rowing banks of Turkish galleys. The former defender of Pamplona refused to be disheartened by evil chance. At length he found a place on an east-bound ship and July 14, 1523 left Venice behind.

Almost two months later, on September 4, the Holy City lay stretched before him; hastening on he passed through the gates of his sacred Jerusalem. With extraordinary devotion and consolation the pilgrim spent long hours in meditation at the tomb of the Redeemer and at every other spot connected by tradition with the Saviour's life. Deeper and deeper developed that personal intimate love of Jesus; more vividly than ever could he now recall the circumstances and events of his Master's sojourn on earth. For a month and a half he stayed in the Holy Land; gladly would he have remained for life. In those days an apostolate among the Mohammedans was much in his thoughts. But the Franciscan Superior, who had jurisdiction over all the Latin Christians in Palestine, decided otherwise, and wisely too. He recognized the zeal of the saintly pilgrim, but just as clearly perceived that it was too inexperienced and too intemperate in the face of the constant threat of Mohammedan fanaticism. Ignatius promptly obeyed an order to return to Europe, refusing even to glance at the document showing the Provincial's official powers. In January 1524 he was back in Venice and two months later once again in Barcelona.

With his pilgrimage completed what steps would he now take to carry out his part in God's service? First of all he must obtain a good education, his experiences had taught him that. Yet he was thirty-two, with literary attainments that amounted to little more than the ability to read and write. Undismayed he set himself to study Latin grammar, taking his place on the benches of a boys' school in Barcelona. It was a desperately heroic course, for it required real courage for a slow thinking ex-soldier to wrestle with the difficulties of the Latin grammar in the midst of nimble-witted lads young enough to be his sons. For two years he kept doggedly at his humiliating task, hoping to get enough command of Latin to enable him to follow philosophical lectures at some Spanish university.

His master, at length satisfied that Ignatius had attained the necessary modicum, advised him to enter the University of Alcalá. This seat of learning, but recently founded by the great Spanish scholar and reformer, Cardinal Ximenes, was in the first vigor of its youth and enjoyed a high reputation. Ignatius, as inept in scholastic matters as he had been in spiritual ways before Manresa, had to learn wisdom in intellectual pursuits similarly by sad experience. In his desire to complete the preparations for his ministry as quickly as possible, he undertook a program of studies out of all proportion to his abilities. He studied philosophy from Soto's *Terms*, physics from St. Albertus Magnus' work, and theology from the book of Peter Lombard. Of course he did poorly and did not progress very far towards his goal, the priesthood.

Both at Barcelona and at Alcalá, Ignatius devoted his free time to apostolic labors, sometimes overdoing them to the detriment of his studies. He lived on alms, taking up his dwelling in a hospital. He taught little children their catechism, gave the Spiritual Exercises to adults, and devoted himself to works of fraternal charity. An important step was taken when he began to seek companions for his enterprise in God's service. Three young men joined him at Barcelona; they followed him to Alcalá, where a fourth youth associated himself with the little group. All wore a common costume, a coarse brown robe, whence they earned the nickname from the common people, "Ensaylados," "Men of the Sackcloth." Some little success rewarded their pious efforts and several good people made Ignatius their confidant. But there had to be opposition, too. The Spaniards of those days, so touchy in matters of Faith, could hardly let pass the spectacle of students strangely garbed, with little learning, entering into theological and spiritual problems. On too many occasions in other lands, similar groups had harbored secret heretics. Suspicions began to be aroused, and it was whispered about that these queer "Ensaylados" were really secret emissaries of the "Alumbrados," fanatical sectaries who held a doctrine of Illuminism and had but recently appeared in Northern Spain. Yet there were not wanting defenders for the ex-soldier and his companions. The suspicions prevailed at length, and Ignatius found himself denounced to the courts of the Inquisition. The judicial process resulted in a complete exoneration from any charges of heresy. After forty days of imprisonment he was released. But cautious Spanish suspicions would not down and three months later a fresh process was instituted, from which again Ignatius came forth with his views and practices vindicated. Before a month was out, charges were again preferred against him, and this time he was lodged in jail for forty-two days. A very searching examination was made of his words and his works. At the end, without any reflection on his doctrine or his character, he was ordered to change his dress for the ordinary garb of the students of Alcalá and to refrain from teaching truths of Faith until he acquired more theology. The same demands were imposed upon his comrades.

The second part of the instructions bore hardest upon Ignatius' zeal and he thought of moving elsewhere to another University. However, he would not act without taking counsel, so towards the end of June he presented himself to the Archbishop of Toledo, Alfonso de Fonseca. The prelate received him kindly and, after listening to his story, advised him to try the University of Salamanca. Ignatius followed his advice, bringing his little group to Salamanca in July or August 1527. Peace was not to be found here either. The sight of unlearned men, strangely garbed, holding forth on matters of Faith and Morals, was also too much for the worthy citizens of this university town. Once again Ignatius was summoned to defend his words and his actions before a tribunal of three Doctors. They questioned him on his teachings, on his knowledge of theology, and on the book of the *Spiritual Exercises*. The three judges marveled at the wisdom of his answers to their questions which had touched upon abstruse points of theology. They knew him to be poorly educated. What were they to do? Condemnation of the doctrine was out of the question; his views satisfied the strictest orthodoxy. But approval of his actions was hardly possible. After twenty-one days in prison, Ignatius was called before them for sentence. They declared him to be innocent in life and orthodox in doctrine, but they ordered him for the future not to meddle in intricate problems of theology. This command was too much for Ignatius. Rather than disobey, he preferred to leave Salamanca, and Spain too, for it was evident to him that in his native land as things then stood he could accomplish little for the good of souls. Considering the circumstances of the times, and in particular the great religious revolutions then going on in many parts of Europe, these Spanish judges scarcely could have acted otherwise than they did. Ordinary men, they were bound to take ordinary precautions. That they failed to recognize a saint is nothing to their discredit.

Ignatius turned his thoughts towards the University of Paris, then the first of all centers of ecclesiastical learning. He talked over his ideas with his companions, and it was decided that he should go ahead of the others to Paris. When he made suitable arrangements, they were to follow. Twenty days after his release, he packed up his books and set off for Barcelona. There his friends, when they heard of his plans, tried to dissuade him, pointing out the dangers from the hostile armies of the French and the Spaniards engaged in one of their frequent wars. Hostile armies had little terrors for the old soldier, so he took the road to Paris, where he arrived February 2, 1528.

At Paris Ignatius began his philosophical studies all over again. The time at Alcalá and Salamanca with impossible schedules, distractions and trials, had been practically wasted. Experienced now, he did not again overburden himself, but patiently and systematically set about his task of acquiring knowledge sufficient to gain a master's degree. He even planned on eventually obtaining the doctorate. For full seven years he worked away at the courses in the University. They were seven years of heroism. What hours and hours of laborious toil did he not have to spend at his advanced age to keep up with younger and keener minds! Then too, his subsistence depended on the alms he begged. That this begging might not interfere with his studies, he tried to accumulate at one time enough to support himself for a year. Thus during summer vacations, he tramped off to Flanders to ask the charity of the wealthy Spanish merchants doing business in Bruges or Antwerp. One year he even crossed over the Channel to seek aid from his countrymen in London. After a while these expatriated merchants perceiving the merits of their fellow Spaniard sent on their help to him in Paris. Sickness too proved an obstacle to his academic advancement; eventually it forced him to relinquish his desire for the doctorate. For the sake of his studies he diminished much of his public activities for souls. Yet even what he did brought him into trouble and persecution. Charges of heresy were brought against him; but when the process was completed, the inquisitors, Matthaeus Ori, O.P. and Thomas Laurentius, O.P., gladly vindicated his orthodoxy. Laurentius in examining the book of the *Spiritual Exercises* was so delighted with what he found therein that he requested of Ignatius a personal copy for himself.

After a year and a half of humanistic studies at the College of Montaigu, Ignatius followed philosophical lectures given by a learned and pious Spaniard, Dr. Juan de la Pena. In Lent of 1533, his course was completed to the extent that he was awarded the master's degree. Two years more were devoted to theology; but weak health brought an end to his scholastic career, forcing him to leave Paris for Spain to seek rest and recovery in his native air. Ignatius never acquired great erudition, still he managed to attain to a fair modicum of learning. From his experience in the three universities, especially in Paris, he obtained a practical knowledge of scholastic organization which was to be of service later on when he came to establish the colleges of his order. Laynez has well characterized the intellectual attainments of Ignatius: "As to study, although Ignatius met with more difficulties than others, yet with his great diligence, he reaped fruit, *ceteris paribus*, equal to or greater than that of his fellow students; he reached an ordinary average in letters, as he showed in his replies in public discussions and in private conversations with his fellow students."

One of Ignatius' reasons in coming to Paris was to prepare a place for the four companions he had left behind in Salamanca. In his absence, however, their interest had waned and eventually they abandoned his leadership. His first attempt at securing co-laborers was thus a failure. Nor was his second attempt, made in Paris, any more successful. In 1529 he won over to his plans three young Spanish students, de Castro, de Peralta and Amador. They made the Spiritual Exercises under his guidance and were so moved that they determined on embracing a life of evangelical perfection. They distributed their possessions among the poor and began to beg alms for their subsistence. Then relatives stepped in, storming and threatening at "such foolish goings-on." When menaces and admonitions failed to move the young fellows, force was resorted to, and an armed band carried off the youths from the Hospital of St. James, where they had taken their lodgings. The law was laid down to them; until they had finished their studies at least, they must live as befitted gentlemen of their station. The pressure of family and surroundings proved too strong, and gradually the three youths forgot their holy ambitions. Ignatius might well have been discouraged. Manresa was seven years behind him and he had little to show, no doctor's degree, no companions and few prospects of ever fulfilling his dreams for God's service.

The change for the better came in that very same year, 1529, when Ignatius made the friendship of two highly chosen souls, the first members of the little band of Parisian students who were to form the nucleus of his future order. When Ignatius began his philosophical studies, he took up his residence in the College of Saint Barbara; there he sought among the students for a tutor who would help him over the difficulties of scholasticism, so hard for one of his age and paucity of training. He found his tutor, and not only a tutor but a faithful friend, his first real companion, in a young Savoyard, Peter Faber (more exactly Favre or le Fevre). Peter Faber was born of humble peasant stock at Villaret (Haute Savoie) in 1506. As a lad he tended his flocks of sheep, and it seemed that he was destined to do so for life; but such evidence did he give of deep piety and intellectual keenness that means were found to send him to the University of Paris. In 1525 he began his philosophical studies and in 1530 he gained the Licentiate. His intellectual attainments were of a high order, but much more remarkable was his virtue. In the midst of all the looseness of Paris student life (conditions in the University through the Middle Ages were frequently pretty bad) Peter lived on faithful to the teachings of his childhood, his life being as pure as the mountain streams of his native land. He was blessed too with a singularly loving and beautiful disposition; indeed of all the Jesuit Saints and Beati, his personality is the most charming. The young Savoyard peasant was at once impressed with the humility of the former Spanish captain, nor was he long in recognizing the worth of the man who so patiently sought his aid. Confidences grew and before long Faber disclosed to his friend the secrets and problems of his soul. Ignatius advised him to make a general confession, to frequent the Sacraments weekly, which in those days was extraordinary, and to make a daily examination of conscience. In the next two years, 1530–1532, Faber achieved marvelous progress spiritually. At last Ignatius was convinced that now he had the co-laborer whom he had sought, and so he disclosed his plans to the saintly young ecclesiastic: the pilgrimage to Jerusalem and the life spent in service of God for souls. The generous-hearted Faber responded enthusiastically. Ordination to the priesthood was conferred on him in 1534; thus he was to be the first priest of the Jesuit order. In the next year, 1535, he made the complete Spiritual Exercises. Until his death Faber preserved his beautiful, lovable character, gracing a life exceptional for piety and zeal. Truly apostolic was his spirit of prayer. It was his custom on approaching a city to address himself to the angel guardians of the town and of the inhabitants. All his later life he kept a list of seven persons and seven cities to be the special objects of his prayers; Luther, Bucer and Melancthon were among the persons, Wittenberg stood first on the list of towns.

Somewhat previous to his meeting with Ignatius, Peter Faber had made the acquaintance and formed a firm friendship with another Basque noble, also a student of Saint Barbara, Francis Xavier. Their friendship ripened into deep attachment; they shared the same room, and together they received the master's degree. Francis Xavier was born on April 7, 1506 in the castle of Xavier, near Sanguesa in Navarre. His parents were Don Juan de Jassu and Donna Maria de Azpilcueta, both of noble blood and excellent in character. The father, as President of the Royal Council of the King of Navarre, served his sovereign loyally in evil days as in good. Francis' meager prospects as the youngest son were diminished by the disasters which came upon his family in consequence of their faithfulness to the unfortunate King of Navarre. They were still further jeopardized by the death of the father when Francis was still a small child. The only avenue of opportunity left to him was in a learned profession. Such a career was in accord with his natural tastes and, ever ambitious to better his fortunes, he embraced it, choosing to make his studies at Paris, the leading university of the time. The year 1528 found him enrolled as a student on the lists of the College of Saint Barbara. Possessed naturally of a strong character, he was still further blessed in making the friendship of Peter Faber; for the influence of the pure-hearted Savoyard must have helped much to preserve him from contamination by the baser elements of the university life. The greater danger for him lay in his tremendously ambitious nature. He was quite influenced by the literary vanities of the Renaissance; once caught up by some of the forces of Humanism, he might have ended as a rather worldly ecclesiastic. Nor were all his acquaintances as orthodox as his faithful Savoyard friend might have wished. There were several proud, heretical minds among the students, and in the ranks of the professors there were holders of various dangerous opinions. Given Xavier's determination and untiring energy, there was no telling whether or not another Calvin might have been developed. It was Ignatius of Loyola who determined it otherwise. At first Xavier rather disapproved of Faber's new-found friend, especially when the shabby ex-soldier sought openings for pious discussions. Ignatius persisted, for there never was a better judge of men; and if it depended on him he would not lose this brilliant fellow country-man. It was a long, difficult struggle; later on the master admitted that Xavier was the hardest material he had ever had to handle. When the young scholar obtained a small lectureship in the College of Beauvais, there was not a more enthusiastic admirer than Ignatius; and his admira-tion took the very practical turn of recruiting students for Xavier's classes. At length persistent kindness won and Ignatius possessed the heart of Xavier. Then could he arouse that brilliant, enthusiastic soul to a higher learning, the intimate knowledge and love of God. Francis went through the Spiritual Exercises and placed himself unreservedly in the hands of Ignatius.

In 1532 new companions came in the persons of two Spanish university men. The elder of the pair, for they presented themselves together, was James Laynez, born at Almazan (Soria) in 1512. It is worth noting that this Spaniard, who was later to be so highly prized by Ignatius, to be one of the outstanding figures at the Council of Trent, and to be the second General of the Order, was one quarter of Jewish blood. Laynez made his earlier studies at Alcalá where in 1532 he took the master's degree. At Alcalá he had known Ignatius by sight, but had never made his acquaint-ance. The younger man was Alonso Salmeron, born at Toledo in 1515. He was gifted with exceptional scholarly talents, which marked him out at Alcalá where he made his course. At the university he met and became a fast friend of Laynez. Both had become deeply interested in the rumors and opinions concerning Ignatius which were current in Alcalá. They decided to see for themselves in Paris, where they also hoped to finish their studies. The very first one whom they met as they dismounted from their horses was the object of their quest. A very short time convinced them that their man deserved all the good accounts which they had heard of him. Both offered themselves to Ignatius to be his companions.

About the same time another recruit was gained in a young Portuguese student, Simon Rodriguez de Azevedo, born at Voucella in the diocese of Vizeu. He was a scholar of the King of Portugal who had been so im-pressed by his talents and virtues that he sent him at royal expense to Paris. When Rodriguez met Ignatius he was in considerable quandary as to the type and state of life in which his ardent nature could best fulfil God's service. When the latter unfolded his own plans to him, the young Portuguese recognized that here was his vocation and placed himself unreservedly under Ignatius' guidance. Still another follower was found in a Spanish student by name Nicholas Alfonso, commonly known as Bobadilla after his birthplace, Bobadilla del Camino in the diocese of Valencia, where he was born in 1507. After some studies at Valladolid and Alcalá, he came to Paris to pursue a course at the university. Having heard that help and support in his studies might be obtained from a fellow countryman, named Ignatius of Loyola, he sought him out. Touched by the generous response that met his request, before long Bobadilla was captivated by the remarkable personality of his benefactor. The circle of the first companions was now completed; they were all to remain faithful, though in later years Rodriguez and Bobadilla were to cause the founder considerable vexation. These first companions of St. Ignatius have thus been characterized by a Protestant historian: "a timid Savoyard, Faber; the influential Portuguese, Rodriguez; four Spaniards, the proud and heroic Xavier, the prudent, statesmanlike James Laynez, the learned Salmeron, the impetuous Bobadilla."

Frequent contact with their spiritual captain left the new companions more than ever impressed with his comprehension of God's service and his burning zeal for souls. Daily they became more and more attached to him. On his part he began to shape and mold their characters. In giving the Spiritual Exercises to Faber as a preparation for the latter's ordination, Ignatius initiated his first companion into his plans, in which the conversion of Mohammedans still played a large part. Later he discussed these plans with the others of the group. All responded most enthusiastically. However, their courses at the university were not yet completed and wisely they determined to remain three years longer at Paris that they might be more thoroughly prepared for future labors. Such a practical decision must have had the direction of Ignatius' experience behind it.

That their plans might not go awry for want of certainty and stability, the companions determined to bind themselves by vows of poverty and chastity, as well as by a third obligation of making a pilgrimage to Jerusalem and of spending the rest of their lives in apostolic labors. Always practical, they further proposed that until their studies were completed their poverty would not preclude possessions sufficient for their support. They determined, moreover, that after ordination their vow should forbid the acceptance of any stipends for works of the sacred ministry. As regards the vow of pilgrimage, the recurrent Turkish wars might prevent its fulfillment. They planned therefore to wait for a year at Venice for shipping; if then the journey proved impossible, they were to go to Rome and offer themselves to the Holy Father for any work to which he might assign them.

The vows were taken on the Feast of the Assumption, August 15, 1534. Early in the morning of that day, Ignatius and his six companions left the city, walking out to the hill of Montmartre, the traditional site of the martyrdom of St. Denis. In the Martyr's chapel, possessed by the Benedictine nuns, they knelt in prayer around the altar, while Peter Faber, the only priest among them, celebrated the Holy Sacrifice. When Communion time came, he turned around and faced them, holding up to them the Sacred Host. Each in turn, beginning with Ignatius, read out to the hidden Christ the formula of the vows. Then Faber gave Holy Communion to each one. He turned back to the altar, read out his own formula, and administered the Holy Sacrament to himself. It was a momentous day in the lives of all the little band. It was as momentous in the life of the Society of Jesus, for on that day were laid the first, if remote, foundations of the order.

The following year on the feast of the Assumption, the companions reassembled in the same chapel to renew their vows. Ignatius alone was not present, for the condition of his health necessitated a sojourn in his native land. On the second anniversary three others knelt with them, Claude Le Jay, Paschase Broët and Jean Codure. Le Jay was a Savoyard, born in 1504 at Mieussy in the diocese of Geneva. He was a friend of Faber and after his own ordination followed him to Paris for further studies. In 1534 he received the Master of Arts degree and was introduced to Ignatius whose followers he straightway joined. At the first renewal of vows in 1535, Le Jay took his place with the little group and pronounced his own vows for the first time. Paschase Broët was a Picard, born at Bretancourt in 1500. His studies were first made at Amiens after which he was ordained in 1523. For ten years he labored as a priest in his native Picardy, then he decided on coming to Paris for further studies. Through Le Jay he was brought into the little group, pronouncing his vows at the renewal of 1536. On that day also another made his first oblation; he was Jean Codure, born in 1508 at Seyne in Provence. Both the philosophical and theological studies of Codure were made at Paris. At the university he came to know Peter Faber, who directed him in making the Spiritual Exercises. He was not yet a priest when he joined himself to the companions. With Ignatius the little group now numbered ten.

Ignatius in 1535 was in Spain trying to regain his shattered health. Going first to his native town of Azpeitia, he stayed there three months, lodging at the Magdalen Hospital in preference to his brother's castle of Loyola. Even in this period of recuperation he could not refrain from preaching to the peasantry, who flocked in such numbers to hear him that the sermons had to be delivered in the open fields. When he felt well enough to travel again, Ignatius visited various cities in the peninsula arranging and settling up the personal affairs of his companions in view of their new status under a vow of poverty. With this business completed, he departed from his native land for Italy, planning to await there his companions' arrival to join him on the pilgrimage to Jerusalem. While sojourning at Bologna, he attempted to resume his studies for the doctorate at the ancient university, but a recurring sickness forced him to relinquish the idea. There was nothing left to do but to set off for Venice, the rendezvous. Once established in the city of the lagoons, he gave himself over to the care of souls. Under his direction several prominent personages made the Spiritual Exercises; one of them Diego de Hoces, a learned Spaniard, joined him as a recruit.

Meanwhile in Paris the companions continued their studies. The fact that they persevered in unity despite the absence of their leader augured well for the future, for their only common bond was the fact that they had taken upon themselves similar obligations. At length, late in 1536 all agreed to tarry no longer in Paris. Though it was winter they resolved to set out for Italy. It was an extremely hazardous journey that lay before them: the passes of the Alps were blocked by snowstorms, and the way passed through country infested by warring bands of the French and the Spanish-Imperial armies. On November 15 they started out and after two months of incredible hardships entered Venice to find Ignatius waiting to greet them.

There was no prospect of a passage to Palestine until the summer. So the group turned to works of charity for the unfortunates of Venice. They devoted themselves especially to the care of the sick in the Hospital of the Incurables and in the Hospital of St. Paul. The attention of the Venetians was soon attracted by the sanctity and zeal of these young ecclesiastics. The attention was not entirely favorable. The old suspicions and calumnies began to circulate once more. Ignatius was denounced to the authorities, but with the usual result, a complete exoneration. In the early spring all but Ignatius set out for Rome to obtain the Papal permission for their journey to the Holy Land, to request leave for ordination for those of their number who were not yet priests, and to lay their future plans before the Pope. Ignatius decided against going to Rome himself, thinking that his presence would be hurtful to the general plan. There were two influential men at Rome, whom he considered as likely to be unfavorable to anything with which he was connected. He had had trouble with each. One was the Cardinal Caraffa, the great reformer, and later Pope Paul IV, and the other was Doctor Juan Ortiz, an important Spanish diplomatic official. At Venice Ignatius had met Cardinal Caraffa, who with St. Cajetan had founded in 1524 the Theatines, the first order of Clerks Regular; Caraffa was most anxious for Ignatius to join his group to the new order, and was quite displeased when he refused to do so. Both had at heart the same thing, the reform of the Church, but they sought it in different ways. At Rome things turned out much better than had been expected. A good welcome awaited the companions, especially from Dr. Ortiz whom they found completely changed and most eager to help them at the Papal court. Nor was the stern Caraffa unfavorable. Pope

Paul on his part, anxious to learn more about these young students, invited them to hold a disputation with some of the Roman theologians in his presence. The Pope was much pleased and impressed with the learning and deportment of the companions. He gladly granted their petitions and dismissed them with his blessings and an alms for their pilgrimage.

After the return to Venice, those who were not priests prepared themselves for their ordination. On June 24, 1537, the feast of St. John the Baptist, Ignatius, Xavier, Salmeron, Rodriguez, Bobadilla, and Codure received the Sacrament of Holy Orders from the hands of Bishop Nigusanti of Arbi. Further days of retreat were spent in preparation for their first Mass, which all but Ignatius celebrated on September 11. He was to wait until the Christmas of 1538. The pilgrimage to Jerusalem was next in order. But of this there was still no prospect; the war between Venice and Turkey had cleared the seas of all Venetian shipping. The companions continued their spiritual retreat at places separated from each other but in close proximity to Venice, so that they would be within easy call if a ship were at last obtained. After a short while, when it became evident that the chances of sailing were remote, Codure came to Vicenza to discuss with Ignatius, Faber and Laynez the advisability of the companions devoting themselves to works of the public ministry during their period of waiting. All responded enthusiastically and armed with faculties from the Nuncio Varallo they distributed themselves throughout the Venetian territory. They walked boldly into the principal streets and squares of the towns, wherever they could congregate a crowd. Waving their hats in the air and crying out invitations to hear the word of God, they preached to the assembled citizens. At first the people greeted the stumbling Italian of these foreigners with derisive laughter, but before long the spirit of the men won the hearts of the simple folk and their preaching bore fruit. Thus the companions began the first apostolic work of the Society of Jesus.

When the year 1537 drew to a close and there was still no hope of peace between Venice and the Sultan Soliman, the obligation of their pilgrimage ceased. The other alternative, the offering of themselves unconditionally to the Pope, called for consideration. It was decided that Ignatius, Faber and Laynez should go to Rome to find out how the situation stood and to make whatever preparations were necessary. The others in the meantime were to betake themselves to the various university towns of Northern Italy, there to devote themselves to the apostolic works of preaching and hearing confessions. They were not to neglect the opportunity of seeking recruits if any of the students appeared favorable to their plans. This last brought up the question as to what name they should bear in case they were asked who they were. In Paris they had been called Iniguistae. Would they retain that name now? Ignatius settled the matter by promptly replying, "You will say that you belong to the Company of Jesus, that will be our name." So originated the name of the new order. So it has remained, despite some attempts to change it, to the present day. Ignatius had in mind by the word "Company" a spiritual organization similar to the military companies in the wars of the late Middle Ages. Usually such companies called themselves after the soldier who led them; the new spiritual soldiers were followers of Christ, under His banner they fought, to Him they were entirely devoted, by His name should their regiment be known. In translating the word "company" into Latin for the official ecclesiastical documents, the word "societas" was used. It was not an accurate rendition, nevertheless it has come to be the common Latin term for the order. The English "society" and the German "Gesellschaft," translations of "societas," are the usual terms for the order among the people who speak these tongues. Only in the Spanish and to some extent in the French and Italian world, is the original still used.

The companions separated. Xavier and Bobadilla went to Bologna, Rodriguez and Le Jay to Ferrara, Salmeron and Broët to Siena, Codure and Hoces to Padua. Ignatius, Faber and Laynez set off on the all-important journey to Rome. They tramped the whole distance on foot. As the three neared the Eternal City, they stopped to pray at a little hermitage in La Storta, the last halting place before the city. Here it was that Ignatius had one of his most important mystical experiences. In an ecstasy, as he later declared, he beheld the Eternal Father and with Him, Jesus carrying His cross. Jesus addressed him with these words: "I will be propitious to you at Rome." What meaning these words could have, Ignatius was unable to fathom; but he was certain of this, so he informed his companions in relating to them his vision, that whatever trials awaited him at Rome, even if it were death, Jesus would be propitious to him. This was the only vision that Ignatius ever related in detail to his companions. Of his spiritual experiences, he was invariably reticent.

Rome was reached in late November 1537. The Holy Father welcomed the three very generously; Laynez and Faber were appointed to lecture in the College of the Sapienza, the former to discourse on theology, the latter to explain the Scriptures. Ignatius employed himself with preaching to the crowds in the streets and in giving the Spiritual Exercises to several prominent persons. Doctor Ortiz sought his guidance; together both retired to the mother-house of the Benedictines, the Abbey of Monte Cassino, to spend a whole month making the entire Spiritual Exercises. Back in Rome, Ignatius astonished his two companions by informing them of the death of Hoces at Padua, a fact which he seems to have learned by a revelation. Hoces, the last to join the original company, died a victim of his zeal, the first of the order to answer the final call.

So favorably had the situation developed in Rome, that in 1538 Ignatius called all the companions to the Eternal City. As they gathered in conference, they had much to report: crowds listening to their sermons, numbers flocking to their confessionals, several young priests and ecclesiastics offering themselves to them for similar service. As they compared the evident success of their apostolic work, Ignatius proposed for their consideration the question whether the time had not come to consolidate their labors by transforming their group into a religious order.

The deliberations did not get very far, for they were interrupted by one of the usual attacks upon Ignatius and his companions. In Italy, in fact in Rome itself, there were to be found several crypto-heretics tirelessly, albeit insidiously, spreading the Lutheran heresies. Frequently secret Protestants were popular preachers, who used the medium of the pulpit to spread their doctrines covertly. One such was an Augustinian preacher, Agostino Piermontese, a man of no little influence. The young priests about Ignatius discovered his secret heterodoxy and in their public sermons began to unmask the hypocrite. To distract attention from himself, Piermontese returned the attack. Aided by powerful friends he raised a perfect storm of calumnies against these priests newly arrived in the city. It was heralded abroad that Ignatius was a condemned heretic, that several tribunals had examined him and had convicted him. His followers, so it was said, were fugitives from Spain, France and Venice. Nor were these the only charges against the companions. Ignatius reacted quickly. There was more at stake than his own personal honor, there was the honor of his followers and most important of all there was the fate of the new order which he was at last about to bring into reality. He had immediate recourse to the courts. Fortunately there happened to be in Rome three judges who at various times had participated in one or other of the former trials of Ignatius. They were Figueroa of Alcalá, Ori, the Dominican Inquisitor from Paris, and Gaspar de Doctis, auditor of the Nunciature at Venice. These now came forth gladly in defense of Ignatius and his companions. Their testimony made his vindication complete. Some damage was repaired, but not all as yet. The opponents sought to bury the whole trial in silence, by preventing the publication of the exonerating sentence. Ignatius knew that a complete and final vindication was necessary for the future success of his new order. Going in person to Paul III he laid the whole case before the Pontiff and begged him to order the public promulgation of the sentence. The Pope recognized the wisdom and justice of the plan and gave the necessary command. On

November 18, 1538 the Governor of Rome published the verdict proclaiming to the world the complete innocence of Ignatius and his companions.

With all the doubts of their orthodoxy set at rest, the group could take up again their discussions. This they did in the Lent of 1539. All without hesitation favored the project of organizing into a religious order. But for a time some could not make up their minds as to the advisability of adding to the vows of chastity and poverty still another, a vow of obedience to an elected superior. After many days of discussion, penance and prayer, all voted to take the vow. With that vital question settled, a few more topics were discussed, such as the nature of their practice of poverty and the proposal of teaching catechism to children and the unlearned. On June 24, 1539 the discussions were brought to an end.

Ignatius now set himself to the task of putting these ideas in form and of composing a sketch or formula of the new institute for presentation to the Holy Father. Cardinal Caspar Contarini, a leader of the Counter-Reformation, agreed to place the formula before the Pope. On September 3, 1539 Paul III received it. As he perused the document he was most favorably impressed; it is said that he remarked: "The finger of God is here." Father Thomas Badia, O.P., to whom the Pontiff presented the plan for a first scrutiny, gave it his hearty approval.

Further detailed examination, however, had to be gone through, and a whole year was to elapse before the official confirmation was finally granted. A commission of Cardinals was appointed to subject the formula to a rigorous scrutiny. The prospect of confirmation was not too favorable. One of the members of the commission was the able and pious Cardinal Guidiccione, who was flatly opposed to any new religious orders. Indeed he thought seriously of amalgamating all existing orders into four and then subjecting the four to the most severe reform. As for the new formula, he would not even look at it. Ignatius sought aid in prayer, offering to God three thousand Masses. At length Cardinal Guidiccione relented and asked to see a copy of the formula. As he read the document, the good Cardinal became most favorably impressed; when he finished he was satisfied that he might in this case make an exception. So he gave his full approval to founding of the new order. The last barrier removed, on September 27, 1540, Paul III promulgated the Bull "Regimini militantis Ecclesiae," canonically establishing as a religious order, the new Society of Jesus.

Two steps remained to complete the organization: the election of a General and the profession of the solemn vows by the first fathers. Several of the companions had been dispersed throughout Italy during the year in which the formula of the institute was being examined. Two, Rodriguez and Xavier, had even left for Portugal to prepare for departure for India. Xavier in fact had gone on to the remote Orient. Ignatius in April, 1541 recalled the companions to Rome. Four could not come: Xavier in India, Rodriguez in Portugal, Faber in Germany (by Papal orders) and Bobadilla in Bisignano (also by Papal command). After several days of prayer Ignatius was elected General, with only one vote, his own, dissenting. He refused to accept the verdict most determinedly. Only after days spent in prayer and at the command of his confessor Father Teodosio, a Franciscan, did he finally yield to the insistence of his companions that he become the superior, the first Father General of the Society of Jesus. His reluctance certainly refutes a rather common misunderstanding that Ignatius, the former officer, had the strongest desire always to lead and command. On April 22, 1541 six companions, Ignatius, Laynez, Salmeron, Le Jay, Broët and Codure met together in the Basilica of St. Paul's Outside-the-Walls. There in the chapel of our Lady, Ignatius said Mass for the group. When he came to the Communion, holding the Blessed Sacrament in his hand he read his own solemn profession; then turning to his companions he held up to each one the Sacred Host as each in turn read out the formula of his own vows. The Society of Jesus was an accomplished fact.

CHAPTER III

THE TRAINING OF THE MEN.
THE SPIRITUAL EXERCISES.

St. Ignatius had gathered around him a small band of men; but they were select men, men of talent and of high aspirations. His next task was to train them for his great and noble purpose. That training was done in the school of the "Spiritual Exercises." A knowledge of these Exercises is of essential importance, if there is to be any comprehension of the history of the Society of Jesus. The order itself sprang from them; its Constitution truly may be said to have been born of them. Not only the first Jesuits, but every Jesuit during the four hundred years of the Society's history has been formed in and through this school of asceticism. The mighty stream of literature which contains what is called "Jesuit Spirituality" has had its source in the Spiritual Exercises.

The Exercises are contained in the book of the *Spiritual Exercises* written by Ignatius in 1522 at Manresa. In later times and in other places, as he acquired a more technical theological knowledge, he improved the wording of the text; he added also a few details, which were natural complements of his original composition. So famous is this book in the history of Christian spirituality, that some have claimed that, judging from the influence it has exercised, it should be assigned the third place in spiritual literature, *Holy Scripture* being the first, the *Imitation of Christ* the second, and the book of the *Exercises* the third. Certainly, much of the reform of morals and the revival of faith and devotion in the Counter-Reformation was based upon it; and to this day a large part of Catholic asceticism has found in it its fountainhead. Truly remarkable is the number of writers, not only Catholics but Protestant, who in recent times have made the book of the *Exercises* the subject of their special investigation. Realizing what an influence the book has had during the last four hundred years, they have been eager to examine its nature and origin.

Some of the writers have found it a "strange book." It is strange, and for many reasons. It is a very small book, the text in print being not more than one hundred and fifty brief pages; one might well call it a pamphlet or a tract rather than a book. Then, it is strange in form. Any one who takes up the book for mere reading will be greatly disappointed. It will seem utterly dry. There is not the least attempt to appeal by means of attractive literary form. In fact, as a prominent Jesuit writer has said: "it is as unliterary as possible." It consists of the plainest, simplest statements of theology and spirituality, with a great deal of directions and minute regulations largely for the "Director" of the retreat. There is no poetry and apparently no enthusiasm—remember the word "apparently," for there will be found many powerful appeals to enthusiasm. There is no rhetoric; in fact a too rhetorical presentation of its considerations in a retreat may spoil its best effects, viz., fruitful meditation. According to St. Ignatius, of all his disciples Bl. Peter Faber was the best Director of retreats—and he was no orator at all. The truths of the Exercises are not new; they are as old as the Gospels. When simply read or heard they sound plain, almost commonplace. But when deeply pondered in their logical sequence and psychological connection, the newness and greatness of the method of St. Ignatius will be realized.

A strange book! A Protestant (Professor Boehmer), who has written much on the Society and has tried to understand it, has not hesitated to say that "it is no book at all in the ordinary sense of the term. For a book is intended to be read; but this one is not meant for reading." In this last statement he is quite right. St. Ignatius did not intend the book for mere reading. The Exercises were not meant to be read, but to be made, to be experienced, to be lived. And they are supposed to be made under a competent director. When during the life time of St. Ignatius the Exercises were violently attacked in Spain and stigmatized as heretical, vigorous defenders arose, among them Bartholomew de Torres, later Bishop of the Canaries. The third of his reasons for defense is pertinent here, and reads as follows: "No one can know the real value of the Exercises unless he has made them. I have made them. I have seen well educated men who understood nothing in them, not even the things that are clear, Catholic, and entirely taken from the Gospel and tradition. Those things would easily have been understood if they had made the Exercises." [1]

A similar judgment might well be passed on certain critics of the Exercises. In all probability their strictures would not have been penned, had the writers gone through the complete Exercises according to the mind and directions of St. Ignatius. To do this would have involved a retreat of thirty days, for the complete Exercises, as composed by Ignatius, were intended to occupy a period of about that duration. A full eight days' retreat at the very least is required to obtain even a fair insight into the nature and methods of the Exercises. It may be well to observe that the eulogies bestowed on the Exercises by Popes and saints, such as St. Charles Borromeo and St. Francis de Sales, refer to the complete Exercises. This

---

[1] Brou, S.J., *Les Exercises Spirituels,* Paris (1922), p. 78.

does not mean that great fruit may not be expected from a much shorter retreat; but a thorough judgment cannot be expressed, except by one who has gone through the Spiritual Exercises in their entirety.

Not a few of the writers on the Exercises have tried to explain them by various comparisons. Some have characterized them as a "Manual of Drill." [2] That is a superficial and entirely misleading idea. The Exercises are something vastly deeper than that, as will appear presently. In the beginning of the chapter, they have been given the title of a "school." For this there are excellent reasons. First, the greatest Jesuit commentators on the Exercises call them a school of spirituality; the last sentence of an excellent modern book on the Spiritual Exercises is: "Essentially, and taken in their entirety, the Exercises of St. Ignatius are a school of sanctity." [3] Secondly, Pope Pius XI in his Encyclical on the Exercises ("Mens Nostra," 1929) calls them a school. Thirdly, St. Ignatius himself describes his own spiritual experiences, which are the basis of the Exercises, as a school. He speaks of the "lessons" which God gave him; [4] again he says, "At this time God treated him (Ignatius) in the same manner in which a school master treats a child whom he instructs." [5]

The Exercises offer a "schooling" in which the principal part is not the mere pouring of information into the pupil's mind but the stimulating of the pupil to the active exercise of his own powers. If there ever was an educator who insisted on "self-activity" it was St. Ignatius in his Exercises. The very title "Exercises" suggests the idea of self-activity. The one who gives the retreat is warned not to do too much for the exercitant but to lead him to find for himself by meditation and reflection what is of importance for his spiritual life. This idea is emphasized in the very beginning of the book.[6] According to Father Rickaby, S.J., the exercitant is "to play the game himself, not to be a mere looker-on or listener . . . he must sweat and toil for himself, think hard and seek God fervently."

The Exercises are not a systematic treatment of spirituality, nor yet a handbook of asceticism. The book gives little theory; it is rather a book of practical guidance.[7] It is a book *sui generis*, to use a philosophical term, a book not belonging to any class, but standing alone, unique in its character. It is evident, then, that the Exercises cannot be explained satis-

---

[2] These writers exaggerate the traces of Ignatius' former military career in the whole structure of the Society.

[3] Brou, S.J., *Les Exercises Spirituels*, p. 230.

[4] *Testament*, no. 25.

[5] *Ibid.*, no. 27.

[6] Annotation, no. 2.

[7] Cf. Suarez: *De Religione Societatis Jesu.* IX, 5, 4. "Opus hoc ex instituto non est ad tradendam doctrinam theologicam . . . continet magis practicam quam speculativam doctrinam, traditam per modum artis magis quam speculativam."

factorily in a few pages. All that is attempted here is to give a meager outline of the leading ideas.

The Exercises are preceded by the well-known prayer *Anima Christi,* "Soul of Christ sanctify me," etc. Formerly it was thought that this beautiful prayer had been composed by St. Ignatius, and it was often called "The Aspirations of St. Ignatius." But it existed long before him; the latest researches have traced it back to the twelfth century. It was a favorite prayer of his, and throughout the Exercises he repeatedly recommends its use. It was through the use of it by St. Ignatius in the Exercises that the prayer became so generally known that finally it has become connected with the name of the Saint.

St. Ignatius says that the complete Exercises are to last about thirty days. He divides these into four parts which he calls "weeks" or stages. Since the word "school" has been taken as descriptive of the Exercises, the term, "four courses of study," may be used appropriately. These four courses, however, are not disparate but are most intimately connected, the one logically and psychologically following the other and all forming one harmonious whole. The Saint here, as in so many things, shows his practical wisdom by saying [8] that the different "weeks" need not be exactly seven or eight days, but may be shortened or lengthened according to the disposition of the individual exercitant. For some more quickly, others more slowly, obtain the goal set in the different weeks.

The Exercises begin with a consideration which is usually called "the Foundation," and is considered by some commentators as a part of the first week, by others as an introduction to it. But it is not merely a "grand portal or vestibule," as some have styled it. Most important is it to consider the very words of St. Ignatius carefully; he calls it "principio y fundamento." The latter word is easily understood: a foundation, on which the whole spiritual edifice, as a mighty tower or a gigantic cathedral, is erected. The other word "principio" or "principle" is taken from the philosophical language of Scholasticism: a great first truth and supreme maxim from which other truths naturally, logically and necessarily follow.

The Foundation is so important that it may well be quoted in a literal translation: "Man was created to praise, do reverence to and serve God our Lord, and thereby to save his soul. And the other things on the face of the earth were created for man's sake and to help him in the following out of the end for which he was created. Hence it follows that man should make use of creatures so far as they do help him towards his end, and should withdraw from them so far as they are a hindrance to him in regard to that end. Wherefore it is necessary to make ourselves indifferent in regard of all created things—in all that is left to the liberty of our free

---

[8] Annotation, no. 4.

choice, and is not forbidden—so that we on our part should not wish for health rather than sickness, for riches rather than poverty, for honor rather than ignominy, for a long life rather than a short life, and so in all other matters solely desiring and choosing those things which may better lead us to the end for which we were created." [9]

In all this there is nothing new. The substance of the individual truths are commonplaces of spirituality. It is the putting them together with their logical connection so clearly and so emphatically brought out, and all at the very beginning of the Exercises, that constitutes the psychological force of the Foundation. There is not much difficulty for the exercitant in the first and second sections. The third and following look more serious. The third speaks of what use must be made of "creatures." By this last term the Saint includes all created things, designating a few by way of example. Creatures are to be used only as means towards the end for which God created man. And here St. Ignatius becomes insistent: they are only to be used if, and so far as they are a help towards that end; they are not to be used, but to be avoided and surrendered, if they are not a help, and so far as they are not a help. In place of the English "so far as," the original Spanish has "tanto-quanto" (or in Latin "tantum-quantum"). These words present the great truth in a more striking fashion and reveal some of the elemental, tremendous force of the great principle. The practical applications of the principle are numberless and at times call for great heroism; a constant and consistent following of the principle constitutes great sanctity. Already it becomes apparent that beneath the very simple words of St. Ignatius are hidden depths of spirituality.

What makes the carrying out of the principle *tantum-quantum* so difficult, are the natural predilections or repulsions, which so often hinder men from forming proper judgments on various creatures. To lessen these propensities, to guard against being swayed by aversion or drawn by attraction, St. Ignatius says that the exercitant should make himself "indifferent" to the creatures that repel or attract. It is to be regretted that there is no English word which exactly expresses what St. Ignatius means by the word "indifferentia." The word "indifferent" will not do, for it is too often used in a somewhat derogatory sense, meaning "mediocre," "unimportant," or "cold," "apathetic," "lacking interest." Cardinal Newman's word, "detachment," though better, is not wholly equivalent. "The more modern word, detachment, expresses a large part of what St. Ignatius means, but not quite the whole." [10] The real meaning is: "to stand above, to be independent of, aversions and attractions" in one's decisions.

[9] Translation in Rickaby, S.J., *The Spiritual Exercises of St. Ignatius Loyola*, London (1923) p. 18.

[10] Longridge, *The Spiritual Exercises*, London (1919) p. 29.

Such an attitude is most logical, but also most difficult, as one naturally does not possess it in most things. It is important to strive after this disposition, so that, and this is the conclusion of the Foundation, "we may solely desire and choose those things which may better lead us to the end for which we were created." The word "better" and similar expressions will appear again in prominent connections.

Plain and homely as the single truths may seem to be, in their logical connection they are a true philosophy of Christian life, and a sublime one. The *tantum-quantum* in particular is what the Creator meant by saying that man should "subdue the earth" [11] and rule over all things, that he should be the master of all creatures and not their slave. The Foundation is the one solution, the correct answer to the two fundamental questions of all true philosophy: "Whence?" and "Whither?" These two tremendous questions which have been asked by all thinking men from the beginning, are solved there. It may now be understood what the real purpose of the Exercises is. St. Ignatius has explained it in the very beginning: "preparing and disposing the soul to remove from it all inordinate attachments, and after their removal to seek and find the Divine will in the laying out of one's life." [12]

To find the Divine will! Forgetting God and His claims, as Father Faber so often proclaimed, is the besetting sin of the day. St. Ignatius has a remedy in the very beginning of his Exercises by making God's will, honor and service the center of all life. Looking back upon the Foundation one must see in it "a system of truths which are so clear, so simple, so forcible, so irresistible and withal so noble and sublime that we can never sufficiently admire them, and shall never be able to fathom their depths. The Foundation is the shortest, but most comprehensive epitome of all natural Christian philosophy. It gives the most complete solution to the question of the destiny of man and of everything on earth." [13]

The Foundation shows God's plan concerning man. But man has a free will; he can frustrate God's plan, repudiating in his actions the practical truths of the Foundation. He can refuse to praise and reverence and serve God; he can use the creatures of this world not as means towards the God-appointed end, but as means of gratifying self in its lust for possessions, power and influence. If he does this, he commits sin. With profound psychological insight St. Ignatius wants the consideration of the Foundation to be followed by meditations on sin and its consequences.

There is a general complaint today that the sense of sin is waning. In many it has practically died out. Intellectual leaders, false prophets of

---

[11] *Genesis* I, 28.

[12] Annotation, no. 1.

[13] Meschler, S.J., *The Spiritual Exercises of St. Ignatius* (English Translation), Woodstock College (1889).

the day in literature and philosophy, make light of it; even an Emerson called sin an inevitable, necessary stage in general human progress. Others ridicule the very idea of sin; to them it is only an undesirable "rag and remnant" of medieval obscurantism, monkish fanaticism and Manicheism, or a part of a "slave morality" which is unworthy of "master minds," of "supermen." Lenient, indeed, is the world's judgment on sin. Against this judgment St. Ignatius in the first meditation places God's infallible verdict on mortal sin, written in the fearful fall of the rebel angels and in the dread consequences of our first parents' transgression. This meditation is to fill the exercitant with a deep sense of shame, arising especially from the thought of his own numerous sins. The next meditation, which consists in weighing the gravity of one's own personal sins, is to rouse a profound sorrow over sin. Lastly comes the meditation on hell which is to produce a firm resolution never to sin again. God's final verdict on mortal sin is delivered in the inextinguishable fire of hell. St. Ignatius wants the exercitant to have an intimate sense of the pains of the damned, "so that if through my fault I should forget the love of the Eternal Lord, at least the fear of the penalty of mortal sin may be an aid to me not to give way to sin in future." [14] That motive has been censured as too low. But St. Ignatius knew the human heart better than his critics; he knew that some temptations may be so strong as almost to blot out the thought of the love of God, and that then the thought of hell may act like a glaring red light in the way, warning against danger and disaster. These meditations are placed before the people in the very much shortened three days' retreat. They also form the main subject of the adaptation of the Exercises in the popular missions. They are powerful means of conversion and of renovation of spiritual life.

They are, however, but the preliminary part of the Exercises of St. Ignatius. These are primarily to be found in the following "weeks," when the efforts of the exercitant are devoted to meditations on Christ with a view to His imitation. Even the Foundation and the meditations of the first week are directed towards this goal. The very name of the Foundation shows such a purpose. The meditations on sin are to remove the obstacles to the complete following of Christ. They are also destined to create the proper disposition for the perfect imitation; they are to knock off, as it were, the crown of pride and self-sufficiency which man in his dream of self-glorification places on his head, so that he may now appear humble and docile before the great guide and exemplar, Jesus Christ.

Henceforth the Exercises are strictly Christo-centric. In the very beginning [15] St. Ignatius declared that the purpose of the Exercises was

---

[14] Fifth Exercise, 2nd Prelude.
[15] Annotation, no. 1.

"to seek and find the Divine will in the laying out of one's life." They are to be a way to the perfect life. The idea of a way was prominent in the Old Testament. In the New Testament the Christian profession is called "the way." [16] St. Paul declares that Christ had shown "a new and living way" [17] to the sanctuary. It became a favorite idea from the beginning of Christian literature; one finds the description of the "two Ways" in one of the earliest specimens of Christian literature, the *Didache,* probably written while St. John was still living. It remained a favorite idea in spiritual writings of succeeding ages; a beautiful example is found in the *Imitation of Christ.*[18] The grandest expression, however, of this great principle is to be found in the words of Christ himself: "I am the way, the truth, and the life. No one goeth to the Father save through Me." [19] "I am the way," *because* "I am the truth and the life." "I am the way" (and the only one) to the Father: "No one goeth to the Father save through me." [20] It is one of the profoundest truths contained in the profoundest of the Gospels.

This is also the leading, the central idea of the Exercises; Christ is the way, the only way to the Father, to salvation of the soul. St. Ignatius does not explicitly refer in the Exercises to Christ's word: "I am the way." But one feels there is a latent reference to it. Moreover, in the eleventh rule of the *Summary of the Constitutions,* where the Saint describes the essence of his order by referring to the high point of the Exercises, the "Third Mode of Humility," he explicitly introduces it in the words: "in all things we must seek to imitate and follow Him, seeing He is 'the true way that leads men to life.' " [21] To follow Christ "as closely as pos-

---

[16] *Acts* XI, 2; XIX, 9.

[17] *Hebrews* X, 20.

[18] *The Imitation of Christ,* Book III, c. 56.

[19] *John* XIV, 6.

[20] Many interpretations have been given of the relation of those three ideas to one another. They are not to be taken as simply coordinate: "I am the way, and the truth, and the life," as many explain them. No, the emphasis is on the way. This is evident from the context. Christ had said: "Whither I go, you know the way." (*John* XIV, 4) The apostles were puzzled by this statement, and said: "Lord, how can we know the way?" It is therefore a question of the way. And Christ answered it by saying: "I am the way"— And why? Because "I am the truth and the life." This interpretation is now given by the foremost Catholic Biblical scholars: Fr. Knabenbauer, S.J., Dr. Tillman, Bishop Keppler, the new Westminster translation, which in the *Gospel according to St. John* (1929) p. 77, reads: "He is the way, because He is 'the truth and the life,' " the truth incarnate and the perfect revealer of God and divine things (see *John* I, 14 and 18)— and the one who possesses life in Himself and communicates it to others—(see *John* I, 14). There is in Christ's words an unmistakable allusion to the ideas contained in St. John's grand prologue.

[21] This is evidently a paraphrase of Christ's words: "I am the way, the truth and the life." It is more or less the interpretation given by St. Augustine: "via vera vitae," "the

sible," to follow Him with "utmost generosity and magnanimity," this is the goal of the Exercises. Whatever place various methods, elections, etc., may occupy in the Exercises, they are only of secondary importance. The very heart and soul of the Exercises and of "Jesuit spirituality" is the close and magnanimous following of Christ. That fact is evident from the beginning of the second week to the end of the fourth, when the meditations are practically all on the life of Christ.

The meditations or contemplations (as the Saint calls them) on the life of Christ are preceded by the famous contemplation on the "Kingdom of Christ." It is not a "second foundation," as it has been called, even though the *Directory*, the official interpretation of the Exercises, speaks of it as "a sort of foundation." It is rather a "help" to the exercitant, as Ignatius calls it himself; it is to assist him to meditate fruitfully on the life of Christ. Only a meager outline of it can be given here.

St. Ignatius first presents a kind of parable. A king calls on his subjects to follow him in a war against the "infidels" to re-conquer from them the territory which they have wrested from the Christians. The king is ready to share with his soldiers all the labors, dangers and sacrifices, and afterwards the victory and its rewards. He then applies this to Christ, the eternal King who calls on men to become soldiers in His army. The "parable" of St. Ignatius is medieval; to be quite exact, the picture is a crusading scene. One thinks of a king in the truest sense of the term, of a St. Louis, that most truly Christian Knight, calling on his subjects to follow him on a crusade. One thinks of the enthusiasm such as was witnessed at Clermont, when Pope Urban had described the sufferings of the Christians in the Holy Land, and listens to tens of thousands raising the enthusiastic shout: "God wills it! The Cross! The Cross!" Here is something like the vision St. Ignatius wants to place before the mind of the exercitant.

An ideal King, so manly, yet so kind, "so generous and so truly human," what will good subjects say and do? Will there be cowards, "shirkers," or "slackers"? St. Ignatius in applying this example to Christ the King manifests a profound knowledge of human nature; he understood well what centuries later was expressed in the words: "Mankind is led far more by ideals than by ideas," by ideals, the concrete embodiment of ideas, rather than by ideas themselves, abstract truths. Man's deepest need is satisfied only by persons. Hence St. Ignatius places before the mind a person, an ideal person, the ideal Person. And what beautiful descriptions can be given, and have been given, of that Person, "so generous, so truly human," as He is portrayed in the contemplations on the Kingdom," "so fair and gracious," as He is called later in the "Two Standards."

true way of life." It is a beautiful interpretation, although not the literal one, as explained in the previous note.

In Him "the goodness and kindness of God our Saviour appeared," [22] the most magnetic character ever seen on earth. It is indeed enthusiasm in the best sense of the word, which St. Ignatius wants to stir up in his meditation, an enthusiasm which is not spent in mere emotion, but proceeds to practical decisions, to resolutions to do more for Christ than what is demanded by God's commandments.

More, much more! St. Ignatius says: "They who will be more desirous to show affection and signalize themselves in the entire service of their Eternal King, will make offerings of greater esteem and greater moment; they will deliberately fight the enemy, the 'infidel' in their own hearts, their self-love, and love of the world; they will desire to imitate Christ in suffering and humiliation, and if it should be the wish of the most sacred Majesty, to embrace even actual poverty." This is the spirit of the following of Christ as conceived by St. Ignatius. It proves that the entirety of the Spiritual Exercises is not meant for all, but for high-souled Christians, souls that are truly "magnanimous," truly generous, a spiritual élite. The thought of generous and magnanimous souls occurs soon again when St. Ignatius speaks of souls that are eager to "signalize" themselves in the service of their king and are ready to make "oblations of greater moment." Does St. Ignatius thereby intend all magnanimous persons to enter religious orders? By no means; although this is one way, and the most excellent, to "distinguish" oneself in the service of God. But he wants all to aim at perfection; and perfection means the spirit of the evangelical counsels, although not necessarily their actual practice. They must have "spiritual poverty," although they may live in a palace. Of St. Thomas More, model of laymen, Chancellor of England, it has been said that in spirit he was a Carthusian. The same idea underlies the "Third Orders" and similar organizations.

Christ, then, is the ideal of St. Ignatius. True, too, He is the ideal of all religious. In the different religious orders and "schools of spirituality" that ideal appears in different forms. In the order of St. Benedict He is the King of glory; and the monks, in their beautiful liturgy, serve Him somewhat as the angels and blessed in heaven do. St. Francis of Assisi had a burning, and yet childlike, love for Christ as He appeared as an infant in the manger and as a sufferer on the Cross. Ignatius' temperament and natural disposition were different from those of St. Francis; he could not approach Christ in the same manner as did the Saint of Assisi. Besides, his was another leading idea: St. Ignatius has chosen as his ideal, Christ primarily as the Founder of the Kingdom of God; as such He clearly appears in the meditation on the Kingdom of Christ and throughout the Exercises. Such an ideal made a special appeal to him. It explains the note

---

[22] *Titus* III, 4.

of "apostolic" labor which is latent in this meditation and in many others.

The meditations or contemplations, as St. Ignatius calls them, of the second week are preceded by a prayer "to obtain an intimate knowledge of the Lord." The petition asks to understand the "mind of Christ" (His spirit, ideas, principles and motives)in order that "I may love Him and follow Him," or as it may be worded, "to know Christ more intimately, to love Him more fervently, and to follow Him more generously." It is a beautiful prayer, showing that Christ is the center of the exercitant's thought, and revealing the spirit, practical and magnanimous, with which the meditation should be made. The daily meditation which Jesuits make is generally to have as its subject-matter the life of Christ and is to be made in the spirit of this prayer. St. Ignatius wants the exercitant to meditate especially on what Christ did, how He suffered poverty, labors, humiliations, death—"and all this for me." Such reflections he would have lead to "some spiritual profit"; as he very well put it on one occasion: "all this He has done and suffered for me, what shall I do and suffer for Him?"

When the meditations have reached the episode of Christ's remaining in the temple without the knowledge of Mary and Joseph, "purely to devote Himself to the service of His heavenly Father," St. Ignatius says it is proper to reflect on the state of religious perfection, and "to seek with God's grace to find in what life or state His Divine Majesty is pleased to make use of us." This introduces the important topic of the "Election," as the Saint calls it. It is in some ways the most important point of the Exercises: to make a decision, of course, as in everything, for Christ. For some it is intended to be a decision concerning their life-work or vocation, as it is called. For others, who previously have made an "immutable" choice and are in the priesthood, in religion, or in the married state, the Election is to determine a "reformation" of life, i.e., in what manner Christian perfection is to be practised in the state of life in which they are placed. The question is not whether to decide for Christ, to follow Him or not—that was settled long before in the first week—but how far, how closely to follow Him. And there can be no question after the meditation on the "Kingdom of Christ" that this must be as closely as possible, "sequar te quam proxime," and that one must be ready to be magnanimous, to be determined to "distinguish oneself" in Christ's service. Of course, the principles of the Foundation, particularly the great *tantum quantum* are a guiding star in the Election. But there is something higher, as will be seen. St. Ignatius gives many detailed rules how an Election can be made safely, wisely, magnanimously. They show the practical wisdom of the Saint and a penetrating psychological insight into the depths of the human soul, especially its intricacies, its tendencies to use subterfuges to escape unpleasant demands, to have excuses and palliations, in short, to play "tricks" on oneself, particularly to allow oneself to be deceived by things under the "appearance of good." As the *Imitation of Christ* says: "Natura callida est," "nature is sly and tricky." And the "enemy of human nature," as Satan is repeatedly called by St. Ignatius, knows how to use this fact, by frauds, deceptions, "snares of the devil," as is said in the prayer at the end of Mass. As a preparation for a good Election St. Ignatius gives a "trilogy" of considerations: the "Two Standards," the "Three Classes," the "Three Modes of Humility." The titles may sound strange but a brief explanation will show that they contain material of the highest importance in the spiritual life.

To open the eyes of the exercitant to these "nets" of Satan, St. Ignatius unveils Satan's methods. He proposes the meditation on the "Two Standards" or "Two Banners." In it he gives two startling, dramatic pictures. On the one side, he describes Babylon, whence Satan, the "bandit-chief," dispatches his emissaries to all countries, places, and individuals to tempt people, not directly to sin, but to "the desire of riches, honor, 'influence and power,' and thereby lead them to pride and then to all kinds of sin and vice." That there is truth in this is proved by experience. It is proved also by Christ's repeated and stern warnings about wealth. That particular teaching of Christ is often weakened; it is said Christ denounced only ill-gotten wealth, or the wrong use of wealth. He did much more; He was far more "radical." He did not, indeed, declare wealth in itself to be wrong; He was no Communist; yet He emphatically proclaimed that wealth in itself was a danger for the soul and its best interests. Wealth so easily begets what is called the spirit of worldliness: love of power, craving for honor, vain display, egotism, self-satisfaction, self-worship, and forgetfulness of God. Hence in the other scene Ignatius depicts Jerusalem and Christ, the true Captain, "fair and gracious," sending forth His apostles and disciples, to commend a desire of humiliation which will lead to true humility—and all this "to imitate Christ better."

To test whether one's motives are sincere and genuine, St. Ignatius proposes the meditation on the "Three Classes of Men." Three men find themselves in a quandary as to the disposal of a sum of money, which, though not acquired wrongfully, is a hindrance to their perfect service of God. The first procrastinates and does nothing; the second is willing to do something but not all; the third alone is consistent, being ready not only to give up all attachment to the money but even to relinquish the very sum itself. But St. Ignatius has something even higher. Before the actual Election he wants the exercitant to study carefully and with fervent prayer the "Three Modes (or Degrees) of Humility." These are dispositions of the soul in order that one's "affections be properly framed towards the true teaching of Christ," "that they take delight in it and be set on fire thereby." (Father Meschler, S.J.) It is the "Third Degree" St. Ignatius aims at. There is no longer question of indifference towards wealth or poverty, honor or humiliation. It is now a matter of positive choice; so that the exercitant will, provided God's glory in any case be equal, actually seek poverty with Christ poor and reproaches and humiliations with Christ humiliated and laden with reproaches.

This is the "peak of the mountain of Perfection"; the Third Degree of Humility is the highest summit of all. (Rickaby, S.J.) Here is the best way of serving God, spoken of in the Foundation, and the noblest use made of creatures; here is the way of "distinguishing oneself" as a knight in the army of the King mentioned in the meditation on the Kingdom of Christ; here is the "closest possible" following of Christ. It is impossible to man unaided by Divine grace, for it requires the sacrifice of all that the human heart holds dear. It is the acme of Christian heroism. The appropriateness of describing the Spiritual Exercises as a "school" now becomes apparent. Such terms as a "system of asceticism," a "course of ethical gymnastics," a "manual of drill," a "training school of abnegation," miss the point, confusing the means with the end. The Exercises are truly a "school of Christian heroism," for they train for a sublimity of sacrifice dictated and inspired by an intense and most generous love of our Lord Jesus Christ.

In the beginning of this chapter it was said that the order founded by St. Ignatius, the Society of Jesus, was born of the spirit of the Exercises. This spirit is most vividly expressed in the eleventh and twelfth rules of the *Summary of the Constitutions* which contain the most forceful expression of the spirit of the Society. "They (the members of the Society) must diligently observe, esteeming it of great importance and of the highest moment . . . how much it helps and contributes to progress in spiritual life, to abhor wholly what the world loves and embraces and to accept and desire with their whole strength whatsoever our Lord loved and embraced . . . seriously to follow Christ . . . for His love and reverence . . . that in all things, as far as by the assistance of God's grace we can, we may seek to imitate and follow Him, seeing He is the true way that leads men to life." "To the end that this degree of perfection, so precious in spiritual life, be better obtained, let it be each one's chief and most earnest endeavor in all things, as far as he can, to seek in the Lord his own greater abnegation and continual mortification." For as the Saint says in the Exercises: "we shall make progress in spiritual matters in proportion as (*tantum-quantum*) we depart from, and renounce, self-will, self-seeking and self-love."

The remainder of the Exercises can be described briefly. The object of the third and fourth week is to confirm the Election, that is to strengthen the exercitant in carrying out the plan of life he has adopted. This is done in the third week by meditations on the suffering of our

Lord. Thereby Christ showed His choice of means to glorify and serve the Father, His love and magnanimity. "Nonne oportebat Christum pati," "ought not Christ to have suffered," He told the discouraged, hopeless disciples on the road to Emmaus.[23] The one who in the Exercises has reached this point, deeply realizes and intensely feels the force of this tremendous "ought to suffer" and applies it to himself. He is told to meditate on these sufferings with deepest sympathy. But it is not a mere sympathy, however sacred, that is the ultimate object of these meditations. An intensely practical sympathy is urged upon the exercitant. He is asked to consider "how all this He suffered for my sins, and what ought I to do and suffer for Him." It is again the spirit of the "Third Degree." Here is verified the profound prophecy of our Lord: "And I, if I be lifted up from the earth, will draw all things to Myself" [24]—all things—above all, loving and generous hearts.

The fourth week presents the Resurrection and the various appearances of our Christ on His mission of strengthening and consoling His followers prior to His Ascension. These meditations are to be made with spiritual joy. "The heart should be like an Easter garden, an Eden filled with spiritual delight and joy." (Fr. Meschler, S.J.) There is to be joy with and for the Risen Saviour; there is to be joy also in the thought that for the sincere follower of the Crucified Saviour there is in store a most wonderful reward. And the certainty of reward will strengthen the soul in its heroic resolutions. It is a motive repeatedly proposed by Almighty God in Holy Scripture; and it is a motive of a most practical nature, especially for times of trial and suffering, when out of a tortured heart the cry arises: "of what use is it all?" And yet, it is not mere selfishness; for the reward will be most intimate union with Christ. "In my Father's house are many mansions . . . And I will come again, and will take you to Myself; that where I am, you also may be." [25] This again implies a motive of love; for it is love's greatest happiness to be with the beloved. Hence the meditations of this week are a lively and joyful "Sursum Corda."

The Exercises close with a "contemplation to obtain love" of God. St. Ignatius explains first what true love is. He says it consists in deeds rather than in words or feelings, and the deeds themselves are an interchange, a mutual sharing, of goods. This gives in very simple words a profound description of deep and genuine love—of a love which appears so strikingly in the "Third Degree." Then the Saint proposes four considerations to excite love for God. First, the exercitant is to meditate "with much affection" on all the blessings and benefits, natural and supernatural,

---

[23] *Luke* XXIV, 26.
[24] *John* XII, 32.
[25] *John* XIV, 2, 3.

which God has given him. The soul's answer to this is love of boundless gratitude. In the second place, he is to consider how close God is to him, actually dwelling in all these gifts to him. The answer again is love, love of desire, which seeks to possess God. Thirdly, he is to consider that God is working in him and in all these gifts to him, and that He worked for him in creation and, above all, in redemption. "He loved me and gave Himself for me." [26] The answer here also is love, active love, active in personal service and sacrifices. Lastly, he is to ponder deeply the final truth: God is the supreme beauty and goodness itself. "God is love." [27] All goodness and beauty proceed from Him, their eternal Source. If creatures can be so beautiful and good, how much more the Creator of them. The answer once more is love, love that desires to be transformed, to be united with the Divine Lover. Hence after each of these points, there arises from the soul spontaneously and powerfully the exclamation: "Sume et suscipe," "Take, o Lord, and receive, all my liberty, my memory, my understanding, and all my will, all I have and possess. Thou hast given it to me. To Thee, O Lord, I return it. All is Thine, dispose of it entirely according to Thy will. Give me Thy love and grace, because that is enough for me." This is the famous prayer "Suscipe." It is a hymn, a hymn of love, a most beautiful psalm.

Not all have understood the Contemplation on Divine Love. In a recent work the "Suscipe" is quoted as an example of a prayer of St. Ignatius without any connection with the Exercises. Others have looked upon the whole meditation as a sort of appendix without much connection with the rest of the Exercises. Quite the contrary is the fact. This meditation is the logical conclusion of the Exercises. It sums them up in a brief compendium. It is the crown of the Exercises. At the same time it advances the exercitant one step, but a great step: "Per Christum Hominem ad Christum Deum," through Christ the Man to Christ who is God, through the "Word that was made flesh" to the "Word which was in the beginning." It is the soul's last will and testament; and the final prayer, the "Suscipe," is the golden seal affixed to this testament. The signs and letters of this seal are: "Gift for gift! Heart for heart! Love for love!"

The essentials only of the Exercises have thus far been described, those parts which form the structure, the "body" of the whole, and which show the steady, systematic progress towards the object aimed at. There are many other details, of considerable importance in the spiritual life: principles of asceticism, and subsidiary practices, found throughout the Exercises in places where they are most useful or needed. A few may be mentioned: directions for the general examination of conscience, and for the particular examination which systematically attacks some sin or fail-

---

[26] *Galatians* II, 20.

[27] I *John* IV, 8.

ing, especially a dominant passion or "pet fault"; the rules concerning the "right conduct in taking food and drink," where the great fundamental principle of the *tantum-quantum*, "insofar as they help or hinder," comes again to the front; the rules "for the discernment of spirits," which are of great help to distinguish "movements of the soul," desires and inclinations, to discover which come from God, and which from the enemy of souls, to see which are prompted by selfish nature, especially by the subtler deception under the "appearance of good," to find out the "nets" and "snares" mentioned in the meditation on the "Two Standards." Connected with these last directions are the "Rules concerning scruples." Then there are numerous directions in regard to prayer. The Exercises are to be a school of prayer. St. Ignatius recommends and gives directions for "Three Methods of Prayer," very fruitful, and yet very simple, which can be used by all, even by people of but meager education.

The Exercises, however, are not only a school of prayer but a time of prayer in a most eminent sense. One of the numerous misrepresentations of Jesuit theology was the charge that it was tainted with Pelagianism, that it attributed too much to man's free will and too little to the grace of God. There is no Pelagianism in the Exercises. The saying is attributed to St. Ignatius that "we should act (work) as if everything depended on us, but pray as if everything depended on God." [28] That is sound practical wisdom, and sound theology too. St. Ignatius expects much of man's cooperation, but more of God's grace. Hence throughout the Exercises there is insistence on prayer to obtain God's grace; prayer as a preparation of every meditation, prayer throughout the meditations, prayer interrupting the reflections, and above all prayer concluding every meditation. During the Election the exercitant is counselled to beseech God for light by frequent and fervent supplications. Some of St. Ignatius' final "Colloquies" are truly most beautiful. "Without prayer the Exercises are a lamp unlit." How important prayer is for the one also who gives the retreat is well illustrated by the words of a religious who is not a Jesuit. Fr. Raimond Dreiling, a Franciscan and at the time Provincial in his order, who had devoted many years to the giving of retreats, declared in 1924: "I would not entrust any one with giving retreats unless I knew that again and again he had gone through the little book of the Exercises of St. Ignatius prayerfully," or as he literally expressed it: "unless he had prayed the Exercises through."

Toward the close of the Spiritual Exercises are found some special rules which demand particular consideration because they reveal the ideals

---

[28] Father Ribadeneira gives it in this form: "Let us work as if success depended on ourselves and not on God. Let us work with energy, but with this conviction in our hearts, that we are doing nothing, that God is doing everything." In the *Select Sentences* the wording is turned differently.

of St. Ignatius, and also because they have been so frequently misunderstood. They are the "Rules for Thinking and Acting in Conformity with the Catholic Church," or as they read in Spanish: "The True Sentiments which we ought to hold in the Church Militant." These rules—sometimes briefly called "Rules of Orthodoxy"—eighteen in number, are the last part added to the Exercises; their addition was made probably at Paris. They show that the Saint was by then fully acquainted with the tenets and influence of the Protestant Reformation, and meant the rules to be a protection, an antidote, against the spirit of heresy. It is too narrow a view to hold that they were directed only against the Reformers. Not a few of the humanists before Luther's attacks, even the great Erasmus, had ridiculed Catholic devotions and practices, as pilgrimages, veneration of relics, etc. The rules were directed against them too and the bad influence they had in Catholic countries. The Reformers had not only rejected many fundamental Catholic doctrines and the whole sacramental system, but particularly by denying the Real Presence had dealt a death blow to many beautiful Catholic devotions; they had ridiculed and denounced as idolatry much that many of their descendants today greatly admire and miss and try to introduce again in the modern attempts at "re-Catholicizing" Protestant worship. St. Ignatius says the Catholic must "praise," that is "stand up for," confession, Communion, hearing of Mass and the whole liturgy, the veneration of the saints and all that it implies, religious life under the vows, fasting and abstinence, and good works generally.

One rule in particular, the thirteenth, has been the object of attack and even ridicule on the part of non-Catholics; it is often quoted in derision: "We ought always to hold by the principle that the white that I see, I would believe to be black, if the Hierarchical Church were so to rule." Let a competent interpreter of the Exercises explain it: "When St. Ignatius speaks of 'black' and 'white,' he is not referring literally to colors—on such physical phenomena the Church never dogmatizes: her dogmas are of faith, and faith is of the unseen. What St. Ignatius had in mind was a proverbial phrase, found in one form or other in most languages." [29] The Saint wished to express the kind of absolute trust that should be given to the utterances of one of whom it is known that he can be and must be believed. St. Ignatius urges a childlike, and as it is expressed sometimes, a blind faith in the teaching of the Church. This faith, however, is not really blind, if its motives are considered. They are given by the Saint: "Believing that between Christ our Lord, the Bridegroom, and the Church, His Bride, there is the same Spirit that governs and guides us to the salvation of our souls: because by the same Spirit

---

[29] Rickaby, *The Spiritual Exercises of St. Ignatius Loyola*, p. 228.

and our Lord who gave the ten commandments our Holy Mother Church is guided and governed." No Catholic can object to this. The principle is as important today as it was when St. Ignatius warned against the false and rebellious spirit of his age. It is especially important in these times when lukewarm Catholics who love to style themselves "liberal" are tempted to yield to "compromising," "minimizing," or, to use a popular expression, "trimming," in regard to the teaching of the Church. In general, "in these principles and practical rules St. Ignatius sketches the genuine Catholic spirit, the spirit of loyalty to the Church, the exact Catholic coloring, which is so often wanting even in Catholics." (Fr. Meschler, S.J.)

Non-Catholic critics have seen in these rules the very essence of the Exercises and their sole aim, viz., to train men in "ecclesiasticism" or "churchliness"—a very modern word—i.e., in servile and blind submission to the power and rule of the Church. This is, of course, a complete misunderstanding of the Exercises in general, and of these rules in particular. That supposed object cannot be the essence of the Exercises; for the rules were added later, as a sort of appendix. These rules have been judged in a rather strange manner even by some modern Catholics. One such sees in them, like most non-Catholics, the real object of the Exercises and the best expression of what he calls "Jesuitical Catholicism." The expression, "Jesuitical Catholicism," is itself a misnomer and an abuse, and commonly has a mischievous and sinister connotation. There is but one kind of loyalty and obedience for all Catholics. It is true that in actual and practical obedience there may be degrees. The Jesuits profess a special degree of obedience in their fourth vow, viz., to go to whatever mission the Holy See sends them, even if no means of support are given them. This is a degree of obedience to which Catholics generally are not bound. But it does not constitute a special kind of "Jesuitical Catholicism." Theirs is the one Catholicism, although they are ready to practice it in an exceptional and magnanimous degree. Here too appears the idea of "magnanimity" so prominent in the Exercises concerning the following of Christ.

Almost the opposite view has been recently expressed by a French religious. He sees in these rules a mere appendix of only temporary import, because in the days of St. Ignatius, in the period of the great Protestant rebellion against the Church, some kind of special warning could not well be omitted. That is a serious underestimation and an essential misunderstanding of the Rules. The Protestant attacks were, indeed, the occasion of the special emphasis. Yet the Rules are not a mere appendix without intrinsic connection with the Exercises. A simple illustration will show their true nature and connection with the Exercises.

Suppose, soon after the publication of a code of laws in a country, some special conditions arise which were not explicitly taken into account in the body of the laws. The remedy would be found in the fundamental principles which are contained in the code and which have only to be applied explicitly to the new conditions. That is exactly the relation of these rules to the Exercises, a practical application of the fundamental ideas of the Exercises. They are an application of the idea contained in "The Kingdom of Christ." Christ did found a kingdom, the Kingdom of God. Here on earth the Church is this Kingdom. Hence loyalty to the Church is demanded "from all who want to be loyal in the service of Christ 'the founder and head of this Kingdom.'" Again consider the meditation of the "Two Standards." The Church is the "Civitas Dei" of St. Augustine which must meet in fearful struggle the forces of the enemy of Christ. Those who are eager to follow Christ will fight in their own hearts whatever comes from the enemy of Christ; but they will also do all in their power to oppose Satan's influence in the souls of others, and will endeavor, in true apostolic spirit, to defend and expand Christ's kingdom. Theirs will be the great motto: "Pro Christo et Ecclesia!"—"For Christ and the Church," which has been the battle cry of chivalrous sons of the Church throughout the ages.

Here is reached the deepest reason for loyalty to the Church and here is revealed the intimate connection of these rules with the very heart of the Exercises. St. Ignatius gives as motive for the obedience to the Church the fact that she is "the true Spouse of Christ." Such is St. Paul's profound declaration: "Husbands love your wives, as Christ also loved the Church, and delivered Himself up for it." [30] He carried His love as far as it would go; it was a generous and magnanimous love. It has been seen that the spirit of the Exercises, their primary object and aim, is a great and magnanimous personal love of Christ. Now anyone who sincerely loves Christ cannot fail to have the greatest reverence, loyalty and affection for His "true Spouse" and will most gladly obey her. Here then is had the true relation of the "Rules of Orthodoxy" with the Exercises, a connection not often pointed out clearly enough. In the same passage of St. Paul there is an even more profound idea. He says Christ loves the Church as His own body.[31] Christ identifies Himself with His Church. To Saul, who persecuted Christ's Church, He cried out before the gates of Damascus: "Saul, Saul, why persecutest thou me?" [32] The Church is truly "the mystical body of Christ." This profound idea, so popular at present with devout Catholics, is equivalently contained in these "Rules for Or-

[30] *Ephesians* V, 25.
[31] *Ephesians* V, 29.
[32] *Acts* IX, 4.

thodoxy." That gives the Rules a value more than temporary, a permanent value as long as the Church lasts. They express for all Catholics the sacred duty of unbounded loyalty to the Holy See.

What St. Ignatius laid down as principles in his Exercises he practised in his life. His burning love for Christ is manifest in his ardent love for the Church and in his enthusiastic devotion to the visible head of the Church. He was the first to introduce into a religious order a special vow of obedience to the Vicar of Christ. His last desire on his deathbed was the wish to receive the blessing of the Holy Father. That wish was a profession of his own personal devotion to the Holy See; it was, at the same time, his last will and testament to his sons, his earnest request that they too should "distinguish themselves" by their loyalty to Christ's Spouse, and to His Vicar on earth.

These are the Spiritual Exercises of St. Ignatius. As was said in the beginning they can be fully understood only by one who has made the complete Exercises. But what has been presented here may give a brief idea of the real nature of the little book. It may suggest that the Roman Breviary is right in calling it an "admirable book." [33] It may explain why so many Popes and saints have considered it a masterpiece of spirituality, a masterpiece of soul guidance and soul formation!

And yet, like everything belonging to and connected with the Society of Jesus, the Spiritual Exercises have met with much criticism. Only a brief mention will be made of the fantastic ideas early Protestants had about them. A Calvinist preacher said: "The Jesuits seduce numbers of people into strange practices which they call spiritual exercises. Their victims, as is credibly reported, are intoxicated by fumes and by other uncanny means so that they believe they see the devil in living shape and they then abjure Christ." [34] There are other similarly absurd stories. Not quite so fantastic, though still much mistaken, are the opinions of many modern non-Catholic writers; the limits of this present work precludes their discussion.[35]

What is more surprising is that so many Catholics have severely criticized the Exercises. During the lifetime of St. Ignatius they were violently attacked by some Spanish religious and secular priests. Even the "indifference," that principle of exalted spirituality, was denounced as heretical. The Exercises, and their whole "spirituality," are criticized in our own time by some Catholics, priests and religious who are loyal and devout members of the Church. This is surprising, after so many Popes have approved the Exercises and their spirituality and have found none

---

[33] July 31, Lect. IV.

[34] Janssen, *History of the German People*, Vol. VIII, p. 230.

[35] Brou, S.J., in his valuable book *Les Exercices Spirituels* gives a number of such strange views on forty pages, 121–162.

of the alleged defects in them, after Popes have bestowed the highest encomiums on them, beginning with Paul III in 1548 down to Pius XI in our own day. It is apropos to mention the principal charges; they are frequently encountered in any reading on the Society. Objections [36] have been made that the Exercises and Jesuit spirituality in general are too "formal," almost "mechanical"; that there is too little of the "love of God" in them; that "mystical contemplation" is neglected; above all that they are too indifferent towards and opposed to the "liturgical" devotions.

From such objections one may turn to judgments of an entirely different character. The Exercises were most highly praised by the foremost leaders of the Catholic Reformation: St. Charles Borromeo, St. Philip Neri, St. Francis de Sales, and many others. To St. Francis de Sales is often attributed the statement that "this precious book has saved more souls than it contains letters." Far more important than the praise of these great Saints is the approval of the Exercises by the Holy See. In 1548 Pope Paul III gave the first Papal approbation to the Exercises. That approbation was not bestowed haphazardly or on the spur of the moment. The Pope had ordered three of the most prominent ecclesiastics in Rome at the time to examine the book of the *Spiritual Exercises*. All three were men of great learning and piety: Cardinal Juan Alvarez de Toledo, O.P., Archbishop of Santiago de Compostella, later Cardinal-Bishop of Albano and Tusculum, and at the time Inquisitor General; Philippo Archinto, Bishop of Borgo San Sepolcro, Vicar of Rome; Egidio Foscarari, O.P., Bishop of Modena, Master of the Sacred Palace, and official censor of books in Rome. The three were also active participants at the Council of Trent. These were men surely capable of passing judgment on the orthodoxy and usefulness of a spiritual book. They declared the book to be "most praiseworthy" and "very useful for the welfare and progress of souls." Pope Paul III adopted this judgment, adding that the Exercises were "filled with piety and sanctity," praised and approved their contents, and recommended their use to all the faithful. This approbation and recommendation of the Exercises was repeated by many Popes, notably Alexander VIII, Benedict XIV, Leo XIII, Pius X, and, in several documents, by Pius XI. The last named Pope declared St. Ignatius patron of all Spiritual Exercises wherever conducted.

Pope Benedict XIV spoke of the *Book of the Exercises* as a "wonderful" one, an expression used also in the Breviary. Now an interesting and important question arises. Whence did Ignatius obtain that knowledge which is found in this remarkable book? One thesis has been maintained by a number of Benedictine writers, viz., that the Exercises of St. Ignatius are largely derived from a book of Cisneros, the pious and zealous abbot

---

[36] A discussion of these objections will be found in Appendix III, "Modern Criticism of the Exercises and Jesuit (or Ignatian) Spirituality."

of Montserrat, which was published in 1500 under the title *Ejercitatorio de la vida espiritual*. It is most probable that St. Ignatius used this book; certain details of the Exercises indeed may have been derived from it. But these are not among the essentials of the Exercises. The most characteristic features of the Exercises, the Foundation, the Kingdom of Christ, the Two Standards, the Three Modes of Humility, the Election, etc., are entirely missing in the book of Cisneros. Besides, the plan, spirit and purpose of the Ignatian Exercises differ greatly from those of Cisneros.

Some have wanted to prove the dependence of the book of Ignatius on that of Cisneros by the very title "Spiritual Exercises," as the book of the Benedictine abbot is called *Ejercitatorio de la vida espiritual*, "Exercises of Spiritual Life." On the other hand, the expression "Spiritual Exercises" was a commonplace long before St. Ignatius. From the days of St. Paul spiritual life was compared to athletic practices, that is exercises. The expression occurs numberless times in medieval books; it is often used in the *Imitation of Christ*. Moreover, alone or with slight additions, it was used as a title of many medieval books of piety, especially of devotional treatises.[37] Possibly, the title may have been suggested to Ignatius by Cisneros' book. On the other hand, he may have obtained it from another source; the expression was, as is said, "in the air." It should be noted that several modern Benedictine authors have rejected any substantial dependence of the book of St. Ignatius on that of Cisneros.

In the previous chapter it was recorded that Ignatius read the *Flos Sanctorum* by the Italian Dominican, Jacopo de Voragine, and the *Life of Christ* by Ludolph, the German Carthusian. From the latter, he seems to have taken some of the methods concerning the meditations on the Life of Christ; he certainly took from him some of the matter for those meditations. At Manresa he began to read the *Imitation of Christ*, which remained a favorite book with him ever after. Some ideas of St. Ignatius remind us of the *Imitation*, although direct quotation cannot be pointed out. Several books written by other representatives of the *Devotio Moderna*, developed by the "Brethren of the Common Life," have been mentioned as "sources." No direct borrowing from these or other possible sources mentioned can be shown. If some critics' theses are to be accepted, young Ignatius, having just left the army, must have been a tremendous reader, a regular "bookworm," as one would say today. And yet some of the works which are supposed to be sources were extant only in Latin, a language which Ignatius began to study years after. That certain similarities are found between the Exercises and older spiritual books is to

---

[37] Compare St. Gertrude; *Exercitia Spiritualia*; Tauler, *Rosetum Exercitiorum Spiritualium*; (Pseudo)—Bonaventure, *Exercitia quaedam Spiritualia*; Thomas à Kempis, *Libellus Spiritualis Exercitii*, and *Brevis Admonitio Spiritualis Exercitii*.

be expected, as all deal with the same general subject, spiritual life. Thus the two opposing camps of Christ and Satan, of Jerusalem and Babylon, are met with in spiritual writings before St. Ignatius. If, however, one examines carefully the use by the older writers and that by Ignatius, one will find that there are differences in detail, often considerable. Above all, the special purpose for which St. Ignatius employs the imagery and the psychological place he assigns to it in the whole structure, are essentially different. To take similarities as proof of origin is rather dangerous reasoning.

The question of dependence, however, is of no great importance. No matter how much St. Ignatius might have taken from others, it was only material which he used in his own peculiar, original way. They were merely the stones he employed for his building. The great plan, the architectural perfection, are his; therein is found his undisputed originality. The idea has been well put by Dr. Pastor.[38] After mentioning certain points of striking similarity between the Exercises and words of former writers—among them even Savonarola—he adds: "These are only single stones. The building taken as a whole is a compact and uniform work of art constructed on new and original lines."

One more question remains about the origin; it is of greater significance than the preceding ones. The question is hinted at in the Breviary (July 31), which says: "A man at that time without any learning (litterarum plane rudis) composed the admirable book of the Exercises." Dr. Pastor puts it more explicitly: [39] "One remarkable phenomenon always remains. Here was a soldier, who had learned no more than to read and write and had only just said farewell to a life adrift among the temptations of the world, who yet was able to compose a spiritual work remarkable for inwardness, lucidity, depth and strength. By Ignatius himself and by his first disciples this was regarded as a special instance of the overruling power of the Spirit of God."

Indeed, one cannot explain it without admitting some supernatural assistance. Of this assistance some earlier disciples of the Saint speak explicitly. Fr. Nadal, intimately acquainted with St. Ignatius, says in one place: "God communicated the Exercises to Ignatius," in another: "God inspired them." Fr. Polanco, for years Ignatius' secretary, writes: "Taught by God he received the Exercises," and in another passage: "taught and enlightened (edoctus et illustratus) by the Lord." The same Father wrote a short preface to the Latin version, the *Vulgata*, in which he states that "Master Ignatius composed them not so much from books as through the unction of the Holy Ghost." This was printed as a preface to an edition which appeared at Rome under the eyes of St. Ignatius with at least

---

[38] Pastor, *History of the Popes*, Vol. XII, p. 16.
[39] *Ibid.*, p. 17.

his tacit approval. This fact leads to the other important point, that the Saint repeatedly indicated his indebtedness to a special supernatural assistance. It was quoted before [40] that St. Ignatius said: "God treated him as a teacher treats a child . . . it was always clear to him God treated him in this manner. If he thought differently, he would believe he offended the Divine Majesty." Again he says: "God gave him special light on certain questions"; and he makes similar assertions in his *Testament*, which indicate clearly enough that he was convinced of having received some supernatural help in the composition of the Exercises. And how can the Exercises be explained without admitting some such assistance?

There is, however, no wish to imply that this supernatural assistance was in the form of a "private revelation," such as has been given to some saints. Much less is there any intention of endorsing the opinion that the Blessed Virgin "dictated" the Exercises to St. Ignatius. This legend does not go back beyond the first part of the seventeenth century; it seems to be contradicted by several statements of St. Ignatius, and is resolutely rejected by the foremost modern Jesuit historians: Astrain, Watrigant, Tacchi-Venturi, among others.

Father Polanco, secretary of St. Ignatius, did not hesitate to say that the giving of the Exercises was the principal ministry of the Society. Their history during the last 400 years has not yet been written, but the partial accounts which have appeared are most impressive. Many non-Catholic historians have recognized and acknowledged their historical significance. Boehmer, who devoted himself for years to the study of the Society, has called the book of the Exercises "a book of human destiny," one which has greatly influenced the course of history. This is particularly evident in the annals of the sixteenth century. It was through the Exercises that a great part of Germany was saved for Catholicism, a fact explicitly affirmed by contemporaries. Writes one: "It is to the Exercises which many of the German magnates (secular and spiritual) performed that we owe almost all the good which was done in Germany later on." [41] Indeed, everywhere the Exercises were one of the principal instruments in the great Catholic reformation of the sixteenth century, which was truly a "new Spring" in the history of the Church. It is particularly this phase of the history of the Exercises which has impressed non-Catholic writers most. The words of one deserve to be quoted: "There is, indeed, no other work of Catholic literature which, for its historical effect, can be compared with Ignatius' little book. Soon the Exercises won recruits throughout the whole Catholic Church. Not only Jesuits, but numerous secular clergy, princes of the Church, scholars and laymen in the most various positions, performed the Exercises, and the system had the most

---

[40] See above, p. 49.

[41] Bl. Peter Faber quoted in Janssen, *History of the German People*, VIII, pp. 228–229.

powerful effect on all types: doubters recovered through it their faith, pleasure-seeking children of the world, famous scholars and influential personalities were moved to repentance. In the most distant lands, the Exercises raised up apostles of Christianity, and many a European prince became, through the Exercises, a devoted champion of the Catholic cause." [42]

Extraordinary were the effects produced in communities of the older religious orders; some were brought back to the primitive discipline, others inspired to new religious fervor and activity.[43] The Venerable Louis Blosius, a celebrated Benedictine Abbot of the sixteenth century, a distinguished writer on spiritual and mystical subjects, often called a "forerunner" of St. Francis de Sales, pays an eloquent tribute to the Exercises and their beneficent influence on his monks. In this connection the words of a famous Friar of our own time deserve to be quoted. The Dominican Father Denifle, whom his Protestant adversaries called "one of the most learned men of modern times," speaks of the influence of the Exercises on religious orders in the following words: "Through the Exercises the Jesuits of olden times were formed and those of our own day are formed. All other religious orders followed their example without giving up an iota of their old statutes. On the contrary, the practice of the Exercises helps them to observe their own rules more faithfully." [44] The same writer then describes the fruit which the laity can derive from the Exercises: "to become better acquainted with the Christian ideal of life, and the way that leads to it, viz., Jesus Christ." It is worth noting, in passing, that the fruit mentioned by the great Dominican is almost identical with that given above as the very heart of the Exercises.[45] In addition the Jesuits have been indefatigable in giving adaptations of the Exercises, especially of its First Week, to hosts of people in the form of missions and retreats.

This study of the Spiritual Exercises may be fittingly closed with the tribute paid to them by Pius XI in his encyclical *Mens Nostra*. "Among all the laudable methods that exist and that are inspired by the sound principles of Catholic asceticism, there is one which has attracted the full and repeated approval of this Apostolic See, which has won fullest praise from saints and masters of the spiritual life, which has reaped great

---

[42] Rene Fülop-Miller, *The Power and Secret of the Jesuits*, New York (1930), p. 16. This is a work not without considerable flaws; on the other hand it capably refutes some common errors about the Society, and in forceful and felicitous language describes many important phases of its history.

[43] Very interesting details are given by Brou, *Les Exercises Spirituels*, pp. 81–102 on the marvelous fruits derived from the Exercises by various religious orders, as well as the secular clergy.

[44] Denifle, *Luther und Luthertum*, Mainz (1904), Vol. I, part I, 2d ed., pp. 176–177.

[45] See above, p. 54.

harvests of holiness for four centuries. We allude to the method of St. Ignatius Loyola, of him whom we love to call the Specialist of the Exercises. His little book of Spiritual Exercises is small in bulk but precious in content. From the day that it was solemnly approved, praised and recommended by Our Predecessor, Paul III of holy memory, from that day (to use the words written by Ourselves before Our Pontificate) the book 'almost instantly established and imposed itself as the wisest and most universal code for the government of souls, as the inexhaustible source of deep and solid piety, as an irresistible stimulus and secure guide to conversion and to the highest spirituality and perfection' . . . In the same thought concur those who attained or increased their spiritual strength in this school of the Exercises, and who (to use the words of Our Predecessor of happy memory, Leo XIII) 'whether for their ascetic doctrine or for sanctity of life have flourished' in the last four centuries.

"The solidity of spiritual teaching, far from the dangers and illusions of the pseudo-mystics, the marvelous adaptations to every class and condition of persons (from souls given to contemplative life to men living in the world), the organic unity of its parts, the remarkable order in which the truths to be meditated are succeeded by spiritual instructions suitable to lead a man from the point where he is freed from sin to the most sublime peaks of spirituality, by the road of abnegation and victory over passion, all these things render the method of St. Ignatius the most commendable and the most effective." [46]

---

[46] *Mens Nostra*, Rome (December 20, 1929).

CHAPTER IV

HEROIC AGE

For sixteen years St. Ignatius of Loyola was to govern the new Society of Jesus, until death closed his career on July 31, 1556. They were important, those years, important as any of his life, for in them he moulded his order into a permanent organization that would live and develop according to his own unique planning. Such an accomplishment he obtained, in part, by his personal government marked by a readiness to undertake any employment desired by the Popes for the Church's good, by a wise and prudent direction of subjects, and by a prayerful spirit permeating all endeavors. But much more did Ignatius achieve the permanent actuality of the Society by composing its Constitutions, in which he set down the definite and documentary provisions for the nature of the order and its processes of operation.

The personal appearance of Ignatius during this period may be learned from a description drawn by the pen of his beloved novice, Ribadeneira: "He was of medium height, or, more accurately, somewhat below the average, with a small frame, although his brothers were tall, and well-formed. His countenance commanded respect, his forehead was high and without wrinkles, his eyes deepset, the eyelids puckered and wrinkled with his many tears, the ears of medium size, the nose high and curved, a somewhat ruddy complexion, his head bald, and his whole aspect venerable. His appearance was joyfully grave and gravely joyful, so that his serenity rejoiced those who looked upon him, while his gravity impressed all about him." [1] Towards the end of his life he thus appeared to a young Flemish scholastic, Franz Coster: "The day before yesterday I saw for the first time the most reverend Father Ignatius, to my indescribable joy and satisfaction. I could not satisfy myself with the sight of him. An old man, he walked in the garden leaning on a stick. Virtue shines in his countenance; he is gentle, friendly and lovable, so that he converses with learned and unlearned, great and small; truly is he a man venerable above all, for whom a great reward in Heaven awaits!" [2]

These years too were the heroic days of the Society. Its ranks filled with

---

[1] Astrain, *A Short Life of St. Ignatius*, Trans. by Hull, p. 113, London (1928).

[2] Duhr, *Geschichte der Jesuiten in den Ländern deutscher Zunge*, Freiburg (1907), Vol. I, p. 563.

veritable apostolic giants; many a one of them seemed to possess the force of an army, as, often alone, he journeyed afar to fan up the graying embers of Catholic faith, to oppose a barrier to the Protestant advance, or to raise aloft the Cross amidst the heathen savages. These early Jesuits exemplified the ideal of the Society of Jesus; they materialized the hopes of St. Ignatius.

Pope Paul III during the remaining nine years of his pontificate continued to lend strong support to the new order; he issued six more important documents in its interest. In one of these documents the original restriction of membership to sixty was removed (1544) and in another permission was granted to admit spiritual coadjutors with simple vows (1546). So great were the opportunities for apostolic labor and so few were there among the numerous applicants who could measure up to Ignatius' high standards for the professed, that the Saint conceived the plan of enlisting many worthy priests as assistants. The idea was entirely new, especially the reckoning of them with their simple vows as true religious. Julius III, the succeeding Pope, continually furthered the order's activities; as Cardinal presiding at Trent, he had been impressed by the work of the Jesuits at the Council. He issued the Bull "Exposcit debitum" of July 21, 1550, which constituted a new and solemn confirmation of the Society's institute and privileges, sanctioning besides the changes and complements which Ignatius had given to the original rule. Likewise he issued in 1552 the Bull of Foundation for the German College, an institution which he generously supported.

The labors of St. Ignatius and his companions for the spiritual good of the Roman populace was a large factor in the Papal good will.[3] The Church of Santa Maria della Strada, the first Church of the order in the Eternal City, became the center of a revival of piety and virtue. From its doors the fathers sallied forth through the streets and alleys to preach and catechise in the open air the children and the neglected poor. When Ignatius preached in the church many important persons came to listen intently to his simple discourses, delivered in a halting Italian with a Spanish idiom. Yet his earnestness and animation held them, and they could not but be impressed when with glowing countenance he invariably concluded: "Let us love God with all our hearts, with all our souls and with all our will!"

Great good was accomplished by the Saint in what today would be called "Social Work." Thus he founded the Casa di Santa Marta for unfortunate street-women, especially for those of them who were married. Though advised that his efforts for wretches so hardened in vice were doomed to failure, he persisted until within three years more than

---

[3] Pastor, *History of the Popes*, Vol. XII, pp. 36–57; XIII, pp. 180–183.

a hundred poor creatures had found shelter in the refuge. He established also the Casa di Santa Caterina dei Funari for maidens whose innocence was endangered by poverty or evil environment, that there they might safely remain until they married or entered a convent. He labored to raise funds for orphanages and similar charitable institutions; while under his direction his brethren ministered to the sick in the hospitals, nursing their bodily ills and providing for their spiritual needs. The welfare and protection of Jewish converts claimed his special care.

When the serious dispute between Paul III and King John of Portugal over the control of the Inquisition came almost to the breaking point, St. Ignatius devoted his best energies, with considerable success, to composing the difficulties. Some writers have inferred that the Saint was opposed in principle to the Inquisition because of his preventing Jesuits from accepting posts on the Tribunal. The contrary was the case. In fact he urged Paul III in 1542 to revive the Inquisition in Italy and he was of the opinion, declared in a letter to Canisius, that the execution of a few of the leading German heretics would have ended the Religious Revolt.[4] Ignatius, as a man of his age and as a Spaniard, quite approved of the Inquisition. His opposition to Jesuits on the Tribunal came from his conviction that the work would interfere with ordinary apostolic labors of the Society and would involve the acceptance of prelacies forbidden by the rule.

Several requests for amalgamation, coming from the Somaschi, the Barnabites and the Theatines, were rejected by the founder of the Jesuits. Ignatius highly regarded these new orders of Clerks Regular, but he was convinced that their purposes and that of his own Society differed too widely to make a combination advisable. Cardinal Caraffa, co-founder of the Theatines, had thought of such a union, but, according to Ribadeneira, came to agree on the whole with the reasons for the Saint's refusal.[5] Ignatius did welcome the invitation of the Carthusians for mutual spiritual assistance and communion in prayer.

More decidedly did he refuse the many requests for the spiritual guidance of women, both of individuals and of convents, being of the opinion that such direction did not fit in with the special apostolic labors of his priests. He was determined that his Society would have no Second Order. Considerable difficulty was occasioned by the attempt of Isabel Roser to affiliate herself and some companions to the Society. This noble Spanish lady had been a generous benefactress of the Saint in his early days at Barcelona. Ignatius was grateful, but his decision was fixed and he refused her request when she came to Rome in 1545. The ladies appealed to Paul III so insistently that the Pontiff ordered Ignatius to receive their solemn vows as their superior. Doña Isabel had little idea of

---

[4] Brodrick, *Saint Peter Canisius*, London (1935), pp. 211 ff.

[5] Pastor, *History of the Popes*, Vol. XII, p. 55.

obedience or the religious life, so difficulties increased. At length Ignatius convinced the Pope of the impossibility of the situation and the Holy Father relieved him of the charge.

Much of the last fifteen years of his life was occupied by Ignatius in the composition of the Constitution of the Society.[6] As the chapter following will offer an analysis of this document, in this only a few historical points will be narrated. All of the early fathers, and none more than Ignatius, recognized the need of a definite and written regulation of the life of the new order, if it were to survive and if its ideals were to be preserved. Several times in the first year the professed fathers in Rome met to work out plans. In 1541 Ignatius and Codure were entrusted with the task; on Codure's death, shortly afterward, the whole labor devolved upon Ignatius. The next six years he spent studying, meditating and praying; then in 1547 he began to write, still carefully reflecting, for it was not until 1550 that he completed the first draft. The Jesuits in Rome were asked to pass upon this preliminary rule. From their suggestions the Saint with the aid of Polanco inserted the alterations he deemed appropriate. Then the document was subjected to the test of experience; Nadal put the new body of law into operation in Spain, Portugal, Germany and Italy; Quadrio introduced it into India. During the four years following, Ignatius weighed the reports of the various experimentations and made here and there the changes he thought advisable. When he died in 1556 the Constitutions were almost entirely completed; in fact, as will be noted later, they were accepted by the First General Congregation of the order with but a few insignificant alterations.

The last year of the Saint's life was clouded with threatening disaster, for with the election of Cardinal Caraffa as Pope Paul IV, Ignatius had good cause to fear the destruction of his life work.[7] The new Pontiff, with all his devoted labors for the Catholic Reformation, was yet a man little tolerant of the ideas of others. Ignatius was but one of several excellent ecclesiastics who felt his displeasure; Cardinal Pole, Cardinal Morone and even Cardinal Ghislieri were among them. The stern Neapolitan for years had been deeply prejudiced against the founder of the Society of Jesus; he had little sympathy for the Roman College and his name, significantly enough, was not on the list of contributors to the support of the German College. Still, in the beginning of his pontificate Paul IV treated Ignatius and the Jesuits kindly; he admired their work for the poor of Rome, sent Salmeron to Poland, sought the advice of Bobadilla in reform problems and valued Laynez highly. The mistrust however would not down. As the disastrous war with Spain developed, yielding to the rumor of arms concealed in the house of the Jesuits, most of whom

---

[6] Pastor, *History of the Popes*, Vol. XII, pp. 58–60.

[7] Pastor, *History of the Popes*, Vol. XIV, pp. 246–250.

were Spaniards, the Pope ordered the premises searched. The officials would have made only a perfunctory inquiry, had not Ignatius insisted on the entire house being examined. Paul IV did not continue Julius III's support of the German College; most of the Cardinals stopped their contributions also. Such a grave loss of funds during a period when neither money nor loans were available, almost ended the institution. Clerical students from Germany had to be turned away; indeed for two years not a single German was maintained in the college. Cardinal Otto Truchsess in his discouragement wished to abandon the whole project. But not Ignatius, who declared his readiness to be sold as a slave rather than give up his Germans. He distributed the German students among the various Italian colleges and ordered their support until a better day would come. The danger lest the Pope might radically change the Constitutions, a thing which Ignatius greatly dreaded, did not arise until the Saint had died.

Of the works of Ignatius' brethren during his generalate none were more outstanding than the labors of the four who assisted in the deliberations of the Council of Trent, Le Jay, Laynez, Salmeron and Canisius.[8] Le Jay, chosen by Cardinal Truchsess as his advisor, was the first to arrive at Trent; he was one of the two theologians commissioned on February 23, 1546, to draft the decree on the Holy Scriptures and Tradition. On Paul III's request for Jesuits to act as Papal theologians at the Council, Ignatius chose Faber, Laynez and Salmeron. He provided them with wise instructions as to their conduct: they were to make the care of souls their first concern; they were to avoid, in preaching, doctrines on which Catholics and Protestants were at variance; they were to end their sermons and instructions with a prayer for the success of the Council and in all their conversations they were to be cautious and unassuming. Faber never reached the Council, for he died on August 1, 1546, a martyr of obedience, a death in keeping with his holy character.[9] The presiding legates, Cardinal del Monte and Cardinal Cervini, accorded Laynez and Salmeron a cordial welcome to Trent. The Spanish Bishops, on the other hand, were a bit ashamed of the youth and shabby clothes of their fellow-countrymen. But not for long; soon they were to be loud in their praise, as was the whole Council, of the virtues and learning of the two priests. On alternate days Le Jay, Laynez and Salmeron said Mass for the people, administered the Sacraments and explained the Faith. Despite the prohibition that neither bishops nor theologians were to preach at Trent, at the request of some of the Fathers of the Council, the Cardinal Legates had Laynez preach on Sundays and feast-days in the Church of S. Maria Maggiore. Large congregations gathered to hear him. The Legates

---

[8] Pastor, *History of the Popes*, Vol. XIII, pp. 78–82.

[9] Faber was beatified by Pius IX in 1872.

ordered both Spanish Jesuits to participate in the discussions of the theologians before the Bishops and Cardinals. So sound and learned were their treatments of the problem of Justification that many members of the Council requested copies of their remarks. An hour was the longest time given to any theologian for the statement of his case; yet the presiding Cardinals permitted Laynez to speak for three hours, and even longer. When the subject of the Sacraments was taken up, Laynez and Salmeron were appointed to summarize the errors of the Protestants and to set down the opposing statements of the Fathers and the Councils; their report was presented by Cardinal Cervini as a basis of negotiation. In the discussions, the same Cardinal made it a practice of having one of the Jesuits among the opening speakers, to explain the status of the question, and of reserving the other until the end, to refute the less correct opinions which had been advanced. Many learned prelates before voting sought their advice.[10] When in 1547 Ignatius wished to send Laynez to Florence in response to the request of the Duchess, Cardinal Cervini declared that he was indispensable to the Council; and Bishop Archinto, the Vicar of Paul III, wrote to the Saint that his sons could not do more good in any place in the world than at Trent. In 1547 Canisius was sent to the Council in the capacity of advisory theologian to Cardinal Truchsess. On the removal of the sessions to Bologna, Laynez and Salmeron followed the Council; Le Jay and Canisius, after delaying at Trent for instructions from Cardinal Truchsess, finally joined their confrères. In the conference on Penance, Laynez again spoke for three hours. Canisius likewise participated in several discussions. The labors of these four Jesuits drew the attention of the Bishops of the Catholic World to the new order. In Spain, according to Araoz, the report of their work did more good for the Society than all the labors of the Spanish Jesuits.

The Italian Bishops at Trent were so impressed with Laynez and his companions that they eagerly sought to obtain Jesuit priests for their dioceses. In a short time fathers of the order were inaugurating a revival of the Faith in almost every important city of the peninsula.[11] The beginning was made in 1545 in Venice where Laynez lectured thrice weekly on the Scriptures; Broët worked at Montepulciano and also at Faenza, where he reconciled numerous feudists and founded the Compagnia della Carita for the sick poor. Salmeron preached at Verona, Belluno and Modena. At the last city, unfortunately, his ardor outran his prudence and brought him into conflict with the zealous Cardinal Morone, who dismissed him from the diocese. Cardinal Morone, however, was always

---

[10] Pastor, *History of the Popes*, Vol. XII, p. 81 quoting "Epistolae Salmeroni" I, 26, 27; Astrain, *Historia de la Compañia de Jesús en la ancien asistencia Hispañia*, Vol. I, pp. 526, 527.

[11] Pastor, *History of the Popes*, Vols. XII, pp. 82–90; XIII, pp. 192–198.

deeply attached to the order, later on insisting on the establishment of a college in Modena. In the Duomo of Florence during the Lent of 1548, congregations numbering 8,000 and 9,000 listened to Laynez's sermons. Padua, Parma, Bologna, Brescia, Pisa, Naples and Reggio were among the Italian cities that received the ministrations of the Jesuits.

The fathers devoted themselves likewise to the poor peasants of the remote districts in the Abruzzi, the Lunigiana, Calabria and Apulia. They found such incredible ignorance and neglect of even the commonest Catholic practices that they were accustomed to speak of these regions as the "Italian Indies." Foremost among the apostolic laborers must be reckoned Silvestro Landini, truly a missionary of the first rank. Thus was he described by a contemporary: "He makes peace between relatives, between neighbors, between communities; he induces runaway monks to return to their convents; he stirs men up to give means of subsistence to convents and to the poor; he procures rules against profane swearing and for the reverent observance of Sunday; he preaches in churches and public places, explains the Catechism, exhorts men to enter religious life; he fasts daily, his food is a coarse bread of millet seed, his drink a little water. Great and small model their lives on his; even if he were not to preach, his example alone would be a constant sermon." [12] Landini later became the Apostle of Corsica, where conditions far worse than in Italy but spurred on his zeal; he died there March 3, 1554, worn out by labors, hardships and privations.

The first members of the order to enter Sicily were Lhost, a Netherlander, who worked at Girgenti, and Laynez, who achieved reforms in Monereale and lectured in its Cathedral. The Spaniard Doménech, the most important of the early Jesuits on the island, came to Palermo in 1547; he was confessor to the Viceroy and his wife, reformed a convent of penitents, labored hard for the erection of orphanages, and established a college in the city in 1549. Just a year before at Messina, on the order of St. Ignatius, was begun the first of the Society's colleges, which from the start were operated exclusively for extern pupils.

The Jesuits were to be found in the forefront of the conflict with Italian heretics. Lutheranism in Italy, because it was hidden, often propagated by apparently orthodox preachers, and strong in the support of certain sections of the intelligentsia, was exceedingly difficult to cope with. The priests of the order, nevertheless, carried a vigilant warfare right into the most active centers of heterodoxy. Broët attacked the teaching of the apostate Ochino at Faenza, Le Jay at Ferrara offset the favor which the Duchess Renée gave to the innovators, and Landini cleared the diocese of Luni of heretical teachings. Salmeron journeyed to Modena

---

[12] *Monumenta Historica S.J., Epistolae Mixtae*, Vol. I, p. 445.

to contravene the influence of its Academy, a body of literati responsible for the dissemination of many doctrinal errors and the virus of free thought; the caustic and acrimonious allusions in his sermons offended many and brought him into conflict with Cardinal Morone, as has been noted. Active heretical groups in Venice, Genoa and Naples were vigorously opposed by other Jesuit preachers. In the last city in 1552 the followers of Valdes, who, though not a heretic, was a man of very dangerous and unorthodox views, raised a storm against the Jesuits. Salmeron's sermons, preached in Naples in the following year, however, won back many to the old Faith.

The most effective means for reviving Catholicism in Italy, as well as for combating heresy there, was found in the colleges for extern students which were begun under the direction of Ignatius during the last years of his life. It would appear that the Saint, though realizing the value for souls of youth education, was some time in coming to look upon it as a labor proper to his Society.[13] Colleges opened up to 1546 were exclusively training schools for the younger members of the order. What first brought Ignatius into the wider field of education may have been the glowing accounts of St. Francis Xavier concerning the results of Jesuits teaching extern pupils in the college of Goa. In that institution, established before their arrival in the city, the fathers were invited to conduct classes in 1543; not, however, until 1549 were they given complete charge. The first Jesuit college to offer instruction to non-Jesuit students was the College of Gandia, founded by St. Francis Borgia as a house of studies for the order in 1545; here in 1546 lectures in philosophy were opened to externs and in 1548 two classes in Latin Grammar were added. In that same year Paul III bestowed university status on the Spanish institution; Gandia was thus both the first college and the first university of the Society of Jesus. The College of Messina, as has been noted above, was the first Jesuit college intended from the start for lay-pupils. The citizens of Messina backed by the Viceroy of Sicily petitioned the founder of the Jesuits to inaugurate a school for boys in their city. Ignatius consented and determined to make it a model college. For its staff he chose ten of his most talented subjects, five Italians, a Spaniard (Nadal, the first rector), a Frenchman, a Savoyard and a German (Canisius); he took special pains in arranging the curriculum, insisting on the methods of the University of Paris as the norm to be followed. The College of Messina opened its doors in 1548.

Within a period of eight years, up to the founder's death, twenty-one

---

[13] Farrell, *The Jesuit Code of Liberal Education*, Milwaukee (1938), pp. 1–153. Cf. Appendix A which contains a list of the thirty-three colleges approved by St. Ignatius and opened before his death, as also a list of the six approved by him but established after his death.

colleges were opened in various Italian cities. Their beginnings were modest indeed; Ignatius desired the institutions to stand on their own resources and grow gradually rather than to start in a great flourish, only to fail miserably later. The poverty and privations which were the lot of almost all these first staffs called for the staunchest heroism. At the head of all stood the Roman College (1551). Ignatius planned it to be the ideal and center of Jesuit education; hence he called to its halls the order's best theologians, philosophers and classicists, the excellency of whose instruction attracted large numbers of students. It had a leading part in extending to Rome and thence to the Catholic world the revival of Scholasticism begun by the Dominicans in Spain.

Next in importance ranked the German College.[14] Cardinal Morone, who in the course of his several nunciatures in Germany had obtained an expert knowledge of religious conditions there, suggested to the founder of the Jesuits the establishment in Rome of a college which would train German ecclesiastical students in learning and piety. He hoped that they might return to their unhappy country to become scholarly and saintly bishops, administrators and professors. At the time there was no place in the Empire where such training might be obtained. Rome could give it; and moreover the daily contacts with the Papacy and the sacred traditions of the City would foster in the hearts of the young German students a deep devotion for the Holy See. Saint Ignatius eagerly responded to the zealous Cardinal's suggestion, offering all the resources of his order for the work. Most of the preliminary steps were Ignatius'; and he it was who drew up for the institution its set of rules and regulations, a masterpiece that has served as model for countless seminaries. Julius III by a solemn Bull of August 31, 1552 formally founded the German College and gave it to the charge of the Society of Jesus. A short time later Ignatius was obliged also to assume the financial support of the institution, a burden which he undertook because of his faith in the project and his deep affection for the German students.

From Spain St. Ignatius received the strongest response in these early years.[15] The Spaniards, just finished with the long crusade against the Moors and girding themselves for the conflict with the Northern Protestants, readily welcomed his ideal of unswerving loyalty to the Catholic Church. The military spirit of the new order carried a special appeal to the fighting and adventuresome race of the Conquistadores. In numbers they offered themselves for the service; capable and learned recruits they were too, for many were doctors or scholars of the flourishing Universities

---

[14] Steinhuber, *Geschichte des Collegium Germanicum in Rom*, 2 Vols. (1906); Pastor, *History of the Popes*, Vol. XIII, pp. 229 ff.

[15] Astrain, *Historia de la Compaña de Jesús en la ancien asistencia de España*, Vol. I, pp. 201–678.

of Salamanca and Alcalá. Soon priests of the Society were in almost every Spanish city, preaching to crowded churches and winning all hearts with their heroic care of the sick. A number of them died nursing the plague-stricken. Their instruction of the young, hitherto considered undignified, gained universal approbation; the people of Toledo blessed God at the sight of the Jesuits ringing bells and marshalling the children through the streets to religious teaching.[16] Colleges, some liberally supported by Spanish nobles, sprang up within a short time in all parts of the land.

The first Jesuit to come to Spain was Araoz, a kinsman of Ignatius, in 1539. At Azpeitia he had to deliver his sermons in the open air to a congregation of 4,000, many of whom climbed the trees and roofs to listen to him. Bl. Peter Faber arrived in 1541; the next year he had to leave for Germany, but in 1544 he returned and joined Araoz in Portugal. Bearing letters of high recommendation from King John III, both journeyed to Valladolid to meet Philip II. At the Spanish court they found several powerful friends: beside the Prince, Cardinal Juan Tavera, the Grand Inquisitor Diego Tavera and the Nuncio Poggio. Araoz accompanied Philip II to Madrid, where his advocacy of frequent Communion aroused considerable comment, favorable and unfavorable, the latter labeling the practice a Jesuit invention. Rapid growth by 1547 justified the erection of a Spanish province, with Araoz as Provincial.

If the successes were great, great too was the opposition. The over-cautious among the Spaniards suspected any new religious movement as a possible recrudescence of the heretical Alumbrados. In Saragossa, where the Prior of the Dominicans had labored hard for the establishment of a Jesuit college, the opposition of some other religious and many of the local clergy for a time defeated his efforts, even though he was supported by the Viceroy, the Inquisitors, the civic council and many nobles. The Primate of Spain, Archbishop Siliceo of Toledo, manifested a strong antipathy to the Society; his order of 1549 forbidding anyone but parish priests to administer Holy Communion in his archdiocese was aimed at the Jesuits, whom he was reported to have labeled as heretics. Two years later the Archbishop caused to be read in every pulpit a document forbidding all official priestly work to the Jesuits. As such an act constituted an attack on the Papal privileges of the order and hence on the honor of the Holy See, Julius III addressed to Siliceo a letter of high praise of the Society, while the Nuncio, Poggio, strongly defended it. When Philip II declared against him, the prelate withdrew his prohibition. The condemnation of fifteen propositions from the *Book of the Spiritual Exercises* in 1553 by a commission appointed by Siliceo, produced little effect in view of the previous approval of the work by Paul III.

A most violent storm broke out in Salamanca when on the proposal of

---

[16] Astrain, *op. cit.*, Vol. II, p. 523.

Cardinal de Mendoza in 1548 a college of the order was begun. The opponents were led by the distinguished Dominican theologian, Melchior Cano, a man of brilliant gifts and deep learning but withal a difficult character. Cano seemed to be convinced that the Jesuits were none other than the forerunners of Anti-Christ. In his sermons in 1548 he attacked them so strongly as to make the fathers objects of such suspicion that many hesitated to be seen conversing with them. They bore their trial in silence, though they did seek out Cano and offer him an explanation of their character and customs. When this proved unavailing, Ignatius appealed to the highest authority of the Dominican Order. The Master-General, Francisco Romeo, responded by issuing in December 1548 a circular letter to all his brethren, generously praising the Jesuits, recommending them to the fraternal charity of the Friars, and forbidding in virtue of holy obedience any attack, public or private, against them. Two of the most outstanding Spanish Dominicans, Luis de Granada and Juan de Peña, also vigorously defended the fathers; de Peña composed an apologia for the Society of Jesus. Paul III came to the order's support by letters in its behalf to the Bishops of Cuença and Salamanca. Before such support the opposition in Salamanca soon disappeared. The eloquent sermons of the Jesuit Estrada and the charity of his confrère, de Torres, for the condemned criminals did much to correct unfavorable impressions. For a time it seemed as though the great Archbishop of Valencia, St. Thomas of Villanova, would join the anti-Jesuits; the innovations in religious life made by St. Ignatius did not appeal to him. When, however, he learned that the changes had Rome's approval he dropped his opposition and became a great benefactor of the order. Trouble arose again in Saragossa in 1555 when the Jesuit college was finally established. A question of the privileges of the older orders was involved, the Augustinians claiming that their rights were infringed upon. The Archbishop supported them, and the populace so turned against the Jesuits that they had to leave the city. The decision was given eventually in their favor and the college in a short time was opened. During these trials the Spanish Jesuits found a true friend in the holy secular priest, Blessed John of Avila, the Apostle of Andalusia.

An offset to all opposition as well as a heightening of the prestige of the new order came in the accession to its ranks of St. Francis Borgia,[17] Viceroy of Catalonia and Duke of Gandia. Borgia came to know the Society of Jesus through a meeting with Bl. Peter Faber. So impressed was he with its purposes that he founded in Gandia a college for the

---

[17] *Monumenta Historica Societatis Jesu, Monumenta Borgiana,* Vols. I–V; Clarke, *The Life of St. Francis Borgia,* London (1900); Suau, *Vie de St. François Borgia,* Paris (1905); Karrer, *Der Heilige Franz von Borja,* Freiburg (1921); Yeo, *The Greatest of the Borgias,* Milwaukee (1931).

order, where, as has been noted, extern pupils were first taught by Jesuits. On the death of his wife, having gone through the Spiritual Exercises, he took a vow to enter the Society of Jesus. Since civic duties and the care of his children prevented its immediate fulfillment, Paul III, at the instance of St. Ignatius, permitted the Duke to pronounce the solemn vows in 1548 and yet to administer his temporal possessions for three years until the future of his family was assured. Such was the fervor of the new recruit that six months after his profession Ignatius was obliged to curtail by half his prayers and penances. In 1550 he went to Rome to be received by the founder; in the following year he returned to Spain to be ordained, May 23, 1551. The step taken by Borgia had been kept from all but a few friends; the sensation, when in 1551 Spain learned of his action, can scarcely be described. It is said that ten thousand came to his first Mass. The new priest took up the work of preaching, especially to the poor and lowly, in many parts of Spain. His fervent utterances and his ascetical appearance deeply impressed the throngs that gathered to hear him. In 1554 Ignatius named him general Superior of the now three Spanish provinces, Castile, Aragon and Andalusia. Under his guidance much of the remarkable progress of the order in Spain was achieved.

It was John III's plea for missionaries for India that brought the first Jesuits to Portugal, St. Francis Xavier and Simon Rodriguez.[18] They arrived in Lisbon in 1540. The ten months of waiting for the East India fleet's sailing they employed with fruitful results in apostolic labors for the Portuguese capital. The King was delighted with the two priests and heard with approval their description of the purposes of the new Society of Jesus; he even desired them to live in the royal palace. They preferred to take up a humbler residence in the Hospital of All Saints. The good they wrought in the populace by their sermons, their devotion to the care of criminals—even the condemned—and the success of their directing the young court nobles in the Spiritual Exercises, had all Lisbon enthusiastic about them. The people loved to call them "The Apostles." King John gave up all idea of the Indies and moved to retain the two Jesuits in his kingdom at home. On St. Ignatius' decision it was at length agreed that one, Xavier, should journey on to the East.

Rodriguez remaining in Portugal continued the labor for souls. To further the work, the King founded a house of studies for the order at Coimbra, while many youths of the noblest families applied for admission into the new organization. The membership by 1546 warranted the establishment of a province. In undertaking this charge Rodriguez, the Provincial, composed rules on a basis given by Ignatius, and obtained from the recruits a measure of piety and discipline which won the ap-

---

[18] Pastor, *History of the Popes*, Vol. XII, pp. 98–101; XIII, pp. 189–192.

proval of Bl. Peter Faber during his visit to the country. The preaching, the zealous administration of the Sacraments and the practice of poverty of the new fathers, gained the highest esteem of the people. Three colleges were begun at Lisbon, Evora and Coimbra. Two of the Jesuits, Gonsalez and Nuñez, in 1548 embarked on the hazardous journey to Morocco to bring the consolations of religion to the Christian slaves; at Tetuan they cared for over five hundred captives. Both returned to Portugal to collect clothes, medicines and alms for these unfortunates. So pleased was King John that he entrusted all care of the Christian slaves to the Jesuits. He wished also to appoint fathers of the Society as judges of the Inquisition, but relinquished the proposal because of the strong opposition of Saint Ignatius.

Yet it was just in this flourishing section that the first internal crisis in the order occurred. Too many novices had been accepted and too little care had been exercised in the choice of them; a striving after independence and a worldliness began to appear, foreboding the most evil consequences. Rodriguez, while a truly saintly character, proved in the long run unsuitable for the office of Provincial; he seemed to wish to develop the province according to his own ideas and not those of St. Ignatius, and to make it somewhat independent of the rest of the order. The founder removed him from office, whereupon an insubordinate element broke out into open dissatisfaction. Ignatius acted in the crisis with inflexible force, sanctioning the drastic act of the new Provincial, Torres, in expelling 130 members. In 1553 only 105 Jesuits remained in the Portuguese province. Rodriguez turned to the Court to seek royal aid for his reinstatement; then the summons came for him to appear in Rome. He obeyed, though on his arrival at the headquarters of the Society he demanded a formal trial. It was granted and the decision went against him. After some hesitancy he submitted. No doubt the fact that the Constitutions had not yet been published in Portugal contributed a good deal to the difficulties. On their promulgation, which occured shortly, the Portuguese province took on a new lease of life.

From 1540, a number of the younger Jesuits had been sent to Paris to make their studies at the University; in 1548 there were eighteen of them living in an annex of the Lombard College. They attracted little attention as they wore the dress of laymen. St. Ignatius had always cherished a desire to set up a definite foundation in France,[19] especially in Paris, the center of ecclesiastical learning. His hope was to be realized only after years of struggle with Gallican-minded officials and ecclesiastics. Even the powerful support of Henry II and of the Cardinal of Lorraine availed little. The conflict started with the endeavor of the Bishop of

[19] Fouqueray, *Compagnie de Jésus en France*, Paris (1910–1922), pp. 1–221; Pastor, *History of the Popes*, Vol. XIII, pp. 203–208.

Clermont, Guillaume du Prat, an ever loyal friend of the Society of Jesus, to turn over to the Jesuits the college which he had founded at Paris for the training of priests to cope with Lutheranism. The transfer required a royal decree, which the King at the request of the Cardinal of Lorraine signed in 1550 and issued again in 1551. The document to possess legal force had to be registered by the Parlement of Paris, most of the members of which were strong Gallicans. Prospects for registration were exceedingly dubious. Matters were made worse when the Jesuit superior in Paris committed the error of presenting the Papal Bull of October 18, 1549, confirming the privileges of the order, to the Royal Council; that body communicated it to the Parlement. The Gallican jurists at once raised the question of Papal privileges in France and declared that the Society of Jesus transgressed the rights of the King, of the Parlement and of the French episcopacy. The Papal document was returned to the fathers and, for a time, the matter rested.

The new Provincial of the French Jesuits, Broët, a native of France and an alumnus of the University of Paris, renewed the attempt to obtain registration towards the end of 1552. Henry II again ordered the Parlement to register his decree, only to be met with an unyielding opposition. A resolution was put forth that before any action the royal patent and the Papal Bull must be submitted to the Bishop of Paris, Eustace du Bellay, and to the theological faculty of the University of Paris. Du Bellay was a thorough-going Gallican and had already refused the Jesuits faculties to hear confessions and to preach in his diocese. As a result of this prohibition only in the exempt Benedictine Abbey of St. Germain-des-Prés and in the neighboring diocese of Soissons were the fathers able to perform their priestly functions. When Broët came to present the Bull to the Bishop, the prelate gave him a very unfriendly reception and in true Gallican fashion assured him that the Pope could give no confirmation for France. The theological faculty's report was made only after a long delay. It was a complete condemnation. The very name, "Society of Jesus," was declared offensive; the fact that the order received everyone without distinction was censored; the innovations in religious life were pronounced blameworthy; and the privileges were held to be contrary to the rights of ecclesiastical and secular personages. In a summary the Society of Jesus was asserted to be dangerous to the Faith, disturbing to the peace of the Church, destructive of religious orders, an organization that pulled down more than it built up. It was a Papal Bull that the authors of the report so thoroughly condemned; yet their report was prefaced by the expression of their "deep veneration for the Holy See."

A great popular excitement against the Jesuits followed, in which sermons were preached assailing the fathers and placards attacking them were nailed up in public places. Bishop du Bellay forbade the priests of the order under pain of excommunication to exercise their priestly duties until the Papal Bull should be confirmed by himself, the faculty of theology and the Parlement. Broët submitted, though at the same time he forwarded an appeal to the Supreme Pontiff.

St. Ignatius himself made no direct reply to the condemnation, though strongly urged to do so, for he did not wish to be drawn into a long conflict with the University of Paris. Rather he chose to take his case to the judgment of the whole Catholic world. Turning to the Catholic princes, lay and clerical, who had observed the fathers laboring in their dominions, and to the universities which had heard them lecturing in their halls, Ignatius asked for expressions of opinion as to the lives, character and works of the Jesuits. The response was immediate: commendation poured in from such princes as John III of Portugal, the Viceroy of Sicily, the Duchess of Tuscany and the Duchess of Ferrara; from the Universities of Valladolid, Coimbra, and Louvain; and from the Inquisitors of Saragossa, Evora, Ferrara and Florence.[20] These testimonials the Saint intended to lay before the Pope, Julius III, whose very primacy, after all, the Paris document had attacked.

The step did not have to be taken. The Cardinal of Lorraine during his visit to Rome in 1555 arranged a meeting between four doctors of the University of Paris, members of his entourage, one of whom had composed the condemnation, and four learned Jesuits. The discussions resulted in the doctors acknowledging their mistake. The condemnatory document, though never formally recalled, was in a short time forgotten. During Ignatius' lifetime, however, only one college was established in France; that was the college founded by Guillaume du Prat, the Bishop of Clermont, at Billom, a city of his diocese, in 1556.

The first Jesuits in the Low Countries [21] were Spanish members of the order who had been students at Paris; the war between Francis I and Charles V forced them in 1542 to leave France. With the intention of completing their studies they settled at Louvain; there they were joined by their first Flemish recruit, Vischaven, a pious priest of great strictness of life, Bl. Peter Faber, during a short stay in the city, so won the hearts of the undergraduates that on the rumor of his departure for Portugal nineteen wished to follow him; he chose nine of them. In 1547 the little group at Louvain elected Vischaven as their superior and drew up a set of regulations for their life which they sent to Ignatius. The Saint approved of their acts, only enjoining on them the duty of seeking the approval of the Bishop of Liége for their corporate existence. Great diffi-

---

[20] These testimonials may be found in the Bollandists' article on St. Ignatius, *Acta Sanctorum, Julii tom.* VII, *Commentarius praevius*, parts 47, 48, pp. 513–518.

[21] Poncelet, *Compagnie de Jésus dans les anciens Pays-Bas*, Brussels (1927), Vol. I, pp. 34–111; Pastor, *History of the Popes*, Vols. XII, p. 102; XIII, pp. 208–209.

culties were experienced in the Low Countries also in obtaining legal authorization; Charles V was prejudiced against the order and two of his most influential officials, Granvelle and van Zwichem, were unfavorable. Ignatius sent Ribadeneira to the Netherlands in 1555 to negotiate for the official recognition. He received a friendly reception from Philip II, attracted much attention by his sermons and gained valuable friends at the Court of Brussels. Shortly after the death of St. Ignatius, Philip II granted the required civil rights.

Two Jesuits, Broët and Salmeron, in 1542 were sent by Paul III as nuncios to the persecuted Church of Ireland.[22] They were to confirm the bishops and the chieftains in the Faith, bring about reforms, open Latin schools, find suitable candidates for the episcopacy and care for the poor. Ignatius ordered them to adapt themselves to the Irish customs and to spend any monies received in their official duties on the poor and for religious objects. The two fathers went by way of Scotland in order to visit James V. At the Scottish court efforts were made to dissuade them from continuing on, for their lives would be imperilled by the agents of Henry VIII who knew of their mission. Broët and Salmeron went on, however, arriving in Ireland in the Lent of 1542. They found everything in chaos; most of the chieftains and bishops had accepted the royal supremacy, although the people were still loyal; the true bishops were in hiding; many of the convents stood deserted and in ruins. The realization of the impossibility of carrying out most of their programme was soon evident to them. Still they tried to do what spiritual good they could for the people. It was not much, for the soldiers were hot on their tracks, and after thirty-four days of constant flight they escaped to Scotland. Of their mission Bellesheim observed: "To outward appearance a failure, this first mission of the Jesuits to Ireland was destined in the course of time to bear much fruit." [23]

Germany in the second half of the sixteenth century was to be the chief battleground of the Jesuits in their conflict with the Protestant Revolutionists; [24] yet it was by an accident that the first Jesuit arrived in that country. Bl. Peter Faber in 1540, on the order of Paul III, was going with the Imperial Ambassador, Ortiz, on his journey to Spain, when word came from Charles V directing his representative to attend the religious conference at Worms. Ortiz took his Jesuit companion with him to Worms and then to Regensburg, whither the conference had been trans-

[22] Hogan, *Ibernia Ignatiana I*, Dublin (1880).

[23] Bellesheim, *Geschichte der kathol. Kirche in Irland*, Mainz (1880), Vol. II, p. 82; Pastor, *History of the Popes*, Vol. XII, pp. 100–101.

[24] Duhr, *Geschichte der Jesuiten in den Ländern Deutscher Zunge*, Freiburg (1909–1928), Vol. I, pp. 1–162; Pastor, *History of the Popes*, Vol. XII, pp. 103–112; XIII, pp. 198–204.

ferred and where an imperial diet was to assemble. Faber busied himself with hearing confessions and in giving the Spiritual Exercises. He alone could not attend to all who wished to make them; so some who already had gone through the Spiritual Exercises, such as the able secular priest, Cochlaeus, imparted them to others. Many ecclesiastical and secular princes took Bl. Peter for their confessor. Faber had to leave for Portugal with Ortiz in 1541, but he was soon to be back again in Germany. In the very next year Paul III sent him, together with Le Jay and Bobadilla, to labor in the Empire under the direction of the Nuncio Morone.

Faber was assigned to the Rhineland to work directly under the Nuncio. At Spires, the Cathedral cantor, Otto Truchsess von Waldburg, soon as Cardinal and Bishop of Augsburg to become one of the chief mainstays of Catholicism in Germany, made the Spiritual Exercises under his guidance. Thence he was sent to Mainz where he rendered valuable help to the Archbishop, Cardinal Albrecht von Brandenburg, in the reform of the clergy. While in this city two of the best prelates in Germany, Bishop Pflug of Naumberg and Bishop Helding, coadjutor of Mainz and later Bishop of Merseburg, were directed through the Exercises by Blessed Peter. His next apostolic labors brought him to Cologne; the Catholics there had been begging repeatedly for his help in their desperate struggle to save the city from being turned over to Protestantism by the Archbishop von Wied, an ignorant and thoroughly worldly ecclesiastic, soon to apostatize and attempt marriage. The University of Cologne led the fight against the false shepherd, who himself was not without strong supporters. Faber readily lent his assistance to the faithful Catholics. He journeyed to Bonn, where the Emperor was interviewing the Archbishop, to present to the Nuncio the petition of the University praying for definite action. The upshot was that Charles V forced the recreant prelate to a temporary betterment of affairs. Soon after, the Catholics of Cologne besought the Nuncio to keep Faber in their city. An order from the Pope made the granting of their petition a certainty. During his stay the saintly scholar preached with marked success and met in disputation Bucer and other heretics. He also secured a house for the seven young Jesuits who had come to study at Cologne, thus establishing the first German foundation of the order. Faber left Germany finally in 1544, having been ordered to Portugal. The sad state of the Faith in the German lands filled the kind heart of Bl. Peter with anguish, for he held the German people in deep affection; never did he cease to pray for them all, Protestant as well as Catholic, even until his death.

Le Jay, who possessed a character quite similar to Faber's and who also believed that more was accomplished by a reform of morals than through contests of theology, was sent by the Nuncio in 1542 to Bavaria and the Upper Danube area. With him as co-laborer went Robert Wauchope, the blind Archbishop of Armagh.[25] They encountered the stiffest opposition, not only from Protestants but from evil-living priests. At Regensburg, when Le Jay sought the removal of a preacher of bad repute, threats were made that he and his companion would be thrown into the Danube; to which Le Jay replied that heaven could be reached as easily by water as by dry land.[26] At Ingolstadt in 1543 the Jesuit lectured on the Sacred Scriptures before the University and gave the Spiritual Exercises to Bishop von Hutten of Eichstätt; then on the order of the Pope he journeyed to Dillingen to work for Cardinal Truchsess. Duke Ernest of Bavaria, Archbishop of Salzburg, brought him to that city, while a provincial synod was being held. Le Jay's advice proved valuable, especially his statement that the denial of the Papal primacy alone made the Protestants heterodox; for it cleared away much of the confusion and misunderstanding that had hampered the Catholic defense in the Salzburg region. He joined Cardinal Truchsess again at Worms where the prelate was participating in an Imperial Diet. King Ferdinand was greatly pleased with Le Jay's sermons, and the bishops present at the Diet sought his advice and invited him to their dioceses.

Bobadilla was used in all sorts of employments. At first he was sent to Vienna to act as assistant to the Nuncio Verallo; while at the Austrian capital, he managed also to lecture on the Epistle to the Romans and to prepare Turks and Jews for Baptism. Then, in the retinue of Verallo, he visited Nuremberg, Spires, Worms and Brussels. At other times he wrote in the Catholic cause, preached in Latin at Passau and Regensburg, ministered to the Italian soldiers of the Imperial army in the Schmalkaldic War, helped in the revision of the curriculum of the University of Cologne and aided the Catholics of that city in their struggle with the apostate Archbishop von Wied. Bishop Nausea of Vienna has well described him as "the most vigilant agent of the Holy See in all Germany." [27] Bobadilla was a rather loquacious individual, not without a touch of braggadocio. He was apt to speak his mind bluntly to rulers, ecclesiastical and secular; and more than once he was discourteous in his frankness. In fact it was his outspokenness that ended his career in Germany; he expressed such sharp disapproval of the "Interim," [28] that the Emperor dismissed him from Augsburg. When he arrived in Rome,

---

[25] Wauchope, a Scotsman and a brilliant scholar of the University of Paris, had been named to the primatial see of Ireland, but because of the persecution was never able to reach his diocese. He was not a Jesuit, though he did participate in the work of the Society in Germany with great zeal, despite his affliction.

[26] *Mon. Hist. S.J., Epistolae P. Pasch. Broeti, Jay,* etc., p. 276.

[27] *Mon. Hist. S.J., Epistolae Mixtae,* Vol. I, p. 368.

[28] The "Interim" was the temporary compromise between the Catholic and Lutheran doctrines, issued by Charles V in the hope of obtaining eventually a religious peace. It pleased neither side.

Ignatius afforded him a frigid reception. Yet withal, Bobadilla, as Canisius later testified, worked hard, braved grave dangers and "put a sturdy shoulder to the wheel" for the Catholic cause in Germany.[29]

The first German Jesuit and the greatest was St. Peter Canisius, Doctor of the Universal Church.[30] St. Peter was born in Nymegen in the present Holland in 1521; his university studies were made at Cologne, where in 1543 he came in contact with the Society of Jesus in the person of Bl. Peter Faber. Under that holy priest's guidance he went through the Spiritual Exercises at Mainz and on May 8, 1543, entered the Society. He returned to Cologne to complete his theological studies and at the same time began his long apostolic career by preaching sermons in Latin to the students and ecclesiastics and giving simple talks in German to the people. He was the first author of the Society to publish, producing in 1543 an edition of the Dominican mystic, Tauler, and in 1546 a three folio patristic work consisting of a Latin translation of writings of St. Cyril of Alexandria together with the writings of St. Leo the Great. Canisius participated most actively in the conflict of the Cologne Catholics with the Archbishop von Wied; sent by the clergy and the University of Cologne, he traveled to the Netherlands to enlist the aid of Charles V and the Papal Nuncio, then to Liége to obtain the help of its Prince-Bishop, and finally to Suabia to seek again the assistance of the Emperor and the Nuncio. From Suabia he was ordered to Trent to be the advisor of Cardinal Truchsess at the Council. Then St. Ignatius called him to Rome personally to train him, and, after having placed him for a year on the first staff of the College of Messina, sent him back to the German apostolate. The proximate reason for Ignatius' command was the request of Paul III that he designate three Jesuit theologians to revive the declining University of Ingolstadt, in compliance with the petition of Duke William IV of Bavaria. With Canisius were appointed Le Jay and Salmeron. On September 2, 1549 after receiving the blessing of the Pope, the three set out on their memorable journey, memorable indeed, for it was the launching of the counter-attack that was to halt the hitherto irresistible onrush of Protestantism.

To most of their contemporaries it must have seemed that the three Jesuits were advancing in a cause already lost. Nearly half of Germany was gone beyond recall and what remained was so hopelessly enmeshed in a chaos of indecision, ignorance and immorality that even the most sanguine might have doubted the possibility of revival. Nadal, who was in Germany during 1555 as Visitor of the order, declared that the work there was considerably more difficult than that in the Indies. If revival

---

[29] *Mon. Hist. S.J., Mon. Ignat.* Ser. IV, i, p. 715.

[30] Braunsberger, *B. Petri Canisi epistulae et acta*, 8 vols., Freiburg (1896–1923); *Petrus Canisius, ein Lebensbild* (1921); Brodrick, *St. Peter Canisius*, London (1936).

was to come, this shrewd observer pointed out, it would have to be achieved through education and literary activity. Colleges furnishing a sound classical and Christian education were vitally needed; yet it was a long time before the princes, who must found and support them, could be convinced of their utility. Only two colleges were established during the lifetime of St. Ignatius: Vienna and Prague; shortly after his death two more, Cologne and Ingolstadt were added. All but the Vienna college owed their beginning to St. Peter Canisius; that of Cologne, which was to become for the North another Roman College, was the reward of his zealous sermons.

The work at Ingolstadt consisted in the lectures of Canisius, Le Jay and Salmeron as members of the faculty of the University. From the outset the prospects were disheartening: the auditors counted up to only fourteen and most of them lacked fundamental preparation, to say nothing of even an interest in theological studies. Le Jay and Salmeron were recalled and Canisius was left to carry on alone. He did, accomplishing much good by his private tutoring of students, by his lectures and by his apostolic labor for the people. St. Peter strove hard to induce the Duke of Bavaria to found a college in the city, without for a long time making much advance. Ignatius in 1555 ordered him to depart for Vienna. Canisius continued to work for the Ingolstadt project, as also for a college in Prague, which was badly needed in the sad condition of the Bohemian Catholics, a condition far worse than that of the Germans. The Prague college became a reality in 1556, that of Ingolstadt in 1558. Vienna itself called for the best efforts of Canisius and his brethren; so desperate were Catholic affairs that, according to Nadal, were it not for the Jesuits the Austrian capital would have become Lutheran. St. Peter stood in the forefront of the defense; he preached with great results in German and Italian, lectured on the *Epistles of St. Paul,* ministered to the prisoners and took care of priestless country parishes in the neighborhood of the city. Ferdinand I wished to nominate him for the bishopric of the city; but Canisius refused the dignity, though he did take over the burdens of administrator for a year.

It was at Vienna that Peter Canisius composed the work which will always be associated with his name, the Catechism.[31] There existed no handy summary of Christian Doctrine suitable to the times, yet nothing was more needed to correct errors and to clear up misunderstandings. In some districts Catholic children actually were being instructed from Lutheran catechisms. To provide a remedy Ferdinand I called upon the Viennese Jesuits to draw up a Catholic summary. The task was intrusted to Canisius in 1552. After two years he was able to place his work before

---

[31] Braunsberger, *Entstehung und erste Entwicklung der Katechismen des sel. Petrus Canisius,* Freiburg (1893).

the King; in 1555 it was published at Vienna under the title *Summa doctrinae christianae*. The first catechism of Canisius was printed in Latin, for it was intended primarily for teachers and young students. A year later he brought out a short extract, which appeared in Latin at Ingolstadt and in German at Dillingen. In 1558 still another catechism, intermediate between the first two, was finished by St. Peter; this was produced at Cologne. The effect of these catechisms can never be fully reckoned. It is no exaggeration to say that they were key-books of the Counter-Reformation; even before their author's death they had gone through more than two hundred editions in twelve languages. Generation after generation learned the principles of the Faith from their pages. Down even into the eighteenth century in many parts of Germany, the term "Canisi" was the synonym for "Catechism"; indeed today the expression is still used in Fribourg.

Not for the good of Europeans alone were the Jesuits to labor; but to strange and far-distant peoples, the cultured heathens of the East and the painted savages of the but recently heard-of West, the members of the order were to carry the light of the Gospel and to preach the salvation of the Crucified. The foreign missions of the Society of Jesus began when St. Francis Xavier sailed from Lisbon in 1541.[32] More than a year later, after a hazardous voyage he landed at Goa. At first his very best efforts were called into a struggle with the degraded morals of the Europeans, many of whom had succumbed to the vicious luxuries of the East. His earnest pleading or his fierce denunciation recalled some from lives that were a scandal even to the pagans. Others were gained by his love of the poor and his friendship for the lepers. But the most, probably, were won by the spectacle of this new black-robed priest, walking through the streets, ringing a bell and surrounded by children whom he was gathering for religious and moral instruction.

Xavier had come to the East primarily, not to reform bad Christians, but to preach the Gospel to the heathen. So he left Goa to work among the poverty-stricken people on the Fishery Coast of Cape Comorin. The natives of these barren stretches were nominally Christian; they had been baptized eight years before; but receiving no further instruction, they were in almost complete ignorance of the Faith. Francis for a whole year went from village to village, preaching and instructing, leaving behind in each place written prayers to be memorized and repeated daily. His voice gave out, so often did he speak, and his arm grew weary from baptizing;[33] more than once he administered the Sacrament to a whole

---

[32] Pastor, *History of the Popes*, Vol. XII, pp. 114–123; Schurhammer, *St. Francis Xavier* (trans. by Eble), London (1928), pp. 65–199; Coleridge, *The Life and Letters of St. Francis Xavier*, London (1912), Vol. I, pp. 109–424; Vol. II, pp. 1–147.

[33] *Mon. Hist. S.J.*, *Mon. Xaver*, Vol. I, pp. 283–286, 293.

village at a time. Along the Coast he built forty-four churches and had at least four native-born Indians ordained priests to be his assistants. Opposition came from the Brahmins; but neither their threats nor their bribes deterred him.

During the next four years Xavier carried his apostolate to other regions of India, to Ceylon, the Malay Straits, the Molucca Islands and the Isle of Amboina, not omitting a return to the Fishery Coast. The fame of his gift of healing and of his raising of the dead, the report of his ecstatic prayer, the sight of his compassionate love for children, for slaves and for sinners, endowed his preaching with an irresistible force. His baptisms continued to an almost incredible number; once, during the course of a month he baptized 10,000 men.[34] The newly-made Christians found in St. Francis a valiant protector against the greedy and cruel Portuguese officials and adventurers; with most outspoken language he begged John III to put an end to the tyrannical treatment of his neophytes.

In ever-increasing numbers Jesuits were sent out to India to assist in the great harvest. In 1549 their numbers warranted the creation of the Indian Province, over which Xavier was named superior. In addition to the Goan houses, colleges were soon started at Bassein, Cochin and Quilon; fathers were working too at Malacca, on the Fishery Coast, in the Molucca Islands and in the island of Socotra. The zealous and unsullied lives of these priests moved the Viceroy to write to Rodriguez that their labors recalled those of the Apostles of old. Especially did Baertz, a Netherlandish Jesuit, prove himself a worthy companion of Francis Xavier; his labors for the Faith and for the reform of morals on the island of Ormuz under most difficult conditions caused Christian and non-Christian to look up to him as a prophet and a wonder-worker. On the Fishery Coast Criminali sealed his testimony with his blood, having been beaten to death with savage cruelty. He was the first martyr of the Society of Jesus.[35]

The priests in India set great store by the thorough instruction of the neophytes. On the advice of St. Ignatius, a catechumenate of three or four months' duration was introduced. Schools where reading, writing and catechism were taught, were opened for native children. As the interpreters, though carefully selected, did not always prove satisfactory, the Jesuits were urged to acquire the languages of their districts. Henriquez was particularly successful with the Tamil tongue, composing the first Tamil grammar. The fathers labored unceasingly too for the protection of their converts not only from the exacting, avaricious European officials but from the murderings and plunderings of the powerful Mohammedans.

---

[34] *Mon. Hist. S.J., Mon. Xaver*, Vol. I, pp. 366–367.
[35] Casters, *The Ven. Anthony Criminali*, Trichinopoly (1926).

India, large as it was, was still not big enough to limit the spirit of St. Francis Xavier. While working at Malacca he came in contact with a Japanese, whose accounts of his native country and his people, in response to the Saint's eager questions, fired Xavier's zeal to raise the Cross in that distant land.[36] When his decision became known to his Portuguese and Indian friends, there was a perfect uproar of protests: his ship most certainly would be lost in the typhoons or wrecked on hidden reefs; even if it survived it would surely be captured by pirates, and that meant horrible torturing and a cruel death. Xavier had reckoned it all, but he would not abandon the project. On June 24, 1549, accompanied by two brothers of his order and a few Japanese converts, he sailed out of Malacca in a Chinese junk, the captain of which was probably as much a pirate as a merchant. Almost two months later, August 15, 1549, Francis stepped on the soil of Japan at Kagoshima.

Xavier began his mission amid conditions most unfavorable to the introduction of Christianity. Anarchy reigned in Japan: the Emperor was the weakest of figureheads and hardly less helpless was the Shogun; the ones who really ruled were the sixty or more petty princes, the Daimios, and they only within their own little states. The perpetual wars which they waged against each other filled the land with turmoil and confusion. The Buddhist monasteries, well organized and possessing strong armed forces, wielded considerable influence; in time they would be a most formidable obstacle to the Christian religion. The universal contempt for foreigners formed another very difficult barrier. Yet the reasoning character of the Japanese and their lively interest in religious questions gave Francis some hope. He drew up a summary of the Christian teaching and had it translated, intending to read it to the audiences that might give him a hearing. The translation, made by a person of no literary talents, only amused the learned; when Xavier tried to read it in the streets, the crowds hooted and laughed at him. Still his very learning, his reputation and the sublime truths evident in the awkward phrases, could not but make an impression. After a year his converts numbered a hundred, and such were the crowds that came to listen to him that the bonzes in alarm obtained a prohibition against conversion. Francis moved to the island of Hirado, where he was able to start a promising mission. He entrusted the work to de Torres when he proceeded onward to the chief island, Honshu.

For a while he resided at Yamaguchi. His main purpose, however, was to visit Meaco (Kioto), the capital, with hope of obtaining in a personal interview with the Emperor the permission to preach in all parts of Japan. Had he understood the real state of affairs and the powerless-

---

[36] Pastor, *History of the Popes*, Vol. XIII, pp. 315–325; Schurhammer, *St. Francis Xavier*, pp. 199–213; Coleridge, *The Life and Letters of St. Francis Xavier*, Vol. II, pp. 148–351, 389–509.

ness of the Emperor, he would never have started out. With a lay-brother he made the trip in the depths of winter. Both had to suffer terribly tramping through the snow-covered country, crossing swollen streams, enduring the privations of wretched country inns and bearing the taunts of the village crowds. In the end the journey was fruitless; Xavier could not obtain an interview with the Emperor, and, even if he had, he could have achieved nothing with that helpless nonentity. Still some valuable lessons were learned: what real power the Daimio of Yamaguchi held; and how much prejudice to the Gospel poverty and mean appearances caused in the eyes of the natives. When on his return St. Francis, in better dress and bearing presents from India presented himself before the Daimio of Yamaguchi, he was warmly received and given full permission to preach. Within a half year he was able to baptize over 500 converts. A most valued assistant was found among these neophytes, a half-blind actor whom Xavier christened Lawrence. Later, as a lay-brother of the order, Lawrence used his gifts of eloquence in countless sermons and disputations, winning thousands of fellow Japanese to Christianity, among them some of the Daimios. Xavier also preached the Gospel in the dominion of Bungo, the Daimio of which had invited him and promised the support of missionaries. Conditions in India necessitating his return, St. Francis had to depart from Japan in 1551. He left the infant church in the charge of de Torres.

One of the things Xavier learned in Japan was the primary importance of China in the Orient. The Japanese respect for the learning and wisdom of China especially impressed him. A determination grew with him to bring this vast nation to Christ; [37] indeed, one of his purposes in journeying to Meaco was to obtain a passport for China from the Emperor. He kept the thought ever in view. When the business at Goa was completed, he felt the time had come, and he set out for Malacca to make preparations for an entry into China. Here precisely was the great difficulty: entrance into the country was strictly forbidden to foreigners; imprisonment and, possibly, even death awaited anyone who put a foot on the Chinese shore. Xavier planned at first to accompany a Portuguese envoy, for an ambassador of the great King John III might not be refused entrance. The commandant of Malacca, however, blocked the venture. The Saint then determined to go it alone. By sailing in a Portuguese merchant ship to the island of Sancian, a trading station not far from Canton, he hoped to reach a spot whence he might be smuggled into the forbidden land. Once within he would face whatever was to come. He arrived at Sancian in the fall of 1552, but could find no one daring enough to convey him across to the mainland. All, Portuguese and Chinese, warned him against the

[37] Schurhammer, *St. Francis Xavier*, pp. 277–311; Coleridge, *Life and Letters of St. Francis Xavier*, Vol. II, pp. 510–578.

attempt. When he would not be dissuaded, they abandoned him to await all alone the opportunity to carry out his enterprise.

The chance never came, for on November 22 he was struck down with a violent fever. For five days he lingered, racked with the sickness, delirious a good part of the time. Only two, a Chinese servant and an East Indian, watched by his side in the wretched straw hut that sheltered him. At two in the morning of November 27, 1552, alone and abandoned save for the two Oriental boys, his great soul went to its rest. His body, sprinkled with lime to hasten its decomposition, was quickly buried. Yet when the coffin was opened, February 17, 1553, the body was discovered perfectly incorrupt. It was carried to Malacca and again buried, this time without a coffin; when six months later it was disinterred once more it was again found incorrupt. The body was conveyed to Goa, where it was finally placed in the convent of Bom Jesus; there it has remained still incorrupt until the present day.[38]

St. Francis Xavier was essentially a man of action gifted with the broadest vision; he longed to go everywhere and to do everything humanly possible for his Lord Jesus, the passion of his soul. If to some his activities should appear feverish and foolhardy, let it be remembered that he looked upon himself not as a lone individual missionary, but as the leader of a band, whose duty it was to go before and survey the lands his followers were to evangelize. He was quite as great a mystic as an apostle of practical deeds; long hours were spent by him in prayer, and his rest, often taken at the foot of the altar, was frequently but a few moments snatched from a night of deep communing with God. Always kindly, his affectionate friendliness won every heart, for he knew how to be all things to all men to gain them for Christ. His relations with ecclesiastical dignitaries were marked by a deep reverence, and towards the members of other religious orders he nourished a warm fraternal charity. Finally, he served God in a spirit of joy and with a merriment that enheartens all who read his life story. Protestants, even men of no religion, deeply cherish his memory. For his fellow-Catholics he is the greatest apostle since St. Paul.

The first African mission of the Society of Jesus was started in the Congo, when in 1547 Rodriguez sent out from Portugal two priests, a scholastic and a lay-brother. They worked with some success until 1555 when they were driven from the country. Causing much wider interest was the attempt to send Jesuit missionaries to Abyssinia.[39] King John III

---

[38] The right arm of the Saint was cut off and carried to Rome in 1614; today it rests in the altar dedicated to his honor in the Church of the Gesu. Missionary bishops and priests are frequent celebrants of Mass on the altar.

[39] Beccari, *Rerum Aethiopicarum Scriptores occidentales, inedite a saeculo XVI ad XIX*, Vols. V and X, Roma (1907, 1910).

had received a letter from the Negus Claudius, asking that the Pope send a Patriarch to his country, as his people were anxious for union with the Holy Father. The Portuguese monarch suggested that a Jesuit be consecrated for the task. St. Ignatius did not oppose the request, though the office was episcopal, since the dignity was one of toil and hardships only. Pope Julius III, because of the remote inaccessibility of the country, decided to consecrate three Jesuits, Nuñez Baretto as Patriarch, and Oviedo and Canero as suffragan-bishops. This was done in 1555; Ignatius died, however, before the work was begun.

Brazil [40] was the first land in the New World to be the scene of Jesuit mission activity. Manoel Nobrega with five companions in 1549 sailed with the Portuguese fleet that was to found Bahia. The fathers began the evangelization of the aborigines at once, striving to win the savages from their roaming life and cannibalism to civilization and the Faith of Christ. By 1553 four settlements were established; in that year the province of Brazil was constituted and Nobrega named as Provincial. Whatever advances were made had to be accomplished in the face of most terrible conditions. The activities of the whites, most of whom were deported criminals, almost completely nullified the labors of the fathers; they forced the natives into slavery, worked them without mercy till they died, and treated the Indian women most shamefully. The missionaries spared no effort to protect the unfortunate aborigines; they pleaded with the masters, denounced their cruelties and refused the obdurate absolution. Their appeals to the King of Portugal brought some relief; but on the whole their efforts were frustrated by powerful colonists. So disgusted was Nobrega that he withdrew himself and his brethren from Bahia, leaving but one father for the instruction of the children. The degraded condition of the natives proved quite as heartbreaking. Roamers of the jungles they were, without fixed abode or government, unstable of character, possessing scarcely a rudimentary morality. In small bands they haunted the deep forests waging continual war on each other. The fathers tried to gather them into settlements, especially those who had been baptized, that they might become accustomed to the ways of civilization. But such efforts were rendered of little avail by the whites who, for their own safety, urged on the aborigines in their inter-tribal slaughter, not excepting cannibalism. The half-breeds wielded an even more sinister influence. It was a miracle of perseverance that the fathers kept to their task in spite of great poverty and the hatred of rich slave-owners. In 1557 the arrival of the noble Men de Sa as Governor marked a change for the better. The missionaries received the strong support of this worthy official.

Back in Rome, the years of Ignatius' generalate were drawing to a

---

[40] Pastor, *History of the Popes*, Vol. XII, p. 516; Vol. XIII, pp. 291–296.

close. His health was so shattered by a serious illness in 1550 that he expressed a desire to relinquish his office. Vigor enough returned to enable him to carry on the government until 1554. In October of that year he named Nadal as his Vicar-General. His strength kept gradually diminishing; sometimes he was too weak even to say Mass. Finally in the summer of 1556 a Roman fever brought him to the end. He died quietly and peacefully two hours after sunrise on July 31, 1556, in his sixty-fifth year. Father Pollen thus summarizes the personality of St. Ignatius: "It is impossible to sketch in brief Ignatius' grand and complex character: ardent yet restrained, fearless, resolute, simple, prudent, strong and loving. The Protestant and Jansenistic conception of him as a restless, bustling pragmatist bears no correspondence at all with the peacefulness and perseverance which characterized the real man. That he was a strong disciplinarian is true. In a young and rapidly growing body that was inevitable; and the age loved strong virtues. But if he believed in discipline as an educative force, he despised any other motives for action except the love of God and man." [41]

---

[41] Pollen, "Ignatius of Loyola," *Catholic Encyclopedia*, Vol. VII, p. 643. De la Torre, S.J. in his introduction to his *Letters of St. Ignatius* has drawn a lengthy, magnificent character-portrait; it may be found in the English translation of Astrain's *A Short Life of St. Ignatius Loyola*, pp. 113–115.

CHAPTER V

THE NEW ORDER AND ITS CONSTITUTIONS

Father Nadal relates that St. Ignatius had asked God for three favors: first, that the Institute of the Society be confirmed by the Holy See; second, that the Spiritual Exercises be approved by the Pope; third, that he be spared to write the Constitutions for his order. These three wishes were granted. In the composition of the Spiritual Exercises St. Ignatius proved himself a great spiritual educator, in the foundation of the Society of Jesus a great organizer, in the writing of the Constitutions a great legislator.

In the previous chapter it was said that the Society and its Constitutions were "born of the Exercises." It was not, however, in the manner imagined by some of the earlier writers on the origin and history of the Society. Some spoke as if at Manresa in 1522 the whole plan of the Society had stood clearly before the mind of St. Ignatius, particularly in the two meditations on the "Kingdom of Christ" and the "Two Standards." Some even have asserted that through a special revelation, God had told the Saint that he was to found an apostolic order and also had shown him the essentials of the structure of that order. The opinion is rejected by leading modern Jesuit historians and spiritual writers and cannot seriously be maintained.[1] The examination of a few historical facts will make this quite evident. In the meditations on the "Kingdom of Christ" and the "Two Standards" there is indeed an atmosphere which presages the foundation of an apostolic order; they contained, as it were, the seed of the future order. St. Ignatius himself must have had some thought and desire in this regard, as he soon after, in Spain and in Paris, began to gather companions. Yet it was all vague. The vows at Montmartre in 1534 have been considered by some the foundation of the Society. Certainly the ideal had become clearer and more definite. But what came into being then was only a sort of brotherhood. Vows of poverty and chastity were taken; but there was no superior, and above all, no vow of obedience, the most essential part of a religious order.

Subsequent events confirm the statement that there was no definite in-

---

[1] The Bollandist van Ortroy, *Analecta Bollandiana*, Brussels (1908), pp. 392–418; Dudon, *Saint Ignace de Loyola*, Paris (1934), pp. 622 ff.; similarly Tacchi-Venturi, Meschler and other Jesuit scholars.

tention of founding an order until 1539. Polanco states explicitly: "When ours arrived in Rome in the spring of 1538, they had not yet any intention of founding a congregation." Statements of Laynez and the words and actions of St. Ignatius also confirm the fact.[2] During 1538 and the early part of 1539 the fathers, in their evening meetings after their priestly labors of the day, debated for weeks the question whether to found a religious order. In the spring of 1539 they finally decided in the affirmative. To Saint Ignatius was assigned the task of drawing up the preliminary plan of a constitution, the first "Formula Instituti," which in a somewhat amplified form constitutes part of the complete "Institute" of the Society. The account of the presentation to Pope Paul III and his official approval of it by the Bull "Regimini militantis ecclesiae" on September 27, 1540, has been related in the previous chapter.

A more detailed constitution than the "Formula" was necessary. Paul III in the Bull of confirmation had declared that they could "freely and licitly write particular constitutions in conformity with the purpose for which the Society was founded." This work, naturally, devolved upon St. Ignatius. He began to commit his work to writing in 1547, assisted by his secretary Polanco. But the greatest help the Saint expected from above; he prayed fervently and often said many Masses over certain points before coming to a decision. In 1550 the first draft of the Constitutions was finished. Ignatius called to Rome the professed fathers who could be easily reached and laid his work before them for examination. Upon their suggestions some alterations were made in the second draft of 1552. From that year on the Constitutions were tested in various provinces. The first General Congregation, meeting in 1558, two years after St. Ignatius' death, confirmed them as the law of the Society. They were presented to Pope Paul IV, who ordered them to be examined by two Cardinals, Scoti and Suavi; according to Sacchini, two other Cardinals were added, the Dominican Ghislieri and the Franciscan Dolera. The Cardinals returned the document to the Pope without one word altered. When the fathers of the First General Congregation were admitted to an audience July 6, 1558, Paul IV, though not any too friendly towards St. Ignatius and the new order, approved and confirmed all the privileges and indults which his predecessors and he himself had given the Society. Under the circumstances this was also an implicit confirmation of the Constitutions. Explicit confirmations have been given by Pope Gregory XIII and several other Popes to the present day.

The assertion that the Council of Trent "most solemnly approved the Society" is not true. The statement is found in the magnificent defense of the order by Archbishop Beaumont of Paris, shortly before the sup-

---

[2] Dudon, St, Ignace de Loyola, p. 24; Pastor, History of the Popes, Vol. XII, pp. 31–32.

pression of the Society, and has been repeated by some Jesuit writers in popular works. Pope Clement XIV in the Brief of Suppression explicitly rejects this claim. And the Pope was right. There was no solemn approbation of the Society issued at Trent, only what may be called an "indirect" approbation. The facts are stated by Pollen:

> Before this Ignatius had asked the Jesuit fathers at Trent to inquire whether it would be possible to obtain from the Council an approbation of the Society. There was no doubt that the Conciliar Fathers had had a good opportunity of seeing how the Jesuits worked; there was no doubt that in many places (Paris for example), where there was perennial jealousy at Papal approbations and privileges, a conciliar approbation would be received without demur. Ignatius' reasons were excellent, but the Jesuit fathers at Trent were not fully satisfied. The Council being rather a legislative than an administrative body, they pointed out that the approbation of an order might appear to some to be beside its functions, so that the application might cause comment and, perhaps, no good. They had so far only consulted one of their friends, who had not been in favour of the project. If, however, Ignatius wished them to go further they would do whatever he should require. Needless to add, Ignatius did not urge his plan. It is interesting to see how free in stating difficulties these sticklers for obedience were, and how sensibly and straightforwardly they explained their case.[3]

The "indirect" approbation occurred in the exception which the Council made to its legislation concerning the one year of novitiate for religious and the acceptance or dismissal of the candidate after that period.[4] The Council stated: "by this the Synod did not want to change or forbid anything, whereby the religious of the Clerics of the Society of Jesus might be prevented from serving the Lord and His Church according to their pious institute which was approved by the Holy See." The words "pious institute" have no special significance; it is a common expression used concerning religious orders and congregations. Astrain, Duhr and other Jesuit historians consider that the Council's words constituted only an "indirect" approbation; Suarez expressed it well when he said the Council gave the Society a "mentio honorifica," i. e., an honorable mention.

The Constitutions form part of what is called the "Institute of the Society of Jesus." This comprises: (1) Papal Bulls and other pontifical documents approving the Society, determining its work and its ecclesiastical standing, beginning with the Bull of Confirmation by Paul III; (2) "the Examen Generale" containing subjects to be explained to postulants and points on which they are to be examined; (3) the Constitutions with "Declarations" (explanations of certain parts); (4) Decrees of General Congregations which have equal authority with the Constitutions; (5) Rules, general and particular; (6) Various instructions etc.; (7) The

---

[3] Pollen, *St. Ignatius Loyola*, pp. 103, 104.

[4] *Concilium Tridentinum*, Freiburg (1924), Tomus 9, p. 1083 (XXV Session, ch. 16).

Book of the Spiritual Exercises; (8) the Ratio Studiorum or "Plan of Studies." It will be sufficient here to examine only the Constitutions.

In the first place it must be stated that the Constitutions are the work of St. Ignatius. One of the many fictions concerning the Society is the one that designates not Ignatius, but his first successor in the generalate, Laynez, as the real author of the document. It has been a favorite thesis of modern non-Catholic writers; but it was proposed long ago and by Catholics too, especially at the time of the Suppression.[5] The modern proponents of the theory judge that only a learned scholar like Laynez could have been the author, and not Ignatius whom they consider incapable of producing such a masterpiece. How little do they know Ignatius! If they had read some of his 6,000 letters to Jesuits, secular priests, prelates, princes (and of his authorship of these letters there can be no doubt), they would have found Ignatius to be a man of extraordinary practical wisdom, possessing a remarkable gift of guiding others, and they would have recognized that the spirit of the letters is identical with that of the Constitutions. St. Ignatius was the sole author of the Constitutions, although he did listen to the suggestions of his companions. For his sole authorship there are numerous and indubitable declarations of his contemporaries. They do not conceal the fact that he accepted suggestions; thus they aver that he took from Laynez the idea of establishing colleges for the training of the young men of the order.[6] That is the sole claim Laynez has in regard to the authorship of the Constitutions.

Did St. Ignatius draw his ideas from any special source? One can dismiss as utterly absurd the thesis that St. Ignatius derived not only the Exercises but also some of the most important features of his organization (the form of government, the nature of obedience, the "initiation," the different classes of members) from Moslem sources.[7] A contemporary tells us that during the time of writing the Constitutions the Saint had in his room only the Missal, another said only the *New Testament* and the *Imitation of Christ*. That does not exclude the possibility of his having used his knowledge of the rules of other orders, some of which he had studied.[8] He had become personally acquainted with the rules and life of two of the older orders: of the Benedictines of Montserrat and Monte Cassino (in the latter monastery he had spent forty days in 1539 while giving the Exercises to Dr. Ortiz, the Imperial Plenipotentiary at Rome);

---

[5] Cardinal Malvezzi, a bitter opponent of the Jesuits, urged Clement XIV "to show courage against the Society, not of St. Ignatius but of Laynez and Aquaviva." Pastor, *Geschichte der Päpste*, Vol. XVI, part 2, p. 205.

[6] Farrell, *The Jesuit Code of Liberal Education*, Milwaukee, (1938), p. 14.

[7] A refutation is had in Dudon, *Saint Ignace de Loyola*, pp. 641–642.

[8] Codina, "Regulae antiquorum ordinum et praeparatio Constitutionum S.J.," *Archivum Historicum S.J.* (1932), Vol. I, pp. 41–72.

of the Dominicans in whose convent at Manresa he had lived some time.[9] Hence that some details of his Constitutions may have been due to reminiscences of the rules and custom of these orders would have been but natural.

Some of Ignatius' rules were "commonplaces" of religious life: thus the rule of the Summary prescribing reading during meals is found almost literally in the rules of other religious orders; so too the practice of reading in community the Summary of the Constitutions and other rules at specified times follows an old Benedictine custom set down in the Rule of St. Benedict (Ch. LXVII). The rule of the Society which says that anyone who notices (outside of confession) grave temptations of others should inform the superior, has been violently stigmatized as "spying" and "mean denunciation." Yet such a practice is explicitly prescribed in the rules of St. Basil and is probably observed in every religious order, as in any respectable family; for if exercised in the spirit of charity (and that is what the rule implies) it is a most necessary means of protecting the honor and preserving the well-being of a community.

Again, the manifestation of conscience to the superior or to the spiritual father, often criticised by non-Jesuits, is mentioned by Cassian as a common practice of old monasticism. So also the rule of prompt obedience, that at the sound of the bell one must not finish even the letter begun, is to be found literally in Cassian's *Institutes* (IV, 12); in fact Cassian adds: "not even the dot on the 'i' is to be finished." Cassian is the foremost of the early monastic writers; with his *Institutes of the Monks* and *Conferences of the Fathers* he exercised a profound influence on many great religious, such as St. Benedict,[10] Cassiodorus, St. Dominic and St. Thomas Aquinas. Hurter, S.J. asserts that: "From the twelfth to the eighteenth century there is scarcely any solid spiritual writer who does not utilize the ideas and examples mentioned by Cassian." There is ample evidence that St. Ignatius was acquainted with, or at least influenced by, this ancient authority, especially in the *Epistle on Obedience*, where the Fathers are quoted thirteen times, three quotations being from Cassian. There is a special beauty in the fact that though different orders have different dress, customs and occupations, a unity of spirit exists which has become fixed in what may be called the monastic tradition. From this St. Ignatius drew, directly or indirectly; and though he deviated more than any other founder from old customs and practices, he did so for very important reasons. Such "borrowings" from the rules of other religious orders were,

---

[9] Grisar, S.J., in "St. Dominikus, Zum siebenhundertjährigen Gedenktag seines Heimganges," *Stimmen der Zeit*, Vol. CII (1922), p. 117, says: "In particular St. Ignatius owes not a little to the example set by the Dominicans."

[10] Cf. Rule of St. Benedict, Ch. LXXIII and the observations of Dom Delatte, O.S.B., *The Rule of St. Benedict*, London (1921), p. ix.

as in the case of the Spiritual Exercises, stones which the Saint used in an original manner in his architectural structure of the Constitutions. Some have denied the originality of the Exercises; no one has done so in regard to the Constitutions and the character of the Society of Jesus. On the contrary, to many Ignatius was altogether too original.

An examination of the Constitutions of the Society is in place: first, for a clear understanding of the nature of the Society, its peculiar character as a religious order, its guiding principles and practical customs; secondly, for a consideration of the numerous criticisms and even flagrant misrepresentations of the Society's laws and practices. It is no exaggeration to say that no body of men has been so severely criticised as the Society of Jesus. In the Constitutions [11] there are ten parts, each of which will be briefly considered.

Part I deals with the admission of candidates: what abilities, mental and physical, what qualities of soul are to be looked for in the applicant; also what defects are to constitute impediments for admission. It is quite evident that very special care must be had in the selection of candidates for the important work ahead.

Part II concerns dismissals: who should be dismissed, for what reasons, by whom and how. Part III treats of the novitiate: by what exercises, bodily and above all spiritual, the novices are to be trained. In all religious orders up to that time the duration of the novitiate lasted for one year; the Society extended the period to two years to prepare the candidates thoroughly before they bound themselves by perpetual vows. The training is given in a special house called the novitiate, under an experienced spiritual guide, called the Master of Novices. The most essential part of the spiritual training is the making of the complete Spiritual Exercises during thirty days. This section contains instruction of supreme spiritual importance on the vows, prayers, abnegation, charity, zeal for souls, etc. The novitiate is to be a school of Christian perfection.

The longest section is Part IV, which was elaborated with special care. Here are treated the studies by which, after the novitiate, the young religious, now called "scholastics," are prepared for the active life of the Society. The colleges and other schools of the order, their officers and form of government, the subjects to be studied and the methods both of teaching and studying are described. Ordinarily after the novitiate, there is a period called the juniorate in which literary studies are followed for one or two years; then follow three years of philosophy with due attention to the important branches of natural science. With the completion of the philosophical course the scholastics are usually employed in teaching for a few years. Then they enter upon a four-year study of theology with

---

[11] A good account of the Constitutions may be had in Pastor, Vol. XII, pp. 54–78. There are a few errors in this translation owing to misunderstandings of the original.

its various branches, dogma, Scripture, moral theology, canon law, ecclesiastical history and liturgy. In scholastic theology St. Thomas is the master to be followed. The teaching of philosophy and theology, as well as the repetitions and disputations which form an important part of the course, are conducted in Latin. During the juniorate, philosophate and theologate there are both instruction and practice in preaching. Ordination takes place after the third year of theology. Besides these regular studies, in modern times some devote two, three or more years to special studies, the various sciences, law, political economy, literature, history, philosophy and theology, as a preparation for teaching or writing. The spiritual development of the scholastics during these years of study is carefully provided for by frequent exhortations and by such spiritual exercises as daily meditation, examinations of conscience (twice every day), weekly confession, frequent (now daily) Communion, spiritual reading and an annual retreat of eight days. The young religious are repeatedly reminded that they must devote themselves zealously to their studies with the pure and religious intention of becoming efficient instruments to work for the greater glory of God and the salvation of souls.[12] In this Part IV are also directions concerning the education of pupils not belonging to the Society. These directions formed the basis of the later Ratio Studiorum, the plan of Jesuit instruction.

After the completion of the studies there follows the "Tertianship" or "Third Year of Probation," called so because it is added to the two years of probation in the novitiate. This was an entirely new feature in religious life, one of St. Ignatius' innovations. During the year the young priest is to renew and deepen the fervor of his spiritual life in readiness for entrance upon active apostolic labors. This is done primarily by the making of the complete Spiritual Exercises of thirty days (for the second time in the Jesuit's life) and by the systematic study of the Institute of the Society.

Such is the training that all Jesuit priests receive; it implies a long period of systematic and harmonious studies, it calls for intense intellectual activity and spiritual development. The candidates entering the novitiate either possess college degrees or have finished at least high school, and usually one or two years of college. The course of the studies, after the novitiate, takes up twelve to fourteen years; at its completion the priests pronounce their final vows.

Part V treats of these vows, their nature and variance. Here is found the description of the different grades in the Society, a feature quite new in the history of religious orders and one which met with considerable

---

[12] An interesting account of life in a scholasticate is to be found in Bernoville, *The Jesuits*, Paris (1937), Ch. V. The author remained at the house of studies at Enghien, Belgium, for some days to obtain first hand experience.

criticism. Part VI deals with the spiritual life of those finally admitted into the Society, particularly of the observance of poverty, chastity and obedience. The last mentioned, because of its singular place in the Institute and in the life of the Jesuits, will receive more detailed treatment presently. Part VII has to do with the various occupations of the Society, especially the missions undertaken on the order or wish of the Pope, and the works of mercy, spiritual and corporal, in which the order engages. Part VIII concerns the means of preserving union among the members, though scattered over many and distant lands, between themselves and with the superiors. It deals also with the supreme legislative body of the Society, the General Congregation, prescribing when it is to be called and who are to take part in it. The method of electing the Father General is likewise treated in this section. Part IX treats of the Father General, specifying his powers and the qualities to be expected in him. Needless to say these qualities call for high standards of intellect, will and character. In no one better than in St. Ignatius himself were these qualities realized. Part X treats of the means of strengthening and preserving the body of the Society in good condition. It contains a summing up of the most important points of the preceding parts. Special warning is set down against ambition. There is included a strict prohibition against the seeking directly or indirectly of any position of authority within the Society; there is an equally severe order not only not to seek but even to refuse any prelacy or dignity outside the Society, unless the same has been commanded by the highest ecclesiastical authority.

These are the Constitutions of the Society of Jesus, the result of intense meditation and prayer on the part of St. Ignatius during almost fifteen years of hidden life. While some of his brethren shone before the Council of Trent by their theological knowledge, while Xavier traversed sea and land as a conqueror for Christ the King, Ignatius, the leader and inspirer, had practically disappeared from the outside world into the little house by the side of the Church of the Blessed Virgin della Strada. But those hidden years were years of the greatest fruitfulness, for in them St. Ignatius produced what has been styled, even by bitter enemies of the order, a rare piece of organizing and legislating wisdom.

Constitutions, "the fundamental organic law or principles of a society embodied in written documents," are usually a body of rather dry enactments and terse regulations. There are sections of the Jesuit Constitutions which are of such a nature, particularly, as is to be expected, the brief "rules" strictly so-called. This fact has been unduly generalized by some Catholic writers, who have contrasted the Jesuit Constitutions with the simpler and warmer spirit, as they term it, of the rules of St. Benedict, St. Francis, or St. Vincent de Paul. There is some truth in the contrast; nevertheless the Constitutions of St. Ignatius contain many passages expressing profound spiritual truths, on which the laws or rules are based, and others glowing with intense religious fervor. All in all, the Ignatian Constitutions are truly a spiritual book of the highest order.

The foregoing describes in brief the whole Constitutions and Institute of the Society of Jesus. There are no secret instructions, no secret Jesuits. It is to be noted with regret that myths of this nature have been propagated by enemies of the Society so successfully that sometimes they have been accepted and cited by writers otherwise learned and credible.[13]

What then, is the nature of this religious body, the Society of Jesus? It might be best first to discuss its name, which was an object of much contention in the past. In the beginning the companions of St. Ignatius were known by several designations: "Iñiguistas," after the Saint's original name of Iñigo; "Theatines," this in Rome, owing to a confusion with another religious order just previously founded; "Reformed Priests," also a Roman appellation; "Apostles," given in Portugal and the East Indies because of St. Francis Xavier, a true apostle, the best known of the Society in those regions. Soon, however, they were called all over the world "Jesuits." It was not the first time the name had been applied; in the fourteenth century the religious body founded by Bl. Giovanni Colombini had been popularly called the "Gesuati"; in the fifteenth century the term "Jesuites" was used of pious persons, given to the frequent use of the name of Jesus, and gradually in a disparaging sense of "pietist" for persons parading their religiousness. The Society did not invent the word "Jesuit" and has never used it in official documents; neither have the Popes, who speak in their Bulls and other pronouncements of the "clerics of the Society of Jesus." As a matter of fact the term was first applied, and in a derogatory sense, to members of the order by Protestant adversaries, as St. Peter Canisius wrote from Cologne in 1545.[14] Suarez in his commentary on the Society says the same, although admitting that the name could be understood in a correct and pious sense and used appropriately enough as a short substitute for the rather long "religious of the Society of Jesus." Soon the members of the order, realizing such appropriateness, began themselves to use the name "Jesuit" outside official documents.[15]

Even the official name "Society of Jesus" met with considerable opposition. The most determined opposition was met in France; the Parlement of Paris was largely responsible for the fact that the Jesuits were recognized in France in 1561 only under the title "Society of the College of

---

[13] A brief account of such myths may be found in Appendix V.

[14] "Obtrectatione, quae nobis etiam Jesuitae nomen dedit," Braunsberger, *Canisii Epistulae et Acta*, Freiburg (1896), Vol. I, p. 1340.

[15] The old Bollandists say the word is a "popular and compendious one," *Acta Sanctorum*, July, Vol. VII, p. 483 (ed. 1868).

Clermont," their first house in Paris; the Jansenists and freethinkers of the eighteenth century in the flood of anti–Jesuit books and pamphlets continually employed the expression "les soi-disant Jésuites" (the self-styled Jesuits).[16] Very zealous Catholics too objected to the name; to them there seemed to be some pride and arrogance in the assumption of the Holy Name.[17] They are not to be criticised too readily; the terms "Society of Jesus" and "Jesuit," so accepted today, were decided novelties in the sixteenth century. Others held that the name was "new and unheard of"; yet in 1458 and 1459 Pius II, in an effort to revive the crusading spirit, instituted a military order with the actual name "Society of Jesus." [18] St. Ignatius very probably did not know of this earlier use of the title. The Popes, from Paul III in 1540, by their confirmations of the Society of Jesus, had at least implicitly approved the name. One Pope, however, Sixtus V, a good and truly great man, objected to the title and wished to change it, though he would have permitted the term "Society of the Jesuits"; Sixtus died before the change was carried out. His successor, Gregory XIV, in his apostolic constitution *Ecclesiae Catholicae* (1591) confirming the Institute of the order, declared explicitly: "the name Society of Jesus by which this praiseworthy order was called by the Apostolic See at its birth, and by which it has been designated hitherto, is to be retained for all times."

The name "Society of Jesus" was chosen by St. Ignatius himself, as has been related in Chapter II.[19] So determined was the Saint on the name that some have concluded that it was revealed to him. But the statements of the early Jesuits are conflicting on this point, and so nothing positive can be asserted.[20] It was neither pride nor arrogance that influenced Ignatius to the choice of the name, but an intense personal love of Jesus. Herein is a most striking example of the relation of the Institute to the Exercises; the very name "Company," for "Society" is an inadequate rendition, recalls vividly the great meditation in which "Christ the King" invites his subjects to follow Him in His great campaign. Yet the

---

[16] Cf. the title of the official condemnation of Parlement in 1762: "*Extraits des assertions dangereuses et pernicieuses en tout genre que les soi-disant Jésuites . . . ont soutenues . . . etc.*"

[17] An excellent answer to the charge of "pride and arrogance" was made by Henry IV of France to one who had made such an objection. He remarked: "Some of my vassals are Knights of the Holy Spirit; there is in the Church an order of the Holy Trinity; and here in Paris is a society of religious women who call themselves 'Daughters of God.' Why, then, object to a 'Society of Jesus'?" Another and a more solid answer was made by Cardinal Hosius to Maximilian II, when he said: "Jesus calls us all 'brethren' and 'sons of God'; these are prouder names than 'companions'; besides, no one can please all."

[18] Pastor, *History of the Popes*, Vol. III, p. 46.

[19] Chapter II, p. 43.

[20] *Analecta Bollandiana*, Vol. XXVII, p. 408.

use of "Company of Jesus" in no way meant that the new order claimed a special place of honor, a privileged position, with or near Christ; such a thought might well have implied pride. Ignatius spoke in a military sense, a company, or in a modern term, a regiment of Christian soldiers. From the sixteenth to the eighteenth centuries many officers, usually noblemen, raised regiments which often carried the name of the officer who recruited them.[21] Somewhat similar but in a spiritual way was the soldier Saint's idea: his order was to be a regiment of picked men, enlisted by Jesus, Jesus Himself being the head, the Captain; their regiment was to fight under Jesus and, as He is also the King, to fight for Jesus.[22] That is the truly noble and inspiring meaning of the name "Society," or rather, "Company of Jesus"; and so the very beginning of the "Formula" or first draft of the Constitutions may be translated: "Whoever desires in this Regiment, which we want to be designated by the name of Jesus, to do battle for God under the banner of the Cross . . ."

This Company of Jesus, as regards its nature, is first a religious order in the strict sense of the word, i. e., a religious body in which solemn vows are taken.[23] It is one of the thirty or more religious orders of the Catholic Church.[24] Secondly, it is an order of Regular Clerics, i. e., an order in which the majority of the members are priests, or preparing for the priesthood.[25] In the introductory chapter various types of religious were noted: monks, canons regular and friars. One of the main differences between these groups was an ever-increasing application to the active apostolic life, which implied that religious were more and more in priestly orders. The monks originally had been mostly laymen, so also were the followers of St. Francis; it is most probable that St. Benedict was only a deacon,[26] it is certain of St. Francis. In St. Dominic's order, the "Friars Preachers," the priesthood was, of course, more necessary. The beginning of the sixteenth century witnessed the rise of a new type of religious, the clerks regular, in which the larger and essential part were priests. Among the first of the new orders were the Theatines, Barnabites and Somaschi; all three were founded before the Jesuits and all three made overtures

---

[21] As examples recall the Regiments of Balderon, Blancart, Chiese, Holstein of the Imperial army in the Thirty Years' War, or Butler's Dragoons of the same force, or the Irish Regiments de Dillon, de Lally and de Walsh in the French Armies at Fontenoy and Yorktown.

[22] Cf. Polanco, *Vita Ignatii Loyolae*, Vol. I, p. 74: "It is not called the Society of Jesus as if ours pretended to be the special companions of Jesus, but the word is taken in a military sense (Compañia) as a regiment of one under whom they do service."

[23] *Codex Iuris Canonici*, c. 488, No. 2.

[24] Cf. Appendix IV for the number of religious orders. The incorrect idea that there are only four or five religious orders has rather wide acceptance.

[25] *Codex Iuris Canonici*, c. 488, No. 4.

[26] Delatte, *The Rule of St. Benedict*, p. 425.

to have their institutes united with that of St. Ignatius, which fusion Ignatius refused.[27] The clerks regular deviated in various ways from the customs of the older orders; the Society of Jesus, of all, went the farthest. A description of these innovations is of importance for an understanding of the Society of Jesus, as also of the strong objections made by other religious to various features of the new order.

One of the first innovations occurred in the "grades" or classes of members in the Society. In the Society, as in most religious orders of men, there is a fundamental distinction between those who are priests, or destined for the priesthood, on the one hand, and those others who while truly Jesuits are not priests nor destined for the priesthood. These members, though laymen, are truly religious in the full sense of the term. They are occupied mostly in the domestic works of the Society, as bookkeepers, accountants, sacristans, caretakers and artisans; some have been artists and architects of distinction. They are known popularly as "lay-brothers," and technically in the Society, as "temporal coadjutors"; they wear the same habit and live substantially the same life as the clerical members. They are divided into three grades: the novice lay-brothers, who spend two years in spiritual training; the approved temporal coadjutors, who take simple but perpetual vows of religion after their novitiate; and the formed temporal coadjutors, who after ten years or so as approved coadjutors receive their final, simple vows.

In the clerical members of the organization, the grades among whom caused some controversies and misunderstandings in the early days, there are further distinctions. First are the scholastic novices,[28] who spend two years of probation and training in preparation for entrance into the Society, which is effected, as in the case of the lay-brothers, by the taking the first simple, perpetual vows. They are now known as approved scholastics and for some years devote themselves to preparation for the priesthood. After ordination and a third year of novitiate, which is commonly known as the "tertianship," they are eligible for the final vows. These final vows are of two kinds and constitute the two final grades in the Society. Some pronounce simple but final vows and are henceforth known as formed spiritual coadjutors. They are eligible for all but a few of the highest offices in the Society, they may be made rectors of colleges or universities; not a few of the ablest rectors, professors, missionaries, preachers and writers were of this grade. Others pronounce four solemn vows, the three essential vows of poverty, chastity and obedience, and a fourth of

---

[27] Pastor, *History of the Popes*, Vol. XII, p. 55.

[28] In the earliest days some were accepted into the Novitiate, without it being definitely determined whether they were to be priests or lay-brothers. They were technically known as "Indifferentes." This grade is listed in the Constitutions, though no longer actually existing.

special obedience to the Pope in regard to the missions. These are known as the professed of four vows; they are eligible for any office in the Society, and through their elected representatives form the General Congregation, the legislative body of the Society. The professed also make a few simple vows, e. g., never to covet or accept any ecclesiastical dignity and never to allow a mitigation of the vow of poverty.[29]

The professed of the four vows [30] form the kernel of the Society; the novices and scholastics are in a preparatory stage and the coadjutors help as auxiliaries. All are truly Jesuits. As regards clothes, food, observance of rules, all Jesuits are alike, no matter of what grade or class; the professed enjoy no special privileges.

Objections were raised against this distinction of the priests into two classes, but the objections were made by outsiders rather than by spiritual coadjutors. Far more vigorous was the criticism against the delay of the final vows. In the older orders the final solemn vows were made immediately after a novitiate of one year. In the Society at the end of two years' novitiate, all made perpetual but simple vows. The solemn vows were made only after the completion of the many years of training. Not a few members of older religious orders declared that those having only simple vows were not religious in the true sense. This opinion went against explicit or implicit declarations of several Popes. The matter was finally settled by Gregory XIII in two solemn Bulls, "Quanto Fructuosius" [31] of 1582 and "Ascendente Domino" [32] of 1584. In the last document the Pope approved of the distinction of spiritual coadjutors and professed. In rather severe language he censured those who, under the pretext of zeal for religion, disturbed the peace of mind and the vocation of others and tried to undermine the institute of the Society, particularly the status of those who had made only simple vows in the order. Gregory XIII then emphatically declared that those who after the novitiate make the simple vows are "truly and in the proper sense religious" (vere et proprie religiosos esse).[33] He further forbade anyone to call in doubt, or to raise

---

[29] The Society was not the first or only order to add other vows to the three essential ones; the Knights of St. John had a vow of serving the sick and defending the Faith; some branches of the Order of the Holy Spirit had a vow of serving the poor as their lords; the Augustinian Canons of the Windesheim Congregation had a vow of observing perpetual enclosure; and the Barnabites had a vow of not aiming at ecclesiastical dignities. Many orders and congregations since the founding of the Society have additional vows, such as a vow to devote one's whole life gratis to the service of the poor, or to teach poor children gratis.

[30] There is another class which so rarely occurs as to need but passing reference: The professed of three vows, who take only the three essential vows in solemn form.

[31] Institutum S.J. Bullarium, p. 87.

[32] Ibid., p. 90.

[33] The decision, that without solemn vows a person could be a religious in the strict

controversies over this and similar points of the Institute of the Society of Jesus.

The new Code of Canon Law of 1917 has also answered the old objection against the Society for putting off the final vows and not making the profession immediately after the novitiate. According to Canon 574: "in all orders and congregations that have perpetual vows, the novices after the novitiate must, before they take perpetual vows, be they solemn or simple, make temporary vows for three years." Further, according to Canon 573 no one can make the profession, if it is perpetual, until the twenty-first year is completed. May not these laws be considered a vindication of St. Ignatius?

One of the innovations of St. Ignatius which encountered strong opposition was the omission of the chanting of the sacred office in choir. Hitherto all orders had followed the practice. Several able and zealous religious, convinced that choir was essential to religious life, strongly and openly disapproved of Ignatius' course. More than one Pope, as will be seen, wished to impose choir on the Society. Their successors invariably revoked the orders. St. Ignatius, had he consulted his own inclinations, would certainly have retained the practice; but he felt that the work of preaching, hearing confessions and teaching, which was to occupy his order so completely, would be seriously impeded if the members had to spend several hours daily in chanting the Divine Office. He did not seek exemption for his priests from the private recitation of the Office; this, together with Mass, a half-hour meditation and two examinations of conscience, occupied some three hours, a period of formal prayer in his judgment sufficient in the day of a priest so wholly devoted to external work for souls.

The body of the Society is divided into provinces, a procedure which was not an innovation, having been first introduced by the military orders and later adopted by the friars. It is almost a necessity in large bodies with central government. Generally the provinces are based on national lines, such as the English, Irish or Portuguese provinces. Where the country is large there are often several provinces; thus there are seven in the United States and five in Spain. The provinces geographically or linguistically related are grouped into assistancies. At present there are eight assistancies: The Italian Assistancy, with the provinces of Rome, Naples, Sicily, Turin and Venice-Milan; the German Assistancy, with the provinces of Austria, Lower Germany, Upper Germany, Eastern Germany, Hungary, the Netherlands, Lithuania and the Mission of Latvia; the French Assistancy, with the provinces of France, Lyons, Champagne and Toulouse; the Spanish Assistancy, with the provinces

sense of the term, was of epochal importance; thereby was raised the stature of all the numerous congregations of simple vows.

of Aragon, Andalusia, Castile, Leon, Toledo and Portugal; the English Assistancy, with the provinces of England, Ireland, Northern Belgium, Southern Belgium, Lower Canada, Upper Canada and the Vice-Province of Australia; the American Assistancy, with provinces of Maryland-New York (soon to be divided), New England, Chicago, Missouri, New Orleans, California and Oregon; the Slavic Assistancy, with the provinces of Greater Poland and Masovia, Lesser Poland, Czechoslovakia, Jugoslavia and the Vice-Province of Roumania; the Latin-American Assistancy, with the provinces of Argentina, Central Brazil, Southern Brazil, Colombia, Mexico and the Vice-Province of Chile. A Father Assistant, representing each Assistancy but possessing no executive power over his Assistancy, resides at the General's curia.

The chief legislative authority resides in the General Congregation. It consists of the General (if alive), the Assistants, the Provincials and two delegates from each province, who must be professed fathers and are elected by the Provincial Congregation. This last congregation is composed of the Provincial, the rectors and a number of the older professed fathers. The General Congregation always meets for the election of a new General; it also elects his Assistants. It has the power of deposing the General for grave reasons, though such an action has never been taken in the four hundred years' history of the order. On a few occasions General Congregations have been called during the life-time of a General to decide very important matters. The General Congregation can issue canons and decrees, i. e., laws which have the force of the Constitutions. Its decrees, however, have been invariably elucidations of the Constitutions, explicit applications of general laws to new conditions, and similar legislation.

At the head of the whole order is the General. The title has no military connotation; the complete official designation, Praepositus Generalis, means Superior General, "generalis" merely signifying "universal" or "over all." There was nothing new in this usage; for centuries the Franciscans had a Minister Generalis and the Dominicans a Magister Generalis, the Theatines and the Somaschi even used the very term Praepositus Generalis. The General is elected for life. This was a departure from the practice of most of the older orders, the Generals of which were and are elected for a certain number of years. The General is the only superior of the Society who is elected; all others, Provincials, rectors and superiors of most houses or residences, are appointed by him. This last also constituted an innovation, as in most other orders Provincials and local superiors are elected. From all this it follows that the form of government in the Society is monarchical, as is explicitly declared in the *Epitome*.[34] Much

---

[34] *Epitome Instituti S.J.*, Rome: (1924), Tit. V, pt. I, 4.

of the government of the other orders is done through the Chapter, the assembly of all or certain members. There is no such chapter in the Society, neither for the whole order, nor for the provinces, nor for the houses. There are consultors for the rectors and the Provincials, as there are Assistants for the General; but theirs are only advisory powers.

The power of the General is great; yet many writers have exaggerated its extent. It has been called despotic; indeed the claim has been made by Canon Littledale that it gives the General "the absolute disposal of members of the Society . . . for every purpose." Such an idea is quite erroneous. The General's power, in reality, is limited and far from arbitrary; he can exercise it only within the limits of the Constitutions, which he cannot change. Then he has around him the Assistants who, if they consider his conduct unworthy of the Society or detrimental to its well-being, can call a General Congregation for his deposal. In addition, he has a personal admonitor, appointed by the General Congregation, whose duty it is to admonish the General if he or the Assistants consider it necessary for grave causes. Lastly for every Jesuit there remains the possibility of appealing from a decision of the General to the highest superior, the Pope.

Attention might be called here to the rather common, but quite absurd, notion of the "Black Pope." The Supreme Pontiff, the "White Pope" (called so from his white cassock) is supposed to be but a venerable figurehead, while the real power behind the throne is the "Black Pope," the black-cassocked General of the Society of Jesus. This is one of the "wild ideas" entertained about Jesuits. That on some ecclesiastical matters a Pope occasionally might consult the head of over 25,000 men, stationed in every part of the world, would not be unnatural. But to ascribe to the General any controlling influence over the Pope is simply too childish. The truth is that some Popes were friendlier to the Society than others, assigning to the members important missions, placing them at the head of various ecclesiastical institutions and the like. But other Popes showed more aloofness, even coolness to the order; a few wanted to introduce important changes in the Constitutions; and one suppressed the whole Society. He had the power to do this. The Society absolutely submitted to his sentence of death, as it was its sacred duty to do so.

In a body so highly centralized as the Society obedience is of paramount importance. The more the principle of local stability was abandoned, and the greater the mobility and the flexibility attained, the more necessary was some kind of bond to hold the members together. That was obedience. On this virtue St. Ignatius insisted most strongly, in the Constitutions (Part III, Ch. 1, No. 23, and especially Part IV, Ch. 1), in a considerable number of rules in the *Summary of the Constitutions*, and more in detail and most eloquently in his celebrated *Epistle on the Virtue of Obedience*.

Yet there is no feature of the Jesuit order more severely or more frequently attacked than its obedience. It is charged that the obedience of the Society is "overdone," that it differs essentially from the obedience of religious orders, that it was an extraordinary and unheard of novelty. As a matter of fact, Jesuit obedience is essentially the same as that of other religious orders; the difference is only one of emphasis, as in the order of St. Francis the emphasis is on poverty. In all religious orders and congregations the most characteristic vow is obedience; in some it is the only vow explicitly made in the profession. The Rule of St. Benedict assigned a paramount importance to obedience; in the Benedictine profession stability and obedience are vowed. Thus speaks Dom Paul Delatte, O.S.B., a foremost authority on the Benedictine Rule: [35] "Let us not be astonished that our form of profession contains no explicit mention of poverty and chastity. This omission is traditional and is found in the diverse branches of the order. Nor have Carthusians, Canons Regular, Carmelites and Dominicans an express mention of the three vows; some have only the vow of obedience." During the violent controversies about poverty among the early Franciscans, Pope John XXII in 1317 in the Decretal "Quorundam Exigit" [36] declared: "Great is poverty, greater is chastity, but greatest is obedience, if kept perfectly. For the first deals with (external) matters, the second with the flesh, but the third with the mind and soul." This declaration but repeats the teaching of St. Thomas Aquinas to the effect that of the three vows that of obedience was the foremost and the greatest.[37] No fault then should be found with St. Ignatius for placing special emphasis on this vow.

The Saint's views were definitely expressed in his *Epistle on Obedience:* "Other religious orders may surpass the Society in fasting and other austerities which according to their institute they piously practice; but in true and perfect obedience and abnegation of will and judgment I greatly desire that those who serve God in this Society should be conspicuous . . . and should be distinguished by this mark." He wanted a most perfect obedience, not only of prompt external execution, but of complete submission of will and intellect. This last phase, "submission of intellect," is one to which most vigorous objection has been made, even by some Catholics.

One accusation made for over a century by non-Catholics is that Jesuit superiors can oblige subjects to do something which is sinful, "to commit

---

[35] Delatte, O.S.B., *The Rule of St. Benedict,* p. 390. Dom Delatte was Abbot of Solesmes and Superior-General of the Congregation of Benedictines of France.

[36] Adopted into the Collection of Pontifical Decrees called *Extravagantes Joannis XXII,* tit. XIV, c. 1, "de verborum significatione." In Freidberg, *Corpus Juris Canonici,* Vol. II, p. 1223.

[37] *Summa Theol.* II, II qu., CLXXXVI, a 8.

sin." It was especially due to Michelet, whose opinion was accepted and spread by other writers. There is in the Constitutions an expression "obligare ad peccatum." It is declared that the rules of the Society do not bind under sin (inducere obligationem ad peccatum) unless they belong to the essence of the vows, or "if the Pope gives an order," or "if a superior according to the institute gives an order in virtue of holy obedience." [38] The expression in question means "to oblige under sin," or "under penalty of committing sin," that is, to invest a command with such gravity that its transgression would be a sin. St. Thomas uses the term often, in one place five times.[39] It is to be found in the Rules for Franciscan Tertiaries, as well as in the Dominican Constitutions. For a thinking person it is impossible to believe that such an abomination could be found in the Constitutions of a great religious order, Constitutions which had been approved and praised by so many Popes after careful examination by their eminent theologians. Only those who see in the Papacy the veritable anti-Christ could accept such a suggestion. Again, from the beginning the Institute of the Society has been subjected to the keenest scrutiny by hostile, albeit able critics; would not these have "pounced" upon such an abomination? Yet not a word about it appears in any early criticism. To remove all doubt, the words of St. Ignatius may be quoted; he uses the expression "ad peccatum" as synonymous with "sub poena peccati." [40] He explicitly states too that: "obedience is to be rendered where there appears no sin." [41] In fact in the same chapter of the Constitutions he remarks: "in all things in which no sin of any kind can be recognized"; thus he forbids obedience if even a venial sin were involved. These important passages have been entirely omitted by the framers of this accusation; a fact which convicts them of dense ignorance or wilful slander.

Certain expressions of St. Ignatius in recommending the most perfect obedience have been ridiculed by non-Catholics and have been criticized even by some Catholics. Thus his admonition to his religious to look upon the Superior's command "as if it were the voice of Christ" has been protested. Yet the Saint's principle has a solid scriptural basis in St. Paul's exhortation for general obedience to all lawful authority: [42] "Be obedient to them that are your temporal lords according to the flesh . . . in the simplicity of your heart, as to Christ . . . as to the Lord and not to man . . ." This has certainly a far more direct application with regard

---

[38] Const. Part VI, c. V. The principle was already in the rules of the order of St. Dominic. Cf. St. Thomas, *Summa Theol.* II, II, qu. CLXXXVI, a. 9.

[39] *Summa Theol.* II, II, qu. CLXXXVI, a. 9: "obligare ad mortale" (peccatum).

[40] Part X; Part IX, c. IV B.

[41] Part III, c. III, also *Summary*, 31; *Epistle on Obedience*, 10.

[42] *Ephesians* VI, 5.

to obedience to spiritual superiors. The principle of Ignatius was a commonplace in the works of the Fathers, the founders of religious orders and spiritual writers.[43] His teaching is so identical with that of St. Basil, St. Benedict, St. Bernard and many others that Suarez does not hesitate to say: "it is clear that Bl. Ignatius either took it from those Fathers or at least spoke in their spirit." These Saints, and with them St. Ignatius, do not hesitate to cite as proof the words of Christ Himself: "He that heareth you, heareth Me"; [44] St. Benedict quotes them in his Rule [45] after he has explicitly stated: "the obedience shown to superiors is indeed given to God."

Critics of St. Ignatius have sharply censured another direction of his, that the perfect obedience should be blind obedience. Connected with this is what St. Ignatius calls the "highest degree of obedience," the submission not only of the will but also of the intellect, so that "what the Superior commands and thinks good, should seem just and reasonable to the inferior." This principle was by no means new with Ignatius; thus St. Gregory said that "true obedience does not judge," and similarly spoke St. Bernard, St. Bonaventure and many other great theologians.[46] St. Nilus, a foremost figure among the first monks, in his *De Monastica Exercitatione* (written about 425), clearly and strongly urges the monk to "obey the superior although what he commands may not seem plausible, submitting his own reasonings to the art of him who is experienced in guiding others, judging that his knowledge is more trustworthy." [47] If the patristic writings were carefully examined the principle of Ignatius probably would appear in quite common acceptance.

This submission of the intellect does not require of the subject the absolute acceptance of the command as the best in itself. St. Ignatius clearly says "the judgment should be that whatsoever the superior commands and thinks good seems just and reasonable to the inferior, insofar, as I have said, as the will by its force can bend the understanding." [48] The Saint wants the subject to make an honest effort to see the wisdom of the superior's command; he is not asking him to stultify his intellect. He is but striving to guard the subject from the delusions of self-love.[49] Nor is representation to a superior prohibited in the Society. St. Ignatius explicitly declares: "Neither are you hindered, if anything occurs to you different from the superior's opinion . . . to propose it unto him." [50]

---

[43] Cf. Suarez, *De religione S.J.*, Bk. IV, C. 15, for a long list of quotations.
[44] *Luke* X, 16.
[45] *The Rule of Saint Benedict* (trans. by Card. Gasquet), London (1936), c. V, p. 24.
[46] Suarez, *De religione S.J.*, Bk. IV c. 15, No. 7.
[47] Migne, *Patrologia Graeca*, Vol. 79, p. 719 ff.
[48] *Epistle on Obedience*, 9.
[49] *Ibid.*, 8, 11, 12.
[50] *Ibid.*, 19.

This type of obedience was exacted in the older orders, at least in some of them. What otherwise could the Fathers have meant by such expressions as that one must "obey as to God," or "as to Christ"? Dom Delatte so explains the obedience of the Rule of St. Benedict.[51]

Much ridicule has been visited on the Ignatian ideal of "blind" obedience, and with much inconsistency; "blind" obedience in a soldier is much extolled, yet in a spiritual warrior is branded as absurd and servile, even unethical. Now it must not be forgotten that the term "blind" obedience is a figurative one, and like other figurative expressions must not be pressed. Indeed, St. Ignatius warns against a too liberal interpretation, saying: "Judgment should be renounced with a kind of blind obedience (caeca quadam obedientia)."[52] He certainly wants the mind open to see if anything sinful be in the command. Nor does he wish to do violence to the intellect, for he observes that this obedience cannot be expected where "the evidence of the known truth is against it."[53]

Similar judgment must be passed on two other expressions of the Saint, illustrating this quality of obedience of the intellect. The subjects, he says: "must suffer themselves to be carried and ruled by Divine Providence in their superiors, as if they were a dead body, which suffers itself to be borne to any place and to be treated in any manner whatever, or like an old man's staff which serves him who holds it in his hand, where and in what use soever he pleases."[54] It is quite clear that these are but figurative expressions, metaphors which must not be pressed. Dom Delatte rightly observes: "when masters of the spiritual life use these expressions they merely wish to express the perfect pliancy of the obedient soul, dead to its own will."[55] St. Ignatius did not originate either expression. The comparison of "the old man's staff" has a parallel in an ancient Greek work, called *Monastic Constitutions*,[56] incorrectly attributed to St. Basil; in this ancient work the figure is of a carpenter's tool. The other more startling expression, "like a dead body," was used by St. Francis of Assisi;[57] but it is of much older origin, having been also employed by St. Nilus.[58] It is not likely that St. Ignatius was acquainted directly with the illustration of St. Nilus; but it is most probable that he knew the one from St. Francis.

In all the Constitutions one note is constantly stressed; it is love, love

---

[51] Delatte, O.S.B., *The Rule of St. Benedict*, p. 90.

[52] *Constitutiones*, Part VI, C. I.

[53] *Epistle*, 9.

[54] *Const.*, Part VI, c. I; *Summary*, 36.

[55] Delatte, *The Rule of St. Benedict*, p. 87.

[56] Quoted in Pastor, *History of the Popes*, Vol. XII, p. 67. It will be found among the works of St. Basil in Migne, *Patrologia Graeca*, Vol. 31, col. 1410.

[57] S. Bonaventure, *Legenda Major S. Francisci*, c. 6.

[58] Migne, *Patrologia Graeca*, Vol. 79, col. 771.

of God, love of the neighbor and love of the fellow members of the order. In the very first rule of the *Summary* one may read: "and on our part the interior law of charity and love, which the Holy Ghost is accustomed to write and imprint in the hearts of men, is to help (in the preservation, government and advance of the Society of Jesus)." Similar citations may be found throughout the Institute. The motive for obeying the superior is declared to be love and not fear; the unity of the order is proposed through fraternal charity. To promote the last St. Ignatius encouraged constant communication between the brethren, no matter how far scattered they might be. St. Francis Xavier summed up the ideal of the order when he wrote: "The Company of Jesus ought to be called the company of love and conformity of souls." [59]

[59] *Ep.*, 12 Jan. 1549.

CHAPTER VI

EARLY PROGRESS

Pressing problems confronted the young order now bereft of its remarkable founder: what was to be done about the Constitutions, completed by Ignatius to be sure, but as yet not accepted by the order; who was to be chosen to take his place, guiding the infant organization in the very difficult first years; how, when and where could the professed be assembled into the First General Congregation for such vital legislation and so important an election? Paul IV's attitude made solutions doubly hard; he quite disapproved of some features of the order, especially the life term of the general and the absence of choir.

On Laynez, who had been elected Vicar-General in 1552, devolved the task of assembling the First General Council in November 1556. Rome would have been the meeting place, but that was prevented by the war between the Pope and Charles V.[1] Suggestions of Spain or France not finding acceptance, the Congregation was postponed until the termination of the war. In the meantime Paul IV began to manifest his unfavorable attitude towards the Society, and ordered Laynez to hand over for examination the Constitutions of the order and the Bulls of confirmation. The Papal action largely arose from the complaints of that difficult character, Bobadilla,[2] who approved neither of the Constitutions as written by Ignatius nor of the election and government of Laynez; according to him the Rule needed revision and alteration, and the Society should be governed by the still living original founders.

Laynez moved energetically to meet the danger. He caused Nadal and other fathers who knew the Constitutions to draw up refutations of Bobadilla's objections, and readily welcomed an investigation of his own conduct. When Cardinal Carpi vindicated his claim to the office of Vicar-General, only advising him to seek the advice of the professed fathers in gravely important questions, Laynez anticipated an appeal of Bobadilla by personally asking the Pope to appoint a Cardinal to investigate the whole affair. Paul IV received Laynez, whom he greatly admired, very kindly and named the Dominican Cardinal Ghislieri for the task. The Cardinal's report was most favorable. The commission of Cardinals desig-

---

[1] Pastor, *History of the Popes*, Vol. XIV, pp. 251–258.
[2] Astrain, *Historia de la C. de J. en la asistencia de España*, Vol. II, pp. 12 ff.

nated to examine the Constitutions and Bulls returned them unaltered.

The First General Congregation finally assembled at Rome on June 19, 1558. Laynez was elected successor of Ignatius, as the second Father General of the Society of Jesus. The Congregation voted to accept the Constitutions in their entirety as written by the founder, making but a few very minor changes. Paul IV, however, asked the fathers to consider the introduction of choir and the limitation of the General's term of office. Such essential departures from St. Ignatius' ideals the Congregation did not wish to make. To the Pope's renewed insistence, they expressed their readiness to obey but also their wish to abide by the original Constitutions; Paul IV had given no express command and there were the official confirmations in the Bulls of Paul III and Julius III. Laynez and Salmeron sought to place the views of the Congregation before the Pope. They received a very severe reception. The Pontiff addressed them in rather heated terms as they knelt before him, declaring Ignatius to be a tyrant and the Jesuits rebels for not introducing choir. When Paul IV's anger cooled, he allowed Laynez to defend the order's position. Nevertheless word was sent to the Congregation to enact legislation providing for choir and a three year term for the General. The Congregation of course obeyed. However, the changes lasted only until the death of the Pontiff. Since Paul IV's orders had not been formally promulgated, the Society on the advice of eminent non-Jesuit canonists [3] gave up the choir. When Laynez came to the end of his third year of government, he offered to resign; on the same principle his resignation was not accepted. Even Bobadilla was reconciled. Pius IV, the succeeding Pope, expressly repealed the decrees and confirmed the Constitutions as they originally stood.

For seven years Laynez zealously directed the rapid growth of the Society. At his death on January 19, 1565, there were eighteen provinces, one hundred and thirty houses and thirty-five hundred members. Four assistancies had also been established: the Italian, the German (including France and Poland), the Portuguese and the Spanish. In the nineteenth century a false thesis advanced by Müller in his *Les origines de la Compagnie de Jésus: Ignace et Laynez*,[4] asserted that the scholarly second General was the principal author of the Constitutions. This opinion was successfully refuted by the Jesuit scholars, Brucker, Hubert and Thurston.[5] Even as the Father General, Laynez continued to labor personally for the wider interest of the Church, lending valuable assistance in the

---

[3] Pastor, *History of the Popes*, Vol. XIV, p. 257.

[4] Paris (1898).

[5] Brucker, *Études*, Vol. 77 (1898), pp. 703–709; Hubert, *Theol. Lit. Zeitung* (1899), pp. 310–311, Thurston, *The Month*, Vol. 94 (1899), pp. 518–526. No doubt St. Ignatius sought Laynez's advice.

founding of new seminaries and taking part in the Conference of Poissy where he opposed the Calvinist leader Beza. Laynez was a saintly priest, a deep scholar and a successful author of theological works.[6]

Pius IV proved a strong friend of the Society of Jesus, a fact which can be attributed in part to his nephew and secretary, St. Charles Borromeo.[7] Once he did display hostility to Laynez and Robera, holding them responsible for what he considered the over-ascetical manner of life adopted by his nephew. Pius granted several privileges to the order, especially the power of conferring philosophical and theological degrees. He entrusted the new Roman Seminary to the fathers. This appointment, the use also of the Jesuits by Cardinal Savelli for the examination of the clergy seeking benefices, and the employment of them by Cardinals Savelli and Farnese in the visitation of the Roman parishes, aroused against the Society a storm which culminated in a book severely attacking the fathers. Pius IV not only came to the support of the Jesuits but wrote letters defending them against the book to the Emperor, the Duke of Bavaria, the three Ecclesiastical Electors and Cardinal Truchsess.[8] On other occasions he sent still other letters commending the order to various princes. Due to Pius IV was the praise which the Council of Trent bestowed upon the Society. He gave strong backing to the Roman College and relieved the hard financial straits of the German College.

In the final sessions of the Council of Trent Jesuit theologians played important roles.[9] Pius IV sought the advice of Laynez on the steps to be taken for its last convocation in 1562. When the Council assembled the Pontiff ordered Laynez, Salmeron, Polanco and Canisius to attend as Papal theologians. Couvillon, a French father, was present as a representative of Bavaria. Laynez addressed the Council on five occasions, once against the concession of the Chalice to the laity and four times in defense of the Papal position and powers. His speech of October 20, 1562 was a masterpiece of learning, clearness and pertinency; Sarpi, the apostate Servite and a bitter enemy of the Pope and the Jesuits, declared that it had made an impression scarcely equalled by any other speech in the whole course of the Council. Laynez, it should be noted, did not hesitate to oppose the position taken so strongly by most of the Spanish Bishops against the Papal power over the episcopacy. In the debate on the concession of the Chalice Salmeron spoke for three hours against the proposal.

---

[6] Boero, *Vita del Servo di Dio P. Giacomo Lainez* (1880); Astrain, *Historia*, Vol. I, pp. 73 ff.; Tacchi-Venturi, *Storia della de C. de G. in Italia*, Vols. I, II, passim; Duhr, *Geschichte der Jesuiten*, Vol. I, passim; *Mon. hist. S.J. Lainii Monumenta*, 8 vols., Madrid (1912–1917).

[7] Pastor, *History of the Popes*, Vol. XV, pp. 87–98.

[8] Pastor, *History of the Popes*, Vol. XVI, p. 88, text and note 4.

[9] *Ibid.*, Vol. XV, pp. 264–365.

Canisius in the beginning thought some mitigation would do good, but later on relinquished that opinion. His greatest service to the Council was the help that he gave in preventing the threatened break between Ferdinand I and the Pope; his efforts went far to save the Council, which in the event very probably would have collapsed. It was owing to the suggestions of Laynez that duelling was forbidden, that the oath to accept the Tridentine decrees was required of all Doctors of Theology on the receipt of their degree, and that some mitigation of the Index was granted by Pius IV. Laynez and all the Society devoted themselves to assisting the Popes in the later carrying out of the Tridentine reforms, especially in the provisions for ecclesiastical education.

To the joy of Pius IV, of Cardinal Ghislieri (soon to be Pius V) and of all participants in the Catholic Reformation, the Second General Congregation elected Francis Borgia, the Spanish Assistant, as the third Father General. The Society owes much to the seven years of his wise and vigorous rule. He devoted himself first to strengthening the internal organization of the rapidly growing order; for this purpose he produced a new Latin edition of the rules, unified and completed the particular rules of the various offices, and improved the methods of administrative reports. Then he took special steps to insure the proper training of the younger members; this end he obtained by the opening of novitiates, separate from the colleges, in each province and by the furtherance of the Roman College. Specially significant were his efforts for deepening the spiritual life of all the members; he defined more definitely the religious exercises, insisted on the preeminence of mental prayer over vocal in the order's spirituality, and lengthened the time of the daily meditation from a half to a full hour. The last change was a departure from the policy of St. Ignatius; but St. Francis Borgia deemed that the circumstances of the order warranted it. Borgia was foremost among the early Generals in the promotion of the foreign missions; especially did he advance the work in Peru, where a province was erected in 1568, and in Mexico, where a province was established in 1572.

It was during the generalate of Borgia that the Society's ranks were blessed with the presence of the holy youth, St. Stanislaus Kostka.[10] St. Stanislaus was born October 10, 1550 at the castle of Rostkow in Masovia, Poland, of an important noble family. At the age of fourteen, together with his brother, he was sent to Vienna that he might be educated at the Jesuit College there. Stanislaus proved himself an excellent student and, even more, a youth of the highest virtue and purity. He was especially devoted to the Blessed Sacrament and to the Mother of God, whom he loved to call "my Mother." Heavenly visitations were vouch-

---

[10] Bartoli, *Della vita e miracoli del B. Stanislaus Kostka*, Rome (1670); Coleridge, *The Story of St. Stanislaus*, 3rd ed., London (1893).

safed him; at one time he received Holy Communion from the hands of an angel, and at another he was honored by an apparition of the Blessed Mother with her Divine Child. Stanislaus was a manly, heroic lad, persisting unflinchingly in his saintly life despite the continued and brutal punishments which his wayward brother inflicted on him in an effort to dissuade him. When his application for acceptance was refused by the Austrian Provincial who dreaded the wrath of the youth's father, the courageous boy, not yet sixteen, fled Vienna and tramped on foot all the way to Augsburg and Dillingen to beg admission from St. Peter Canisius. Saint recognized Saint and Canisius received Stanislaus into the order. After a short while the holy novice was sent to Rome to be welcomed in the novitate of San Andrea by still another Saint, Francis Borgia. Stanislaus' life in the Society was of brief duration; after ten months during which all hearts were won by his beautiful life and character, he died on August 15, 1568. The Church beatified this saintly novice in 1670 and canonized him in 1726. His native Poland declared him heavenly patron of his country in 1671. St. Stanislaus is venerated throughout the world as a patron of youth.

Borgia was not long in office when Cardinal Ghislieri was elected Pope Pius V. On the day of his coronation the holy Pontiff manifested in an extraordinary way his regard for the Father General and the Society; halting the procession on its way to the Lateran at the Professed House of the Jesuits, he embraced Francis Borgia, who with his brethren was standing on the steps to greet the Holy Father as he passed by.

The Pontiff bestowed many favors on the order: he employed the Jesuits as pontifical preachers, had them translate the Catechism of Trent into German and French, bestowed on them the confessionals of St. Peter's by organizing the College of Penitentiaries of the Vatican, endowed the fathers with the right to teach in universities and to confer degrees, sanctioned their exemption from capitular government, and declared the Society a mendicant order with the consequent privileges.

Yet St. Pius V could not accept entirely some of the innovations of St. Ignatius, especially the absence of choir and the system of grades (scholastics and coadjutors with simple vows). By this last system religious without solemn vows received ordination, something previously unknown. In 1567 the Pope ordered the Jesuits to offer the Congregation of the Council a justification for the simple vows of the scholastics and for the lack of choir. With the reasons given for the simple vows Pius V declared himself satisfied. In regard to the choir he was willing to grant exemption to most in the order because of their active duties in the care of souls or in the studies; but he felt it his duty to introduce the practice in brief form, to the extent that in certain churches (not connected with colleges) at least two fathers should recite the Office together. In consequence choir was begun at the Roman Professed House in 1568. Pius V's command being oral did not formally annul the earlier Papal concessions; hence with Papal authorization the choir could be relinquished, which was actually done after a short period.

The difficulty concerning grades was not yet ended.[11] On October 14, 1568 appeared a decree which insisted on solemn vows as a necessity in the ordination of religious. Borgia appealed to the Congregation of Cardinals to find out if in view of the Bulls of Paul III and Julius III the legislation affected the Society. He was told that the Jesuits might continue to ordain scholastics with simple vows, but with the obligation of providing for dismissed priests who might be in serious want. The answer satisfied neither St. Pius V nor St. Francis Borgia. The Pope asked for a reconsideration; and, when the Cardinals yet persisted in their decision, the Holy Father finally made the decree applicable to all religious orders. The situation for the Society was precarious: one of the most fundamental points of the Constitutions was to be altered and the Society, as St. Ignatius conceived it, with its policy of strict selection, would certainly disappear in a few years. The General sought the advice of the Provincials and of eminent Jesuits, how far the Constitutions might be adhered to in keeping with obedience to the Papal command. It was recommended that all be admitted to the three solemn vows before ordination but that only those who had pronounced the fourth vow of obedience to the Pope be eligible to sit in a General Congregation.

The application of the general legislation to the Society gave rise to difficulties within and to hostility without the order. When the innovations of the Constitutions would now be objected to by those who did not recognize the purposes of St. Ignatius, it would be no longer possible to appeal to the wisdom of the Saint and to the confirmations of Papal bulls. The door was open to all sorts of essential changes. Enemies of the order loudly asserted that the saintly Pope was hostile to the Society and was preparing to alter it completely,[12] if not to suppress it. Such was far from the fact, as the many privileges and letters of endorsement and praise by St. Pius V proved.[13]

The Pontiff employed the abilities of the saintly General on Alexandrini's legateship in Spain, Portugal and France, to arouse the Catholic princes to crusade against the Turkish menace. In all three royal courts he was received with every mark of respect. In the French court Borgia strove hard to prevent the "Marriage of Religions" between Marguerite of Valois and Henry of Navarre, a fact which helps to dispose of the

---

[11] Pastor, *History of the Popes*, Vol. XVII, pp. 277 ff.

[12] Pastor, *History of the Popes*, Vol. XVII, pp. 277 ff.

[13] *Ibid.*, pp. 282–283.

charge of complicity in the massacre of St. Bartholomew.[14] On the return journey the Saint fell sick unto death and was just barely brought to Rome, where he died on October 1, 1572. St. Francis Borgia was a leader of the reawakened Catholicism and a providential champion of the Society.[15] He has often been portrayed as a harsh ascetic. He was a severe man; but largely his severity was with himself, with others he was paternally kind. The Church beatified him in 1624 and canonized him in 1671.

In the last year of Borgia's generalate Gregory XIII was elected Pope; during his pontificate which lasted through the administration of the next General, Mercurian, and for four years of Aquaviva's, he so supported the Society of Jesus as to be considered by many the order's greatest benefactor. One of his first acts was the appointment of a commission, of which St. Charles Borromeo was a member, to examine the changes in the Constitutions made by St. Pius V. On the report of the commission, Gregory XIII, on February 28, 1573, issued the Bull "Ex sedis apostolicae," revoking the obligation of choir and permitting the ordination of Jesuits with simple vows. The Bull also granted a new and solemn confirmation of the Society and its privileges. Later, on May 25, 1584, the Pontiff issued still another Bull of confirmation, "Ascendente Domino," which among other provisions contained the most important decision that scholastics and coadjutors with simple vows were true religious. Gregory XIII's love of the Society arose from his admiration of the work of its colleges for the revival of the Faith; the colleges he never tired of praising and recommending to princes and bishops everywhere. His affection was most practical; he continually bestowed abundant financial support on these institutions, several of which in Germany, Switzerland, Italy and even in Japan owed their origin to him. The seminaries of Vienna, Prague, Gratz, Olmütz, Braunsberg, Fulda and Dillingen, the Universities of Wilna and Pont-à-Mousson, were in great part also due to this Pontiff. To the Collegium Germanicum and the Roman College Gregory XIII was lavishly generous in financial support, academic privileges and the erection of buildings; he has been called the second Founder of the Germanicum, and the Roman College today is known as the Gregorian University. The English College, the Greek College and the Hungarian College (later joined by him to the Germanicum) were entrusted by this Pontiff to the Society. Gregory XIII in his reform of the calendar employed the service of the Jesuit mathematician, Clavius, who composed

---

[14] Duhr, *Jesuiten Fabeln*, p. 797.

[15] *Mon. Hist. S.J. Mon. Borgiana*, 5 vols., Madrid (1894–1911); Suau, *Histoire de St. François Borgia*, Paris (1910); Yeo, *The Greatest of the Borgias*, Milwaukee (1936); Karrer, *Der heilige Franz von Borgia*, Freiburg (1921).

the final draft in 1578 and later in 1603 issued a strong defense of the epochal change.

When the Third General Congregation met to select a successor to St. Francis Borgia, Pope Gregory XIII expressed the wish, though leaving the fathers free, that someone other than a Spaniard be selected for the Generalate. Everard Mercurian,[16] a native of Belgian Luxemburg, was chosen to be the fourth Father General. The new superior had held many important offices in the Society, vice-rector of San Andrea (on the appointment of St. Ignatius), Provincial of Lower Germany, Assistant for Germany and Visitor of Aquitaine and France. During the seven years of Mercurian's generalate, the order's remarkable growth continued: three new provinces, Poland, Milan, and Venice, brought the number of provinces to 21 with a total of 5,650 members in 144 colleges and 33 residences; the English and Maronite missions were also begun. The Belgian Father General successfully withstood Philip II's desire to use the Jesuits in the reform of the older orders in Spain, a course which would have brought untold ill-feeling upon the new order. In Spain too Mercurian had to act in a rather delicate situation that had arisen among the Jesuits over the subject of mysticism. A small group, followers of Balthasar Alvarez [17] (possibly the leading Jesuit mystic, and also a confessor of St. Theresa), wished for a practice of mystical prayer which the majority considered not in keeping with the apostolic life of the Society. Alvarez, though the group had acted against his advice in the matter, incurred much criticism. The General ordered him to submit an account of his method of prayer; after an examination Mercurian approved of it for Alvarez himself, but discountenanced it as a general practice. Mercurian died on August 1, 1580. A few months previously the Society lost by death one of the ablest of the early Jesuits, Jerome Nadal.[18] Nadal, as founder of several colleges and as visitor of many provinces, introducing the Constitutions into practice, may be included among the real founders of the order.

During the administrations of Laynez, Borgia and Mercurian, the order throughout Italy developed strongly and steadily, unhampered by any serious or continued persecution. In 1558 three provinces, Naples, Tuscany and Lombardy were established, and within twenty years Lombardy was divided into Venice and Milan. In 1584 the Italian Assistancy included 1,689 members with 41 colleges, 20 more than in 1556. St. Charles Borromeo was a most ardent promoter of the Jesuit colleges;

---

[16] Manare, *De vita et moribus Everardi Mercurian Praecep. Gen. S.J. commentarius*, Brussels (1882).

[17] De Ponte, *Vida del P. Balthasar Alvarez, Religioso de la Comp. de Jesus*, Madrid (1615); Astrain, *Historia*, Vol. II, pp. 189–195; III, pp. 477–480, 538–540.

[18] *Mon. hist. S.J., Epistolae P. Hier. Nadal*, Vols. I–IV; Astrain, *Historia*, Vols. I–III.

several institutions were begun at his urging, though some had to be relinquished later because their close proximity hindered their proper development. The fathers Palmio, Perucci, Adorno and Gagliardo were valued assistants of the great Archbishop by their sermons, by their advice and help in his visitations and synods, and by their labors for his educational projects. Unfortunately one Jesuit, Mazzinario, became so involved in the quarrel between St. Charles and the Spanish governor of Milan as to forget himself and to attack the saintly Cardinal. The offending priest was cited to Rome, suspended from preaching for two years, and forced to beg the Saint's pardon. The Italian fathers worked vigorously against the cryptic, yet exceedingly dangerous, Italian Protestantism both in the north and at Naples. Possevino, who was to become the much trusted agent of the Popes, entered the order in 1559 and the very next year began his apostolic career by successfully preaching against the Calvinists in Savoy. Salmeron zealously opposed the Reformers in Naples, and Christopher Rodriguez brought heresy to an end in Calabria in 1566. Very fruitful were the sermons of the priests who worked out from the Roman College in the various dioceses of Italy; their sermon courses were an anticipation of the popular missions soon to be established. Similar success came to the pulpit labors of Palmio in Naples.

It was at this time in the Roman College that the original Sodality of the Blessed Virgin was established.[19] Jean Leunis, a Belgian scholastic and a teacher of grammar in the institution, was the founder. In 1563 he formed the pupils of his class into a sodality. The object of the confraternity was personal perfection in virtues and studies, as well as works of charity and of zeal for souls, under the invocation and special protection of the Blessed Virgin Mary. Six years later a division was made into a sodality for the older boys and one for the younger lads. The older boys' sodality was solemnly recognized by Gregory XIII in the Bull "Omnipotentis Dei" of 1584. The Prima Primaria, as this sodality was known, received powers to affiliate other sodalities or to erect new ones, and to share with them its rich indulgences and spiritual privileges. Wherever the Jesuits went, in the schools and parishes, they organized sodalities, which received a warm welcome from the people. Such was the growth of these organizations that within 13 years there were 30,000 sodalists; in some cities the various sodalities of students, laborers, merchants, professional men and priests numbered from seven to twenty. Later on hundreds of thousands were enrolled in the sodalities and from their ranks came canonized saints, Popes, princes, ecclesiastics, army officers and statesmen.

---

[19] Mullan, *The Sodality of our Lady studied in the Documents*, New York (1912); Loffler, *Die marianischen Congregationen*, Freiburg (1924); Delaplace, *Histoire des Congrégations de la Sainte Vierge*, Bruges (1884); Beringer, *De Congregationibus Marianis Documenta et Leges*, Vienna (1909).

The good done in strengthening and deepening the Faith, as well as in all kinds of charitable endeavors never can be calculated. The fierce hatred with which the enemies of the Church pursued the sodalities is a striking testimony of their worth.

The Society of Jesus in Spain and Portugal also continued its steady development.[20] Much of its progress was due to St. Francis Borgia. In 1554 he was appointed Commissary general of the order in the peninsula; and two years later he was placed over all the foreign missions of the Society whether in the Orient or New World, they being all either Spanish or Portuguese. During his seven years as Commissary general the Spanish provinces were transformed; he found them lacking in both subjects and foundations, he left them with well-filled ranks and many apostolic employments. To his novitiate at Simancas came numerous doctors of the flourishing Spanish universities and also representatives of the leading Spanish families. Borgia's sanctity, especially his asceticism and his devotion to the poor, his eager initiative, his influence with the Regent of Castile, all contributed much to such happy results.

Charles V in his retreat at Yuste sought his counsel, entrusted him with negotiations concerning the Portuguese succession and named him one of the executors of his will. It was St. Francis Borgia who preached the eulogy of the great monarch at solemn obsequies in Valladolid. But with the successes were failures too: the last years of the Commissary general in Spain were embittered by disappointments; there were misunderstandings and discontent among some of the members who considered him not forceful enough in their defense and at the same time too little considerate of them; there were the aversion and disfavor of Philip II; and there was the affair of his book being placed on the Index.[21] The personal sufferings Borgia bore courageously; the resentment of Philip II at his going to labor in Portugal he ignored. At length the Saint was called to Rome for work in a far wider field.

Five colleges were founded at Trigueros, Lisbon (by Cardinal Henry), Madrid, Villagarcia and Alcalá respectively. The students increased in the two decades from 300 to 5,800. These institutions of learning not only produced zealous ecclesiastics and worthy laymen, but became the source of the army of Spanish and Portuguese missionaries that spread through the pagan world, East and West. Two fathers, Gonçalez and Serges, were chosen tutors of the Portuguese Crown Prince, Sebastian.

---

[20] Astrain, *Historia*, Vol. II, in toto; III, pp. 1–181.

[21] A heretical tract had been bound into the same volume with the Saint's work *Obras del Christiano compeustas por D. Franc. de Borgia, Duque de Gandia*. Borgia was absolutely innocent; the action of the printer may have been malicious, as the practice was a not uncommon trick of heretical printers for the spreading of their doctrines. Astrain, *Historia*, Vol. II, pp. 110–113.

Serges, though it was against his advice that Sebastian launched a crusade in Africa, accompanied his royal master and died with him at Alcassar in 1578.

In apostolic labors the Spanish and Portuguese fathers worked zealously. Bustamente preached with success at Trigueros; Ramirez at Madrid and Salamanca, in which place numbers of his student-auditors entered religious life. In the rebellion of the Moors in 1569, Jesuit chaplains accompanied the army of Don Juan and the fleet of Requesens; afterwards the members of the Society took upon themselves the protection of the defeated Moors. Even ten years previously the order had opened a house for converted Moors at Granada. Four fathers and four brothers served with the Christian fleet at Lepanto. In nursing the plague-stricken the Jesuits of the two countries achieved a noble service; in 1558 twenty died in Aragon caring for the sick, in 1563 five more lost their lives, in 1569 eighteen at Lisbon made the supreme sacrifice, and in 1579 and 1580 in the same city several more became martyrs of charity. The priests of the order gave loyal assistance to the Spanish and Portuguese Bishops in carrying out the Tridentine reforms.

One reform project, however, brought much trouble and obloquy upon the Society; it occurred in connection with the correction of abuses in the religious orders.[22] Ormaneto, the Papal Legate and a truly zealous reformer, impatient with the unsatisfactory means of securing information, suggested to Philip II that the Jesuits be employed to obtain surreptitiously the required data. Philip II agreed and appointed Melendez, the rector of Madrid College, for the task. Melendez and his Provincial, Cardeses, vigorously refused the unwelcome employment; but when Philip II insisted and Ormaneto imposed obedience with the threat of ecclesiastical censures, Melendez had to begin. The Jesuit superiors, especially in view of the fact that other such projects were in contemplation, appealed to the Father General, Mercurian, who on his part forbade further action until the matter was laid before Pope Gregory XIII. The Pontiff acquiesced in the Jesuits' refusal. But the countermand came too late to save Melendez; a storm of protest arose against him and forced him to leave Spain. Quite naturally the unfortunate affair bred resentment against the new order in many quarters.

Nor was this the only difficulty of the Society in the peninsula. The order had been too far extended and had begun to suffer in consequence. Signs too of the future troubles over the powers of the General, the method of his election and the inequality of grades, appeared. A pamphlet was published which proclaimed the alleged discontent of the Jesuits themselves. One Jesuit indeed made the demand for a Spanish head of

[22] Astrain, *Historia*, Vol. III, pp. 57-59.

the Society. Ribadeneira, on the order of Mercurian, stepped forth as a champion of the Ignatian ideal and produced a printed refutation of the charges. Still on the whole the Society in Spain and Portugal continued to prosper and to enjoy the good opinion of many holy men, especially the saintly secular priest, Bl. John of Avila, the Apostle of Andalusia.

In France civil recognition was at last obtained but only after the hardest struggle.[23] The Gallicans and Calvinists, through the agency of the Parlement and the University of Paris, were still able for some time to frustrate the French King's good intentions towards the Society. In 1560 the Jesuits once more pressed for recognition. Yet four times within the space of a year the Parlement refused to register the royal decree; it was supported in its opposition by the University and for a time by the Bishop of Paris, du Bellay. The reason, that the Society of Jesus had been recognized neither by a general council nor by even a provincial council, was typically Gallican; the solemn Bulls of the Popes were studiously ignored. The friends of the Jesuits, among whom were the Cardinals Tournon, Lorraine, Armagnac and Guise, increased notably after the Conference of Poissy; the very boldness of the Protestant champions opened the eyes of many to the value of an order already noted for its defense of the old religion and of the Apostolic See. At length the Parlement on February 13, 1562 yielded so far as to recognize the Society with reservations; the name had to be changed to the Society of College of Clermont, and the privileges of the Papal Bulls had to be renounced. Legal existence was now a fact. The restrictions after a short while were cancelled; and the Parlement even began to afford the Jesuits its protection.

The University continued obdurate; its opposition stiffened, in fact, with the success of the recently opened Jesuit college of Paris. This college, to which the Rector of the University had given his consent, the fathers determined to make an outstanding institution of learning; and so they called to its staff their ablest professors. Foremost among these was the Spaniard Maldonatus, a distinguished Scriptural authority; at Paris, however, he gave his best effort to lecturing in philosophy and theology. Unbelief was rife in the upper classes of French society; to meet this unfortunate situation Maldonatus, casting aside all useless speculation, discussed learnedly and brilliantly the vital topics of God's existence and the soul's immortality. His lectures became a sensation. Students flocked to hear him in such numbers that the large lecture hall, capable of holding a thousand, could not contain all the auditors; some were turned away, others to secure a seat came two and three hours in advance. His success and that of his colleagues resulted in a falling off in the classes of the University. The professors, some of whom were Huguenots,

---

[23] Pastor, *History of the Popes*, Vol. XVI, pp. 204–210; Fouqueray, *Compagnie de Jésus en France*, Vol. I, pp. 221–331.

sought to close the new college on the score that the faculty for lecturing given the Jesuits was defective in form. The Jesuits Provincial ordered the lectures suspended for a time, a decision which the students greeted with such manifestations of displeasure that the Parlement commanded their resumption. The University party then besought the able jurist, du Moulin, a Protestant and a strong enemy of the Jesuits, to put in form a legal opinion of their case. His report was of course decidedly adverse to the order. Stimulated by it the University condemned the Society on October 8, 1564. The Jesuits now sought incorporation in the University, waiving all claims to dignities, rights of conferring degrees, or acceptance of honorary academic positions, and promising complete obedience to the Rector and the statutes, as far as the Constitutions permitted. The University's reply was a renewed prohibition of their teaching and a threat of the deprivation of all rights and privileges for those students who continued to attend the Jesuits' lectures.

The fathers appealed for the protection of Parlement, an act which brought down upon their heads a storm so great as to dismay their most sanguine supporters. The Jesuits were overwhelmed with satires and lampoons; simultaneously in twelve of the city's churches they were assailed from the pulpit; while not one of them dared appear in the University quarter lest he be stoned. The hostile speech of Étienne Pasquier during the legal proceedings inflicted the greatest harm on the Society. Though his charges were a tissue of lies and misrepresentations, borrowed largely from the Lutheran Chemnitz, this clever advocate put them forth so audaciously and with such an air of conviction, posing as the champion of religion and law against the foes of progress, that his invectives prejudiced many minds then and for centuries to come. His real reason was revealed in his attacks on Pope Paul III and on the fourth vow of the professed; it was Gallican enmity of the Papacy. Parlement took no definite stand, contenting itself with a declaration on April 5, 1565 that the Jesuits' affairs were to remain in statu quo. Later however, on July 1, Possevino obtained letters patent allowing the order to resume its name and to open colleges in all parts of France. With this event the hostility of the University was silenced until 1594.

Despite all the hue and cry against the Society, the numbers of the French Jesuits increased until in 1564 the erection of a second province, that of Aquitaine, was justified. The colleges also multiplied, especially after the legal recognition. At the death of Mercurian they counted fifteen. The maintenance of these educational institutions called for courageous persistence in the face of poverty and actual want, for many of them were insufficiently endowed and often the help promised by civil authorities or benefactors failed to materialize. The sacrifices were gladly made and the privations endured that a Catholic youth might be trained for France. The Cardinal of Lorraine proved himself a most worthy cooperator in the order's educational work when he founded the University of Pont-à-Mousson and entrusted it to Jesuits. Gregory XIII created its university status in 1572 by the Bull "In supereminentis." Pont-à-Mousson was not long developing into a mighty source of Christian education, especially in the training of future priests for France, and for Scotland too.

The apostolic labors of the Jesuits of these decades in reviving the faith of the French Catholics were truly inspiring. The work of Laynez at the Conference of Poissy has already been noted; by his side was Polanco. Foremost among the French fathers should be counted Edmond Auger.[24] At Toulouse in 1566 distinguished citizens and a thousand students, many of them tinged by Calvinism, listened with rapt attention to Auger's sermons; the University of Toulouse wished to confer on him the doctorate, the city magistrate besought his return for the following Lent. In Paris similarly crowded congregations followed his discourses and the Court summoned him to preach in the royal chapel. Later in Lyons not only the churches, but the hospitals and the prisons heard his voice; 2,000 converts were gained, and a society of noble ladies organized to visit twice weekly the hospitals. At Marseilles the prisoners in the galleys were the recipients of his zealous charity. Henry III made him his confessor and sought his elevation to the purple, a dignity which the humble religious escaped by fleeing the court. Auger labored quite as effectively with his pen; besides ascetical and polemical works he wrote two catechisms, which did for France what St. Peter Canisius' catechism did for Germany. In the course of eight years 38,000 copies of one of his catechisms were disposed of at Paris alone.

Perpinien's eloquent orations to the youth of Paris in 1566 aroused them to a renewed loyalty for the old Faith. In 1570 Possevino arrived in Dieppe to find Catholicism prostrate; in a few days he won back 2,500 Huguenots. Manare, his successor, converted 4,000 more. The combined labors of the two Jesuits in a few months transformed the city into a Catholic stronghold. Possevino continued his apostolate in Lyons and at Marseilles where he preached not only in the cathedral but in the orphanages of the city. Maldonatus left his lecture hall in Paris to go with five companions preaching and catechising through the western country of France, especially in Poitou where the Calvinists were very strong. Two fathers every morning and evening gave simple conferences, while Maldonatus twice daily delivered more learned discourses to the better educated and the students. The confessionals were so besieged during Holy Week that, had the priests numbered fifty, they would not have

---

[24] Bailly, *Historia vitae P. Edmundi Augerii*, Paris (1652); Fouqueray, *Histoire*, Vols. I, II; Sommervogel, *Bibliothèque*, Vol. I, pp. 632–642.

been sufficient. The ministry of the plague-stricken brought the fathers to risk their lives four times, in 1562, 1563, 1577 and 1580; on the first occasion Paschasius Broët, one of the first companions of St. Ignatius, made the supreme sacrifice, a martyr of charity.

It was for the very existence of Catholicism in the German lands that the German Jesuits had to battle during these years.[25] They gave themselves unrestrainedly to the defense of the old Faith, counting neither cost nor sacrifice. Of their devoted efforts the Papal Legate, Cardinal Commendone declared: "According to that which I also have seen in Lower Germany and in Upper Germany, this Society of Jesus through their exemplary lives, through their continual preaching and the education of youth have rendered the greatest service to religion." [26] His opinion was repeated by other nuncios and legates, Frangipani, Lippomano and Ninguarda, in their reports to Rome; one, Delfino, affirmed his belief that if the Jesuits were expelled from Germany, with them would go the Catholic religion.[27]

First and ever in the van fought St. Peter Canisius.[28] He seemed to do everything, preach in great cathedrals, catechise in lonely country churches, write all kinds of polemical and theological books, erect colleges, direct universities, govern and visit provinces of the order, assist Papal nuncios, and act himself in the capacity of a legate for the Holy See. He seemed to be everywhere, in Austria, Bavaria and Upper Germany, the Rhineland and Lower Germany, Franconia, Bohemia, Poland, Italy and Switzerland. Though he opposed Lutheranism with every ounce of his strength, yet always did he act with singular freedom from bitterness; once he wrote: "In defending the truth we must observe charity, considerateness and moderation." [29] The vast majority of Protestants, in the Saint's opinion, erred not through malice but through lack of knowledge.[30] Canisius believed that more would be achieved by the simple explanation of Catholic teaching than by belligerent controversy. Thus when he came to Straubing (1558) to revive the faith of the people, almost lost because of a fallen-away priest, he preached a whole Lenten course only on the sufferings of our Lord's sacred Passion. The prayer for the common interests of Christianity, which this apostolic man composed, revealed the beautiful charity of his soul; it is still said after Sunday Mass in many places.

[25] Duhr, *Geschichte der Jesuiten in den Ländern deutscher Zunge*, Vol. I; Janssen, *History of the German People*, Vol. VIII.

[26] Baberini LXII, 58 f., 145, quoted in Duhr, *Geschichte*, Vol. I, p. 845.

[27] Schellhass, *Nuntiaturberichte* (1896), p. 376, A. 2. Schreiben from Feb. 13, 1574 (*ibid.*), quoted in Duhr, *Geschichte*, Vol. I, p. 846.

[28] Brodrick, *St. Peter Canisius*, London (1935).

[29] Janssen, *History of the German People*, Vol. VIII, p. 237.

[30] *Ibid.*, p. 235.

Of the hundreds of Jesuits who followed the inspiring lead of St. Peter Canisius, only a few can be named here: Hoffaeus, Provincial of Upper Germany, Visitor and German Assistant, an excellent executive, a preacher, writer and devoted friend of the poor and the sick; Rhetius, a reformer, preacher, historian, translator of the Greek Fathers, hagiographer and author of school text books; Scherer, preacher to both the lowly and the great, confessor at Court and also in humble churches, who practically alone won back the Duchy of Baden-Baden; Priscianensis, a laborer with lasting success at that most difficult and delicate task, the reform of religious houses. Among the very many authors, mention should be made of Peltan, Pisan, Thyraeus, Torres, and Gretser. The Jesuit writers against the German heretics, it can be said, for the most part followed Canisius' example of mildness; there were exceptions, however; some replied bitterly to the abusive torrent unleashed against them.

All the Papal legates who worked so valiantly to remedy the almost hopeless state of the German church, prelates like Bonhomini, Commendone, Delfino, Gropper, Lippomano, Ninguarda and Portia, looked upon the fathers of the Society as their most valued assistants and advisers, as has been noted. Zealous German ecclesiastical princes, as Cardinal Otto Truchsess von Waldburg, Bishop of Augsburg, Archbishop Brendel of Mainz, Bishop von Mespelbrunn of Würzburg and Balthasar von Dernbach, Abbot of Fulda, found in the Jesuits loyal and efficient helpers in their efforts to introduce the Tridentine reforms, to save the Faith of their flocks, and to overcome the menacings of the Protestant preachers and nobles. After the Peace of Augsburg (1555) when the Emperor Ferdinand I in the Hapsburg lands, the Dukes Albrecht V and Wilhelm V in Bavaria applied the *jus reformandi*, as the Lutheran princes did in their territories, these Catholic princes employed the priests of the order, but only for the specific works of spiritual regeneration.

The most effective labor of the German Jesuits in the Catholic Reformation was accomplished in their educational endeavors. Almost from the start theologians of the Society lectured in the universities: thus Dietrich Canisius, half-brother of the Saint, and Lambert Auer taught at Vienna, where Ferdinand I gave to the order *in perpetuum* two positions on the theological faculty; fathers of the Lower German Province lectured on theology, mathematics and astronomy at Cologne; the Jesuits were placed in charge of the University of Ingolstadt almost at the beginning of their work in the Empire. But it was their own colleges which were the most important element in their battle for the Faith. Cardinal Commendone affirmed: "It is a fact that in the Church in Germany I have found no stronger nor greater bulwark for the Catholic religion than the colleges of the Jesuits." [31] During the twenty years under review twenty-one col-

---

[31] Pogiani, Epp. III, 307 f., quoted in Duhr, *Geschichte*, Vol. I, p. 845.

leges were founded in various parts of the Empire, almost one a year. Most of these colleges were secondary schools, though some were of university rank as Dillingen, Braunsberg, Fulda and Würzburg. In connection with the last institution its founder, Bishop von Mespelbrunn, established a major seminary, a preparatory seminary, and a school for poor boys, all to be conducted by the Jesuits. The very maintenance of these colleges called for heroic efforts and sacrifices on the part of the fathers. Sometimes their founding brought difficulties upon the order, from the tendency of ecclesiastical and secular authorities to transfer to their support the properties of monasteries or convents which had been abandoned, or in which only a handful of religious remained. The older orders naturally resented the transfers. But, while some Jesuits were perhaps too forward in accepting them, St. Francis Borgia as Father General was opposed to the practice.[32]

The Jesuit colleges played a most vital role in the elevation of the German clergy according to the ideals of the Council of Trent. Some of the colleges served the purpose of preparatory seminaries; others, especially those of university grade, included major seminaries. The well-trained alumni of the German College at Rome, more and more as the years passed on, occupied leading positions in the hierarchy of their native land. Superiors of the older religious orders sent their young religious to study at the Jesuit colleges.[33] Young monks and friars, Benedictines, Cistercians, Canons Regular, Premonstratentians, Franciscans, Dominicans and Carmelites attended the classes at Mainz, Munich, Würzburg, Regensburg, Braunsberg, Ingolstadt and Dillingen. Each of the last two institutions maintained a house for the religious students, where they lived a community life, even to the regular performance of the office of choir. The care of the faith and virtues of the lay scholars, the bulk of the students of the colleges, was held a primary duty by the fathers; one of the chief agencies for the work were the sodalities erected in every college of the order.

It need hardly be said that from the very start the Jesuits encountered a determined, widespread, almost overwhelming opposition, which grew in intensity and formidableness as the Reformers came to realize the importance of the new recruits in the Church's ranks. Melancthon, Chemnitz and Flacius led the vehement attack of the preachers and writers, some of whom descended to most absurd calumnies and vitriolic abuse.[34] The Lutheran nobles in the Catholic states strove to force their Catholic lords to banish the order, while the Protestant princes again and again in the national diets tried to obtain the expulsion of the Society from the Empire.

---

[32] Duhr, *Geschichte*, Vol. I, pp. 379, 385.

[33] *Ibid.*, pp. 499–502.

[34] Janssen, *History of the German People*, Vol. VIII, pp. 237–242, 285–292.

Opposition too arose on the Catholic side. But with few exceptions, such as the zealous Franciscan Nas, Coadjutor-Bishop of Brixen, who honestly acted through misapprehension,[35] most of the opposition came from unworthy priests and vicious, half heretical canons who resented the assistance given by the Jesuits to the bishops' efforts for reform. Despite all opposition, the German fathers of the order even in the two decades being discussed had obtained an appreciable measure of reform among Catholics and had brought the irresistible advance of Protestantism to a standstill.

In Switzerland the Society labored with similar results in three localities. In the South, as has been noted, they cooperated in the visitations and reforms of St. Charles Borromeo and at his request undertook the charge of the Helvetian College at Milan, which he had founded to be the source of a worthy priesthood for the Swiss. At Lucerne, whose citizens would not be put off until the General granted their repeated requests for a college, the fathers opened a house in 1574 and three years later the much sought for college. Their apostolic labors in and around the city, as well as their teaching in the college, made Lucerne a stronghold of Catholicism in the central part of the country. To Fribourg in 1580 came St. Peter Canisius for his last great work, the founding of a college there; his labors and those of his brethren made Fribourg a bulwark for the old Faith in the West.

It was during this period that the first steps of the Society were taken in Hungary at the invitation of the Archbishop Olahaus of Esztergom (Gran) in 1559. In 1561 he gave over to them the conduct of the seminary at Nagyszombat (Tyrnau). At Rome in 1578, at the instance of the Jesuit Szántó and Cardinal Santori, Gregory XIII founded the Hungarian College which he soon united with the German College. Stephen Báthory brought the Polish Jesuits to Transylvania in 1570, and in 1579 founded a college for them at Klausenberg. The course of the Society in both regions was beset with constant hindrances and actual persecution by the Calvinists, so that for some years the fathers obtained little apparent success.

The precarious state of Polish Catholicism forty years after Luther's religious revolt is something hard to imagine today. Yet in the middle decades of the sixteenth century, despite the devout loyalty of the bulk of the Polish common people, the fate of the old religion hung in the balance. The country was overrun with reforming preachers, often of the most fanatical and persistent type, for Poland proved a haven for all sorts of religious innovators. The numerous and powerful landed gentry, the Schlacta, in great part having embraced the new views, were impatient

---

[35] Pastor, *History of the Popes*, Vol. XX, pp. 58–61.

to destroy the Catholic religion after the manner of the neighboring junkers of Prussia and Saxony. Lastly, the King, Sigismund Augustus, though remaining a Catholic, through weakness of character found it difficult to resist the pressing demands of the Protestant factions. Three things, besides the piety of the people, saved Poland for the ancient Faith: the work of Stanislaus Hosius, the Polish Cardinal, the efforts of the Papal nuncios, and the labors of the Society of Jesus.[36] The first fathers of the order came to Poland as advisors of the nuncios, Salmeron in 1555 with Lippomano, and Canisius in 1558 with Mentuato. The reports of both Jesuits offered a gloomy picture; Canisius, however, was able to render good service to the cause at the Diet of Petrikau. Six years later the Society obtained a permanent foundation in the country when Cardinal Hosius erected for them the college of Braunsberg; this was followed by the establishment of other colleges at Pultusk (1566), Jaroslaw (1568), Wilna (1570) and Posen (1571). A province independent of Austria was set up in 1576. The vigor with which the fathers turned to the work filled the Nuncio Ruggieri with joyful hopes.

The good expectations of the Pope's representative were more than realized in a short while, especially during the reign of King Stephan Báthory (1576–1586) who wholeheartedly supported the Society. This King cherished the friendship of the eloquent Polish Jesuit Skarga, made another father, Laterna, his confessor, and generously helped financially and in many other ways the colleges of the order. At the outset the priests of the Society directed their efforts to stopping the Protestant advance and to strengthening the Catholic ranks; later they also turned to achieving the reunion of the Ruthenian schismatics.

Striking and practical sermons, copious writings, excellent teaching, exemplary conduct and sincere piety brought results in some parts of Poland that were almost miraculous; in Gostyn the entire population returned to Catholicism. Learned lectures on important sections of the Holy Scriptures, intended for the educated class, were given two and three times a week in the larger cities; corresponding talks explanatory of the Catechism for simpler folks were delivered as regularly in the small towns. People of all classes and creeds, Lutherans, Zwinglians, Calvinists and Anabaptists, mingling with devout or negligent Catholics, listened to the Jesuit priests setting forth the clear and coherent doctrines of the Catholic Church. So sought after were the fathers, particularly in the confessional, that they were frequently forced to remain in the churches from three in the morning until seven in the evening. Public disputations held in the 'seventies at Wilna and Posen and in the 'eighties at Lublin

---

[36] Pastor, *History of the Popes*, Vol. XIV, pp. 333–336; XVI, p. 152; XVIII, p. 306; XX, pp. 395–405; Rostowski, *Lituanicarum Societatis Jesu historiarum libri decem*, reprint, Paris (1877).

helped to gain back many converts to the Catholic fold. Confraternities for works of practical charity or for the veneration of the Blessed Sacrament, which were conducted by the priests of the order, attracted many souls and proved the best refutation of the charges of the innovators. Among the Ruthenian schismatics, marked success was achieved by Herbest and Nahai who made numerous conversions among the lower classes of the people. There was of course no lack of vigorous opposition, but the attacks of the heretical pastors and the threats of their supporters among the nobles failed to deter the Polish Jesuits.

The colleges, as elsewhere, constituted the most important agency for the renewal of Catholicism. But a few years after their inception, and they were sending forth a steady stream of Polish youth imbued with a strictly Catholic spirit and devoted passionately to the ancient Faith. Nowhere in Europe did the Jesuit schools receive large enrollments more quickly; and this was all the more remarkable in view of the foreign nationality of most of the early professors. The excellent teaching and the painstaking care for the students' intellectual and moral welfare won the approbation of Catholic parents. Even many Protestant families sent their sons to the Jesuit colleges, despite the vehement protests of their own pastors. The sons of noblemen, then so influential, frequented the classes in large number; at Pultusk in 1588 almost all the four hundred students were nobles. The education of the children of the poor was not forgotten either; at Wilna and Pultusk free schools for poor Ruthenians were maintained, while at Braunsberg a school for the sons of German workmen was established. At the death of Stephan Báthory in 1586, the Polish Jesuits were conducting a university at Wilna and another at Braunsberg, eight secondary colleges and one preparatory school. This monarch and Pope Gregory XIII were responsible for the origins of many of these Polish colleges of the order. The Holy Father made special use of the Italian Jesuit Possevino for his educational projects in Poland. Wilna, which, on the suggestion of Báthory, Gregory XIII had established as a university in 1579, developed into the chief center of renewed Catholic life in the east of Poland, as also of the reunion movement among the Ruthenians. The university of Braunsberg became in the west of the country a light for the whole of Northern Europe; to its halls journeyed students from Poland, Lithuania, Livonia, Prussia, Pomerania, Hungary, Sweden, Norway and Denmark; its theological faculty was one of the foremost of the times.[37]

---

[37] Duhr, *Geschichte*, Vol. I, p. 182. The student rolls of Braunsberg list Germans, Prussians, Poles, Swedes, Norwegians, Danes, Finns, Russians, Courlanders, Estonians, Letts, Galicians, Poles, Moravians, Hungarians, Transylvanians, Carinthians, Irish, Scots, Italians and even Tartars.

Of the numerous zealous Polish Jesuits who effected the redemption of the Faith, one, the eloquent Peter Skarga, deserves special mention; he was in a scarcely less degree for Poland what Peter Canisius was for Germany. Skarga was born at Grojec in Masovia in 1536. Even as a young theological student at Lemberg in 1564, his gifts of oratory attracted attention. In 1569 he entered the Roman novitiate of the order, San Andrea, only six months after the holy death of his countryman, St. Stanislaus Kostka. Two years later, back in Poland, he was assigned first to Pultusk, then in 1573 to Wilna, where he was made vice-rector in the following year. The sad religious condition which he found convinced him, to use his own expression, that his India was his native land. His unwavering devotion to the cause of Polish Catholicity throughout his long life has made him one of the great characters of Poland. Skarga was a magnificent orator, the Polish Bossuet he has been called; for years he continued to hold audiences, crowded with foes as well as friends, spellbound with his burning eloquence, his moving expression of pathos, his forceful presentation of Truth. He labored just as zealously with the pen, producing a long series of Latin and Polish works, among which may be noted a catechism, a defense of the Blessed Sacrament, a very valuable volume on the Unity of the Church (later of decisive influence with many Ruthenians), and Lives of the Saints that went through many Polish editions. Like St. Peter Canisius, Peter Skarga in the treatment of heretics was averse to all unkindness and violence; by love and good example he would convert them back to the old Faith. Once he intervened to save a Calvinist, who had assaulted him, from a most severe physical punishment. Skarga was still to labor for several years during the next generalate, that of Father Aquaviva.

For the restoration of Sweden [38] to Catholic unity, a project much desired by him, Gregory XIII employed as his agent the Italian Jesuit, Possevino. Before Possevino's advent two other Jesuits had entered that country, Warszewski, a Pole, in 1573, and Nilssön, a Norwegian convert, in 1576. The first soon returned to report some meager hopes for the re-Catholicizing of the nation. These expectations were based upon the tried and true Catholicity of the Queen, a Polish princess, and the favorable dispositions of the King, John III, who was ambitioning election to the Polish throne. The second priest remained in Sweden, in disguise on the advice of the King lest the Lutherans discover his character and mission. He did manage, despite grave difficulties, to conduct a small school in Stockholm preparing a few Swedish Catholic lads for the German College in Rome. A request of John III for Jesuit missionaries aroused Gregory XIII's highest hopes, and he determined to send a

---

[38] Pastor, *History of the Popes*, Vol. XX, pp. 430–432.

learned father to deal with the Swedish monarch. His choice was Possevino.

The Holy Father proposed the mission to the father on the occasion of the latter's accompanying Father General Mercurian in a routine visit. Possevino hesitated when he learned that political negotiations for a Swedish-Spanish alliance were included in the task; he accepted, however, when the Pope assured him that the alliance was a necessity for the successful outcome of the main purpose, the conversion of the Swedish King and his people. Antonio Possevino [39] was one of the ablest Jesuits of the first century. Born at Mantua in 1534, he came to Rome at the age of eighteen and before long was chosen by Cardinal Ercole Gonzaga as his secretary. A great career seemed certain, yet its bright prospects were renounced by Possevino when in 1559 he entered the Society of Jesus. The success of his labors in Savoy against the Calvinists and of his ten years' apostolate in France, which has already been noted, established his reputation as a preacher, missionary, scholar, writer and diplomat. Mercurian had made him his secretary, recognizing in Possevino a man of large ideas, persistent application, great missionary zeal and high principles. It is little wonder that Gregory XIII chose him for the difficult mission.

Possevino, after a wearisome journey, arrived at Stockholm December 19, 1577. He appeared in secular garb, for dressed in his religious habit he could never have passed the frontier. The situation proved even more complicated than had been expected; Nilssön, eager for the conversion of Sweden, in all sincerity had assured the King of the possibility of obtaining the Chalice for the laity and other concessions which he sought. There really was very little probability of such concessions, and the Pope's agent had to correct the misapprehension at once. Possevino then addressed himself to his principal task, the convincing the King of the truths of Catholic doctrine. It called for much patience, since he had to keep answering the ruler's difficulties in discussions which dragged through the months until May 1558. Even then he had to make certain of the King's sincerity; just before absolution Possevino asked the royal convert whether or not he was ready to accept any decision of the Pope in regard to the Chalice. An affirmative answer was given. Thereupon Possevino received John III into the Church and administered to him the Sacraments of Penance and Holy Eucharist. All had to be done in the greatest secrecy, for if the news had gotten abroad, popular tumults would have made a quick end of all the good hopes.

Possevino had then to return to Rome with his report and the con-

---

[39] Kartunen, *Biography of Possevino*, Rome (1908); Theiner, *Schweden und seine Stellung zum Heiligen Stuhl*, Augsburg (1838).

cessions which John III had requested. He left Sweden, commissioned by the King not only to declare the royal position to the Pope but also to negotiate for the Spanish treaty and for the Polish throne. While the father had been in Sweden he was able to do some positive work for the Faith by distributing Catholic books, especially a Swedish translation of Canisius' catechism. His observations however convinced him that the conversion of the country could be achieved only through native priests; hence he brought back with him a number of young Swedes and Finns to be trained as missionaries. At his suggestion two pontifical seminaries for this purpose were established, at the University of Braunsberg in 1578 and at Olmütz in 1579. On this return journey Possevino at Warsaw and Prague did what was possible in promoting the Swedish King's interests.

Finally, on September 27, 1578, the Jesuit arrived at Rome. Gregory XIII appointed a commission of Cardinals to examine his report and especially to pass upon the concessions asked for by the Swedish King. The commission's reply was not too promising; five out of twelve concessions were rejected as ungrantable. Further light on the Swedish prospects was sought from Possevino, when he returned from Naples where he had been working for John III's cause in Poland. The refusal of the five concessions was maintained.

Gregory XIII, believing still in the possibility of Sweden's return to the old Faith, decided to send back his envoy as a Papal Nuncio provided with the widest powers as Vicar-Apostolic for the whole of Scandinavia, Moscovia, Lithuania, Hungary, Pomerania and Saxony. Possevino departed from Rome in the spring of 1579 for the North, stopping at the Imperial and Polish courts to further the candidacy of John III. On August 7, 1579 he entered Stockholm, this time courageously wearing his religious dress. The Catholic cause during his absence had diminished considerably owing to John III's hesitancies and his renewed insistence on concessions which formerly he had been willing to forego. Possevino found that he could accomplish little with the royal opportunist, whose policy seemed to shift with the varying fortunes of Spain. After a year of disappointments he finally left Sweden. On his departure, persuaded more than ever that Catholicism would return to the Scandinavian world only through the apostolate of native priests, he brought with him fifteen more youths for Braunsberg and Olmütz. The failure of the mission was not his; it is now clear that in the circumstances he was attempting the impossible. Some may criticise Possevino for his political negotiations; but it should be remembered that in themselves they were not wrong and that he undertook them reluctantly, only on Gregory XIII's wish and on the Pope's insistence that they were essential to the great project of Sweden's conversion.

In the Low Countries [40] Philip II in 1556 accorded the Society of Jesus civil recognition and the permission to erect establishments. The fathers already had been working at Louvain, where also their younger brethren were in studies, and at Tournai. In the latter town the first college for externs was opened in 1562; others followed in the next few years in seven cities of the country. At first the houses formed part of the Rhenish Province, but in 1564 St. Francis Borgia grouped them into a separate jurisdiction, the Belgian province. Twenty years of varying fortunes were to pass before the Flemish and Walloon Jesuits could obtain that solid position which was to make their labors among the most successful in the old Society. This retardation was due, on the one hand, to the mistrust of Philip II and the antipathy of his lieutenant, the Duke of Alba, and, on the other, to the insurrections, riotings and anarchy of the religious wars of William the Silent and his followers.

The Jesuits threw themselves wholeheartedly into the battle during these desperate crises for the old Faith in the Low Countries. In some districts where the danger was not so proximate, as in the principality of Liége, they renewed the religion of the people by their sermons and catechetical instructions and strengthened the life of the clergy by the Spiritual Exercises. In the more threatened sections, fearless of mob violence they preached against Calvinism, reconciling many heretics, and at the same time inspiring the Catholics to a staunch defense of the Faith. Dupont at Cambrai converted many of the innovators; van Asten journeyed to Harlem, Zutphen and Deventer at grave personal danger to preach for the Catholic cause; Coster at Antwerp deliberately chose for his bold and forceful attacks on the Reformed religion the church of St. Walburga, because it was situated right in the midst of the largest Calvinist neighborhood. Such outspoken activities of the Netherlandish Jesuits, indeed, created a profound impression, but they also aroused the furious hatred of the Calvinists, the Gueux and all the followers of William the Silent. Wherever the latter's soldiers obtained the upper hand, or his officers came into control of a city or province, the Jesuits were immediately marked for attack and expulsion. After the Pacification of Ghent when the members of the order refused the oath against Philip II, convinced not only that it was disloyal but also that it meant the destruction of Catholicism, they were expelled from Antwerp, Maastricht, Tournai, Cambrai and Bruges. In the expulsion from Antwerp, William the Silent secretly sought to have the whole Jesuit community murdered; [41] his plan was frustrated only by the timely arrival of a cavalry escort sent by the Archduke Matthias. At Antwerp, Maastricht, Cambrai and Douai the Jesuits were insulted by William's soldiers or by howling

[40] Poncelet, *Compagnie de Jésus dans les anciens Pays-Bas*, Vol. I, pp. 111–327.
[41] *Ibid.*, Vol. I, pp. 304–305.

mobs of Calvinist fanatics. The prompt action of the Catholics of St. Omer just in the nick of time saved the fathers from being driven from that city. Liége under the rule of its Prince-Bishop, van Groesbeck, offered a safe haven for the exiled religious; the Bishop received the fathers with a truly paternal kindness and supported their works in spite of a strong local opposition.

The Jesuits found other friends too in the Low Countries: the bishops, the loyal Catholics, and above all the three regents, Requesens, Don Juan of Austria and Alexander Farnese. Farnese, who had been baptized by St. Ignatius and with whose family the support of the Jesuits was a tradition, restored the order wherever he was victorious; as a result the fathers were soon back in all the cities from which they had been driven. When Duke Ernest of Bavaria became Prince-Bishop of Liége, one of his first acts was the foundation of a Jesuit college (1580).

It was during the years 1570 to 1576 that St. Robert Bellarmine, at Louvain, accomplished his first work for the defense of Catholicism. Sent originally as a student to the northern university that he might obtain first-hand knowledge of the new heresies, it was not long before his sermons and lectures against the teachings of the Reformers attracted wide attention. For six years crowded audiences regularly followed his discourses; even Protestant students came from Germany and England to listen to his presentations. Bellarmine not only opposed Luther and Calvin but also attacked the false theories of Baianism, that peculiarly dangerous system which the pious and learned Michael de Bay had evolved in his honest effort to reconcile the Protestants. Twelve of Bellarmine's brethren of the Low Countries in another field proved their heroism, dying as martyrs of charity in the service of the plague-stricken.

The Jesuits in the British Isles were but a handful, yet their daring wrote a glorious chapter in the Society's history. The first was the Irish father, David Woulfe,[42] sent to Ireland as Papal Nuncio by Pius IV to strengthen the princes and the bishops, to labor for reform by suggesting suitable candidates for the episcopacy and by forwarding ecclesiastical discipline, and to watch over the preaching and the administration of the Sacraments. He was to perform his official duties with the greatest simplicity, of course in disguise, and was to receive neither payments nor alms. The good priest actually suffered grievous want in the beginning by his over-strict interpretation of his instructions. Woulfe arrived in Ireland in 1560 and for seven years carried out his task in all parts except the Pale where it was impossible for him to venture. Crowds of people, many of them the poorest of the poor, flocked to receive his ministrations and to settle their affairs of conscience; many who had more or less lis-

---

[42] Hogan, *Distinguished Irishmen of the Sixteenth Century*, London (1880), pp. 5–16.

tened to the new doctrines were brought back, the greatest victory being achieved in the public abjuration of the Protestant Bishop of Limerick, a lapsed priest. On the father's recommendation the Holy See raised six worthy priests to Irish bishoprics. In the face of the might of the persecuting English government, nothing could be done for the erection of colleges and seminaries, although the nuncio was able to send several Irish youths to Rome for their sacerdotal studies. At length, in 1567, after several times eluding the priest-hunters, Woulfe was captured and imprisoned in the Dublin Castle, along with his friend, Archbishop Creagh of Armagh. If his sufferings even approached those of the Archbishop's, which have become known, they must have been terrible indeed. With the aid of friends, after five years in the loathsome dungeon, Woulfe managed to escape to Spain. On the continent he labored much for the Church in his native land and later, on two occasions, succeeded in getting back to the persecuted flock. One of Woulfe's companions, Edmund O'Donnell, was captured and cruelly executed by the Elizabethans at Cork in 1575. He was the first Irish Jesuit to die for the Faith.

To Scotland another Jesuit was sent as Papal Nuncio in 1562.[43] He was Nicholas Floris, more commonly known as Goudano from his birthplace in Gouda, Holland. His mission was the outcome of the wish of Pius IV to help Mary, Queen of Scots, in her very difficult position. With the Pope's representative went Edmund Hay, a Scottish priest and later to become a distinguished member of the Society. Despite the utmost secrecy news of the embassy leaked out. Angry excitement greeted the report in Edinburgh and John Knox thundered against this diabolical emissary of Baal and Beelzebub. After a month in hiding, Goudano at last obtained an interview with the Queen, and then only with the greatest stealth. The conversation only proved Mary's good intentions and her inability to do more than desperately to retain the old Faith in a precarious existence. She could not even guarantee safe conduct to the Nuncio. The Jesuit had hardly any greater success with the Bishops; only one of them dared to receive him, and then in a remote spot and on the pretext of his being a merchant. Finally Goudano made his escape in a Flemish ship from an unfrequented part of the Scottish coast. About the only tangible result of the mission was that a group of young Scots returned with Edmund Hay to enter with him into the Society of Jesus. Later they returned at the risk of their lives to keep the old religion alive in their native land.

The first official contact of the Society of Jesus with the persecuted English Catholics came with the appointment of two fathers to the newly

---

[43] Pastor, History of the Popes, Vol. XVII, p. 277; Thurston, "Studies on the History of Mary Queen of Scots. The Mission of Father Nicholas of Gouda." The Month, Vol. XCVI (1900), pp. 167–176.

opened English college at Rome in 1578. In the conflict between the Welsh and English students, the latter had asked that the college be entrusted to the Jesuits. The Society was rather reluctant, but eventually the first Jesuit rector, Agazzari, was named.[44] Cardinal Allen, the venerable patriarch of the English Catholics, in 1579 made the request that Jesuits also be sent to England.[45] Father General Mercurian was able to comply, for Englishmen from 1573 had been entering the order. Bl. Edmund Campion and Robert Persons, both brilliant scholars and both exiles for conscience' sake, were the two Jesuits chosen for the perilous mission. Blessed Edmund,[46] born in London in 1540, had distinguished himself at Oxford as a humanist and an orator. At the University he had so far conformed as to take the Oath of Supremacy and to accept deacon's orders in the Establishment; but that very last act struck him with such remorse that he abandoned his prospects and fled to Ireland. After a short while he crossed to the continent and made his abjuration at Douai in 1571. Two years later he applied and was received into the Society of Jesus. His novitiate was made at Prague and Brünn; then he taught at Prague and was ordained priest there in 1578. In his one year of priestly ministry he had won all hearts by his preaching and pastoral work. Robert Persons,[47] born in Somerset of yeoman stock in 1546, also gained a distinguished name at Oxford for his intellectual gifts. Partly for his strong Catholic leanings and partly through college quarrels he was obliged to leave the University. On the continent in 1574 he was reconciled to the Church and in the following year accepted into the order at Rome. He was one of the first to suggest the English mission, and contributed also to the settlement of the difficulties of the English College, for a short time acting as its pro-rector. To Persons was owing the "mission-oath."

Mercurian drew up most prudent instructions for the project, especially insisting on complete abstention from politics, even forbidding any adverse criticisms of Queen Elizabeth. The two fathers themselves petitioned the Holy See for some mitigation of the hard position of English Catholics prohibited by the Bull of Excommunication from rendering allegiance to the Queen. Gregory XIII in response included in the faculties the provision that in view of the state of affairs, until the Bull was publicly enforced, English Catholics were exempt from its effects.

---

[44] Pastor, *History of the Popes*, Vol. XIX, pp. 382–384; Pollen, *The English Catholics in the Reign of Queen Elizabeth*, London (1920), pp. 271–282.

[45] Pastor, *History of the Popes*, Vol. XIX, pp. 388–402; Pollen, *The English Catholics in the Reign of Queen Elizabeth*, pp. 331–372.

[46] Simpson, *The Life of Edmund Campion S.J.*, London (1886); Waugh, *Edmund Campion*, New York (1935).

[47] Persons, *Memoirs* (Catholic Record Society), Vols. II, IV, London (1906–1907); Pollen, "Robert Persons," *Cath. Encycl.*, Vol. XI, pp. 729–731.

Campion and Persons with ten seminary priests or students and a lay-brother at last left Rome in 1580. The journey was known to the English government, whose agents and spies at the British ports awaited their arrival. Several of the party were arrested almost on landing; but despite all vigilance Persons, disguised as an officer, and Campion, in the dress of a jeweler, eluded detection to arrive safely in London.

Catholic friends came to offer cooperation; a group of young gentlemen organized by George Gilbert, who later died in the Society, offered their aid at the risk of life and fortune to guide the missionaries about and to help them escape the growing pack of priest-hunters. The two Jesuits decided to separate that they might reach more Catholics in different parts of England. Riding through the countryside from one secret meeting of Catholics to another, saying Mass by stealth, absolving and reconciling, inspiriting timid souls, they brought back in the one short year of their hazardous apostolate at least 10,000 souls. Some have placed the number much higher. They lived all the days dangerously; capture, they knew, could be but a matter of weeks at the most. Yet they were not to be the first English Jesuit martyrs; for two secular priests, Bl. Thomas Woodhouse in 1573 and Bl. John Nelson in 1578, awaiting execution, petitioned for reception into the Society of Jesus and were granted the vows before their deaths.

Campion and Persons before their separation had been asked to prepare a statement of their purpose in coming to England, so that when they were imprisoned the government's false charges could be refuted. The request came from Thomas Pound, a Catholic layman who was spending thirty years in prison for the Faith and who before his death was admitted to the vows of the Society. Persons wrote a routine summary. But Campion extended his statement into a letter to the Privy Council, declaring in measured terms that he was a priest and Jesuit, that he had come to England to fight only sin and ignorance, that he had no concern with politics and that he wished, trusting in the Scriptures and the truth of his doctrine, to meet the Protestant divines in a public disputation. Pound was so elated by Campion's statement that he could not hold it back from friends; it was not long before it was spread abroad and all England was stirred with the force of Campion's challenge. The very fury of the replies and their term for the modest document, "Campion's Brag," only revealed how much the blow had struck home. Campion's defense was a truly significant document: it established the loyalty of Catholics, it turned upon the Reformers their own favorite weapon by its appeal to the Scriptures, and it brought the conflict right to the Royalist theologians with its request for the disputation. One thing was clear to all Elizabethan England, court and close, town and manor: Catholics no longer were timorously on the defensive. From Campion's pen, even as he journeyed about in Lancashire, came another document, a more golden one still, the *Decem Rationes*,[48] or in its full English title, *Ten Reasons, relying on which, he offered to the Ministers of the Church of England a Disputation in the Cause of the Faith*. The *Decem Rationes* went through fifty editions and became the fundamental book of the Catholic Reaction.

If there was excitement before, there was a perfect furore now. The priest-hunters redoubled the pursuit. It could not last much longer. A spy and a traitor ran Campion down at Lyford Grange, Berkshire, on July 17, 1581. He was dragged to London and cast into the most terrible dungeon of the Tower. Large promises were offered him, if he would embrace Anglicanism; these spurned, he was menaced with torture. Tortured he was, and most cruelly on the rack. Then when his memory was weakened and his vigor impaired, he was given his disputation. Denied preparation, deprived even of notes, forced to stand without support, weakened though he was, he faced his opponents with their armory of books through four long conferences, undefeated. Then followed his trial for treason. He magnificently refuted every allegation; but, of course, he was convicted. He was hanged, drawn and quartered on December 1, 1581. With him died two priests, recently received into the Society, Bl. Ralph Sherwin and Bl. Alexander Briant. The vast crowd, assembled to witness his death, was deeply moved by his heroism, as was all England. Cardinal Allen declared that Campion by his death did more for the Catholic cause than if he had continued to labor for many years. Bl. Edmund Campion was truly the noblest character among all the brilliant figures of Elizabeth's England. The priest-hunters failed to apprehend Persons, but they made his labors in England impossible; he escaped to the continent to work through many years for the persecuted Church of his native land.

The European losses of Catholicism were counter-balanced by the wide conversions among the heathen of the Far East and the aborigines of the New World. A new missionary epoch dawned, in which Friars and Jesuits brought whole tribes and nations into the Christian fold. Much of the remarkable success of the Society was due to the organizing and directing of St. Francis Borgia. His instructions to the missionaries (March 1567) were a model of practical wisdom: they were to give first consideration to the new Christians, solidifying their faith to insure its perseverance; then, in the conversion of the pagans they were to advance gradually and prudently, neither undertaking burdens impossible to sustain, nor wandering far afield to baptize large numbers for whom they never could care, nor recklessly exposing their lives, since the common good suffered when the sparse ranks of the missionaries lost priests not easily replace-

---

[48] Morris, "Blessed Edmund Campion and his 'Ten Reasons.'" *The Month*, Vol. LXVI (1889), pp. 372–383.

able. It was at Borgia's suggestion that St. Pius V formed a commission
of Cardinals to supervise the work of converting the infidels; [49] from this
commission eventually developed the Congregation of the Propaganda.

In India [50] in the face of the obstacles arising from Brahminism with
its caste-system, Mohammedanism with its bitter hatred of Christianity,
and the cupidity and immorality of many Portuguese, such progress was
made that in 1560 the Jesuits could count around Goa alone, 12,967
baptisms. Goa was the headquarters of the Society in the East; here were
maintained a college, a seminary for young Indians, a special house for
catechumens, a professed house and a novitiate. The bright prospects were
seriously threatened by losses in the sparse ranks of the missionaries, in
consequence of their heroic deaths in the care of the victims of the frequent pestilences. The situation was remedied in 1574 with the arrival of
forty-four Jesuits, of whom twenty-six were priests. They came under the
leadership of Alessandro Valignani whom Father General Mercurian
had appointed Visitor of all the eastern missions. So well and for so many
years did Valignani perform his task of governing and providing for the
work in India, China and Japan, that he has been called with justice the
"Apostle of the East," ranking second only to St. Francis Xavier. One of
his first acts in India after the visitation of the missions, was the holding
of a provincial congregation which gave better organization to the labors
of the fathers. He recommended the learning of the native tongues for
a more satisfactory approach to the native mind, and made answer to the
question of having only Portuguese Jesuits in India by inviting fathers
and brothers of all nationalities to come to the East.

Hitherto the labors of the Jesuits had been confined to the coasts of
India; but in 1579 the opportunity of reaching into the interior, even to
the northern parts, came with the invitation of Akbar, the Grand Mogul,
that priests be sent to explain the doctrine of Christ and to bring with
them the sacred books of the Christians.[51] In his search for a single religion this renowned monarch was accustomed to hold religious discussions at his court to which he brought Hindoos, Mohammedans and
Parsees. Three fathers were chosen: Bl. Rudolph Aquaviva, an excellent
theologian and a kindly, courtly nobleman; Monserrat, also a distinguished character; and Henriquez, a convert from Mohammedanism
and a fluent speaker in Persian. After a three months' journey, the Jesuits
reached the court, near Agra. They held frequent disputations with
learned Mohammedans and Brahmins in the presence of the Grand
Mogul. In the course of these discussions, Aquaviva's attacks on Mo-
hammed almost gained him the martyr's crown, his life being saved only

[49] Pastor, *History of the Popes*, Vol. XVIII, p. 350.

[50] *Ibid.*, Vol. XVIII, p. 347; XX, pp. 473–478.

[51] Maclagen, *The Jesuits and the Great Mogul*, London (1932).

by Akbar himself. Abul Fazil, the chief minister, warmly supported the Christian priests, urging his sovereign to accept Christianity as the only single religion possible, since the Hindoos could never embrace the religion of their Mohammedan oppressors. Akbar admired Christianity, even allowing his second son to receive instructions; but his pride and unrestrained morals prevented the Grand Mogul from bowing to the yoke of Christ. Nevertheless he wished to retain Aquaviva at his court and, when the priest had to depart, sought to bestow gifts of gold and precious jewels upon him. Aquaviva declined the rich presents, asking only for the liberation of some Christian slaves. In 1583 the Jesuit was back in Goa, with only the freed Christians as the tangible result of his mission.

For thirty years after St. Francis Xavier's death, his Jesuit brethren tried vainly again and again to gain a permanent footing in China.[52] Nuñez Baretto in 1555 reached Canton but could remain only for a month; no better success rewarded the efforts of Perez in 1565, of Ribera in 1568, or of da Costa in 1575. It was to Valignani that the first effective steps were due, although he himself did not make the entry. On his voyage to Japan in 1577, the Visitor was obliged to stay for ten months at Macao, a Portuguese settlement on the Chinese coast, where the Jesuits had been established since 1565. Engaging both Portuguese and Chinese in conversations, Valignani sought all possible information on the problem. From his findings he drew up instructions which emphasized the need of acquiring the Chinese language and of conformity to Chinese customs and usages. Unable to postpone his journey to Japan, he left the instructions for another Italian Jesuit, Ruggieri, who was his choice for the task and who was on his way to Macao. Ruggieri arrived in the town in 1579; a skilled linguist, he devoted himself at once to the acquiring of a knowledge of the Chinese tongue and to the composing of a catechism in the language. Three years, however, were to pass before he could obtain the permanent entry.

The flourishing state of the Japanese Christians certainly must have cheered Valignani when he landed in the island kingdom in 1579.[53] During the thirty years since St. Francis Xavier's departure, their ranks had been continuously increasing. The growth was slower in the first two decades than in the third; though in 1571, when Vilela returned to India, worn out after twenty years of toiling, the number of the Christians was estimated at 30,000 and it was believed that they were to be found in every one of the sixty-three principalities. Most of the converts were of the lower classes, yet one daimio and a few learned scholars had embraced the Cross. The zeal of the Japanese converts for the Faith and their attachment to its devotions, left nothing to be desired. Their charity for the sick and unfortunate as well as their love for each other, recalled the days of

[52] Pastor, *History of the Popes*, Vol. XX, pp. 466–468.
[53] Pastor, *History of the Popes*, Vol. XX, pp. 448–458.

the early Christians. Hostility but proved their constancy; when the Daimio of Hirado in 1560 persecuted the Church, many readily forfeited their properties and cheerfully took the road to exile. Such excellent results were obtained by but a handful of missionaries; up to 1563 there were never more than 9 Jesuits in Japan; in the year following, 7 priests and 8 lay-brothers, including 3 Japanese, increased the ranks; in 1570, 2 more priests came to aid the work. The missionaries won the rich harvest by persevering through years of toil that showed no visible results, by refusing to be discouraged when a change of rulers or the whim of a petty tyrant swept away their hard-earned gains. Their noble lives and their generous, self-sacrificing devotion to the sick, made a deep impression on the shrewd Japanese; such virtues were in sharp contrast with the viciousness and selfish ease of the pagan bonzes.

The early advances were made in places of secondary importance. The several attempts of Vilela and his native coadjutor to convert Meaco (Kioto), then the political and religious center of the kingdom, were rather fruitless owing partly to the hatred of the bonzes and partly to disturbed political conditions. Vilela kept at his task in the districts outside the city so persistently that he gained the popular respect and was able to erect seven churches. Truly heroic was his apostolate, especially in its loneliness; for six years he did not gaze upon a single European face, and for three years he had not even the consolation of saying Mass.

The greatest advance came after the powerful Nobunaga had seized the imperial throne in 1565. This new ruler favored the Christians, removing the barriers against them. Mass conversions were effected in Omura and Meaco; many nobles and important dignitaries in Bungo and Meaco sought Baptism. In 1579 the Christians numbered 150,000. Such were the prospects that the optimistic looked for the total conversion of Japan within ten years. The visitation of the zealous yet prudent Valignani was most opportune; he would encourage the best efforts and would restrain the "ill-considered projects," for after all there were only fifty-nine missionaries, and but twenty-three of these were priests. Under his direction Catholic Japan was divided into three districts: Bungo, Meaco and Higen; two seminaries were started in the hope that native youths would be found worthy for the priesthood; a college was erected at Funau and a house of probation opened at Iquisenqui. Valignani wisely insisted on the adoption of the customs of the country as far as possible. He was able to retain the good will of Nobunaga, though he could not effect the conversion of the haughty ruler, whose dreams were solely of earthly glory and power.

Jesuit mission activities in Africa during this period were largely unsuccessful. The high hopes for Abyssinia failed to materialize; [54] the Pa-

---

[54] Pastor, *History of the Popes*, Vol. XVIII, p. 346; XX, p. 481.

triarch Nuñez Baretto died at Goa in 1562 without ever having set foot in his diocese, while Turkish corsairs prevented any help from reaching the few Jesuits isolated in the country. Their labors were restricted to the small number of Portuguese, owing to the opposition of the Negus. So impossible was the outlook that the abandonment of the mission was considered; it was retained, but only on the insistence of Gregory XIII. The evangelization of the negroes of Angola in West Africa was begun in 1560; little, however, was achieved until the coming of Barreira in 1579. More auspiciously was a start made in the same year in East Africa near the Zambesi by Gonçalvo da Silveira; [55] in a short time 400 blacks were baptized and, following that, 300 more with their king in the neighboring region of Monomotapa. But in the next year the whole mission was destroyed and da Silveira slain in a murderous inroad of the Mussulmans.

To the Lebanon in 1578 Gregory XIII sent two Jesuits, Raggio and Eliano, the latter an accomplished scholar in Hebrew, Arabic and in Oriental religious problems, to assist the Maronites in clearing up matters of discipline and doctrine.[56] They returned to Rome to present their report and to obtain wider faculties; along with them they brought two Maronite youths to study for the priesthood in Peter's city. One immediate result was the setting up in Rome of a Syriac press to furnish good religious books in that language, especially the Syriac catechism which the Jesuits had composed. In 1580 Eliano, accompanied by a fellow religious, Bruno, went back to the Lebanon. There they participated in the synod held at the monastery of Quannobin and assisted in the visitations which followed. Later the Jesuits journeyed to Damascus to visit the Greek Patriarch of Alexandria in the hope of bringing him into reunion with Rome; though received with every courtesy, the fathers were unable to obtain any practical result. The journey itself was made amidst great hardships and dangers; several times the two Jesuits were held prisoners by the Mohammedans. Eventually Bruno returned to Rome, while Eliano traveled to the Copts of Egypt.

The first American apostolate of the Society of Jesus, the mission of Brazil, was in existence seventeen years when Bl. Ignatius Azevedo, a zealous Portuguese Jesuit, arrived as the Visitor, sent by St. Francis Borgia to introduce the Constitutions and to examine the labors of the fathers.[57] The mission he found full of promise but woefully lacking in priests; a native clergy at the time was out of the question, some of the European priests had proven not too satisfactory, and the Jesuits were too few and too scattered. The plan of the Visitor was to bring capable youths from Europe to Brazil and there on the spot to give them their sacerdotal and

---

[55] Chadwick, *Life of Ven. Gonçalvo da Silveira*, London (1910).

[56] Pastor, *History of the Popes*, Vol. XV, pp. 492–495.

[57] Pastor, *History of the Popes*, Vol. XVIII, pp. 326–330; XX, pp. 509–510.

missionary training and to impart to them the knowledge of the Indian tongues. He wished also to bring out zealous artisans for the material help of the missions. With this in view de Azevedo returned to Europe. Preaching in all parts of Portugal and Spain, with burning words he fired the enthusiasm of many young men to offer themselves for the distant harvest field. He was able to choose about sixty young Jesuits to go out with him to the colony, the largest group of missionaries of the order yet to leave for the foreign missions. Passage was secured in a fleet of three ships which left Portugal, June 7, 1569. Not one of the Jesuits who sailed was to reach Brazil. Off the Canary Islands the ship carrying de Azevedo and forty of his companions, was captured by a Huguenot corsair, Jean Sourie, who, though sparing the lives of the crew and the soldiers, brutally treated the Jesuits and finally drowned them in the sea. One Jesuit, who seems to have offered to act as a cook, was exempted; whereupon the son of the captain clothed himself in the habit of one of the murdered Jesuits and cheerfully went to his death. Of the two remaining ships but one was able to return to Europe, and this too was captured by a Huguenot sea-rover, Cadaville. The pirate captain killed three of the Jesuits immediately and cast seven others into the sea. It is of interest to know that many of these young religious were but sixteen and seventeen years of age, some even were only fourteen and fifteen.

The difficulties of the Brazilian mission, which were increased by the avarice and cruel harshness of the Portuguese traders, became so great that some of the Jesuits despaired of any successful outcome. Others, more hopeful, gathered the natives into villages remote from the white settlements, and there strove to teach the savages the Faith and the usages of civilization. Eloquent of the tyranny of the European colonists was an incident occurring in 1575, when the mere rumor of the approach of the Portuguese caused the natives to scatter from the settlement on the Rio Real. The self-sacrificing charity of the Jesuits in nursing the Indian victims of the plagues of 1577 and 1581, won the hearts of the poor aborigines and gained many converts. By 1581 the mission had so grown, despite the obstacles, as to possess two colleges and five houses.

The next outstanding missionary in Brazil, indeed one of the foremost apostolic men in the Society of Jesus, was the Ven. José de Anchieta.[58] Such were his labors from his arrival in the Portuguese colony in 1553 until his death in 1597, that he has been called the "Apostle of Brazil." Protestants as well as Catholics have recognized his accomplishments for the Christianization of the aborigines. Thus Southey in his *History of Brazil* has drawn the picture of this tireless missionary: "Bare-footed, with a crucifix, and a rosary round his neck, with staff and breviary in hand, his

---

[58] *Life of Anchieta*, Oratorian Series, London (1849).

shoulders weighed down with the burden of the requirements for his altar, this missionary penetrated the forests, swam across the streams, climbed the most rugged mountain districts, was lost in deserts, faced the wild beasts, and overcame all these dangers and labors in order to win souls." [59] The reports made by Anchieta are a valuable source for the history and knowledge of Brazil. In his study of the native language he produced a grammar of the Tupi tongue, which modern philologists value for its scientific worth. Such was his reputation for the performance of miracles that he was known as the "Thaumaturgus of Brazil."

It was at the request of Philip II that the Spanish Jesuits came to labor in the Vice-royalty of Peru. [60] In response to the King's request, St. Francis Borgia ordered each of the four Spanish provinces to choose two priests for the venture. Philip II followed up his request by liberal provisions for the missionaries, a generosity which he continued as long as he lived. The Jesuits arrived in Peru in 1568 and established themselves first at Lima and Cuzco. Their labors, without neglecting the whites, were to be especially for the Indians; in the beginning, however, they showed some hesitancy in accepting parishes among the Indians, an arrangement which had been a constant source of trouble before their coming. It was not long before the fathers were literally searching the continent for the Indians; thus Zuñiga before his death in 1577 had penetrated into wildest parts of the Andes, and Barzana in 1585 had travelled across these mountains to the valleys of the eastern slope. The early Spanish Jesuits in Peru rendered remarkable services for the knowledge of the Indian languages. Zuñiga was noted for his zeal in acquiring the native tongues. Barzana, while in Upper Peru (modern Bolivia), mastered the Puquina speech and, after his arrival on the eastern side of the Andes, so learned the local tongues as not only to preach with facility in them but to compose a grammar, lexicon and prayerbook in five dialects; his name became also authoritative for the Quichua speech. Holguin was another apostolic linguist; he lived for years in the Jesuit college at Juli on the shores of Lake Titicaca and attained such proficiency that the Viceroy appointed him interpreter-in-chief for the Quichua, Puquina and Aymara tongues; his grammar and vocabulary of Quichua are still of value. Holguin was also named by the Viceroy as the defender and advocate of the Indians. The Jesuits at the college of Juli operated a printing press which brought out the works of Holguin, a grammar, a vocabulary and a Life of Our Lord in the Aymara language. According to Tschudi in his *Organismus der Khetsua-Sprache*,[61] the publications of this press were superior in accuracy and production to the output of the Peruvian presses of the second half of the nineteenth cen-

---

[59] Southey, *History of Brazil*, London (1810), p. 310 seq.

[60] Astrain, *Historia*, Vol. II, pp. 304–316; III, pp. 154–181.

[61] Quoted in Pastor, *History of the Popes*, Vol. XX, p. 506.

tury. De Torres Rubio taught Quichua and kindred dialects at the college of Chuquisacha and to him the Bishops of Peru entrusted the correction and the new edition of the catechism. Other Jesuits made important contributions to the knowledge of Peruvian history and ethnology, notably de Acosta and Blas Valera, who was a descendent on his mother's side of the Incas. The Jesuit colleges of Peru helped much in the education of a native clergy.

Mexico became the scene of Jesuit activity in 1572, when twelve fathers under the leadership of Sanchez and sent by St. Francis Borgia landed at Vera Cruz.[62] They began at once to preach in that city and in Puebla de los Angeles and with such success that the inhabitants of both cities wished to retain them. But as their orders directed them to set up their foundation in Mexico City, the fathers proceeded to the capital, where in 1573 they established a college. Within a few years colleges were being conducted by the Jesuits in five other Mexican cities; in these, as in the institution in Mexico City, sodalities were conducted to the great spiritual good of the students. The labors of the fathers for all races, whites, negroes and redmen, gained the expressed approval of the Archbishop and of the Viceroy. Their conduct during the plagues of 1575 and 1576, their knowledge of the Mexican language and their zeal for the poor natives, won for them the affection of the Indians. During the years under review, the Mexican fathers laid the foundations for the glorious missionary work that was soon to follow.

From Havana, which was part of the Mexican province, went the Jesuits who attempted the mission of Florida, three in 1566 and ten in 1568, under the leadership of Martinez and Segura.[63] Martinez was slain by savages in 1566. Segura labored under the most difficult conditions to organize the mission; in an attempt to locate a new station, unprotected by Spanish soldiers, he reached as far north as the Rappahannock, where he and seven companions were murdered in 1571. The remaining Jesuits were recalled to Havana in the following year. Florida was the only failure of the Mexican Jesuits.

The twenty-five years of the generalates of Laynez, St. Francis Borgia and Mercurian proved beyond a doubt that St. Ignatius' work was not a pious dream but a most potent reality. Under their guidance the fathers of the Society stopped the seemingly unconquerable advance of Protestantism, fired the hearts of Catholics with a new loyalty to the old Faith and to the Popes, and spread the Gospel in the far lands of heathen darkness. The opponents of the Faith recognized them as the devoted soldiers of the Papacy; their Catholic brethren welcomed them as valiant companions-in-arms.

---

[62] Astrain, *Historia*, Vol. III, pp. 125–154.

[63] Kenny, *The Romance of the Floridas*, Milwaukee (1934).

CHAPTER VII

TRIUMPHS AND TRIALS

Claudius Aquaviva, who was the almost unanimous choice of the Fourth General Congregation on February 19, 1581 for the office of General, was to become, next to St. Ignatius, the most important member of the Society of Jesus.[1] If the Jesuit order honors Loyola as its founder, it must acknowledge Aquaviva as its preserver, for in these early days of its history, he it was who brought it through storms fraught with such disasters as were only surpassed by those which accomplished its temporary suppression two hundred years later. Under no other General, save again St. Ignatius, did the order make such progress, further extend its activities, and beget so many holy sons. During the thirty years of Aquaviva's government, the Society of Jesus grew from 21 provinces to 32, from 10 professed houses to 23, from 12 novitiates to 41, from 144 colleges to 372, from 33 residences to 123, from 5,165 members to 13,112. In the foreign mission fields not only were the older works more solidly established but new ventures for Christ were undertaken in Canada, Chili, the Philippines, China and Paraguay, in which last place the famous Jesuit Reductions were begun at Aquaviva's suggestion. The *Ratio Studiorum*, the plan of teaching which gave to Jesuit education that system of definitely purposed and well organized studies which made its colleges the best and most popular in Europe, was worked out under his personal supervision. During his generalate, among the scholars of the Society were to be found such men as Vasquez, Orlandini, Sanchez, Possevino, Skarga, Suarez, Lessius, Becan, Gretser, Tanner, Laymann, and first of all, St. Robert Bellarmine, Doctor of the Church. In these years too the progress in things of the spirit kept pace with the intellectual advances; the study of the Spiritual Exercises was promoted, the best methods of giving them were collected together, combined and published in a document called the "Directorium." The Ignatian ideals of sanctity reached their highest development in the lives of nine Saints and eighteen Beati who were members of the order under Claudius Aquaviva. This chapter will offer a survey of the long and fruitful government of Aquaviva; other topics, as

[1] Jouvancy, *Hist. S.J.*, Vol. II; Pastor, *Hist. of the Popes*, Vols. XX–XXIV; *Cath. Encyl.* I, p. 109; Astrain, *Historia*, Vols. III, IV; Santagata, *Istoria della Prov. di Napoli d.C. d.G.*, Vol. III, pp. 546–588.

education, foreign missions, and the work in the Counter-Reformation, will receive more detailed treatment in subsequent chapters.

The greatest work of Aquaviva for the Society of Jesus was his defense of the Institute against the attacks of certain malcontents among the Spanish Jesuits.[2] Backed by the powerful influence of Philip II and the Spanish Inquisition, a small but exceedingly resourceful clique tried to subvert the essential ideals of St. Ignatius and to overturn or paralyse the government of Aquaviva, at least as far as the Spanish provinces were concerned. His defense was made all the harder by the fact that the attack was launched during the pontificates of Sixtus V and Clement VIII, who were not over-favorable to certain innovations in the religious life which St. Ignatius had introduced. It was well for the order and its Institute that the supreme office in this crisis was in the hands of a man of keen intellect and unwavering resolution. Alonso Sanchez spoke with exaggeration, yet he indicated the caliber of the new General, when he said that if eight or ten of the most able Jesuits were fused into one man, such a man yet would not be another Aquaviva. As striking is the tribute of Maximilian of Bavaria, the leader of the Catholic cause in the Thirty Years' War. From his personal knowledge of Aquaviva, he said: "I cannot praise him enough; one is forced, so to speak, to fall in love with him, and to look to him alone." For thirty years and more Aquaviva fought steadily and unflinchingly for the ideals of the founder, always in a prayerful spirit and with such moderation that in his countless writings and correspondences, he never abandoned his dignity and self-control.

Claudius Aquaviva[3] was born in Naples in 1543, the younger son of the Duke of Atri; in his twenty-fourth year he entered the Society of Jesus. Before his election to the generalate he had given presage of his executive abilities in the office of Provincial of the province of Naples. His first years in the supreme office came within the last part of the pontificate of Gregory XIII, who continued to manifest his affection for the sons of St. Ignatius, especially by the two solemn confirmations of the order, the Bulls, "Quanto Fructuosius" and "Ascendente Domino." It was during these early years too that Aquaviva organized the studies of the Jesuit colleges and produced the *Ratio Studiorum*. Sixtus V, the succeeding Pope, while not unfriendly to the order, for he strongly supported its labors, especially in the colleges and in the foreign missions, yet did not approve of certain features of the Constitutions. He was a member of one of the older religious orders and accustomed to the viewpoints of medieval re-

---

[2] Astrain, *Historia*, Vol. III, lib. 2 (1925).

[3] Campbell, "Claudius Acquaviva," *Cath. Encyl.*, Vol. I, pp. 109–110; Koch, "Claudius Acquaviva," *Jesuiten-Lexikon*, Paderborn (1934), p. 81–83; Sommervogel, *Bibliothéque de la Compagnie de Jésus*, Paris (1890), pp. 480–491.

ligious life; it was not strange that the innovations of St. Ignatius did not appeal to him. These and the title with its use of the Holy Name, he wished to see changed. It was particularly unfortunate that in his pontificate the Spanish intriguers should have made their attack against some of the very points which displeased the Pope. Sixtus V was motivated by the highest purposes; the same cannot be said of the Spanish malcontents.

The Society of Jesus was not long in existence when dissatisfaction with St. Ignatius' ideals of government began to be manifested by certain of the Spanish brethren.[4] Though never important numerically, these malcontents, because of the outside influence which they were able to command, were especially troublesome. There had been too much frequentation of the court and the upper circles of society; and when the General insisted on a stricter adherence to the Constitutions, the opinion arose among some that his powers were excessive. Demands were made for a Vice-General for Spain, a proposition which the distrust of many Spaniards for anything emanating from Rome greatly fostered. The election of subordinate superiors by a majority vote was also urged, and doubts were cast upon the advisability of the distinction between the professed and the formed spiritual coadjutors. There was no stint in the praise of St. Ignatius, but it was more than once ventured that his ideals were beyond the capacities of ordinary mortals. Few of the complainants, it may be of interest to note, were conspicuous lights of religious observance.

Previous to Aquaviva's generalate two memorials begging for changes, drawn up by two Jesuits who had not the courage to append their names, had been presented to the Nuncio at Madrid. Other attacks followed and the matter came to a crisis when, in March 1586, on the complaint of the Jesuit Diego Hernandez, the Inquisition arrested several Spanish Jesuits, including one of the Provincials, Antonio Marcen. The charge against Marcen was that he had encroached upon the jurisdiction of the Inquisition in dealing with one of his subjects. The affair developed from a case against an individual to an attack upon the Institute of the Society of Jesus, involving too the Papal power, for the whole Institute had had the solemn approval of several Pontiffs. The Inquisition was annoyed by Aquaviva's appeal to the Pope and ignored the Papal letter seeking further information. When Sixtus V learned that the Inquisition had ordered the Jesuits to hand over all printed copies of Papal Bulls confirming the order's privileges, he at once ordered the Grand Inquisitor to restore them and to proceed no further with the trial of the Jesuits.

But the malcontents were not to be outdone. Two of them, Vasquez and Enriquez, succeeded through the Inquisition in obtaining from Philip II an order greatly hampering the Provincials in sending their subjects out

---

[4] Astrain, *Historia*, Vol. III, pp. 357–713.

of Spain, not only the ones destined for apostolic work in Transylvania but the delegates elected for the Procurators' Congregation in Rome. Such interference with free communication with Rome incensed Sixtus V and again he ordered the Grand Inquisitor to return the sequestered documents and to send the minutes of the Jesuits' trial to Rome. The records were not sent, since the trial had ended in an acquittal. Pulpit attacks on the order, however, continued, as did the petitioning of the Inquisition for changes in the order.

Vasquez appealed to the Society in Spain for a national congregation, only to receive a flat refusal. Only in the provincial congregation of Castile, where he had some influence, did Vasquez achieve anything. The fathers there assembled petitioned for a General Congregation and a special representative of the General for the Spanish provinces. Both petitions were rejected by the Procurators' Congregation then assembled in Rome.

For a second time the intervention of Philip II was procured. On this occasion the monarch requested a visitation of the Spanish provinces by a prelate not of the order, but one either chosen or approved by himself. Sixtus V acquiesced somewhat reluctantly; his misgivings were more than justified when the Visitor's instructions were found out, for these directed him to inquire not only into the lives of the individual Spanish Jesuits but into the very Institute of the Society of Jesus. Aquaviva quickly and skillfully acted to save the order: he directed the Provincials of Spain and Portugal to draw up memorials counter to those of the malcontents; he pointed out to the Pope the real purpose of the agitation, the withdrawal of the Spanish Jesuits from Roman dependence and the settlement of all problems in Spain where the King's influence was paramount; he objected too to the fitness of the particular Visitor chosen. Sixtus V, impressed by his arguments, revoked the order for the visitation. There yet remained the much more difficult task of dissuading Philip II. The General expressed to the monarch his willingness for a visitation, provided that the Visitor were a Jesuit. To the discredit of the malcontents, he was able to prove to the King that the overwhelming majority of the most eminent Spanish and Portuguese Jesuits considered the visitation of an extern a calamity. After some hesitancy the king abandoned his plan and Acosta, just returned from sixteen years' sojourn in the Jesuit missions of Peru, was appointed Visitor.

The last recourse of the disturbers was to the Pope himself, who, according to a common report, was not too favorable towards the Society of Jesus. Despite his assistance to the order in many of its undertakings, Sixtus could not bring himself to approve certain innovations of St. Ignatius in the practice of religious life. By 1588 the letters of the malcontents had made such an impression on the Pontiff that he ordered the Roman

Inquisition to choose two learned theologians who, with the aid of a Jesuit, would examine the Constitutions and remedy their defects.

Aquaviva in defense of the order sought from nuncios, bishops and Catholic princes, far and near, testimonial letters as to the good labors of the Jesuits, and also as to the joy of the heretics and the sorrow of Catholics at the attacks on their Constitutions. Letters poured into Rome from the highest Catholic personages, so impressing the Pope that he wrote to Germany that his intention was not to change the Constitutions but only to correct the defects of a few Jesuits. Meanwhile, the work of the commission was bidding fair to turn out so favorably for the order that the members hesitated to place the results before the Pontiff. Though somewhat disturbed by the delay Sixtus seemed determined to abide by his promise not to change the Constitutions. On one point however he was adamant, the change in the name. Moreover, he decided that the change should be effected not by an order of his own but by a decree of the General. Aquaviva could not but comply, and so he composed and presented the decree to the Pope for his approval. It never was published for the death of Sixtus V on August 27, 1590 ended the matter. Gregory XIV, the second successor of Sixtus V, ignoring the vehement protests of the Spanish ambassador, went beyond his original intention of forbidding further attacks on the Jesuit Constitutions and published two most solemn confirmations of the Society's Institute in the Bulls "Ecclesiae Catholicae" (June 28, 1591) and "Exponi Nobis" (July 1591). Ignatius' ideals and Aquaviva's government were vindicated. It was not long before a more friendly attitude was adopted by the Spanish Inquisition.

The last of the Spanish troubles had not yet been heard; they were to reappear a few years later in the reign of Clement VIII, a Pontiff not too favorably disposed towards the order. Clement VIII was not an enemy of the Jesuits; he bestowed many favors on them, raised Toletus and Bellarmine to the cardinalate, highly valued the work of their foreign missionaries, and labored with special devotion in the defense of the order in France. Still, through most of his pontificate, he maintained an attitude of cold reserve towards the members of the Society. To him some of the Jesuits seemed too proud and some too ready to mix in matters that did not pertain to them, especially in the field of politics. No doubt he was affected by the feeling against the Society which had grown up in certain quarters, and his misgivings were confirmed by the faults of certain prominent members of the order. These faults were human misconceptions of policies, almost to be expected as accompanying the great successes of the order. They were the failings of individuals; the ranks of the Jesuits were filled with men of the highest sanctity, indeed the vast majority labored with unceasing zeal in God's cause. It was, then, unfortunate that the Spanish troubles should have been revived in the reign of a Pope so disposed as Clement VIII was. The presence of Toletus [5] in the College of Cardinals was not a help, for the first Jesuit Cardinal was no friend of Aquaviva and more than once used his great influence with the Pope against the best interests of the Society of Jesus.

The malcontents this time directed their attacks against Aquaviva and sought to lessen the powers of the General. Their ranks were strengthened by the accession of the capable Acosta, disappointed because he had not received an appointment as Provincial. Again they had the support of Philip II. On December 2, 1592, Acosta arrived in Rome, and without the knowledge of Aquaviva sought and obtained through the Spanish ambassador an audience with Clement VIII. He presented to the Pope the case for the limitation of the General's powers and petitioned that a General Congregation be summoned. The Pontiff agreed to call one himself, if the Jesuit General refused. Aquaviva opposed with every bit of his power the General Congregation, for he saw in it the ruin of Ignatius' work. The Saint had set the greatest store on the office of General; he made every possible provision for the choice of a capable and zealous superior and endowed him with great powers. The permanence of such a superior, Loyola felt, would be the best guarantee against the order's decadence. There was nothing to do, however, but send out the summons for the Congregation. The outlook was indeed ominous, for Aquaviva had opposed to him the power of Philip II, the ability of Cardinal Toletus and the dispositions towards the Jesuits of Clement VIII.

The first ray of hope appeared when the result of the elections for delegates to the General Congregation became known; the malcontents suffered a complete defeat, not even in the Spanish provinces were they able to secure the election of a single delegate. However, Philip II brought such pressure to bear that Acosta had to be admitted into the General Congregation and had to be accorded a vote. The King sought further concessions, but he failed to obtain them owing to the intervention of Clement VIII; during the whole course of the troubles, despite his personal views, the Pope made it a point that the Jesuits should receive justice and freedom of action.

The first business was the examination into the charges laid against Aquaviva. Some of the delegates would have refused to sit in judgment on the General, but Aquaviva insisted on the scrutiny of his conduct. A committee of five fathers spent a whole month at the task; their decision amounted to an almost complete vindication. The only stricture they

---

[5] Nieremberg, *Varones ilustres de la C. de J.*, Bilbao (1890); Koch, "Francisco de Toledo," *Jesuiten-Lexikon*, 1760–1761; Goyena, "Francisco Toledo," *Cath. Encyl.*, Vol. XIV, pp. 766–771; Hurter, *Nomenclator literarius theol. Cath.*, Innsbruck (1871–1886), Vol. III, pp. 247–256.

made on the General's conduct was that he clung too tenaciously to his opinions, and that he favored some more than was fitting. Aquaviva in person brought the findings of the committee to Clement VIII, who was so favorably impressed that he remarked: "They sought a culprit and they found a saint."

Philip II determined on more active intervention. Five of his demands concerning relations with the Inquisition, as they encroached on no vital point, were accepted by the Congregation; but the memorial of Sessa, his ambassador, asking for constitutional changes was unanimously rejected. Sessa carried his case to the Pope, who directed the fathers to discuss the proposal pertaining to the final vows. The fathers, out of deference to the Holy Father, discussed the article, but resolved to adhere to the legislation of their founder. Their determination was disquieting to Clement VIII, who looked on such conduct as a sort of defiance which would consider no change at all. On January 24, 1594, he personally addressed the fathers assembled in the Roman Professed House. After speaking on humility and pride, the Pope blamed the Jesuits for meddling in matters which did not concern them, for censuring the doctrines of others, for having no regard for the opinions of prince, king or emperor, for discussing whether the Pope had a right to do this or that, for despising monachism, for looking on their own Constitutions as perfect and unimprovable, with need neither of visitation nor reform. The Pontiff spoke with gravity and in a friendly manner, but warned the fathers that if they did not effect some remedy, he himself would take a hand.

The fathers were thunderstruck. What possible remedies could be adopted? Decrees had already been passed against divergence of doctrine and for adherence to St. Thomas Aquinas. What part of the Constitutions, they asked themselves, could be changed that would guarantee more respect for the King of Spain and for monastic orders? As for humility, their founder had insisted that the members consider their society as the least among the religious orders. It was at length decided to have recourse to the Pope and to ask him to point out what changes ought to be made. Toletus, to whom they brought their request asking him to present it to the Holy Father, met the fathers with a flat refusal. As a matter of fact, according to his own admission, two days before the Pope's allocution, he had presented to Clement VIII nine points for the emendation of the order.

The Pontiff was not desirous of making any changes himself, so he offered the fathers four considerations for their discussion: the three year term of office for superiors, the account which Provincials should render at the end of their term, the acceptance of the Papal reservations on certain sins, and the right of decision for the Assistants in certain cases. There was no hesitancy in accepting the first three proposals. In regard to the fourth the fathers unanimously voted that, though allowing for five exceptions, they considered the restriction inopportune.

Toletus, Sessa and Acosta demanded that the Congregation come to a decision on the calling of another General Congregation in the sixth year following and on the proposal to change all the Assistants except the lately-appointed German Assistant. Opportunity for expressing any opinion was not permitted since Toletus carried to the Congregation the Papal order for acceptance. The new Assistants were elected January 18, 1594, and with that last act the Fifth General Congregation came to a close.

The malcontents in their main objectives had been defeated; Aquaviva had been justified and no essential change had been made in the Constitutions. Afterwards Clement VIII himself mitigated some of the unwonted legislation. The regulations for the holding of General Congregations at stated intervals was abrogated some years later. The Spanish Inquisition adopted a more favorable attitude towards the Society and Philip II declared himself satisfied. Acosta, an able and truly zealous man, was reconciled with Aquaviva. Many saw in the beatification of St. Ignatius Loyola in 1609 a new approbation on what was his principal work, the Constitutions of the Society of Jesus. Clement VIII, however, was not yet done with the idea of changing the life-term of the General. A proposal was set on foot to remove Aquaviva by making him the Archbishop of Naples, an honor which the General, both from motives of humility and from a desire to prevent change in the life-tenure of the supreme office, strongly opposed. The fathers of the Society too were most anxious that the plan would not succeed. But it seemed as if nothing could stop the proposal; Toletus, to whom the Jesuits appealed, refused to consider their petition. At last the Portuguese Assistant found a way to prevent the calamity. If Aquaviva must be made an Archbishop, then why not let him be elevated to the rank of Cardinal? There would be no difficulty in obtaining this honor since many Catholic princes, especially those in Germany, would be only too glad to petition for it. Once Toletus was faced with Aquaviva in the Sacred College, there would be little need of apprehension as to which of the Jesuit Cardinals would succeed in managing the affairs of the order. Toletus evidently did not relish the prospect, for before long he persuaded the Pope to drop Aquaviva's bishopric.

Three events may be said to have ended the intrigues of the Spanish malcontents. The first was the issuance of the brief of Paul V, "Quantum religio," on September 4, 1606, which contained a major confirmation of the Institute and an approbation of the three decrees of the Fifth Congregation. These decrees dealt with agitators in the order, a prohibition against meddling in politics and secular business, and the continuance of superiors in office for a definite time. The second event was the holding of the Sixth General Congregation, February 20 to March 29, 1608, for a renewal of the spiritual life and the discipline of the order, and for the enactment of special legislation against the disturbers of the peace within the Society. The third event was the beatification of Ignatius, with the implications already mentioned. The Spanish internal trouble disappeared without a trace, as its superficial character warranted; at no time was the number of the intriguers more than thirty.

One of the most difficult problems which faced Aquaviva during a large part of his generalate was the controversy with the Dominican theologians on the subject of supernatural grace, the controversy "de auxiliis," as it is known.[6] The limitations of this work permit scarcely more than a chronological summary of the dispute. Recourse to manuals of theology and to histories of dogma must be had for a more adequate knowledge of the points at issue and the interaction of both parties in the long disputation. The question concerned the extremely difficult problem of the relation of God's grace and man's cooperation with that grace for his eternal salvation. Luther and Calvin had brought the problem into general interest by their complete denial of man's free will and their teaching that God, without any cooperation on the part of man, saved or damned him eternally. This repudiation of the free will and this doctrine of unconditional predestination, every Catholic theologian denied unequivocally. Divergence among Catholic divines arose over the problem of reconciling God's omnipotence and omniscience, which all held, with man's free will, which all likewise held. The problem was not new; long before, it had troubled Catholic doctors, even in the days of the fifth century Pelagians. It may be said that the Jesuit theologians explained better the free will, while the Dominican theologians explained better the omnipotence and omniscience of God.

The controversy started in 1585 in Spain with the publication, by one of the ablest of the Jesuit theologians, Luis de Molina, of a work entitled, *Concordia liberi arbitrii cum gratiae donis*. The book was attacked by one of the foremost of the Dominican theologians, Domingo Bañez. Theologians, tribunals of the Inquisition, and the Spanish Universities entered the lists, the controversy developing with great acrimony despite the efforts of the Dominican and Jesuit Generals to preserve harmony. The dispute dragged on for some years until Clement VIII decided to bring the controversy to Rome for decision. The Pope had hoped to end the matter in short order; he accomplished little, however, and the struggle of theological doctrines continued for nine more years into the reign of Paul V. At first, the Generals of both orders were cited to ap-

---

[6] Cf. works of Serry, O.P., de Mayer, S.J., Billuart, O.P., de Regnon, S.J., Dummermuth, O.P. and Frins, S.J. A very good account in English may be had in Brodrick's *Life of Blessed Robert Cardinal Bellarmine*, II, pp. 1-69.

pear before the Pope and work for a solution, but after many a session nothing much was accomplished. Then in 1602 Clement VIII sought to have the matter settled by a commission before whom the chosen theologians of both orders should defend their respective teachings. Again no speedy ending was effected, despite the personal presence and participation of the Pontiff. Paul V in 1605 bent his efforts to closing the endless debates. It was not until August 28, 1607 that he finally brought about the end of the long controversy. His decision was a compromise; both sides might hold their own particular teachings, but neither was to censure, brand with the term heretical, the holders of the opposite opinion. In the view of Paul V, the time had not yet come for a dogmatic decision. The regrettable feature about the whole controversy was the bitterness and mutual recrimination incident to the long debates. Yet this must be said: the dispute was no scholastic quibble; it dealt with the most vital points of Faith. The Jesuits really feared that the opposite teaching would lead to Calvinism, while the Dominicans just as sincerely feared that their opponents' doctrine tended to Pelagianism. During the controversy and especially in the years that followed, the superiors of both orders strove earnestly and successfully for mutual understanding and good will between the brethren of both societies.

In the struggle between Paul V and the Venetian Republic, the Jesuits suffered severely for their loyalty to the Holy Father. An element hostile to the rights of the Papacy obtained the rule of the Republic; their opposition was confirmed by the machinations of the ex-Servite friar, Paolo Sarpi, an absolute heretic whose one purpose was the destruction of Italian Catholicism. The ruling clique in Venice in their turn protected the apostate. When Paul V at last laid Venice under an interdict, the Jesuits stationed in various parts of the Republic's territories observed the prescriptions of the Papal censure in the face of all the threats of the government. The Venetian rulers determined to rid the Republic once and for all of a body so devoted to the Holy See. Sarpi, who hated the Jesuits with an especial venom, urged on the warfare against the Society of Jesus. The order was banished *in perpetuum* from the territories of the Republic, its revenues were seized, and those Venetians who dared to write to a Jesuit, or who refused to withdraw their sons from the Jesuit colleges abroad, were threatened with exile or even slavery in the galleys. The carrying out of all these measures caused the fathers and their friends the greatest sufferings. Nor did the peace between the Pope and the Republic in 1607 end the trials of the order in Venice, since one of the conditions insisted on by the Venetian negotiators was that the Jesuits were not to be recalled. Paul V loyally stood by the Society until Aquaviva, in the interest of peace, persuaded him to abandon the question of the Jesuits' return. Even after the resumption of relations, the

Pope continued to work for the return of the Society; yet such was the antipathy of the governing class towards the Jesuits, that fifty years were to pass before the members of the order were again permitted to labor in the territories of the Venetian Republic.

In the rest of Italy, in Spain and in Portugal, countries little affected by the titanic struggle with Protestantism, the Jesuits of Aquaviva's time labored efficiently, if quietly, and with marked success in popular missions in the cities and through the country districts. Especially noteworthy was the work of the Turin Jesuits under the direction of St. Charles Borromeo in the Alpine valleys of his jurisdiction. In 1584 this heroic Saint died in the arms of his confessor, Father Adorno, S.J. In the Pyrenees the Spanish brethren performed similar labors bringing the consolations of religion to the people of the remote mountain districts.

The educational work, now definitely organized by the *Ratio Studiorum*, became in a sense the most important occupation of the Jesuits of the three countries. Not only did the older schools expand in the quality of their teaching and in the numbers of their students, but new colleges came into existence, eleven in Italy and eight in Spain. Both in the churches and in the colleges of the order, the Sodality of the Blessed Virgin proved a most efficacious means of deepening faith and extending charitable endeavors. Typical of many sodalities were the four conducted in connection with the college of Ascoli; the first was comprised of noblemen, the second of merchants and artisans, the third of the older students, and the fourth of the younger pupils. At Naples there was organized a sodality for secular priests which at the beginning in 1611 had 30 members, and after a century possessed a roll of 462 members of the diocesan clergy.

The number of Saints who lived during the administration of Aquaviva, is one of the most outstanding features of his period of government. They constitute a majority of all the canonized Saints of the Society of Jesus. The sanctity of each of them was the fruit of the asceticism of the Spiritual Exercises.

First among these saintly Jesuits to run his course, was Saint Aloysius Gonzaga.[7] Royal courts and princely palaces are not usually the seed ground of sanctity, yet it was in just such environment that this holy youth was reared and in which he began the first steps of his saintly career. Aloysius Gonzaga was born at Castiglione, March 9, 1568, a scion of the Gonzagas, the Dukes of Mantua. Early in his youth a great spiritual force entered into the life of Aloysius when he came under the influence of the saintly Cardinal Archbishop of Milan, St. Charles Borromeo, from whose hands he received his First Holy Communion.

---

[7] Meschler, *Life of St. Aloysius,* Eng. trans. London (1911).

It was in Spain, where he had gone to serve as a page for the sons of Philip II, that Aloysius first formed the idea of entering religious life in the ranks of the Jesuit order. The strongest opposition to his ambition arose when he sought his father's consent that he might resign his inheritance and follow his vocation. At length, when the Duke was won over and the consent of the Emperor to the resignation of his position was obtained, Aloysius presented himself at the novitiate of the Society of Jesus in Rome, November 25, 1585. The sight of the son of the Gonzagas, one of the oldest of the princely houses of Italy, abandoning his patrimony with all its brilliant prospects and adopting the lowly and difficult life of a Jesuit novice, caused a veritable sensation not only in Italy, but in Spain and the Empire. When five years later he appeared in his native Castiglione and was permitted to preach there, though not yet a priest, thousands flocked to see and hear him, and many were moved to confession. Remarkable as were his humility and his spirit of sacrifice, his angelic purity of life was his outstanding characteristic. His practice of the severest asceticism proved him to be a strong-hearted, virile soul, totally unlike the impossible, insipid character given him by some artists and hagiographers. His gifts of prayer marked him for a saint of the highest mysticism. No one recognized this more clearly than his spiritual father at the Roman College, St. Robert Bellarmine. After the novitiate, Aloysius entered immediately upon the study of theology, for he had completed his philosophical course while yet a layman in Spain. But the Saint was destined never to ascend the altar. In his fourth year, before his ordination, a virulent plague swept over Italy in 1591. Delicate though he was, the holy youth volunteered to care for the victims of the pestilence. On March 3, Aloysius fell a victim to the disease and, on June 21, 1591, died a martyr of charity. Thirty years after his death Gregory XV beatified him and in 1726 Benedict XIII raised him to the altars of the Universal Church. Because of his great holiness, and especially for his extraordinary chastity, the Church has designated St. Aloysius the patron Saint of youth.

The three Saints who followed St. Aloysius were the Japanese Martyrs, Sts. Paul Miki, John de Goto and James Kisai.[8] In the same year, 1597, in which they made the supreme sacrifice, there came to an end the long and most fruitful career of St. Peter Canisius.[9] It is hard to write with restraint about this holy man, so tireless in labors, so varied in accomplishments, so beautiful in character. A brief summarization of his life must suffice. Nine colleges owe their actual founding to him, although, as his latest biographer, Brodrick, remarks, almost all of the

---

[8] A further reference will be made to them in the chapter on the foreign missions.

[9] Braunsberger, *Beati Patri Canisii Societatis Jesu Epistolae et Acta*, 8 vols., Freiburg (1896–1923); Brodrick, *St. Peter Canisius*, London (1935).

forty Jesuit colleges operating in the German lands were directly or indirectly traceable to him. He served for a time as the Rector of the University of Ingolstadt, as the administrator of the University of Dillingen, and as professor in the University of Vienna. Time and again he upheld the Catholic side in disputations with the Reformers at Cologne, Worms, Regensburg (twice) and Augsburg (twice). In his pulpit labors, he was at different times court preacher at Vienna, cathedral preacher at Regensburg, Worms, Strasburg, Würzburg and for seven years at Augsburg; with even more eagerness he exhorted and catechised the children, servants and the simple peasant folk in the abandoned country districts of Lower Austria, Alsace, Franconia and other regions of rural Germany. To illustrate the multiplicity of his labors, it may be noted that he was the agent of the people and the University of Cologne in obtaining the aid of Emperor Charles V and the Nuncio against the apostate Archbishop of Cologne; that he was the companion to a Papal Nuncio to Poland; that he was for a year the administrator of the diocese of Vienna, which see he thrice refused; that for thirteen years he was the Provincial of the Upper German province of his order; that twice he acted as a theologian at the Council of Trent; that on one occasion he helped to save the Council when its continuance was jeopardized by a quarrel between Ferdinand I and Pope Pius IV; that he was the confidential agent of the Pope to bring the Tridentine decrees to the German princes and Bishops, and to urge on them the establishment of seminaries and colleges. In a previous chapter, his great literary work, the Catechism, has been discussed; that work, however, was but one of many which came from his pen. He composed a partial refutation of the Centuriators of Magdeburg, a five volume treatise on the Blessed Virgin, the Mother of God, as well as many other books on theology, history, patrology, asceticism, hagiography, popular devotions, and even an adaptation of a Latin grammar. The list of his literary works with their various editions and translations covers sixty pages in Sommervogel's *Bibliothèque de la Compagnie de Jésus;* and yet the list is incomplete. One of the most appealing things about St. Peter Canisius was his beautiful character; he loved the poor, he was devoted to the temporal as well as the spiritual welfare of his brethren, he was charitable to everyone, even to the bitterest of his Protestant opponents. Good works, prayer and gentle kindliness were his weapons against the religious rebels. He was beatified by Pius IX in 1896, and on May 5, 1925 Pius XI canonized him and at the same time proclaimed him a Doctor of the Church. So important was his part in the Counter-Reformation in the German lands, that St. Peter Canisius has been popularly acclaimed as "The Second Boniface," "The Hammer of the Heretics," "The Watchdog of Germany."

In far different scenes labored the next Saint of the Society of Jesus, a humble lay-brother, busy with the uneventful yet unending duties of porter in the quiet corridors of the remote college of Palma in Majorca, St. Alphonsus Rodriguez.[10] St. Alphonsus was born in Segovia July 25, 1532, the son of honorable tradespeople. After leading a noble Christian life as a layman, he entered the Society on the death of his wife and children, in the grade of lay-brother. In a short time he was sent to Palma in the Balearic Islands; there for forty-six years he answered the bell and tended the door of the college. By the example of his saintly life and by his words of advice, St. Alphonsus exercised a remarkable influence, not only over his religious brethren but also over a great number of lay people with whom he came in contact in the course of his duties. One young Jesuit was indebted to him, at least in part, for his own life work, the Apostle of the Negro slaves in the New World, St. Peter Claver. As the years went by St. Alphonsus justly attained a high reputation for sanctity because of his penitential practices and his gifts of prayer. At the command of his superior he set down on paper his thoughts and experiences; after his death these were collected and eventually published; they manifested a correct doctrine and a profound spirituality. He helped to popularize the "Little Office of the Immaculate Conception." The holy brother died on October 31, 1617; he was beatified in 1825 and canonized in 1887.

Another youthful Saint entered the ranks of the Society during this period, shortly after the death of Aquaviva. He was a young Belgian, St. John Berchmans.[11] St. John was born at Diest in Brabant, March 13, 1599. In his youth, even in his childhood, John was marked among his companions for his gentle and affectionate kindness and for his conscientious sense of duty. His devotion to his invalid mother in her long sickness displayed too a characteristic virtue. But above all was his manly and genuine piety, manifested especially in his devotion to Mary, the Mother of God. After some time spent with the Jesuits as a student of their college at Mechlin, he entered the order in that city, September 24, 1616. Following the two years of novitiate, he was first sent to Antwerp for his philosophical studies; but his stay there was very brief for his superiors decided to send him to the Roman College for his course. The young Flemish scholastic made the journey on foot, arriving at the Roman College, December 31, 1618. The two years of philosophical studies were accomplished with such success that in the third year he was chosen for the post of defender in the scholastic disputations held in the Greek College, then under the charge of the Domini-

---

[10] Cassanuova, *Saint Alonso Rodriguez*, Eng. trans. London (1932).

[11] Delehaye, *St. John Berchmans*, Eng. trans., New York (1926); Daly, *St. John Berchmans*, New York (1921).

cans. It was on returning from these disputations that he was seized with a violent fever from which he died, August 13, 1621. St. John Berchmans' sanctity consisted not in the practice of great austerities nor in special gifts of prayer, but in the perfection with which he fulfilled the duties of the religious state. He was especially devoted to the Rule. St. John consciously determined to become a saint; and the path to that goal, he was convinced, lay in the perfect observation of the Rule. It is hardly too much to say that in his canonization, the Rule was canonized. Yet with all his native sanctity, he found the observance difficult: "My greatest mortification is common life," he once remarked. That he was successful in his complete and exact obedience, is testified to by all his spiritual directors. St. John was beatified in 1865 and canonized in 1888.

Foremost among the scholars of the order was the Saint who was next to complete his earthly pilgrimage, St. Robert Bellarmine, Cardinal and Doctor of the Church.[12] Robert Bellarmine was born of an ancient noble family at Montepulciano in Tuscany, October 4, 1542. His mother was the sister of Cardinal Cervini, later Pope Marcellus II. The lad became one of the first students of the recently opened Jesuit college of his native town, and attracted by the example of the fathers determined to join their ranks. He entered the order at Rome on September 9, 1560. At the completion of his philosophical studies he taught the classics for four years, first at Florence and later at Mondovi. His theological course was begun at Padua; but in 1567 it was decided to send him to Louvain for its completion, in order that he might obtain a first hand knowledge of the heresies then prevalent in the North. In 1570, St. Robert received the priesthood; for the next six years he lectured with such success in the classroom and preached with such eloquence in the pulpit that crowds flocked to hear him, Protestants as well as Catholics among them, some auditors even journeying from distant parts. In the controversies over Baianism he played a leading part. Recalled to Rome by Gregory XIII, the young professor was appointed to the chair of Controversial Theology at the Roman College. This was to be the greatest work of his life; for twelve years his classroom was to be the center of defense for the Counter-Reformation. In course of time he published his lectures in three volumes, *Disputationes de Controversiis Christianae Fidei Adversus Hujus Temporis Haereticos*. The *De Controversiis* is the greatest literary defense issued by Catholics during the whole period of the Reformation; in whole or in part it has gone into at least forty

---

[12] Brodrick, *The Life and Work of Bl. Robert Cardinal Bellarmine*, 2 vols., London (1928); other biographies by von Frentz, Freiburg (1921); Mendes, Porto (1930); Fiocchi, Rome (1930); Tacchi-Venturi, II, *B. Rob. Bellarmine, Esame della nuove accuse contro sua santità*, Rome (1923); Sommervogel, *Bibliothèque* I, pp. 1151–1254.

editions. It became the handbook of the Catholic controversialists on every front of the Protestant Reformation. The Protestants themselves considered it the most dangerous blow struck at their cause; not only did they forbid the reading of it, but in over one hundred books they attempted to answer it. In some of their universities they even founded chairs, anti-Bellarmine professorships, for its continual refutation.

In 1588, St. Robert left the classroom to become the spiritual director of the Jesuit students of the Roman College. He loved the work, in the course of which he became the guide of the soul of St. Aloysius, assisting that holy youth in his last hour. For two years, 1592–1594, St. Robert governed the Roman College as its rector; then he was sent to the Neapolitan province to be its provincial superior for three years. At the request of Clement VIII he was recalled to Rome and in 1599 was raised by the Pontiff to the Cardinalate, despite the opposition of Cardinal Toletus. As a superior he had been kind, even affectionate, and an able administrator as well.

Clement VIII had raised St. Robert to the purple in order that he might have the benefit of his advice in theological problems. He remained the adviser of all the Popes under whom he served until his death. One of his first tasks was to participate in the controversy "de auxiliis"; his suggestion was that the point of doctrine be left to the schools for further discussion and that the disputants be enjoined against mutual censurings. This, indeed, was the final solution, yet it did not please Clement VIII and the new Cardinal was removed from Rome by consecration as Archbishop of Capua. In his new see St. Robert forgot Rome, its honors and its controversies, devoting himself entirely to the welfare of his diocese. He induced new life into the ecclesiastical institutions, presenting the world with the spectacle of a zealous shepherd of his flock, especially of the poor. After the death of Clement VIII, both in the conclave which elected Leo XI and in the conclave which chose Paul V, the saintly Cardinal's name, much to his own discomfort, was considered.

Paul V recalled St. Robert to Rome. The Saint, however, was not at peace until he was officially relieved of his diocese, for he could not bear the thought of being an absentee shepherd. He was appointed to the Holy Office and to several other congregations. In the conflict of the Pope with Venice, St. Robert rose to the defense of the rights of the Holy See writing against the protagonists of the Republic, Giovanni Masiglio and the apostate friar, Paolo Sarpi. In 1606 he entered his famous controversy with James I of England concerning the power of the Papacy. It was in his writings in this dispute that he enunciated the principles of government which many Americans feel to be basic in their own political life. His opposition in this case to the absolutism of kings earned for him the enmity of the French regalists and Gallicans. The saintly Cardinal also took part in the earlier phases of the controversy over Galileo, with whom he was on friendly terms. After the election of Gregory XV in 1621, as his health was beginning to fail, St. Robert retired to the Jesuit novitiate of Sant' Andrea to prepare for the end. Death came to him on September 17, 1621.

St. Robert Bellarmine's character was a noble and winning one, his nature was kind and loving, his heart was ever open to the poor. He was a tireless warrior in God's cause, as the many labors of his long years prove, none more so than the large number of writings which came from his pen. Contemporary accounts reveal him as a man of prayer and of singular purity of conscience. His prompt beatification was generally expected, but obstacle after obstacle arose, particularly from regalistic politicians. At length Pius XI determined to overcome the opposition which still persisted even in modern days; on May 13, 1923 he declared the venerable Cardinal Blessed, on June 29, 1930 he raised him to the altar, and on September 9, 1931 he proclaimed St. Robert Bellarmine a Doctor of the Church.

Of other saintly Jesuits who labored in the Society during the time of Aquaviva over twenty-five have been beatified. All but one suffered martyrdom either in the Far East, in England, in France, or in Hungary; notice of them will be given in other chapters. The one *Beatus* who was not martyred was Blessed Bernardino Realini,[13] the apostle and patron of Lecce. Bernardino was born at Capri, December 1, 1530, studied medicine and law at Modena and Bologna, and after a successful governmental career, entered the Society of Jesus at the age of thirty-four. After ordination he worked so zealously at Naples that he was venerated as a saint. In 1574 Bernardino was sent to Lecce in Apulia to found a college; in that city he remained until his death, July 2, 1616. His holy life, courteousness, humility and charity caused him to be held in the estimation of the people as the "Father" of the city. Popes, kings, and the Emperor recommended themselves to his prayers or sought his advice. When he was about to die, a delegation of the citizens waited on him to beseech him to be the patron of the city and of the people in Heaven. In him natural virtue was elevated to truest sanctity. Blessed Bernardino Realini was beatified September 9, 1895.

It was the lives of these holy men which constituted a triumph most consoling for Aquaviva in the midst of the machinations of the malcontents and the attacks of extern enemies. Their sanctity, flowering from the Spiritual Exercises and guided by the prescriptions of the Institute, was the best proof of the value of both. These Saints bespoke holy brethren, fervent fellow religious, zealous companions, sure evidences of the healthy vigor of the order.

---

[13] Biography by Venturi, Rome (1895).

CHAPTER VIII

ROLLING BACK THE PROTESTANT TIDE

If today Austria, Hungary, Czecho-Slovakia, Poland, Lithuania, large parts of Southern Germany and Switzerland, almost the whole of the Rhineland, all of Westphalia, all of Belguim and a third at least of Holland, are considered Catholic lands, with a total Catholic population well over seventy million, the fact is due principally to the labors of the Jesuits in the Catholic Restoration, inaccurately called "The Counter Reformation." Up to the third quarter of the sixteenth century, the advance of the Protestants seemed irresistible. Much of the territory just cited was definitely in their hands; it seemed but a question of a few more years before the rest would be completely under their control. But then St. Peter Canisius appeared, leading a handful of Jesuits in a forlorn hope. Well might contemporaries have reckoned impossible his salvaging of anything; yet before the century was out, he and his brethren, waging a tireless warfare in classroom, in pulpit and in the arena of books, had won back province after province. The tide had been turned. It is rather strange that this great accomplishment of the Jesuits has often been but poorly appreciated by Catholic, even by Jesuit, writers, especially seeing that it has made a tremendous impression on Protestant writers, such as von Ranke and Macaulay. In lasting results it was greater even than the accomplishments of St. Francis Xavier.[1]

After the Religious Peace of Augsburg (1555) the Catholic princes determined to defend the ancient Faith of their territories by the very same means which they had been forced to concede to the Protestant princes in the latters' efforts to eject Catholicism and Catholics from their own states. If there was to be no toleration for the old religion in Hesse and Saxony, then neither was there to be toleration for the new creed in Austria and Bavaria. The Catholic princes in consequence forbade the public worship of the Lutherans and Calvinists, banished their ministers and admitted only the strictest Catholics to the canonries of the Cathedral chapters. Much more important was the task remaining, the revivifying, the rekindling, if need be, of the Catholic Faith. For that labor the princes and the bishops called upon the Jesuits and the

---

[1] Duhr, *Geschichte der Jesuiten in den Ländern deutscher Zunge*, Vols. I, II.

174

Capuchins. The Jesuits, because of their greater numbers and the wider diversity of their works, were able to take up a larger share of the task; the efforts of the Capuchins, however, formed a very important part of the Catholic Restoration.[2]

The first in effectiveness of the labors of the Jesuits, was the educational work of their thirty or more colleges. Of the products of these colleges Pastor observes: "A new era had opened when the highest offices, both in the Church and State, began to be filled by that new generation, which principally educated in the schools of the Jesuits, had received a strictly Catholic education and solid instruction, and with it clear principles and a strength of character which enabled them to comply with the tasks of the changed times and to maintain the inevitable struggle against their adversaries."[3] Now especially did the value of such educational institutions as the Collegium Germanicum and the College of Braunsberg become apparent. A new day had dawned for the old religion when the alumni of the Jesuit institutions became the occupants or the administrators of sees in all parts of the north, or the holders of the all-important canonries of the cathedral chapters.

In the equally vital literary field the Jesuit writers produced an impressive number of books and treatises in German and Latin; works on controversy, theology, asceticism, hagiography; besides collections of sermons, manuals of devotion, literary essays and scientific tractates. The works of St. Peter Canisius have already been noted. By his side in the apostolate of the pen labored Rethius, Hoffaeus, Scherer, Gretser, Tanner, his half-brother Dietrich Canisius, Thyraeus, Brillmacher, Peltan, Pontanus, the Italian Maggio, and the Spaniards, Gregory of Valentia and Torres. The literary output of many of them was in extent alone truly astonishing.

The educational and literary activities of the German Jesuits were equalled by their pastoral labors and the assistance which they rendered to the nuncios and the bishops in the reforming of the clergy and the laity. Much of their success in winning secular and regular clergy to a holier life came from their use of the Spiritual Exercises. Several fathers were called upon to be confessors to the Catholic princes and their families. It was a task accepted with the greatest reluctance and only after all sorts of regulations had been laid down to obviate entanglements in political and courtly affairs. The truly saintly lives of several members of the Austrian and Bavarian princely families stand as a tribute to their Jesuit confessors.[4]

---

[2] Cuthbert, O.S.F.C., *The Capuchins*, 2 Vols., London (1928).

[3] Pastor, *History of the Popes*, Vol. XXIII, p. 343.

[4] Duhr, *Geschichte der Jesuiten in den Ländern deutscher Zunge*, Vol. I, 685–712; II, part II, 205–299.

From 1588 onward occurred the restoration of the Faith in the Hapsburg lands of Upper and Lower Austria, Styria, Carinthia, Carniola and the Tyrol. The last district alone was strongly Catholic; elsewhere the Archduke Ferdinand encountered the bitterest opposition in his application of the Religious Peace of Augsburg. The Jesuits' part lay solely in the training of a better clergy and in the instruction of the laity. The case of Klagenfurt offers a measure of their success; that city in the beginning of the seventeenth century could count scarce a dozen Catholics, yet within forty years it had acquired a reputation as a stronghold of Catholicism. New colleges founded at Laybach (1588), Klagenfurt (1604), Innsbruck (1606) and Yagreb (1608) had an important influence on the restoration, as did the fact that all the higher education of the Tyrol was placed under the direction of the Jesuits. The University of Gratz (1536) with its higher school, its secondary school, and its college for poor students, became one of the strongest centers of the movement. The Crown-lands of Bohemia proved the hardest field for the Jesuits' endeavors; yet their efforts were not without results in the colleges of Prague, Brünn, Krumlau (1588) and Glatz (1597), nor were their numerous sermons preached both in Czech and German fruitless. Sodalities proved of special help; the pupils who had been sodalists in the colleges, later on during the Thirty Years' War almost to a man remained staunch champions of Catholicism.

In Bavaria the order attained its highest successes, owing to the support of Duke William, who among other gifts built for the Society a large college and the magnificent church of St. Michael in Munich. A new college was opened at Constance (1604), the University of Dillingen was founded for the Jesuits by Bishop Henry von Knöringen in 1607, and the seminary at Eichstatt was given to the fathers by Bishop von Gemmingen about the same time. At Ingolstadt the two leaders of the Catholic cause in the Thirty Years' War, the future Emperor Ferdinand II and Duke Maximilian the Great of Bavaria, were pupils of the Jesuits. The restoration of Catholicism in Donauwörth, one of the occasions of the Thirty Years' War, was the work of monks who had been trained for the most part by the Jesuits, and of the members of the Society themselves.

Franconia was another scene of the successful labors of the order. Here they assisted the Bishops of Würtzburg and Bamberg, and the Abbot of Fulda in the restoration of the Catholic religion in central Germany. It was largely owing to the missions of the Jesuits both in the cities and in the country districts that these regions became staunchly Catholic. In the Southwest of Germany, in Pfalz-Neuburg and in Alsace, the Catholics were strengthened and their ranks multiplied by the numbers converted by the zeal of the fathers. Colleges were established at

Molsheim (1593), Neuburg (1613), Hagenau (1615) and Ensisheim (1615). At Worms the opposition of the Protestants within the city and in the neighboring states to the introduction of the Jesuits was overcome by the protection of the Nuncio and the support of the Catholic residents of the city.

In the Rhineland, with the exception of the Lower Palatinate, a definitely Calvinistic state, the Faith had been preserved; though for a long period it stood in the greatest danger from the machinations of the apostate Archbishop of Cologne, Gebhard Truchsess, and his allies. The task of the Jesuits was to confirm the Catholics in their loyalty. They accomplished this to the extent that the Faith of the Rhinelanders has become proverbial. The colleges at Aachen, Trier, Cologne, Mainz, Coblenz and Heiligenstadt, and the seminary at Cologne were most active sources of the Catholic defense.

In Westphalia the dubious outlook for the old religion was only changed when staunch Catholic Bishops occupied the sees of Münster, Osnabrück and Paderborn. These prelates employed the Jesuits as their chief agents in the revivification of Catholicism; and in no place in the German lands were the pastoral efforts of the fathers more intensive and more successful. The colleges at Münster (1587), Paderborn (1597) and Hildesheim (1601) played their part in the restoration. The college of Münster in 1592 had 1,000 students; the college of Paderborn, refounded by Bishop von Fürstenberg in 1604, was in 1614 raised to the status of a university.

All these labors of the Jesuits were carried on in the teeth of the stiffest opposition. Once the Protestants realized that their foremost adversaries were to be found in these new religious, they left nothing undone to frustrate the Jesuits' efforts, if not to destroy the order completely. The banishment of the Jesuits was demanded in the Diets; street tumults were raised against them in Bohemia and in Aachen; the strongest pressure was brought to bear on Catholic princes to prevent their introducing the new order in their territories. Relentless and bitter attacks in press and pulpit raged unceasingly to discredit the Jesuit schools and to fix upon the members of the Society the evil reputation for the vilest crimes. This literary attack was answered pamphlet for pamphlet, though not always with the moderation which St. Peter Canisius continuously urged and which he himself practised. Opposition within the fold was not very great; and almost all of it came from worldly-minded or half-heretical ecclesiastics, who opposed their bishops in the matter of the Jesuits as they did in about everything else.

In Switzerland the Jesuits proved valued assistants to the Nuncios and the bishops in the task of reform and restoration. Particularly was it their privilege to labor with St. Francis de Sales, a former pupil of the

Jesuit college of Paris; under his direction the fathers established a college and a refuge at Thonon. The college at Lucerne, for which the citizens persisted in their request until the superiors yielded, was a success from the beginning. No less blessed were the pastoral labors of the fathers in the canton of Lucerne and in the neighboring districts, crowds flocked to their sermons and large numbers thronged the Communion rail. The five colleges at Lucern, Fribourg, Pruntrut, Constance and Thonon nourished the Faith of the Swiss youth. The secular priests trained by the Jesuits in the Swiss College of Milan, founded by St. Charles Borromeo, played a salutary part in the revival. The opposition of the Swiss Protestants against the Society was particularly strong: one canton forbade under pain of death the attendance of any Protestants at Jesuit colleges; while in the Valletillina the presence of Catholics at any Jesuit college in or out of the country was proscribed. The Bishop of Chur was prevented from bringing the Jesuits into his diocese. But the opposition always failed wherever the order obtained a foothold.

The part of Hungary free from Turkish domination at the end of the sixteenth century was practically a Protestant land. Before the end of the third decade of the next century, it was to be strongly Catholic again. The change came about largely through the educational and pastoral labors of the Jesuits. Archbishop Olahaus, Primate of Hungary, called the fathers to his side in 1559; colleges were established at Nagyszombat (1561) and Thurocz (1586). A most furious opposition arose on the part of the ascendent Calvinists; the Jesuit colleges were closed, their properties confiscated, and they themselves driven from the land. The fathers would not be turned from their task; at length after long struggles they were able, with the aid of the re-inspirited Hungarian Catholics and of the Hapsburg rulers to establish themselves permanently. The experiences of the college and seminary of Klausenberg (1584), with its checkered career of closings and openings depending on the fortunes of the Protestant or Catholic arms, were typical.

As in Germany and in Poland, one Jesuit stood out in the Catholic Restoration in Hungary; by an odd coincidence this defender of the Papacy like the other two bore the name of Peter. Peter Pázmány [5] was born October 4, 1570, at Nagyvarad, a Protestant; in 1583, owing to the influence of his Catholic stepmother and his Jesuit teachers, he became a Catholic. He entered the Society of Jesus four years later and after his noviceship was sent to the Roman College for his major studies. It was providential that he had as a professor, St. Robert Bellarmine, whose lectures on the *Controversies* were to serve him so well in later years. After three years of lecturing on philosophy and theology at Graz,

---

[5] Harney, S.J., "Cardinal Peter Pázmány," *Thought* (1936), Vol. XI, pp. 225–237.

Pázmány was sent to his native land at the request of the zealous Bishop Forgacs. Here he labored from 1601 to 1603 assisting the prelate in the pulpit and by his controversial writings. The next four years found him again lecturing at Graz; yet, despite the calls of the classroom, he managed to keep in the Hungarian conflict by his writings and translations. In 1607 Pázmány was permanently assigned to his native land as the helper and trusted advisor of the new Archbishop of Esztergom and Primate of Hungary, Forgacs. Almost at once he achieved such a reputation by his sermons as to merit the appellation, "The Hungarian Cicero"; his controversial works increased in volume and importance; and his defense of his order before the Diet of Pressburg was successful. Few of his labors had such important results for the Catholic Restoration as his apostolate among the Hungarian princely families, the apostacy of large numbers of which had caused such serious losses to Catholicism. Pázmány won back more than thirty of the foremost families among the Magyar magnates. In 1616 Pázmány left the Society of Jesus on his elevation to the burdensome position of Archbishop of Esztergom and Primate of Hungary. As he has always been listed as a son of St. Ignatius and since as Archbishop he chose his former brethren to be his chief auxiliaries, his subsequent labors deserve mention. In his new office he so inspired the Hungarian Catholics that at last they were able to obtain a majority in the national Diet. Two colleges, a seminary and a university were founded by him and entrusted to the Jesuits. The colleges were at Nagyszombat (1619) and Pozsony (1624); the seminary (1623) was the renowned Pazmaneum of Vienna, in which Hungarian clerics were to receive their training; the university was the Pázmány University, located first at Nagyszombat (1635) and later, after the liberation of Budapest, at that capital where it flourishes to this day. No one among the German or Hungarian hierarchies was more devoted to the Collegium Germanicum-Hungaricum than Archbishop Pázmány. He was assiduous in carrying out the decrees of the Council of Trent, in holding local and national synods, and in providing for the decent support of impoverished diocesan clergy. Urban VIII marked his approval of Pázmány's work by raising him to the Cardinalate on November 19, 1629. Controversy was one of Pázmány's constant occupations before his elevation to the primatial see. He wrote not only good doctrine but with such a style as to have exercised an asknowledged influence on Hungarian prose. Of all his books, *The Guide for Divine Truth* is the most important; such was its effect upon Magyar Lutherans that they sought the aid of their German co-religionists for a champion. The foreign apologist took ten years in composing a reply, to which Pázmány furnished a very prompt answer. The cardinal died March 19, 1637. The result of his apostolate has been summed up by one writer in these words: "He was born in Protestant Hungary and he died in Catholic Hungary"; [6] to him above all others, was such a result due.

In Poland the Jesuits continued in the forefront of the Catholic restoration. The support of King Stephan Báthory was continued by Sigismund III, one of their pupils. So numerous had the Polish Jesuits become—there was scarcely an important town in the land which did not possess a house of the Society—that in 1608 a division was made into the Polish and the Lithuanian provinces. In 1616 the former province maintained nine colleges, five residences and a novitiate; the latter province, two universities and eight colleges. These educational institutions extended their influence in an ever widening circle, since the leading state functionaries and the higher clergy, largely recruited from their alumni, brought the virile Catholicism of their college days into the conduct of the affairs of church and state to the great benefit of the old Faith.

The priestly labors of the Polish fathers continued to be fruitful. Sodalities, both of scholars and of citizens, were used by them for the deepening of faith and the intensifying of charity. Missions were preached in the remote frontiers of the Carpathians, Silesia, Hungary, Livonia and White Russia. A leading part was taken in the reunion of the Ruthenians, particularly by the faculty of the University of Vilna. In 1616 participation in the renovation of the Basilian monks occupied the fathers. St. Josaphat, Archimandrite of the reformed order, later Archbishop of Polozk, and finally a martyr, was a pupil of the Jesuits; as was William Rutski, the Archbishop of Kiev, another leading promoter of reunion.

The Polish Jesuits were not without their share of opposition. The Protestants of Danzig, Thorn and Riga sought by every means to stop the Society; as did their Polish confrères, whose diminishing numbers only intensified their hostility. In 1606 a most threatening attack was made by the party of Rokosz; it was only defeated when the venerable Skarga rose to the defense of his order. In 1614 there appeared in Cracow one of the most notorious of the attacks on the Society of Jesus, the "Monita Secreta Societatis Jesu," [7] which purported to reveal the secret instructions directing the machinations of the Jesuits. It was a palpable forgery, the work of revenge of an ex-Jesuit, Zahorowski. A complete refutation was made by Gretser in 1618. However, it has seen much service in all parts of Europe, despite the fact that not one reputable historian has anything but contempt for the forgery. Peter Skarga to the end was the leading champion of the Catholic cause. All Poland

---

[6] Bangha, "Pázmány," Cath. Encyl., Vol. XI, p. 596.

[7] Cf. Appendix V, "Alleged Secret Intructions of the Jesuits."

mourned when death came to him September 24, 1612; his eulogist, the Dominican Berkowski, hailed him as another Elias. To this day his memory is held in reverence by his countrymen.

Russia was the scene of Jesuit endeavors in the early years of Aquaviva's generalate. Gregory XIII sought to mediate between Stephen Báthory and Ivan the Terrible in the hope of furthering his cherished plans for defense against the Turks and for reunion of the Russian schismatics. For the difficult negotiations he chose Possevino as the man best informed on Baltic affairs.[8] In 1581 the Jesuit journeyed to the Northeast, overcame Báthory's prejudices and distrust of his mission, and crossed into the dominion of the Tsar. Six interviews with Ivan the Terrible and his advisors convinced Possevino that the question of reunion depended on the conclusion of a peace with Poland. The peace discussions took place in a remote frontier town under the greatest handicaps, not the least of which was the intense cold of a bitter Russian winter. Hardships and sufferings bore down upon Possevino; but as the moving spirit of the conference, he kept to the task until a ten years' armistice was agreed upon. Braving still further the rigors of the climate, the Papal envoy then hastened to the court of the Tsar to present the armistice and to press for the reunion. For all his pains, he received nothing but empty promises; indeed, personally, he had to withstand the rage of the terrible Tsar. During the debate on reunion held in the Kremlin, February 21, 1582, the Tsar in the presence of his court began to speak in a most insulting manner of the Pope. Possevino's calm answers only infuriated Ivan so that he raised his scepter, the very scepter with which he had killed his own son a few months before, against the Pope's representative. Possevino was not to be frightened, he stood his ground and faced out the unbridled passion of the brutal bully. At the conclusion of the interviews, all that could be obtained was a meaningless embassy to the Pope.

Some years later, after the death of Ivan the Terrible, when the False Demetrius made his bid for the Russian throne, two Jesuits were chaplains with the Polish troops of his army. This fact has given rise to the false assertion that the Jesuits and the Pope used the impostor as a puppet to further their ambitions. The fact of the matter is that the Pope and the Jesuits, as many others in Europe, were completely taken in by the pretender's claims and were really convinced of his legitimacy. They supported him in the hope that with a Catholic Tsar the much desired reunion would be achieved.[9]

The better fortunes of Catholicism in the Low Countries, following

---

[8] Pierling, *Antonii Possevini missio moscovitica*, Paris (1883); *Le Saint Siège, la Pologne et Moscou*, Paris (1885).

[9] Pastor, *History of the Popes*, Vol. XXVI, p. 220.

upon the advent of Alexander Farnese as Viceroy, were advanced by the labors of the Jesuits.[10] In the towns and cities won back from the Calvinists, colleges and residences were reopened and the fathers again vigorously labored for the restoration of the old Faith in the peoples' hearts. In the armies of the Viceroy, himself a devoted friend of the order, several Jesuits served as chaplains. The Belgian hierarchy, especially the Prince Bishop of Liége, von Grosbeck, and his successor, Duke Ernest of Bavaria, welcomed the cooperation of the fathers in the work of reform. As elsewhere, members of the order placed special emphasis on catechetical instruction. As early as 1566, Coster had translated the Catechism of St. Peter Canisius, in 1609 Makeblyde produced at Antwerp his own catechism in Flemish. The pupils of the Jesuits shared in the good work, the students of one college instructing poor children in as many as thirty or forty classes. The Flemish Jesuits embraced the ministry of preaching with such zeal that in one year 15,206 sermons were delivered by them.

Such labors increased even more under the rule of the pious sovereigns, the Archduke Albert and the Archduchess Isabella. New colleges and new residences were opened in all parts of the Catholic Netherlands. In 1616 a division of the province had to be made, consisting of the Flandro-Belgic province for the Flemish regions, with 617 members and 15 houses, and the Franco-Belgic province for the Walloon sections, with 653 members and 16 houses. Almost all of these houses were colleges, the educational work of which proved most efficacious for the Catholic Restoration. The Jesuits enjoyed a high reputation as teachers; to their classes came practically all the sons of the nobility and of the well-to-do middle classes. Yet poor and destitute students took their places by the side of the more fortunate, for the fathers made generous provisions for their education. Douai at this period had an enrollment of 1,600 students, among whom were to be found 400 in the Arts, 600 in Philosophy and 100 in Theology. Each college usually maintained 4 sodalities, 1 for the pupils, 1 for younger children, 1 for youths and 1 for adults. Large memberships testified to the popularity of these pious confraternities, while the numerous good works undertaken proved their value. The colleges established along the French border became effective barriers against the inroads of Calvinism.

In the revival of Catholic art which succeeded upon the victories of Farnese, the Jesuits participated especially in the erection of several fine churches. The fact that here as elsewhere most of the Jesuit churches were erected in the Baroque style, has led to the misnomer of the "Jesuit" style of architecture and to the fiction of the Jesuits deliberately

---

[10] Poncelet, *C. de J. dans les Anciens Pays-Bas*, Vols. I, II.

using Baroque as part of the Catholic propaganda. The frequent use of Baroque in Jesuit churches was merely coincidental, since most of these edifices were built when that style was enjoying wide popularity. That the fathers of the Society had no exclusive predilection for Baroque, is proven by the beautiful Gothic churches erected by them at Münster, Coblenz, and Molsheim.

Much of the order's progress in the Low Countries was owing to the wise guidance and farseeing rule of Oliver Manare. After valuable service in Italy, France and Germany, Manare, a native of Douai, returned to his home country as Visitor of the Belgian province; from 1585 until his death his labors as Visitor, Provincial and subject, in founding colleges, strengthening the order, and providing for the spiritual and intellectual development of the younger brethren justly merited for him the name: "Father of the Belgian province." Among his associates, who wrought so successfully by voice and pen against the Calvinists, must be listed Franz Coster, controversialist; Charles Scribani, writer; Herman Hugo, ascetical writer; Herbert Rosweyde, forerunner of the Bollandists; the Spaniard, Martin del Rio, jurist and theologian; and above all, Leonard Lessius, one of the outstanding theologians of the Jesuit order.

The successes of the Flemish Catholics were balanced by the unhappy fate of the Dutch Catholics, who were forced to endure most violent persecutions. The Mass was proscribed; the severest penalties were visited on any one daring to harbor a priest; while the sending of children abroad to Catholic and Jesuit schools was absolutely prohibited. The Dutch Catholics were driven to the catacombs; yet for all their trials, their faith burned only the stronger. In 1592, two Dutch Jesuits, Leonius and Duyst, began, at the risk of their lives, to labor in the United Provinces. Obliged to steal from place to place in disguise, they had to say Mass and administer the Sacraments at night. One priest was forced to change his residence eight times in twelve days. In 1611 the Dutch mission was organized; it consisted of 14 fathers, dispersed in 12 places. Notwithstanding the difficulties and perils of their wandering existence, these fathers were able to reap a glorious harvest, one of them converting 200 Anabaptists, another 300.

The French Jesuits of the period persevered through the bitterest storms of Huguenot and Gallican opposition to become a most potent element in the Catholic Restoration.[11] In the struggle between Henry IV and the Holy League they were placed in a most difficult position; whatever action they took would bring down the enmity of one side or the other. The League's cause seemed the natural choice; yet Auger,

---

[11] Fouqueray, *C. de J. en France*, Vols. II and III.

the foremost French Jesuit, strove to keep his brethren aloof from all parties, fearing the disastrous consequences of political connections. Aquaviva strongly warned the French fathers against mixing in political concerns and punished severely two of the most eminent among them, Mathieu and Sammier, when their zeal for the League overstepped the proper bounds. With few exceptions the fathers faithfully adhered to their rule and to the commands of the General, those at Bordeaux preferring exile to disobedience.

Gallican enemies of the order sought to implicate the Jesuits in Jean Chastel's attempt on the life of Henry IV (December 24, 1595). There was not even a shadow of complicity. To the end, despite torture and even more despicable means, Chastel maintained that he had acted alone. All that could be said was that once Chastel had attended lectures of the Jesuits. Without an opportunity for defense the Society was banished from France, its properties ordered confiscated, and attendance at Jesuit schools abroad forbidden. Something more was needed, however, to bolster up the charges; the sight of a Jesuit on the scaffold would give concrete embodiment to the allegations. A victim was found in the former teacher of Chastel, Father Guignard,[12] the librarian of the College of Clermont, in whose room books on tyrannicide had been found. The innocence of the priest was beyond doubt; yet Guignard was condemned and executed on the very same day. There was to be no delay that might possibly frustrate the judicial murder. Henry IV did not believe in the complicity of the order; still he took no steps to prevent its condemnation. Many influential Frenchmen, however, did protest openly against the outrage. Pope Clement VIII thought seriously of breaking off the negotiations for the reconciliation of Henry IV, a course from which he was dissuaded by Aquaviva. The General begged the Pontiff to ignore the persecution of the order, lest the good of the Church might be jeopardized in the failure of the reconciliation.

The battle over the Jesuits was fought in the literary arena as well as in the courts. Étienne Pasquier wrote against the members of the Society as the enemies of France; Antoine Arnauld assailed them as authors of doctrines hostile to the state and as teachers contemptuous of real learning. The replies of the Fathers Richeome and Armand attracted the interest of Henry IV; but he was especially impressed by the defense made by the celebrated Jesuit controversialist and preacher, Pierre Coton, whom he highly esteemed. At length the King agreed to the recall of the Jesuits and issued a decree to that effect, September 1, 1603.

So many restrictions were placed upon the activities of the order in the

---

[12] Pastor, *History of the Popes*, Vol. XXIII, pp. 115-117; Fouqueray, *C. de J. en France*, Vol. II, pp. 379-411.

decree, that Aquaviva hesitated to accept it and only the earnest pleas of the Nuncio and Coton induced him to trust the monarch. His confidence was not misplaced. Henry IV adopted a more favorable attitude toward the order; he chose Coton not only as the court preacher but as his own confessor, he contributed very generously to the founding of the College of La Flèche, and gave his permission for the establishment of four other colleges. When the Parliament of Paris protested to him against his favorable treatment of the Jesuits, the monarch answered with his celebrated defense of the Society of Jesus.

The assassination of Henry IV by Ravillac, on May 14, 1610, afforded the Gallican-Huguenot clique another opportunity in their warfare against the order. This time the teachings of the Jesuits were alleged as making them accomplices in the deed. In proof the book of the Spanish Jesuit, Mariana, *De Rege et Regis Institutione* (Toledo 1599), was cited, for in it the author had put forth, but only as his own personal opinion, that a tyrant might lawfully be assassinated. The book meant nothing to Ravillac since he was unable to read Latin. As a matter of fact in the very year of its publication, Aquaviva had condemned the work and had ordered its destruction. That there might be no question as to the attitude of the Society of Jesus, the General, on July 6, 1610, forbade under pain of excommunication any member of the order to maintain either publicly or privately, either as a teacher or as an advisor, either by word of mouth or in writing, that a private person of whatsoever condition, could, on any plea whatsoever, either kill kings or princes, or make any attempt on their life. On August 14, he followed this with a prohibition of all discussion whatsoever of Mariana's book. The General's condemnation was of course completely ignored by the enemies of the order. A prolonged warfare of pamphlets raged over the guilt of the order. The Society's cause was successfully defended by Coton in his *Lettre déclaratoire de la doctrine des Jésuites* and by his *Déclaration de l'Institute des Jésuites*.

That the enemies of the order aimed at the Jesuits only as a point of attack against a greater objective, the Papacy, became evident when their agent, the Parlement of Paris, condemned St. Robert Bellarmine's treatise on the Pope's power in temporal matters, written in refutation of Barclay's book against the Papacy. This last book, though on the Index, was permitted free circulation in France. The attacks on the order increased to such vehemence by 1612 as to frighten some of the French Jesuits into the weak expedient of placating Parlement. The Provincial of the province of France, Baltazar, and six other Jesuits issued a declaration stating that they conformed to the doctrines of the School of the Sorbonne even in that which concerned the sacred person of the kings, the maintaining of the royal authority and the Gallican liberties guarded through all time in the kingdom.[13] Aquaviva sharply rebuked Baltazar for his pusillanimity. On the other hand, French Jesuit writers, such as Eudaemon-Joannes, Gaultier and Sirmond, labored unceasingly with their pens in the defense of the Papacy. Coton continued by his preachings and his writings to be a tower of strength for the order.

The Gallicans eventually defeated their own purposes; their very bitterness served to win for the Jesuits the esteem of large sections of the French people. The best elements of Catholic France, Cardinals and members of the hierarchy rallied to their support. Several bishops requested Jesuits to accompany them on the visitations of their diocese and to conduct popular missions in their jurisdictions. Missions given in remote districts often resulted in the restoration of the Faith in regions where it had seemed destined to disappear; the work of the Jesuits in the Cervennes, in the diocese of Mende, is an instance. Throughout France the fathers worked with marked success in the converting of Calvinists, especially by disputations with the Calvinist ministers. In this field Coton stood foremost. Two Jesuits, one a priest, Blessed James Salès, and the other a lay-brother, William Saultemouche, made the supreme sacrifice of their lives in defense of their belief in the Blessed Sacrament, when they were done to death by a Calvinistic mob at Aubenas on February 6, 1593. The writings of Gontry, Veron, de Bordes, du Duc, Richeome, Arnoux and, above all, Coton, contributed much not only to the defense of Catholicism, but to the rich revival of piety and asceticism which flourished in the France of the early seventeenth century. Worthy of mention also is the work of Coton as the royal confessor to Louis XIII; that this King's life was more blameless than that of any French monarch since St. Louis, was largely owing to the wise guidance of his youth by Coton.

In France too the Jesuit educational work was an outstanding factor in the Catholic revival. The improvement in morals and the increase of popular devotions were in a large measure attributable to the good priests who as boys had been trained in the colleges of the Jesuits. One need seek no further than St. Francis de Sales for an example. The successes of the French Jesuits in their schools resulted first from the *Ratio Studiorum* and then from the devotion of priests and non-priests to the apostolate of the classroom. In the sad state of higher studies, a consequence of the terrible Huguenot wars—a decline especially marked in the University of Paris—the continued existence of one university, that of Bourges, was owing to the fathers. The rapid increase of the French houses of the Society warranted the grouping of the French provinces into a fifth Assistancy. The extent of the work of the French

---

[13] Fouqueray, *C. de J. en France*, Vol. III, p. 289 ff.

Jesuits may be gauged from the statistics of 1616 when there were 5 provinces: France with 9 colleges and 3 residences, Aquitaine with 7 colleges and 1 residence, Lyons with 12 colleges, Toulouse with 10 colleges, and Champagne with 9 colleges and 1 residence.

The English Jesuits waged their desperate battle for the Faith in the very shadow of the gallows.[14] Seven fathers, Bl. Thomas Cottam, Bl. Robert Southwell, Bl. Hugh Walpole, Bl. Francis Page, Bl. Edward Oldcorne, Bl. Ralph Ashley, Bl. Thomas Garnet, and one lay-brother, Bl. Ralph Owen, were martyred after excruciating tortures. Many others of the Society were held for long periods in prison where death brought relief to the torturings and the unspeakable conditions of their confinement. The journal of one of these priests, John Gerard, who managed to escape to the Continent, offers a vivid picture of the hazards of the perilous English mission.[15]

On the continent Persons labored untiringly for the restoration of Catholicism in his native land. His efforts were not always wise nor opportune; but of their sincerity there can be no question. Like Cardinal Allen and several other exiles, who placed faith above nationalism, Persons looked for help through foreign intervention; he favored the Armada and became a leader of the pro-Spanish party. As the years passed on and he grew more and more out of touch with the home situation, his plans became less suited to the situation; but not for a moment did his zeal for the old Faith of England abate. Owing to him, colleges for the training of English priests were founded at Valladolid, Seville and Madrid.[16] To him also must be credited the renowned college of St. Omer's where the sons of English gentlemen obtained the learning denied to them at home. The work of St. Omer's can scarcely be overestimated; many of the leading English, Irish and American Catholics of the seventeenth and eighteenth centuries received their education within its walls; Persons rendered good service in composing the difficulties which arose between the students of the English seminaries and their Latin Jesuit masters, difficulties largely the result of different viewpoints and temperaments. On April 15, 1610 Robert Persons died at Rome. Whatever were his mistakes, his labors and devotion have made him one of the foremost English champions of the Catholic cause.[17]

In the lamentable divisions which split the ranks of English Catholics

---

[14] Foley, *Records of the English Province*, London (1877).

[15] Morris, *The Life of Father John Gerard of the Society of Jesus*, London (1881).

[16] Hicks, "Father Persons, S.J., and the Seminaries in Spain," *The Month* (1931), Vol. CLVII, CLVIII.

[17] Pollen, "Robert Persons, S.J.," *Cath. Encyl.*, Vol. XI, pp. 729–731. Unfortunately there exists no biography of Persons.

at home, the Jesuits were unfortunately entangled. This should be said for all parties, that it is understandable how the tenacity with which these brave men clung to the Faith of their fathers would extend to their personal views as to the methods best suited for its preservation. Opposition to the leading part played by the Jesuits led to the formation of two factions, the Jesuit party and the secular priests' party. It should be noted that most of the secular priests supported the Jesuit policies.[18] The factions clashed bitterly twice in the reign of Elizabeth, first in the disputes of the priest prisoners of Wisbeach, and secondly in the strife over the office of the Archpriest Blackwell. The last quarrel deserves some notice. The death of Cardinal Allen left the English Catholics leaderless. There were no bishops who naturally would have taken command. Persons, despite the contrary statement often made, labored for the appointment of bishops; [19] and so too did the party of the secular priests, who hoped in the appointment of one of their number to increase their influence at the expense of the Jesuits. Clement VIII deemed the times inauspicious for the appointment of a bishop and created the office of an archpriest, who was to reside in England, to govern with the aid of a council and to confer on matters of policy with the superior of the Jesuits. In 1593 George Blackwell, a secular priest and a friend of the Jesuits, was selected for the position.[20] The strongest opposition to Blackwell, to his conduct of the office and to the influence of the Jesuits arose among a minority of the secular priests, known as the "Appellents"; some of the extremest among them did not hesitate to seek aid even of the Elizabethan government. Numerous pamphlets from both sides added fuel to the fire, the bitterness of the secular minority being matched by the intemperateness of the Jesuit, Lister. Persons, too, unfortunately wrote his replies in a rancorous spirit. The quarrel was carried to Rome, where in 1602 the Roman Inquisition handed down its decision: the charge of schism against the Appellents was declared unfounded, the Archpriest in the future had not to seek the advice of the Jesuits, nor was his office to be abolished, the Jesuits were not to be recalled, nor was the Society to be removed from its English colleges on the continent, and all negotiations with the heretics to the injury of Catholics were prohibited. Henry Garnet, the Jesuit superior, issued a circular asking his brethren to live in peace and concord with the secular clergy.

The advent of James I brought no relief to Catholics. Several of the

[18] Hicks, "Blessed John Southworth and His Times," *The Month* (1930), Vol. CLV, p. 352.

[19] Pollen, "The Politics of English Catholics during the Reign of Queen Elizabeth," *The Month* (1902), Vol. C, p. 183.

[20] Pollen, *The Institution of the Archpriest Blackwell*, London (1916).

persecuted body, despairing of any ending of their intolerable burdens, began to think of violent remedies. The Jesuits under Garnet, even at the loss of their popularity, strove to dissuade their suffering co-religionists from such courses. Hardly a year was to pass before Garnet was innocently to be involved in just such a violent attempt, the Gunpowder Plot. Knowledge of the conspiracy came to him principally through the confessional; Catesby, one of the plotters, revealed the conspiracy to a Jesuit in confession, granting the priest the permission to consult his superior. Both priests felt themselves powerless to act in the case, persuaded that the danger of breaking the seal of confession prevented disclosure on their part. On the discovery of the plot, Garnet was arrested; after a trial which was a complete mockery of justice, the Jesuit superior was condemned and executed on May 3, 1606.[21]

The Jesuits were foremost in opposition to the efforts of James I to impose on his Catholic subjects an oath of allegiance which in conscience they could not take. This heretical oath, drawn up by an apostate priest and an ex-Jesuit, Christopher Perkins, was so phrased as to give the appearance of orthodoxy. Non-theologians might not perceive its true meaning, disputes would arise; and all the time, the government could hypocritically repudiate any intention of injuring the Faith of Catholics. The oath did attain one objective, it split the ranks of the Catholics into two bitter factions. The Archpriest Blackwell, when pressure was brought to bear upon him after his arrest, sought to temporize, even to the extent of approving the oath after its condemnation by Rome. A second condemnation came from the Papacy; and Paul V directed St. Robert Bellarmine and Persons to send earnest exhortations to Blackwell against the oath. James I, who fancied himself a great theologian, attempted a refutation of the two Papal briefs and the letter of Bellarmine, roundly boasting that he had given the great Catholic controversialist a sound thrashing. The Cardinal's answer easily disposed of the ridiculous effusion, revealing its distortions and deliberate falsehoods.[22] The royal thinker, heedless of the cautions of his best friends, returned to the lists and in his second venture not only defended the oath to his own satisfaction, but wandered afield to attack several Catholic doctrines and to prove that the Pope was Anti-Christ. At the request of Paul V, St. Robert made a second reply, much to the discomfiture of the disputatious monarch. During the rest of James' reign,

---

[21] Pastor, *History of the Popes*, XXVI, pp. 129–157; Foley, *Records of the English Province S.J.*, Vol. IV, pp. 1–192; Pollen, "The Gunpowder Plot," *Cath. Encycl.*, Vol. VII, pp. 81–84; Kurtscheid, *A History of the Seal of Confession* (Eng. trans. by Marks), St. Louis (1927), pp. 156–161, discussion of Garnet and the Seal.

[22] Brodrick, *Blessed Robert Bellarmine*, Vol. II, c. XXII, XXIII, XXIV. The whole question of the oath is treated.

the English Jesuits were forced to pursue their ministry in constant fear of the pursuivants, by whose discovery they faced the certainty of long imprisonment or of a cruel death.

The Scotch Jesuits had to brave even greater perils than their English brethren; anyone in Scotland might arrest a Jesuit and even kill him if he resisted. Yet several of them faced out the hatred of the Presbyterian majority and remained to strengthen their fellow Catholics. Others in the Scots College at Pont-à-Mousson, trained priests to keep alive the Faith in the kingdom of the north. The most notable among the Scotch Jesuits was Bl. John Ogilvie, the martyr.[23] In the nine short months in which he labored in Scotland, he gained back many to the old religion. He was apprehended, tortured most cruelly, and hanged as a traitor at Glasgow, March 10, 1615. His patience, courage and gaiety in the midst of his excruciating torturings, wrung admiration even from his judges.

Truly inspiring is the heroic devotion of the Irish Jesuits,[24] whether daily risking their lives to keep the people true to the heritage of St. Patrick, or training with unflagging zeal in their continental schools the lads who were to return as priests to their native land. Among them the most striking character was the lay-brother Dominic O'Collins, a nobleman by birth, the head of his clan, who, when dispossessed of his lands because of his loyalty to his Faith and Motherland, enlisted as an officer in the armies of the League and of Spain that he might fight in the defense of Catholicism. Towards middle life, he abandoned the brilliant prospects of his military career to enter the Society of Jesus as a humble lay-brother. Everyone was edified by the sight of the handsome former officer and nobleman serving the table of the College of Santiago de Compostela. In 1602 he was sent to his native land, but hardly had he arrived when he was captured at Dunboy, tortured and executed at Youghal, October 31, 1602. Some of the Irish Jesuits had to spend long years in prison; others led the hunted life of fugitive priests on the barren mountains or in the bogs.

In the all important work of keeping alive the race of priests, the Irish Jesuits played an important part by their colleges at Lisbon, Salamanca, Valladolid, Santiago, and Seville. How effective the work of these colleges was, may be judged from the record of the students of the first thirty years of the college of Salamanca: from the ranks of these exiled scholars came a primate of all Ireland, 4 Archbishops, 5 bishops, 9 provincials of religious orders, 30 martyrs, 120 distinguished writers and 40 doctors of divinity and professors. It is worth a passing notice

---

[23] Brown, *John Ogilvie*, London (1925).

[24] Hogan, *Ibernia Ignatiana*, Dublin (1880); *Distinguished Irishmen of the Sixteenth Century*, London (1894).

that not only the Spanish royalty and the nobility contributed to the support of these colleges, but also the poor of Spain. The fishermen of Galicia were granted permission to fish on six Sundays and holydays in the year so that the proceeds from the sale of their catch might be devoted to the Irish colleges. In 1616, the number of Irish Jesuits totaled 82; of whom 38 were in Ireland, 18 in Spain, 9 in Portugal, 7 in Belgium, and 1 each in Mexico, Paraguay, Austria, Bavaria, Italy and France.

In summary, the Jesuits fought in all parts of the far-flung battle-line of the Catholic Restoration. They saved Southern and Western Germany, Hungary, Bohemia, Poland and Belgium to the Faith; they led the Papal cause in France; they strengthened the Catholic minorities in the dark hour of persecution in Holland, England and Scotland; they helped in the preservation of Catholicism in Ireland.

CHAPTER IX

EDUCATION AND LEARNING

In the previous chapters the origins and the early development of the educational work of the Society of Jesus have been described. It was seen that although, in his original idea, St. Ignatius had not contemplated the founding of an order of teaching religious, yet before he had finished with the writing of the Constitutions, he had made the education of youth one of the primary works of his sons. Thus did he declare that among the labors especially proper to the Society of Jesus were the teaching of catechism to children and to the ignorant, the lecturing on philosophy and theology in universities, and the instructing of youths in grammar schools and colleges. The fourth part of the Constitution was devoted by him to the subject of education; it is the longest and the most perfectly arranged division of the document. The College of Messina, coming near the close of St. Ignatius' life, was one of the first ventures of his order in the field of secular education; in its staff and organization the founder took a very special interest. The remarkable increase of the Jesuit colleges has already been noted: how the demand far exceeded the resources of the fathers, and how, at the end of the sixteenth century, in Europe alone, Jesuits were educating boys and young men in over a hundred colleges. It is now in place to describe the organization of the studies of these colleges and the composing of the educational code of the Jesuits, the *Ratio Studiorum*, which was to make their colleges the most efficient educational institutions of the next two centuries.[1] In the beginning no uniform system of studies was followed, but the plan of instruction in each school was adapted to the traditions of the locality in which it stood. Some improvements were made in keeping with the principles of the Fourth Part of the Constitutions; but these were considered not to be enough and the demand for a common code of studies and methods arose on all sides from both teachers and superiors.

It is worth noting, in passing, that the assignment of a large part of the members of the order exclusively to the teaching of youth made the Society of Jesus the first religious order to adopt this education of youth

---

[1] Cf. Bibliography for literature on the Ratio Studiorum and Jesuit Education.

as a special ministry whereby it might attain its end, the glory of God and the salvation of souls. Other orders, long before the Jesuits, had engaged in the work of education, but their participation was accidental to the primary object of their particular institutes. Marvelous things had been accomplished by the Benedictine monks and the Irish monks, not only in the preservation of the culture of the past and in the forwarding of it in their learned studies, but also in their teaching in the monastic schools. Educational work, however, was not the first purpose of their existence; in fact most monasteries in the late Middle Ages maintained no extern schools at all. The Order of Preachers adopted teaching more explicitly as a part of their apostolate, but their educational work was restricted to the higher fields of theology and philosophy, in which their accomplishments have been unsurpassed. St. Ignatius went further when he placed the teacher of literature or science on a par with the preacher, the confessor or the missionary. His sons in this new apostolate have so carried out the wishes of their founder as to warrant Professor Paulsen's observation that the Society of Jesus in a special sense is a teaching order or a school order.

The fourth part of the Constitutions contained only general regulations as regards the education of secular students. St. Ignatius promised that a more complete system would be devised later on: "A number of points will be treated of separately in some document approved by the General Superior." [2] Claudius Aquaviva was to give that promise actuality in the *Ratio Studiorum*.

In the Fourth General Congregation (1581) twelve fathers representing various nationalities were delegated to carry out the prescription of St. Ignatius. Little however seems to have been accomplished. Three years later Aquaviva took the positive step of calling to Rome six experienced schoolmen for the specific task of drawing up a uniform schedule of studies. The members of the commission were: Juan Azor (Spain), Gaspar Gonzalez (Portugal), Peter Buys (Austria), Antonio Guisani (Upper Germany), Stephan Tucci (Rome) and James Tyre (France); [3] different provinces and nationalities were thus represented that due consideration might be given to the special problems of each country. The committee spent nine months at their task, devoting as much as three hours a day to discussion. Every source was drawn upon: the best authors on education were consulted; the regulations and customs of universities and colleges, particularly those of the Roman College, were studiously examined; and the observations and recommendations sent in from all parts of the Society were carefully considered. At

---

[2] Const., P. IV, c. CIII, Decl. A.

[3] It is of passing interest to note that the representative of France, James Tyre, was a Scotsman by birth.

least three complete plans of studies previously drawn up by Jesuits, were of the greatest assistance to the fathers. The first scheme was the composition of Nadal, made from 1548–1552 for the College of Messina; as St. Ignatius was alive when it was drawn up it may be surmised that he had some share in its elaboration. Nadal's talents, his prudence, above all, his education at the University of Paris, lent weight to the plan. The second document was an adaptation of the above plan which had been sent to the Roman College. The last program was the most important of the three; it was the fruit of the genius of Ledesma, the prefect of the Roman College, a scholar of Alcalá, Paris and Louvain, a teacher for twelve years in the Roman College. Ledesma's plan contained in outline practically all the provisions for classical studies later to be set down in the *Ratio Studiorum*. These schemata were not the only ones considered; still extant are some fragmentary schedules which had been already worked out for individual Jesuit colleges in Italy, France, Spain, Portugal and Germany, one of which has been attributed to St. Peter Canisius. The basis of all planning and discussion was always Part IV of the Constitutions.

In August 1585, after nine months of unremitting toil, the tentative plan was ready. Aquaviva submitted the document to the criticism of the professors of the Roman College, as well as to his own and the Assistants' examination. The more searching test of actual experiment then followed. The scheme was sent to each Provincial with a letter ordering him to choose at least five eminent and experienced scholars of his jurisdiction to examine and criticise the proposed program. Each member of these various provincial committees was first to consider the provisions of the document privately and then meet with the other members for joint examination at least three times a week. After thorough scrutiny and experimentation, each provincial committee was to send to Rome a summary of their opinions. This first document was in the nature of a sketch or treatise rather than a code of rules and practices, which the final edition of the *Ratio* was to be.

As the reports and suggestions came into Rome, they were examined by the leading professors of the Roman College and by three of the original commission. A second plan was then drawn up and, after examination by the General and the Assistants, was sent in 1591 to the provinces for experimentation. This document was entitled *Ratio atque Institutio Studiorum*; it was the first real Ratio. The Provincials and the delegates to the Fifth General Congregation (1593–1594) reported on the merits of this later plan; among the changes asked, was the abridgment of the program. At last, in 1599, after every effort had been made to fashion as perfect a system as was possible, fifteen years after the inception of the task, the final plan was approved and published, the

Ratio atque Institutio Studiorum, as it has become generally known.

The *Ratio* presents a code of rules divided into four categories: the rules for executives, for professors of theology, for professors of philosophy, and for professors of literature. The rules for executives comprise the regulations for the Provincial, the rector of the college and the prefect of studies. The entire management of the college with all powers of government is placed in the hands of the rector, thus securing the benefits of firm rule and single policy. Yet to forestall arbitrariness, the rector must seek the advice of the consultors; and all, teachers, masters and students, have free recourse to the Provincial. The direct charge of the classes, the curricula and the students is given to the prefect of studies, whose task is to see that the system operates with the best possible efficiency. In the rules for the professors, whether of higher or of lower studies, there are sets of common regulations and series of specific prescriptions for the individual professors of the various classes.

Organization of studies, the primary virtue of the Ratio, made for a definite objective; that was the education of the whole man on a Christian basis. The fault of the university education of the later Middle Ages was an overemphasis on philosophical speculation; the fault of the education of the Renaissance was an exaggeration of humanistic studies. St. Ignatius and the authors of the Ratio sought to combine the best features of both systems in their programme: the lower classes would impart a cultural training according to the best traditions of Christian humanism, the higher classes would train the intellect according to the best thought of Aristotle and St. Thomas. A consideration of the proximate purposes of each class will show how these ends were attained. In the lower divisions Latin and Greek were the basis of the studies; geography and history were treated, but only as complements of the classics. There were usually five classes which with their specific objectives were: Lower Grammar (a knowledge of rudiments and elements of the languages); Middle Grammar (a wider knowledge of grammar, with simple readings); Superior Grammar (a complete knowledge of the grammar, with more advanced readings and with practice in versification); Humanities (advanced readings for fluency and command of the languages as a preparation for eloquence, with some erudition and a preliminary training in rhetorical precepts); Rhetoric (a complete study of rhetoric with oratorical and poetic composition). This plan of classical studies was not an iron-bound prescription to be followed slavishly, but admitted of adaptations to suit the varying needs of place and time. The superiors in their rules were instructed to make such changes when they were warranted.

The Ratio has received its share of gainsaying. Critics often allege that it overemphasizes Latin and neglects the mother tongue, that it makes scarcely any provision for history, and that it completely ignores elementary education. Many of such complaints arise from the mistake of reading modern ideas into the minds of the people of the centuries past.

The emphasis which the Ratio of 1599 placed on Latin certainly would be undue in a modern curriculum, but in the sixteenth and seventeenth centuries it was quite fitting. Then Latin was the universal language of Western civilization, particularly the language of diplomacy and of the law codes. So vital was Latin in the life of the times, that for anyone who lacked a fluency in it, a career either in the State or in the Church, or any participation in the life of the higher intellectual circles, was unthinkable. The best Protestant schools of the day set a similar value on Latin, conducting academic exercises and dramatic performances in that language, even sometimes levying fines against the use of the vernacular. The charge of neglecting the mother tongue might as easily be levelled at the Protestant educational systems as at the Ratio. The fact of the matter is that in the Jesuit colleges taken as a whole and over the period of years to the Suppression, the mother tongue was not neglected; as the demand warranted it, it received greater consideration. As early as 1560 Nadal urged the Cologne Jesuits to cultivate diligently the German language and to seek out the best means of teaching it; [4] in 1567 he repeated the same advice to the fathers at Mainz. The Bohemian Jesuits in 1600 opened a private academy for the study of Czech.[5] Several German Jesuits in the early decades of the seventeenth century proposed the establishment of a society for the improvement of their native language. It was only the advent of the Thirty Years' War that prevented the accomplishment of their plan. Rules for the writing of French verse have been found in a course of rhetoric which dates back to the French Jesuits of 1663.[6] The number of great writers of French, German, Italian and Portuguese literature, who were trained in the schools of the Jesuits, would seem to indicate that the mother tongue was not completely passed over in their classrooms.

Other critics complain of the neglect of history and geography in the prescriptions of the Ratio. Some grow quite indignant that history should have been treated as a mere accessory of the classical text. Yet where in the sixteenth century, was there a school, Protestant or Catholic, which placed any great emphasis on history? History had not developed enough to warrant great treatment. Gradually, with the advance of time, history obtained a place of honor among the literary studies of the

---

[4] Duhr, *Die Studienordnung der Gesellschaft Jesu*, Freiburg (1890), p. 109.

[5] *Ibid.*, p. 110.

[6] Chossat, *Les Jésuites et leurs oeuvres à Avignon, 1553–1768*, Avignon (1896).

Ratio. It certainly was highly valued in the French Jesuit colleges of the early eighteenth century.[7] The schedule followed in the colleges of the Upper German province of the same time, provided for the separate study of history in each class and offered in the course of the six years a survey of universal history.[8] Geography received full treatment only in the philosophical course in connection with the study of astronomy; elsewhere it was considered in the category of erudition explanatory of the classical text. For the times such treatment was adequate enough; when the interest in the subject grew more widespread and the need of geographical knowledge became more urgent, the Jesuits increased the attention which they gave to it. Before the middle of the seventeenth century, there were courses in geography in all the French colleges.[9] Few men of those days did more for geography than the missionaries of the order by their explorations and their mapmaking, Jesuits such as Martini in China and Kino in Mexico.

Another point of objection is that the Ratio contains no provision for elementary education; an indication, it is asserted, that the Jesuits were indifferent to this most fundamental branch of learning. Elementary education received little consideration for the reason that the Jesuits had neither men nor means sufficient for the task; they were unable to answer even the demands of their own colleges. A choice had to be made, and they felt that it should be for the secondary and higher education, since by their training they were better fitted for such fields. That the Society viewed elementary education with indifference can hardly be asserted in the face of the primary instruction imparted by Jesuits in the Reductions of Paraguay, and even in some parts of Europe.

It may be of interest to note, in passing, the time devoted to class hours in the Jesuit colleges. Usually two hours and a half in the morning and two hours and a half in the afternoon were the lengths of the school sessions. In the rhetoric class, the half hour was dropped both in the morning and in the afternoon so that the pupils might have more leisure for personal study and for the practice of composition. A holiday usually came in the middle of the week, Wednesday or Thursday, for it was felt that more than four class days in succession would dull the pupil's keenness and dampen his enthusiasm for study. Frequently the weekly holiday was spent by all the pupils together in a

---

[7] Daniel, Les Jésuites instituteurs de la Jeunesse au XVII siècle et au XVIII siècle, Paris (1880); Rochemonteix, Le Collège Henry IV de la Flèche, Le Mans (1889), Vol. IV, pp. 123–147.

[8] Duhr, Studienordnung der Gesellschaft Jesu, pp. 104–106; Pachtler, Mon. Ger. Paed. IV, p. 105 seq.

[9] Daniel, "La geographie dans les collèges des Jésuites aux XVII et XVIII siècles." Etudes, Series 6, Vol. III (1879), pp. 801–826.

country house, called the "Villa," where the lads might refresh themselves from the drudgery of books by games or tramps across the fields and woods. The principle, "Mens sana in corpore sano," was fully subscribed to by these early Jesuits; only it was applied by them not to a handful of picked athletes, but to all the pupils of the college.

For the demands of higher education the Ratio provided philosophical and theological courses. The theological faculties of the universities can be dismissed with the notice that St. Thomas Aquinas was the basis of instruction and that the useless subtilties of the pre-Reformation days were avoided.[10] Philosophy was taught to the student at the end of his humanistic studies, when his mind, enriched by the treasures of Latin and Greek literature, would be better prepared to comprehend its problems. A three year course was provided: in the first year after an introduction to philosophical studies, minor and major logic were the subjects considered; in the second year, metaphysics; in the third year, special metaphysics, rational psychology and ethics. The scholastic method of lecture and disputation was followed throughout. In philosophy Aristotle was accepted as the standard author, though not blindly, for his false opinions were corrected in the light of revealed truth; St. Thomas too was greatly honored except in those points in which he was deemed incorrect. The Ratio has had to stand criticism for not having followed St. Thomas as rigorously as some would demand.[11] It was during these years that the scientific studies, physics, astronomy and the mathematical studies were made. The authors of the Ratio felt that such studies should come after the literary, at a time when minds were more mature and could better appreciate scientific problems. The high esteem in which mathematics was held by the early Jesuits may be learned from the memorial of the greatest Jesuit mathematician, Clavius, in which he speaks of the utility, advantages and place of mathematics, and in which he pleads for the careful choice and special training of the mathematical professors. The names of Clavius, Ricci, Grimaldi, Saccheri, Scheiner and Kircher, all Jesuits and all Jesuit trained, exemplify still further the value set on mathematics in the Jesuit curricula. Physics in the modern sense was still a thing of the future; yet the physics of the day was not neglected and efforts were made to keep abreast of the advances of the science, as is witnessed to by the physical cabinets and the lists of experiments of many of the eighteenth century Jesuit colleges. The Ratio, with all its insistence on the classical education, did not take a one-sided view; in the higher classes it provided as carefully for the scientific studies as it had for the literary in the lower classes.

The authors of the Ratio laid no claim to having invented an entirely

---

[10] *Ratio Stud.*, Reg. Professoris Scholasticae Theologiae, 2.

[11] *Ibid.*, Reg. Professoris Philosophiae, 2, 6.

new system of education. They borrowed much from the studies of the past and prudently sought an adaptation of the educational methods in vogue before the establishment of their order. Fundamentally the roots of their system were to be found in Scholasticism. St. Ignatius, his first companions, and all the early Jesuits were Scholastics. It is not strange, then, that the fashioners of the Jesuit system of education should have assigned the first place in theology to St. Thomas and the first place in philosophy to Aristotle. More proximate sources of the Ratio were the universities of the times and the classical schools of the Netherlands. The Universities of Paris and Louvain, and to a lesser degree, those of Alcalá and Salamanca, influenced the minds of the early Jesuits; the schedule of studies and the methods of instruction employed in these seats of learning, were the models adopted by the fashioners of the Ratio. It is probable that St. Ignatius made his division of studies (Languages, Arts, Philosophy, and Theology) from the customs of Paris; the further division of Language into Grammar, Humanities and Rhetoric is that also of Paris. The school exercises, particularly the method of scholastic disputation came from the same source; Polanco expressly states that the disputations held in the colleges at Messina and Vienna were conducted after the manner of the University of Paris.[12] Louvain also had considerable influence in the formation of the Ratio; it was highly thought of by St. Ignatius and several of the early scholars of the Society received their education in its halls. The exercises in the liberal arts of the Collegium Germanicum in which St. Ignatius took such an interest, were, on his own statement, modeled after those of Paris and Louvain.[13] The plans of Nadal and Ledesma, as has been noted before, were the groundwork of the Ratio; both men drew their experience from their many years of study at Paris, and Ledesma also from the courses which he had followed at Louvain.

Second only to the influence of the universities was the part the classical schools of the Netherlands, the educational institutions founded by the Brothers of Common Life, played in the making of the Jesuit system of education. These teachers of the fifteenth century represented the best in Christian humanism; St. Ignatius, who detested the works of the pagan humanists, entertained the highest regard for the literary achievements of the Brothers and their pupils. He himself had been a student at the Collège de Montagu in Paris, originally a foundation of this learned and pious fraternity. Several of the early Jesuits had received their education in these schools of the Low Countries; Ribadeneira enumerated fifty-three Jesuit writers before 1600 who had come from this region. Trained in these Christian-humanistic Schools were Coster and

---

[12] Duhr, *Studienordnung der Gesellschaft Jesu*, p. 5.
[13] *Mon. Hist. S.J.* (Mon. Ignatiana), Madrid (1906), Series I, tom. IV, p. 653.

Buys, both cooperators in the fashioning of the Ratio, St. Peter Canisius, the founder of so many Jesuit colleges, and Leonard Kessel, the rector of the college of Cologne. Just prior to the Reformation the most renowned of all the schools of the Netherlands was the school of Liége. To its customs may be traced many of the methods of instruction and many of the stimuli of study to be found in the *Ratio*.[14] The preponderance of Cicero in the Latin studies finds its origin in the practices of this school.

Certain other systems have been incorrectly assigned as sources of the Jesuit plan of studies. It has been said that the educators of the order merely copied from the system of the Strasburg school founded by the great Protestant educator, Jacob Sturm. The similarity that does exist between the two programs arises from an identity of sources; Sturm, like so many of the early Jesuits, had been a student at Liége, Louvain and Paris. Professor Paulsen, a foremost Protestant educational authority, is of the opinion that any dependence of the Jesuits on Sturm's plan is most improbable.[15] The educational projects of Luis Vives, the Spanish humanist, are also incorrectly assigned as a source of the Ratio. Much of the similarity here can be traced to the fact of Vives having been a student at Paris and of having lived for many years in the Netherlands. The one chance meeting at Bruges between St. Ignatius and Vives could hardly explain the origin of the Ratio. Moreover the practices which Vives advocated, infrequency of punishment, physical care, systematic teaching of Latin, all of which are to be found in the Jesuit system, were part of the common tradition of Christian education, in vogue among Christian masters long before Vives or the Jesuits were thought of.[16] If it be granted that the authors of the Ratio borrowed much from the educational practices of the past, it must also be granted that they relied to a great extent on their own experience and that of their fellow-Jesuits from 1540 to 1599, and also on their own painstaking efforts in the fifteen years during which they elaborated the Jesuit program of studies. One thing they did not borrow from any other system, and that is the wonderful unity and organization which are the Ratio's chief characteristics. A perfectly attainable goal in education was set up and the paths to that goal clearly marked out by the prescription of a definite work and a definite method for each class. It was a system so well organized that it could carry an even mediocre teacher to successful results.

Systems of education, as of anything else, remain magnificently conceived plans, unless those who carry them out are actuated by the highest ideals. The *Ratio Studiorum* obtained its great success because the

---

[14] Schwickerath, *Jesuit Education*, St. Louis (1904), p. 139.

[15] Paulsen, *Geschichte des gelehrten Unterrichts*, Vol. I, p. 412.

[16] Kayser, "Johannes Ludwig Vives," *Historisches Jahrbuch* (1894), Vol. XV, p. 350.

Jesuit teachers felt that it was the most effective means of obtaining the glory of God, and accordingly devoted themselves wholeheartedly to its use. Professor Paulsen says that the secret of the success of the Jesuits was their conviction that they were the chosen instruments for the saving of the Church. It was more than that; the Jesuits employed the *Ratio Studiorum* in their schools not only to oppose Protestantism, but to increase in others the love and worship of God, which after all is the basis of all human learning, culture and existence.

So numerous and so popular did the Jesuit educational institutions become that in the period before the suppression of the order in 1773 literally hundreds of thousands of young men had been trained by the fathers of the Society. Many of these colleges came into being in the first century of the order's history; their founding has already been noticed in previous chapters. A summary of the whole development is all that can be given in such a work as the present. In 1615, at the death of Aquaviva, the colleges numbered 372; a century later in 1710 their number had almost doubled to 612; when the movement for the suppression of the order commenced they totaled 621. These colleges were distributed among the various assistancies as follows: Italian Assistancy, 125; Portuguese Assistancy (including Asiatic provinces), 52; Spanish Assistancy (including Latin-America and the Philippines), 196; French Assistancy, 89; German Assistancy (including Poland, the Low Countries and England), 199. Most of these educational institutions were what would be called today "academies" or German "Gymnasien." Less than a third were pensionats—boarding schools—and in these the boarding pupils usually formed a small percentage of the whole. The early Jesuits were quite reluctant to take over the management of pensionats for the students, and often it was only the force of circumstances that moved them to do so. It would be extremely difficult and too lengthy a process to give the number of students educated by the fathers, but a few instances will indicate the general trend. In the 18 colleges of the Paris province in 1643, at the beginning of the reign of Louis XIV, there were in attendance, 13,000 students. In the 100 colleges in the Empire in 1626, the enrollment usually averaged well over 600, in some it went even to more than 1,000. The 34 colleges of the Low Countries numbered their scholars in the same proportions. The students were drawn from the ranks of nobility and of the middle classes, although ample provisions were made for poor lads who were talented and ambitious. In some of the German colleges at least one-quarter to one-third were charity scholars, their support being obtained from the alms begged by the fathers for them and by the sermons preached for the same purpose. St. Peter Canisius, Fathers Volk and Lanoy were especially devoted to the education of needy scholars. The presence of these poor lads on the same benches with young princes and nobles and with the sons of the wealthy burghers, is sufficient answer to the false impression that the Jesuits devoted themselves exclusively to the educating of aristocrats.[17]

The Society also took part in the work of higher education to the extent that, at the time of the suppression, the fathers were teaching in twenty-four universities. The theological and philosophical faculties of the Universities of Ingolstadt, Vienna, Prague, Cologne, Breslau, Freiburg-im-Breisgau and Heidelberg were either partly or wholly in their hands; while the entire Universities of Gratz, Dillingen, Paderborn, Fulda, Braunsberg, Vilna, Würzburg, Pont-à-Mousson, Tyrnau, Olmütz, Dijon, Tournon, Quito and Sucre, were completely in the charge of the Jesuits. In the beginning, the work in the universities met with considerable opposition, notably at Vienna, Paris (in connection with the Collège de Clermont), Louvain, Cracow and in Mexico and Peru. The fathers eventually had to leave the University of Louvain; and they never succeeded in establishing an institution of university grade at Cracow.

The Jesuits exercised a very large share in the education of the clergy. At the time of the suppression, 176 seminaries were staffed by members of the order. These seminaries were to be found: 20 in the Italian Assistancy, 10 in the Portuguese, 33 in the Spanish, 32 in the French, and 81 in the German. As has been noted in a previous chapter, the model for these institutions of clerical training, as well as for all the seminaries which arose as one of the greatest fruits of the Council of Trent, was the Collegium Germanicum-Hungaricum in Rome. In Rome too stood the leading college maintained by the Jesuit Order, the Roman College, today known as the Gregorian University. On its staff were to be found the choicest professors of the Society. Even as early as 1584 it had a student enrollment of 2,017. The Jesuits in the Eternal City had charge also of the Greco-Ruthenian College, the English College, the Irish College, the Scots College and the Maronite College. The work of preparing priests for the martyr-missions of the British Isles was carried on by the Jesuits also at the Irish Colleges of Lisbon, Santiago, Salamanca, Seville and Poitiers, at the English Colleges at Valladolid, Seville and Madrid, at the Scots Colleges at Madrid and Douai, and at the University of Pont-à-Mousson.

All this vast educational work would have been an impossibility were it not for the thousands of generous benefactors who came to the support of the fathers. The Jesuits, since they belonged to a mendicant order, had to teach gratuitously. It was the numberless gifts of pious

---

[17] Duhr, *Geschichte der Jesuiten in den Ländern deutscher Zunge*, Vol. I, c. 5, 6, 7.

Catholics which made possible the erection of the buildings, the dwelling-places for the professors, the hostels for the poor scholars, and the foundations that assured the permanence of these educational institutions. The Popes, especially Gregory XIII, were particularly generous; so too were the Emperors, Ferdinand I and Ferdinand II; the Dukes of Bavaria, Albrecht V, Wilhelm V, and Maximilian I; the Kings, John II of Portugal and Henry IV of France. Cardinals such as Farnese, Ludovici, Truchsess, Hosius and Pázmány, Bishops such as Frederick von Fürstenberg and Guillaume du Prat, erected and endowed colleges for the fathers. Their example was followed by hundreds of the nobility and of the well-to-do burghers of the cities of Catholic Europe, who made the more than eight hundred Jesuit educational institutions permanent actualities.

The literary activities of the Jesuits constituted one of their principal achievements in the intellectual defense of Catholicism.[18] In every field of learning writers of the order produced works of lasting value. The number of the authors alone astonishes one: Southwell, even in his early day, could enumerate 2,237, while in our own time an estimate based on Sommervogel's *Bibliothèque des Ecrivains de la Compagnie de Jésus,* would place the number at eighteen thousand at least. Truly prodigious too was the literary output of many of the early fathers: Becanus composed 52 works, Sirmond 56, Stengel 80, Kedd 66, Nieremberg 57, Faurer 66, Raynaud 100, Bolland 61, Labbe 83, Hazart 87, Menestrier 164, Hardouin 108, Kraus 70, Neumayr 112, Cordara 71, Boscovich 151. Jacob Gretser was the most prolific with a literary output of 234 books or pamphlets, which have been bound in 17 folio volumes.

Naturally, the first fields of Jesuit literary activity were theology and philosophy; there the fathers devoted themselves to the revival of Scholasticism, basing their works upon Aristotle in philosophy and St. Thomas Aquinas in theology. Francis Suarez, "Doctor Eximius," was the first of all Jesuit theologians, as he was also one of the greatest theologians of all time; his works fill twenty-three folio volumes in the Venice edition of 1740. With him must be placed: Cardinal Toletus; Fonseca, the Aristotle of Portugal; Molina, whose works on Grace precipitated the famous controversy, also a leading Jesuit commentator on St. Thomas; Gregory of Valentia, a renowned professor of theology at Dillingen, Ingolstadt and Rome; Vasquez; St. Robert Bellarmine;

---

[18] References for the following pages may be found in: Sommervogel, *Bibliothèque des Ecrivains de la Compagnie de Jésus,* Bruxelles-Paris (1890–1909); *Supplement* to the same by Rivière, Toulouse (1911–1930); Heimbucher, *Orden und Kongregationen der Katholischen Kirche,* Vol. II, pp. 235–287, "Die Jesuiten als Schriftsteller und Förderer der Wissenschaften," 3rd edition, Paderborn (1934); Koch, *Jesuiten-Lexikon,* Paderborn (1934).

Lessius; Becanus; Granado, Ruiz de Montoya, commentator on St. Thomas; Tanner, author of a complete course of Scholastic theology; de Coninck; Ripalda; Perez; Amico, author of an eight volume course of theology according to the method in vogue in the Jesuit schools; Mendoza; Petavius; Dicastillo; Cardinal de Lugo; Arriaga; Artieda; Platel, known for his textbook on theology, *Synopsis cursus theologici;* Viva; Mayr; and the Wirceburgensians, a common name for the former Jesuit theologians of the University of Würzburg, Holtzclau, Kilber, Munier and Neubaur, who produced in the years just preceding the Suppression, a fourteen volume complete cursus of theology, the *Theologia Wirceburgensis,* a work outstanding for clarity, thoroughness and methodical treatment.

The study of the Sacred Scriptures and their correct interpretation occupied many scholarly Jesuits. Among these, the two outstanding writers are Maldonatus, whose commentary on the Gospels is valued even to this day, and Cardinal Toletus, who wrote a commentary on the first twelve chapters of the *Gospel of St. Luke,* on the *Gospel of St. John* and on the *Epistle to the Romans.* Other distinguished Jesuit biblical scholars were: Salmeron, author of an excellent explanation of the *New Testament;* Ribera, writer on the twelve lesser prophets, *St. John's Gospel,* the *Apocalypse* and the *Epistle to the Hebrews;* Prado, who with Villalpando produced a large commentary on *Ezechiel;* Emmanuel Sa, expositor in brief form of difficult passages of the Scriptures and composer of a catena of the Gospels; Serarius, a Scriptural commentator, whom Baronius called "The Light of the Church in Germany"; Alcazar, known for his explanation of the *Apocalypse;* St. Robert Bellarmine, who in his controversies showed himself to be an expert exegete and who wrote an exposition of the *Psalms* and a Hebrew Grammar; Giustiniani, who completed a commentary on all the *Epistles of St. Paul,* and on the Catholic *Epistle of St. James;* Sanchez, commentator on most of the books of the *Old Testament* and also on the *Acts of the Apostles;* Cornelius à Lapide, whose commentaries covering almost all of the Scriptures have often been reproduced and are highly thought of even today; Bonfrère, author of an explanation of the *Pentateuch, Judges, Ruth* etc., also worthwhile lectures on Biblical Interpretation and Word-Signification, and a catalogue of places in the Scriptures. Translations of the Bible were also produced by Jesuit writers: as Azevedo and Caldeira in Ethiopian, Duhan and Desvignes in Persian, Wujek in Polish, Kaldi in Hungarian, Bouhours in French (*New Testament*), the Prague Jesuits in Czech. Jesuits wrote likewise in the field of Christian archeology; Gretser was first, with his five volume work on the Cross of Christ and his other archeological investigations; Donati composed works on Old and New Rome; Nicquetius treated of the inscriptions of the Cross, also of the names and paintings of the Mother of God; Gumppenberg drew up the frequently reprinted and translated *Atlas Marianus;* and Pettinati wrote on the pilgrim shrines of Styria dedicated to Mary.

The fathers of the Society of Jesus accomplished a great deal in the development and exposition of moral theology; many of the leading moralists of the sixteenth and seventeenth centuries were Jesuits. Laymann and Busembaum may be considered outstanding in this field. Laymann taught for twenty-nine years at Ingolstadt, Munich and Dillingen; at Munich in 1625 he brought out his frequently reprinted *Theologia Moralis* in six volumes, a work which ranked him with the leading moralists. Busembaum wrote the *Medulla Theologiae Moralis,*[19] which merited more than two hundred editions and gained the approval of St. Alphonsus. Among the other distinguished Jesuit moralists may be noted: Azor, whose *Institutiones Morales* belonged to the best in the field and has frequently been reprinted; Sanchez, renowned for his work on the Sacrament of Marriage; Figliucci; Reginaldus (Regnault), the author of several treatises on the administration of the Sacrament of Penance—St. Alphonsus declared him to be the classic author on the subject; Badelli; Cardinal de Lugo, who because of his work, *De Iustitia et Jure,* was numbered by St. Alphonsus as the greatest theologian after St. Thomas; Escobar y Mendoza, whose work on moral theology was singled out by Pascal for his calumnious attacks against the Jesuit moralists; Cardenas, also numbered among the classic moralists by St. Alphonsus; Lacroix, whose *Theologia Moralis* has been reissued twenty-five times; Reuter, the author of *Neoconfessarius, Theologia Moralis,* and *Casus Conscientiae,* all of which have been frequently reprinted.

A foremost Jesuit writer in Canon Law is Schmalzgruber whose reputation stands to the present day. His *Ius Ecclesiasticum Universum,* a seven folio work, first appeared in 1717. Laymann has been already noticed for his work in moral theology, he was equally renowned in the domain of Canon Law. Pirhing, the author of a folio, *Ius Canonicum,* and Wiestner, the composer of a five-volume treatise on the subject, which won the approval of Benedict XIV, wrote with distinction on canonical problems.

In polemics, because of the part which the order played in the so-called "Counter-Reformation," Jesuit writers have had a foremost place. St.

---

[19] This work is often used as the basis for the perennial calumny of the Jesuits teaching that the end justifies the means. The approbation of St. Alphonsus and the Church's approval of the more than two hundred editions (up to 1845) of Busembaum's work would never have been given, if the work had contained so gravely immoral a doctrine. Busembaum's actual opinion was: "A negative precept of the natural law which prohibits a thing intrinsically evil can never be lawfully transgressed not even under the influence of the fear of death." Lib. I, tr. II, C. IV, dub. 2, n. 1.

Robert Bellarmine, Doctor of the Church, is *facile princeps;* his *Disputationes de controversiis Christianae Fidei adversus hujus temporis haereticos* is recognized as the greatest controversial work ever written; it has gone through innumerable editions; Protestants established anti-Bellarmine chairs against it in German and English universities. St. Robert composed several other controversial works; especially noteworthy are his replies to Masiglio and Sarpi, protagonists of the Venetian Republic in its quarrel with the Pope, and also his answers to Barclay and James I. Louis Richeome, because of his valuable writings against the French Calvinists, also takes a leading place. So too does Petavius, the author of many treatises on chronology, history, philosophy, polemics, patristics and the history of dogma; the full list of their various editions occupies twenty columns in Sommervogel. Petavius has been called "The Father of the History of Dogma"; his ability as a controversialist was quite on a par with his patristic attainments. Among the other leading Jesuit controversialists must be considered: St. Peter Canisius, whose great contribution has already been noted; Gregory of Valentia; Skarga, whose writings and sermons made him the leader of the Catholic Restoration in Poland; Becanus; Gretser; Cardinal Pázmány, the author of the polemical works so responsible for the revival of Catholicism in Hungary; Raynaud; Berthier, whose *Journal de Trévoux* proved a strong refutation of the errors of the Encyclopedists; de Barruel, the opponent of Infidelism and Secret Societies.

Jesuit authors have produced works in pastoral theology which have merited several printings. Such treatises were: Agostini's *Directions for the Administration of the Sacrament of Penance,* Lohner's eleven volumes, Agnelli's *Manual for the Pastoral Office,* and Andrucci's *Directions for Confessors.* In the treatment of liturgical subjects worthwhile contributions have come from the pens of von Balinghem, Guyetus, Baldassari and Azevedo.

Much of the work of the Society had been in the ministry of the pulpit. To provide for the proper equipment of the preachers, writers of the order produced a copious supply of sermon-literature. The most important of all such writers is Faber with his *Concionum opus Tripartitum* which appeared in three folios in 1631, and has been frequently brought out since, the last edition coming in 1866. Other noteworthy writers for the sacred pulpit were: Skarga; Labata with his subject-concordance; Lingendes; Oliva, the eleventh General of the order; Lohner, author of the frequently reproduced *Bibliotheca Manualis Concionatoria;* Vieira; Bourdaloue; Aguilar; Houdry; Hunolt; de Isla; Tschupik; and Merz, writer of several volumes of sermons against the "Enlightenment" of the eighteenth century. Textbooks for training in both profane and sacred eloquence were composed by St. Francis Borgia, Regius, Pelletier, Caussin, Bodler, Bonucci and de Colonia.

The topic of asceticism has been greatly enriched by the writings of the Jesuits. On the foundations laid down by St. Ignatius in the *Book of the Spiritual Exercises,* his sons have produced a veritable literature on holiness. The first of all the Jesuit ascetical writers is Rodriguez; his three volume work, *Christian Perfection,* ranks as one of the classics of Christian ascetical literature; it has gone through 126 editions in almost every European language and in several Oriental tongues. Though written originally for his Jesuit brethren, Rodriguez' work has come to be used by countless religious of all orders and congregations and by large numbers of the laity. Next in importance stands de la Puente, known through his *Meditations on the Mysteries of Our Holy Faith,* a work that has merited many translations, his *Spiritual Directory for Confessions* and his *On the Perfection of a Christian.* With these two writers must also be placed Scaramelli with his *Discernment of Spirits, Guide for Mystical Theology* and *Directorium Asceticum.* Among the other noteworthy authors of ascetical works must be listed: Alvarez de Paz; St. Robert Bellarmine, who wrote *The Elevation of the Spirit to God, The Eternal Blessedness of the Saints, The Seven Last Words of Christ on the Cross* and the *Art of Dying Well;* le Gaudier, whose work *De Perfectione Vitae Spiritualis* is in use even today; Lallemant, writer of the important *Instructions in the Spiritual Life;* Drexel, the author of the *Golden Book* and of *The School of the Cross of Love,* writings which have been often reprinted and have been eagerly read even by Protestants; Saint-Jure, whose *L'homme religieux* has been numbered amongst the best ascetical works; Nieremberg, who composed many solid spiritual books that have merited frequent translations; Druzbicki; Nouet; Bl. Claude de la Colombière; Rogacci; Judde; Pergmayr; and Grou, author of excellent spiritual treatises that have gained considerable renown.

In the domain of history, both secular and profane, the members of the order have rendered distinguished service by scholarly editions of the Fathers, by the publication of the acts of the Councils, by histories of the Church, both universal and provincial, by critical studies of the lives of the saints, particularly in the work of the Bollandists, by numerous hagiographies of their own saints and distinguished men, by the reports of their laborers in the foreign mission lands, and by national and local histories. In editing the Fathers and in preparing for publication the Acts of the Councils, as well as other materials of the early Church, the best work done by Jesuits was that accomplished by Labbe. This scholar, because of his *De Byzantinae Historiae Scriptoribus,* is considered one of the founders of the study of Byzantine history; he produced too *Nova bibliotheca Mss. Librorum* (in two volumes), *Biblioteca bibliothecarum, Concordia chronologica, technica et historica* (in five volumes), *Sanctorum Patrum, Theologorum Scriptorumque ecclesiasticorum utriusque Testamenti Bibliotheca chronologica*. He also began a monumental work of eighteen folios on the Councils which was completed by his colleague, Cossart. Quite as important were the labors of Sirmond who searched through the most renowned libraries of France and Italy for works of the Fathers, many of which he published for the first time; he likewise edited in three folios the history of the ancient Gallican councils. Cardinal Sforza Pallavicino ranks high with his *Istoria del Concilio di Trento*. Other Jesuits who did noteworthy work in this special field are: St. Peter Canisius; de Duc; Gretser; Garnier, editor of the *Liber diurnus Romanorum Pontificum;* Hardouin, the author of 108 publications of which the most famous is the *Acta Conciliorum et Epistolae decretales ac Constitutiones Summorum Pontificum;* Hartzheim, who produced a valuable collection of the German councils and the *Bibliotheca Colonensis*.

The most renowned contribution of the Jesuit historians is the *Acta Sanctorum* of the Bollandists, an enormous work (to date sixty-three volumes and yet incomplete) on the lives of the Saints of the Roman Martyrology.[20] The treatment of each saint includes a history critically written, any ancient accounts still extant, an evaluation of the source material, and a discussion of his miracles and of the veneration which has been paid to him. Rosweyde, a Jesuit from the Low Countries, was the first to conceive this monumental project. Neither he nor his immediate successors realized in the beginning what an enormous task they had set for themselves; only St. Robert Bellarmine seemed to have guessed it, for on his perusal of Rosweyde's prospectus he made the remark that his brother religious must have been expecting to live for two hundred years. Rosweyde accomplished little more than the collection of an enormous amount of manuscript material from the Low Countries, northwestern Germany and northern France. On his death in 1629, Jan Bolland, of the same province, was entrusted with the documents. Bolland changed Rosweyde's plan of treatment considerably, searched further abroad for material, and began the editing of the sources and the actual writing of the lives. His name has been attached to the fathers who have carried on his work, so that up to the present day they have been known as the Bollandists. With few exceptions they have been Jesuits from the Low Countries; the non-Jesuits were the young Benedictines whom the fathers trained to carry on the work at the time of the Suppression of the

---

[20] Delehaye, *The Works of the Bollandists through Three Centuries 1615–1915* (Translated from the French), Princeton University Press (1922)

Society and one secular priest who labored during that period also. However, as the work was suspended shortly after the Suppression and was renewed again in 1837 by Jesuits only, the Bollandists' labors were almost exclusively the work of the Society of Jesus. Bolland called on the aid of the Jesuit houses for manuscripts, ancient books and Latin publications; whatever was collected was housed at Antwerp in a hagiographical museum, which the leader had erected and in which he and his companions worked. It was not long before this museum had become one of the best historical libraries in Europe. In 1643 appeared the first two volumes, which dealt with the Saints of January and were the exclusive work of Bolland. Shortly, two able assistants, Henschen and Papenbroech, both consummate scholars and indefatigable workers, were given to the director. After the appearance of three volumes dealing with the Saints of February, the assistants were sent to Rome for the purpose of gathering material from the great libraries of the Eternal City. The two writers everywhere received a warm welcome, and not only from their fellow Jesuits, but from members of other religious orders, from the Cardinals and from Pope Alexander VII. Libraries were opened to them, copyists were provided to work under their direction; as a result, on their return from their journeying through Europe they brought back to Antwerp an enormous supply of materials from the archives of Rome, Italy, Germany and France. The work went steadily on and the folios continued to appear until 1773 when the fiftieth was published. 3 volumes are devoted to the Saints of March, 3 to those of April, 7 each to those of May, June, July and August, 8 to those of September, 14 to those of October and 4 to those of November 1 to 8. As the years passed on other scholars took the place of the pioneers; notable among them were, Cuypers, Pinius, editor of the Mozarabic Liturgy, Stiltink, and Ghesquière. But in effort none of these surpassed Henschen, who toiled for forty-six years at the task, nor Papenbroeck who devoted fifty years to the critical study of the lives of the saints. At the Suppression Maria Theresa supplied funds and means that the work might be carried on; while the Bollandists offered to train Benedictine monks to continue the work. However, Joseph II, "the Sacristan Emperor," interfered in this as in so many other ecclesiastical matters; and when the Bollandists or their successors failed to produce a folio a year as he had ordered, he suppressed the foundations. It was asserted then that really educated men were little interested in the work, a rather amusing statement in view of the esteem in which the Bollandists have been and are held today by historians, Protestant or unbelieving. Catholic scholars recall the encomium of Alexander VII, that no one had undertaken a more useful or a more honorable work for the Church.

Jesuits in other parts of the world contributed much to historical knowledge by their writings on the lives of particular saints or groups of saints. Thus Rader produced a three volume work on the Bavarian Saints; Macedo treated of the Patron Saints of the countries and cities of Christendom; Strunk wrote the lives of the Saints of Westphalia; Cepari composed striking biographies of Sts. Aloysius, Berchmans, Frances of Rome and Mary Magdalene de' Pazzi; Prilesky wrote the *Acta Sanctorum Hungariae.*

The Jesuit contribution to the writing of profane history, on the whole, was not of so great importance. Still several of the fathers produced works of real value. Among such historians may be listed: Juan Mariana with his *Historiae Hispaniae* in thirty volumes; Strada, who wrote in beautiful Latin the history of the wars in the Low Countries; Brunner, celebrated as the Livy of Bavaria, author of the *Annales virtutis et fortunae Bajorum;* Blas Valera, a descendent of the Incas, who wrote authoritatively on the antiquities of Peru; Balbinus, whose researches in Bohemian history have proven of great value for the knowledge of the Czech sources; Daniel, the royal librarian and royal historiographer, with his *Histoire de France;* Bougeant, author of a history of the Thirty Years' War; Naruszewicz, known for his ten volume history of Poland; Lozano, who wrote of the La Plata lands in his *Historia de las Revoluciones de la Provincia de Paraguay;* de Mailla and Gaubil, both Far-Eastern missionaries, who brought out valuable works on the history of China; and Xavier de Feller, whose *Dictionnaire Historique* has been highly esteemed in biographical studies.

For the advancement of the exact sciences, mathematics, physics and astronomy, Jesuit scholars performed remarkable services. Astronomy was the first science to attract the attention of the savants of the order, though many of them also gained well-earned reputations in mathematics and physics. Colleges erected and maintained great observatories at Marseilles, Lisbon, Prague, Vienna, Milan, Florence, Parma, Pont-à-Mousson, Graz, Lemberg and Tyrnau; members of the order were entrusted with the observatories at Peking, Vienna, Wilna, Schwetzingen and Mannheim. Among the Jesuits who rendered outstanding scientific services should be noted: Ricci, whose fifteen volumes, partly mathematical, partly philosophical, written in Chinese, are still held in honor in China; Clavius, called the "Euclid of the Sixteenth Century," to whom Gregory XIII entrusted much of the task on the improvement of the calendar; Guldin, whose work, *Centrobaryca,* originated the Guldin's Rule; Scheiner, the founder of solar physics and famous for many discoveries, such as the sun-spots, the refraction of the atmosphere, the pantograph, the lunar-map; Grienberger; de la Faille; Cyast, who observed the comets and the passage of Mercury, and was the first to report on the Nebula of Orion; Grimaldi, who studied the lunar-spots, discovered the diffraction and dispersion of light and prepared the way for the theory of undulations. At the same time in far-off China at the Imperial Court of Peking, Jesuits worked with equal success in the scientific field; their astronomical instruments are to this day one of the sights of the former Chinese capital. Schall lectured on mathematics, and from 1645 was President of the Mathematical Tribunal at the Imperial Court; with Rho, a Milanese Jesuit, he composed in Chinese several valuable works on mathematics and astronomy. Verbiest, Philip Grimaldi, Kogler, von Hallerstein, Rocha and d'Espincha were elected at various times to the presidency of the Mathematical Tribunal. Among the other Jesuit scientists at Peking may be listed the astronomers, Kastner, Slaviczeck and Gaubil. Back in Europe through the seventeenth and eighteenth centuries, Jesuit scholars continued to enrich scientific pursuits with their discoveries. Foremost among them stands Athanasius Kircher, of such a universal genius as to merit the name "Doctor of a Hundred Arts." Kircher was born at Geisa near Fulda in 1602; taught mathematics and other sciences at Würzburg, Avignon, and Rome; invented one of the earliest counting machines, a speaking tube, the aeolian harp and the magic lantern; founded the Museo Kircheriano, still frequented in Rome; thirty-nine folios on mathematics, linguistics (including the first steps in the study of hieroglyphics), music, medicine, and history. Roger Joseph Boscovich follows Kircher only in time; he was certainly a far greater scientist. To his studies are credited sixty-six treatises on astronomy, pure mathematics and speculative science; to his practical abilities are due such works as the preservation of the dome of St. Peter's, the surveying of the Papal States and the invention of the ring micrometer. Popes, scholars and learned societies in all parts of Europe, even the Royal Society of London, celebrated the scientific attainments of Boscovich. Other Jesuit scientists who rendered special service to science are: Zupi, the first to observe the phases of Mercury; Zucci, from whom came the idea of the mirror-telescope; Riccioli, who discovered lunarspots and produced a new and more scientific lunar-map; Fabri, a renowned physicist and author of thirty-one scientific treatises; Sarrabat, the first to examine comets by means of the telescope, and Maximilian Hell, who for thirty-five years was the director of the Imperial Observatory of Vienna.

Mention must be made of the Jesuit contribution to the science of geography. The missionaries of the order gained almost as much renown for their explorations and discoveries as for their apostolic labors. Marquette, though a most zealous missionary, is remembered largely in connection with the exploration of the Mississippi. Acosta's *Historia Natural y Moral de las Indias* is considered even to this day as a most valuable work on the geography and ethnography of the aborigines of

Latin America; a similar value has been accorded to du Halde's descriptions of Mongolia and China. Several Jesuits were distinguished as cartographers. The first map of China to be issued in Europe was the work of Martini, who has been called the "Father of Chinese Geography." It was a worthy forerunner of that great map of China, Tartary and Tibet, called by Wegener "the greatest production in the whole history of Cartography," the joint work of Regis, Bouvet, Jartoux, Cardoso, du Tartre, de Mailla and Bonjour, O.S.A. The first maps of New Mexico, Arizona and Lower California were produced by that remarkable missionary, traveller, rancher and geographer, Eusebio Kino. Other distinguished Jesuit cartographers and their works were: Verbiest, a map of China and a world-map; Fritz, a map of the Amazon; Gilg, a map of the Mexican Sierra; Almeida, a map of Ethiopia; Adrian, a map of Carinthia; Dechalles, a map of the Mediterranean. A Jesuit, König, produced the first known textbook on geography, his *Institutio Geographiae Elementalis.*

Philology and literature owe much to the industry of Jesuit writers. Many of the languages of the aborigines of Asia and America were first reduced to written form by the Jesuit missionaries; grammars and vocabularies too were worked out for these strange tongues by the same agency. Sinology, the investigation and study of the Chinese speech and literature, was particularly a Jesuit work in the seventeenth and eighteenth centuries.

The prominence afforded Latin, Greek and Hebrew in the Jesuit colleges naturally produced a large number of classicists. Among such scholars may be listed: Perpiñá, renowned for his Latin orations; Alvarez, the author of that most widely-used Latin grammar, *De Institutione Grammatica,* in three volumes, a work which was used even in the last century at Harvard; Torsellini, who produced an often-reprinted work in four volumes on the Latin particles; Delrio, a commentator on Claudian, Seneca, Livy and other Latin classical writers; Mayr, a distinguished Hebraist, author of a Hebrew grammar and translator of the New Testament and the smaller catechism of Canisius into that ancient tongue; Gretser, who wrote a Greek grammar still in use, a Latin-Greek-German Lexicon, and a translation of several of the Greek Fathers; Spanmüller (Pontanus), considered by many to be the greatest Jesuit classicist, author of the frequently reproduced *Progymnasmata Latinitatis,* commentator on Virgil, Ovid, and Cyril of Alexandria, a poet, and author of a most remarkable memorial on the cultivation and improvement of humanistic studies; de la Cerda, a Virgilian scholar and editor of Tertullian; Perzivales, a Greek Jesuit from Crete, renowned as a Hellenist; Sanadon, a commentator on Horace; de Colonia, author of several theological, historical and dramatic works, one of which, his *Ars Rhetorica,* has been republished several times; Porée, renowned as a rhetorician and as the teacher of Voltaire; Bayr, author of a Greek grammar and several valuable lexicons; Desbillons, famous for his edition of the fables of Aesop and Phaedrus.

Notable literary works of a more general nature were produced by: Tiraboschi, author of a well-known Italian History of Literature, *Vetera Humiliatorum Monumenta,* in four volumes, *Biblioteca Modenese* in six volumes, *Memoire Storiche Modenesi* in six volumes, and the editor of the *Nuovo Giornale de' Letterati d' Italia* in forty-three volumes; Zaccaria, who wrote, besides his numerous theological works, a history of Italian Literature; von Klein, the author of *Deutsches Provinzialwörtbuch, Leben und Bildnisse der Grossen Deutschen,* and *Super Opinione Lessingi de Tragoedia Historica et super Emilia Galotti.* Nor must there be forgotten the Spanish Jesuit, de Isla, whose satirical romance, *Historia del famoso Predicador Gerundio de Campazas, alias Zotes,* has merited frequent editions and translations into German, English and French. This work and other satirical pieces have won for de Isla a high place in Spanish literature. The French Jesuits from 1701 to 1767 edited the excellent literary journal, *Mémoires Pour Servir à l'Histoire des Sciences et des Beaux-Arts,* familiarly known as the *Journal de Trévoux,*[21] which not only carried many outstanding articles on contemporary literature, but from 1745 onward waged war against the Encyclopedists.

In the study and development of native languages in the foreign mission fields, Jesuit scholars rendered most valuable services. The Portuguese fathers in India erected printing presses at Goa, Rachol and Ambalacatta in Cochin, from which came a veritable stream of translations of the Bible, catechisms, the life of Our Lord, the lives of the Saints, and religious books, as well as grammars and dictionaries composed by the fathers. In the Tamil language, good work was done by the Jesuits, Henriquez, Gonsalvez, de Proença, Faraz, Balthasar d'Acosta, d'Aguilar, Cattaneo, Pereira, de Maya and Beschi, the last writing Tamil poetry of a high order. For the study of Konkani, a similar service was performed by Stephens, Ribeira and Przikril. In Sanskrit, worthy of note are the labors of de Nobili, Roth, Hanleden, Pimental, Calmette and du Pons.

In Chinese language and literature, Matteo Ricci was the leading Jesuit scholar. He was the author of *Tien-hio-schei,* which was of such merit as a work of Chinese literature, that Kiang-lung included it in a collection of Chinese classics. Ricci translated Euclid into Chinese and

---

[21] Dumas, *Histoire du Journal de Trévoux depuis 1701–jusqu'en 1762,* Paris (1936); Palmer, "The French Jesuits in the Age of Enlightenment," *The American Hist. Review,* Vol. XLV (1939), pp. 44–58.

in that language composed an arithmetic, a geometry, a treatise on European Script, a book on Controversies, a dialogue on Friendship and finally a dictionary. Verbiest wrote the valuable *Kiao-li-siang-kiai*, a statement of the fundamental teachings of Christianity, which became the basis of much of the Christian Chinese religious literature; besides he composed works on astronomy, geography and a Manchu grammar; in all, over thirty books. Other Jesuits brought out in Chinese works on every subject from religion to music; some of the more notable among them were: Cattaneo, Diaz, Pantoja, Schall, Buglio, Couplet, Herdtrich, Gerbillon, Rougemont, de Prémare, Parrenin, Dentrecolles, Visdelou and de Mailla. An Annamite-Portuguese dictionary, as well as a catechism for catechumens in Latin and Cochin-Chinese, came from the pen of de Rhodes.

Despite the relatively short period during which they were in Japan, the Jesuits were able to accomplish much in the use of Japanese. The first grammar and lexicon were produced by the lay-brother Fernandez; two grammars were composed by Rodriguez; a Japanese-Latin-Portuguese lexicon was brought out by the fathers of the college of Amacusa in 1595; eight years later this was followed by a great Japanese-Portuguese dictionary. Baretto, Gomez and others wrote catechisms and ascetical works in the tongue of the islands. Even an effort to introduce the Latin script was attempted. To the south in the Philippine Islands the Jesuits achieved marked success with the chief dialects. Bobadilla produced one of the best Tagalog grammars; Noceda composed a large Tagalog dictionary with the aid of Sanlucar, and by himself translated the Psalms into that tongue; Tejada achieved similar successes in the use of Visayan.

In the Spanish and Portuguese colonies of the New World the Jesuits displayed a like aptitude in the use of the native languages. In Peru, Blas Valera wrote extensively and authoritatively on the religions, customs and antiquities of the pre-Christian Peruvians. So too did Molina. Among the Jesuit scholars in this linguistic field the following were especially successful: Acosta, author of a catechism in the Quechua and Aymara tongues; Barzena, publisher of a grammar, a lexicon, a confessional manual and a prayer book in five native dialects; Holguin, composer of a grammar and dictionary in the Quechua speech; Torres-Rubio, producer of grammars in the Aymara, the Quechua and the Guarani languages; Bertonio, author of a Spanish-Aymarac, Aymarac-Spanish Dictionary. Similar services were done for the Tucuman speech by Anasco and others. Many of these works were printed at the press set up in the Jesuit college at Juli on the shores of Lake Titicaca.

In Chile, de Vega, Valdivia, Santisteban, Febres and Havestadt worked in the Araukani tongue; in Bolivia, Chomé, author of a large dictionary, and Camano labored with marked results in the Chiquito language. In Paraguay, Sanchez produced a lexicon for the Ubjaren speech, Marban for the Moxos tongue, while Brigniel issued a grammar, dictionary and catechism in the Abiponir language. Brazil honors Ven. José Anchieta not only as a remarkable missionary but also as a distinguished linguist, for he was the author of a classic work in the Tupi speech; a similar accomplishment was achieved by his colleague, Figueira. Anchieta also produced a great and a small catechism and a dictionary in the Tupi language. Grammars, vocabularies or catechism came from the pens of Ruiz de Montoya, Restivo, d'Aragona, Samaniege and Insauralde; the latter's book on the proper employment of time is the greatest work in Guarani. The Galibi speech was served by Pelleprat, Lombard and de la Mousse; even the French-Negro dialects of the Antilles received a dictionary and a dialogue book by the zeal of Ducoeurjoly.

In Mexico the language of the Aztecs and other native tribes received the attention of the Jesuits. A grammar with a vocabulary of the Cahita dialect was published by an unknown Jesuit in the eighteenth century; Ortega composed a grammar, vocabulary, catechism and a confessional manual, and later a lexicon for the Cora tongue; Figueroa got out a similar work in both the Tepehuana and the Tarahumara languages. Fonte and Rinaldini were authors of valuable works in Tepehuana; de Guadelaxara, Roa, Victorino and Steffl made similar contributions in Tarahumara. The speech of the Pimas of Sinaloa and Sonora was treated by Bonifaz, Velasco, Mercado and Sedlmayr; that of the Optata by Aguirre, and that of the Tequima by Lombardo.

In Canada the language of the Iroquois was studied by Bruyas; that of the Hurons by Chaumont, St. Jean de Brébeuf, de Carheil and le Caron; that of the Illinois by Gravier and le Boulanger; that of the Abnaki by Rasles; that of the Chippewa and Ojibway by Ferrand; that of the Montagnais by Laure and Le Brosse; that of other Algonquin tribes by several Jesuits. Even in Maryland, though but a short time there and with the care of the white settlers on his hands, Andrew White wrote a grammar, vocabulary and a catechism in the native dialect.

The knowledge of these distant lands and of their peoples were considerably advanced by the writings of the Jesuit missionaries. The fathers, by the journals of their travels and by their reports to their superiors, made Europe acquainted with the customs, usages and traditions of the strange peoples to whom they brought the light of the Gospel. Their observations became sources for the history, ethnography and geography of the new countries; the value of the *Jesuit Relations*, written by the French missionaries of Canada, is known to all. They were, however, but one collection of hundreds of similar documents, such as the reports and writings of Paez, d'Almeida, Mendez and Lobo on Abyssinia; of Sicard on Egypt; of Cordeyro on the Azores; of Barradas on the lands of the Tigris; of Tieffentaller on Hindustan; of Tachard on Siam; of Koeffler on Cochin-China; of de Andrade, de Semedo, du Halde, Gerbillon, Legobien, Gaubil and von Laimbeckhoven on China and its neighbors, Mongolia, Korea, and Tibet. The *Mémoires concernant la Chine* and the *Lettres Édifiantes et Curieuses* of the French Jesuits laboring in China, if not so well known as the Canadian *Relations*, are quite as important. Lafiteau and Charlevoix wrote authoritatively on the Indian tribes of Canada; Acosta with great distinction on the lands and peoples of South America; Valera and Eder on Peru; Molina on Chile; Dobrizhoffer on the Paraguay Reductions; Eckart on Brazil; Salvatierra, Kino and Baegert on Mexico; Combes on Mindinao and the Philippines.

Poetry and prose received many worthwhile contributions from the pens of Jesuit writers. Latin poetry, as was natural in the times and the circumstances, benefited the most: Anchieta wrote two thousand and eighty-six distichs in honor of the Mother of God; Bidermann, the foremost author of school-dramas, composed a three volume work of Latin epigrams, a satirical work on Utopia, and German abstracts of his Latin plays. The best known of all the Jesuit Latin poets is Balde, a kindly and pleasing poet whose works have merited translation. Masen besides writing several school-dramas, historical and ascetical works, as well as a treatise on Eloquence, was the author of the poem *Sarcotis*, which has been frequently translated and had some influence on Milton in his writing of *Paradise Lost*. Other Jesuits who wrote Latin poetry with success are: Sarbiewski, Rapin, LaRue, Ceva, Bougeant, Carpani, Cunichio and Zamagna.

Nor in the poetry of their mother-tongues were good poets lacking among the Jesuit writers. Frederick von Spe was especially noteworthy; his *Trutz-Nachtigal* and his *Goldenes Tugendbuch* contain many charming and beautiful songs. Balde wrote as beautiful poems in German on our Lady as he did in Latin; the songs of Nakatenus have merited publication even in our day; Haschka wrote the words of the hymn which Haydn set to music for the Austrian national anthem; Blessed Robert Southwell's poems are treasures of English literature. In Hungarian Faludi exercised considerable influence on the Magyar poetry, as did Naruszewicz in Polish and Bettinelli in Italian.

In their native prose, Jesuits wrote with success. A few of the more noteworthy of the Jesuit prose-writers are: Campion and Persons in English; Bartoli, the elder Segneri, Strada, Pallavicino and Bresciani in Italian; Ribadeneira, Mariana and de Isla in Spanish; Bourdaloue and Bouhours in French; Pázmány in Hungarian. Gracián introduced the *estilo culto* into Spanish prose. As literary critics, de Cygne, Brumoy, Tournemine, Jouvancy and Bouhours were highly honored.

The dramas written for production by the pupils of their colleges must be listed among the foremost literary achievements of the Jesuits.[22] So numerous were these plays and such was their influence that they have merited the study of leading scholars of the dramatic art. Their primary purpose, however, was not the advancement of the drama, but the cultural education and moral instruction of the pupils. To afford an exercise for eloquence and rhetoric, to bring home the principles of the classic drama, to help towards a greater fluency in Latin speech, these were the primary pedagogical objectives. To foster piety, to guard youth against the corrupting influence of evil society by the portrayal of vice as something essentially despicable, to arouse a veritable crusade for virtue by the sight of the inspiring example of the saints, these were the primary moral objectives. Yet these school-dramas were not without considerable influence on the development of the theatre, particularly in the technique of production, the use of scenery and the employment of music. According to Trautmann, the Jesuits sought to unite all arts for the service of the drama.

The themes of the school-dramas were drawn from Biblical episodes, the lives and legends of the saints and the events of profane history; in the treatment of purely secular subjects, the plots were spiritually serious, deeply tragic and morally important. Comic drama was written also, striking at those shortcomings and foibles of human nature which could be portrayed without offense to conscience. It need scarcely be said that vulgarity and low comedy were ruled out. The titles of some of the productions will give an idea of the general run of the themes: *The Prodigal Son, Joseph in Egypt, Christ the Judge, Saul and David, Elias, Constantine, Belisarius, Godfrey de Bouillion, The Conversion of St. Benno.*

The productions were often given before the public; indeed, one of the purposes of the Jesuit school-dramas came to be the edification and training of the people. In 1614 the students of the College of La Fléche acted their play on a most elaborate scale before Louis XIII and his court. But nowhere were the plays given before larger audiences and with greater splendor than in Munich, especially in the years 1574, 1577 and 1597.[23] The Bavarian Dukes cooperated in a most generous way and the people flocked from all the nearby country to the outdoor performances, thronging the square, crowding the balconies and even the

---

[22] Muller, *Das Jesuitendrama in den Ländern deutscher Zunge*, 2 vols., Augsburg (1930); Janssen, *History of the German People*, Vol. XIII, pp. 185–208; Baumgartner, *Geschichte der Welt-literatur*, Vol. IV, pp. 623–637.

[23] Duhr, *Geschichte der Jesuiten in den Ländern deutscher Zunge*, Vol. I, pp. 325–356.

roofs of the adjoining houses. *Constantine* was the tragedy offered in 1574. The performance was two days in its presentation, over one thousand actors took part and the whole city was decorated for the occasion. In the victorious entry into Rome after the defeat of Maxentius, Constantine drove four span of horses, surrounded by four hundred horsemen in shining armor. The visible sign of the Redemption was carried through the streets amidst the spirited cheering of the populace, deeply stirred by the impressive spectacle. For the performance of the tragedy *Esther* in 1577, the ducal court loaned the costumes, jewels and plate of the palace treasury; over one hundred characters participated in the great banquet scene. The dedication of St. Michael's Church, the gift of Duke William to the Jesuits, in 1597, was the occasion of a tremendous pageant-drama, *The Triumph of St. Michael;* 900 singers formed the choir for the musical parts. Even the devils were represented in large numbers, for at the conclusion of the piece St. Michael gathered about him his hosts and drove 300 devils into the mounting flames of hell. In the beginning, and for a long time, the dramas were given in Latin; in fact the use of that language had been prescribed by the *Ratio.* However, for the benefit of those who did not understand Latin, translations were often supplied; while for the grand pageants, before each act a narrator explained in the native speech the story and the action which was to come. The people were satisfied; indeed the very force of the incidents held their attention and the themes were usually familiar to them. After 1700, presentations in the vernacular became more common. The plays had most salutary effects on the observers; Guarinoni, an Italian physician, declared that they did more good than a sermon; a spectator of the play *Cenodoxus the Doctor of Paris, or The Conversion of St. Benno,* even raised the value to a hundred sermons. It is good to note that the Jesuit writers abstained from writing low polemics and eschewed all insulting abuse and invective against the Protestants, in marked contrast to the writers of the school-dramas of the sects.[24] This is admitted by several Protestant critics.

The drama was used successfully not only in Europe but in the foreign mission fields of Paraguay, Japan, Ceylon and India. In these lands they possessed a special efficacy in teaching the truths of religion and in depicting the history of Christianity. Of course, the Jesuit school-dramas ought not to be judged too strictly according to the canons of great dramatic art. Their primary purpose, as has been said, was education and edification. Still they were not without merit and they helped toward the advance of culture, encouraging a taste for the theatre and for its subsidiary arts. Jesuits contributed to the technique of the drama in such

---

[24] Janssen, *History of the German People,* Vol. XIII, pp. 186–190.

writings as those of Jouvancy in his *Ratio Docendi*, of Masen in his *Palaestra Eloquentiae Ligatae Dramatica*, and of Lang in his *Dissertatio de Actione Scenica*. Goethe, who witnessed a production of the Jesuit school-drama at Regensburg, praised not only the play he saw but the artistic methods of the Jesuit writers.[25]

St. Ignatius had entered the field of education because he saw therein great opportunities for the glory of God and the good of souls. From his initiative his sons produced a system of learning, established in a short time hundreds of colleges, and began to occupy an acknowledged place among scholars. Such were their activities and accomplishments, indicated above, that many came to consider them primarily as a teaching order. Certainly they had made education one of the chief works of the Society of Jesus.

---

[25] Goethe, *Travels in Italy*, p. 3 (Translation, London, 1883).

CHAPTER X

THE FOREIGN MISSION FIELD

Inspiring indeed is the record of the seemingly endless labors of the Jesuits in pulpit and chancel, in classroom and lecture hall during the Counter-Reformation. Yet just as inspiring are the toilings of those other Jesuits, who, leaving Europe, journeyed afar amidst diverse perils to bring the light of the Faith to heathen Hindus, Chinese and Japanese, to savage Africans and Red-Indians. Their missions benefited as much from Aquaviva's genius for government as did the home provinces; the work of the older stations was more solidly grounded and many new peoples were evangelized, often in the face of the bitterest opposition and even of martyrdom. The history of the Jesuit missions after the great general's death is largely an account of the following out of the plans and methods set down in his time.

The African missions had at least their full measure of heroism if not of success. Abyssinia [1] in 1580 seemed a hopeless proposition; the handful of Jesuits could effect little in conversions and there was small hope for European recruits with the Mohammedan corsairs infesting the trade routes. In 1589 two fathers, Montserrat and Paez, fell into Mussulman hands and were doomed to the slavery of the galleys; in 1595 a Maronite Jesuit, de Georgiis, did succeed in landing at Massawah, only to be slain by the sword. Two years later, on the death of Lopez, not a single Jesuit remained in the dominions of the Negus. The mission was not abandoned; Paez after his release from the galleys entered the country in 1603, to be followed shortly afterwards by five of his brethren, one a converted Brahmin from India. A period of prosperity for Catholics ensued. Paez, the superior, won the good will of the Negus, especially by his knowledge of medicine and of architecture; the great royal palace at Gondar was built by him. A catechism was composed in the Ethiopian tongue, disputations were held with the Monophysite clergy, a college was established, and mission stations were set up even among the frontier tribes. Just before his own death in 1623, Paez received the Negus into the Church. More recruits came to labor on the mission, despite the dangers from the Turks who captured and decapitated two of them, Machado and Pereira. By 1625 over twenty-five thousand

---

[1] Beccari, *Rerum Aethiop. Scriptores Occidentales inediti* (14 vols.), Rome (1903–14),

heathens had been baptized and many thousand heretics brought back to the fold; in the following year Catholicism was declared the state religion. But the prosperity was short-lived; in 1532 a new Negus, Basilides, a vicious profligate, hating the religion which opposed his polygamy, launched a bitter persecution. Priests were imprisoned, hanged or stoned to death, and the Abyssinian Mission was destroyed. More successful were the Jesuits who evangelized the negroes of Angola, Guinea and the Congo. In Angola by 1590 Barreira could report twenty thousand converts, a college at Loanda, two residences and a mission station; in 1604 the same missionary raised the Cross on the shores of Sierra Leone, baptizing the native potentate and many of his subjects. The negroes found in Barreira and his confrères, Vogado and Veres, staunch protectors against the slave-traders. In Europe at the same time the missionaries' brethren, Molina and Sanchez, were teaching the unlawfulness and injustice of slavery. The mission in Mozambique eventually possessed a college and six residences. All these apostolic labors in Angola, Guinea, the Congo and Mozambique, were successfully operated by the fathers until the suppression of the order.

India furnished another proof that the blood of the martyrs is the seed of the Church, in the deaths at Cuncolim in Salsette on July 15, 1583 of Bl. Rudolph Aquaviva, a nephew of the General, and of his four companions Bl. Alphonsus Pacheco, Bl. Antonio Francisco, Bl. Peter Berno and Bl. Francisco Aranha.[2] In the very next year, 1,500 pagans became Christians; in 1589, 3,800 were baptized, whilst a college and a seminary were erected near the site of the martyrdom. About the same time in Southeastern India, the Jesuits were assisting the Archbishop of Goa, Alexius Menezes, in his successful efforts for the reunion of the Nestorians of Malabar, the so-called Thomas Christians, taking part with the Archbishop and the Malabar priests in the synod of Diamper at which the unification was accomplished. Pope Clement VIII appointed Father Roz, as one sympathetic with the Malabarese and fully acquainted with their liturgy, to be their Bishop in the see of Angamale; later the Pope transferred him to the newly-created archiepiscopal see of Cranganore where he was able to complete the work of reunion.[3]

The Madura mission for the heathens of this part of India was begun in 1595 by Gonsalvo Fernandez. Relatively few conversions, and these only among the pariahs, or the casteless people, were all that this devoted missionary could show after years of effort. No impression whatsoever was made upon the Brahmins, who deigned not even a curious

[2] Goldie, *First Christian Mission to the Great Mogul; The Blessed Martyrs of Cuncolim*, London (1897).

[3] Bertrand, *La Mission du Madure d'après des documents inédits*, 4 vols. Paris (1847–1854), pp. 848–854.

interest in Christianity, which for them was not merely an inferior philosophy from the barbaric West but a vulgar superstition fitted only for the untouchables. A change for the better came with the arrival on the Madura mission in 1605 of Robert de' Nobili, an Italian Jesuit and a nephew of St. Robert Bellarmine. De' Nobili's solution of the problem was, to say the least, most revolutionary: he proposed to reach the influential Brahmins by becoming, as far as it was possible for a Christian, a Brahmin himself, one who could expound the Gospel to them in their own language and according to their accustomed method of presentation. Fortified with the approval of the Archbishop of Cranganore and of his own Provincial, Laerzio, he began to lead the life of a Hindu recluse, cutting himself off completely from any connections with the Portuguese, even from Fernandez, the apostle of the lower castes; with these last he likewise avoided every contact. His dress was that of a Brahmin noble, his customs those of the Saniassi, Hindu ascetics held in the highest veneration. The first lonely days and weeks, spent in uninterrupted solitude, were employed in obtaining a mastery of Sanskrit and of the Tamil and Telingas speech, as well as in seeking a penetrating knowledge of Indian philosophy. The curiosity of the Brahmins was aroused over this mysterious hermit, interviews were sought which, when the strange recluse felt he had sufficient facility in the native tongue, were graciously accorded. In the first meetings philosophy and science were the exclusive topics of conversation; but eventually de' Nobili led on to the exposition of Christianity, offering its truths as a development or a realization of the best Indian thought. The reserve of the Brahmins was broken and before long some of them were even seeking Baptism; for these the Jesuit composed apologetical works couched in the Hindu manner of presentation. Against the native customs no line was drawn, excepting, of course, those incompatible with Christianity, such as polygamy and idolatrous superstitions. De' Nobili allowed the differences of caste, considering them to be purely civil institutions and even permitted the use of the distinctive marks to the newly baptized. His success was amazing; large numbers of Brahmins became catechumens, and their conversion, as subsequent persecution proved, was genuine.

Opposition to such unique and revolutionary practices was soon forthcoming from all sides. The recriminations of the jealous Brahmins were to be expected; yet they effected little, for converts continued to be made. The brethren of de' Nobili, especially Fernandez, as well as other Catholics, so sharply and effectively criticised him that his works were brought to a standstill for ten years. Complaints were carried to Goa, and from Goa to Rome. Some of the charges not only misunderstood but grossly misrepresented the pioneer missionary; one rumor in Rome had it that he had apostatized. De' Nobili in his own defense composed an exhaustive apology; this with other important documents were sent to Rome for the commission which Paul V had set up to inquire into the whole problem. In the meantime an ecclesiastical assembly at Goa, previously hostile, changed to a more favorable opinion. The Roman decision was on the whole favorable to de' Nobili, even to allowing the use of caste symbols; however certain precautions were insisted on to eliminate heathen superstitions.

For forty-two years de' Nobili labored on the Madura mission. Though attaining most remarkable successes, he did not lack a full share of crosses; at one time from 1640–1642 he was held a prisoner in Madura. He died with a reputation for sanctity at Mylapore on January 16, 1656. Such were his services that he has been hailed as the "Second Apostle of India" and as the "Apostle of the Brahmins." [4]

His co-laborers and their successors carried on in his methods, founding missions not only in Madura but in Carnate, Mogor and Ceylon. Of these zealous priests one became a martyr, Bl. John de Britto,[5] who was beheaded in a persecution aroused by his opposition to polygamy. Other outstanding laborers were: de Vico; Martius; de Maya, a fellow prisoner with de' Nobili; Laynez, later Bishop of Mylapore; da Costa, who entered one of the castes permitted to treat with all groups and was thus able to gain many souls among the lower castes; Bouchet, who in twelve years converted 20,000 souls; Beschi, known for his works in Tamil and his controversial writings against the Lutherans, who first came to Madura in 1706; Deistermann and Tieffentaller. So blessed were the endeavors of the Madura missionaries that usually 5,000 converts were made in a year; even in persecution times 3,000 was the annual total. Towards the end of the seventeenth century the Christians numbered over 150,000. This figure is remarkable in view of the fact that the Jesuits on the mission were usually seven or eight, the highest number was fourteen in 1746; and it is noteworthy too for the reason that the Madura mission was outside of and remote from the Portuguese possessions, protected neither by military force nor political influence. At the banishment of the order from the Portuguese dominions the mission suffered in the loss of the Portuguese priests; still, those of other nationalities carried on until the general suppression; and even then they continued to labor under the Paris Foreign Mission priests until their deaths.

About the beginning of the eighteenth century the Jesuit mission

---

[4] Dahmen, *Ein Beitrag zur Geschichte der Missions-methode und der Indologie*, Münster (1924); *Robert de' Nobili, l'Apôtre des Brahmes, Première apologie* (1610), trans. Paris (1931).

[5] *The Life of Ven. John Britto*, Oratory Series, London (1851); Haupert, *John de Britto*, Trichinopoly (1924).

among the Brahmins had to pass through a serious crisis arising out of the toleration of the native customs, the controversy over the Malabar Rites.[6] For eighty years after Gregory XV's decision, de' Nobili and his successors continued unmolested to permit certain native customs and practices, and themselves to wear the distinctive Brahmin dress. The difficulty of administering the Sacraments separately to the various castes was solved by the practice of some of the Jesuits adopting the caste of the padaram, a group which was allowed intercourse with all castes. It should be noted that de' Nobili himself secretly administered to the pariahs, as did some of his brethren who like him had adopted the usages of the Saniassi, the highest Hindu ascetics. In 1704 opposition broke out afresh. Complaints were lodged at Rome against the Jesuits' procedure; and the Papal Legate, Charles-Thomas-Maillard de Tournon, who had been sent by Clement XI as legatus a latere to visit the Christian mission of the East, especially of China, decided to adjudicate the problem. During an eight months' stay at Pondicherry awaiting passage to China, the legate examined the charges. It must be said that his procedure was neither thorough nor prudent; hindered by sickness, he did not visit any part of the inland missions; his inquiries were made of Capuchins, the complainants, who had not visited the interior either, and from a few natives, the latter being questioned through interpreters; his consultation of the Jesuits seems to have been very cursory. At length he issued a decree of sixteen articles legislating on practices in use or supposed to be in use among the neophytes of Madura, Mysore and the Carnatic; these practices were condemned and prohibited as defiling the purity of religion and faith, and the missionaries were forbidden under threat of heavy censures from permitting them among their converts. The decree was dated June 23, 1704; yet the Jesuit superiors were not informed until July 8, just three days before Tournon's departure. The fathers were dismayed, yet in the short time left strove to impress on the legate the insufficiency of his information and the disaster for Christianity which impended. Tournon yielded so far as orally to remove the censures and provisionally to suspend the prescription requiring all the missionaries to give spiritual assistance to sick pariahs not only in their churches but in their dwellings.

The decree when it reached Rome was received with reserve. On January 7, 1706, Clement XI ordered a provisional confirmation to be sent to him, decreeing its execution until the Holy See might provide otherwise, after having heard those who might wish to speak in objection. The Holy Father however informed the Procurator of the Madura mission that the missionaries were to observe the decree "in so far as

---

[6] Bertrand, *La Mission du Madure d'après des documents inédits*; cf. Bibliography in *Cath. Encyc.* Article "Malabar Rites."

the Divine glory and the salvation of souls would permit." The objections and the suggested corrections of the missionaries were carefully examined during the pontificates of Clement XI, Innocent XIII, and Benedict XIII. The last mentioned Pope enjoined on the bishops and the missionaries of the district the execution of Tournon's decree. It is highly possible that this decision did not have force in India, for shortly afterwards Clement XII, Benedict's successor, ordered the whole case reopened. The final disposition came when the Cardinals of the Holy Office drew up an instruction on the Tournon decree and Clement XII by a Brief of August 24, 1734 sanctioned their decision and prescribed an oath for the missionaries that bound them to the observance of the Brief of August 24 and obliged them to obtain a similar obedience from their neophytes. In the regulations of 1734 there were mitigations of many hard prescriptions of Tournon's decree, some being replaced by mere counsel and advice. The most difficult point retained was that which imposed on the missionaries the public administration of the sacraments to sick pariahs in their dwellings. The Jesuits submitted as their vows and spirit demanded, even though it was hard for them to suppress their misgivings for the future of Christianity among the high caste Brahmins.

The enemies of the Society have used the question of the Malabar Rites, and also of the contemporaneous Chinese Rites, to accuse the Jesuits of knowingly accepting for themselves, or deliberately permitting to their neophytes idolatrous or superstitious practices. Such a charge is both unjust and absurd. De' Nobili and his brethren were not so stupid as to have undergone the perils and hardships of the missions of Madura, Mysore and the Carnatic and to have incurred the certainty of eternal damnation, just for the sake of establishing a spurious and false Christianity. The Popes who disapproved of some of the Malabar usages, never questioned the good faith of the Jesuit missionaries. The beatification of Bl. John de Britto, who practised the rites, proved the confidence of the Popes in the good intention of the fathers. It was fundamentally a question of that tolerance of native customs which every missionary must make. To say that some of the Jesuits of the Madura mission carried their toleration too far, in no way impugns either their sincerity or their honesty.

In the north of India the Jesuits appeared again at the court of the Grand Mogul in 1595 when Jerome Xavier, a kinsman of the saint, and two other Jesuits were received by Akbar.[7] In the freedom which the Indian potentate extended to the fathers, flourishing missions were established at Lahore and Agra, while numerous and notable conversions

---

[7] Maclagan, *The Jesuits and the Great Mogul*, London (1932).

followed. Akbar, though he showed himself more than favorable to the Christian priests, reading with interest the life of Christ translated into the Persian by Xavier, remained a sceptic to the end. His successor, Djehangir, at first manifested little good will towards the missionaries, but later so changed his attitude as to allow the Baptism of his brother's three sons, a ceremony which was performed with the greatest splendor and solemnity. So bright were the Church's prospects in 1612 that the Jesuits felt justified in opening a college at Agra and a house at Patna. A reversal of good fortune came in 1616; then so bad became the affairs of the Christians that the missionaries proposed to abandon the field. This surrender the General, Vitelleschi, refused to consider. One of the companions of Xavier, the lay-brother Benedict de Goes, left the north of India in 1602 in search of a land route to China; he penetrated into Tibet, probably the earliest modern European to reach the kingdom of the Grand Lama.[8] Two of his brethren, priests of the Society, de Andrade and Marquez, in 1624 arrived at Ladak where they were received by the friendly local ruler. Two other Jesuits, Grueber and d'Orville, starting out later in 1661, after six months of perilous journeying from Peking, reached Lasha. There they remained two months and descended through Nepal to Agra, where d'Orville died. In the early eighteenth century Desideri and Freyre worked at Lasha from 1716–1729, when the Capuchins took over the mission.

The Jesuits labored with the Spanish Dominicans and later with the Paris Foreign Mission Fathers in the extremely hazardous missions of Cochin-China and Tonkin.[9] St. Francis Xavier's name is forever connected with Malacca; there in 1649 his brethren founded a college. Some thirty years earlier, in 1615, two fathers of the Society, Buzoni and Carvalho, began an apostolate in Cochin-China which was so successful that within twenty years they converted 12,000 heathens. The increase in the number of the Christians became especially notable after the arrival of de Rhodes [10] in 1624; over thirty churches were erected, while the yearly average of converts up to 1663 was 2,000. Soon after, a long-enduring persecution broke out which had its corps of martyrs, especially about the year 1700. The Jesuits remained until 1755. To Tonkin came de Rhodes and Marques in 1627 to help the Spanish Dominicans; the response to their preaching was most heartening, the sister and seventeen relatives of the king sought Baptism. Yet persecution in 1630 forced the missionaries to leave and brought death to many native Christians. Four Jesuits went to North Annam to answer the appeal which the Christians of this land had made to Pope Urban VIII.

---

[8] Wessels, *Early Jesuit Travellers in Central Asia*, The Hague (1924).

[9] Demontezon, *Mission de la Cochinchine et du Tonkin*, Paris (1858).

[10] *Voyages et Missions du P. Rhodes*, Paris (1653), Lille (1884).

From North Annam they were able again to enter Tonkin and to reap a rich harvest; by 1661 the Tonkinese Christians numbered 300,000 with 386 churches. Tonkin however was destined to be a land of martyrs. In 1658 persecution commenced and lasted with more or less rigor for a hundred years; the missionaries were frequently banished, only to return each time shortly afterwards; and the native Christians, though of the proverbially fickle Annamite stock, suffered martyrdom by the thousands. In 1721 and in 1723 four Jesuits were killed, Alvarez, de Abreu, de Cunha and Messari; in 1737 two more were put to death, Bucherelli and Kratz. Yet in that very year seven fathers, including three natives, labored on this dangerous mission. The warfare against the Society in Portugal helped to bring to an end the Jesuit missions in Indo-China; two fathers, Gietl and le Clerc however came to Tonkin in 1772. Of all the mission lands, here were more native priests; and here, too, were congregations of native nuns. Both native priests and native nuns achieved wonders in keeping the Faith alive amidst the most terrible persecutions.

The first Jesuit to obtain a permanent residence in China was Michael Ruggieri who arrived at Canton in 1582, where in the next year he was joined by Francisco Pasio and Matteo Ricci.[11] The Viceroy of Kwang-tung received the Jesuits with benevolent kindness, assigning the fathers a house in Tschao-King. In 1585 Ruggieri and a companion visited the provinces of the interior, leaving Ricci to maintain the work at Tschao-King. Matteo Ricci, the father of modern Chinese Christianity, was born at Macerta in the March of Ancona in 1552; after following the classical course at the Jesuit college in Ancona and the study of law in Rome, he entered the Society of Jesus, 1571. Gifted with a special aptitude for the sciences, it was Ricci's good fortune to have had Clavius as his professor in astronomy and mathematics; the scientific knowledge then acquired under such a master was now to serve the pupil well, gaining for him an entrée into the circles of the Chinese literati. Right from the start these learned Chinese were impressed by the industrious and well-ordered lives of the kindly foreign priests, so markedly in contrast with that of their own bonzes. The house at Tschao-King with its oil paintings was an object of keenest interest to the mandarins. Ricci was especially happy in his ability to embody foreign ideas in a form easily understandable by his inquirers; from geographical and astronomical explanations he proceeded eventually to an exposition of the fundamental truths of Christian belief and morals. His initial progress, it is true, was very slow; no converts were made among the learned, in fact only one poor abandoned incurable sought Baptism. But Ricci would

[11] Tacchi-Venturi, *L'Apostolato del P. M. Ricci C. de J. in Cina secondo i suoi scritti inedti*, Rome (1910); P. Matteo Ricci, S.J., *Commentari della Cina dall'autografo' inedito*, Macerata (1911).

not be discouraged, though after six years he could count only sixty Christians. Unfamiliarity with the language and the consequent need of interpreters proved a serious drawback; to overcome this, though forty years of age, the zealous Italian began the study of Chinese. Ricci was quite as gifted a linguist as a scientist, and he obtained such a grasp of the language that in 1595 he wrote in Chinese a work *The True Doctrine of God*, which has merited to be included by Khuan-Lung in a collection of Chinese classics. Other works in the native tongue appeared from his pen, treatises on religion, arithmetic, astronomy, geography, music and philosophy.

The enmity of the new Viceroy interrupted for a while the good work and forced the fathers to leave their home. The storm was short in passing and soon the Jesuits were back in Tschao-King. Despite the persecution of the bonzes, the house became a gathering place for the mandarins and the scholars who delighted in the conferences with the Western priests. More to accommodate themselves to the native idea of a learned savant, as well as to avoid confusion with the despised bonzes, the Jesuits decided to adopt the costume of the Chinese scholars and to don the silken robes of the mandarins. The experienced Valignani approved of this step, as later did both the General and the Pope. Ricci was ever a practical man; realizing how much the approval of the Emperor would mean to the mission, he determined to make the journey to distant Peking and there to seek the acquiescence of that potentate. He first travelled to Nanking in 1595; though unable at once to set up a Christian community there, he did find means of obtaining his ultimate object when the Governor decided to take him along to Peking that he might assist in the improvement of the Chinese calendar. His stay in the imperial city on this first arrival was of short duration. On his return to Nanking he found things had so improved that more than ever he was able to obtain the favorable attention of the intellectuals. It was in this city that in 1603 the cause of Christianity received a decided impetus by the conversion of a foremost civil official and scholar, Paul Siu.

On his appointment as superior of the mission, Ricci again became eager for the settlement of Peking. A second time he set out for the capital which he reached after a journey of indescribable hardships, January 24, 1601. This time the Emperor Wang-li, ignoring the strongest opposition, granted the Occidental priest permission to establish a residence. The monarch was especially delighted with the presents which Ricci had brought to him: striking clocks, astronomical instruments, a universal geographical map, copper engravings and oil paintings of the Redeemer and of the Madonna. The imperial good will and the welcome of the eminent statesmen and scholars more than counter-balanced the hostility aroused against the Christian savant. Ricci was able to build a house and even to establish a novitiate in Peking, August 27, 1605. The number of converts in the beginning was not very great, after 25 years they counted only 2,000; yet the paucity of numbers was made up for by the constant character of the neophytes and by their importance as highly placed civil-servants or learned men. The Chinese Mission suffered a staggering loss in the premature death of Matteo Ricci on May 11, 1610, in his fifty-eighth year. The Emperor, to show his esteem for the dead missionary, himself provided a place for the burial, a mark of distinction reserved only for men who had rendered outstanding service to the state.

The Chinese mission continued to make progress; in Nanking one of the fathers, Vagnoni, was emboldened to preach Christianity openly, and in 1611 a church could be ceremoniously consecrated. To forestall the evil effects of banishment, an ever-present possibility, the Jesuits strove hard for the formation of a native clergy and for a liturgy in harmony with Chinese ideas. They petitioned Rome for the extraordinary privilege of substituting Chinese for Latin in the ceremonies. Paul V in 1615, acting on a favorable decision of the Roman Inquisition and with the advice of St. Robert Bellarmine, allowed the employment of Chinese, specifying, however, that only the language of the scholars was to be used.

The persecution which broke out in 1617 threatened to destroy completely the advantages hitherto achieved. On February 4 of that year an imperial edict banished the missionaries; the two in Nanking were thrown into a wooden cage and transported to Canton, where the fathers from Peking were joined to them, and all were brought to Macao. In this exile a ray of hope broke for the missionaries, when in 1619 several new laborers arrived bearing three Papal Briefs authorizing the use of Chinese in the Mass, in the Breviary and in the administration of the Sacraments, as well as the translation of the Sacred Scriptures and the covering of the head during the Sacrifice of the Mass. With the fall in 1622 of Shin, the mandarin most responsible for the persecution, the mission was restored and entered upon a most flourishing period. Five years later, at the death of the Emperor Hi-tsong, there were twenty-six fathers in twelve residences scattered through eight provinces.

Success continued still to increase during the reign of Tsong-Tsching, 1627–1644, owing largely to the work of Father Adam Schall.[12] Johann Adam Schall von Bell was born in Cologne in 1591; after his studies and ordination in the Society, his plea for the Chinese mission was accepted and he arrived at Macao in 1619. When the persecution of Shin

---

[12] Werfer, *Leben des P. Joh. Adam Schall und sein Wirken in China*, Schaffhausen (1854).

had abated, he worked for some years at Si-ngan-fu, the capital of Shen-si, until 1631, in which year he was summoned to Peking to work on the correction of the Chinese calendar, a project already started by the convert mandarin Paul Li and the Jesuits Longobardi and Schreck. The major part of the work was to be Schall's. The Chinese were accustomed to arrange the calendar every year and for this task there existed a Mathematical Tribunal of two hundred scholars. It was with this body that Schall and his Jesuit assistant had to work; no easy task was it, for they not only had to make numerous mathematical corrections, but they had also to convince the Chinese of their errors, make them understand the changes and prove to them the necessity of the changes and the truth of the principles upon which they were based. To do this the Jesuits had to give courses in astronomy and the underlying mathematical sciences; in pursuance of the last task the fathers composed 137 scientific treatises in Chinese, of which one hundred were published.

Their work in a strict sense might not look evangelical; but it was nevertheless of the utmost importance to the advance of Christianity, for its success won the good will of the emperor and of his high officials throughout China towards the new religion. For this purpose alone did Schall devote himself to the task.

The revolt of the Manchus, which ended the Ming dynasty, did not change the prospects of the mission. When the rebels entered Peking with fire and sword, strangely enough, they left the Jesuit house unmolested. Several members of the fallen dynasty, after their flight to Kwang-si, were baptized by the Jesuit Koffler; among such were the Empress Helena and the Crown Prince Constantine. The first Manchu Emperor, Shun-che, showed himself most favorable to Schall and his brethren. When Schall correctly predicted the solar eclipse of September 1, 1664 and the lunar eclipse of February 10, 1645, the new Emperor named him to the presidency of the Mathematical Tribunal and made him a Mandarin of the First Class. Only the orders of superiors convinced the Jesuit scientist that he should accept the last honor; his acceptance received Papal approval later. Shun-che even waived the strict etiquette of the Chinese court to visit intimately the missionary in his own house and there to spend hours discussing astronomical problems. The whole of China followed the Emperor's favor, hailing John Adam, "T'ang-Jo-Wang," as a great teacher. The growth of the mission under this first Manchu ruler may be judged from the following statistics: in 1617 there were 13,000 Christians, in 1650 they had increased to 150,000 and in 1664 they reached the total of 237,000, ministered to by the Jesuits in 49 residences with 159 churches.

During the minority of Kang-hi, a very severe persecution was directed against the Jesuits by the Chinese pagans at the instance of the astronomer Yang-kiang-sien who attacked "the revolutionary, evil learning and false astronomy of the missionaries." Schall, Verbiest, Buglio and Magalhaens were cast into prison and sentenced to be strangled. A high judicial court found the sentence too light and ordered Schall to be cut into bits while still alive. The old missionary, almost entirely incapacitated by paralysis, was unable to make himself understood in his defense; his colleague Verbiest, though himself heavily chained, interpreted his replies and made an heroic and fiery defense of his stricken leader. The sentence was never carried out, owing to the superstitious terror of the Chinese at an earthquake and fire which destroyed the very part of the palace chosen for the execution. Shortly after his release, the old missionary died, in 1666; his end was possibly hastened by his sufferings. Adam Schall was a saintly missionary, a great scientist, a lovable character, and the second great figure of the Jesuit Chinese Mission.

Ferdinand Verbiest, born at Courtrai in Belgium, October 9, 1623, was the third great missionary of China.[13] His complete defeat of Yang-kiang-sien and the heathen astronomical systems, won for him the good will of the new Emperor Kang-hi, who made him first a member of the Mathematical Tribunal and later its president. Buglio and Magal-haens too were welcomed back; other missionaries returned in 1667, in which year the converts numbered twenty thousand. In 1674 Verbiest constructed the great bronze astronomical instruments which even to this day constitute one of the sights for the tourists in Peking; he also cast over 132 cannons for the imperial army, instruments far superior to the Chinese weapons, and invented a more efficient type of gun carriage. What pleased the Emperor especially was the table of all the solar and lunar eclipses for the next two thousand years which Verbiest had drawn up. These scientific achievements gained such favor for the mission that several princes and princesses, many mandarins and scholars became Catholics. The number of the native Christians cared for by the Jesuits mounted to 300,000, with 208 churches; the complete roll of Chinese Catholics, administered to by Jesuits, Dominicans and fathers of the Missions Étrangères, counted up to 800,000 in 1,200 communities. On March 22, 1692 the Jesuits Thomas and Pereira obtained from Kang-hi an edict of complete toleration for the Christian religion. When Verbiest died, January 27, 1688, the Emperor caused a noble tomb to be erected over his grave. The Papacy too honored this zealous missionary-scientist, when Innocent XI in a Brief of December 3, 1681 bestowed on him the highest praise.

During the years 1697 to 1717 an internal storm almost wrecked

---

[13] Carton, *Notice Biog. sur le P. F. Verbiest, Missionaire a la Chine,* Bruges (1839); Bosmans, "Ferdinand Verbiest," *Revue des Quest. Scientif.* (1912).

the mission, the controversy over the Chinese Rites.[14] The difficulties arose out of the efforts to bring into harmony the local traditions and practices of the neophytes with the Christian Faith. As was said before, it was a problem that has faced every missionary to heathen people; St. Patrick was especially happy in the solution by which he retained for his converts everything Gaelic except that which was essentially idolatrous or immoral. The particular question in China concerned the honors paid to Confucius and to ancestors, as well as the words used in designating the Deity. The Jesuits with hardly an exception believed that these rites could have a purely secular significance, and hence permitted their use by their converts. To have prohibited the practices would have practically closed the door to any converts from among the mandarins and the scholars, who in their official duties were obliged to perform them. There can be no question of the sincerity of the fathers in making these concessions; they were all learned men, Ricci, Schall, Verbiest and their confrères; they knew intimately the traditions of the Chinese literati; they had suffered much and they were prepared to suffer even death for the Christian Faith; finally, they were not the type to concoct a degenerate Christianity. Yet sincere missionaries, Dominicans, Franciscans and priests of the Missions Étrangères believed that the concessions had gone too far and that the practices were really idolatrous. One Jesuit, Longobardi, the successor of Ricci as superior, was opposed to the customs, while the Dominican Gregorio Lopez, Bishop of Basilea and Vicar-Apostolic of Nanking, upheld them, sending a memorial to the Sacred Congregation in favor of the Jesuits. Unfortunately a nationalistic element complicated the controversy; the Jesuits were for the most part Portuguese looking to Macao for support, while the Dominicans were Spanish depending on Manila.

The matter was carried to Rome and in 1645 Innocent X condemned seventeen propositions concerning the Chinese Rites. However, in 1656 Alexander VII by a decree of the Congregation of the Index permitted the use of some of the customs, provided they were purely civil ceremonies, all paganism being avoided, and provided that they could not be relinquished without grave injury to the Christians. The dispute did not come to an end; indeed, with the arrival of French missionaries, Jesuits and fathers of the Missions Étrangères, the controversy was much further increased by another nationalistic element and by the repercussions of the burning struggles in France between the Jesuits and the Gallicans and Jansenists. Matters reached a crisis when the Vicar-Apostolic of Fu-kien, Charles Maigrot, in 1693 issued a mandate forbidding the reverence of Confucius and of the ancestors,

---

[14] Huonder, *Der Chinesische Ritenstreit*, Aachen (1921); Schmidlin-Braun, *Catholic Mission History*, Techny (1933), p. 474 ff.

and also the use of the words "Tien" and "Shang-Ti" for God. The Jesuits protested the command and the Vicar-Apostolic sent a representative to Rome in 1696 to present his case. A special congregation of Cardinals and theologians was set up by Innocent XII for the settlement of the dispute. On November 24, 1704 the Holy Office issued a decree prohibiting the Chinese ceremonies; Clement XI dispatched an order for its carrying out to Cardinal de Tournon, Titular Patriarch of Antioch, whom he had already sent to the East to investigate the matter on the spot. The Emperor Kang-hi himself in a letter to the Pope declared that the usages were purely political; further he threatened with the severest penalties anyone who preached against them. Considering the Jesuits to be better informed, Kang-hi, who was friendly to them, finally ordered de Tournon to leave Peking and banished Maigrot. One Jesuit, Visdelou, it is interesting to note, sided with the Legate. At Nanking in 1707 de Tournon issued the mandate prohibiting the Chinese Rites; he was arrested and handed over to the Portuguese of Macao, who cast him into prison where he died June 8, 1710. The new legate, Mezzabarba, made some mitigations which Innocent XII, however, forbade in 1723. The final decision came on July 11, 1742, with the Bull "Ex quo singulari" of Benedict XIV. By this document the Pope ordered all missionaries to suppress heathenish usages and to take an oath binding them to the observance of the decrees. Rome had spoken, there was nothing left but to obey.

The successor of Kang-hi, Yung-cheng, was an enemy of the Christians; during his reign a fierce persecution raged in which 300 churches were destroyed and several Jesuits attacked. Among them was Hinderer who had labored thirty-seven years in China and who had introduced the devotion to the Sacred Heart. Exceptions from the persecutions were made for those Jesuits who held official positions in connection with the Mathematical Tribunal. The succeeding Emperor, Kien-lung, was won to a more favorable attitude by the artistic skill of the lay-brothers, Attiret and Castiglione and their successor, the priest Sickelpart, in the painting and decorating of the imperial palace, as well as by the ability in mathematics, music and linguistics of Amiot. Though the lot of the Jesuits in Peking improved—there were twenty-nine members of the order in three houses—yet in the provinces the imperial agents continued the persecution. At Su-chow on September 13, 1748, de Attimis and Henriquez met martyrs' deaths.

The destruction of the Jesuits in the Portuguese dominions dealt the Mission a severe blow. The French Jesuits continued on until the general suppression; their mission had always been independent of the Portuguese province. In 1773 the Jesuit mission of China finally came to an end. The ex-Jesuits continued to labor as best they could until death claimed them; among these were Rocha who died in 1781, d'Espincha who died in 1788, both members of the Mathematical Tribunal, and de Almeida who died in 1805. The last Jesuit of the old Society in China was de Poirot, whose end came in 1815. Over 456 Jesuits, priests and lay-brothers, labored on the Chinese Mission; they were of various nationalities, Portuguese, Italian, Spanish, German, Swiss, French and Chinese, the latter numbering 81 of whom 48 were priests. Besides, more than one hundred Jesuits died en route to China, many of them the victims of their charity to their fever-stricken fellow passengers.

In another part of the Far East, during the generalate of Aquaviva, the Jesuits established a new foundation for their work. This was in the Philippine Islands,[15] whither they had been called by a Dominican prelate, Bishop de Salaza. The fathers arrived in 1581 for the beginning of their very fruitful apostolate on the Islands; five years later the mission became a vice-province under Mexico; and in 1605 was designated an independent unit. The Jesuits within ten years increased to 100, and in the beginning of the eighteenth century to 165; at the time of the Suppression the fathers cared for 208,798 Catholics in 86 pueblos. Their foundations included 3 colleges, a university (since 1621) at Manila, 4 seminaries and boarding schools, 15 residences and 6 mission stations. The missionaries not only cared for the spiritual and intellectual welfare of the natives, but trained them as well in agriculture, house-construction and in the culture of the silk worm. The fathers from the Philippines evangelized the aborigines of Mindanao, of the Caroline, Ladone and Mariana Islands. The "Apostle of the Marianas" was Luis Sanvitores, who came to the region in 1668; he baptized 50,000 natives in the 13 islands and sealed his labors by a martyr's death. Several German Jesuits worked in these remote islands; two were slain by savages, Borango and Strobach.

No better proof of the flourishing condition of the Japanese mission, at the beginning of the period being treated, could be had than the embassy of the Christian Japanese nobles to the Pope in 1585.[16] Valignani, the Visitor of the Jesuit missions of the Far East, conceived the idea of such an embassy, which would afford concrete justification of the zeal of Gregory XIII for the missions and likewise furnish an actual realization of the greatness of Western culture to the Japanese. The Christian daimios welcomed the proposal, designating their own relatives as the ambassadors. A party of five Japanese princes and high nobles, accompanied by Jesuit interpreters, set out on their long and dangerous jour-

---

[15] Astrain, *Historia de la C. de J. en la Asistencia de España*, Vol. IV, c. 3, 4; V, c. 16; VI, c. 15; VII, c. 18; for Mariana Islands, VI, c. 16; VII, c. 19; Repetti, *The Philippine Mission*, Manila (1938); *The Philippine Vice-Province*, Manila (1938).

[16] Pastor, *History of the Popes*, Vol. XX, pp. 460-465.

ney, February 20, 1582. After two and a half years' travel, going to India and around the Cape of Good Hope, the embassy at last landed at Lisbon, August 10, 1584. Everywhere in Portugal, Spain and Italy great welcomes awaited them; Philip II at Madrid received them with the highest honors of his court, as did the Grand Duke of Tuscany when they passed through his territory. As the Japanese nobles journeyed on, opportunities were afforded them to view the best accomplishments of Western art and architecture; in particular did they marvel at the glories of the Cathedrals of Pisa, Florence and Siena. But the heartiest and the most magnificent welcome of all awaited the Oriental princes at Rome, where they arrived on March 22, 1585. Enormous crowds flocked through the streets to catch a glimpse of these yellow-skinned, almond-eyed strangers from the mysterious islands of the farthest East; Cardinal Farnese made himself their host and Gregory XIII received them in solemn consistory. At this consistory the Japanese princes appeared in their national costume and took part in the elaborate ceremonies with such courtesy and modesty that all the Papal court and the ambassadors of the Catholic powers were deeply touched. No one was more profoundly affected than the aged Pontiff, as he beheld kneeling at his feet these newly-born children of the Faith, who had journeyed from the ends of the earth to offer him, their father, the homage of their people. All Rome was edified with the piety and reverence of the Japanese nobles when weekly they approached the Sacred Table. Sixtus V continued the favor of his predecessor to the Japanese envoys, conferring on them Papal knighthoods on the eve of their departure for their native land. Catholic cities and states showered honors upon them as they travelled through Southern Europe on their homeward journey.

When again they stood on Japanese soil in June 1590, the returned travellers found a very different situation for Catholicism than what had existed when they had started forth. The hour of trial for Christianity had already come.[17] Taikosama, the supreme ruler, had launched a fierce persecution against the Catholic Faith in 1587, because Christian maidens and matrons had refused to submit themselves to his demands. The imprudent behavior of the superior of the mission, Coelho, has been said also to have been a cause of the ruler's enmity. The Law of Christ was prohibited, twenty-two churches were destroyed and three lay-brothers, two native and one European, were martyred. By 1594 six Jesuit priests met their death in the persecution. The fathers refused to flee the Islands, but hid themselves until Valignani in 1591, accredited as the envoy of the Viceroy of India, dared to enter the court of Taikosama and to win the ruler over to halting the persecution and permitting

[17] Delplace, *Le Catholicisme en Japan 1540–93*, Mechlin (1908); Pages, *Histoire de la Religion chrétienne au Japan 1598–1651*, Paris (1869).

the Jesuits to stay in Japan, even though the public functions of the Christian religion remained under ban. The missionaries came forth from their hiding places and continued their apostolate, obtaining numerous conversions. Taikosama in 1596 even received with cordiality the Christian Bishop of Japan, Pedro Martinez, S.J. and gave leave to all Christian priests to do as they pleased in the Islands. These priests now included the Franciscan fathers who had come to Japan three years before. Things did not always go harmoniously with the two groups of religious; unfortunately their disputes were further enflamed by nationalistic differences: the Jesuits were Portuguese and the Franciscans were Spaniards. Unfortunately too Taikosama's good dispositions were not lasting. The increase of the native Christians and the continual arrival of foreign priests aroused his fears of foreign invasion or of domestic revolution. The ridiculous and false boastings of a stranded Spanish sea-captain as to the designs of the Spanish King confirmed the Japanese ruler's apprehensions. Persecution was renewed. Among the Christians put to death at Nagasaki on February 5, 1597, were three native Jesuits, the scholastics, St. Paul Miki and St. John de Goto, and the lay-brother, St. James Kisai.[18] The Jesuits again retired into hiding until the death of Taikosama in the next year brought an end to their afflictions.

As the new ruler, Daifusama, was favorable to the Christian religion, the missionaries could again begin their apostolate. Despite local persecutions the number of the Christians increased to one million in 1614. The first Japanese to reach the priesthood in the Jesuit order was ordained in 1601. Nagasaki, with its five parishes maintained by native priests and the several churches of the Jesuits, Dominicans and Franciscans, became the most important Christian center. The Jesuits displayed great literary activity, producing books such as a Japanese-Portuguese dictionary and a Japanese grammar. Unfortunately for the best interests of the mission, the Jesuits failed to avail themselves of the cooperation of the native secular clergy; European methods did not fit the situation. Much progress was made under the ruler Tjejasu, who was well disposed towards the Catholic religion until his mind was turned against its adherents by the calumnies and false insinuations of the Dutch and English merchants. These adventurers hoped to wrest the trade of Japan from the Spaniards and the Portuguese; and, bitterly hating the Catholic religion, they played upon the Emperor's fear that the European priests were but the advance agents of Spanish conquest. Such insinuations added weight to other causes and moved Tjejasu to commence a severe persecution of Catholics in 1614. The Era of Martyrs

[18] Boero, *Istoria della vita e del martirio dei Santi Giapponesi, Paolo Michi, etc.*, Rome (1862).

had come for the Christians of Japan; most of them met it with heroic constancy.

On January 24, 1614 an edict, banishing all priests and ordering the destruction of all churches, was proclaimed. The succeeding Emperor, Jjemetsu, increased the persecution, trying by wholesale martyrdoms to annihilate Christianity. Thousands were put to death, some being buried alive, others being burned at the stake. Yet in the brief respites which occurred between the persecutions, the surviving priests made many conversions; in 1625 after ten years of violent attacks the Christians totaled 300,000. The combats of the Japanese martyrs and their clergy, both European and native, rival anything read of in the annals of the Martyrs of the Catacombs. The most frightful tortures—being laid on beds of burning coals, being cast into sulphurous waters, hanging head downwards over sulphurous pits—these and other terrible sufferings failed to shake the constancy of these Oriental heroes.

Of the Jesuits, 87 laid down their lives for Christ; 47 priests, of whom 10 were Japanese, and 40 non-priests, scholastics and lay-brothers, of whom 34 were natives. Bl. Juan Machado was slain in 1617; two years later the lay-brother, Bl. Leonard Kimura, was slowly roasted to death. In the "Great Martyrdom" of Nagasaki, September 10, 1622, Bl. Sebastian Kimura, Bl. Charles Spinola and 7 scholastics, after several years of imprisonment, in company with 43 other Christians, gained the crown at the stake. A few days later on September 15, Bl. Camillus Costanzo met death by fire; in the same year on November 1, Bl. Paul Navarro and 3 lay-brothers made the supreme sacrifice. Bl. Jerome de Angelis and Bl. Simon Yempo were killed in 1623; in the next year on February 22, Bl. James Carvalho and 7 companions were slowly burned to death. This terrible form of death was the portion of Bl. Francis Pacheco, Bl. Giovanni Zola, Bl. Balthasar de Torres, 5 scholastics and a lay-brother on June 20, 1626, and Bl. Thomas Tzugi with 2 companions in 1627. In the next year on Christmas Day the lay-brother, Michael Nagaxima, gained the martyr's palm after heroically undergoing eight different forms of torture. The martyred Jesuits of the year 1633 numbered 24.

This year, 1633, saw the beginning of the horrible torture of the "Pit"; the first to die was the lay-brother Nicholas Fucananga, who was hung head downward over the sulphurous pit for almost four days; a few weeks later Father Borges and two novices died in the same terrible fashion; on October 2, after seven days of such agony, death came to the priests Fernandez and Saito. So excruciating was this torture that the Provincial, Ferreira, after five hours of agony apostatized; yet Ferreira was a man who had labored heroically on the Mission for twenty-three years. Twenty years later the apostate returned and willingly suffered the agonies of the pit until death. Nakura, Adami and de Souza, priests, with two lay-brothers, remained steadfast at the time of Ferreira's apostacy. When the news of the unfortunate man's fall reached Europe, thirty-three members of the order under the leadership of Marcello Mastrilli prepared to leave for Japan, there to make reparation by their own deaths. In the meantime the priest, Vieira, and three lay-brothers were martyred in 1634. Father Mastrilli had hardly landed when he was arrested and condemned to the "Pit" where he suffered from October 5 to 17. The last native Jesuit priests, Casui and Porro, were put to death in 1639. The priests, Rubina in 1642 and Marquez in 1643, each with four companions, in an attempt to land in Japan to aid the shepherdless flocks, were captured and slain.

To make certain that Japan would be entirely cut off from the outside world, all travel in foreign lands was forbidden. A few Dutch and Chinese traders were allowed to remain on an island near Nagasaki, but only as sort of half-prisoners; while all other foreigners were prohibited from even landing in the Islands. The Jesuits never abandoned hope of entering Japan once again. Three of them in 1749 actually effected an entry, but what their fate was, no one has ever learned. The actual organization of the Japanese province was kept up until the Suppression. Nothing but praise has been given to the Jesuits for the solid grounding in the Faith which they gave to their Japanese neophytes; the heroic constancy of the Japanese Christians in the hour of martyrdom was its fruit. There has been some criticism of them for the long interval prior to the establishment of a hierarchy and for the little attention given to the formation of a native clergy. The Jesuits had petitioned for a bishop and one arrived eventually but only after a long delay which was the result of circumstances beyond the competence of the Jesuits. There were more grounds for complaint in regard to the native clergy. Yet this must be borne in mind that the whole mission problem, the native clergy included, was a new thing to all Europeans of the sixteenth century. There were ten Japanese Jesuit priests and several native scholastics among the martyrs, which shows that some beginning was made.

In the Near East during the period, the Jesuits were frequently employed by the Popes in their efforts for the reunion of the Eastern schismatics and heretics.[19] Fathers di S. Angelo, Cassa, Lanzea and Sasso visited the various Monophysite sects and the Greek Melchites. If their efforts were not over successful, that fact was due to no lack of endeavor on their part but to the obstinacy which they encountered, for beside the Maronites, who were already Uniates, very few of the Easterners really desired reunion. In 1603 at Caffa on the Black Sea a

---

[19] Carayon, *Relations inédites des missions de la Comp. de Jésus à Constantinople et dans le Levant au XVIIᵉ Siècle*, Paris (1864).

mission was started for the Tartars by Zogda; and in 1614 his brethren
began to work among the isolated Christians of Mingrelia and Georgia.
Members of the order preached missions throughout the islands of the
Aegean, along the Illyrian coast and cooperated with the Franciscans
in Bosnia and Herzegovina. The opening of a Jesuit house in Constantinople, in November 1583, marked the beginning of an important
mission. The fathers obtained entrance into the Turkish capital through
the good offices of the French and the Venetian governments; they were
to devote themselves to the care of the Christian captives, to work for
the reunion of the Greeks and to oppose the Protestants. Mancinelli
labored unsparingly for the Christian slaves of the Turkish galleys. The
work of the Jesuits was temporarily halted when the plague in 1586 carried off all the brethren as its victims. Twenty-three years later in 1609,
thanks to the efforts of the French and Austrian rulers, the Jesuits were
again permitted to open an establishment in Constantinople; and it was
not long before a school, in which instruction was given partly in Greek
and partly in Latin, was started. The Jesuits were in Constantinople primarily as chaplains of the French Embassy; but before long they extended their activities to the Christians of the city, the suburbs, and even
to those in the nearby parts of Asia Minor. In a number of localities
they erected schools which were given over to the direction of nuns,
opened chapels, looked after the spiritual needs of the foreigners, mostly
sailors from the ships in the port, and devoted themselves to reconciling
schismatics. From Constantinople the fathers ventured forth to care for
Christian communities in Saloniki, Naxos, Santoria, Tenos, Syros and
Chios. A mission was established in the Crimea and another at Erzerum
in Armenia, the last in 1688. Even in the kingdom of Persia in the middle of the seventeenth century the members of the order founded at
Ispahan and at Resch Christian settlements which endured until the
bloody persecutions of Nadir Shah, 1736–1747. Among the laborers at
Constantinople Cachod deserves special mention because of the numer-
ous conversions which he made among the schismatics; in the year 1712
alone he reconciled four hundred. This zealous priest likewise devoted
himself to the Christian galley-slaves, and died a martyr of charity in
1726. Of the other apostolic men there should be mentioned: among the
Greeks, Lovina, Erdschlager (another martyr of charity), Keller and
Lichtle; and among the Persians, Roux. In Syria the priests Chikelio,
Manilier, Sella, Beugen and Lambert labored for the reunion of the
Jacobites at Aleppo, Damascus and Saida; in the Lebanon at Antura,
Lambert carried on a similar apostolate. In the year 1750 the "Mission
des Orients," as the whole work in the Levant was known, numbered 7
stations in the Grecian Archipelago, 6 stations in Syria and Egypt, and
2 in Persia.

In the New World, the Jesuits under Aquaviva continued the development and expansion of the missions in Brazil, Peru and Mexico; under his successors they extended their zealous works to all parts of the Western Hemisphere. In Brazil [20] Ven. José Anchieta brought his long and remarkable life to a close in 1597. On the Maranhao River Francisco Pinto met his death at the hands of the savages in January 1608. The work on the Maranhao so increased that in 1629 the region was set off from Brazil as a province. In 1640, Vieira [21] began his zealous apostolate along the Amazon, working out from Maranhao. This missionary, second only to Anchieta, was born in Lisbon in 1580 and was brought to Brazil when still a child. After ordination to the priesthood in the Jesuit order, his gift of eloquence in the pulpits of Brazil, Portugal and Rome and his prose-writings rated him with Bossuet and Bourdaloue. He served Portugal so well as a patriot and a diplomat that Southey calls him one of the greatest statesmen of his country. Vieira's first labors with the aborigines lasted but a year; in 1641 he was called to Portugal to be the confessor and adviser of John IV. His heart always remained with the poor natives of the Amazon valley, so that after eleven years he managed again to be sent to the Maranhao mission. There his journeyings took him over hundreds of miles along the Amazon and its tributaries, amidst tribes of the fiercest savages. He founded fifty villages in which he induced the wandering Indians to settle, translated the catechism into their rude dialects, and trained them in the arts of peace as well as in the truths and practices of Christianity. By the year 1663 there were over 56,000 baptized natives in the Amazon region. So resolutely did Vieira protect the neophytes from slavery and white oppression that twice he was driven from the mission field and once, in 1661, he was banished to Portugal. Twenty-one years were to pass before he again preached and baptized among his beloved Indians; this return was to be permanent, for he remained with them until his death, July 17, 1697. Though persecuted to the end and misunderstood, even in his own order, this zealous priest remained unshaken in his devotion to the natives. It was but fitting that the chief mourners at his funeral should be the slaves and the poor. Vieira's heroic defense of the Indians inspired his brethren to be constant in their petitioning the Portuguese King in behalf of the aborigines; it was largely owing to their efforts that Joseph I on June 6, 1755 granted freedom to all native-born Brazilians. The unceasing battle of the Jesuit missionaries

---

[20] Rodriquez, *Historia de la Comp. de Jesus na Assistencia de Portugal*, 2 vols., Porto (1931); de Azevedo, *Os Jesuitas no Grão Pará, suas missioes e a colonisação*, Coimbra (1930).

[21] Cabral, *Vieira, Pregador*, Porto (1901); *Une grande figure de Prêtre, Vieira*, Paris (1900).

against the enslavement and oppression of their Indian flock, brought on them the hatred of those colonists and merchants, both in Brazil and Portugal, who had invested in the slave trade. Such people gave the strongest support to Pombal when he set out to destroy the Society of Jesus. At the time of this destruction, in 1750, there were in Brazil 445 Jesuits, of whom 228 were priests. These fathers maintained 69 foundations which included 7 colleges in the principal cities, a seminary, 32 houses or residences and 28 mission stations. In addition 145 Jesuits, of whom 88 were priests, labored in the province of Maranhao, supporting 44 foundations, of which 2 were colleges and 42 residences or mission stations. Among the Brazilian Jesuits must be recorded Roelandsz, a laborer for twenty years among the wild Tapuyas; Bourel; Szentmatonyi and Malagrida, who was juridically murdered by Pombal in Portugal after an apostolate of eighteen years among the Brazilian Indians. Baron de Rio Branco, a distinguished Brazilian statesman of the last century, pays this tribute to the Jesuit pioneers of his native land: "One cannot fail to recognize that they rendered the greatest service to the land of Brazil. The occupation and colonization of Portuguese America in the sixteenth and seventeenth centuries is for the greater part their work. As missionaries they imparted civilization to many thousands of Indians, and thanks to their self-sacrificing work the native race has taken a considerable part in the development of the Brazilian people. They were always the champions of the freedom of the Indians and the teachers of the Brazilian youth desirous of education. Brazil owes to the Jesuit schools nearly all the great names of her literary history of the sixteenth to the eighteenth century."

In Peru [22] the numbers of the Jesuits under Aquaviva had increased to such an extent that the districts of Chile, Ecuador, Paraguay and New Granada were erected into independent missions and eventually into separate provinces. For the first few generations the focal point of Jesuit activities in Peru were the towns. This does not mean that the evangelization of the aborigines was only incidental to the care of the Spaniards. With the work of the colleges was combined the labor for the Indians and the Negroes; each college was constituted a base for missionary activity. In fact such was the absorption in the task of converting the tribesmen that one Provincial, the distinguished ascetical writer and theologian, Alvarez de Paz, complained that studies and discipline were suffering. As elsewhere, the Indians found in the Jesuits their constant protectors against the greed of the colonists. Luis Valdivia [23] and Diego de Torres fought unceasingly for justice and kind treatment of the na-

---

[22] Astrain, *Historia*, Vol. IV, lib. III, c. 5, 6; V, lib. II, c. 5; VI, lib. III, c. 6; VII, lib. II, c. 4.

[23] Astrain, *Historia*, Vol. IV, lib. III, c. 12; V, lib. II, c. 14.

tives; it was owing to the efforts of these two Jesuits that the Araucani were rescued from complete extermination. Valdivia in 1593 crossed the ocean to Spain to lay before Philip III the sad plight of the Indians. Philip sent him back with a royal decree sanctioning the liberty and guaranteeing protection of the natives. The promulgation of this decree meant much for the missions; and if any colonist ventured to violate it, he found an unyielding and successful opponent in Valdivia.

In the early part of the seventeenth century the Peruvian Jesuits began to settle among the Indian tribes.[24] In 1631 Urrea founded three settlements for converted tribesmen, which after twenty years were handed over to the secular priests. The Chiquitos mission in the present confines of Bolivia was started in 1692 by de Arce, who met a martyr's death in 1718. Some years earlier than the foundation of the Chiquitos mission, in 1674, Baraza and the lay-brother Castillo with a few Indian guides made a twelve day journey down the Marmore River to reach the Moxos tribes.[25] The priest lived for four years with these aborigines, acquiring a proficiency in their language and gaining their confidence. After a short respite in Peru to rebuild his shattered health, he returned to open the first Reduction among the Maxos in 1686. Within ten years aided by his brethren, Marban and Orellana, Baraza was able to erect six great Reductions for twenty thousand Indians. During twenty-seven years this heroic missionary labored among the Moxos, penetrating to every part of their territories, instructing them in the truths of Christianity and baptizing about 40,000, teaching them agriculture and manual arts, directing them in the erecting of churches that rivalled those in Peru. At length, on September 16, 1702, Baraza met his death at the hands of heathen Indians. Other distinguished missionaries of the Peruvian province were: Sebastian; Arlet, who converted six tribes, among them the fierce Canicianos; von Leyder; Borinie, who enjoyed an especial success in teaching the savages the arts of civilization.

Pursuing wandering wild tribes, as Urrea, Ferrer and Ruess did, was an extremely difficult task; it was a dangerous one too, as the death toll of four missionaries from 1596–1629 would indicate. The Jesuits of Peru, whether in the colleges or on the missions, enjoyed the good will of the government, the clergy and the best elements of the people. True, there were a few difficulties, such as the trouble with the University of Lima, and that with the Archbishop Saint Alfonso Turibio; arising as these contests did from misunderstandings, they were eventually composed. In 1750 the province of Peru numbered 306 priests among its 526 members and had charge of 24 foundations including 15 colleges, 4 seminaries and 3 residences. In addition, there were the In-

---

[24] Astrain, *Historia*, Vol. IV, lib. III, c. 10.
[25] Astrain, *Historia*, Vol. VI, lib. III, c. 7; VII, lib. II, c. 5.

dian missions on the upper tributaries of the Amazon and among the Maxos tribes; these missions in 1752 counted 21 Reductions, comprehending 31,349 natives, served by 48 priests. When the Spanish Jesuits were dispersed in 1767, the members laboring in Peru ministered altogether to 55,000 Indians.

The Jesuit foundations in Chile were separated from Peru and erected into a vice-province in 1607, and later raised to the status of a province in 1684.[26] As early as 1593, seven Jesuits led by Pinas came to Santiago to labor both for the Spaniards and for the Indians. The progress was certain though slow, for the Chilean settlements were in constant peril for almost two hundred years owing to the persistent attacks of the Araucani, the ablest and most successful Indian fighters in the Western Hemisphere. The native missions suffered severely in the protracted struggle. At one time eleven foundations were destroyed by the savages; two priests, de'Aranda and de Vecchi, and a lay-brother, Montalbán, were slain at Elicura in 1612. The most outstanding missionary among the Jesuits of Chile was Valdivia, whose work for the conversion and defense of the Indians of Peru was continued for the natives of Chile. Of immense value was the dictionary and grammar of the Araucani tongue, which de Vega succeeded in producing in 1605. Missionary expeditions of Astorga, Rosales and de Pozo to the Chiloe Islands were especially fruitful in baptisms. Mascardi penetrated far to the South to the Patagonians, where in 1763 he was slain by savages. In the year 1750 there were 242 members of the province of Chile, of these the priests were 130; while the foundations of the province were 23, including a university, 9 colleges, a seminary and 12 residences. The missions in 1767 cared for 7,718 Christian Indians, Araucani, the tribes of Chiloe Islands, and the Puelches and the Patagonians.

In the last years of the sixteenth century Jesuits came north from Peru to find a new field for their zeal in Ecuador.[27] At Quito their priestly labors were markedly successful; flourishing sodalities were maintained for priests, Spanish gentlemen, Spanish ladies, students, Mestizos, Indians and Negroes; a college was opened, later a full university was begun and the direction of a seminary undertaken. Advances were made to bring the Gospel to the wild tribes of the Andes and on the western headwaters of the Amazon. After the initial successes, which warranted separation from Peru in 1608, the progress was slow, owing to the paucity of reinforcements as well from Ecuador as from Spain. It was only in 1696 that the province of Quito was established. In the

---

[26] Astrain, *Historia*, Vol. IV, lib. III, c. 11; V, lib. II, c. 15; VI, lib. III, c. 13, 14; VII, lib. II, c. 16, 17.

[27] Astrain, *Historia*, Vols. IV, lib. III, c. 7; V, lib. II, c. 6; VI, lib. III, c. 8; VII, lib. II, c. 6.

next generation internal dissensions for a few years caused the new province considerable embarrassment, though even during this period an overwhelming majority of the province were truly zealous men. Nothing proves this last fact more than the labors of the Quito Jesuits among the aborigines. The evangelization of the native tribes began about 1600, when Ferrer commenced his toil among the Amobagacuas, the Caronados and the Cofanes in the eastern part of Ecuador. After an apostolate of incredible hardships during which he succeeded in founding three Christian settlements, Ferrer was slain by the Cofanes in 1611. Fruitful were the labors begun in 1637 by Gugia and Cueva with the tribes at the headwaters of the Amazon; [28] the former worked among the Indians for fifteen years, the latter for thirty-four years. Richter, who was murdered by wild savages in 1696, had succeeded in establishing nine Reductions for the tribes of these regions, besides composing a dictionary and catechism in the barbaric dialects and writing a description of the Rio Ucayli and the peoples who dwelt upon its banks. Samuel Fritz spent forty-three years in this district, establishing forty Reductions. In 1689 he travelled in a skiff the whole length of the Amazon from the slopes of the Eastern Andes to Para, that he might complete the map of the mighty river. The labors of the fathers in inducing the wild rovers of the forests to settle down to an ordered civilized life, an extremely difficult task at the best, was further complicated by the raids of the Brazilian slave-hunters. In 1750 the Quito province counted 286 members, of whom 117 were priests; the province maintained 11 colleges, 2 seminaries and 4 residences, besides taking care of 14,500 Indians in 33 Reductions on the Upper Amazon and 7,588 other Christian Indians, chiefly among the Maynas tribes.

The Jesuit Reductions of Paraguay,[29] the most remarkable missionary achievement of the Old Society, were begun at the instigation of Aquaviva. The first Jesuits to labor in this part of the Spanish Indies were Francisco Angulo and Alonso Barzena, the apostle of Tucuman, who began their evangelical toilings in 1586 as wandering missionaries among the Guarani tribes. Despite a nomad existence these fathers reaped a great fruit of souls; Barzena is said to have baptized 20,000 heathens in the space of four months. Other Jesuits followed them into the territory. Fronte, to care for the spiritual good of the Spanish colonists, founded in 1595 a college at Asunción, an institution soon to be

---

[28] Astrain, *Historia*, Vol. VI, lib. III, c. 9; VII, lib. II, c. 7.

[29] Astrain, *Historia*, Vol. IV, lib. III, c. 9; V, lib. II, c. 9, 10; VI, lib. III, c. 11, 12; VII, lib. II, c. 10; Pastells, *Compañia de Jesús, Provincia del Paraguay*, 4 vols., Madrid (1912–1923); Hernandez, *Organizacion social de las doctrinas Guaranies de la Comp. de Jesús*, 2 vols., Barcelona (1913); Charlevoix, *Histoire de Paraguay*, Paris (1756), London (1769); Cunninghame Graham, *A Vanished Arcadia*, New York (1924).

followed by other colleges or small foundations at Buenos Aires, Santa Fé, Cordova, Rioja, Santiago del Estero, S. Miguel de Tucuman, Balta, Tarija and Corrientes. The number of the foundations of the mission warranted separation from Peru; accordingly, in 1606 a new province of Paraguay consisting of Paraguay, Tucumania and Chile was erected. Aquaviva, dissatisfied with the more or less ephemeral results of the wandering missions, instructed the fathers to establish permanent settlements for the neophytes. The first Provincial of Paraguay, Diego de Torres, the staunch defender of the Indians, gave himself wholeheartedly to the undertaking. Two great obstacles had hindered the Christianizing of the Indians: one was the custom of establishing the conquered natives in locations, which too often resulted in their enslavement; the other was the bad example of the whites. De Torres was convinced that the salvation of the aborigines depended on their freedom and their isolation; he sought and obtained from Philip III an autographed letter guaranteeing the liberty of the natives and forbidding the entrance of Spaniards into the Indian settlements about to be founded.

These colonies of native Christians were to be self-governing, were to possess their own churches and public buildings, and were to be almost completely independent of the neighboring Spanish settlements. Cataldino and Maceta, both Italian Jesuits, in the year 1609 led a group of 200 baptized Guarani families to a spot where the Piraga River enters the Paranápanema and there founded the village of Our Lady of Loreto, the first of the Paraguay Reductions. A large picture of the Crucifixion, sheltered under a thatched roof, marked the center of the community and the spot where later the village church was to be erected. In the next year a second Reduction was established at S. Ignacio-Miri; others followed until there were thirty Reductions in existence. The intense opposition of Spanish colonists and of even a part of the clergy, proved unavailing before the royal ordinances and the zeal of the Jesuits.

The worst enemies of the Reductions were the Brazilian slave-hunters, the "Mamelucos," who in their nefarious trade did not hesitate to make incursions across the frontier into the Spanish territories.[30] Such a scourge were they to the Indians of the Reductions, that in 1630 alone they murdered or carried off 30,000 Guarani. Safety lay only in flight, and so, led by the Jesuit Maceta, the neophytes fled to the lands beyond the Uruguay River, between that river and the Paraná, where the Jesuits had established other Reductions. Maceta's guidance of the tribes on the trek through the primeval forests was a skilful accomplishment; but the hardships entailed exacted such a toll that only 12,000 Indians reached their new home. The new mission of the Guarani so prospered

---

[30] Astrain, *Historia*, Vol. V, lib. II, c. 11.

that eventually 33 Reductions were set up, which harbored at one time 150,000 souls. Further to the north, after 1692, the Chiquitos Reductions were founded among the Mocobias, Tobas and Abipones tribes; in 1767 these settlements counted 23,288 native Christians. Between the Guarani and the Chiquitos, the Taruma mission contained 3 Reductions which in 1767 cared for 3,777 souls. To the west of the Paraná in the Gran Chaco, 15 Reductions, built between 1735 and 1767, contained 5,000 Indians of the mountain tribes. In Tucuman a Reduction was founded among the Chiriguanos and the Mataguayas, and in northern Patagonia still another. How fruitful the spiritual labors of the Jesuits were in the Reductions may be judged from the fact that from 1610–1768 on the Guarani mission 702,086 Indians were baptized.

The difficulties to be overcome in settling wild wanderers in a stable community and in teaching them the pursuits of peace, were truly incredible. The fathers, in quest of the fierce tribesmen, plunged into the primeval forests, crossed turbulent streams and treacherous swamps, faced death from ravenous wild animals, poisonous snakes and savage humans. They carried with them only their breviaries and their cross-topped staffs; their sole companions were a handful of native guides and interpreters. In the beginning, on a few occasions, a small body of troops went with them for protection. Once the nomads were settled on the reductions, other problems arose: the perseverance of their fickle charges had to be obtained, time and again the wild children of Nature ran away from the ordered village life, and the fathers had to follow after them into the forests and plead with them to return; polygamy and other vices of the savages, as well as the sinister power of the sorcerers, had to be overcome; mistrust for the whites, often only too justified, had to be removed; finally, protection from the oppression and bad example of the worst elements among the Spaniards and from the attacks of the heathen aborigines had to be provided. It is not surprising that in this enormous task thirty Jesuits were martyred, three of whom have been beatified, Bl. Roque Gonzales, Bl. Alonso Rodriguez and Bl. Juan del Castillo, and that several others fell victims of fevers and privations to die as martyrs of charity.

All the planning of the villages, the laying out of the streets, the erection of the churches, homes, work-shops and store-houses, all this devolved upon the fathers. It meant that they had to instruct their neophytes in such manual arts as carpentry, masonry, black-smithing, tin-smithing, and in such fine arts as painting and sculpturing. As agriculture was the economic basis of the communities, the fathers likewise were required to instruct their simple folk in farming, fruit-culture and cattle-raising. What infinite pains were called for to train a people by nature indolent, capricious, and not a generation from the aimless roaming of the forest, can well be imagined. Yet Cunninghame Graham has called the result of their labors an "Arcadia."

A brief description of a Paraguay Reduction will not be out of place. On a site, chosen usually in a high and healthy spot, the new foundation was laid out around the four sides of a great central plaza. On three sides, east, south and west, on streets leading from the plaza, were built the Indians' houses, tile-roofed and, in the beginning, of simple material, later of stone or adobe. On the north side was erected the church. To its left stood the priests' house and to its right the well-kept cemetery, then the widows' home, the refuge and the hospital for crippled children. At the back of the church were located the workshops and storerooms, while behind the dwellings of the natives stretched the farms. At each of the four corners of the plaza stood a high wooden cross; and before the street entering from the south usually there was placed a statue of the Mother of God. In the plaza also was to be found the village well. The pride of each village was its church, a noble edifice with a fine façade, a magnificent vestibule and a great belfry; its interior would possess three to five altars, would be adorned with rich gilded decorations, and would have several statues quite worthy of the whole. Friends and foes alike have wondered how such glorious buildings could have been erected by such people in so remote districts. Their ruins today still win the admiration of travellers. The sacred vestments and the church plate were in keeping with the beauty of the churches. Singing and music were made much of; and Jesuits, such as Vaes, Sipp and Baucke, instructed the Indians in these arts, composing vocal and instrumental pieces for them. Almost every village possessed a choir and an orchestra of forty men, who not only played but learned how to make their own instruments. Cattano declared that the Indian violinist played the most difficult pieces of Italian masters with rare skill. Processions on Saints' days were truly gorgeous affairs; nor did the fathers fail to employ the dramatic art, frequently presenting the miracle and mystery plays. Schools, where at least elementary education was imparted, stood in every village; while in three Reductions, Loreto, Santa Maria la Mayor and San Francisco Xavier, printing presses were set up. Sports were encouraged and games too, except those of chance, which had to be prohibited in view of the Indians' weakness for gambling.

The soil and property belonged to the community; a sort of communism was necessitated in the training of such primitive people. Yet it was a communism directed and governed by the fathers, much in the manner and methods of religious orders. Private property was not excluded; private fields, the products of which remained the free possession of their owners, were permitted. Business was restricted to the sale of the products of the fields, wheat, rice, sugar-cane, cotton, Paraguay tea, etc., and was intended only for obtaining such supplies as salt and metals, which could not be had on the reductions, and for the payment of the royal tax. Whites were usually excluded from the Reductions, for the reasons which the sad experiences of missionaries the world over could justify; yet their exclusion was not complete; in every village a house, called St. Isadore's House, was set aside for white visitors and travellers. To protect the Reductions from the inroads of the Mamelucos and the heathen Indians, eventually a militia was organized, armed and trained by Spanish officers, but led for the most part by the native caciques.

The Paraguay Reductions have won unstinted praise from the most diverse sources. Bishop Don Pedro Farardo, O.SS.Trin. of Buenos Aires, writing to the Pope in 1725, declared that purity among these Indians, who by nature were inclined to all sorts of vice, had become so habitual that he believed that in the Reductions in the course of a year not a mortal sin was committed, since the watchfulness of the shepherds foresaw and prevented the slightest fault. The testimony of Bishop Farardo was but one of numerous encomiums of Spanish bishops and crown officials. No less a person than Voltaire called the accomplishment of the Jesuits in Paraguay "a triumph of humanity." So also wrote Buffon, Montesquieu, Chateaubriand, Dalla, von Haller, von Müller, Robertson, Macaulay, Southey, Cunninghame Graham and numerous others. In view of all this laudatory tribute, how ridiculous are the charges of enormous wealth which the Jesuits are accused of having amassed in the Reductions! The real poverty of the fathers was only too evident to the despoilers at the time of the Suppression, when no other loot was found but the plate and ornaments of the churches. Of the same nature are the legends of the hidden gold mines which the Jesuits of the Reductions were said to have worked; those who have searched the sites of the Reductions for them time and again in vain, can refute such fairy stories. All these and many other calumnies were but part of the literary warfare which helped to bring about the destruction of the Society of Jesus. The Suppression of the order was a death blow to the most glorious achievement of the Catholic missions. At the time of this catastrophe, in the Paraguay province there were 564 Jesuits working in 12 colleges, 1 university, 3 houses of retreat, 2 residences and 57 reductions in which 113,716 Indians were being cared for.

New Granada, the present lands of Columbia, Panama and Venezuela, became the scene of Jesuit activity in the year 1604, from which time many richly spiritual works were undertaken, especially at Cartagena, Bogotá and among the Indian tribes.[31] The mission was raised to the

---

[31] Astrain, *Historia*, Vol. IV, lib. III, c. 8; V, lib. II, c. 7; VI, lib. III, c. 8, 9.

status of a province in 1696; in 1750 it comprised 196 members, of whom 120 were priests and supported 16 foundations, among which were 9 colleges, a seminary and 5 residences. The fathers of New Granada emulated the rest of their South American brethren in the care of the Indians; in the year 1750 they maintained 3 great missions, Llanos, della Meta and Orinoco, ministering to 6,594 natives. Three Jesuits, Beck, Fiol and Toebast made the supreme sacrifice when, on October 15, 1684, they were murdered by the savages.

The glory of the New Granada province is the apostolate of St. Peter Claver among the negro slaves at Cartagena.[32] St. Peter was born in Catalonia in 1581 and entered the Society of Jesus in 1602. While making his studies at Majorca, he became the fast friend of the holy lay-brother, St. Alonso Rodriguez, who foretold to him that his field of labor was to be in America. The young religious, not yet a priest, was sent to New Granada in 1610; six years later he received Holy Orders. Trained by an illustrious missionary, Sandoval, St. Peter began his glorious missionary career. One of his first acts was to add to his four solemn vows of profession a fifth vow, forever to be the slave of the negro slaves, a bond which he kept perfectly to the end. There were pressing opportunities for his zeal at Cartagena, then the chief slave-mart of the New World. At times, over a thousand unfortunate blacks were landed every month in the most awful conditions, moral and physical, with only a terrible future of cruelty and degradation before them. For almost forty years St. Peter devoted himself unreservedly to these wretched beings; he met every slave-ship, carrying food, delicacies and medicines; he made the poor, crazed and brutalized unfortunates realize that he was their friend and father; later in the compounds he nursed the wretched sick and diseased, never shrinking from the most disgusting and loathsome sores; then he instructed them in the truths of Christianity, in the consolations of the Cross, and, when they were prepared, he baptized them Christians. In the long course of his apostolate St. Peter baptized three hundred thousand negroes. The opposition which so often and so seriously oppressed him, came not from the slave-dealers only, but from fastidious Catholics who looked with suspicion and disdain upon his labors for the unfortunate blacks, and even from some of his brethren who could not gauge the zeal of the Saint. St. Peter accepted all criticism quietly, redoubled his bodily austerities, and went on steadily with his work. The Church placed her approval on his labors when Leo XIII canonized him and declared St. Peter Claver to be the patron of all missions to the Negroes.

---

[32] Astrain, *Historia*, Vol. V, lib. II, c. 8; Laures, *Der Sklave der Negersklaven*, Einsiedeln (1923); Lunn, *A Saint of the Slave Trade*, London (1935).

Jesuits labored in scattered missions throughout the Caribbean area.[33] In Guiana especially was their work successful. Here in 1643 a mission was inaugurated among the Galibis; thirty years later Grillet and Bechamel penetrated to the tribes of the interior, and shortly afterwards de Crivelly, who died in 1718, began his thirty-three years of fruitful labor. With a similar zeal Lombardi and Ramette after 1710 devoted themselves to the Guiana mission. From the middle of the sixteenth century the fathers worked at Havana, spending themselves in the usual employments with such strenuous effort that within a period of forty years fifty-six Jesuits succumbed before their time. The conversion of the Caribs of St. Vincent in 1650 by Dejan and the missionary activities in Central America of Mesland, who died in 1672, deserve special mention. In the Lesser Antilles, especially at St. Kitts, the Irish Jesuit, Bathe,[34] devoted himself to his unfortunate countrymen and countrywomen who had been sold into slavery by the Cromwellians. He came in 1652 and for five years brought the consolations of religion to the miserable Irish slaves. Bathe was frequently forced to go about disguised and to perform his ministrations by stealth, for his freedom, if not his life, was always in jeopardy.

The first years of the Society of Jesus in Mexico were devoted largely to the ministry among the Spaniards and the sedentary Indians and to the founding of colleges.[35] These institutions multiplied rapidly, attaining great success among the whites and the natives; for the latter exclusively several colleges were established. It is well to keep in mind, when following the more dramatic history of the missions, that these educational and pastoral labors were always zealously maintained. The first native mission was among the Chichimecos, a fierce tribe of central Mexico, whom the fathers Christianized and trained in civilized life. This mission opened the way to a greater field, the far-extending Nueva Viscaya, stretching northward from Zacatecas for a thousand miles to the Colorado and the Rio Grande Rivers, including what are today the states of Durango, Chihuahua, Sinaloa, Sonora, Lower California and part of Arizona. It was a hard country, high plateau, higher mountains, cut with deep canyons, and a rocky coast; the barrenness of this mountain land reached its worst in the hot, rocky peninsula of Lower California. So identified did the missionaries become in the next century and three-quarters with this vast area that it has been called "Jesuit

---

[33] Demontezon, *Missions de Cayenne*, Paris (1857); Mury, *Les Jésuites à Cayenne*, Strasbourg (1895).

[34] Hogan, *Distinguished Irishmen of the Sixteenth Century*, London (1894).

[35] Astrain, *Historia*, Vol. IV, lib. III, c. 1, 2; V, lib. II, c. 1, 2; VI, lib. III, c. 4, 5; Vol. VII, lib. II, c. 1, 2, 3; Jacobsen, *Educational Foundations of the Jesuits in the Sixteenth Century New Spain*, California (1938).

Land." Dr. Bolton, who has done so much to make the accomplishments of these Jesuits known, thus describes their campaign: "River by river, valley by valley, canyon by canyon, tribe by tribe, these harbingers of Christian civilization advanced into the realms of heathendom. They gathered the natives from villages, indoctrinated them into the Faith, trained them in agriculture and the simpler crafts, and in schools and seminaries taught many of them reading, writing and music. Under the tutelage of the patient Jesuits, barbarians who formerly had constructed only the meanest huts now built substantial temples, some of which still stand as Christian monuments. The natives were generally well-disposed toward the missionaries. But secular Spaniards exploited their labor in the mines and haciendas; and native priests were jealous of their white competitors. The result was a series of periodic Indian revolts in which a score or more of the Black Robes in New Spain won the crown of Martyrdom. But the march went on!" [36]

The first advance into Nueva Viscaya was made in 1691 by Gonzalo [37] and Perez among the Tapia Indians. Perez baptized two thousand of them and Gonzalo settled five thousand of these untamed savages in Christian pueblos, so identifying himself with the tribesmen as to obtain the surname "de Tapia." Gonzalo de Tapia sealed his mission with his blood in Sinaloa in 1594. About 1600 Santarén's evangelization of the mountain tribes in the Sierra Madre was begun. Among the Acaxes in Tapia and the Xiximenes, Santarén and Ruiz heroically worked in the very face of an Indian uprising; with the Tepehuanes toiled Fonte and Ramirez; to the Laguna tribes of Coahuila came other Jesuits to found, in spite of plague and sickness, most successful missions. Shortly afterwards, the advance along the coast in Sinaloa was made, when Ribas, Mendez, Villalta commenced the conversion of the Suaquis, Sinaloas and Tehuecos. Then followed the Christianizing of the Mayos by Mendez, with a harvest of twenty thousand souls. In the mountains to the East in 1616, the Tepehuanes, led by a fanatical Indian claiming to be a messiah, broke out into a bloody revolt which resulted in the assassination of eight Jesuits, including the patriarchal Santarén. Martyrdom was an ever-present possibility for these Jesuits; in an attempt to bring the Faith to the Chinipas in the Sierra Madre, Pascual and Martinez were slain. The coast missions, however, continued to prosper; in 1617 Ribas brought into the Christian fold those unconquerable warriors, the Yaquis; in 1620 Mendez and Azpilcueto raised the Cross among the Lower Pimas and the Opatas. Castano, laboring among the

---

[36] Bolton, "The Jesuits in New Spain," *The American Cath. Hist. Review* (1937), Vol. XXI.

[37] Shiels, *Gonzalo de Tapia (1561–1594), Founder of the First Permanent Jesuit Mission in North America*, New York (1934).

Opatas in 1638, baptized 3,000. The seven Jesuits ministering to the Coastal Indians by 1646 were able to settle 14 pueblos and to count more than 20,000 baptized natives. In summary, in the 600 miles of territory west of the Sierra and along the coast, in 1645 there were about 100 mission villages with fine churches, prosperous ranches and well-stocked farms. The number of Baptisms in less than a half-century totalled up to 300,000. The presence of only forty-six Spanish soldiers in the principal garrison, speaks eloquently of the missionaries' success.

The advance was again resumed among the mountain Indians when Figueroa and Pascual in 1639 started the evangelization of the Tarahumaras; others of their brethren followed to penetrate into the Tarahumara Alta. Incursions of the savage Tobosas and the uprisings of the Tarahumaras destroyed most of the mission; Godinez and Basili gained the martyr's crown. For several years work was restricted to the southern part of the missions until 1673 when Tardá and Guadalajara reopened the Tarahumara Alta mission. It was an almost impassable mountain region and severely cold in winter, yet in five years' time eight Jesuits ministered to four thousand Indians. Two sanguinary revolts, in which Foronda and Sanchez met their deaths, for a time wiped out a portion of the mission. In 1676 the Jesuits, Prado and Pecoro, renewed the labors among the Chinipas and within four years had 4,000 baptized neophytes living in pueblos. It was in this field that Salvatierra gained his first experience as a missionary; Ordraz and Illing were two outstanding toilers among the Chinipas.

The peninsula of Lower California and the land of Pimeria Alta on the northeast coast of the Gulf next became the scene of Jesuit activities. In these regions worked Kino, Campos, Salvatierra, Ugarte, priests who rank with the greatest missionaries of the Society. Eusebio Kino [38] was born in 1644 in the Tyrol and entered the order in 1665; in 1680 he arrived in Mexico and shortly afterwards began the mission of Lower California. Seven years later he came to Pimeria Alta, the scene of his great labors. For twenty-four years Kino worked for the conversion of the natives, baptizing personally 4,500 Indians. He established many mission pueblos where his brethren brought the tribesmen into the fold; and he supported these stations by maintaining prosperous ranches. In his search for souls and in pursuit of the business of the mission, he is said to have travelled 20,000 miles on horseback. He achieved distinction as an explorer, proving the fact, hitherto disputed, that Lower California is a peninsula and discovering the Casa Grande in Arizona. Similarly his maps of the districts explored by him have won for him a

---

[38] Bolton, *Kino's Historical Memoir of Pimeria Alta*, 2 Vols., Trans., Cleveland (1919); *Rim of Christendom: A Biography of Eusebio Francisco Kino*, New York (1936).

reputation as a cartographer; and his writings about the natives of his missions have established him as an ethnologist and an historian. But with all his accomplishments he was first an apostle and defender of his Indian children. He died March 15, 1711.

Salvatierra [39] became the evangelist of Lower California; his labors to establish and support the missions in this barren waste were truly heroic; at his death seven missions were flourishing. It was Salvatierra who established, for the support of the missions, the famous "Pious Fund." His colleague, Ugarte, erected stations in the southern part of the peninsula; there later Carranco and Tamaral were murdered by the savages. Altogether, more than fifty Jesuits toiled in Lower California and, in this most unpromising field, within seventy years established about twenty successful pueblos for several thousand Indians.

In the eighteenth century a large number of the missionaries came from Germany and Italy. Hellen and Sedelmayr carried on Kino's work, as did Konsag and Linck. Rhuen and Tello were killed in the Pima Revolt. Gummersbach, who died in 1736 with a reputation for holiness and who was known as the "Father of the Indians," founded a refuge for Indian maidens in the Convent of Corpus Christi in Mexico, and in the literary field translated several spiritual works into the native tongue. Ratkay and Kratzhoffer were also among the Jesuits martyred by the savages. The lay-brother Steinhofer, who was skilled as an apothecary and a surgeon, is known for his book, *Manual of Medical Botany*.

Throughout all their years in Mexico the Jesuits of the old Society enjoyed the good will of the Mexican hierarchy, with the one exception of Juan de Palafox, Bishop of Puebla.[40] The misunderstandings arose over the question of faculties; the Bishop had pronounced views on the question of jurisdiction, views which earlier had brought him into conflict with the Dominicans, Franciscans and Augustinians. The trouble with the Jesuits lasted several years and was aired in Mexico, Spain and Rome. Innocent X in a Brief of 1648 sustained the Bishop's claims but urged him to be kind and lenient with the Jesuits; again in a second Brief of 1653 he confirmed the previous decision. The affair would have merited little consideration, were it not for the use made by the Jansenists and other enemies of the order of two letters written by the Bishop in presenting his case to Rome. There is some doubt as to the authenticity of the second letter; and, indeed, Bishop Palafox later in Spain repudiated its contents. The letter contains wildly exaggerated

---

[39] Venegas-Wilbur, *Juan Maria de Salvatierra*, trans. and ed. by Wilbur, Cleveland (1929).

[40] Astrain, *Historia*, Vol. V, lib. II, c. 3, 4; Cuevas, *Historia de la Iglesia en Mejico*, El Paso (1924), Vol. III, pp. 283–313.

charges concerning the wealth of the Mexican Jesuits; that the fathers owned large farms and numerous herds and six big sugar plantations, that they engaged in mining on a great scale. Whatever farms, herds or plantations were owned, were the property of the missions, used solely for their support; the actual poverty of the Mexican Jesuits has been amply proved by Astrain. And further, as a matter of fact, the members of the Society in Mexico never engaged in any mining operations. The enemies of the order hoped that the beatification of Bishop Palafox would be a sanctioning of the charges contained in his letter; his cause was discussed during the great campaign which led to the Suppression. Bishop Palafox was a saintly man and a zealous bishop; his beatification would have placed a seal of approval upon his virtues, not upon the exaggerations which in the heat of a controversy he may have written.

At the time of the Suppression there were three hundred and fifty priests among the five hundred and seventy-two members of the Mexican Province. The foundations of the province included twenty-three colleges, eight seminaries, four residences, and eight missions, beside the missions of Lower California, Sonora with twenty-three pueblos, and Tarahumara. The number of Indians cared for by the Mexican Jesuits in 1767 amounted to 122,000.

Few Jesuit missionary activities have gained greater renown than the labors of the French fathers in Canada.[41] Protestant and Catholic alike have rendered glowing tributes to these heroic apostles, explorers and martyrs. Massé and Biard were the first French Jesuits to come to America; their work, however, at Port Royal in Acadia and at St. Sauveur in the present state of Maine, from 1611–1613, was but transitory, owing to the destruction of the mission by the English from Virginia. After twelve years, on the invitation of the Recollects, the Jesuits again came to New France; five of them, under the leadership of Charles Lalemant, landed at Quebec June 19, 1625. Among the number were Massé and St. Jean de Brébeuf; all remained in the ministry of the whites and the redmen at Quebec and its environments, except St. Jean, who set out through the forests to live with the Indians, following them in their wanderings and dwelling in their wigwams. With his savage companions he travelled almost to the site of the present Toronto. Again the whole mission had to be abandoned, when the English captured Quebec in 1625. But after the French had recovered Canada by the Treaty of St. Germaine in 1632, the Jesuits Le Jeune, Noué and Davost resumed the interrupted labors. The next year saw Massé and St. Jean

---

[41] Charlevoix, *Histoire et déscription generale de la Nouvelle France*, Paris (1744), English translation, New York (1866); Thwaites, *The Jesuit Relations and Allied Documents*, Cleveland (1896); Rochemontoix, *Les Jésuites et la Nouvelle France au XVIIe siècle*, Paris (1895); *Les Jésuites et la Nouvelle France au XVIIIe siècle*, Paris (1906).

de Brébeuf returning, and after that, help came regularly from France. In 1635 the College of Quebec was founded; it remained until the end the educational home for the youth of the Province.

The main work of the Canadian Jesuits was to be with the aboriginal tribes. In 1634 was begun the Huron mission, among the members of that tribe living on the shores of Georgian Bay, Lake Huron. Severest privations, to say nothing of the ever-present threat of death from the fierce Iroquois, were the lot of these heroic priests. Yet twenty-five Jesuits hesitated not to face the terrible dangers; among them were St. Jean de Brébeuf, Chaumonot, St. Antoine Daniel, Davost, St. Isaac Jogues, Bressani, St. Charles Garnier, Le Moyne, Pijart, Raymbault, Raguenau and St. Noël Chabanel. Within six years more than two thousand Indians were baptized, and five chief, and thirty minor, mission stations were established, with the mission of St. Ignace at the central point. But the whole of the good work was swept away in a maelstrom of fire and blood, when in 1648 and 1649 the ferocious Iroquois ravaged the country of the Hurons, burning fifteen Christian villages, slaughtering all the warriors and dragging the women and children off into slavery. Five of the fathers were martyred, butchered with refinements of cruelty that only wolfish men could invent; they were St. Jean de Brébeuf, St. Noël Chabanel, St. Antoine Daniel, St. Charles Garnier and St. Gabriel Lalemant.[42]

They were not however the first martyrs at the hands of the Iroquois. In 1642 St. Isaac Jogues [43] and a lay-brother, St. René Goupil, were captured by the Mohawks and brought to Ossernenon, now Auriesville, New York, where after fiendish torturing they were condemned to slavery. St. René was killed for making the sign of the Cross on the forehead of an Indian child. St. Isaac made his escape through the help of the Dutch of New Netherlands, who enabled him to reach Europe. He returned to Canada and in 1646 once more braved the savage Mohawks; this time he was accompanied by a layman, St. Jean de la Lande. Both were captured and, after excruciating agonies, were murdered, October 19, 1646. The rest of the missionaries led the remnants of the Hurons to the safe proximity of Montreal and Quebec, where settlements were made on the Isle of Orleans, at St. Michel, Loreto, Prairie de la Madeleine and Sault St. Louis.

After the destruction of the Huron mission, the French Jesuits, undaunted, seemed to extend their activities to the four points of the compass. Even the most unimaginative must be astonished at the lengths of their journeys, by canoe through distant rivers to far-distant lakes, by foot or on snowshoes through the virgin forests a thousand miles and

[42] Wynne, *The Jesuit Martyrs of North America*, New York (1925).
[43] Talbot, *Saint Among Savages*, New York (1935).

more from Montreal or Quebec. To the North they sought out the Algonquins and the Montagnais, ranging over a vast territory from Labrador to Hudson Bay, which Albanel reached in 1670. From 1640–1682 twenty-four fathers, operating out of Tadoussac as the principal station, labored among these tribes; Bailloquet became especially the apostle of the Montagnais. The northern Indians were docile and readily accepted Christianity; but the mission among them was extremely difficult, for the terrible cold of the winter and the hardships of the trackless forests wore down the strength of the hardiest missionary.

In the West the Jesuits established missions among the Ottowas and a residue of the Hurons camping on the shores of Lake Superior and Lake Michigan. Important stations were set up at Sault Ste. Marie, Michilimackinac and Green Bay to minister not only to the Ottowas, Hurons and Algonquins, but also to the Sac and Fox, the Illinois and the eastern Sioux. With these tribes Allouez, Dablon and Druillettes labored; Ménard, in search of the Dakotahs, met his death in 1661. The most distinguished missionary in the territory was James Marquette.[44] It was from the mission of St. Xavier that, in 1673, in company with the explorer Joliet, Marquette set out on that memorable journey which led to the exploration of the Mississippi. The little party paddled their canoes down the Wisconsin River to enter the great river, then down its course to the confluence of the Arkansas, and finally back again to St. Xavier, a journey of 2,500 miles in 120 days. Marquette died on the eastern shores of Lake Michigan in 1675. Other Jesuits established the mission of Kaskaskia, or pushed further west on the upper Mississippi to reach the Sioux, as did Guignas in 1727 and 1735. Messeiger in 1731 sought the Crees and the Assiniboine; five years later, on Massacre Island, Lake of the Woods, Aulneau was slain by the Sioux.

To the South in Lower Louisiana the Jesuits brought the Gospel to the Yazoo, Natchez and Alibamon Indians, and for a short time maintained chaplaincies at Mobile and Biloxi.[45] After 1726 the tribes on both sides of the Mississippi were evangelized by the fathers of the order; among the aborigines were the Choctaws, Alibamons and the Arkansas. The southern missions had their quota of martyrs; Du Poisson, a missionary to the Arkansas, was killed at Natchez in 1729, Souel was murdered by the Yazoos in 1729 and Senat was slain at the stake by the Chickasaws in 1736.

Back in the East of Canada, in the present Maine, New Brunswick and Nova Scotia dwelt the Abenaki tribes, like the Montagnais, docile and ready to accept Christianity. Druillettes and other Jesuits labored

---

[44] Thwaites, *Father Marquette*, New York (1902).
[45] Delanglez, *The French Jesuits in Lower Louisiana 1700–1763*, New Orleans (1935).

among them with marked success from 1650 to 1660. Journeys were made by the fathers through many sections of northern and western New England and contacts were made with several tribes. In the year 1694 Bigot and Rasle began their fruitful apostolate; the Indian tribe of Norridgewock became entirely Christian. Sebastian Rasle sealed his love and devotion for his native flock by a cruel death at the hands of Puritan ruffians in 1724.

The last missionary labors of the Canadian Jesuits were to be for their cruelest foes, the murderers of eight of their brethren, the Iroquois. The mission was frequently interrupted by the wars between the French and the English. In the struggle the Five Nations played an important role, mostly on the side of the English, but not always, a fact which enabled the missionaries to work among them. The first attempt was from 1654–1658, particularly among the Onondagas, with whom labored Le Moyne, Chaumonot, Ragueneau and Du Peron. An outbreak of the Mohawks, in which the lay-brother Liégeois and the priest Garreau were killed, ended the mission for a time. Seven years later it was opened when six fathers, among whom were Pierron and Frémin, came at the plea of the ambassadors of the cantons. During this period the Christian settlement of Iroquois at Caughnawaga, on the opposite bank of the St. Lawrence from Montreal, was established. There it was that Kateri Tekakwitha, the Lily of the Mohawks, died in 1680; such was the virtue of this child of the forest that her cause for beatification is under way. Hostilities brought the second mission to a close in 1686. The last phase began in 1702, when the Jesuits came at the appeal of the sachems. They remained with the Five Nations for seven years, until 1709, when the mission was finally abandoned. In the years that followed, a considerable number of the Christian Indians from time to time migrated to Caughnawaga.

Beside all the hardships, privations and perils of their far-flung mission-field, the French fathers had to contend with continued opposition in the settlements. The purveyors of whiskey to the Indians hated the priests who strenuously opposed their abominable traffic; the regalistic officials and a section of the clergy, tainted with Gallicanism or Jansenism, had little use for the members of the Society of Jesus. But the fathers were not deterred from the work before them and they carried on until the Suppression. Their numbers were never very large; in 1720 there were only twenty-four Jesuits in Canada, in 1757 there were but thirteen.

The English Colonies,[46] with two exceptions, held only persecution

---

[46] Hughes, *The History of the Society of Jesus in North America, Colonial and Federal*, 2 Vols. Text, 2 Vols. Documents, New York (1906–1917); *The Woodstock Letters*, passim.

or death for any Jesuits who might venture into their territories. The exceptions were Maryland and Pennsylvania. Two Jesuits, White and Altham, came with the first settlers of Maryland in 1634; they were to care for the needs of the Catholics who formed an important part of the colonists. White also devoted himself to the neighboring Indians, baptized many of them and wrote a catechism in Patuxent; however, the mission among the Indians did not progress far, owing partly to misunderstandings between the priests and the white authorities. Protestants from Virginia overthrew the Catholic government; and after 1676 the penal laws merely tolerated the Catholics, whose lot became so bad that emigration was thought of as the only possible relief. The Jesuits remained at their posts, more or less secretly ministering to the Catholic colonists in Maryland and Virginia. Some of the well-to-do planters' sons were sent to St. Omer's College in Belgium and not a few entered the Society. Pennsylvania gave a larger measure of liberty to Catholics than any other colony; only in the Quaker Commonwealth could Mass be said openly. As in Maryland, all the priests were Jesuits; English fathers served at Philadelphia where St. Joseph's Church was opened in 1730 by Greaton, and German fathers served in the southern counties about Conewago. Among the distinguished Jesuits of Maryland and Pennsylvania may be listed: White, Copley, Greaton, Carroll, L. Neale, the last two Archbishops of Baltimore, Schneider, who had been rector of the University of Heidelberg, Pellentz, Graessel and Farmer (Steinmayr). At the Suppression there were twenty-three priests laboring in the two provinces.

The mission work of the Society was largely undertaken by the Portuguese, Spanish and French provinces; this was so because Portugal, Spain and France were the Catholic colonizing nations in the sixteenth, seventeenth and eighteenth centuries. But it ought to be noted that a very large number of the missionaries came from Germany, Italy and the Low Countries. These Jesuits volunteered to leave their provinces that they might devote themselves to the conversion of the heathen. The Italian missionaries were especially prominent in the Orient, the German missionaries in South America and Mexico.

CHAPTER XI

STEADY STREAMS AND CROSS CURRENTS

The period from the end of Aquaviva's generalate until the first movements for the Suppression of the Society constitutes roughly the second century of the history of the Society of Jesus. It was a time of quiet and steady development of the good works already established. If the labors of the members were not seemingly as grand as those of the first century, the heroic age, they were none the less quite as intense. The accomplishments in education and learning have been detailed in a previous chapter, so too have the achievements in the foreign missions. There remain the non-educational activities of the European Jesuits during the last three-quarters of the seventeenth century and the first quarter of the eighteenth. The full stream of noble deeds flowed steadily onward during these years, yet by no means in unruffled tranquillity. Cross currents, boisterous and perilous, rose to block its progress. They were energetically met and overcome; yet forces deriving from them eventually combined for the destruction of the order.

Twelve Fathers General guided the destinies of the Society of Jesus during these years: Mutius Vitelleschi, a Roman, 1615–1645; Vincent Caraffa, a Neapolitan, 1646–1649; Francis Piccolomini, a Sienese, 1649–1651; Aloysius Gottifredi, a Roman, 1652; Goswin Nickel, a German, 1652–1664; John Paul Oliva, a Genoese, 1664–1681; Charles de Noyelle, a Belgian, 1682–1686; Thyrsus Gonzalez, a Spaniard, 1687–1705; Michaelangelo Tamburini, a Modenese, 1706–1730; Francis Retz, an Austrian, 1730–1750; Ignatius Visconti, a Milanese, 1751–1755; Aloysius Centurioni, a Genoese, 1755–1757. During the terms of office of these men, the Jesuits continued to enjoy the esteem and good will of the Sovereign Pontiffs, half of whom were their former students. There were only four occasions when exceptions occurred in this favorable attitude. Just before the election of Caraffa (1646), Innocent X by his Brief, "Prospero felicique statui," ordained the assembling of a General Congregation every ninth year and also a three year term of office for all superiors, excepting the Master of Novices. The second ordinance was revoked by the next Pope, Alexander VII, in 1658; the first remained in force, though frequently dispensed from, until 1746 when it was abolished by Benedict XIV. During Noyelle's adminstration Innocent XI was so displeased with the French Jesuits, either because of their attitude during the controversy on the Chinese Rites or because of the position some took towards the Gallican "Déclaration du Clergé de France" (the reason has not yet been determined), that he forbade for two years their reception of novices. Innocent XI also supported Gonzalez in his efforts to force Probabiliorism on the Society; and it was this Pontiff who condemned certain laxist propositions of a few Jesuit moralists who pushed the principle of Probabilism too far. Previously, Alexander VII had issued condemnations of such propositions. During the discussions over the Chinese Rites, a story was spread that the Jesuits were resisting even the orders of the Holy See. This calumny Tamburini, the General at the time, vigorously combated. At his command the Congregation of Procurators, then meeting in Rome and representing every province of the order, drew up a solemn declaration of unconditional submission and most faithful adherence, which Tamburini on November 20, 1711 presented to Clement XI.

A most dangerous internal crisis was precipitated by Gonzalez' determination to force the abandonment of the Society's almost universally held doctrine of Probabilism for his own views of Probabiliorism.[1] Probabilism is a doctrine in Moral Theology which holds that, when there is question solely of the lawfulness or unlawfulness of an action, it is permissible to follow a solidly probable opinion in favor of liberty, even though the opposing view is more probable. Probabiliorism, on the other hand, teaches that it is not lawful to act on the less safe opinion unless it is more probable than the safe opinion. Both systems were formulated about the sixteenth century, although great theologians in previous times can be cited as holding or acting on one or other of the two doctrines. Medina, a Dominican theologian, was the first to teach explicitly the doctrine of Probabilism; his system won the acceptance of the majority of theologians in the last half of the sixteenth century, including such divines as Toletus, Bañez, Vasquez, Lessius and Suarez. Reaction to the rigorism of the Jansenists caused some moralists to go too far in the opposite direction, developing a doctrine which cannot properly be called Probabilism, but must be designated Laxism. The Popes, Alexander VII and Innocent XI, condemned several propositions of such moralists. A reaction to this Laxism resulted in a widespread revival of Probabiliorism; however, almost all the Jesuit theologians held to the system of Probabilism. There was one outstanding exception, Thyrsus Gonzalez, a former professor of philosophy and theology at Salamanca and subsequently a devoted preacher of popular missions. In advocacy of his opinions he had even written a book against Probabilism, to which the Gen-

---

[1] Astrain, *Historia*, Vol. VI, Lib. II, "Probabilismo," pp. 119–372; Slater, *A Short History of Moral Theology*, New York (1909); Lehmkuhl, *Probabilismus Vindicatus*, Freiburg (1906).

eral, Oliva, in 1674 refused the permission for publication because of the unanimous rejection by the censors of the order. Innocent XI, who favored Probabiliorism, on his ascent of the Papal throne lent his support to Gonzalez by issuing to the Jesuit superiors a decree ordering them to allow all professors freedom to teach either doctrine. This liberty had already been accorded. Gonzalez now hoped that the General Congregation, to which he had been delegated, or the new General (about to be elected) would decree that henceforth Probabiliorism should be the sole doctrine of the Society. Of course the Congregation, strongly in favor of Probabilism, did no such thing. When, however, owing to the recommendation of Innocent XI, Gonzalez was elected General, he felt convinced that his choice was God's manifestation that he should suppress Probabilism completely. Jesuit Probabiliorists were called to fill the important teaching positions in the order, while their opponents were restrained in various ways. The rejected book could now be published, so Gonzalez thought; and a modified edition of the work actually was printed at Dillingen in 1691. The Fathers–Assistant blocked its appearance; they dreaded the consequences if the General should force his private opinions on the whole order against its will, and this to the detriment of its freedom of teaching. Both sides appealed to Pope Innocent XII for mediation. Segneri, the distinguished preacher, earnestly besought the General not to shame his subjects before the whole world to the joy of the Jansenists. His plea was unheeded by Gonzalez who was bent on going through with his purpose. After a new examination on the order of the Pope and with many corrections, the book, *Fundamentum theologiae moralis de recto usu opinionum probabilium*, finally appeared in 1691. Bossuet, himself a probabiliorist, declared that nothing more formidable had ever been written against Probabilism; St. Alphonsus Ligouri found in it exaggerations of rigoristic tendencies. The Assistants, fearing for the Society's future now more than ever, laid before the Procurators' Congregation of 1693 a proposal for the calling of a General Congregation. Their proposal was accepted; Gonzalez, trusting in the aid of the Pope, strove to make the decision ineffectual. An assembling of a General Congregation, however, could not be put off indefinitely, since there still stood the Constitution of Innocent X ordering its convocation every ninth year. In 1696 accordingly the Fourteenth General Congregation came into session. The Assistants requested the delegates to make an investigation of the conduct of office both of themselves and of the General. As all parties and the Sovereign Pontiff too were desirous of peace, a satisfactory solution which assured the liberty of the theologians of the order was arrived at. Until the present day the Jesuits have continued as the foremost proponents of Probabilism.

The second century for the Italian Jesuits was a period of solid accomplishment. In 1656, at the plea of Pope Alexander VII, the long banishment from Venice was brought to an end, and the fathers resumed their educational and spiritual works in the towns of the Republic. Jesuits, particularly Mastrilli, helped the Grandmaster Lascaris in restoring discipline among the Knights of Malta; though for a while, owing to the machinations of a faction among the knights, they were expelled from the island. A similar experience was the lot of the Sicilian fathers when, in the early eighteenth century, because of their championing the cause of the bishops, the Viceroy, Maffei, banished them. When Austria obtained possession of Sicily, the Jesuits were allowed to return.

The fathers of the Italian provinces achieved an immense amount of good through the preaching of popular missions. Most successful of all was Segneri (1624–1694),[2] considered by many the greatest Italian orator after St. Bernardine and Savonarola; his vigor of reasoning and richness of imagination, his fire and priestly unction, justify such opinions. The example of his eloquence reformed the Italian pulpit. At first Segneri preached in the great cathedrals; but later for twenty-seven years he gave himself to the work of popular missions. His success was such that townsfolk and peasants, rich and poor, everywhere in Tuscany, the Papal States and the chief Italian cities, flocked to his instructions. To him belongs the credit of introducing the modern method of conducting popular missions, when he based his discourses on the Spiritual Exercises, especially on the meditations of the First Week. The preceptor of Segneri, Oliva, later General of the Society, was himself a distinguished pulpit-orator, having occupied the post of Apostolic Preacher of the Palace under four Popes, Innocent X, Alexander VII, Clement IX and Clement X. A companion of Segneri, Pinamonti, toiled with him on the popular missions for twenty-six years, not only assisting in the pulpit but helping in the composition of the valuable ascetical writings of the great orator. Another zealous companion of these missions, Fontana, deserves mention for his tireless labors.

Of these popular preachers one has received the highest honors of canonization, St. Francis de Geronimo.[3] St. Francis was born at Grottaglia, near Tarento, December 17, 1642; after his studies, made under the Jesuits, and his ordination, he entered the Society July 1, 1670. Though his most ardent desire was the foreign missions, his superiors, recognizing his talents, bade him prepare for the work of the pulpit. He did so and for forty years (1676–1716) labored so tirelessly and with such fruit in the churches and through the streets of Naples that he de-

---

[2] Massei, Translation of his Italian biography of Segneri in No. 27 of the Oratory Series, London (1851); Hallam, *Introduction to the Literature of Europe*, Vol. II, p. 26, New York (1841).

[3] Clarke, *Life of St. Francis de Geronimo*, New York (1891).

served the title, "The Apostle of Naples." Among his great triumphs was the General Communion held by him in the Gesù Nuovo on every third Sunday of the month. For days he would preach in the streets and squares, often in the alleys of the lowest quarters, short, energetically eloquent sermons urging attendance at the Communion. In answer to his pleadings, thirteen thousand to fifteen thousand communicants would come to the Gesù Nuovo on the third Sunday. In the times between, he worked on the popular missions in all sections of Naples and in the villages and hamlets of the neighboring countryside. Crowds filled the churches, or flocked across the fields and through the country lanes to listen to St. Francis, as he preached with all the fervor of a southern Italian. His very ascetical appearance strengthened his message and conquered the heart of many a degraded sinner. Especially eloquent would he become when he preached on the Blessed Virgin; for twenty years every Tuesday night in the Neapolitan Church of Saint Mary of Constantinople he proclaimed her glory. Christians were not the sole object of his zeal; the Turks and the Moorish galley-slaves were sought out by him, and he won many converts from among them. St. Francis devoted himself also to the establishment of social relief works for the benefit of the Neapolitan poor. In his missions and labors for the General Communion, the saint received much aid from a society of laymen connected with Gesù Nuovo, the "Oratorio della Missione"; the duties of these men consisted in maintaining order at open-air sermons and in urging recalcitrants to the sacraments. For this zealous society the saint founded a Mons Pietatis, a Christian loan shop, and developed their sick-benefit and funeral-insurance organizations. Much attention was given by this apostolic priest to the spiritual and temporal welfare of the penitent women who crowded the two refuges of Naples as the result of his preaching; more than twenty-two of them later embraced religious life. Nor did he forget the abandoned street-waifs; for these he provided shelters that guarded them from the temptations of their lot. His place in the hearts of the Neapolitans was amply attested by the tremendous outpouring of all classes at his funeral. St. Francis de Geronimo was canonized May 5, 1839.

Another Italian missionary who was raised to the altars was Bl. Anthony Baldinucci (1665–1717).[4] Frascati, Viterbo and the surrounding districts were the scenes of the popular missions which he preached almost incessantly for twenty years. His methods at times were unusual, even startling; yet they were in keeping with the ideas of the people of the times and places of his labors; and his harvest of souls was enormous. Leo XIII beatified Anthony Baldinucci on April 6, 1893. Deserving of mention for labors in another field is the lay-brother, Andrew

---

[4] Goldie, *Life of Bl. Anthony Baldinucci,* London (1894).

Pozzo (1642–1709), a master of architecture and of the fresco painting of the Baroque period. To him are due the decorations of San Ignazio in Rome, and those of the University Church in Vienna, and the altar of St. Ignatius in the Gesù, Rome.

To the Italian Jesuits, especially to Segneri, is due the unmasking of Quietism. That sinister and false mysticism was propagated in Rome by the Spaniard Molinos; under the outward appearances of the deepest piety the evil system led to the most abominable immoralities. Many good people, as highly placed in the Church as Cardinal Petrucci, were so deceived that when the Jesuits and Dominicans, perceiving the real harm of Molinos' teachings, attacked him in 1662, they encountered the stiffest opposition. The first decisions went somewhat in the favor of the pseudo-mystic, despite the vigorous warfare of Segneri against him; even the works of Segneri and his colleague Belluomo were for a time condemned. The Jesuits, supported by many bishops, persisted in their opposition until Innocent X ordered a more thorough investigation. The real and abhorrent character of Molinos' system was then completely exposed and in 1687 his Quietism was definitely and severely condemned.

Nowhere more than in Spain and Portugal did the works of the Jesuits of the period flow along more steadily in quiet channels.[5] The greatest accomplishments of the members of these provinces were in the foreign missions, far-extended in all parts of Asia and Latin America. Their numerous colleges, while not producing as many great names as in the first century, still regularly obtained the good results of solidly founded institutions. Sacerdotal labors, dispensing the Sacraments, preaching, catechising children and the unlearned, caring for the sick in the hospitals, all these received the complete devotion of hundreds of Spanish and Portuguese Jesuits of the second century. Popular missions especially flourished with such preachers as Padial in Granada, Calatayud in Castile, Vieira, Moreira and da Cruz in Portugal. Many of the Jesuit preachers and ascetical writers devoted themselves to the spread of devotion to the Sacred Heart. None labored more zealously or more successfully than Bernard de Hoyos (1711–1735), a mystic who in his short life of twenty-four years achieved great heights of contemplative prayer.[6]

The patriotism of the Portuguese Jesuits in the events which brought an end to the union with Spain, won for them the confidence of the House of Braganza. There were many burdensome consequences to this royal favor; not only were the Jesuits named as court confessors, but some, especially Vieira, were repeatedly sent on diplomatic missions. John IV appointed Fernandes to the Council of State and tried in vain to have him accept the position of Grand Inquisitor. The limit was reached

---

[5] Astrain, *Historia*, Vol. V, lib. I; VII, lib. I.

[6] Uriarte, *Vida del P. Bern. Fr. de Hoyos de la C. de J.* (1888).

when Dom Pedro, the Regent for his brother Alphonsus VI, in 1678 named Fernandes a member of the Cortes. The General, Oliva, acted with dispatch, threatening the father with suspension if he took his seat; Fernandes immediately resigned his mandate.

In Spain a similar royal favor was given to the Jesuits by Philip IV and his Queen, Maria Anna of Austria, especially to the Queen's confessor, Nidhard.[7] In 1666 this father was appointed to the Council of State, which honor he accepted only on the order of Pope Alexander VII. The good accomplished by Nidhard was somewhat negatived by court intrigues; in fact it was owing to the machinations of Don Juan of Austria, half-brother of the King, that he was forced to leave Spain in 1669. He was sent as ambassador to Rome, where in 1672 he was raised to the Cardinalate. The Bourbon kings of Spain retained Jesuits as confessors and tutors; prominent among their confessors was Daubreton. Of all the Jesuits who labored in the Iberian Peninsula, those whose duties called them to the royal courts were few; the vast majority carried on the more congenial works of the teacher, the preacher and the writer, spending themselves for souls with a faithful devotion. The numbers of the Spanish and Portuguese Jesuits who died in the service of the plague-stricken, are truly inspiring.

In Germany [8] at the beginning of this period, the Counter-Reformation was in full advance, with the Jesuits almost everywhere in the van. They enjoyed the confidence and the support of the Catholic princes, lay and clerical, such as the Emperor Ferdinand II, the Duke Maximilian of Bavaria, the three Rhenish Electors, the Bishops of Paderborn and Würzburg, and the Abbot of Fulda. The membership had so increased that in 1623 Bohemia was created a province, and in 1626 the Upper Rhine and the Lower Rhine provinces were set up; these with Austria and Upper Germany brought the provinces of the Empire to five. So the number remained until 1755 when the province of Silesia was established. More and more, as the enemies of Catholicism came to realize that their most active adversaries were Jesuits, did they turn against the members of the order the full force of their attack of systematic persecution, calumny and exile. In 1605 the Reformers in the Palatinate and in 1608 the Protestant delegates to the Imperial Diet demanded the banishment of the Society from the Empire. Actual expulsion came later, from Aachen in 1611, from Danzig in 1612, from Bohemia, Moravia and Silesia in 1618.

Then broke the Thirty Years' War with all its horror and destruction, so terrible that some parts of Germany were reduced to deserted

---

[7] Astrain, *Historia*, Vol. VI, c. 6; Duhr, *Geschichte*, Vol. III, pp. 823 ff.

[8] Duhr, *Geschichte der Jesuiten in den Ländern deutscher Zunge*, Vol. II, parts 1, 2; Vol. III; Vol. IV, parts 1, 2.

wastes which took a century and a half in recovery. The initial success of the Catholic armies under Tilly and Wallenstein in the first ten years opened up new fields for the Jesuits in the areas recovered for Catholicism. The Edict of Restitution of June 1629 gave Ferdinand II the distribution of much of the recovered church properties; he possessed likewise the Papal permission for their disposal. To the Society the Emperor made large grants of such holdings; but the gifts often brought only trouble and controversies with the older orders who were the ancient possessors. Most of the acquisitions were soon lost in the disastrous turn of the war, caused by the entry of Gustavus Adolphus and Cardinal Richelieu on the Protestant side. The Lutherans, as much as the Calvinists, were now rallied to the new champion of Protestantism, and the Catholic lands were overrun by the Swedes and their allies. The Jesuits, as the most outstanding group among the supporters of the Catholic cause, were made the special object of attack. The very fact that the Catholic victories had been gained by their former pupils, Maximilian the Great, Tilly and Piccolomini, served but to deepen the fierce antipathy against them. Gustavus Adolphus, at the height of his victory in 1631, proposed to drive the Jesuits forever from Germany; in the same year the Protestant princes determined that their price of peace would include the banishment of the order. Two years later just such a demand was made at Frankfort. The hatred of the Jesuits aroused in the dark days of the Thirty Years' War has remained a heritage in the German Protestant mind to the present. Hunger, sickness, extortion, banishment, imprisonment and even violent death, the agonies of this long drawn-out war, struck the Jesuits with terrible force, robbed them of the fruits of their labors of a century, and, for some time, plunged both the fathers and their projects into hopeless misery. Many colleges in Central and South Germany were plundered by the Swedes, who more than once hesitated not to torture the members of the order. The lay-brother Schölling was slain at Ebersberg, June 1, 1632; the priests Passoki and Cramer were murdered by a Protestant soldier, November 2, 1642, after the Battle of Leipsic. Louis XIII interceded with his ally, the Swedish field marshal, Baner, to have his soldiers treat the Jesuits with consideration. The admonition was really needed, for the Swedes nourished a special hatred for the Society; a Jesuit found in their homeland would have been executed. It is not surprising that they meted out terrible treatment to the Jesuits and levied the hardest contributions on their churches and colleges. Several of the fathers died victims of pestilence; of the eighteen Jesuits who accompanied the armies of Maximilian of Bavaria, six succumbed while tending the plague-stricken soldiers. The province of the Upper Rhine lost seventy-seven priests, who died either in the field hospitals or on the battlefields. The Jesuits played a very positive role in the Catholic defense. A large number of the fathers served as chaplains; often in a beleaguered city they were the soul of the defense. They turned their colleges and residences into hospitals in which fathers, scholastics and brothers vied with each other in the care of the wounded and dying. In the conquered areas they strove to win back the people to the ancient Faith; the court confessors among them, like Lamormaini, encouraged and preserved the Catholic princes in the defense of their religion. In the very last action of the war, the siege of Prague in 1648, a decisive part in the defense was the fighting of the student corps, organized and trained by Plachy, a father of the Prague college. In connection with the Peace of Westphalia, it has been charged that the Jesuits deliberately delayed its conclusion and in union with the Papal Legate, Chigi, rendered the transactions more difficult so that the Papacy might obtain the greatest possible advantage. The charge is but an unproved suspicion of the enemies of the order. Such a course would have been contrary to the known sympathy of the Jesuits for the people's sufferings in that long and dreadful conflict, a sympathy so evident in the writings and lives of Jesuits such as von Spe, Brunner and Balde.[9]

One bright light shining through the gloom of those terrible years was the continued effort of the poet-priest, Friedrich von Spe, to bring an end to the witch persecutions, a curse in Germany since the middle of the fifteenth century.[10] With the advent of the religious revolution the mania increased to alarming proportions, due to the anarchy of belief and the unhealthy emphasis which Luther and his colleagues were continually placing on the devil and his works. This increase spread later to Catholic districts and in some of them eventually approached the terrible limits prevailing in the Lutheran and Calvinistic districts. Throughout the land by the thousands, unfortunate wretches were subjected to the most excruciating tortures to wring from them a confession of their alleged accomplices; by the thousands they perished with horrible agonies in the flames of the stake. Many of the poor beings were innocent victims of mere suspicions. How men, otherwise reasonable and kind, could have so far departed from their senses, could have so blunted their feelings, is hard to understand; except that a sinister spirit of the age swept over men's minds and hearts. The Jesuits had no common attitude towards the witch persecutions; some, children of their age, approved of

[9] Duhr, *Geschichte*, Vol. II, part 1, pp. 474–493. For the conduct of Chigi and the Jesuits, confer Pastor, *History of the Popes*, Vol. XXX, pp. 94–136. The Nuncio and the fathers opposed peace-concessions only when such proposals would have greviously damaged the Catholic Faith.

[10] Duhr, *Geschichte*, Vol. I, c. 21; II, part 2, c. 10; Duhr, *Die Stellung der Jesuiten in den deutschen Hexenprozessen*, Freiburg (1900).

them, others viewed them with suspicion, others still opposed them entirely.[11] The order itself had taken no stand; not a single mention of "possession" or of "exorcism" is to be found in the Constitutions or in the ordinances of the Generals. St. Peter Canisius acted somewhat in accordance with the ideas of his times; yet in his smaller catechism, for the use of the common people, he avoided all mention of the devil; even in his larger catechism he seldom speaks of Satan and then only as the author of sin. All this is in marked contrast with the repeated references to the devil and to his power over humans to be found in Luther's works. St. Francis Borgia. Hoffaeus and Bader, the last two, important Provincials in the German provinces, were sceptical and wished the fathers to leave the witch affairs alone. This may be said to have been the general attitude of the Jesuit superiors from the beginning. The Jesuits at Trier for a time displayed a regrettable attitude towards the witchcraft trials; indeed, it has been asserted that the Trier Jesuits used the charge of witchcraft to have Protestants put to death, a charge rejected by Burr, a foremost American authority on the matter.[12] It is good to know that the fathers in Coblenz and in Mainz heartily disapproved of the course adopted at Trier. Unfortunate were the writings of those otherwise able theologians, Gergory of Valentia and Delrio, in defense of the punishment of the witches; still they were more than balanced by the works of Tanner and Laymann; Tanner, whose proposal would have practically done away with the trials, courageously braved the threats of persecution as a witch's accomplice.

It was in 1631 that von Spe delivered his telling blow against this horrible mania, by writing the famous *Cautio Criminalis*,[13] or to give its full title in English, *Caution in criminal processes, or a book on witch trials at this time necessary for the magistrates of Germany, and most useful for the councillors and confessors of princes, inquisitors, judges, lawyers, confessors of the accused, preachers and others. Written by an unknown Roman theologian.* Friedrich Spe von Langenfeld was born near Düsseldorf, Rhineland, in 1591 and died at Trier in 1635, having caught an infection from wounded soldiers whom he had been nursing. He had taught moral theology at Paderborn, Cologne and Trier and had achieved a deserved reputation as a poet by his *Trutznachtigal* and his *Goldenes Tugendbuch*, the latter a work much loved by Leibniz. His life in the Society was not always a happy one, for he had to bear the

---

[11] Schwickerath, "Attitude of the Jesuits in the Trials for Witchcraft," *The American Catholic Quarterly Review*, Vol. XXVII (1902), pp. 475–516.

[12] Cf. Duhr, *Jesuiten Fabeln*, p. 386, Freiburg (1899); Janssen, *History of the German People*, Vol. XVI, p. 441 for Burr's opinion.

[13] Schröder, "Die Cautio criminalis" in *Literaturw. Jahrbuch der Görresges*, 3 (1928), pp. 134–150.

cross of misunderstanding with superiors. Von Spe, like many Jesuits of the times, heard the confessions of the unfortunate victims of the witch persecutions and assisted them in their last hours. These confessions convinced him of the innocence of the poor wretches; in the *Cautio* he makes this definite statement: "I assert and confirm under oath that I never found one of the accused guilty; and yet I have taken all possible means to ascertain the truth." His hair had grown prematurely gray at the experiences of assisting so many innocent victims in their horrible execution. The *Cautio Criminalis* did not propose immediate abolition of the trials, but advocated such reforms in procedure as would have put a quick end to the witch persecutions. The most effective parts of the book were the cuttingly sarcastic descriptions of the horrible abuses in the legal procedures, especially in the use of torture. The author spared no one, neither prince nor ecclesiastic, neither judge nor peasant. The *Cautio Criminalis* has won the approbation of men of all creeds.

The members of his order on the whole showed themselves favorable to von Spe's work. The General, Vittelleschi, assured him in writing not to worry over the efforts of a Cologne Jesuit, Roestius, to have the *Cautio* placed on the Index. Many of the criticisms which did arise came either from prejudice or from the fear of the consequences, if the officials attacked should turn upon the order; some of these jurists had in fact demanded the expulsion of the Society. More serious was the fact that the book was published anonymously and without the sanction of superiors. Von Spe had given the manuscript to friends and they had published it without his consent. There was a grave suspicion in the minds of several that von Spe was not wholly unaware of the action being taken by his friends; if that were true he would have been guilty of a most grievous breach of the rule and would have been deserving of expulsion. The General was most anxious about the accusation; after some correspondence with the Provincial of the Lower Rhine province and with von Spe, Vittelleschi wrote the author a mild rebuke in view of the dubious method of its publication.[14] Von Spe's book did not bring an end to the witch persecutions; but it effected their abolition in many places and led to their eventual suppression.

For some time after the Thirty Years' War, the German Jesuits were occupied in recouping their losses, and then in developing the foundations already established. The Counter-Reformation had more or less spent its force. That fact and the delimitation of Catholic and Protestant regions by the Peace of Westphalia, prevented anything like the sweeping victories of the late sixteenth century. In the now definitely Catholic lands of the Empire the fathers continued their educational works and

---

[14] Duhr, *Geschichte*, Vol. II, part 2, p. 760.

their labors for souls; it was largely due to their work that classical education did not fail. The Upper Rhine province suffered greatly in the wars of Louis XIV; four colleges were destroyed when the soldiers of the Grand Monarch burned the towns of Ettlingen, Baden, Speyer and Worms.

One glorious result of the Jesuit labors during this period was the numerous individual conversions. Even while the Thirty Years' War was on, the fathers every year brought large numbers of converts into the Catholic fold. Huneken, a Saxon Jesuit, alone reconciled several thousand; while Metsch, a priest of great charity and eloquence, was credited with having made 10,000 converts, including 9 ministers and 109 apostates. From 1666–1678 in Silesia, Moravia and Bohemia the number gained back to Catholicism by the priests of the order counted up to 29,588. Konias, who died in 1760, worked with remarkable success in winning conversions in Bohemia. The parish clergy and the priests of other orders were inspired to zealous emulation; the constant use of the Spiritual Exercises strengthened all to work together for a renewal of Catholic life.

During these years several Jesuits of the Lower Rhine province devoted themselves to the scattered brethren of their Faith in the Protestant North, the Diaspora, as the German Catholics call the region. From 1651 there were fathers laboring at Königsberg, even earlier at Glückstadt and Bremen, and from 1660 in Copenhagen. During the same period other priests of the order from Hildesheim rendered special service in the Hanoverian towns. In the beginning of the eighteenth century members of the Society founded a permanent mission in Schwerin, which they maintained even as ex-Jesuits until 1806. In Prussia the first successes were rather slight owing to the hostility of the Great Elector, Friedrich Wilhelm, who refused the Jesuits permission for landed properties as well as the rights of preaching and instructing the youth. Better days came under his son, Friedrich I, and increased under the latter's successor, Friedrich II, the Great; the last ruler frequently interceded for the fathers and sought to influence the Emperor Joseph II to afford them his protection. Some very notable conversions were made among the princes of Germany: such especially were Friedrich August I of Saxony, later King of Poland; his heir, Friedrich August II; the Count Palatine Edward von Wittelsbach and his sister, the Countess Luisa. It may be noted here that almost every Catholic German prince in the eighteenth century had Jesuit confessors and tutors at his court.

Missions to the people of the towns and through the country hamlets, was a much sought-for work among the German Jesuits of these times. Among the earlier missionaries of the seventeenth century Jeninger labored with remarkable success for thirty years in Southern Germany. Towards the end of the century the Italian Jesuit, Fontana, was brought to Germany to instruct his brethren in the methods of the popular missions invented by Segneri. Thus trained, Herdigen and Loferer became the founders of the popular missions in Germany and Austria; for years they travelled over all parts of the Empire and were listened to everywhere by eager crowds. Similar good work was accomplished in Switzerland and in Bohemia by Maillordoz. Numerous other Jesuits followed in the footsteps of these pioneers of the popular mission. In the Austrian province alone, in 1732, eighteen priests were set aside for this work. Here also should be noticed the labors of Merz, the cathedral preacher of Southern Germany, of Wurz of the Austrian pulpit, but above all, of Hunolt, who has been rated as one of the best preachers of the eighteenth century and whose many volumes of sermons are in demand even to this day. In Austria in the same period the Jesuits organized confraternities for catechetical instruction; Parhamer worked most untiringly in this apostolate. In 1768 there were twelve catechetical missionaries among the Austrian fathers. At the time of the Suppression, in 1774, there were in the German lands 5,340 Jesuits, who operated 117 colleges, 32 seminaries, 51 residences and 58 mission-stations.

The society in Hungary in the early part of the seventeenth century had to endure many difficult trials at the hands of the Calvinists, who almost succeeded in making both Hungary and Transylvania Protestant. Their failure was due largely to the Jesuits, to one especially, Pázmány, as has been noted.[15] The order was brought back to Hungary by the Emperor-King Matthias, only to be driven out in the rebellion of Bethlan Gabor in 1619. At Kaschau on Sept. 8, 1619, two Jesuits, Bl. Stefan Pongracz and Bl. Melchior Grodecz, with the Bl. Canon Stefan Crisinus, were murdered by the Calvinist soldiers. This terrible deed was but the outcome of the bitter campaign directed against the order, especially by Alvinczy in his *Querelae Hungariae*.

With the Catholic victory and the expulsion of the Turks the Jesuits both in Hungary and in Transylvania pursued peacefully and with solid profit the vocations of teachers, preachers and writers. Hevenesy and Baranyi brought into reunion with Rome many schismatics among the Wallachians and the Rumanians. In 1767 there were in Hungary and Transylvania 900 Jesuits who maintained 17 colleges, 20 smaller foundations and 11 missions.

The Polish Jesuits in the second century of the order found their chief work in their fifty-one colleges, not only in the teaching of the

---

[15] Cf. Ch. VIII, pp. 178–180.

classics but in the developing of the Christian character of their students, especially through the sodalities of the Blessed Virgin Mary.[16] In their schools they did not forget the Polish language, even though as elsewhere the basis of instruction was the classical literature; the names of Skarga, Wujek, translator of the Bible, Naruszewcz and Albertrandy prove their interest in their mother tongue. The charge that the Jesuits were responsible for the downfall of Poland is quite ridiculous; in their schools and in all their activities the Polish fathers strove always to instil a true love of country. As in other lands, among the most fruitful labors of the times were the popular missions; Jesuit preachers traversed the entire land even to the frontiers and beyond, to Hungary, Transylvania, Silesia and Russia, bringing to hundreds of thousands of people this form of the Spiritual Exercises. The Polish fathers at various times maintained missions in Russia, the Crimea, Constantinople and Persia.

Opposition from several quarters was encountered; a sharp struggle with the University of Cracow lasted for a long time and ended with the closing of the Jesuit college; the attacks of the Protestant Swedes, the Russian schismatics, the Tartars and the Turks did an immense amount of harm to the Catholic Church in Poland, and in her sufferings the Society had its share. Among the schismatics the work of reunion was carried on with marked success by fathers such as Przeborowski, Vota, Mancinelli and St. Andrew Bobola. These victories for Christian unity however were obtained at a bloody price; about thirty Polish Jesuits were slain by Cossacks or other schismatics. Foremost among those martyrs stands St. Andrew Bobola.[17] St. Andrew was born in Sandomir, Poland, in 1590 and at the age of twenty-one entered the Society of Jesus. After the completion of his course he was sent to Bobruisk in 1630, where he achieved marvels by his preaching, winning the hearts of all by his devotion to the plague-stricken. Six years later on being sent to Lithuania he gained similar successes with the popular missions and in the reconciliation of heretics. His numerous conversions made him the object of special hatred for the recalcitrant schismatics who sought in every way to hinder him, not hesitating even at personal violence. On May 16, 1657, two Cossacks seized the Saint and, after severely beating him, dragged him tied to their saddles to Jarnow. There he was tortured most fiendishly. No horror in the passions of the early martyrs, nor in the sufferings of the victims of the Indian savages, surpassed what was inflicted on his living body; he was burned, half-strangled, partly flayed alive,

---

[16] Zaleski, *Jezuici w. Polsce*, 5 vols., Lemberg (1896–1906); Bednarski, "Declin et Rénaissance de L'Enseignment de Jésuites en Pologne," *Archiv. Hist. S.J.*, Vol. II (1933), pp. 199–233.

[17] De Buck, *Essai historique sur le B. A. Bobola*, Brussels (1855); Gallagher and Donovan, *The Life of St. Andrew Bobola*, Boston (1939).

and finally dispatched by a saber cut. St. Andrew Bobola was canonized by Pius XI on Easter Sunday 1938.

Polish Jesuits also were frequently employed as confessors to the kings and tutors of the princes. One of the Polish members of the order actually ascended the royal throne; he was John Casimir, a brother of the King of Poland, who entered the Society in 1643, was raised to the cardinalate by Innocent X in 1645, and was crowned King of Poland in 1648. As John Casimir had not received the priesthood, there was nothing to prevent his election as King; of course his immediate connection with the order had ceased when he became a Cardinal. The Society in Poland enjoyed the confidence of Jan Sobieski; indeed it was owing partly to the pleas of his confessor, Vota, that he made his celebrated march to the relief of Vienna in 1683. In 1755 the Polish Assistancy was erected, consisting of four provinces, Greater Poland, Lesser Poland, Lithuania and Masovia; in the very year of the Suppression a fifth province was established, that of White Russia, a providential occurrence, for in this province the Society of Jesus was to be preserved. The Polish Jesuits at the time of the Suppression numbered 3,386, and were in charge of 52 colleges, 15 residences and 93 mission-stations.

The foundations which the Society was able to establish in Russia enjoyed only a precarious existence. In 1684 a Jesuit, Schmid, came to Moscow as the chaplain of the Imperial Embassy; and about the same time the Grand Duchess Sophie, at the Emperor's intercession, permitted the erection of a small house and a college. The next year the Pope dispatched another Jesuit, Debois, on an embassy to the Grand Duchess; and Jan Sobieski sent still another of the fathers, Vota, to Moscow as his representative. A popular tumult on the occasion of Peter the Great's assuming the governing power, in 1689, forced the closing of the Moscow venture. A few years later, however, Peter allowed the erection of a Catholic church and the recall of the Jesuits, who remained until 1719 when the Tsar quarreled with the Emperor. At the turn of the century several missions were undertaken by the Jesuits in White Russia. With the first partition of Poland in 1772, not a few Jesuit colleges and foundations passed under the Russian Crown; it was in these institutions that the Society was able to maintain its existence after the Suppression.

In Sweden, any Jesuit who dared to enter the country, except in the retinue of a Catholic ambassador, faced a sentence of death.[18] An attempt was made however in 1623 by a Jesuit, Schact, himself a convert; the courageous priest was forced to the rather incongruous disguise of a dealer in mousetraps. The secretary of King Gustavus Adolphus, Ursinus, and the Burgomaster, Anthelius von Telge, gave him their assist-

---

[18] Duhr, *Geschichte*, Vol. II, part 2, 75 ff.

ance; on the pretence of being von Telge's servant, he was able to dispense the Sacraments. The Jesuit was not long undiscovered. An Italian renegade, whom Schact had nursed when the traitor was plague-stricken, betrayed all three men. The two Swedes were put to death; while the priest, after seven months' imprisonment during which he was thrice tortured, was banished from the realm. The fact that he was a foreigner saved his life. The conversion of the Queen of Sweden, Christina, the daughter and heiress of Gustavus Adolphus, may be said to have started in her frequent conversations on religion with Macedo, the Jesuit chaplain of the Portuguese Ambassador. At the request of the Queen, the General sent her two theologians, Malines, a professor of theology in Turin, and Casati, a professor of theology in Rome. No light task awaited them; Christina was shrewd, clear-sighted and learned; she had been making a study of religion for five years. After long discussions the royal lady was satisfied; and at Brussels in 1655, Christina, the daughter of the Protestant Champion of the Thirty Years' War, gladly forfeited her throne that she might become a Catholic. In 1664 the Jesuit Sterck, chaplain of the Imperial Embassy, was arrested and sentenced to death because, after the Ambassador's death, he had held services for the Spanish residents. Only the most strenuous exertions of the Spanish ambassador saved the priest; the sentence was commuted to banishment. The work of the Jesuits in Sweden and Norway in the next century, except in the chaplaincies, was practically nil. The establishment of the Nordicum, a seminary for Scandinavian converts, at Linz in Austria in 1698 by the Jesuit Gottseer, was a praiseworthy effort to prepare a clergy for the Northern Nations.

In Flanders and in other parts of the Netherlands under Catholic rule the fathers of the Society put the quiet years of the period to good advantage in the developing of all their works, but especially that of education. The Missio Castrensis and the Missio Navalis (founded in 1623) afforded a glorious opportunity for the zeal of many chaplains, not a few of whom met death on the battlefield or in the pest-ridden military hospitals. One of the chief accomplishments of the Flemish Jesuits was their catechetical apostolate. Few provinces could compare with them, either in the number and enthusiasm of the catechists, or in the successes achieved. Priests, scholastics and novices joined in the task of instructing the young children whom they gathered together on Sundays and holydays. Solid grounding in the fundamentals of Faith was guaranteed by the use of Canisius' shorter Catechism or of Coster's Flemish translation of the small Roman Catechism. In 1640 the catechists of the Flandro-Belgic province numbered 200, giving instruction to 32,500 children; in Antwerp alone, some years previously, 5,000 little folk were taught their religion by the Jesuits. Lay cooperation, either in the form of organizations supporting the work or in actual participation as teachers, was welcomed by the fathers. So highly esteemed was the catechetical apostolate that the civil, as well as the ecclesiastical authorities, gladly manifested their endorsement by their presence at its festal celebrations. Except for the Jansenist controversy, which will be treated later, the Jesuits of the Catholic Netherlands experienced little opposition to their varied works in the second century of the order. At the Suppression the Belgian Jesuits counted 1,013, in charge of 36 colleges, 4 seminaries, 3 residences and 7 missions.

To the north during these years the Dutch Jesuits had to face the severest persecutions. Except that they had not to dread the death penalty, their sufferings were quite on a par with those of their English brethren, in fines, imprisonments and exile. Yet the Dutch fathers, along with their confrères among the secular priests and the Capuchins, carried on their apostolate undismayed. Often they were forced to go about disguised as merchants or doctors. The scattered flocks were assembled in secret, the ignorant were instructed, the faint-hearted were encouraged, the Sacraments were dispensed even though God's service had to be held in the depth of the night or in hidden places. There were a few martyrs of blood, such as the priests, Boddey and Paesman, and the lay-brother, Noltin, all three of whom were slain by the Calvinists at Utrecht on July 30, 1638; but the common lot was the suffering of privation and prison. After the Peace of Westphalia some mitigation eased the position of Catholics and gave freer opportunities to the priests. The Dutch mission increased steadily; in 1622 there were 17 stations; in 1636, 31; after the Peace of Westphalia, 40. In 1618 there were 20 Jesuits; in 1634, 63; in 1654, 90. Regrettable controversies arose on the points of jurisdiction and faculties between the Vicars Apostolic, who ruled the Dutch Catholics, and the Jesuits; eventually the problems were settled by Urban VIII. Far more disastrous was the struggle with the Dutch Jansenists. Unfortunately a considerable section of the clergy had embraced Jansenistic ideas in their seminary days; and the United Provinces afforded a refuge for the Jansenists driven from France and Flanders. When Peter Codde fell away, eighty-one priests left the Catholic Church to form the Jansenist sect of Utrecht. All along, the Dutch Jesuits had been uncompromising in their warfare on Jansenism; now they had to bear the brunt of the united attack of the Jansenists and the Calvinists, who only too readily rallied to the support of any enemy of Rome. Members of the Society were expelled from twenty-two stations in the province of Holland; later they were driven from other stations, so that at the Suppression there were only thirty Jesuits laboring in eighteen stations in the United Provinces.

Across the Channel in the British Isles the Jesuits in the second century of the Society, except for one brief moment in England and another in Ireland, led the life of the catacombs.[19] Yet in the very face of persecution the English Jesuits increased: in 1606 a novitiate was opened in Louvain, which was later translated to Liége and finally located at Watten in Flanders; a house of studies was maintained at Liége and even a tertianship at Ghent; in 1623 the mission was erected into a province, which in 1636 reached its maximum number of 374 subjects. It was, in a way, a strange province, for all its permanent foundations were on the continent or in the Maryland mission. In England the work was organized according to districts known as "Colleges"; there were nine such "Colleges," as well as six smaller posts, all governed by the Provincial from the continent, where he usually resided. During the reign of Charles I, only one Jesuit was put to death, Bl. Edmund Arrowsmith, a noble Lancashire priest, who was betrayed by false friends and executed in 1628. In the dread days of Cromwell ten Jesuits were slain or died in jail, victims of prison brutalities. Charles II seemed personally favorable to the Society; yet it was during his reign in 1679 that the Oates Plot [20] took the toll of twenty-one deaths among the Jesuits, eight on the scaffold and thirteen in prison. Titus Oates, the arch-liar of history, after a discreditable career as a Protestant, managed to have himself received into the Church as a repentant prodigal. The Jesuit Provincial, Strange, was persuaded to give him a place in the English College at Valladolid, from which he was soon expelled. The Provincial was again persuaded to give him a second chance at St. Omers; but it was not long before he was expelled from that college also. Whether he had ever been a true Catholic, or was just a sham convert, as he himself later asserted, would be a question hard to decide. One thing at least is certain, he had learned enough of Catholic practices and terms to give color to his infamous lies. It would be wearisome and useless to detail all the machinations and the terrible deeds which in his charges he attributed to the Jesuits. They were all a farrago of lies, yet they sent many holy and noble men to terrible deaths. The Jesuits who were martyred were: Bl. William Ireland, Bl. Thomas Whitbread, Bl. William Harcourt, Bl. John Fenwick, Bl. John Gavin, Bl. Anthony Turner, Bl. Philip Evans, Bl. David Lewis. Several more fathers were cast into prison, among them being Bl. Claude de la Colombière; of these imprisoned priests thirteen died either in jail or as a result of their confinement.

With the advent of the Catholic James II, a brief moment of peace came for the English Jesuits. The king chose as his confessor the Jesuit

---

[19] Foley, *Records of the English Province of the Society of Jesus*, 8 Vols., London (1873–1883).

[20] Foley, *Records of the English Province*, Vol. 5, pp. 8–109; Duhr, *Jesuiten Fabeln*, p. 805,

Warner; while another Jesuit, Petre, he made a member of his Privy Council. James had sought also to have Petre raised to the episcopacy and even to be named a Cardinal. This Jesuit's appointment did the Stuart king only harm because of the opportunities it gave his enemies to visit on him all their anti-Jesuit hatred. Despite many charges against Petre, evidence seems to prove that he conducted himself well in office. A college was begun in London in 1687 under the rectorship of Charles Poulton; and an open chapel was established where sermons and controversial lectures were held. The future was bright with hope. But the expectation was short-lived; for no sooner had William of Orange been seated on the English throne by the Revolution of 1688, than college and chapel were closed and the persecution of Catholics and Jesuits renewed. This last persecution was not to blood; but it included every other means of repression, and with such effect as to render impossible any notable advancing of the Catholic cause. Chaplaincies in the houses of Catholic noblemen were the only opportunity for most of the eighteenth-century English Jesuits to exist and to carry on their sacerdotal work. About one hundred fathers were thus employed, serving not only the nobleman's family, but also the Catholic peasantry of the neighborhood. At the time of the Suppression there were 274 Jesuits in the English province, of whom 140 were resident in England.

During the period under consideration, differences and misunderstandings continued to plague the relations between the Jesuits and the secular priests. With the establishment of an Apostolic Vicar in 1625, a quarrel over jurisdiction arose; the second Vicar, Dr. Richard Smith, not wishing to recognize the exemptions of religious, sought to introduce episcopal approbation of confessors. The Brief "Brittania" of 1631 decided that the faculties of regular missionaries should continue to be obtained immediately from the Holy See. However, after the increase of the Vicars-Apostolic to four in 1685, the regulars were obliged to obtain episcopal approbation. Finally in 1753 came the Constitution "Apostolicum Ministerium" of Benedict XIV, which by its Regulae Missionis definitely established the relations of the regulars with the Vicars-Apostolic.

The oath question in the time of the Commonwealth again caused difficulties. The representatives of the Catholic clergy, secular and religious, were called on short notice to give their subscription to a document dealing with their allegiance, called the "Three Questions." With the other priests, More, the Jesuit representative, accepted the proposals; he considered that the reasons in the preamble sufficiently qualified the text of the proffered oath. He was quickly recalled to the continent and punished for his imprudence. The differences between the seculars and the Jesuits were sometimes further complicated by the Gallican and

Jansenist controversies in France, where many of both groups had obtained their clerical education, and possibly also by a too persistent clinging to exemptions and privileges. As had been said in a previous chapter, these differences were between good men whose strong characters on the one hand led them to a noble loyalty for the Faith and on the other to an exaggerated tenacity of their own ideas.

The Scotch Jesuits, though but a handful, fought a glorious battle for the old Faith. In 1640 there were six fathers on the mission, serving as chaplains in the castles of Catholic nobles or wandering as missionaries among the clans of the Highlands. When James II ascended the throne of England and Scotland, two fathers, Forbes and Patterson, were called to be chaplains at Holyrood, and permission was given for the opening of a school. All these good plans collapsed with the advent of William of Orange; and the Scotch fathers were forced back to their hidden and perilous apostolate.

The Irish Jesuits enjoyed a few years of peaceful happiness during the domination of the Confederation of Kilkenny, 1642–1654. The Irish mission attained its greatest expansion with thirteen residences, including one or two schools. The bloody days of Cromwell brought these foundations to a swift ending; yet eighteen fathers stayed at their posts to brave the storms of Puritan fanaticism. Two, Robert Netterville and Bathe, were slain in the massacre of Drogheda; another, Boyton, was martyred by Puritans at Mary's altar on the Rock of Cashel; the rest had to endure terrible sufferings and constant perils, as Christopher Netterville, who for one whole year hid in his father's tomb, or Galosse who was hunted like a wolf by the Cromwellians. In the dark days following the surrender of Limerick, the Irish Jesuits continued amid dangers and privations, often in the direst poverty, to minister to the poor of the towns or to the downtrodden peasantry of the mountains and the boglands. Alleviation began to appear only shortly before the Suppression; yet in this brief time one father, Austin, opened a school in Dublin. Irish Jesuits outside of Ireland achieved much for education and for souls in the second century of the order; the more notable among them were Luke Wadding,[21] Comerford, Sherlock, and Richard Lynch in Spain; Ambrose Wadding and Peter Wadding in Germany; Duiggin and Lombard in the Low Countries; Kelly, Bathe and Routh in France; O'Fiehily in Paraguay; Michael Wadding, missionary and mystic, in Mexico; and Thomas Lynch, Provincial at the time of the Suppression, in Brazil.

The steady streams and cross currents in the second century of Jesuit

---

[21] Not to be confused with his cousin, the distinguished Irish Franciscan of the same name. Peter, Michael and the Jesuit Luke were brothers; Ambrose was their cousin and brother of the Franciscan Luke.

history were especially evident in the record of the French provinces.[22] The membership in 1610 reached 1,135; in 23 years' time it had trebled. It included 3,350 Jesuits in 5 provinces, France, Aquitaine, Lyons, Toulouse and Champagne, and in 7 missions, Carribean Islands, Canada, Greece, Syria, Persia, India and China. The work on the missions has already been considered and so, too, have the labors in the colleges; yet it may be in place to remark that nowhere were the Jesuits' schools more numerously attended and nowhere had they greater influence in the diffusion of culture. Nineteen Jesuits were called to fill the extremely delicate office of royal confessor; expecially noteworthy among them were Auger, Caussin, Sirmond, Ferrier, la Chaise, le Tellier and de Linières. How far their influence went beyond the confessional, it would be hard to say; certainly they did accomplish much in opposition to Jansenism and in the furtherance of the foreign missions. On the other hand they incurred much jealousy and misunderstanding; and they had to bear much blame for such royal acts as the destruction of Port Royal, the Revocation of the Edict of Nantes and the persecution of the Huguenots, though their direct responsibility has not been proved. La Chaise, the confessor of Louis XIV for thirty-four years, despite the fact that he fulfilled his difficult duties conscientiously, became the object of several calumnies; modern criticism has cast them upon the rubbish heap.[23] The sources of these stories are: the letters of Lisolette, Duchess of Orleans, whose hatred for priests renders her testimony valueless; the letters and memoirs of Madame de Maintenon, which have been shown either to have been falsified or based on misinformation; and other writings of a similar character. The worst accusation against Père la Chaise is that he connived at the King's liaison with the Marquise de Montespan. Quite the opposite is the truth; the Jesuit played an important part in the breaking up of the affair. Nor is there any proof to substantiate another charge that la Chaise advised the Revocation of the Edict of Nantes, although no doubt he approved of it as did most Frenchmen of his day. The Pope believed that he did not urge the King strongly enough in certain religious problems, not realizing that Louis XIV paid little attention to his confessor once he considered the affair at hand to be a purely state concern. La Chaise's fault was in being too conciliatory; it was his tendency to try and save a situation if it were at all possible.

The influential position of the confessors aroused the jealousy of the powerful Cardinal Richelieu. At his order they were frequently changed; and a few of them had to bear the brunt of his anger. Particularly was

---

[22] Carayon, *Documents inédits concernant la Comp. de Jésus*, 23 Vols., Poitiers and Paris (1863–1868).

[23] Charitelarize, *Le Père de la Chaise, confesseur de Louis XIV*, Paris et Lyons (1859); Koch, "Franz d'Aix de la Chaise S.J.," *Jesuiten-Lexikon*, 314, 315.

this the case with Caussin; in 1637 with great courage he presented to Louis XIII a memorial against the continuance of the Thirty Years' War, citing especially the hardships which the people had to endure during this protracted conflict.[24] Richelieu not only had Caussin banished to Quimper, where he was kept under surveillance like a political prisoner, but he even calumniated the priest before the French officialdom and to his religious superiors. Caussin's fate was to be a warning to other Jesuit confessors that they were to confine their activities solely to the confessional. Monod and Suffern were two other confessors who were made to feel the Cardinal's displeasure. The ire of this powerful political ecclesiastic was further stirred by some of the writings of Jesuits: notably the pamphlets, *Mysteria Politica* and the *Admonitio ad Regem,* which attacked his support of the German Protestants, and which, though published anonymously, were usually ascribed to the French Jesuit Garasse and to the Munich rector, Keller. The work of Santarelli on the Papal and regal power also angered the Cardinal. In fact this last book raised such a storm among the Gallicans that the French superiors obtained protection only by a declaration against Santarelli's teaching on the divine right of kings, and by the promise to support the censures of the Sorbonne and never to advocate anything contrary to that body in such matters.[25] This yielding was too abject, and Urban VIII was rightly displeased with the French Jesuits. Aside from these incidents, Richelieu, to whom consistency was of small concern, gave his support to the order both in France and on the foreign missions. His favor to the Jesuits at home was due to his realization of the force which the Society exerted against Protestantism and Gallicanism; the latter movement, whenever it menaced his power, found no partisan in the Cardinal.

The most boisterous and also the most devastating cross current that struggled to hinder the steady progress of the French Jesuits was Jansenism.[26] The intense antagonism of the conflict was but to be expected, since Jansenism was hardly less than a cryptic Calvinism insinuating itself into Catholic life. The French Jesuits, piercing its rigoristic piety, perceived its true nature and fought it relentlessly. This was particularly true with regard to the Jansenists' opposition to frequent Communion, a practice which they intensely abhorred. To them Christ in the Blessed Sacrament was a remote, awesome Deity, to be worshipped from afar, not the loving God-man whose Eucharistic presence is the outcome of His desire to be with the sons of men. They demanded an almost im-

---

[24] Rochemonteix, *Nic. Caussin et le Cardinal Richelieu,* Paris (1911); Pastor, *History of the Popes,* Vol. XXVIII, pp. 389–391.

[25] Fouqueray, *Histoire,* Vol. IV, pp. 166–172.

[26] Rapin, *Histoire de Jansénisme dépuis ses origines jusqu'en 1644,* Paris (1861); *Dict. Theol. Cath.* VIII, pp. 318–529.

possible goodness in those who were to receive Holy Communion, and thus they excluded many from the Sacrament for long periods of time together. Such views were diametrically opposed to the whole Jesuit position, and the fathers fought them most strenuously. Ignatian asceticism, emphasizing warm, personal and intimate love of God, had always made much of the frequent reception of the Blessed Sacrament. Indeed the priests of the Society had always been conspicuous for their advocacy of the practice, the justification for which they found in the decrees of the Council of Trent. In the controversy under discussion there was hardly a point on which the Jansenists and the Jesuits clashed more sharply. Since that time the views of the Catholic world have come to the universal acceptance of frequent Communion. Pius X made this acceptance complete by his decree in which he urged all to receive the Blessed Eucharist frequently, and if possible, even daily. It was the final justification of the Jesuits' stand against the Jansenists.

Cornelius Jansenius (Jansen), from whom the heresy takes its name, was a Louvain scholar and Bishop of Ypres; he had become convinced that the Church for centuries had departed in teaching and in discipline from her original simplicity. In union with a friend, Jean du Vergier de Huranne, more commonly known as Abbé St. Cyran, from a benefice later conferred upon him, Jansenius planned the reform of the Church by the abandonment of Scholasticism and by a return to what both he and his friend considered the teachings of St. Augustine. Jansenius gave the movement its theological basis; as he had been greatly influenced by Baius, his teaching, which he professed to draw from St. Augustine, was semi-heretical and quasi-Calvinistic. Du Vergier, or St. Cyran, developed the moral and ascetical side, especially in regard to questions of virtue, the reception of the Blessed Sacrament, and church discipline. It was a chilling rigorism that he produced and advocated. Both men were opposed to the Society of Jesus because of its persistent opposition to Baianism. Jansenius possibly had other reasons; his application for entrance into the Society had been rejected, and he had been the advocate later at Madrid of the University of Louvain in its quarrel with the Belgian Jesuits. The doctrinal founder of the movement for some time had been embodying his ideas in a book to be called *Augustinus,* since it purported to contain the true teachings of the great Doctor of the early Church, when death brought an end to his labors on May 6, 1638. Before he died Jansenius made a complete submission to any decision of the Holy See regarding his book, in the event that it should ever be published.

Two years later came the actual publication of the *Augustinus,* and this in spite of the determined opposition of the Belgian Jesuits who had recognized its truly heretical character. St. Cyran prepared a second edition, which was published at Paris in 1641, thus bringing the conflict to France. Paris, not Louvain, was henceforth to be the chief battleground. In the French capital St. Cyran gained recruits among the rigoristic-minded, especially from the circle of the Arnaulds, a powerful regalistic family, Gallican to the core and stubbornly perverse in their adherence to the new semi-Calvinism. None were more stubborn than Mère Angelique Arnauld, the superioress of the Convent of Port Royal, and her nuns, whom De Péréfixe, Archbishop of Paris, characterized as being pure as angels but proud as devils. A few bishops, a mere handful among the French hierarchy of the day, also lent their support to the new teachings. Cardinal Richelieu, always dogmatically orthodox, kept St. Cyran and his group pretty much in check, though he was unable to prevent the spread of Jansenistic ideas and Jansenistic rigorism in the pulpit and in religious books.

The two French Jesuits who first assailed the new heresy in their writings, were Sirmond [27] and Petau; [28] the former's *Praedestinatus* answered the Calvinistic teachings of the Jansenists on the salvation of the human race, the latter's *De libero arbitrio* refuted the historical, philosophical and theological statements of the *Augustinus*. Petau in his historical-dogmatic work on Pelagianism carried still further the refutation, by his examination of St. Augustine's real teaching. Answers and counter-answers poured forth from both sides. In the meantime Rome had been examining the book and the controversy it had aroused. In 1641 came a decree of the Holy Office condemning the *Augustinus*, which condemnation received more solemn form in the Bull "In Eminenti" of Urban VIII. The Jansenists were determined not to yield, as the publication in 1643 of Antoine Arnauld's work against frequent Communion clearly indicated. At the earnest request of many bishops Rome set up a special commission which worked for two years in examining the *Augustinus*. The result was a final and definite condemnation of five propositions of Jansenius by the Bull "Cum Occasione" of Innocent X in May 1653. There is not space in a work such as the present volume to recount all the dodges and artifices by which the Jansenists endeavored to hold to their doctrines and yet to worm out of a condemnation as heretics. They did waste much of their time in diatribes against the Jesuits, whom they recognized as their essential enemies.

The first Jansenist apologists will never be remembered for the brilliancy of their attack. But now there arose among them a most able literary champion, Blaise Pascal. [29] A great physicist and mathematician,

---

[27] Hurter, *Nomenclator litterarum theologiae catholicae*, Vol. III, pp. 1073 to 1081.

[28] Fouqueray, *Histoire*, Vol. V, pp. 279–281.

[29] Strowski, *Pascal et son temps*, 3 Vols., Paris (1907).

and a pious but morbidly scrupulous individual, Pascal by his very reputation was a tremendous asset to the movement. He wrote excellent prose
and his writings against the Jesuits, the *Provincial Letters,* dealt the
Society a grievous blow that it has felt even to the present day. The celebrated work was begun in defense of Arnauld and to forestall the condemnations of some of his works; but in Jansenist fashion it developed
into an intensive attack on the Jesuits. On January 23, 1656, the first of
the letters appeared; others followed at intervals until March 27, 1657,
to the number of nineteen. They caught the fancy of many and enjoyed
a great popularity despite the condemnations of Rome and of the French
government. The letters, published under a nom de plume, purported
to be the writings of a certain Louis de Montalte to a friend in the
country; their full title ran: *Les Provinciales, ou Lettres écrites par
Louis de Montalte à un provincial de ses amis et aux RR.PP. Jésuites
sur le sujet de la morale et la politique de ces pères.*[30] The first four dealt
with the question of grace and liberty, the dogmatic problem of Jansenism, and were intended to be a defense of Arnauld; so too did the seventeenth and the eighteenth; the nineteenth was never finished. The rest,
from the fifth to the sixteenth, attacked the moral teachings of the
Jesuits and the practice of their moral principles in the confessional, in
the schools, in their writings, and on their missions. Their doctrine of
Probabilism and their practice of casuistry were asserted to be the cause of
many and great evils. The Jesuits in their striving after power for themselves and for Rome were depicted as excusing, conceding and permitting wrong, all to the degeneration of the Christian ideal of life and
to the endangering of the purity of Faith.

There can be no question of the literary merit of the *Provincial Letters.* The satire and the raillery were couched in studiously polite and
moderate terms; the humor was extremely clever. But the contents were
an almost complete misrepresentation of Jesuit teachings, a conglomera-
tion of interpolations, omissions, citations lifted from their context, and
falsified texts. The limits of this chapter will not permit an examination
of all, or even a part of these tamperings and falsifications; Dr. Karl
Weiss of Gratz has done it admirably in his *P. Antonio de Escobar y
Mendoza als Moraltheologe in Pascals Beleuchtung und in Lichte der
Wahrheit.*[31] A few facts may give some idea of the *Letters:* three decisions of Jesuit casuists are wrongly quoted; of errors of detail scholars
have found more than two hundred; of suppressions of texts one hun-

---

[30] Brou, *Les Jésuites de la Légende,* Vol. I, p. 308; Duhr, *Jesuiten Fabeln,* pp. 434,
453, 477.

[31] Weiss, *P. Antonio de Escobar . . . Warheit auf Grund der Quellen,* Klagenfurt
(1908); new edition, Freiburg (1911).

dred more. It has been said that Pascal never intentionally falsified, though it is admitted that he did not consult the Jesuit authors whom he attacked, but accepted on their face value alleged quotations from the Jesuit moralists supplied to him by his fellow Jansenists, and on them based his embittered accusations. If that be the case, then to accuse and condemn men in such vital matters without further investigation is a sad reflection on one who claimed to be the champion of virtue. As for the use of Probabilism, this may be said that it has been the moral doctrine of many of the ablest and holiest Catholic theologians, outside the Society of Jesus. In regard to casuistry, the practice of solving supposititious cases, certainly it is evident how essential such procedure is for the judicial and legal training necessary to the sacerdotal confessor; it is for the priest what the case system is for the lawyer.

The Jesuits hastened to the defense of their order. Among the best efforts were Nouet's *Impostures et Réponses*, Annat's *Réponses* and Daniel's *Entretiens de Cléandre et d'Eudoxe sur les Lettres au Provincial*. These were detailed and solid refutations, and for that very reason could not repair all the damage done. The thoughtless throng which applauded Pascal's clever falsities had neither the patience nor the ability to weigh the factual rebuttal. As the old saying has it: "Calumny runs on the wings of the wind, refutation limps painfully after." The *Provincial Letters* have passed into the anti-Jesuit legend; even today they are cited by those who have never read them, or by those who have never bothered to find out if the condemned men ever had a defense.

Pascal's work and its refutation were but the high lights in the bitter controversy; the warfare of books and pulpits continued for generations. Boutauld, Bouhours and le Moyne were among the leading Jesuit champions; against them appeared an eight-volume work of a hermit of Port Royal, the Abbé de Ponchateau, *La Morale Practique des Jésuites*. In the next century the Jansenist, Zorn, attacked le Tellier who had written much against the sect. After the final condemnation of the Popes, the really heretical Jansenists and their close sympathizers were comparatively few; but unfortunately there was a large and widespread element among French Catholics, including many priests and several bishops, who were affected by Jansenist rigoristic tendencies. This manifested itself in moral teaching and practice. Jansenistic rigorism spread from France to Italy, Austria and Germany, and aided considerably in the Suppression of the order, which remained ever inimical even to tendencies towards Jansenism.

In the last decades of the seventeenth century and in the first part of the eighteenth, Jansenism experienced a revival, due to the activities of Pasquier Quesnel, an ex-Oratorian, who had been dismissed from his Congregation for his heretical views. In 1694 on the death of Arnauld, he became the leader of the sect; shortly before this he had brought out a work, *The New Testament in French with Moral Reflections on Each Verse*. It was a Jansenistic book and the Jesuits accordingly attacked it. They were not alone in this; several bishops, Pope Clement XI in 1708, and the Paris Parlement in 1711 placed it under the ban. Unfortunately, the Archbishop of Paris, Cardinal de Noailles, when he was Bishop of Chalons, had approved of Quesnel's work. The prelate always denied the charge of Jansenism; nevertheless some of his views certainly approached Jansenism, and he refused for a long time to receive the Bull "Unigenitus" which had condemned Quesnel. He was so hostile to the Society that for thirteen years, until shortly before his death, he withheld the sacerdotal faculties from the priests of the order.

Truly providential in the period of these conflicts was the revelation of the devotion of the Sacred Heart,[32] coming in the last quarter of the seventeenth century. The warm love of Christ's human Heart for men which is the object of the devotion, and the responding warm love of men's hearts for Christ which the devotion generated, proved to be the best antidotes for the frigid rigorism resulting from Jansenist principles. The Jesuits were chosen for a large part in the spread of the veneration of the Sacred Heart. St. Margaret Mary informed Bl. Claude de la Colombière,[33] the rector of the house at Paray-la-Monial and her adviser, that in the great revelation of 1675 she had been instructed that he was to be her assistant in the task of establishing the devotion. The holy priest dedicated himself by vow to this divinely appointed duty. He gained the cooperation of the priest, Gallifet, who was to extend the devotion to Catholics in European countries, in both Americas, and in the Orient. When Bl. de la Colombière died, he was succeeded in his office of director of St. Margaret Mary by Croiset, who was also to become a leading promoter. In 1688 St. Margaret Mary informed the fathers that in the revelations of that year the furtherance of the devotion was in a special way entrusted to the fathers of the Society. The Jesuits accepted the trust; in the colleges, in the popular missions, in the foreign fields, wherever they had influence, they preached and wrote tirelessly of Christ's loving Heart. Rolin, de Hoyos, Duhan, Schauenberg, Faure, Marquez were the leaders in stirring men's hearts to respond to the Divine Love. As said before, the devotion to the Sacred Heart was the best antidote for Jansenism. The Jansenists on their part pursued the devotion with the hatred which they harbored for the Society of Jesus; to them it was the Jesuit devotion, and that was enough to gain for it their utmost hostility.

The second foe whom the French Jesuits had to battle were the Gal-

[32] Hamon, *Histoire de la Dévotion au S. Coeur*, 4 Vols., Paris (1923-1931).

[33] Seguin, *The Life of the Ven. Claude de la Colombière*, trans. London (1905).

licans, an enemy of old and continual conflict. In the days of Louis XIV's absolutism, Gallicanism reached its peak. In such circumstances warfare with the Society of Jesus, bound by special tie to the Sovereign Pontiff of Rome, was inevitable.[34] The struggle was made all the more difficult for the French Jesuits because of the friendship which Louis XIV bore for them, the aid which he gave to their foreign missions, and the support which he lent them in their conflict with the Jansenists. Besides, their legitimate patriotism made doubly hard opposing the Grand Monarch in whom was centered all the glory of the France of that Golden Age. It is consequently quite understandable that in a few instances some of the French fathers faltered a bit in the battle with Gallicanism. Their true spirit, however, was manifested on such an occasion as the public defense of the Papal infallibility in Paris in 1661, to the angry dismay of the Gallicans and the Jansenists, as also by the fact that after the Declaration of the Gallican Rights of 1682 the Jesuit schools of divinity were practically the only places in France where the propositions of that document were not taught.

This Declaration of the Gallican Rights came as a climax to the struggle between Louis XIV and Innocent XI over the "Regalia." The "Regalia" were certain rights claimed by the French monarchs, by which the king could appropriate the revenues of certain bishoprics during vacancies and also by which he could confer certain benefices, generally bestowed by bishops. Louis XIV planned to extend his claims of appropriation to all bishoprics during vacancy and to take a larger share in the distribution of benefices. Innocent XI flatly rejected his pretensions; the Pope possessed an inflexible character that was more than a match for all the power of the "Sun-King." Louis tried to ignore the Papal protests; and the Brief of January 1681, dealing with the points at issue, was suppressed by the order of Parlement. The Holy Father turned to the French Jesuits to procure its publication. With one exception they had all been loyal to the Papacy; that unfortunate individual was Maimbourg who so defended the royal pretentions that he was expelled. The Papal request put the French Jesuits in a most difficult position; by profession they were most devoted to the Holy Father, not one of them had openly countenanced the King's claims; yet they knew that a Papal decree without the sanction of Parlement would have no force in France, and they truly feared that any attempt to publish the one in question would certainly lead to schism. In dread of the last catastrophe they refrained from publishing the Papal Brief. It was not the action to be expected from Jesuits, and Innocent XI was very displeased. Yet the French fathers did not forfeit his confidence; when, because of the seiz-

---

[34] Pastor, *Geschichte der Päpste*, Vol. XIV, part 2, c. 4, 5.

ure of Avignon by the French troops, the Holy Father determined on the excommunication of Louis XIV, he entrusted the sentence to a French Jesuit, Dez. The French fathers begged the General to lay before the Pope the real danger of schism if the sentence were published. After a conference with the General, Innocent XI recalled Dez and relinquished his idea of punishing the French monarch.

In 1682, at the request of the Paris Parlement and of several bishops, a general assembly of the clergy of France was called to act in the controversy. Though many French bishops were opposed to Louis XIV, enough support among the hierarchy was found to enact on March 19, 1682 the famous Declaration of the Rights of the Gallican Church. These Gallican Rights, there were four in number, maintained: (1) the Pope has not the power to depose sovereigns nor to dispense their subjects from the oath of allegiance; (2) the Church represented by a General Council is superior to the Pope; (3) the exercise of the Pope's authority should be regulated by canons; (4) the Pope's decisions are only binding when sanctioned by the Church. The Declaration was proclaimed by royal decree, March 23, 1682. In this statement of the Rights of the Gallican Church was finally formulated all the anti-papalism and Caesaro-papism that ever since the Western Schism had been developing in France. Several of the French Episcopacy refused to accept the Declaration, as did the Faculty of the Sorbonne. But Louis XIV was bent on having it accepted as the official doctrine of the French Church. By persuasion or threat he forced it on all the secular clergy and on the religious orders; at his command it was to be taught in every seminary. One exception was tolerated: the Jesuits were not asked for their assent to the Four Gallican Articles, nor did they offer it. Unfortunately some of them did not take as decided a stand for Rome as they should have, but tried to effect a reconciliation of the opposing parties. La Chaise, the king's confessor, suggested that in all Jesuit colleges attached to universities and in the order's own University of Pont-à-Mousson, the Gallican Articles be explained not as dogmas but as opinions.[35] The General, of course, refused that. In a letter to the General, La Chaise offered the consideration that concession on the part of the Pope was both desirable and urgent. No wonder Innocent XI was provoked with the French Jesuits. What made them waver? The very real dread of a national schism and its fearful consequences, is the answer. Their true, permanent loyalty to the Sovereign Pontiff, as has been noted before, was manifested by the fact that in their theological schools the Gallican Articles were never taught nor countenanced.

Though Louis XIV did not press the Jesuits to accept the Gallican

---

[35] Pastor, *Geschichte der Päpste*, Vol. XVI, part 2, pp. 880–882.

Articles, he did formulate plans to dominate the Society, or failing in that, to separate the French Assistancy from the rest of the order. When the General, Gonzalez, refused to consider his plan of obtaining a preponderance in the councils of the Society by a new division of the assistancies, the King in 1688 ordered the French Assistant, Fontaine, and all the French Jesuits in Rome to return to France. Further, all correspondence with the General was forbidden and an effort was made to have a separate superior, or vicar-general, residing in France for the Jesuits who were the King's subjects. Again Gonzalez refused the desire of Louis XIV. The five French Provincials on their part begged their sovereign to desist from his plans. After two years, in 1690, Louis XIV abandoned his scheme and for the future allowed the Jesuits of his dominion to follow their institute unmolested.

Of all the works of zeal of the French fathers, none were more fruitful than the labors of the popular missonaries. Of the numerous fathers who gave themselves to the exacting toil of the home missions, only a few can here be noticed. First among all stands St. John Francis Regis,[36] an apostle both of the crowded towns and of the remote mountain villages of the South of France. St. John Francis Regis was born January 31, 1597 at Fontcouvert (Aude), entered the Society in 1616, was ordained in 1631, and died after nine years of unremitting labor in 1640. His personal holiness early reached a high level from which he never permitted it to recede. The ten short years of his priesthood were given exclusively to popular missions. The first year he spent at Toulouse, tending the plague-stricken; the next two years he labored about Montpellier as a center, converting Huguenots, administering to the sick in the hospitals and to the needy, rescuing unfortunate girls, preaching and teaching religion to the children and the uninstructed; the last seven years he devoted to the evangelizing of the country villages, fifty of them in le Viverais, le Ferez and le Velay. His superiors had refused his request for the Canadian mission with its perils and privations; so when they did grant his prayer that he might devote himself for six months in the year to the missions in the mountain valleys, he chose the months of the winter that he might bear his share of the sufferings of the Cross. Never faltering in the bitterest weather, in snow, sleet and cold, St. John Francis would plod on from one lonely hamlet to another, bringing the strength of God's sacraments and the comfort of His word to the poor mountainfolk. The rest of the year would find him in the hot streets and alleys of the cities, teaching, preaching, absolving and rescuing broken souls. More than one dissolute villain, enraged by the conversion of his companion, openly threatened the Saint's life, only to be disarmed by

[36] Cros, *St. Jean François Regis*, Paris (1902); Holland, *St. Jean François Regis*, Chicago (1922).

his calm gentleness. Nor was St. John Francis deterred by the harder cross of misunderstanding on the part of his own. Seventy years after his death an enemy of the Society spread the story that St. John Francis Regis had been officially expelled from the Society, at least that his dismissal papers had arrived just subsequent to his death. Two Papal commissions, one in 1712, and one in 1879, with full access to the Jesuit archives, have proven the falsity of the calumny. The holy missionary was stricken in the lonely hamlet of la Louvesc in the mountains of Ardèche; after two days' illness, on December 31, 1640, he was called to his reward. Almost immediately steps were taken for his beatification, which occurred, May 18, 1716; finally, on April 5, 1737, St. John Francis Regis was raised to the full honors of sainthood.

A life of similar accomplishments was that of Julien Maunoir,[37] in the land of Brittany. Maunoir was born in 1606 at St. Georges de Reintembault in the diocese of Rennes and entered the order in 1625. Even before ordination the Bretons had gained his interest; he began at once to learn their language that he might be of service to them. At the time they were practically a forgotten people; many of their clergy were so indifferent as not to bother learning the speech of the people. In 1640 Maunoir began his life work determined not only to instruct the laity but to elevate the clergy; he succeeded so well that the proverbial faith of the Breton, priest or peasant, flourished once more. The method of his apostolate was to hold religious services in the towns or villages for weeks, during which besides frequent sermons and instructions there was much singing of hymns. On the last practice the missionary set great store for the inculcating of religious truths. Vast numbers of confessions were heard and Communion was distributed to thousands. The exercises were brought to a grand conclusion by festal processions and dramatic presentations of the mysteries of the Faith. Maunoir helped his cause very much by the catechism, the hymns and the books of devotion which he himself translated into Breton. Great care was given by the zealous father to the education and training of the clergy. The priests responded to his exhortations in such numbers that over one thousand were at his disposal, and he was able to employ as many as forty at a time in the mission work. One of the first houses for closed retreats was opened by him at Quimper, where he had the consolation of seeing one thousand priests and laymen annually making eight-day retreats. After forty-three years of labor the apostolic man died on a missionary journey at Flevin, January 28, 1683. The foundation of retreat houses owes much to another French Jesuit, Huby (1608–1693); at his death almost every city of importance in France possessed a house for closed retreats.

---

[37] Sejourne, *Histoire du Ven. Julien Maunoir*, 2 Vols., Paris (1895).

The glory of the Jesuit pulpit in France was Louis Bourdaloue,[38] as someone has called him, "king of preachers and preacher of kings." Bourdaloue was born in 1632, entered the order in 1647, and after his course was appointed to teach philosophy and later moral theology at Bourges. Occasional sermons revealed his great talents; so in 1665 he was assigned exclusively to the work of the pulpit. Four years later he was brought to Paris where for over three decades his eloquent voice was heard in the pulpits of Notre Dame, of the Jesuit church and of the royal chapel. The great virtue of his style was clear, solid presentation; he worked on his sermons with the utmost care, writing out almost every one. Such was his power over the hearts of the people that at some of his great sermons places had to be secured at daybreak; none admired him more than his contemporary and friend, Bossuet. In his court-sermons Bourdaloue spoke with straightforward honesty, but not with the reckless imprudence which popular legend has credited to him; however one of his discourses has been found of use even by modern Socialists. That he was one of the world's greatest orators is the opinion of many critics and writers, among them, Voltaire, Nisard, Taine, Lord Brougham and Sainte-Beuve. Bourdaloue was much more than a world orator; he was a zealous priest, faithful to the drudgery of the confessional and sincerely devoted to the poor. It has been remarked that his evident goodness, piety, modesty, love of the poor, mildness towards repentant sinners, yet apostolic freedom in the pulpit, was the completest answer to Blaise Pascal. The great orator worked until within two days of his death, which came to him in his seventy-second year, May 13, 1704.

In this chapter and in the two preceding, the record of the Jesuits in the second century of the Society's history has been set down. In the classroom, at the scholar's desk, in the untrodden mission lands, on the battlefield, by the plague-victim's bed, in the cathedral pulpit, in the chancel of the humble village churches, finally on the martyr's scaffold, the sons of St. Ignatius proved themselves worthy of their father. Except for the glorious pioneering in the foreign missions, most of their labors were the quiet development and steady increase of the foundations of the first generations. Some have been led to see in the later Jesuits a retrogression, even an internal falling off from the high standard of the original fathers. The achievements chronicled in these last three chapters prove the contrary. There never was a time in the second century when the Society as a whole did not steadily increase in numbers and in foundations. In regard to holiness, this period had its canonized saints and beati, while the roll of its martyrs is far longer than that of the first years. The work in Paraguay, in the rest of South America, in

---

[38] *Oeuvres complètes*, Besançon (1823); Reville, *Herald of Christ, Louis Bourdaloue, S.J.*, New York (1922).

Mexico, in Canada and in China is, all things considered, the equal of the accomplishments of the first missionaries. To the Jesuits of these times is due the development of the popular mission that bore such fruit in Italy, Spain, Germany and France; to them also must be credited the numerous retreat houses not only of Europe but especially of South America. There were no marked victories against Protestantism as in the first century, for definite limitations had been set both for Catholicism and for Protestantism by the Treaty of Westphalia. Within those limits the Jesuits had to be content to work. If, accordingly, they met the external foes of the Faith only in desultory combat, they must not be considered to have rested on their arms; for they fought to the uttermost of their strength against the internal enemies of the Church, the Jansenists, the Gallicans, the Quietists and the "Philosophers." The Jesuits of the first century engaged in no more important battles, in no more bitterly contested conflicts.

It has been said that once the *Ratio Studiorum* had been completed the Jesuits adhered too rigidly to this accepted plan. But why should they have departed from it? The basis for secondary and higher education in those days was the classical tradition; for that there was no better plan than the *Ratio*. Some changes were admitted in the eighteenth century, in the teaching of the mother tongue and in the sciences; but these were relatively small and the Jesuits rightly devoted themselves to bringing out the perfect product of the *Ratio Studiorum*. As for learned men, aside from the theologians and philosophers, in whom the first century was preeminent, the Society of the second century produced superior mathematicians, scientists, litterateurs and historians, such for example as Boscovich, Hell, Mayr, von Schank, Schall, Verbiest, Denis, Tiraboschi, Zaccaria, Faludi, de Feller, von Spe, de Isla, Bolland, Papenbröch and Henschius. No orators of the early Society were the equals of Segneri and Bourdaloue. It must be remembered that the first Jesuits in their time stood out in contrast to the ignorant and, too often, vicious clergy of the Reformation days; their superiority as learned and zealous priests was easily marked. It was not so with their successors. By the side of the later Jesuits stood numerous companions in arms, worthy and scholarly priests, both secular and religious, the revivified clergy of the Catholic Reformation. It would seem in the providence of God that in all religious orders, as in most religious movements, the first age is the heroic age, the age that sets the standard. It is for the subsequent generations to keep their zeal and virtue at the high level of the first, an accomplishment usually to be obtained in steady, quiet labors. The Jesuits of the second century were faithful to the inheritance of Ignatius, they were worthy brethren of Xavier and Canisius.

CHAPTER XII

GATHERING STORMS

On June 16, 1769, d'Alembert, leader of the French freethinkers and an editor of the Encyclopedia, wrote to Frederick the Great: "It would be madness for the Pope to destroy his bodyguard to please the Catholic princes. . . . It is strange that their most Catholic Majesties want to annihilate these staunch defenders of the Holy See and that your most Heretical Majesty is the only one to defend them." [1] The Prussian monarch replied that spite, cabals and interested motives had prompted the destruction of the Jesuits. In that bit of correspondence may be found the fundamental reason for the suppression of the Society of Jesus. During two hundred years, the order had been favored by Pope after Pope, several of the Pontiffs had given it their solemn approbation, numerous Catholic rulers had praised its work and afforded it their protection. Now within a generation, this same Society found itself the target of every type of intrigue, scurrility and calumny, its existence forbidden in turn in Portugal, France, Spain, Naples and Parma by the apparently Catholic governments of these states, its organization and life finally suppressed throughout the whole Catholic world by the Pope himself. In overwhelming disaster everything of the Company of Jesus was swept away: its educational activities in hundreds of noble colleges; its vast missionary labors in every part of the globe; and all its other works, whether in scientific circles, in catechetical centers, or in pious sodalities.

How explain so tremendous a catastrophe? [2] Had the Society of Jesus proven false to the ideals of St. Ignatius, had its organization lapsed into decadence? Books, pamphlets and fly-sheets, a perfect deluge of them, vociferously asserted all manner of charges: it had foregone its spirit; it had become enormously wealthy; it cared neither for priest, nor bishop, nor Pope; it maintained an arrogant attitude towards the religious of other orders and towards the secular clergy; it encouraged its members to dabble in politics; it suffered its professors and teachers to fall behind the times; it permitted its moralists to teach and its confessors to prac-

---

[1] D'Alembert, *Oeuvres philosophiques d'Alembert, Correspondence*, t. XVIII, quoted in Crètineau-Joly, *Histoire de la Compagnie de Jésus*, Paris (1844–1846), Vol. V, p. 269.

[2] Koch, *Jesuiten Lexikon*, a good discussion of the causes in the article "Aufhebung" (Suppression), cols. 120–126.

tice scandalous laxism. In this congeries of accusations, what was the truth?

The Jesuits were human beings; at the time in question there were 22,589 of them; among these and among the tens of thousands of their predecessors back to the first fathers, some deficient brethren were to be expected. Had the defects of such religious become so important and so common as to have vitiated the whole body? In the two hundred years of its existence the order had never had a reform. If there had been need, the stern post-Tridentine Popes would have imposed it. On the eve of suppression the Society was far from manifesting symptoms of decadence, but rather gave numerous indications of vigorous health: brisk building construction, prolific and voluminous literary production, marked success of popular missions and retreats, large-scale foreign mission activities, educational reform, at least in Italy, Germany and Austria, new foundations such as the Theresianum in Vienna. Of course there was the perennial charge of enormous wealth, to which the faults of La Valette gave a plausibility. Beneath such a charge lies the prepossession that all who dwell in great colleges and who maintain grand churches must be rich. The staffs of any educational or charitable institution will be only too painfully aware of the contrary of that illusion. The records of the financing of their institutions by the Jesuits, as found in the works of Duhr and Foley, prove that when all the expenses of maintaining and educating the pupils had been paid, when all other customary bills had been met, there was precious little left to promise luxurious lives for the Jesuits. Outside of the case of La Valette, there is no trace of the "negotiatio" forbidden to priests by Canon Law, i. e., the buying of goods at a lower price and the selling of them at a higher price for the purpose of acquiring gain. On the missions a special license sometimes was given by Rome enabling the fathers to sell, together with the products of their own fields, the harvests of their neophytes; but this was given for the protection of the natives from dishonest traders. Thus there would be no exchange of valuable property for trinkets, strings of beads, or a pair of trousers, after the fashion in which land had sometimes been purchased from simple natives in Manhattan and in New England. However imposing the college buildings may have been, whatever were the revenues which maintained them, how far soever the mission plantations extended, the fact is that the individual Jesuits in the seventeenth and eighteenth centuries lived no better than the worthy secular priests of their times, and that was a rather modest existence.

If there had been no decadence, then what bred the hostility to the Society within the Catholic Church? One may pass over the enmity of the Jansenists, the Gallicans and the sycophantic court clerics; their hatred was a badge of honor. That there were good Catholics opposed to the Jesuits, even to the extent of wishing for their suppression, cannot be denied. They were, relatively, not numerous; yet their sincerity must be respected. Their opposition may be traced to three sources: controversies, propaganda and the faults of Jesuits themselves. The controversies on grace, Probabilism and mission methods, as well as the minor disputes in Canon Law, history and pedagogy, had been fought with great heat. How well intentioned the disputants may have been, when they felt keenly about vital issues, especially in an age noted for its belligerency, they were certain to wage a warfare that would leave its scars. If Jesuits be reproached for clinging to privileges too tenaciously, it is well to remember that such a course is but natural and that all religious orders and all groups of secular priests have striven to their utmost to retain what they have honestly believed were their just privileges. That Catholic opponents of the order were affected by the anti-Jesuit propaganda, goes without saying; so widespread, so immense, so clever and so plausible was it, that they would have been scarcely human, if they could have disregarded it. Nor can it be denied that some Catholics were alienated by the faults and mistakes of individual Jesuits. Again let it be repeated, the Jesuits were human beings, burdened with the frailties of human nature. In following out the ideal of St. Ignatius that his order be a flying company ready at all times to give their utmost in all things for the Church, it was to be expected that some of his followers would outreach prudent limits in their zeal and that some would entangle themselves in affairs scarcely in keeping with their calling. Again, exaggeration of a military spirit has its danger: impatience with others, blindness to one's own faults, stubbornness in remaining on a certain line of march. From an immoderate esprit de corps some Jesuits composed too fulsome eulogies of their brethren, or made a one-sided defense of their position in controversy. Others criticised their opponents too sharply, or displayed an inconsiderate desire to attack all who did not agree with their views. Others still maintained an ill-guarded feeling of superiority to all that was not Jesuit. These were the ones who brought on their brethren the frequently repeated charge of "Jesuit Pride."

A word in regard to this so-called "Jesuit Pride" [3] is in place. Pride may be corporate or individual; it may be honest or false. Certainly it can never be maintained that the Society of Jesus, either in its legislation or in its spirit, has bred in its members a false pride. In the Constitutions, in the Spiritual Exercises, in the general rules, in the specific rules for each grade and for each official, humility is insisted on continually.

---

[3] Koch, "Stolz" (Pride), *Jesuiten Lexikon*, cols. 1698–1702.

No other virtue, save obedience, receives greater emphasis; and obedience after all is founded in humility. St. Ignatius never tired of reiterating that the individual member must make it his duty to be humble with the humble Christ; if the candidate were unwilling to strive for the Third Degree of Humility, of the Second Week of the Spiritual Exercises, he was to be dismissed. In the intention of the founder the whole order as a body was to pursue this duty of humility; he would have them consider their own order in reference to other religious orders as the youngest and the least. Since his time, such an attitude has been the recommendation of every Father General to the members of the Society.

In the individual, more specifically, pride may be honest or it may be false. Rejoicing in the glorious deeds of one's ancestors or of one's brethren, celebrating such achievements, drawing inspiration from them, surely such a pride is not reprehensible. Every religious order, every group of secular priests, every unit of civic or political life, has always cherished a pride in such traditions. The Jesuits ought not to be criticised for so doing. Of course, the manifestations of such praise may have been couched in the flamboyant style of a special period, as the Baroque; such was the case with *Imago Primi Saeculi* of the Belgian Jesuits. But as long as such expressions are understood in the proper spirit and are kept within domestic bounds, they hardly warrant adverse criticism. Such pride only becomes vitiated and false when it extends to odious comparisons with others, to unfair criticism, to assumed superiority, to aggrandizing monopoly, to exaggerated self-importance. Then, indeed, is it truly reprehensible. To assert that individual Jesuits have not been guilty of such pride, would be ridiculous. What human can claim freedom from the temptations of false pride? The Jesuits who failed markedly in this matter of pride, when one gets down to actual individual cases, are found to be few; and their failures were in direct contradiction to the training in humility which the Society of Jesus had given them and to the lowliness of spirit which it expected from them.

As a proof that the Jesuits had fallen from their ideals, Boehmer alleges that at their suppression the learned classes rejoiced and the common people remained indifferent, that hardly a protest was raised in all Catholic Europe. Such universal silence might have proved that the people regarded the departure of the Jesuits as good riddance; or it might have proved only the efficiency of the anti-Jesuit propaganda. Indeed, what need would there have been for such a bitter, widespread and voluminous attack, if the order stood so in the bad graces of Catholics? On January 7, 1767, when the enemies of the Jesuits were sweeping along in the full tide of victory, having encompassed the destruction of the order in Portugal, France and Spain, Pope Clement XIII issued the

Bull "Apostolicum pascendi munus" not only to defend the Society of Jesus but to give it a new and solemn confirmation.[4] It is worth noting that congratulations for his action came from numerous bishops throughout the Catholic world. Such was the opinion of the order among the shepherds of the flock that de Ravignan could cite the names of nearly two hundred bishops who by their deeds and their writings rallied to the support of the Jesuits in their hour of trial.[5] Early in the year 1761 when the attack of the French "Philosophers" was threatening the Society, twenty-seven members of the French Hierarchy protested against the persecution of the fathers; later in the same year fifty French bishops testified in their favor to the royal officials.[6] The overwhelming majority of the College of Cardinals to the end were set against the Suppression; the "Zelanti," as the more devout among them were known, were most strongly opposed to it.[7] The sorrow of Clement XIV himself during and after the great trial was significant. To these evidences of ecclesiastical opposition to the fall of the Jesuits, may be added the petitions of Catholic princes and states in Germany, the long, purposely delaying tactics of Louis XV, the almost universal public rejoicing in Portugal at the arrest of Pombal, the Jesuits' most brutal persecutor, the popular demand of the Spanish people for the return of the order, the kind benevolence everywhere exhibited to the Jesuits in their sufferings and exile. Such instances manifest the real sentiments of the people. That they were not more vocal at the times of the various suppressions was owing to the power of the absolute governments, which brooked not the slightest opposition, and to the tyranny of such brutal ministers as Pombal and Tanucci. When the Pope suppressed the order, respect for his person and office, as well as fear of the censures appended to the document, silenced any dissenting opinions among Catholics.

The explanation for the destruction of the order is not to be found in its decadence, for there was none. After the Suppression the enemies of the order had in their hands all the archives, all the correspondence and records of the Society of Jesus; they ransacked them for proofs to substantiate their allegations. So far, they have never given to the world a justification of their charges; the reason is simple enough, they found none. The ex-General Ricci[8] in his prison was examined again and again, yet nothing incriminating either in him or in the order was dis-

---

[4] Pastor, *Geschichte der Päpste*, Vol. XVI, part I, pp. 921–922.

[5] De Ravignan, *Clément XIII et Clément XIV*, Paris (1856), Vol. I, pp. 405–420, 426–434, 453–457; Vol. II, pp. 64–199, 222–372.

[6] Crétineau-Joly, *Histoire*, Vol. V, p. 203.

[7] Smith, "The Suppression of the Society of Jesus," *The Month*, London (Feb. 1902–Aug. 1903), Vols. XCIX–CII.

[8] Lorenzo Ricci, a Florentine, elected May 21, 1758, the last Father General of the old Society.

covered. The record of the ex-Jesuits after the Suppression affords ample proof of the high standards of the organization which gave them spiritual and sacerdotal formation: fifty-five former members were raised to the episcopal rank,[9] many others were chosen vicars-general of dioceses, and a large number of them were appointed professors of theology in seminaries; some were instrumental in the founding of religious congregations, such for instance as the Religious of the Sacred Heart and the Sisters of Notre Dame de Namur; twenty-three ex-Jesuits, who were martyred in the French Revolution in 1792, have been beatified by the Church. The recent beatification of Bl. Joseph Pignatelli,[10] who was a member of the old and may be considered a member of the restored Society, and who was the leader of the Spanish Jesuits at the time of their expulsion from their native land, has been considered by many to be a vindication of the suppressed Society of Jesus. But could one ask for a greater vindication than the Restoration by Pius VII in 1814?

The real cause of the warfare against the Jesuit order is to be found in the hatred of the Papacy and in the hatred of the Catholic Church itself. The death struggle of the Society of Jesus was but an outstanding episode in the far greater war aimed at the very existence of Catholicism. The 22,589 Jesuits, with their 11,393 priests, their 670 colleges, their 176 seminaries, their 273 missions, stood as a learned, disciplined, well organized army across the advance of the enemies of the Faith. D'Alembert recognized them as the "body guard" of the Pope, as the "staunch defenders of the Holy See." All the enemies of Catholicism joined in the attack. The Jansenists sought to pay off the old scores of a century of conflict in which the order had frustrated their attempt to impose crypto-Calvinism on the dogma of the Church. The Gallicans hoped to crush the organization which for two centuries had blocked their efforts at reducing the Pope to a harmless president of a federation of national churches. Certain regalistic and absolutistic Catholic politicians, whose persistent encroachments in the Church's domain had been fought by the Society, swung into action against it. But these three parties were not enough, they had been worsted time and again by the Jesuits; there was need of a stronger force, a more ruthless foe. That was found in French Infidel Philosophy.

Infidelism had spread far and wide among the pseudo-intellectuals and the social dilettanti of eighteenth century France. It had become the fashion to pose as a "Philosopher," to be a disciple of "Enlightenment," to scoff at revelation, to be skeptical of religion. For Catholicism these

---

[9] Kratz, "Exjesuiten als Bischöfe (1773–1822)," *Archiv. Hist. S.J.*, Vol. VI, pp. 182–215.

[10] Hanley, *Bl. Joseph Pignatelli*, New York (1937); Novell, *El ven. P. Jos. M. Pignatelli y la Compañia de Jesús en su extinción y restablecimiento*, Manresa (1893–1894).

"Philosophers" nourished the perfect hate; their leader Voltaire had given them their watch-word: "Crush out the infamous thing." In pursuance of that hate they assailed Catholicism on every side. In science and letters they produced the *Encyclopedia,* which through many of its articles constituted an enormous attack on the Faith, and many other works composed in the same spirit. In politics they possessed for themselves the strong places in almost every European government; almost all the ministers-in-chief were "Philosophers," Pombal in Portugal, de Choiseul in France, d'Aranda in Spain, Tanucci in Naples and Kaunitz in Austria. Thus they held the material means that would serve them to carry out their war against the Pope and the Church. In the path of the Infidel "Philosophers," too, lay the Jesuit forces: indeed, they had already found that their most active opponents in France were the fathers with their *Journal de Trévoux.* The Society of Jesus had to be wiped out; Voltaire wrote to his fellow "Philosopher," Helvetius: "Once we have destroyed the Jesuits, we shall have it all our own way with the infamous thing." [11]

By the second quarter of the eighteenth century definite plans for the destruction of the Jesuits were being formulated. Alvise Mocenigo, at one time Doge of Venice, assured Father General Ricci that, when he was Venetian Ambassador in France during the ministry of Cardinal Fleury, the fall of the order had been planned, and only the opposition of that powerful minister, who feared for the internal peace of the realm, prevented it. In 1739 the Jesuit Kampmiller informed Father General Retz of a sworn plot to destroy the Society. The Count Christiani assured the theologian and historian, Zaccaria, that in 1750 he had been invited to join in a compact aiming at the suppression of the Jesuits, for which the sum of 20,000 scudi had been offered to him.[12]

The first blow was delivered in Portugal [13] by the all-powerful Minister of State, Sebastian Joseph Carvalho e Mello, Marquis of Pombal. It is by the last title that he is usually known, although he did not obtain it until 1770. Though a capable administrator, he was yet an unscrupulous, ambitious man and a tyrannical savage in cruelty. His ascendency over the weak Joseph I made him the absolute ruler of the Portuguese dominions; all classes were cowed into a terrified acquiescence by his ruthless brutality, which respected neither law nor justice. He never assembled the Cortes; and he turned the Inquisition into a

---

[11] Cf. Preface to Weld's *Suppression of the Society of Jesus in the Portuguese Dominions,* p. xviii, London (1877).

[12] Koch, "Aufhebung," *Jesuiten-Lexikon,* Cols. 125–126.

[13] Pastor, *Geschichte der Päpste,* Vol. XVI, part 1, pp. 574–601; Weld, *The Suppression of the Society of Jesus in the Portuguese Dominions,* London (1877); Smith, "The Suppression," *The Month,* Vol. XCIX, pp. 113–130.

department of state. Perpetual imprisonment, exile, or death effectively
checked any criticism of his policies; no wonder that there was general
rejoicing at his downfall.

For the Jesuits, Pombal was a most ruthless enemy. Yet it has been
said that he owed his office partly to the intervention of the court confessor, Moreira; if that be true, then never was meddling in political
matters more terribly punished. A clash was bound to come between a
politician so avaricious for power and an order possessing such influence
at court and held in such veneration by the people. The roots of the conflict lay far deeper. Pombal was considerably influenced by the regalistic
and Jansenistic ideas then current; but more, he was a disciple of the
French "Philosophism." He bore a special hostility towards the Pope
and true Catholicism; seemingly he assumed their responsibility for the
economic and material inferiority of Catholic countries of the period. As
a remedy he would reduce the Church to that subservience to the throne
which obtained in Protestant England and Prussia. The Jesuits, devoted
defenders of Rome, had already frustrated some of his projects pointing
towards such a goal. His plan for the marrying of the royal heiress, the
future Catholic Queen of Portugal, to the Protestant Duke of Cumber-
land, the "Bloody Duke of Culloden," came to naught because of the
opposition of the fathers. They had earned his enmity further by their
accusations against his brother, the Governor of Northern Brazil, for
the outrages of which he had been guilty in that colony.

The New World was to witness Pombal's first attack upon the Society
of Jesus. In 1750, Spain and Portugal entered into a treaty for the re-
arrangement of the boundaries of their possessions along the Uruguay
River; Portugal, in exchange for the colony of San Sacramento on the
La Plata, received the seven Indian Reductions on the left bank of the
Uruguay (part of the present Brazilian State of Rio Grande do Sul).
The treaty had been negotiated in secrecy at Madrid, with little thought
for the opinions of the colonials. No consideration whatsoever had been
given for the rights of the thirty thousand Indians inhabiting the Reductions, despite the fact that their quasi-independent republic was under
Spanish protection and had been frequently guaranteed to them by various Spanish monarchs. Indeed, according to the terms of the document
the entire Indian population was to be uprooted and transplanted into
Spanish territory. It was an act of injustice which Southey has characterized as one of the most tyrannical commands that was ever issued in
the recklessness of unfeeling power. It was a crime too of avaricious
greed. Pombal and his satellites planned to possess themselves of the gold
and silver mines which, vague rumors alleged, existed in the Reductions
and were worked in secret by the Jesuits. It was asserted that the reason
behind the fathers' anxiety for the exclusion of white men from the Re-

ductions was their desire to hoard the wealth unto themselves. The expulsion of the Indians was intended that a clear field might be afforded the Portuguese gold-seekers. Any claims the Indians might have to their own lands, were rudely brushed aside.

Though the protests of both secular and religious authorities in South America were ignored by both governments, the Jesuits determined to defend to the utmost of their power the rights of their Indian flocks, to save for them the fields and the homes which, after one hundred and fifty years of patient toil, their native disciples possessed. The fathers sought to delay the execution of the treaty, at least as regards the banishment of the Indians. At last, only too sadly did the priests realize that their efforts were in vain and that they must bring the Indians to accept the inevitable. With difficulty did they face their flocks and ask them to abandon their fields and firesides, the possession of which had been assured these natives by so many royal proclamations, and to leave them to an enemy from whom in the past the Mamelucos slave-captors had come. Though most of the Indians listened to the fathers, some freer spirits, goaded beyond bearing, broke out in a revolt, "The War of the Seven Reductions." [14] It was a hopeless demonstration; after one battle and a long guerilla campaign, the unhappy natives were crushed.

With the territory of the seven Reductions cleared of inhabitants, the Portuguese engineers combed mountains, rivers and forests in a vain search for the gold mines. There were none to be found; they simply did not exist. The exasperation of the disillusioned Pombal but deepened his hatred of the Jesuits, whom as a "Philosopher" he despised anyway. Against his better knowledge he sought to throw the blame for the "War of the Seven Reductions" on the missionaries of the order. At his instigation a whole wave of defamatory pamphlets and falsified documents were spread broadcast in Portugal and throughout the rest of Europe. There were fables about a Jesuit Empire of Paraguay,[15] of a Jesuit King, Nicholas I,[16] of an Indian-Jesuit army that clashed in open battle with the soldiers of Portugal and Spain; there were lies about the frightful rule of the Jesuits in the Reductions; there were calumnies accusing the Jesuits of illegal, uncanonical commercial transactions.[17] Historians long ago have proved these fabrications to be unhistorical falsifications; even at the time, the French Infidel brethren of Pombal sneeringly dismissed them as crude inventions. Yet the tribe of the gullible, of those who want to believe such calumnies, then as now, was large; so the falsehoods found a ready acceptance in many circles. One of the worst of these ca-

---

[14] Astrain, *Historia*, Vol. XI, c. 11, 12, 13.
[15] Duhr, *Jesuiten Fabeln*, p. 203.
[16] *Ibid.*, p. 220.
[17] *Ibid.*, p. 587.

lumnious writings, one which Pombal had distributed on all sides, was the work of the ex-Capuchin Norbert, *Mémoires historiques sur les affairs des Jésuites;* in this screed the charges of illegal commercial transactions especially were put forward. Norbert was characterized by his former Capuchin superior as "a man without faith or probity." [18] Yet his libel found an entry into the Vatican, where it was welcomed by an official close to Benedict XIV, Cardinal Passionei. Passionei was sympathetic to the Jansenists and was hostile to all religious orders, but especially to the Jesuits. He was on the commission which examined Norbert's work. When not a single well established accusation was found, such was the Cardinal's antipathy to the order that he made the absurd defense that the ex-friar had not intended to accuse the Jesuits of commercial transactions, but had simply presented the quotations of others in the matter. Pombal used the charge of uncanonical trading, made in his own inspired pamphlets, to proceed against the Jesuits in the Portuguese colonies and to decree in 1759 their banishment or imprisonment.

At home in Portugal, in the meantime, the powerful minister had moved against the Society. On November 1, 1755, a terrible earthquake laid Lisbon in ruins and 20,000 persons were killed; of the Jesuits 200 were buried in the ruins of their colleges. The surviving fathers and brothers with all their strength devoted themselves to succoring the stricken citizens. The gratitude of the people but deepened their veneration for the men to whom they turned now, more than ever, for courage in their overwhelming sorrows. Of all the Jesuit preachers, the most revered was the venerable Gabriel Malagrida, an Italian, who had spent thirty years in the Brazilian missions. He was esteemed as a saint by all classes from the humblest workmen to the royal family. To the deeply stirred people, the holy old man preached penance as well as consolation, telling them that the terrible catastrophe was a divine visitation on the sins and injustices of the Portuguese. Pombal was furious, considering the remark a reflection on his own policies, especially in Paraguay. When the King expressed a wish to make the Spiritual Exercises under Malagrida, the angry minister, jealous of the saintly old priest, had him banished to Setubal. Determined further that no Jesuit would again threaten his hold on the King, he cleared the court of all the Jesuit confessors. A deliberate effort was made to poison the King's mind against the order; writings against him, allegedly composed by Jesuits were circulated about the country.

On October 8, 1757, Pombal took a more definite step against the Society when he addressed to Benedict XIV an indictment accusing the Portuguese fathers of laxity, and a demand for a visitation and a reform.

---

[18] Letter of Rev. Father Thomas of Poitiers, Superior-General of the Capuchin missionaries of Madras to the Nuncio in France, cited in Weld, pp. 107, 108.

The petition sorely tried the aged and sick Pontiff; he admired the Jesuits and was exceedingly sceptical of the charges. Still, one of his aides was Cardinal Passionei, who with great insistence kept urging that the minister's request be granted. At length the dying Pope gave in and on April 1, 1758 signed the Brief authorizing the visitation of the Society's houses in Portugal and in the Indies and calling for a report on the alleged abuses. Benedict XIV took care to hedge the investigation with many precautions so that the rights of the order might be protected. Cardinal Saldanha, one of Pombal's creatures, was to be the Visitor. There were several Portuguese prelates far better equipped; but to the minister they were unavailable because of their friendship for the Jesuits. Several of them, including the Archbishop of Evora, that very year had written to the Father General of their admiration for the fervor and zeal of their Jesuit compatriots. The death of Benedict XIV left Pombal and Saldanha without a restraining hand in the investigation. The orders of the Papal instructions were: that a minute investigation be made, that extreme discretion and gentleness be used, that the Visitor hold himself aloof from politicians, that strict silence be maintained on accusations, that no decision be given but that all matter of serious import be referred back to the Pope. These were the wishes of the dead Pope. Saldanha, however, had another master to obey, one who had predetermined the destruction of the Society of Jesus; so he violated every one of Benedict's prescriptions. The visitation was carried out in haste and with violence; it was begun on May 15, and before a fortnight had passed, it was finished; the Brief of Visitation was published throughout the kingdom, giving the impression of the actual guilt of the order; the thorough house to house investigation, which had been ordered, was omitted; the Visitor took his orders in all things from Pombal. On May 21, Saldanha visited the Professed House of Lisbon but examined nothing; a few days later a document was issued, signed as of May 15, charging the Jesuits with illicit, public, and scandalous commerce both in Portugal and in the colonies. Not a single Jesuit had been questioned. The aged Patriarch of Lisbon, de Atalaya, a friend of the Society, was ordered to suppress all Jesuit houses and organizations in his patriarchate; he resisted for five hours before yielding, and died of grief a month later.

In Rome, the Father General Ricci appealed to the new Pope, Clement XIII. In moderate terms the General asserted that the Portuguese Jesuits had been condemned unheard and untried; he asked only for a fair examination of their case. Clement received the superior kindly and assured him of his sympathy. The answer of the tyrannical minister in Lisbon was to republish the old charges and to add newly invented accusations. They had to be inventions; for though Pombal and his protégé, Saldanha, whom he had made Patriarch of Lisbon, had all the Jesuit papers, correspondence and accounts in their hands and though they turned the records upside down, they had found no justification for their charges. But the order's fate had been already settled; so on January 19, 1759 the Society of Jesus was legally suppressed in all Portuguese dominions. It is worth noting that it was about this time that almost two hundred and fifty Bishops and several Cardinals entreated Clement XIII to protect the order from its persecutors.

Some months before the actual suppression, a mysterious attack on the King afforded Pombal the opportunity of giving to the final blow the appearance of a just punishment for murderous conspiracy, as also to pay off some old scores against the Jesuits and the great nobles, whom he likewise hated.[19] On the night of September 3, 1758, the coach of the royal chamberlain, Texeiras, was attacked and the King, who was within returning from a nocturnal love adventure, was slightly wounded. Pombal cast the blame on the powerful noble family of Tavora. They had had a private grievance against the King; but there exists no proof that they were parties to the attempt on the King's life. It has been suggested that the whole affair was one of Pombal's concoctions to terrorize the greater nobility of Portugal, who were stumbling-blocks to his power, by the terrible fate of the House of Tavora. In defiance of all legality, the minister himself presided over the violent and illegal trial at which the victims were tortured and condemned. The Duke of Aveiro, many members of the Tavora family, including the noble old Marchioness, and several servants were publicly put to death with horrible cruelty, January 13, 1759.

After the execution of the Tavoras, Pombal proclaimed the Jesuits as their accomplices in the alleged plot against the King's life, and arrested the fathers, Henriques, da Costa and Malagrida. There was no question at all of their innocence; all that could be said was that they were friends of some of the unfortunate Tavoras. But a public execution of Jesuit regicides ought to bolster up the minister's all too weak case against the Society of Jesus. Malagrida, so venerated by the people yet so hated by Pombal, was chosen for the victim.[20] There had to be a conviction, so honest officials of the Inquisition were removed, to be replaced by enemies of the order; Paul Carvalho, the minister's brother was made President. It was by a court so constituted that the saintly old missionary was condemned to death as a heretic. Two visionary treatises on St. Anne and on the Antichrist, alleged to have been written by him while in prison, were presented as evidence. Malagrida's authorship has never been proved; the extravagances in the works could hardly have been

---

[19] Weld, *Suppression*, pp. 184–224.
[20] Pastor, *Geschichte der Päpste*, Vol. XVI, part I, pp. 594–595.

written by him, unless his reason had been lost in the horrors of his two and a half years' imprisonment. Nevertheless, the aged and saintly old man was publicly strangled to death and his body burned at Lisbon, September 21, 1761. Clement XIII hailed him as a martyr; even Voltaire protested against his judicial murder. More than a century later the citizens of his birthplace in Italy, Managgio, raised a monument in their town to his memory.

Meanwhile the work of confiscation and banishment was being rapidly carried out. The decree of Joseph I, declaring the Society guilty of complicity in the attempt on his life and ordering the forfeiture of all its goods and properties, appeared on January 19, 1759. Straightway began the seizure of colleges, churches and other holdings everywhere throughout Portugal, Brazil and India, wherever the Portuguese king ruled. The University of Coimbra was handed over to the Jansenists; even the use of the Latin Grammar of Alvarez was proscribed. Joseph I wrote to Pope Clement XIII, on April 20, of his intentions for the expulsion of the Jesuits. The Holy Father in reply begged for justice for the fathers and warned the King against condemning a whole order for the unproved charges against some of its members. But not even the Pope could deter Joseph I, or rather, Pombal. The Jesuits were kept at the colleges incommunicado, when they were not thrown into prison. The first departure was on September 1 from the College of Elvas, where the townspeople in tears thronged about the building to bid the fathers a sad farewell. At Evora they were joined with Jesuits from several other communities; thence, scholastics and the lay-brothers having been left behind, the priests, guarded by soldiers like war-prisoners, were marched six days over hard roads and under the burning September sun to the Tagus. There they were cast into the hold of a ship that had been waiting for them since April. When the communities of Lisbon and Santorem were joined to them, the vessel set sail for Civita Vecchia in the Papal States. The voyage of exile had begun. The Jesuits of Coimbra were forced to make their departure under a military guard in the dead of night, September 30; yet despite the hour and a heavy rainstorm the whole city turned out to bid Godspeed to the venerated fathers. At the Tagus, ships were waiting to take them into exile. The constancy of the young scholastics at Coimbra and Evora was truly inspiring. Without the support or guidance of their superiors or of the older fathers, all of whom were either in prison or on the road to banishment, these young scions of Ignatius Loyola refused even to listen to the fair promises or the sinister threats with which both Pombal and Saldanha pressed them. They elected a superior from among themselves, a young priest who had not yet taken his final vows, to whom they gave their obedience. All continued in prayer for one another's perseverance.

Castro, an officer of the King, was sent to these stout-hearted lads, for many of them were yet in their teens, to threaten them, not with exile to Italy, but with abandonment on the savage African coast. Only two weakened, and these even the soldiers treated with contempt. Eventually, all the 300 scholastics of the Portuguese province were ordered into exile. Those in Coimbra, 145 in number, on October 24 received Holy Communion for the last time in the college chapel and after Benediction stood ready to depart. Over the rough roads they were marched to Oporto, where one last effort was made to break their fidelity; they were deprived of the necessities of life, they were forced to suffer hunger, and at the same time they were bombarded with messages from Saldanha. Only three gave up, all the rest remained loyal in their vocation. Clement XIII in admiration at the constancy of these young heroes exclaimed: "they have also proved how much more efficacious is divine grace than any human power.[21]

At Civita Vecchia a kindly welcome awaited all the Jesuit exiles. Clement XIII did everything in his power to make their hard lot bearable; while the Father General Ricci devoted his best efforts to their care. The people of the town, the priests, secular and religious, especially the Dominican fathers, lavished their charity on the exiled priests. In the Dominican church of Civita Vecchia a tablet has been placed to commemorate the fraternal kindness of the sons of St. Dominic to the sons of St. Ignatius in their hour of bitter trial.

In the course of a year most of the missionaries from Brazil, Africa, India and Macao were arrested, expelled from their missions, and transported to Lisbon, where they were either cast into loathsome dungeons or transshipped to the Papal States. The sufferings of these missionaries were especially severe: there was the heartbreak of looking for the last time on their beloved missions and of raising their hands in a last blessing on their inconsolable neophytes; there was the arduous journey to the coast with its hunger and thirst and fatigue, with its tramping and tramping for hundreds of miles over mountains or through the jungles; there was the ever present indignity of the guard, as though they were abandoned, criminal wretches; there was the terrible voyage across the ocean, or oceans for those who were brought from the East, the overcrowding in crazy, leaky tubs, the herding together below decks, the stench, the vermin; and then, at the end, for some there were the foul dungeons of Pombal.

Some one hundred and eighty fathers were imprisoned by the brutal minister in the underground dungeons of São Juliao, Belem, São Jorge, and Almeida. Of all, São Juliao was the most horrible; many of its cells

---

[21] Weld, *Suppression*, p. 297.

were below the level of the sea. The sufferings of the incarcerated victims were terrible beyond words: the semi-gloom of their cells was never broken by the bright sunlight; perpetual dampness sapped their vigor and rotted the clothes on their backs until they had scarce rags enough to cover themselves; the poor and scanty fare was hardly enough to sustain life, and sometimes half of it was stolen by the villainous jailors. To their physical tortures there were added spiritual sufferings, for the Sacraments were denied the unfortunate priests, except at the hour of death. Some of the Jesuit prisoners were foreigners; most of these were eventually released at the intervention of Maria Theresa for the fathers of German nationality, and of the French government for the fathers from France. Of the rest, many languished in these frightful underground holes for seventeen years; several lost their reason and seventy-nine died in the prisons. Only when Pombal fell from power were the doors of freedom opened for the sixty survivors.

Even with the destruction of the order Pombal's hatred was not yet satiated. He actively participated in the intrigues of the Society's enemies in other countries, and he forced the Portuguese Bishops to condemn the Jesuits in Portugal and to praise his work. When Clement XIII, refusing to fall in with his plans against the fathers, complained strongly against the treatment of the Jesuits, the Minister expelled the Nuncio, Acciajuoli, and broke off all relations of Portugal with the Holy See, June 17, 1760. After that the bishops were forced to exercise functions reserved to the Pope; and Pombal had attained his goal, a semi-schismatical church with himself as virtual head. For the next ten years Portugal had no official representative at Rome; yet Pombal's influence was active enough there, through his intrigues with the ambassadors of the Bourbon courts and by the continual issuance of his anti-Jesuit flysheets. One of the last, the bi-weekly, "Jesuit Anecdotes," reached even into the Vatican.

The dissolution of the Society of Jesus in France came next.[22] Through the second quarter of the eighteenth century the tide of opposition to the Jesuits had steadily risen in the realm of Louis XV. Jansenists, Gallicans, Regalists and Infidel Philosophers were united by a common hatred into a practical alliance for the war against the Society. The leadership was assumed by the "Philosophers," who aimed much further than their allies, even to the destruction of Catholicism. Among the literati, the freethinkers counted many warriors to carry on a widespread, unending literary attack; at the court, they relied on the chief minister and his friends to dominate the reluctant, weak-willed King. Toward

---

[22] Pastor, *Geschichte der Päpste*, Vol. XVI, part I, pp. 602–696; Crétineau-Joly, *Histoire*, Vol. V, pp. 172–248; Smith, "Suppression of the Society of Jesus," *The Month*, Vol. XCIX, pp. 263–279, 346–368, 497–517.

their immediate objective, the dissolution of the Jesuit order, with insistent perseverance they bent every energy of their own and of their allies. Their purpose was stated in d'Alembert's observation to Voltaire: "The most difficult task will be accomplished when philosophy is rid of the grenadiers of fanaticism and intolerance." There was an individual leader of the French anti-Jesuit allies, as there had been of the Portuguese enemies of the order; this captain was the Duc de Choiseul, the chief minister of State, a clever, cynical politician, who had purchased his advancement from the king's mistress, Madame de Pompadour, by a malodorous intrigue in her favor. De Choiseul's plans for the destruction of the Jesuits contemplated no prisons, no executions, no martyrs; the brutal bludgeoning of Pombal was repugnant to his more finical nature. Vilifying the fathers, destroying their organization, sequestrating their possessions, by such means would he achieve his purpose. His great power at court enabled him to nullify the protests of the French Episcopacy; his alliance with Madame de Pompadour helped him to offset the efforts of the Queen and the Dauphin to protect the Society.

The enmity of Madame de Pompadour gave impetus to the campaign against the Jesuits. In 1752, this notorious courtesan sought absolution from the Jesuit father, de Sacy. The priest naturally demanded that she abandon her sinful way of life; when she would give no promise, he refused her the absolution, as was his duty.[23] It was not in a contrite spirit that the designing mistress had made her request; what she aimed to obtain was an increase of her power and influence at the expense of the Queen and the Dauphin by the prestige which would accrue from the public, if hypocritical, performance of her Catholic duties. Pompadour was not to be deterred by one refusal; for two years the Jesuit confessors, de Sacy, Desmolitz, and Percesseau were importuned, now with entreaties, now with threats, to bestow absolution. Always, of course, their answer was the same, absolution only after repentance. Infuriated by the repeated refusals, the mistress turned in her hate to the enemies of these priests. She proved a most powerful ally, for when the weak-souled Louis XV seemed to be bestirring himself in the Jesuits' defense, this evil woman silenced the promptings of his better nature.

Damiens' attempt on the life of the King, January 5, 1757, afforded the anti-Jesuits a long-sought pretext to strike a blow against the Society.

It mattered not that the culprit was a Jansenist; the fact that he had been once employed by the Jesuits was enough to unloose a flood of pamphlets reviving the old cry of regicide. The Parlements of Paris and Rouen condemned the Moral Theologies of Busembaum and La Croix

---

[23] Crétineau-Joly, *Histoire*, Vol. V, p. 180; Sainte Priest, *Chute des Jésuites*; de Ravignan, *Clément XIII et Clément XIV*, Vol. I, pp. 93–96 (for enmity of Madame de Pompadour).

to be burned. A mob stirred up by calumnies of the fathers' complicity, threatened to burn down the Collège de Clermont; three hundred soldiers had to guard the Jesuit house on the day of the would-be assassin's execution.

The affair of Damiens was hardly more than an opening skirmish. The real opportunity soon came to the "Philosophers" and their allies, and that from the misfortunes and errors of one of the Jesuits themselves, La Valette, the superior of the mission of Martinique.[24] Antoine La Valette had gone to the Lesser Antilles as a missionary in 1741; five years later he was appointed procurator charged with the financial support of the mission; and in 1753 he was made superior of Martinique and Prefect Apostolic. As a procurator he had achieved considerable success in bettering the sad financial condition of the mission, especially by his skilful management of the sugar and coffee plantations, the revenue of which supported the works of the fathers. His successes led him to embark on larger schemes in the purchase and development of more plantations. The French Colonial authorities looked with approval on his plans since they meant the wider settlement of the islands and the greater exploitation of their natural resources. Yet the permission to carry on the work was only granted cautiously; whatever the Jesuit attempted was to be at his own risk. Hurson, Governor of Martinique, wrote to the home government a letter of warm praise for La Valette's work and in his defense, when the priest had been called to Paris to answer charges of trading with foreign countries. La Valette cleared himself and returned to the islands armed with governmental permission for newer plans. To work out his schemes, he had to borrow large sums of money; ordinarily there would have been little risk, but a disastrous storm destroyed the ships carrying the produce of the plantations to France. To cover his debts, La Valette began to borrow more heavily, to speculate, and to buy goods to sell later at a higher price. The last was the "negotiatio" forbidden to priests by Canon Law, and to the members of the Society of Jesus by their Constitutions. The crash came at last. One disaster followed another for the unfortunate man; an epidemic swept away a greater part of the slaves who worked the plantations, and ships carrying his produce and merchandise were captured by English privateers in the Seven Years' War, with a loss on one occasion of 600,000 livres.

The banking house of Lioncy Frères et Gouffre of Marseilles, from which La Valette had borrowed so extensively, failed February 19, 1756. The creditors of the bank demanded that the French Jesuits make good

---

[24] Rochemonteix, *Ant. Lavalette à la Martinique, d'après beaucoup de documents inédits*, Paris (1907); Brou, *Les Jésuites de la Legende*, Vol. II, p. 136; Duhr, *Jesuiten-Fabeln*, pp. 696 ff.; Pastor, *Geschichte der Päpste*, Vol. XVI, part I, pp. 611 ff.

their losses, or that they be permitted to indemnify themselves with the goods of the order. De Sacy, the financial procurator of the Paris province, to which the mission of the Lesser Antilles belonged, once before had covered losses incurred by La Valette; now again he was prepared to make arrangements to meet the new losses, the liability for which had been undertaken without his knowledge. Other creditors put in their claims, which finally totalled the indebtedness to the sum of four and a half million livres, although La Valette affirmed that at the highest it should have been not more than two and a half millions. It was a common opinion that a part of the great debt was not just. Certainly the payment of the whole sum would have well nigh ruined the Jesuits, not only of the Paris province but of the whole French Assistancy. In strict legality the Jesuits of the French Assistancy had no obligation to pay; for according to the Church Law, recognized by the State, each house, mission or province stood financially as a separate legal person. La Valette's debts were those of his mission. In the long run it would perhaps have been better if the fathers had assumed the full burden, tremendous as it was; but its very tremendousness frightened them and they chose to fight the case. The courts in 1760 decided against them and granted the creditors redress, even from the properties of all the Jesuits in France. The action, up to this, had been heard in the lower courts, from which an appeal might be carried to the royal commission established by Louis XIV for just such cases, or to the highest court of the Paris Parlement. The latter course was fraught with danger because of the number of bitter enemies of the Jesuits among the jurists of the Paris Parlement. Nevertheless the Provincial of the Paris province, without consulting the other French Provincials, made the appeal to the Grand Chamber of the Paris Parlement. It was a fatal step, for it put the order in France in the hands of its most determined foes.

Here it might be well to remark that in all his illicit transactions La Valette had acted alone; later he freely issued a statement declaring that what he had done had been done without the knowledge or the approval of his superiors.[25] His very position, as local superior in so remote a mission, enabled him to conceal his negotiations. The European superiors, especially Father General Ricci, took every possible step to remedy the situation, when the news of it finally reached them. But the circumstances of the times: the troubles in Paraguay, the campaign of Pombal in Portugal, and the controversy over the Asiatic missions, to say nothing of the world-wide Seven Years' War in which France and England were the principal colonial contestants, blocked every attempt at remedying the trouble. Four times Father General Ricci named a Visitor for the

---

[25] *Crétineau-Joly, Histoire,* Vol. V, pp. 192–193.

mission in vain; either the letters were lost, or the designated Visitor was unable to reach his goal. At last the fifth named, de la Marche, succeeded in landing at Martinique but only on a British passport, the island having been captured by the English. His arrival was too late.

The Grand Chamber of the Paris Parlement gave its decision on May 5, 1761, sustaining the decision of the lower courts that the whole body of the French Jesuits was liable for La Valette's debts. But there was more to come. During the discussion of the case, the Parlement asked that a copy of the Jesuit Constitutions be submitted to it. It was an ominous request; for it meant that this high judicial body had in mind something more than the settlement of a legal appeal, nothing less than the complete investigation of the Society of Jesus with a view to its outlawry in the French dominions. Louis XV, wishing to protect the Society and being alarmed by the turn the investigations were taking, endeavored to have the Jesuits conciliate their opponents by the setting-up of a French Vicar-General. The fathers refused, for such a change would disrupt their order. Clement XIII also rejected the change when it was presented to him, with the words: "Sint ut sunt aut non sint"—"Let them be as they are, or let them not be at all." [26] The Holy Father, during all the French crisis, never ceased his defense of the Society and by continual letters and admonitions begged royal and episcopal support for the order. Only too well did he realize that the designs of their enemies went far beyond the destruction of the Jesuits. The King did make an effort at reserving the case to himself and forbidding Parlement all further steps for a year. His prohibitions were ignored. On August 6, Parlement declared that the decrees of the Jesuit General Congregations were encroachments on the Church and on the State, and condemned twenty-four writings of Jesuit authors, including the works of St. Robert Bellarmine and Busembaum, to be burned by the public hangman. The incompetence of a purely secular body in condemning theological teachings, a function peculiar to a clerical court, never seemed to have bothered the legal experts of the Parlement. Two weeks later, August 19, the Parlement by a decree prohibited French subjects from entering the Society of Jesus, restrained Jesuits from all public and private theological teaching, and forbade attendance of French pupils at Jesuit schools. Again the King tried to take the Jesuits' part by suspending the decree for a year; but the Parlement yielded only in the revoking of the prohibition on teaching.

It was about this time that the Paris Parlement issued the *Extraits des assertions*, or to give its full title in English, *Extracts from the thoroughly dangerous and pernicious doctrines which the so-called Jesuits*

---

[26] De Ravignan, *Clément XIII et Clément XIV*, Vol. I, p. 90.

always and persistently have maintained, taught and published in their
books with the approbation of their superiors and their generals. The
contents did not fall short of the formidableness of the title; in them the
Jesuits were accused of every possible heresy and crime. In vain did the
fathers produce a three-volume reply demonstrating that the *Extraits*
were just a mass of fabrications, even listing 758 falsifications. No hearing could be expected from judges who fabricated an edict of Henry IV
and knowingly cited a falsified edition of Busembaum.[27]

The warfare against the order continued unrelenting; especially did
the anti-Jesuit press feverishly cover the country with pamphlets and fly-
sheets against the Society, while the allies drove blow after blow at the
fathers and at those who would protect them, the Bishops and the weak,
reluctant King. On December 30, 1761 an assembly of the French Bishops, convened by Louis to consider the case of the Jesuits, made their
report; [28] forty-five out of the fifty Bishops present gave their unquali-
fied justification to the fathers; four wished for some changes in the
Constitutions, though approving the Society in general; only one spoke
against the order, a Jansenist-minded prelate, Fitz-James of Soissons,
and even he proclaimed "the good morals of the Jesuits." The King and
some of the Bishops, in the hope of allaying the storm, urged the fathers
to sign a declaration of adhesion to the Gallican Articles of 1682, and of
renunciation of the order's privileges. The Provincial of Paris, de la
Croix, and 116 of the priests of his jurisdiction yielded and on December 19 signed the declaration.[29] It was an act of weakness, a betrayal of
the whole Jesuit position in regard to the Holy See; and it soon brought
on the signatories the condemnation of their brethren in the rest of
France and throughout the Society. The Pope and the General did not
openly join their voices to the censuring which followed; though in
private both expressed their displeasure. Realizing the desperate condition of the fathers, the allies pushed on their assault all the more relentlessly, now that they saw their victims weakening. The Parlement of
Rouen on February 12, 1762 declared the rule of the order to be irreligious; forbade all Frenchmen to observe it, to go to a Jesuit school,
or to maintain correspondence with the General; decreed the confiscation
of the Society's properties; and ordered the burning of twenty-nine writings of Jesuits. Other parlements followed the lead of Rouen. The King
endeavored to prevent the registration of the decrees; but he was pre-

---

[27] Cf. Duhr, *Jesuiten-Fabeln*, p. 436 for Döllinger's adverse judgment on the *Extraits;*
Smith, *The Month*, Vol. XCIX, p. 514 (for summary of errors).

[28] Pastor, *Geschichte der Päpste*, Vol. XVI, part I, pp. 634, 635.

[29] Pastor, *Geschichte der Päpste*, Vol. XIV, part I, pp. 636–641; Rochemonteix, *Le
Père Ant. La Valette à la Martinique*, pp. 219 ff.; de Ravignan, *Clément XIII et Clément
XIV*, t. I, pp. 115 ff.; t. II, Chap. IV, pp. 203–216.

vailed upon to relinquish his purpose by Choiseul and Madame de Pompadour. The Paris Parlement on April 1 closed all the Jesuit colleges within its jurisdiction, eight in number, and, three weeks later, ordered the confiscation of the properties. The friends of the Society in the hierarchy did not give up the battle; in May an assembly of the French Clergy sent the Archbishop of Narbonne, de la Roche-Aymon, to present to the King their petition, begging Louis to save the Society. The royal weakling waved away the prelates' plea by asking that the question be set aside.

Nothing now was left but to deliver the final blow. That was done by the decree of August 6, 1762, which condemned the Society of Jesus to extinction. The fashioners of the decree outdid themselves in their denunciations of the Society: they asserted that the Constitutions of the order were contrary to the natural law and dangerous to the spiritual and temporal authorities; they declared that the Jesuit doctrines contained the errors of Arius, Nestorius, Luther, Calvin, Wycliffe, Pelagius and other heresiarchs, were blasphemous, outrageous and insulting to the Blessed Virgin and to the saints, were destructive of the Divinity of Christ, were favorable to the Epicureans and to the Deists, encouraged murder, parricide, usury, vengeance and cruelty, destroyed filial piety and threatened the safety of princes, and finally were contrary to the decisions of the Church, to the Divine law, to peace and good order. That was all. The authors forgot to charge the Jesuits with Mohammedanism, Shamanism, and demon-worship; but then one cannot think of everything. The decree was as thorough in its provisions as in its accusations: the Jesuits were declared incapable of exercising the sacred ministry; they were forbidden to wear the habit, to live in community, or to correspond with one another; they were to lose all their possessions, their churches and libraries; the professed fathers were allotted the munificent pension of one franc a day; the priests might reside in France as private individuals, providing they took an oath to defend the Gallican Articles; none of them were ever under any pretext to observe the rules of the Society; finally they were required to recognize the truth of the calumnies in the *Extraits des assertions*.

Louis XV in a flare-up of courage suspended the operation of the decree for eight months. Clement XIII, in a secret consistory of September 3, voiced his indignation, characterizing the decree of suppression as "the most blasphemous attack of worldly powers on the sanctity of the Church and on learning." In letters to the French clergy the Holy Father again and again reiterated his indignation at the treatment of the Jesuits and expressed his conviction that the blow was eventually aimed at Catholicism itself.

But the allies were not to be deterred from completing the destruction.

Other parlements followed the lead of Paris; although in some, notably those of Bordeaux, Rennes, Toulouse, Pau, Grenoble, Perpignan, Aix, and Rousillon, the stiffest opposition was made by the jurist friends of the Jesuits. Only the parlements of Alsace, Lorraine, Flanders, Artois and Besançon refused to condemn the Society; in their jurisdictions the order was able to exist for a few more years. Early in 1763 the Paris Parlement clashed with the Archbishop of Paris, the saintly Christophe de Beaumont, who, disdaining to remain silent, issued a pastoral refuting the charges against the Jesuits.[30] The tribunal answered by having the pastoral condemned to the flames and by citing the heroic prelate before its court. Louis XV intervened to cancel this last indignity and changed the order to one of exile at La Trappe.

The eight months of suspension having elapsed, Louis XV on April 1, 1763 relinquished his opposition to the decree of the Paris Parlement. A month previously a new order had been issued, demanding from every Jesuit under pain of banishment the renunciation of his vows and the acceptance of a declaration that the Society of Jesus was "perverted, worthy of punishment and ruinous to the State and to the Church." Of the 3,500 Jesuits, only 25, a few priests and a handful of scholastics and brothers acceded. Toward the end of the year, on December 1, 1764, Louis XV, with the most evident reluctance, signed the final decree which destroyed the order in every part of his dominions. The last word was not said until Clement XIII on January 8, 1765, by his Bull "Apostolicum pascendi munus" issued his ringing protest against all that had been done to the Society of Jesus; the Pontiff with the greatest praise confirmed anew the order, its Constitutions and privileges.

The lot of the dispersed French Jesuits was hard indeed, despite the kindnesses of most of the bishops and the practical manifestations of sympathy bestowed on them by all true French Catholics. The Father General Ricci gave to the Provincials the widest powers for arranging the future of their subjects, the priests were permitted to live in private houses and to accept the care of souls. Yet with all their properties confiscated and the payment of the meager pensions made dependent on the repudiation of their order, a large number, being without resources, were forced to take the road to exile. Their enemies in France were still unsatisfied; they now turned their forces and energies towards effecting the complete religious suppression.

The next immediate objective was the destruction of the Society of Jesus in Spain.[31] Because of the high esteem in which the Jesuits were

---

[30] *Documents, Historiques, Critiques, Apologétiques concernant La Compagnie de Jésus,* Paris (1830), t. III, no. 18, 19.

[31] Pastor, *Geschichte der Päpste,* Vol. XVI, part I, pp. 697–849; Smith, "Suppression of the Society of Jesus," *The Month,* Vol. XCIX, 626–650; C, 20–34, 126–152; Crétineau-Joly, Histoire, Vol. V, pp. 227–248.

held by the great bulk of the Spanish clergy and people, the suppression promised to be an extremely difficult task; yet it was accomplished with such dispatch that in a single night the order's existence was stamped out in every part of the wide-spread Spanish dominions. The intrigue of Infidel "Philosophic" ministers of an autocratic king explains the fact. Up to the very year of the suppression, a casual observer would never have dreamt that before a twelvemonth had passed not a single Jesuit would be found in Spain. The anti-Jesuit warfare of Pombal and Choiseul across the borders made no very great impression; in fact there was scarcely any opposition when several of the propaganda pieces inspired by Pombal were publicly burned by the order of the Grand Inquisitor. At the court the Queen Mother, Elizabeth Farnese, proved a strong protectress for the order; as was evidenced by her letter of 1759 to a Spanish Provincial, in which she declared that the Jesuits were innocent of any participation in the Indian revolt in Paraguay and at the same time expressed her admiration for the zeal and charity of the fathers. Charles III himself entrusted the education of the heir apparent, the Prince of the Asturias, to the Jesuit Wendlingen. However, not all in the royal circle were so friendly; in the reign of Ferdinand IV (1746–1759), his Queen, the Portuguese princess Barbara, supported Pombal's colonial policy in South America and succeeded also in having her husband's Jesuit confessor, Ravago, dismissed from the court in 1755. But until the death of the firm-minded Queen Mother, little real harm could be done to the Society. In other Spanish circles there existed elements disaffected towards the Jesuits; the outstanding position of the order in public life had aroused the jealousy of some, the satires of de Isla had provoked resentment among the monastic orders, and the criticism of the writings of Cardinal Noris had affected the sentiments of his Augustinian brethren. Still, it seems hardly credible that such Spaniards would ever have approved the terrible fate that was to be visited on their Jesuit countrymen. The unanimous and urgent appeal of the Spanish hierarchy to Clement XIII in defense of the Society of Jesus against its persecutors, mirrored the true and final sentiments of the Spanish people.

The blow against the Society was planned by a clique of freethinking ministers. Among these politicians may be noted Count d'Aranda, the chief minister, de Roda, Campomanés, Grimaldi, Moñino and the Duke of Alva. All were "Philosophers," disciples of Voltaire and followers of de Choiseul; hence all were bitter enemies of the Society of Jesus. With them must be included Richard Wall, a Spanish statesman of Irish nationality, a bitter enemy of the Jesuits, and the Neapolitan chief minister, Tanucci, a "Philosopher" and self-proclaimed opponent of the Church. This cabal worked upon the suspicions of Charles III, whose mentality was not of the highest order; he was incapable of an independent judgment and, properly prepared, could be made to believe anything. They convinced him of the nefariousness of the Jesuits, and succeeded in turning him from a friend into a most relentless foe of the order. Already while Charles was King of Naples, which crown he held until 1759, Tanucci had begun to work on the fears of the credulous monarch against the Jesuits, and to infect him, though unwittingly on the King's part, with his own anti-clericalism, especially in questions of conflicting Papal and regal rights. Even after Charles' departure for Spain, the Neapolitan's evil influence continued. Tanucci kept on playing upon the King's suspicious credulity to further his own anti-clerical schemes; he found ready cooperators in the freethinking Spanish ministers. The King was told that the Jesuits were the opponents of all that he most desired; their popularity was declared inimical to his autocratic government; their devotion to the Roman Pontiff, a hindrance to his royal prerogatives; their efforts against the beatification of Palafox, which he wished for, an insult. Gradually Charles III was brought to a state of mind in which he was ready to believe the Jesuits capable of high treason, if the opportunity offered.

Charles III's government was by no means popular with the Spanish people. The Minister of Finance, Marquis de Squillace, an Italian, was particularly obnoxious because of his exactions and his foreign nationality. The dissatisfaction, which had been manifested by lampoons, squibs and derogatory pamphlets, finally broke out into a bloody rioting, known as "The Revolt of the Capes and the Sombreros," on March 26, 1766 in Madrid. Apparently the tumult was a demonstration against the hated Italian minister because of his decree prohibiting the wearing of the national costume, the wide-brimmed hat and the long cloak; actually it was a flare-up of the populace against the minister's poor financial policy. The riotings were so serious that the King was obliged to fly to Aranjuez, some of his guards were killed, and the fighting spread through the whole of Spain. The people were finally calmed down by the priests, especially the Jesuits. A strange reward was being prepared for their pains. The anti-clerical ministers, who met in an extraordinary secret council to investigate the causes of the troubles, saw an opportunity for incriminating the hated Society of Jesus. Advices from Tanucci spurred them on. It began to be hinted about that people as simple as the rioters could never have written the anti-government pamphlets. Secret agents were sent to all corners of Spain to gather evidence of the Jesuits' complicity in the insurrection and of their designs on the King's own person. Lies, vague rumors, total exaggerations, anything and everything, were raked in to make such a plausible indictment of the order as would impress the monarch's gullibility. The case was cleverly worked up, and it succeeded in frightening Charles III into consenting to the extinction of the Society of Jesus in Spain. No Jesuit was ever arrested; no Jesuit was ever questioned in a judicial trial as to his own or his order's innocence or guilt. Such simple justice had to be refused, lest the flimsiness of the charges be made apparent. The Society was to be destroyed by the edict of the King, the deluded victim of political knaves. The extraordinary council labored on, silently and steadily. On January 29, 1767, Campomanés charged the Jesuits with high treason in endeavoring to seduce the people from their allegiance, and pronounced the judgment of banishment from the realm. A month later, February 27, Charles III signed the document which condemned almost six thousand of his subjects to exile.

Not an inkling of what had been decided reached the people, so secretly was everything done. The Jesuits however began to feel that some terrible disaster was drawing upon them. Their worst forebodings would have been more than realized, had they but known the contents of the secret orders which were being sent to the alcaldes of every town of the Spanish domains in which they dwelt. According to these documents, at midnight, April 2, the houses of the Jesuits were to be invaded, all the inmates were to be arrested and marched under guard to the nearest coast where they were to be embarked on ships and transported to the Papal States, the papers of every house were to be seized and sealed, and all the goods of the Society were to be confiscated. The alcaldes themselves knew not the contents of the dispatches, for they were forbidden under penalty of death to open the orders before midnight of the fateful April 2.

The blow fell like a thunderbolt. The plans so carefully thought out worked smoothly and, before the morning of April 2 was over, 6,000 Jesuits were being marched like convicts to the coast. They were allowed to take nothing with them but the necessary linen, and the priests, their breviaries. At the various Spanish ports, ships lay at anchor waiting for the banished religious; into these they were hustled and in a brief time the overcrowded craft were carrying all into exile. Persistent efforts were made to detach the scholastics from the fathers, but in vain; almost to a man they preferred to share the bread of exile with their elder brethren. Especially was this true of two young priests of noble blood, the Pignatellis, grandnephews of Pope Innocent XII; d'Aranda, fearing the anger of the Spanish nobility at their harsh fate, tried by every inducement to make them abandon the Society. The elder, Joseph, though seriously sick, insisted on embarking with the rest of the Jesuits, remarking to those who would dissuade him: "My resolution is unshaken. It matters little whether my body becomes the prey of fishes or worms. What I desire above all is to die in the company of the Jesuits, my brethren." His wish was granted; but death came to him only long afterwards, as a member of the restored Society. Such were his virtues that the Church honored him with beatification, May 21, 1933. As has been said before, many look on the sanction of the veneration of Bl. Joseph Pignatelli as a justification of the suppressed Society of Jesus.

During the summer of 1767 the banishment of the Jesuit missionaries from the Spanish colonies took place. All the 2,617, regardless of nationality (there were over two hundred and fifty Germans alone), were first shipped to Spain. The orders to the colonial governors were sufficiently explicit: "After the fathers were placed on board ship, if there should remain a single Jesuit within your jurisdiction, even should he be sick or dying, you shall be punished by death." The missionaries were, as a consequence, herded into the ships; it is little wonder that several of the captives in these overcrowded, unseaworthy hulks, died on the ocean crossing. A far harder cross for these missionaries was the abandonment of their native flocks; by the irreligious act of the suppression some 304,-896 Christian Indians (122,000 in Mexico, 55,000 in Peru, 7,586 in Chile, 113,716 in Paraguay and 6,594 in New Granada) through numerous Reductions, were deprived of their shepherds and the fathers of their souls. The Indians were heart-broken and furiously indignant. In Paraguay, one word from the fathers and they would have risen in rebellion for their priests, who had been to them not only spiritual guides but protectors from the greed and slavery of the whites. Such an uprising would have engaged all the resources of Spain. But the word never came. Calmly and courageously the fathers accepted their share of the Cross.

There had to be a justification, of course. Some pretence at explanation had to be made to the world why six thousand men had been condemned and exiled without trial, charge or defense. The excuse was published, April 3, the day after the destruction had become an accomplished fact; it was a bare statement by Charles III that he had dissolved the Society of Jesus and had banished its members from his realm because of important considerations, which considerations he would always keep a secret in his heart. Clement XIII, on being informed by the King of his condemnation of the Jesuits, wrote to him a most touching appeal, which contained the following two significant statements: "Of all the blows that have wounded us during the nine sorrowful years of our pontificate, the most painful to our paternal heart is the one which your majesty has announced to us . . . We attest before God and men that the body, the institution, the spirit of the Society of Jesus are innocent; nay, that this Society is not only innocent, but pious, useful and holy in its object, its laws and its teachings." [32] The only answer that Charles

---

[32] Pastor, *Geschichte der Päpste*, Vol. XVI, part I, pp. 805–807.

made to the Pope's plea was that even to His Holiness he could not reveal his secret reason. With such an evasion Clement would not rest content; again rising to the defense of the order, he issued a Brief in which he declared that the King imperilled the salvation of his soul by his conduct towards the Jesuits, and in which once more he affirmed: "the body and the spirit are pure, and even suppose that some individual members were guilty, they should not have been treated with severity before having been accused and duly convicted." No stronger condemnation of Charles III, of d'Aranda and his "Philosophic" colleagues could have been penned.

The King's secret reason was simply his conviction that the Jesuits were implicated in the insurrection and in the plots against his life.[33] He shrouded it in secrecy to forestall the interferences of Pope Clement XIII and to prevent a judicial trial of any or all of the Spanish Jesuits. There was to be no Papal action in a field which this absolutist monarch considered his own.[34] His ministers had persuaded him against the trial, knowing full well that their flimsy allegations would not stand the light of day. As a matter of fact, Charles III disclosed his secret reason to the Spanish Ambassador at Rome, Mgr. Azpuru, to Tanucci and to the French Ambassador, the Marquis d'Ossun, who communicated it to his government. In all cases it was the alleged connection of the Jesuits with the insurrection and the plots against the King's life. His secrecy was not owing to his reluctance to discuss the allegation that the Jesuits had spread stories impugning his mother's honor and his own legitimacy. This explanation and the fantastic stories of the ministerial schemes of planting letters of such purport in Jesuit houses or in the baggage of travelling Jesuits are romantic inventions.[35]

As for the charges against the fathers contained in the *Consulta* of January 29, 1767, which moved the King to his act, and in the *Memoria Ministerial*, a document issued in defense of the ministers on November 30, 1768, they have been shown to be groundless by the documents collected by Francisco Guitierrez de la Huerta,[36] Antonio Ferrer del Rio,[37] and Danvilla y Collado.[38] The charges were made to rest largely on five trials and an accumulation of irresponsible hearsay. Three of the trials

---

[33] Smith, "The Suppression of the Society of Jesus," *The Month*, Vol. C, pp. 20–34.

[34] *Ibid.*, pp. 126–152.

[35] Pastor, *Geschichte der Päpste*, XVI, part I, pp. 798–801.

[36] Francisco Guitierrez de la Huerta, *Exposicion y dictamen de el fiscal et de el conseyo y camera* (issued in 1811 as a result of an investigation into the guilt of the Jesuits, when the question of their return to Spain was being considered).

[37] Antonio Ferrer del Rio, *Historia del Rienado de Carlos III in España*, Madrid (1856), (his anti-Jesuit bias does not affect the value of his documents).

[38] Danvilla y Collado, *Reinado de Carlos III*, Madrid (1891–1894), (excellent for its documentary evidence).

were of men supposedly guilty of the plots and friendly to the Jesuits. The innocence of the three is beyond doubt; their guilt could not be proven by the ministers. Of the other two trials, the first was of a moral reprobate who changed his confession to an unfavorable statement against the Jesuits, but only on the day on which their banishment was determined and under circumstances which could not have influenced that decision. The other trial was that of a fanatic, who under torture failed to implicate the order, or any member of it.[39]

D'Aranda and the clique had all of the Jesuit archives in their hands now; but thumb them as they would, not an iota of justification for their slanders, their accusations and their persecutions could they find. They took care however to silence the protests of the people by issuing on October 18 a decree which rendered opposition impossible: any criticism of the King's measure, or any attempt to work for the Jesuits, was declared a civil offense; all Jesuits were threatened with imprisonment and death if they ever set foot on Spanish soil. Yet not all voices could be forever silenced. A year and a half after the dissolution of the Society of Jesus, November 4, 1768, when Charles III in the celebration of his feast day stepped out upon the balcony of the royal palace to receive the congratulatory cheers of his people and, as was the custom, to grant them a favor, he was greeted with a general cry demanding the restoration of the Jesuits. Needless to say it was not granted, but it bespoke the true sentiments of the people.

The misfortunes of the banished Jesuits had but begun. When the ships of the exiles reached the Papal States, they were not permitted to disembark the exiles. It was impossible for the Pope with the meager revenues of his civil domain to provide for them; he was already supporting 4,000 Portuguese Jesuits and there was a possibility that he might have the care of many French fathers. To care for 6,000 more was simply out of the question. Sore at heart for the refusal which he had to give, Clement XIII did what he could by obtaining a refuge for the persecuted religious in Corsica. The stay of the exiles on the island was accompanied with many hardships; it was to last but a year. On May 15, 1768, Corsica came under the control of France, and de Choiseul immediately set about banishing the Spanish fathers. Where they would go next, no one could say. Eventually they found refuge in Genoa, Ferrara and other Northern Italian cities.

The small states of Naples [40] and Parma,[41] dependencies of Spain, soon followed her example in destroying the Jesuit order within their domains. There was no question but that such a course was to be the case

[39] Smith, "The Suppression of the Society of Jesus," *The Month*, Vol. C, pp. 138–140.
[40] Pastor, *Geschichte der Päpste*, Vol. XVI, part I, pp. 850–876.
[41] *Ibid.*, pp. 876–883, 887–919.

in the Kingdom of Naples, where Tanucci, the bitter anti-clerical "Philosopher," was chief minister and the real and sole power. Tanucci already had had an important part in the Spanish tragedy; now he prepared to enact one of his own in the Two Sicilies. First he forbade under the gravest penalties the reading of the Bull "Apostolicum pascendi munus"; then, acting on the Spanish model, he had the Jesuit houses seized at midnight, February 8, 1768, and the inmates, without accusation or trial, marched across the border into the Papal States as exiles. Even the twenty Jesuits on the Island of Malta did not escape, for Tanucci forced the Grand Master of the Knights, Pedro de Fonseca, a vassal of Sicily, to expel them.[42] In the small principality of Parma, a fief of the Papal Throne but at the time under the rule of a Bourbon prince, the minister, du Tillot de Ferino, matched, if he did not exceed, the anti-clericalism of Tanucci. He issued an order, January 16, 1768, that a commission be set up for the investigation of the charters of the monasteries. Clement XIII, as liege lord of the state, in a Brief known as "The Monitorium to Parma," declared the commission invalid and warned all who took part in its formation or in its works that they would incur ecclesiastical censures. Du Tillot gave his answer by expelling the Jesuits during the night of February 7–8. The next morning, a decree appeared suppressing the Society of Jesus and attempting to secularize the non-professed. France, Spain and Naples took the side of Parma against the Pope, forbidding the publication of the Brief and occupying parts of the Papal territories with their troops. Clement was forced to recall the "Monitorium"; nor was there anything that he could do for the Society; its destruction was an accomplished fact in the duchy of Parma. The Bourbon governments and Portugal had won their national war against the Society of Jesus; now they turned to the wider field of the universal Church and began the six years' campaign to force Rome to decree the total destruction of the order.

---

[42] Pastor, *Geschichte der Päpste*, Vol. XVI, part I, 883–887.

CHAPTER XIII

CATASTROPHE

Up to date the enemies had destroyed about half of the Society's organization. It exasperated them beyond measure to realize that 13 provinces of the order still functioned, that 10,959 Jesuits continued to labor in 266 colleges, 103 seminaries and 81 residences. And further, there was little chance that the authorities of the Papal States, Northern Italy, Austria, Hungary, Bohemia, Poland, Russia, Switzerland, the Low Countries, even of England and her colonies would follow their example. In the changes of parties and in the fall of ministries, it was not impossible that the 12,000 exiled Jesuits of Portugal, Spain, France and Naples might be recalled to their home countries. Many in these lands and throughout Europe, many non-Jesuits too, expected such a reversal. Such an eventuality the Bourbon courts and Portugal determined must never be allowed to happen; the only certain way to prevent its realization was a complete ecclesiastical suppression on the order of the Pope.[1] To force the Sovereign Pontiff into such an action, then, became the first objective of the Courts. On January 18, 20 and 21, 1769, Spain and Naples on the urging of Portugal presented to Clement XIII a petition asking for the total suppression of the Society of Jesus. Accompanying the demand was the threat of further seizure of Papal territory and, far worse, the menacing of schism, such as was already the fact in Portugal. The Pope refused to be moved either by threats or menaces.

Clement XIII's death, February 2, 1769, however, put a new face on affairs; and the Bourbon Courts now sought the opportunity of obtaining a Pope who would be certain to bring about the suppression. The ministers began to lay the most thorough plans for the obtaining of that desired end. Seldom, if ever, have the meetings of the Sacred College for the election of a Supreme Pontiff been subjected to such unwarranted pressure and ille-

---

[1] For the entire history of the Papal Suppression: Pastor, *Geschichte der Päpste*, Vol. XVI, part I, pp. 919–955; part II, pp. 1–275; Duhr, *Geschichte*, Vol. IV, part II, c. 14; Heimbucher, *Orden und Kongregationen der Katholischen Kirche*, Vol. II, pp. 190–196; Koch, *Jesuiten-Lexikon*, cols. 126–129; Cordara-Albertotti, *De suppressione Soc. Jesu comentarii*; Theiner, *Histoire du Pontificat de Clément XIV*; de Ravignan, *Clément XIII et Clément XIV*; Smith, "The Suppression of the Society of Jesus," *The Month*, Vols. C, CI, CII.

gal interferences.[2] The solemn prescriptions of secrecy and isolation, the explicit safeguards for the independence of the conclave, set down by Julius II, Paul IV, Gregory XV and Clement XI, were violated time and again by the ministers and ambassadors of Spain, France, and Naples, as well as by certain of the court Cardinals. The French ministry ordered Cardinals de Bernis and de Luynes to establish with the French Ambassador, d'Aubeterre, an understanding in regard to all points connected with the conclave and the election and to receive communications from him both before and during the conclave. D'Aubeterre, the French Ambassador, from without and Cardinal Orsini from within were to head the campaign; the others in the intrigue were to take their orders from them.[3] Orsini from his entrance almost to the end of the conclave maintained a regular correspondence with d'Aubeterre, giving most detailed information of what was occurring. In turn he and certain other members of his party hesitated not to receive the instructions of the Ambassador.[4] De Bernis throughout conducted himself in a similar manner.[5] All such proceedings were gross violations of the conclave-oath, to which these Cardinals had sworn their faith.

On February 15, 1769 the Senate of the Church began its deliberations. The more numerous group by far among the Cardinals desired a Pope of the type of the late Pontiff, one who in defense of the Society of Jesus would face out the menacings of the Bourbon ministers; these Cardinals were known as the "Zelanti." In opposition to them was the party that looked for a Pope who would be ready to conciliate the Bourbon governments. Some of these latter Cardinals were honestly persuaded that peace for the Church could only be obtained by the widest concessions in the matter of the Jesuits; but others among them were actuated only by the desire to bring to actuality the dictation of their own governments. Such political ecclesiastics were called the "Crown Cardinals." At the opening of the conclave one of their leaders, de Bernis, could see little hope for the success of their efforts; as he wrote to de Choiseul: "It is easy to foresee the difficulties of our negotiations on a stage where more than three-fourths of the actors are against us." To overcome the great disparity in numbers the "Crown Cardinals" resorted to the threat of schism [6] if the "Zelanti" dared to choose a Pontiff lacking the approval of the Bourbon governments. It was no idle gesture. Ten years had now passed since Pombal had cut off Portugal from all communication with Rome;

---

[2] For the Conclave cf. Pastor, *Geschichte der Päpste*, Vol. XVI, part II, c. 1; Smith, "The Suppression," *The Month*, Vol. C, pp. 517–536, 581–591; CI, pp. 48–61.

[3] Pastor publishes in Appendix 9 of Vol. XVI, part II, p. 421, the text of the *Plan de conduite approuvé par les Cardinaux de Luynes, Orsini et de Bernis.*

[4] Smith, "The Suppression," *The Month*, Vol. C, p. 527.

[5] Smith, "The Suppression," *The Month*, Vol. C, p. 527.

[6] Smith, "The Suppression," *The Month*, Vol. C, pp. 523, 536.

that was an ever-present misfortune which the most independent Cardinal could not ignore.

Orsini, de Bernis and their coterie took care in the beginning to bring forth no names, but contented themselves with a policy of exclusion. First of all they insisted that the conclave must await the arrival of the foreign Cardinals, intimating that any early choice would never receive the recognition of the Bourbon rulers. Even in the very opening days the "Zelanti" learned that hardly anyone whom they might favor would be acceptable; when on the first scrutiny, Cardinal Chigi, one of their number, received eighteen votes, Cardinal Orsini acting for the King of Naples registered a protest against his name. Throughout the discussions and negotiations the "Crown Cardinals" continued to speak piously enough and with studied delicacy of their not wishing to force the election of anyone on the conclave, but they never failed to make the hidden hint of schism clear. They declared no explicit exclusion; but they drew out and, as it were, killed off all the candidates disagreeable to the crowns merely by insinuating that their election might not be recognized by the ministers of the sovereigns. This method was most efficacious, and at the same time it was least odious. It was also inexhaustible. The last consideration was important, for the Veto, which France, Spain and Austria could use, might only be applied once during a conclave. Such a policy of exclusion limited the choice to about five Cardinals. A list prepared for the "Crown Cardinals" placed the members of the Sacred College under four headings; "good," "indifferent," "doubtful," and "very bad." [7] By this classification 21 out of 43 Cardinals were definitely excluded. Of the remaining Cardinals, about 10, because of health or age, and 5, for various other reasons, could not be considered.

To make doubly certain the ultimate goal d'Aubeterre, inspired by Azparu, the Spanish Ambassador, proposed to de Bernis that a formal promise in writing be obtained from the future Pope that if elected he would suppress the Society of Jesus.[8] Such an arrangement would have rendered the election practically simoniacal. De Bernis refused to give it consideration, declaring that it would be a flagrant violation of Canon Law. Orsini likewise refused, concurring with the view of his French colleague.[9] Both Ambassadors were taken back by the very definite refusals; to d'Aubeterre it seemed ridiculous to boggle over Canon Law and simony, when reason plainly called for the abolition of the Jesuits for the peace of the world. The idea of this pre-election pledge was not yet abandoned. It again appeared in the instructions of the Spanish Cardinals, de Solis and de la Cerda, whose absence had held up the election so long.

---

[7] Danvila, *Historia del Reinado de Carlos III*, Vol. III, pp. 310–311.

[8] Pastor, *Geschichte der Päpste*, Vol. XVI, part II, p. 31.

[9] Smith, "The Suppression," *The Month*, Vol. C, p. 591.

Both ecclesiastics entered the conclave at the end of April. In a meeting of the "Crown Cardinals" held in the cell of Orsini, de Solis read the instructions which he had brought from Madrid and took it upon himself to urge the obtaining of the written engagement, which course was contained in these instructions. Once again de Bernis, de Luynes and Orsini rejected the proposal as simoniacal, useless and repugnant to their conscience. De Solis strove in vain to change them, even suggesting that the promise need not be given in writing, but only orally in the presence of the "Crown Cardinals." This expedient was rejected just as firmly, and the idea of a pre-election promise had to be abandoned. Whether the Spanish Cardinals completely gave up, cannot be stated for certain; but it can be said that they never ventured so far as to propose the promise to a single Cardinal.[10]

Orsini, in rejecting the pre-election engagement, declared that the only course open to the "Crown Cardinals" was to work for a candidate whom they could feel when Pope would be willing to satisfy the desires of the sovereigns. Of the five Cardinals surviving the exclusions, the one who really stood first was Cardinal Lorenzo Ganganelli.[11] Yet it was not certain how he was affected towards the Society of Jesus, for throughout the conclave he had committed himself to neither party and had kept his opinions studiously to himself. De Solis and de Bernis determined to sound him out. He was asked if he recognized in the Sovereign Pontiff the right to extinguish with a good conscience the Company of Jesus, provided he observed the Canon Law, and if he considered it desirable that the Pope should do everything in his power to satisfy the wishes of the Crowns. He gave an affirmative answer to both questions. It is possible too that he may have put his signature to written replies for de Solis. If such a document existed, it is nowhere to be found; although it is testified to by de Bernis in letters of July 28 and November 30 to de Choiseul. It is important to note that Cardinal Ganganelli never gave a promise, either in writing or verbally, to suppress the Society of Jesus.[12] Crétineau-Joly's assertion that he did, has now been disproved by the statements of the Spanish Ambassador, Azparu, written on May 18: "None of the Cardinals have gone so far as to propose to anyone that the suppression should be secured by a written or spoken promise," and on May 25: "Ganganelli neither made a promise, nor refused it." [13] The questions had been put to him as a theologian and in such a capacity he had answered honestly what he believed, i. e., that the Pope could canonically

---

[10] Azparu to Grimaldi, in Danvila, *Reinado de Carlos III*, Vol. III, p. 327.

[11] Pastor, *Geschichte der Päpste*, Vol. XVI, part II, pp. 46–47.

[12] Pastor, *Geschichte der Päpste*, Vol. XVI, part II, pp. 58–60; Smith, "The Suppression," *The Month*, Vol. CI, pp. 60–61.

[13] Danvila, *Reinado de Carlos III*, Vol. III, pp. 330–340, where the matter is discussed.

suppress the Society of Jesus and that its suppression could be most advantageous for the peace of the Church with the Bourbon courts. Yet Cardinal Ganganelli so worded his answers as to guarantee the future freedom of his actions in any contingency.

The "Crown Cardinals," now reassured, bent their endeavors to secure the election of Cardinal Ganganelli. The "Zelanti" were not unwilling to accept him; he was a learned ecclesiastic and one of blameless life; his exact views were not known, it was possible that he might carry on as they would wish. It was certainly clear to them that they could not elect any one of their own party. Their attitude was expressed by Cardinal J. F. Albani: "We could not make a good Pope as we wished; and we did not want to make a bad one; so we made the best we could find among the doubtful candidates." [14] On May 19, 1769 Cardinal Ganganelli was elected Pope by all but one vote, his own, which he cast for one of the "Zelanti." His choice of the name of his predecessor, "Clement," encouraged the friends of the Jesuits.

The new Pontiff was known to be an excellent ecclesiastic.[15] As a friar he had been a fervent, pure religious, attached to the poverty of his order and devoted to the observance of its rules; as Cardinal, and later as Pope, he continued these good qualities, especially in the simplicity of his life and in the practice of poverty. He made no use of his high position to advance the fortunes of his family. He bore a deserved reputation for his talents and judgment, for his scholarly tastes and for his industry. Possessing a pleasing personality, he was noted for his cordiality and heartiness with his associates. Cordara, the Jesuit historian, who was an intimate friend of many of the leading figures of the Rome of that day and who wrote an interesting account of the Suppression, declared that Cardinal Ganganelli "would have been an excellent Pope had his lot fallen on happier times." But the times were such as demanded a heroic Pope who would stand fearlessly before the might of secular sovereigns, a strong Pontiff who would not be coerced by their threats, an experienced and skilled ruler who would not be deceived by the wiles and maneuverings of politicians, and one whose tenacity to the line of duty intriguers would be obliged to recognize. Unfortunately the Pontiff was weak in just these qualities; and more unfortunately still, he chose to act with great secretiveness, seeking to manage the complicated affairs alone, refusing to avail himself of the counsels of the more experienced Cardinals.

As for his relations with the Jesuits, Cardinal Ganganelli's attitude seemed to have changed from friendship to indifference, if not to hostility.

---

[14] Smith, "The Suppression," *The Month*, Vol. CI, p. 54.

[15] Pastor, *Geschichte der Päpste*, Vol. XVI, part II, pp. 62–71; de Ravignan, *Clément XIII et Clément XIV;* "Clément XIV," *Dict. Theol. Cath.*, III, 124 ff.; Smith, "The Suppression," *The Month*, Vol. CI, pp. 178–183.

Originally he was on the best of terms with the fathers; from them he had received his first education at Rimini. Later, as a friar, in the various towns in which he had lived with them he had been most cordial. When Clement XIII raised him to the Cardinalate, he spoke of him as "a Jesuit in a Franciscan habit." For some time the Cardinal remained friendly; but at length he seemed to change. His intimacy with the circle of the Spanish Ambassador, Don Manuel de Roda, may explain his different attitude. The house of de Roda had the reputation of being the center of the anti-Jesuit intrigue in Rome; and it would have been difficult for him not to have been influenced by the multitudinous charges and rumors against the Jesuits circulating in that quarter. His connection with the de Roda circle possibly explains why Clement XIII during the last years of his pontificate ceased to employ his services. It seems significant that he should have been appointed the promoter of the cause of the beatification of Bishop Palafox, and also that he should have become a correspondent of Mgr. Jarente, the Jansenistic Bishop of Orleans, a determined enemy of the order. At the time of his election the future Pope was apparently not well-disposed towards the Society of Jesus; though he could not have been actively hostile, for Tanucci opposed his election to the last.

Peace for the Church by composing the differences of the Courts with the Holy See, Clement XIV made the first object of his pontificate. Accordingly in the very beginning he made several friendly gestures towards the Bourbon princes, at the same time displaying a reserved attitude to the Jesuits, twice refusing Father Ricci the usual audiences. Still the ambassadors in their receptions were given no inkling of any positive steps towards the suppression of the Society. For almost two months both camps remained in suspense; the Jesuits and their friends trying to calm their forebodings by hoping for the best; the anti-Jesuits apprehending the possibility of a last-minute failure of their plans, for they held no promise of the order's destruction. The situation broke on July 12 with the issuance of the Brief "Coelestium munerum," which contained faculties for the granting of a plenary indulgence in the Jesuit popular missions.[16] It was a routine document, a mere renewal of faculties, for which every ten years the Procurator-General made request; the highly laudatory expressions which it contained were in the customary form of such papers. A hundred or so copies had to be printed for presentation to the diocesan authorities wherever the missions were to be preached. In consideration of the Society's situation, the General ordered that the document be divulged only when necessary. The printer, however, seeing a chance for gain in the publication of such a document with

---

[16] Pastor, *Geschichte der Päpste*, Vol. XVI, part II, pp. 106–107.

its high praise of the Society of Jesus, struck off and sold several hundred copies.

The Bourbon Courts, furious at the praise and the publicity, determined on immediate action to force the Pope's hand. On July 22 de Bernis on behalf of the three Bourbon Kings presented to the Pope a joint memorial demanding the suppression of the order.[17] Clement XIV replied that he had his conscience and his honor to consult and asked for delay. De Bernis, according to further instructions, pressed the Pontiff for a written promise to carry out the Courts' demand. Such a commitment Clement XIV was by no means willing to make. De Choiseul, through de Bernis, dispatched a warning that the Society must be suppressed within two months or relations would be severed.[18] The Pope expressed the wish to satisfy the Powers for the sake of peace, but still asked for time for the needed preparations and for the overcoming of the opposition of the Cardinals, averring that in this business he had to work alone and in secret; he declared he was even willing to call a general council to settle the matter.

In addition Clement XIV adopted an inimical attitude towards the Society; he kept all fathers from his presence and would listen to no defense of the Jesuits by their friends; more than once he professed a personal dislike for the order, as given to domineering and intrigue. In several ways he restricted its activities. At Loretto the Spanish confessorship was given to the Franciscans; at Frascati, the episcopal seminary and part of the college were taken away from them by the Cardinal of York; in Rome the Jesuits were forbidden to preach the Jubilee in their own churches. But nothing that the Pope might do could turn the Courts from their purpose; the pressure and threats of schism were continued, until Clement XIV came to the conclusion that the suppression was the least of all evils. On September 30 the Pontiff made the promise, though very vague in its wording, to Louis XV; [19] on November 30, under the strong pressure of Azparu he gave a written engagement to Charles III to submit to his Majesty a scheme for the absolute extinction of the Society.[20] That was the decisive step; Clement XIV had bound himself; from that written pledge the Bourbon Kings and their ministers would never permit a retreat.

The end was not yet, however. For two years more the Pope continued to struggle against taking the final step. What could have been the reasons for his numerous delays and his evident reluctance to bring about the extinction of the order? It has been suggested by some that at heart

---

[17] Text in Pastor, *Geschichte der Päpste*, Vol. XVI, part II, pp. 108–109.
[18] *Ibid.*, p. 113.
[19] Text in Pastor, *Geschichte der Päpste*, Vol. XVI, part II, p. 119, note 5.
[20] Text in Pastor, *op. cit.*, p. 127.

Clement XIV favored the Jesuits and that in his own procrastinating and in the petty persecution, which he permitted towards the end, he was in reality desperately fighting for time in the hope that some fortunate turn of circumstances or of politics might change or defeat the enemies of the Society. It is a plausible explanation and there is something to be said for it. Yet it is hard to doubt that the Pope's dislike for the order was real, when one considers the adverse statements against the Jesuits which he made in the beginning of his pontificate; and he may have sincerely believed that the Jesuits were capable of vindictive schemes against a Pope who would destroy them. This much all must admit: whatever were his personal dislikes and fears, Clement XIV worked to decide the fate of the Society on higher principles and according to the prescriptions of Canon Law.

Another explanation,[21] advanced by Sidney Smith, S.J., in the English Jesuit publication, *The Month* (1901–1902), appears to have far greater plausibility: it is that Clement XIV's opinions changed in regard to the suppression as he addressed himself to the task of achieving it. At the time of his election Clement XIV was convinced, and very rightly, that the extinction of a religious order was warranted if thereby the necessary peace for the Church might be obtained, since religious orders are in no way essential. In applying this conviction to the case of the Jesuits he did not hesitate too much, for apparently he was not favorably disposed towards them. But after his election he came to a very real appreciation of what terrible disasters their suppression would really entail. There would be the patent contradiction of so many Sovereign Pontiffs, especially of his immediate predecessor, Clement XIII, who had solemnly approved of the order just a short time before. There would be the ignoring of the wishes of several Catholic princes and of numerous bishops, who were devoted to the Society, as well as the scandalizing of vast numbers of the faithful in condemning as corrupt an order which up till then the Holy See had recommended to them for their spiritual guidance. There would be the injustice of attaching a stigma to so many individual religious whose entire personal innocence even the Courts admitted, especially by their failure to give the proofs of their accusations. Finally there would be the destruction of a multitude of schools, missions and other good works, a destruction for the most part beyond remedying. Appalled by the thought of such overwhelming disaster Clement XIV drew back, determined either to postpone the suppression with the possibility of preventing it, or at least to achieve it in such a form as would best obviate the evils consequent. It is a conjecture at the most; but it does offer the best explanation of the two long years of delaying of Clement XIV.

---

[21] Smith, "The Suppression," *The Month*, Vol. CI, pp. 260–261.

The Bourbon Courts were willing to tolerate delays, at least for a while; they held the written promise which really counted. That is not to say that they gave the Pope any respite from their importunities or that they relented at all in their anti-Jesuit campaign. Thus on January 23, 1770, a new demand for the suppression was presented to the Pope on behalf of France, Spain, Naples and Portugal. The occasion of the last demand was an attempt upon the life of the King of Portugal, who had been clubbed by an enraged peasant and wounded. It goes without saying that at once the Jesuits were accused of complicity, although the only Jesuits in the kingdom were the poor human scarecrows in the Portuguese dungeons. On another occasion even the name of St. Paul of the Cross was dragged into the anti-Jesuit campaign. He was quoted as warning the Pope to watch his kitchen lest his food be poisoned. What the real sentiments of the saintly founder of the Passionists were may be gathered from his own statement: "Be sure that I feel much the extreme afflictions to which the illustrious Society of Jesus is subjected. The sole thought of so many calamities makes me groan and weep, seeing as I do so many innocent religious persecuted in so many ways . . . I continually pray . . . that God who gives death and life will in His own good time raise this Society to life again with still greater glory; this has ever been and still is my feeling." [22]

Clement XIV sought to gain time by counter-proposals, such as a reform of the order, a long and gradual suppression, or a postponement until the death of Father General Ricci, when no new election would be permitted. Negotiations with Catholic sovereigns not favorable to the Bourbon project helped to hold back matters for a time. Several of the German Catholic princes were of the same mind, as Prince Hohenlohe-Schillingsfürst who later petitioned the Holy See for the restoration of the Society. The Empress Maria Theresa [23] was regarded as the special protectress of the Jesuits; yet before the year 1770 was out, the pressure of the Bourbons and of her own children, Joseph II and Maria Carolina, Queen of Naples, brought her to abandon the order's cause. Towards the end of the year de Choiseul fell from power, and the hope arose among the members of the Society and their friends that the tide against them would turn with the new ministry. This was not to be; for France, needing the Spanish Alliance, refused to thwart Charles III in his pet aversion for the Society of Jesus.

The year 1771 passed, as did 1770, in promises, excuses and delays on the part of the Pope and in constant pressure for the suppression on the

---

[22] Letter quoted in de Ravignan, *Clément XIII et Clément XIV*, 2nd edition, Vol. I, p. 255.

[23] For the calumny of a Jesuit betraying the confession of Maria Theresa, cf. Duhr, *Jesuiten-Fabeln*, pp. 34 ff.

part of the ambassadors. To further their efforts these worthies continually consulted together but without much apparent success. The flippant Portuguese Ambassador, Almada, pictured their meetings: de Bernis seated in the middle intoning "Per omnia saecula saeculorum," with Orsini and Azparu on either side of him responding "Amen."

Some time previously Clement XIV had taken into his service in the affair of the Jesuits, a Mgr. Marefoschi, whom Tanucci declared to be "the one prelate who understood the intrigue of the Jesuits and of other orders of Friars, and who had few dealings with cloistered orders." [24] To Mgr. Marefoschi possibly may be ascribed the petty persecution to which the Jesuits were submitted from now on until the end for the purpose of ruining their credit in the eyes of the Roman people. Clement XIV knew of it and permitted it; but whether he was acquainted with the full extent of the vexations inflicted, it would be hard to say. This much is true, Marefoschi claimed the credit for suggesting such a course of action to the Pontiff.[25] The Seminary at Frascati was taken from the Society and given to the Bishop, the Cardinal of York; the members of the Society were forbidden to give missions in the monastery of Santa Clara, or to receive any special favors from the Congregation of Indulgences. The Bishops of the Papal States were recommended to deprive the fathers of the faculties of preaching and hearing confessions in their dioceses. With much show of hostility the Jesuits were ejected from their colleges at Frascati, Ferrara, Ravenna, Bologna, Modena and Macerata. An Apostolic Visitation of the Irish College, then in charge of the Jesuits, was undertaken by a hostile commission of which Marefoschi was the moving spirit.[26] The finances of the college for a long time had been in an unsatisfactory state, a fact which several previous Apostolic Visitors, after careful inquiry, had attributed to current economic conditions. In this investigation the ordinary procedures were disregarded and no opportunity for defence was permitted; then a judgment of negligence, defalcation and other crimes were rendered against the fathers. A similar treatment was meted out to the Jesuits who directed the Roman Seminary. As a result of Marefoschi's visitation the papers of the institution were turned over to a certain Smurraglia, whose name became a byword in Rome. After a private examination and several months' delay he brought in the charge that the Jesuits had diverted 300,000 scudi from the funds of the institution to their own treasury. Those who were simple enough

---

[24] Tanucci to Losada, quoted by Smith, "Suppression," *The Month*, Vol. CI, p. 269.

[25] Smith, "Suppression," *The Month*, Vol. CI, p. 272 (note 2).

[26] For Visitation of the Irish College and the Roman Seminary, Pastor, *Geschichte der Päpste*, Vol. XVI, part II, pp. 141–142; also Smith, "Suppression," *The Month*, Vol. CI, p. 272.

believed the charge; but no one of robust intelligence put any credence in it.[27]

Charles III, exasperated by the repeated procrastinations, made up his mind to send to Rome an Ambassador who would apply intimidation and the threat of schism relentlessly until the Pope capitulated. He found his envoy in Don José Moñino, a stubborn, hard man and a bully, if he felt the occasion called for it. According to the Auditor of the Madrid Nunciature the new Ambassador was hostile to Rome and to the Pontifical authority, and no one was more set upon the annihilation of the Jesuits. His reputation preceded him to Rome; Clement XIV, who was definitely in poor health, dreaded his coming. The first audience was granted on July 12. The Pope expressed to the envoy a long standing dislike for the Jesuits and gave him the assurance of his intention of suppressing the order. Still, he asserted, delay was unavoidable since the Curia was not in sympathy and all the work devolved upon himself alone. Moñino in reply warned the Holy Father that his sovereign was a resolute prince, not tolerant of too many delays, and that it would be unfortunate for the Pope if he lost the King's confidence. Several weeks were to pass before the ambassador could obtain the next interview. In the meantime his attitude was not improved by the assurance, received from Mgr. Macedonio, that the Pope had repented of his promises and that it was merely in the hope of evading their fulfilment that he kept repeating his excuses for delays.

Six months more of silence passed and then Clement XIV sent word to Moñino that he was ready to grant him a series of weekly audiences. Before these took place Moñino and de Bernis came to an understanding as to a common plan of attack: the Spaniard was to drive the Pope by threats and menaces, even to browbeat him, if necessary, to accept his proposals, while the French ecclesiastic was to approach the sorely tried Pontiff in the guise of a friend and, once possessing his confidence, to advise him that the wisest course would be to yield to Moñino's importunities. In these audiences, which were held every Sunday from August 16 to September 20, Moñino certainly succeeded in terrorizing the perplexed Pontiff with the vehemence of his onslaughts,[28] with the threat of the destruction of all religious orders in Spain, and of the cutting off of the Spanish Church from the Apostolic See. The ruthless envoy hesitated not to offer the Pope the bribe of the return of Avignon and Benevento once the suppression was decreed. That was more than the Holy Father would stand, and he sharply rejected the offer. Clement XIV could not be

---

[27] Pastor, *Geschichte der Päpste*, Vol. XVI, part II, pp. 153, 154 and note 1 of p. 154.

[28] Letter of Vasquez to Roda in Fraile Migueles *Jansenismo en España*, p. 342, cited by Smith, "The Suppression," *The Month*, Vol. CI, p. 387 (note 3).

purchased. Unfortunately he could be, and was, terrorized into capitulation by the terrible prospect of Spain, Naples, France and Portugal outside the True Fold. He asked to see the plan of suppression which Moñino had devised.[29]

Yet when the audiences were ended by the Pope's villeggiatura at Castel Gondolfo, Moñino disappointedly had to admit that he was still without the document of suppression. He informed de Bernis that if, after the return from the villa, the Pope was still hesitant, he would give up and let the Courts adopt whatever measures they deemed expedient. This observation was meant to be relayed to the Pontiff, an action which de Bernis took good care to do himself. The first two audiences after the return afforded the Spanish envoy little satisfaction: the first was only obtained on expressed solicitation, and was so fruitless that Moñino suggested that Tanucci reassert Naples' claim to Castro and Ronciglione; the second offered such little result that the Ambassador in its closing made the observation that whatever was to be done should be done within a month, as the patience of the Spanish monarch would not last much longer. In this last audience the Pope suggested that the Jesuit generalate might be made vacant by the elevation of Father Ricci to the cardinalate, in which case he would forbid the election of another General. Moñino, aghast at the very thought of Ricci in the College of Cardinals, when he got his breath back, hastened to offer an alternative: would it not be enough to make him an archbishop, or just a bishop? The Pontiff replied in the negative, averring that Ricci would never accept a miter, and the matter was dropped. It is pertinent to note that if Father General Ricci were worthy enough to be considered for such exalted offices, his guilt and that of his order could be very justly doubted.

The threats of Moñino and the professedly friendly counsels of de Bernis were at last successful, for on November 22 Clement XIV read to the Spaniard a preamble for the Brief of Suppression and authorized him to communicate the same to his sovereign. A few weeks later on December 13 the Pope appointed Mgr. Zelada to assist Moñino in the composition of such a Brief. The result was the Brief "Dominus ac redemptor," which followed largely the plan shown by Moñino to the Pontiff. Indeed its authorship was largely the Spanish envoy's; for he had not only sketched the outline, but furnished the facts and provisions and even directed the writing of the text. Zelada's part was largely that of a secretary. Clement XIV gave to the document little more than his authority. It was signed by the Pope on June 8, although officially dated July 21.

In the meantime during the period of the Brief's composition, while it was being cast into shape, amended and submitted to the approval of the

---

[29] Pastor, *Geschichte der Päpste*, Vol. XVI, part II, p. 174.

Courts, the campaign "necessary to destroy the feeling in favor of the Jesuits," was not being omitted. The Archbishop of Bologna, Cardinal Malvezzi, on February 10 was commissioned by a Brief to institute a visitation of the Jesuit houses in his diocese and was empowered by the same document to secularize any member of the order who might request such a favor. The visitation was carried out in the following month in a ruthless fashion.[30] Cardinal Malvezzi called the superiors of the various houses together and ordered them to cease from all spiritual ministries and to shut up their churches, to stop all educational work and send the pupils home, to dismiss all the novices and scholastics. No accusation whatever was announced to them; nor were they offered any explanations for such extraordinary commands. On one point only did the Jesuits hesitate, that was the nullification of the vows of the scholastics; only the Pope, or one delegated by him with such authority, could grant the dispensations. The chief superior, Belgrado, as in duty bound, respectfully requested the Cardinal to show him the Brief granting this power. When the superior, after the Cardinal's refusal, persisted in the plea that he was unable otherwise to dismiss the scholastics, he was imprisoned on the charge of contumacy. Then Cardinal Malvezzi himself undertook to dismiss the young religious, having first forcibly divested them of their Jesuit garb.[31]

Before the official promulgation of the Brief, it was deemed necessary to impart its contents to the various princes to ascertain their reactions. This was done by Charles III, who for his part considered the Brief as "according to the principles of justice and equity." The approval of the King of Naples and of the Queen-Regent of Naples came as a matter of course. The French monarch replied with such affected indifference that the Spanish Court was quite exasperated; Louis XV simply transmitted the contents, merely declaring that he "was delighted to hear that (his Catholic Majesty) was satisfied" and he felt confident that "the Brief sent would restore to the dominions of your Majesty the tranquillity which I desire for them no less than does your Majesty." The Empress Maria Theresa in her answer wrote that, though she had no cause of complaint against the Jesuits in her dominions, if the Pope thought that it was for the benefit of the Catholic religion to suppress them, she would place no obstacle in his way. She made however the declaration that she would never consent that the Pope should deprive her of the power of disposing of the persons and the property of the Jesuits who were her subjects.

Clement XIV still strove desperately to postpone the ultimate action. Only after sharp remonstrance from Moñino could he be brought to sign

---

[30] Pastor, *Geschichte der Päpste*, Vol. XVI, part II, pp. 195–201.
[31] Pastor, *Geschichte der Päpste*, Vol. XVI, part II, p. 200.

the Brief, June 8; [32] even then he would not leave the document out of his hands and kept insisting on the necessity of preliminaries being completed. To preserve the property and the archives of the Society from destruction or removal, on June 25 he ordered Mgr. Alfani to affix the Papal seal on the archives of the novitiate at Rome, urging also the various legates in the Papal States to do the same in the Jesuit houses within their jurisdictions. When Moñino again pressed for action, the Pontiff promised to issue a Brief establishing a commission for carrying out the suppression. Another month, however, was to pass before the five Cardinals of the commission, Marefoschi, Casali, Zelada, Corsini and Caraffa, were officially notified of their appointment. All through July the Pontiff still held out on one plea or another: before the 12th it was the necessity of finding out what properties the Society actually possessed; before the 21st it was the propriety of allowing the Jesuits to celebrate together for the last time the feast of St. Ignatius, and the expediency of not interrupting the studies of their colleges before the end of the school term; before the 28th it was the necessity of getting the Brief printed and of informing the Empress that the alterations on which she had insisted had been made. Moñino once more intervened with a sharp remonstrance which obtained on July 29 the printed copies of the Brief, dated for August 16. These copies were at once sent to the courts of Madrid, Versailles, Naples, Lisbon and Vienna. All that remained now was the official promulgation, for which the special commission of the five Cardinals held their first meeting, August 9. To secure secrecy there was adopted a regulation to publish the Brief separately in each house of the Society throughout the world and not in the usual way, "urbi et orbi," a regulation which later on led to unexpected results. Also, contrary to the established custom, when the Brief was published, it was neither solemnly proclaimed in the Campo dei Fiori nor affixed to the gates of the Vatican.

The contents of the Brief of Suppression, "Dominus ac redemptor," because of the limitation of space, can be indicated only briefly here.[33] In the opening paragraphs the motive of the Pope's action is indicated, the restoration of peace and tranquillity in the Church, even if for the sake of this it be necessary to destroy things most dear to him. Then follows the statement that the Holy See in the past has reformed and suppressed religious orders which no longer answered their purpose, and an array of precedents are cited. After this the case of the Society of Jesus is examined. The many complaints against it are cited: the controversies among the members themselves, with other religious orders, with the

---

[32] Smith, "The Suppression," *The Month*, Vol. CI, p. 401 and note 4.

[33] *The Month* for July 1903, Vol. CII, pp. 46–63 contains a complete examination of the contents of the Brief. There is also a summary in Pastor, *Geschichte der Päpste*, Vol. XVI, part II, pp. 210–212.

secular priests, with theological schools, and with the Bishops; the charges of amassing wealth, of mixing in worldly affairs, of tolerating heathenish practices in the missions. The actions of former Popes, before whom these complaints had been laid, in endeavoring to adjudicate them are then instanced. Finally, it is asserted that the unrest in regard to the order had risen to such heights that the Kings of France, Spain, Portugal and Sicily banished the Jesuits from their realms and petitioned the Popes for the suppression of the Society. Clement XIV then declares that after mature reflexion he has come to the conviction that the Society could no longer bring forth the rich fruit for which it had been founded and that by its continuance a true and lasting peace in the Church could scarcely exist. Therefore, and for reasons which he kept secret in his heart, in virtue of the plenitude of apostolic power, he suppressed the Society of Jesus completely. In consequence the members of the order, whom he loved with a paternal love, would be freed from all oppressive controversy, disquietness and anguish and could labor in the vineyard with richer fruit. The actual decree of suppression and the various provisions for carrying out and regulating its consequences follow and complete the document.

The regulations disposing of the members of the order are of special interest. The scholastics were permitted to remain in houses of the extinct order for the space of not more than a year; having been released from their vows, they were free to embrace any state of life they might choose. All the priests were given the option of joining another religious order or the secular clergy under the bishop in whose diocese they were residing; their maintenance was to be drawn either from benefices which they were enabled to receive or from the revenues of the houses of the Society in which they dwelt. In the case of those of the professed for whom such maintenance could not be found, who had no place to go, or who were enfeebled from sickness and infirmities, license was granted for their living together in some house of the former Society, but under the government of a secular priest and not wearing the garb of the Jesuits. Bishops, if they so wished, might employ the ex-Jesuits in preaching and hearing confessions, with the exception of those who still lived in the houses of the old Society. The ex-Jesuits might engage in teaching in schools and colleges, providing they gave no offense by their opinions. The Pope reserved for himself the future administration of the foreign missions of the fathers. It may be asked why the Society of Jesus was suppressed by a simple Brief and not by a solemn Bull. Some have suggested that a Brief was used because it could be more easily recalled; others are of the opinion that since so few could be taken into confidence in the fashioning of the document, owing to the opposition of a large number of the Cardinals, a Brief was the easier to compose.

With its long list of allegations against the Society, there is no denying that the tone of the Brief is very adverse to the Jesuits. Yet the document does not condemn the Constitutions and Rules of the order; neither does it lay any blame on the personal conduct of the members; nor does it impugn the orthodoxy of their doctrines.[34] The numerous charges are cited categorically; but there is no definite statement that they had been proved. One looks in vain for the vigorous and direct language which former Popes used in the suppression of the Humiliati and of other orders. The purpose of the long citation of allegations seems to have been to represent the order as the source of perpetual strife, contradiction and trouble and therefore to indicate that its suppression was necessary for the sake of peace. It is most important to note that it was not a judicial sentence based on a judicial inquiry but purely an administrative measure of Clement XIV. Cordara, the Jesuit historian and a contemporary of Clement XIV, has very wisely observed: "I think that we should not condemn the Pontiff who, after so many hesitations, has judged it his duty to suppress the Society of Jesus. I love my order as much as any man, yet had I been in the Pope's place, I should probably have acted as he did. The Company, founded and maintained for the good of the Church, perished for the same good; it could not have ended more gloriously." [35] In the similar sentiments of St. Alphonsus Liguori all Jesuits concur: "Poor Pope, what could he do in the circumstances in which he was placed, with all the sovereigns conspiring to demand the suppression. As for ourselves, we must keep silent, respect the secret judgment of God and hold ourselves in peace." [36]

The fatal August 16 came at last, and in the evening agents of the commission, accompanied by detachments of troops and police, occupied the various Jesuit houses in Rome.[37] Mgr. Macedonio at the Gesu, where the General resided, treated the fathers with unwarranted harshness and indignity; the beds were dragged out into the corridors, and there the priests were forced to spend the night, each one guarded by a soldier, Father Ricci by eight. All night long the house was ransacked from top to bottom, the sacristy, the library, the living rooms, then the cellar. There had been stories abroad about the vast wealth drawn from the missions and concealed in this, the chief house of the order. All that was

---

[34] On the question of the guilt of the order cf. Pastor, *Geschichte der Päpste*, Vol. XVI, part II, p. 213; Cordara, *De suppressione Societatis Jesu Commentarii*, edited by Albertotti, Padua (1923–1925); Smith, *The Month*, Vol. CII, pp. 171 ff.; Duhr, *Jesuiten Fabeln*, passim.

[35] Cordara, *De suppressione Societatis Jesu Commentarii.*

[36] Smith, "The Suppression," *The Month*, Vol. CI, p. 516.

[37] For details of the carrying out of the Suppression: Pastor, *Geschichte der Päpste*, Vol. XVI, part II, pp. 227–275; de Ravignan, *Clément XIII et Clément XIV*, Vol. II (2nd ed.), pp. 477–482; Theiner, *Histoire du pontificat de Clément XIV*, Vol. II, pp. 338–340; Smith, "The Suppression," *The Month*, Vol. CI, pp. 498–517, 604–623.

found however was 40,000 scudi, most of which had been accumulated for the expenses of certain canonizations. This was seized; and all the papers, account-books and correspondence in the archives were placed under seal.

In the morning when the Father General and all the community were assembled together, the entire text of the Brief "Dominus ac redemptor" was read to them. When the reader had ceased, the venerable superior bowing his head protested that he and his brethren accepted their destruction and stood ready to obey, entirely and respectfully, the command of the Holy Father. In the evening of the same day Cardinal Corsini, one of the commission, sent his carriage to the Gesu with an apparently friendly invitation for Father Ricci to seek refuge in the English College. He accepted only to find on his arrival at the College that he was to be virtually a prisoner, forbidden to hold communication with anyone but the brother who was confined with him. A month later, on September 23, he was transferred to the Castel Sant' Angelo, where he was to be kept a close prisoner until his death.[38] In this fortress too were imprisoned the five Assistants, Gorgo (Italy), de Montes (Spain), de Gusman (Portugal), Rhomberg (Germany), Koricki (Poland), Camolli, the Secretary General, and a few other important fathers. The Jesuits remaining at the Gesu and the other Roman houses were after eight days dismissed, to face the world with the yet unfulfilled promise of twenty crowns. Even for the scanty pittance which was to be distributed periodically to these priests, for whose innocence even their enemies had borne testimony, each applicant had to bring an attestation of good conduct from the curé of the parish in which he resided. For a time they were condemned to an objectless existence by the decree of the commission, forbidding bishops to grant them faculties for preaching and hearing confessions until they had obtained the permission of the Holy See. Such a decree was contrary to the provisions of the Brief of Suppression.

The commission forwarded the Brief to the nuncios and bishops throughout the world with directions to publish it in each house of the order in their jurisdictions and to take possession of all goods of the Society in the name of the Holy See. The extinction of the order in the Papal States was carried out on the whole with the same harshness as at Rome. In Portugal Pombal ordered festive celebrations, the ringing of bells and the firing of cannon to hail the news of the Jesuits' destruction. Because it was not a solemn Bull, the Brief received a grudging reception at the Courts of Spain and Naples. Charles III himself considered the document too lenient since it condemned neither the doctrine, the morals, nor the discipline of the Jesuits. The publication of the Brief was for-

---

[38] De Ravignan, *Clément XIII et Clément XIV*, Vol. II, pp. 482–484.

bidden in Spain, Naples and France. In other lands the Suppression was received with varying sentiments; scarcely anywhere was there the jubilation looked for by the anti-Jesuits. On the contrary, as Huber in his *Der Jesuiten-Orden* declares: "The news of the Suppression of the order, as was expected, was an unheard of sensation; among the clergy and the people, where the order had the greatest sympathy, were very many disapprovals and bitter censures." Several of the French Bishops omitted to publish the Brief. The magistrates in many cities, such as Lucerne, Fribourg and Solothurn, besought the bishops not to make the promulgation and would not allow the fathers to relinquish their schools. In Germany and in Austria the document was soon published. The Empress Maria Theresa in a letter to her cabinet secretary praised the members of the order, and in one to a personal friend paid them this glowing tribute: "I have been inconsolable because of the Jesuits and in despair. All my life I have loved and esteemed them and have seen nothing but what was edifying in them." In her domains the ex-Jesuits were allowed to continue to live in their houses as secular priests. In Augsburg the fathers conducted their *Gymnasium* until 1807. The properties of the Bavarian Jesuits were taken over for a newly erected branch of the Knights of Malta; as a result the priests suffered much from want and from a lack of shelter, although the charity of the Bavarian townspeople and country-folk tried to meet their more essential needs. The rulers of Prussia and Russia positively forbade the publication of the Brief.

With the Society of Jesus suppressed, its enemies now strove to justify their charges by the conviction of the General and his Assistants. If the individual members were of good life, then it was vital to establish the guilt of the superiors of the order. Otherwise the case against them would collapse completely. With this in view the anti-Jesuits bent their efforts to keep Father Ricci a perpetual prisoner in the Castel Sant' Angelo. The treatment meted out to this venerable old priest, who was over eighty, was truly outrageous.[39] His food was always served to him cold and, despite his years, no fire, not even in the dead of winter, was permitted in his prison room. He was deprived of all materials for writing and of all books for reading. At all times a sentinel stood guard before his door, while neither with this soldier nor with anyone else was he allowed to exchange a word. Even worse was the lot of the Assistants in the dark, damp and rat-infested cells in which they were confined. All such treatment was in flat contradiction of the provisions of the Brief of Suppression which enjoined a paternal care for every member of the extinct Society without distinction. It is most certain that Clement XIV

---

[39] Smith, "The Suppression," *The Month*, Vol. CI, pp. 509–510.

knew nothing of the cruel fate of these priests; his isolation and his sickness kept from him the true state of affairs.

The trial-procedures then in vogue called for (1) collection and investigation of evidence; (2) interrogatories of the accused on the basis of such evidence and the recording of his answers; (3) prompt completion of the procès with the pronouncement of innocence and release or the presentation of the guilty one to his judges. Since the commission had full possession of the archives and records of the General's office and, very probably, other documentary material besides, the members had every opportunity to make out a most damaging case against the Jesuits, if such a case did exist.

In the interrogatories [40] Ricci was questioned on three points: alleged attempts to maintain the Society's existence in spite of the Brief of Suppression, alleged concealment of vast sums of money, and the state of the order under his generalship. In support of the first interrogatories it was said that Ricci had appointed a Vicar-General, had granted faculties to the Sicilian Jesuits, had urged the Spanish Jesuits to refuse secularization, and had written to the King of Prussia begging him to maintain the Jesuits in his territories. In answer the former General was able to show: that the appointment of a Vicar-General was a routine practice made in the beginning of every generalate, and was done secretly without the knowledge of the appointee; that he (the General) had destroyed the packet containing the name when the Society was about to be suppressed; that the faculties of the Sicilian Jesuits were granted at the time of their civil suppression and were for the extension of their choice of confessors and for the use of money for their support; that the advice to the Spanish Jesuits related to the time of their civil suppression and was an exhortation to them to remain faithful to the Society then still existing; that the letter in question to Frederick the Great was not his but an unauthorized epistle of a Viennese Jesuit, and that any other letters to that monarch were requests for his aid in certain serious law suits in which the Silesian fathers were involved.

In support of the second interrogatories the General was told that the Jesuits were believed to have hidden fifty million scudi and also to have sent money out of Rome. In answer to these rumors he was able to show: that nothing was hidden in secret vaults; that very little money was sent to Rome, only what was required for the support of the General

---

[40] De Ravignan, *Clément XIII et Clément XIV*, Vol. I, pp. 467–470, "Extraites de pièces à charge concernant l'abbé Ricci, ex-Général des jésuites"; *ibid.*, Vol. II, pp. 484–497, "Procès fait au P. Laurent Ricci, ex-Général des jésuites, d'après l'original écrit par le Père Ricci lui-même (Traduit de l'italien)"; Pastor, *Geschichte der Päpste*, Vol. XVI, part II, pp. 239–243; Smith, "The Suppression," *The Month*, Vol. CI, pp. 613 ff.

and his curia and for the common expenses of the whole order; that as a matter of actual fact the Society was so poor that in order to support the exiled Portuguese fathers he had to petition Clement XIII for the permission to sell churchplate belonging to the order; that an examination of the Society's account books would reveal the financial straits of the Jesuits of the suppressed provinces; finally that the money sent out of Rome had been certain sums dispatched to Venice to be forwarded to the particular foreign missions to which they belonged, and that the totals of the amounts could be found in the books of the Procurator-General.

In regard to the third interrogatory, when he was asked what defects existed in the order during his rule, Ricci made his noteworthy reply: "None, by the mercy of God, which were in any way common; and that, on the contrary, there had been exhibited much regularity, much piety, much zeal, and in particular, much union and charity"; and that "there had, of course, been those occasional defects in individuals which would never be wanting whilst human nature remained what it is, but that these had been met by the proper remedies." [41] In conclusion he was asked if he believed that he still retained any authority over the Society now suppressed, and what authority would he imagine himself to possess if the Pope had merely altered the Constitutions. To the first, he answered that now he had no authority whatsoever; to the second, whatever powers His Holiness would have granted to him.

These interrogatories ended in the middle of January 1774. So trivial had been the questions addressed to him that the former General expected a prompt release. As the days passed by and no dismissal was in sight, he made the request that at least he be informed of the accusations against him and that he be brought to trial. The commission merely vouchsafed the reply that the matter should be attended to. Even this was not done. The interrogatories of the Assistants were briefer and even more trivial than those of their former superior. Comolli, the Secretary, was asked about the existence of secret treasury vaults; he knew of none. De Gusman, who was seventy-eight and bed-ridden, apparently was not asked any questions. De Montes, who was over ninety, was told he was under arrest not for any charge but only that his person might be secured. Koricki may not have been questioned, the fact is not known. Rhomberg, whom Ricci had named in petto as his Vicar-General, was asked if he knew of his appointment (he did not), and was also assured that he was not accused of anything and probably would soon be released. Gorgo was examined principally on the support and employment of the Spanish and Portuguese exiled Jesuits. Months passed on in which not a step was taken either to dismiss the prisoners or to complete the procès. The evi-

---

[41] Response to Interrogation 15, Ricci's procès, cf. de Ravignan, *Clément XIII et Clément XIV*, Vol. II, pp. 489–490.

dent purpose of the commission and of Moñino, now Count Florida Blanca, who dominated it, was to keep the victims in perpetual imprisonment. If the ex-Jesuit superiors could not be convicted of grave crimes, at least by keeping the procès indefinitely pending, the impression would gain currency that it had been completed and had gone against them.[42] At the death of Clement XIV, more than a year had elapsed since the Suppression, more than eight months since the termination of the interrogatories, and more than six months since Ricci had asked for his release.

Clement XIV died September 22, 1774, worn out with sickness and trials. In the thirteen months from the Suppression he had suffered almost continually from grave physical ills and deep depression of spirits. At times he seemed to be crushed under the weight of his sorrows, realizing only too keenly that his sacrifice of the Jesuits had brought little peace to the Church. The anti-Jesuits continued to press him right to the end; the Cardinals of that party besought him to name to the purple certain prelates of their faction, whom he was known to have reserved in petto. The dying Pontiff refused; he would not thus strengthen their hands in the coming conclave. Indeed it was rumored at the time that he had composed a Brief, recalling the Brief "Dominus ac redemptor," and had entrusted this second Brief to his confessor who was to give it to the succeeding Pope. Such an action is mentioned in the ex-Jesuit Wolf's *Allgemeine Geschichte der Jesuiten*, published at Zurich in 1789. The report was never contradicted by Pius VI. Still the existence of such a document has never been proved and it must be treated at the most as a possibility. The quick decomposition of the body of the late Pope afforded an opportunity for the spreading of a rumor that the Jesuits had poisoned Clement XIV. Such a calumny would have been circulated anyway, no matter what were the circumstances of the Pontiff's decease. The report of an official autopsy, made in the presence of several witnesses, *Relazione medica contro il presto veleno del Papa Clemente XIV, Nov. 12, 1774,* proves beyond doubt that the death came in the natural course of the Pope's disease. Such also was the testimony of the Pope's confessor and of many contemporaries; and it has been accepted by all the leading historians of the subject, Walch, Scholl, Lafuente, Theiner, Masson and Reumont.[43]

The new Pontiff, Pius VI, would have restored the Society of Jesus at once, if the circumstances had permitted it; but the Bourbon Courts were still too strong to permit any consideration of the project. Pius VI therefore turned his efforts to relieving the hard lot of the ex-Jesuit prisoners in the Castel Sant' Angelo and to bringing the procès against

---

[42] Smith, "The Suppression," *The Month*, Vol. CI, p. 515.

[43] Duhr, *Jesuiten-Fabeln*, pp. 62 ff.; Pastor, *Geschichte der Päpste*, Vol. XVI, part II, pp. 386–390.

them to a quick conclusion. The bitter anti-Jesuits, Macedonio and Alfani, were dismissed from the commission, and the remaining members and their assistants were ordered to complete the investigation with the promptest dispatch. At the end of April all the papers were placed in the hands of Florida Blanca for his examination and report. It would seem that Pius VI wanted to force the ruthless Spaniard into an admission of the complete lack of evidence for his allegations. The ambassador's reply at least accomplished just that, for his vague charges and conciliatory statements only too clearly revealed his bankruptcy of facts. That he did not prove his case is the opinion of the Spanish historian Manrique, the author of the *Historia Imparcial de la legislation española* and, incidentally, one who strongly approved of the expulsion of the Spanish Jesuits. In a *supplicia* written in August 1775, Ricci complained to the new Pope of the injustice of his imprisonment and the rigor of his treatment. Pius VI again insisted on the speedy termination of the procès and took what measure he could to ease the hardships of the former General's confinement. It must be remembered that the ambassadors of the Courts kept declaring that the honor of their sovereigns demanded the detention of the prisoners.

When it became evident to Florida Blanca that despite all his efforts his victims were soon to be released, he hurried to the Pope to insist that the ex-General and the ex-Assistants be forbidden to meet together after their release, or to communicate with each other, or to talk about the Suppression; that they be placed under an oath of secrecy; that they be interned in separate localities and be kept under perpetual surveillance. His anxiety over Father Ricci was wasted, for on November 24, 1775 death brought an end to the long and bitter trials of the last General of the old Society.

Five days before his death Father Ricci called for Holy Viaticum and, while the ministering priest held up the Blessed Sacrament before him, read to the Vice-Governor of the Castel Sant' Angelo and to several other witnesses a solemn protestation of the innocence of the Society of Jesus. This truly moving document in part reads: "Believing that the time has now come when I must stand before the tribunal of infallible truth and justice—for such is the tribunal of God—after having long and maturely reflected, and after having humbly begged my merciful Redeemer and terrible Judge not to let me be swayed by passion, or bitterness of spirit, or of any unholy affection or object—solely because I judge it my duty to render justice to truth and innocence, I make these two declarations and protestations. 1. I declare and protest that the suppressed Society of Jesuits gave no grounds whatever for its suppression. I declare and protest this with the moral certainty that a superior can have who was well informed as to the state of his order. 2. I declare and protest that I have given no grounds whatever, not even the slightest, for my imprisonment. I declare and protest this with the absolute certainty and evidence which each man has concerning his own actions. And I make this second protestation solely because it is required to vindicate the good name of the suppressed Society of Jesus, of which I was the Superior-General." [44] The dying priest then finished with a statement imputing blame to no one of the authors of the Suppression and pardoning all who had wrought the ruin of himself and his brethren.

Pius VI was very much afflicted by the death of Father Ricci, especially since the end had come before his vindication. He sent the dying priest his blessing. Further Pius VI ordered the most solemn obsequies in the Church of St. John of the Florentines, where the body of the ex-General was placed in state, and its transference with the highest honors to the Gesù for burial in the vault reserved for the Generals of the order. Lorenzo Ricci was a man of spotless life, of wide culture, of solid piety, a beautiful, noble soul whose share of the Cross in trials and sorrows was such as few men are called to bear.[45]

---

[44] Smith, "The Suppression," *The Month*, Vol. CI, p. 622.

[45] Carayon, *Le Père Ricci et la suppression de la Compagnie de Jésus*, Paris (1869) (Documents inédits); for an appreciation of Ricci's character cf. Miguelez, O.S.F., *Jansenisme en España*, p. 301.

CHAPTER XIV

INTERIM AND RESTORATION

With the Suppression of the order the question naturally arises, what was the fate of the 23,000 ex-Jesuits? The priests among them, almost entirely, were received into the ranks of the diocesan clergy; in Austria and in Germany they were even permitted to live and teach in their old colleges but under the superiorship of secular priests. A comprehensive statement about the non-priests would be difficult to make, although it may be supposed as more than likely that a great number of them continued in their sacerdotal studies. For all, the first years were extremely hard, despite the almost universal sympathy and kindness of their fellow-priests, secular and regular, and of the devout Catholic laity everywhere. Their world had collapsed all about them, their cherished brotherhood was broken and dispersed, and their mother, for so they looked upon the Society which had nurtured and trained them, was dead. Their discouragement and sorrowful dismay has been well described by Father John Carroll, a professed father of the old Society and later the first Bishop of Baltimore, patriarch of Catholicism in the United States, in a letter written from Bruges to his brother in Maryland: "I am not, and perhaps never shall be, recovered from the shock of this dreadful intelligence. The greatest blessing which in my estimation I could receive from God, would be immediate death; but if He deny me this, may His holy and adorable designs on me be wholly fulfilled." [1]

Even more eloquent of the sorrow of the average Jesuit is the letter of a simple missionary, Father Mosely, written from his lonely and remote mission station on the Eastern Shore of Maryland to his sister in England.[2] Though a bit lengthy it will repay insertion.

Maryland, 3rd of Oct. 1774.

. . . Yes, Dear Sister, I had heard before I wrote to you that our total Dissolution was much dreaded by us, yet it was not executed even at Rome when I wrote to you in July. It was little to the purpose to mention it to you, as I imagined you was an entire stranger to the cause; and to let you into it would only give you Trouble to learn how we have been used: and now I mention it, I can't do it without tears in my eyes. Yes, Dear Sister, our Body or Factory is dissolved, of which your two

---

[1] J. G. Shea, *Life and Times of Archbishop John Carroll*, N.Y. (1888), p. 39.
[2] *Woodstock Letters*, Vol. XXXIII, p. 376.

brothers are members, and for myself I know I am an unworthy one, when I see so many worthy, saintly, pious, learned, laborious Miss . . . s dead and alive been members of the same, thro' the last two ages. I know no fault that we are guilty of. I am convinced that our labours are pure, upright and sincere, for God's honour and our Neighbour's Good. What our Supreme Judge on Earth may think of our Labours is a Mystery to me. He has hurt his own cause, not us. It's true he has stigmatized us through the World with Infamy, and declared us unfit for our Business, or his service. Our dissolution is known thro' the world; it's in every Newspaper, which makes me ashamed to show my face. Ah, I can say now, what I never before thought of: I am willing now to retire and quit my Post, as I believe most of my Brethren are. A retired private life would suit me best, where I could attend only to myself, after 17 years Dissipation in this Harvest. As we're judged unserviceable, we labour with little heart, and, what is worse, by no Rule. To my great sorrow, the Society is abolished; with it must die all that zeal that was founded and raised on it. Labour for Neighbour is a Jesuit's pleasure; destroy the Jesuit, and labour is painful and disagreeable. I must allow with Truth, that what was my pleasure is now irksome; every fatigue I underwent caused a secret and inward satisfaction; it's now unpleasant and disagreeable; every visit to the Sick was done with a good will, it's now done with as bad a one. I disregarded this unhealthy climate, and all its Agues and Fevers, which have really paid me to my Heart's Content, for sake of my Rule, the Night was agreeable as the Day, Frost and Cold as a warm Fire or a soft bed, the excessive Heats as welcome as a cool Shade or pleasant Breezes— but now the scene is changed; the Jesuit is metamorphised into I know not what; he is a Monster, a Scare-Crow in my Ideas. With joy I impaired my health and broke my constitution in the care of my flock. It was the Jesuit's Call, it was his whole aim and business. The Jesuit is no more; he now endeavours to repair his little remains of Health and his shattered Constitution, as he has no Rule calling him to expose it. In me, the Jesuit and the Missioner was always combined together; if one falls, the other must of consequence fall with it. As the Jesuit is judged unfit by his H . . . ness for a Mission, I think that it is high time for me to retire to a private life, to spend the rest of my days in Peace and Quiet. I should be sorry to be quite inactive, and doing no good; but a small employ would now content my zeal. If I could hear of a vacant place in your neighbourhood for a Chaplain, if my mind don't change, and times don't alter, I believe I should accept it. . . . . While I was actuated with the old spirit, I could seek my Neighbour's good in any corner of the world, where I could procure it; but as now that noble Spirit is abolished by Authority, I don't care how soon I see my native soil, and leave my place to younger and healthier Hands, which I never would have designed, while I could stand or walk, could I have remained on the same footing. We are now like dispersed Sheep, or disbanded Soldiers; what man could live in such a confused distracted state, without some danger to himself? . . .

Yr ever affectionate and Loving Brother,

Jos. Mosley, S.J. . . . for ever, as I think, and hope.

The very human reactions of this good priest must be remembered in the light of the overwhelming disaster which had fallen upon him. His truly noble character was manifested by the fact that he did not return to the happy refuge of his native England, but remained faithful to his lonely distant mission in Talbot County, Maryland, until his death fourteen years later.

Several of the ex-Jesuits in Europe achieved notable success as preachers, Beauregard, Mazzarelli, Alexander and Lanfant, or as writers, de Feller, Zaccaria and Ximenes. In a previous chapter it was noted that many were chosen to be professors in seminaries, or vicars-general of dioceses, that 55 were raised to the episcopate, and that 23 out of 44 who were put to death in the French Revolution have been beatified.

In three countries, France, Prussia and Russia, definite efforts were made to save the Society from the effects of the Brief of Suppression. It need hardly be added that these measures did not come from the Jesuits themselves. In France, Madame Louise de France, a Carmelite nun, the saintly daughter of Louis XV, worked out a scheme for the re-establishment of the French Jesuits in six provinces under the jurisdiction of the French hierarchy.[3] The plan was defeated by Cardinal de Bernis who obtained a new Brief requesting him to see to it that each French bishop in his own diocese carried out the Brief "Dominus ac redemptor."

Frederick II [4] actually forbade the publication of the Brief of Suppression in his dominions. As early as three years before the destruction of the order, on two occasions, June 6 and September 9, 1770, he had his representative inform Clement XIV that he wished the Jesuits in his lands not included in any suppression of the order. When that event actually came about, Frederick II through his minister Carmer on August 30, 1773 announced to the Jesuit Provincial in Silesia that he intended to conserve the Society in the dominions under his rule. A week later, September 6, the governments of Silesia, East Prussia, West Prussia and Cleves, all received instructions ordering them to prevent the proclamation of the Brief. When the Auxiliary-Bishop Strachwitz of Breslau sent the Prussian Monarch a copy of the Brief with a request for the requisite permission to publish it, the document was returned to him with the comment that the King had already declared by word of mouth that the Brief was not to be promulgated nor carried out in his dominions. What could have motivated Frederick the Great, a Protestant, indeed a freethinker, to take such a course? Principally it was his determination not to lose the services of the teachers whom he considered the best and most willing in all the lands under his scepter; the various Jesuit colleges and their University of Breslau occupied a most important position in the secondary and higher

---

[3] Smith, "The Suppression," *The Month*, Vol. CI, p. 513.

[4] For Frederick II and the ex-Jesuits cf. Duhr, *Geschichte*, Vol. IV, part I, p. 402 ff.; Witte, *Friedrich d. Gr. und die Jesuiten* (1892); Kratz, "Ungedruckte Briefe Friedrichs des Grossen," *Archiv. Hist. S.J.*, Vol. I, pp. 281–291; Pastor, *Geschichte der Päpste*, Vol. XVI, part III, pp. 130–150.

education of the Silesian and Prussian Catholics. Frederick II was wont to consider that the furtherance of education was his life's chief goal.

For a while the Prussian King even thought of forming and maintaining a union of the Jesuits, not only in Silesia, East and West Prussia, and Cleves, but those also in the Palatinate, Holland and England. Affairs came to a crisis, when Bishop Strachwitz, desiring to obey the Pope, refused to ordain the Jesuit scholastics and sought further to prevent the spiritual labors of the fathers. Frederick II turned to immediate negotiations with Pius VI. The result was that the Pope verbally approved of the motives of the King in retaining such excellent educators for his Silesian subjects and advised the Prussian Bishops to accommodate themselves to his wishes; but the Pontiff also provided that the Jesuits were to use their powers, not as members of a religious order, but only as individuals and under the jurisdiction of the bishops. Frederick II declared himself content with the decision, which made certain the Suppression of the Jesuits in Silesia and Prussia but gave him the use of their services as teachers, living and working together in their old colleges. By the order of Frederick II they were to be known as "Priests of the Royal Schools Institute." As long as this monarch lived the ex-Jesuits enjoyed his royal protection; but with the advent of Frederick William II to a large extent this favor ceased. Nevertheless they retained the possession of their schools and of the University of Breslau even into the nineteenth century, all the time however working as secular priests and never at any time being permitted to accept novices.

In Russia no promulgation of the Brief "Dominus ac redemptor" was ever allowed. The result was truly remarkable in that the Society of Jesus never wholly ceased to exist but lived on in the small remnant in White Russia and Lithuania, until forty years later when Pius VII solemnly restored the order throughout the whole world.[5] The existence of this small, remote fraction of the Society for a long time was most precarious, only the adverse circumstances of the times preventing its annihilation in the first ten years. Then by a verbal approbation Pius VI protected its life for the next two decades until 1801, when its status in Russia was officially and explicitly guaranteed by a Brief of Pius VII.

Shortly after the issuance of the Brief of Suppression in 1773 the Tsarina Catherine of Russia forbade its publication in all her dominions, a prohibition affecting largely those parts of Poland which she had obtained through the Partition of 1772. In those regions there labored 201 Jesuits, of whom 96 were priests, maintaining 4 colleges, at Polotsk, Vitebsk, Orscha and Dünaburg, 2 residences at Mohilew and Mscislaw and 14 mission stations. They constituted the Society of Jesus which never

[5] Zalenski, *Les Jésuites de la Russie-Blanche*, translated from the Polish by Vivier, 2 Vols., Paris (1888); Pastor, *Geschichte der Päpste*, Vol. XVI, part III, pp. 150–238.

ceased to exist. The superior was the rector of the college at Polotsk, Stanislaus Czerniewicz.[6] He had been informed by the last Provincial of Masovia, to whose jurisdiction White Russia belonged, that in case the legal existence of the Society was continued—owing to the action of the Empress—he was to be the superior of all the Jesuits there and that since he was the rector of a Collegium Maximum, he was to possess the rights and privileges of a Vice-Provincial.

Before the Suppression even Catherine had come to esteem the Jesuits of White Russia because of their work in education; in 1772 when Czerniewicz petitioned for the recognition of the Jesuits, she responded by revoking the decree of banishment against them issued by Peter the Great in 1719. Her confidence was increased by the fact that the Jesuits remained at their posts when the Bishop of Polotsk and many of the Cathedral clergy left the city and went to Poland as a protest against Russian rule. It was further augmented when the rector of Polotsk in his own name and in that of his brethren declared their submission to the new government. The Brief of Suppression, then, found the Empress favorable to the Society of Jesus for several reasons, of which the principal one was their educational services. She now determined to oppose the Suppression of the Jesuits to prevent not only the grave disaster to learning in her Catholic dominions, which would follow on the closing of their colleges, but also to save for all her lands the abilities of these teachers through whom she was planning to elevate the whole system of Russian education.

When the news of the Russian Tsarina's action got abroad, the Nuncio at Warsaw addressed to her the strongest representation urging her to recall her prohibition. His efforts met with no success. In fact on September 19, 1773 in view of the realities of the situation, the Apostolic Delegate for Russia, Bishop Ignatius Massalski of Wilna, ordered all the superiors of the Jesuit houses in virtue of holy obedience to provide that no member was to leave the order's houses nor withdraw from the customary work until he (the Bishop of Wilna) had proceeded to the publication and the carrying out of the Brief of Suppression.[7] This final step he never took, nor did his successor, Stanislaus Siestrzencewicz, the Archbishop of Mohilew. The Jesuits themselves sent a petition to the Empress requesting her to allow the carrying out of the Brief "Dominus ac redemptor"; towards the end of 1773 Czerniewicz, accompanied by two fathers, Lienkiewicz and Katerbring, journeyed to St. Petersburg to present this petition.[8] Catherine refused their plea definitely, declaring to the three Jesuits that her wish was to employ the order for the spread-

---

[6] Koch, "Czerniewicz," *Jesuiten-Lexikon.*

[7] Text of document in Zalenski, *Les Jésuites de la Russie-Blanche,* Document J, Vol. I, p. 451.

[8] Pastor, *Geschichte der Päpste,* Vol. XVI, part III, pp. 155–156.

ing of culture through the Russian territories. There was then nothing left for the Jesuits to do but to carry on as heretofore. Their position was perfectly legal; they could not be affected by a document which for them had never been promulgated. Far different would it have been if the Brief "Dominus ac redemptor" had been published at Rome, "urbi et orbi," with the customary formalities; then there would have been no course left for them but to dissolve themselves. But in the place of the ordinary forms, the Brief had substituted promulgation by the various bishops in the houses of the Society standing in their jurisdictions. The White Russian Jesuits were bound to await the action of their local bishop. And any other course would have been uncanonical, unauthorized, and pregnant with grave disaster to the general welfare of the Catholic Church in those regions, by very reason of the dispersal of the largest body of active priests.

Thus did the old Society live on in this small fraction; although its existence for some years was perilously uncertain. The Nuncio at Warsaw, Archetti, offered many an obstacle to its continuance; as an example there might be cited his forbidding the ordination of the Jesuit scholastics to the priesthood. The Vice-Provincial Czerniewicz had asked the Archbishop of Mohilew to confer the priesthood on twenty young Jesuits; the prelate, hesitating as to what course ought to be taken, sought information from the Nuncio. When after a long delay no answer was forthcoming, the Archbishop decided to ordain the candidates, and did so in November 1776. Shortly afterwards a letter arrived from Warsaw instructing the Archbishop not to bestow Holy Orders on the Jesuit scholastics and further informing him that he was to forbid the Jesuits spiritual employment. The matter was carried to Rome. When the possible evil results were considered, the Secretary of State, Cardinal Pallavicini, acquiesced in the Archbishop's action and even permitted further ordinations.[9]

This permission was highly significant. Yet it did not solve the dilemma which challenged the Russian Jesuits: was the Society of Jesus in White Russia merely existing until the death of its last member, or was it still in the possession of the powers of self-perpetuation of the Constitutions, the maintenance of a novitiate and the holding of General Congregations. An appeal to Rome was not easy and, owing to the still strong pressure of the Bourbon Courts, almost certainly would have brought an unfavorable reply. The Jesuits felt, with much justice, especially after the Pallavicini decision, that Pius VI was personally favorable to their existence. Furthermore was there any need for such an appeal? If, because

---

[9] Pastor, *Geschichte der Päpste*, Vol. XVI, part III, pp. 171–173. In note 1 on page 172 is the reply of the eminent canonist Monsagrati to Cardinal Pallavicini declaring the Jesuits in White Russia not refractory, because the Brief of Suppression had to be proclaimed in each house.

of the non-promulgation of the Brief "Dominus ac redemptor," their part of the Society had not been suppressed, then might they not argue that, at least in their regard, neither had its Constitutions been destroyed? In 1778 the Archbishop of Mohilew received from Pius VI complete powers over the religious orders in White Russia; on the strength of these powers and at the instance of the Empress Catherine, he granted permission to the Jesuits to erect a novitiate at Polotsk in 1780 [10] and to hold a General Congregation in the same city in 1782. [11] At this Congregation Czerniewicz was elected General; out of deference to certain claims of the Archbishop, the new superior contented himself with the lesser title of Perpetual Vicar-General.

The news of these two actions, when it got out to the rest of Europe, caused a sensation everywhere. The Bourbon Courts hastened to register angry protests with the Cardinal Secretary of State, with the result that Cardinal Pallavicini had to summon the Nuncio at Warsaw to demand the dissolution of the novitiate and to insist with Archbishop Siestrzencewicz on the recalling of his permission. Once again the intervention of the Empress Catherine saved the situation, a very desperate one as far as the remnant of the Jesuits was concerned. Not only did the Tsarina refuse to comply with the Nuncio's requests, even though he travelled to St. Petersburg to present them personally to her, but she sent her agent Benislawski to Rome to obtain from Pius VI an official sanction for all that had occurred with regard to the Jesuits in her dominions.

The Pope's position was truly difficult. The Bourbon Courts were watching jealously every development in the Russian survival; with them stood the "Sacristan Emperor," Joseph II, whose ecclesiastical meddlings were causing Pius VI many heartaches; and with them also were several officials of the Roman Curia who had profited by the downfall of the Jesuits. It was no wonder then that the Pontiff refused to meet the Empress Catherine's requests, at least openly. Yet Pius VI dreaded rejecting entirely the Tsarina's petition, for he feared her wrath might vent itself in the persecution of the Catholics of Russia; moreover for himself he dearly wished the Society's restoration. He agreed to receive the proposals but with the stipulation that the mission must be conducted with the strictest secrecy. When the course of the Russian Jesuits was placed before him, Pius VI gave it his verbal approval, thrice repeating the word, "Approbo." [12] That was all the harassed Pontiff could do at the

---

[10] Pastor, *Geschichte der Päpste*, Vol. XVI, part III, p. 178; Zalenski, *Les Jésuites de la Russie-Blanche*, Vol. I, p. 457, Document L (the appointment of Siestrzcencewicz as Apostolic Visitor of all religious orders in White Russia).

[11] Pastor, *Geschichte der Päpste*, Vol. XVI, part III, pp. 204, 205.

[12] Pastor, *Geschichte der Päpste*, Vol. XVI, part III, p. 210. Cf. also in note 2 on the same page (Written and sealed statement of Benislawski).

time; a written document was simply out of the question. On March 12, 1783 the answers were conveyed to Benislawski, who relayed them to the Empress and, later on, to the Jesuits. The Bourbon Courts were not to be outdone; whether or not they suspected any verbal commendation, they pressed Pius VI to issue a declaration, June 27, 1783, in which he protested that he had not revoked the Brief of Suppression and that he regarded as an abuse anything done against it, but that the Empress Catherine would not allow him to act freely. The statements did not cancel the answers given to Benislawski; for the answers merely declared that the position of the Russian Jesuits was not schismatical and that the Pope approved of their continuing in the way they had been going. In the circumstances this verbal approbation was sufficient to justify the fathers of White Russia in continuing not only their existence but in planning for their future development.

The first task which lay before the surviving Jesuits was the educational labor in their own schools and in cooperation with the Imperial authorities. What Catherine expected from the fathers in the first instance was a superior education for the Russian youth free from the spirit of French Philosophism, then the current fad in Europe. In the second instance both the Tsarina and her minister, Potemkin, desired a type of training in which great emphasis and abundant treatment would be given to mathematical and physical studies. One of the principal objectives of a three months' conference, in which Czerniewicz took part shortly after his election as Vicar-General, was educational reform. An important result was the establishment at the Polotsk college of a polytechnical institute for the training of teachers of science, under the direction of an eminent Jesuit scientist, Gabriel Gruber. In 1785 its first graduates were ready to begin their work, and before many years Gruber's school became the pride of Russia. In all this development, as in all the difficulties of the survival, the Vicar-General Czerniewicz directed the course of action patiently and prudently until his death on July 20, 1785. He left to his successor 6 colleges instead of 4 and 172 subjects of whom 95 were priests.

The Second General Congregation of the Russian Jesuits, meeting at Polotsk in September 9, 1785, elected Gabriel Lienkiewicz,[13] a Lithuanian, to the office of Perpetual Vicar-General. His years of office were marked by the first expansion of the surviving Society of Jesus. Requests for receptions poured in from all parts of Europe. Individual ex-Jesuits, overjoyed at the news that their beloved Society still existed, sought incorporation; but only to those who were able to come and live in White Russia could this boon be granted. A corporate group, the Society of the Most Sacred Heart, of which greater mention will be made later, made

---

[13] Koch, "Lienkiewicz," *Jesuiten-Lexikon*, col. 1093.

a plan for acceptance by the Russian Jesuits; for various reasons this common desire could not at the time be granted.

The most notable extension was the revival of the Society of Jesus in the Duchy of Parma.[14] The Duke Ferdinand, a Bourbon prince, while yet a minor under the dominance of a "Philosophical" regency and owing to the influence of Charles III of Spain, had participated in the Suppression of the Jesuits. But once Charles III had died and the power of Florida Blanca had waned, the young Duke, now of age, sought earnestly from Pius VI for permission to restore the order in his state. The Pope gladly gave his verbal consent to the prince's request and his approval also to the Vicar-General's sending three fathers from White Russia to Parma.[15] The province of Italy was erected and Misserati, one of the three Jesuits from Polotsk, was named as the first Provincial.

No one rejoiced more at this event than did the leader of the Spanish ex-Jesuit exiles, Bl. Joseph Pignatelli. Indeed even before the saintly priest had learned of the Duke of Parma's project, he had made application for reception by the Jesuits of White Russia; he had been accepted and was preparing to depart for Polotsk. This step he had not taken until personally he had asked Pius VI concerning the status of the Russian Jesuits and had received the answer from the Pontiff's own lips that the Russian Jesuits were truly Jesuits.[16] Yet even with the restoration of the order in Parma, two considerations forced Bl. Joseph Pignatelli to postpone his accession. One was the necessity of remaining in Naples to prevent the King's plan of organizing the Neapolitan ex-Jesuits into a band of secular priests under the sole jurisdiction of the Neapolitan bishops and of the King, but with the name "Society of Jesus." He was successful in his efforts. The second was the care of the Spanish ex-Jesuits in Italy. At the time, permission to return to their native land as individuals had been accorded them, a favor which Pignatelli rather mistrusted. His scepticism was soon justified by the new expulsion which came in the following year. At length Blessed Joseph was free to enter into the restored Society, and on July 6, 1797 at Parma he had the happiness of renewing his solemn vows into the hands of the second Provincial of the revived Italian Jesuits, Pannizoni. Pius VI, in giving his consent to the restoration of the order in Parma, also approved of the establishment of a novitiate. The first novitiate of the restored Society was established at Colorno in the Duchy of Parma. For the position of novice master there could have been

---

[14] Pastor, *Geschichte der Päpste*, Vol. XVI, part III, pp. 231–232; Zalenski, *Les Jésuites de la Russie-Blanche*, Vol. II, p. 373, Document X.

[15] Pastor, *Geschichte der Päpste*, Vol. XV, part III, p. 231, n. 8.

[16] Hanly, *Blessed Joseph Pignatelli*, New York (1937), statement of Father Mozzi, a companion of Pignatelli, p. 219.

but one choice, and that was made when the Provincial appointed Bl. Joseph Pignatelli to the office.

In White Russia the order continued its steady development. Especially did the reputation of the College of Polotsk increase in every part of Russia. The new Tsar, Paul I, promised to continue the favor of his mother, a promise which he kept. At the death of the Vicar-General Lienkiewicz on November 11, 1798 the Jesuits in Russia and in Parma had increased to a total of 250. Francis Xavier Karew was chosen Perpetual Vicar-General by the Third General Congregation at Polotsk on February 2, 1799; under his rule the Society of Jesus was to attain its highest point of development in Russia. It was also obliged to face the formidable opposition of the Archbishop of Mohilew, who refused to recognize the exemption of the order.[17] Shortly after his election Karew had to send his ablest and most renowned subject, Gabriel Gruber, to Moscow to protect the interests of the order. Probably on account of his great labors for scientific education in Russia as well as his high personal character, Gruber won the confidence of the Tsar. Paul I extended to the Society even greater favor than had his mother. He founded an imperial college and pensionnat for noble students at St. Petersburg and gave them both over to the Jesuits, to whom also he entrusted the parish church at St. Catherine in the capital city; he replaced the Archbishop of Mohilew, Siestrzencewicz, in the department of Catholic affairs of the Ministry of Religion by Bishop Benislawski, a devoted friend of the order. The greatest service, however, was done when on August 11, 1800 Paul I addressed in his own hand the following letter to Pope Pius VII proposing the explicit confirmation of the Society of Jesus in Russia:

Most Holy Father,

The Reverend Father Gruber, the superior of the Jesuits in my states, has expressed to me the wish of the members of the Society of Jesus that I might obtain from Your Holiness their public recognition. I believe that I ought not to hesitate from such a duty, to beg for this order, for which I hold a special predilection, the explicit approval of Your Holiness.[18]

Paul I.

Pius VII was only too glad to accede to the Emperor's petition and in answer issued on March 7, 1801 the Brief "Catholicae Fidei" which furnished the full and formal confirmation of the Society of Jesus in White Russia.[19] Henceforth no one could call into dispute the canonical stand-

---

[17] Pastor, *Geschichte der Päpste*, Vol. XVI, part III, pp. 223–224.

[18] Zalenski, *Les Jésuites de la Russie-Blanche*, Vol. II, p. 84.

[19] *Institutum S.J.*, Vol. I, p. 332; Zalenski, *Les Jésuites de la Russie-Blanche*, Vol. II, Document AG.

ing of the Jesuits in that region and in Parma. A long time was to pass, owing to the arbitrary delays of the imperial agent and the assassination of Paul I, before the Brief was delivered to the Jesuit superior. In fact the Vicar-General Karew died on July 30, 1802 without having seen the official copy. At last, on September 9, 1802, the Russian Chancellor Kotschaubei placed in Gruber's hands the precious Brief, a document which constituted the greatest step toward the general restoration of the order.

Especially significant was the taking of the title, "General of the Society of Jesus in Russia," by Gruber on his election to supreme office by the Fourth General Congregation at Polotsk, October 10, 1802. Gabriel Gruber was a remarkable scholar and scientist.[20] He was born in Vienna in 1740 and after entering the Society made his studies at Gratz, where later he taught Latin for several years; he was the last of the Austrian province to make his profession before the Suppression. After that event for the next eleven years he was professor of mathematics and hydraulics in the University of Laibach, serving on a commission for the regulation of Save; in 1784 he relinquished his good prospects to journey to White Russia in order that he might reenter the Society of Jesus. His varied gifts as an instructor in technical sciences, mechanics, engineering, chemistry, architecture and painting, as well as his linguistic ability in German, Russian, Italian and French, were invaluable for the educational work of the fathers at Polotsk and later at St. Petersburg. The fame of the college of Polotsk and of its scientific academy has already been noted; its physical cabinet, which Gruber had enriched with many machines of his own construction, and its chemical laboratory, also developed by him, became a favorite excursion point for the Russian nobility. Gruber's excellent character was appreciated by native and foreign savants in Russia, as was witnessed by the high value which the Count de Maistre, while he was an ambassador at St. Petersburg, set upon his friendship. With the Empress Catherine and with the Emperor Paul, Gruber labored assiduously in planning the reform and improvement of Russian education. It is hardly too much to say that it was due to his educational work that the struggling remnant of the Society of Jesus received the all-important protection of these two monarchs.

The first task of the new General was to continue the development of the order's activity in Russia. Conditions had become less favorable; the Tsar Alexander was under the influence of a freethinking adviser, although it must be said that for some years the Tsar did not seriously alter the hitherto friendly attitude of the Court. Serious trouble continued to come from the Archbishop of Mohilew, who displayed a schismatical at-

---

[20] Koch, "Gruber," *Jesuiten-Lexikon*; Zalenski, *Les Jésuites de la Russie-Blanche*, Vol. II, pp. 115–138.

titude in his intrigues against the Society of Jesus; he was the first in 1815 to advise their banishment. Gruber did not live to endure that trouble; nor did he expect it, for, an optimist by nature, he never ceased to hope for the ultimate victory of Catholicism in spite of the growing anti-Roman tendencies of the Tsar. The labors of the foreign missions were resumed when Jesuit priests were sent to Odessa, to the Caucasus and to Siberia.[21] Especially fruitful for souls was the work of the ten fathers who worked under the leadership of Landes among the German immigrants at Saratow on the Volga from 1803–1820.[22] In White Russia the excellent work in the colleges was carried on, and so also the spiritual labors of the priests in the residences and at the out-stations.

The second and perhaps the most important task of Father General Gruber was the extension of the order in various parts of Europe and America. In 1803 the ex-Jesuits of England and in 1805 those in the United States sought and obtained affiliation with their former brethren in White Russia. These reunions will be treated at greater length later. Many members of the Fathers of the Faith of Jesus, an organization founded to prepare for the restoration of the Society of Jesus, entered the order in Russia; at one time twenty-five priests from this congregation came to the newly erected novitiate at Dünaburg. Truly significant was the reintroduction of the Society into the Kingdom of the Two Sicilies.[23] Under the ministry of Tanucci, Naples had played a persistent, ruthless part in the destruction of the Society of Jesus; yet the whirlwind of the French Revolution and the usages of hard fate had changed the viewpoint of Ferdinand IV and his Queen, Maria Carolina. Now the King petitioned Pius VII for the reestablishment of the order in his dominions. Father Gruber dispatched an Italian Jesuit, Angiolini, to assist in the negotiations which resulted in the Brief "Per Alias"[24] of July 30, 1804, by which Pius VII canonically restored the Jesuit order in the Neapolitan domain under the superiorship of Father Gruber, as "General for Russia and Naples." The populace of Naples jubilantly welcomed back the Jesuits, as under Bl. Joseph Pignatelli, now Provincial of Italy, the fathers took up again the former labors for souls at their old Church of the Gesù.

Death brought an end to the long and useful career of Father Gruber on March 26, 1805. The last General Congregation to be held at Polotsk elected Thaddeus Brzozowski[25] his successor, September 2, 1805. The new General brought to his office a wealth of experience, for he had been

[21] Zalenski, Les Jésuites de la Russie-Blanche, Vol. II, pp. 119–121.
[22] Pastor, Geschichte der Päpste, Vol. XVI, part III, pp. 222–223.
[23] Zalenski, Les Jésuites de la Russie-Blanche, Vol. II, pp. 124–133.
[24] Institutum S.J., Vol. I, p. 335.
[25] Koch, "Brzozowski," Jesuiten-Lexikon.

secretary in turn to Fathers Lienkiewicz, Karew, and Gruber; he possessed too a spirit of deep piety and warm charity. His special work was to fuse the newer and older elements in the order and to gain respect for the Society in the extern world. In Russia the Emperor Alexander, despite the freethinkers about him, did not yet withdraw his favor; indeed he planned on an even greater employment of the Jesuits in his schemes for educational improvements. While he failed to redeem the promise of Paul I to give the University of Wilna to the Society, he did raise the college at Polotsk to university grade. Missionaries continued to go to Siberia and to the Caucasus, and, in addition, to the Crimea; in all places they achieved remarkable successes. Napoleon's Russian invasion of 1812 forced a part of the Jesuits into flight, among them a young Dutch priest, John Roothaan, then a student at Polotsk and later to be the foremost General of the restored Society. Fourteen of the fathers died in the service of the sick and wounded prisoners of that fateful campaign. Almost at the beginning of Father General Brzozowski's rule, the Neapolitan restoration, which had started so auspiciously, collapsed when the armies of Napoleon invaded the kingdom. Some of the Jesuits were able to remain in the island of Sicily; but most of them were obliged to seek refuge in the Papal States, where at Rome, Frascati, Anagni, Orvieto and Tivoli, with the sanction of Pius VII, they were allowed to open colleges or residences. As long as Napoleon dominated the scene the corporate existence of the Italian Jesuits was exceedingly precarious. A great blow was suffered when, on November 11, 1811, Bl. Joseph Pignatelli died. For years he had been the leading spirit of the Italian organization, comforting, sustaining and animating the Italian brethren in the dark hours of their many heavy trials. During the last years of his life his sanctity and, above all, his charity to the poor of Rome, endeared him to the people. He was beatified May 21, 1933.

The Russian survival, while it preserved the life and organization of the Society of Jesus without interruption, was always a very small affair; and for most Europeans until 1801, it remained as dubious as it was remote. For Catholics a more pressing problem presented itself: what substitute could be obtained which would fill up the wide gap left by the Suppression of the Jesuits in the field of learning and the care of souls. Two of the solutions merit consideration. They were the attempts, one in Belgium and the other in Rome, to found a congregation which would follow the Jesuit rule, would work in the spirit of the Society of Jesus, and would prepare for the eventual restoration of the order. The first congregation, the Society of the Most Sacred Heart of Jesus,[26] was

---

[26] Spell, P. *Léonor Franz von Tournély und die Gesellschaft des hlst. Herzens Jesu,* Breslau (1864); Pastor, *Geschichte der Päpste,* Vol. XVI, part III, p. 233; Burnichon, *La Compagnie de Jésus en France,* Vol. I, pp. 8–14.

founded by two French priests, Francis de Tournély and Charles de Broglie, at Louvain, May 8, 1794. Before long a group of zealous priests associated themselves with the new foundation, among them of special importance were Charles LeBlanc and Joseph Varin. The internal spirit of the little society gave great promise, although its existence was menaced at the very beginning by external dangers. The sweep of the French Revolutionary armies over the Netherlands forced the fathers to seek asylum in Germany and Austria, in which last country they received the protection of the Emperor's sister, the Archduchess Maria Anna. Thus they were enabled to take over the Castle of Hagenbrünn as a head-quarters and as a place for the training of their scholastics in 1797. In that very year the youthful and saintly de Tournély died, and the congregation was merged with the Society of the Fathers of the Faith of Jesus.

This second congregation was founded by a pious Italian cleric, Nicola Paccanari, from whom its members received the more familiar name of "Paccanarists." [27] A few priests, among them two French ex-Jesuits, Epinette and Halnat, joined him; with the permission of the Cardinal-Vicar, della Smugglia, the first vows were pronounced in the Oratory of Caravita in Rome, August 15, 1797. Not long afterwards Paccanari in an audience with Pius VII laid before the Pontiff the plans of his organization, especially their purpose to prepare the way for the restoration of the Society of Jesus. Pope Pius not only gave his approval, merely changing the name from "The Fathers of the Holy Faith" to "The Fathers of the Faith of Jesus," but also bestowed on Paccanari and his brethren several privileges, such as the right to receive ex-Jesuits and to use the Breviary of the Society of Jesus. The next step of the founder was to achieve a union with the Fathers of the Sacred Heart. This last congregation had eighty members, half of whom were learned and able priests, two well established foundations and a good working system of education for its scholastics; the Paccanarists, on the other hand could count but nineteen members, of whom three only were priests, and owned neither house nor means of support. Still they possessed the all-important approval of the Pope, as well as the special privileges mentioned above. For these reasons the fathers of the Society of the Most Sacred Heart under the leadership of Varin submitted themselves to Paccanari, relinquishing their special name for the common title of "Society of the Faith of Jesus." The union was effected April 8, 1799.

The good works of the united congregation developed rapidly. In the very year 1799 some of the fathers began to labor in the military hospitals on the German and Italian battlefronts. In the following year various members undertook different types of spiritual work in many parts of

---

[27] Pfulf, *Die Anfänge der deutschen Provinz der neu erstanden G.J.* (1922); Pastor, *Geschichte der Päpste*, Vol. XVI, part III, p. 234.

Europe: Varin and Roger in France, Rozaven and de Broglie in London, Kohlmann in Amsterdam, Cuénet in Spoleto, where he revived the original Paccanarist foundation. Further a novitiate and scholasticate were opened at Rome, and also a college for noble youth. By 1804 the Paccanarists numbered 110 members, of whom 36 were scholastic novices.

Despite their successes serious dissensions arose among the Fathers of the Faith. The original purpose of the restoration of the Society of Jesus seemed in danger of being lost sight of, especially on the part of the founder who looked with little favor on a union with the actual Society in White Russia. In 1799 he declared his readiness to accept the obedience of the Russian Jesuits, but his own unwillingness to put himself or his associates under their rule. There were also several complaints that his government was domineering; one thing was certain, the good man did not possess the qualities necessary for the ruling of a religious order.

The Papal recognition of the Jesuits in White Russia and Naples brought matters to a head; those anxious for immediate reunion and those dissatisfied with Paccanari left the rule of the latter. Grivel in 1803 departed for Polotsk to be the first Paccanarist to enter the Society of Jesus; in the following year Rozaven, who had seen in England the reunion of the English ex-Jesuits with the order in White Russia, led a group of twenty-five Paccanarists to the novitiate at Dünaburg; Anthony Kohlmann journeyed from Amsterdam to Russia to enroll among the Jesuits; several of the Italian members entered the restored Society in Naples. The French Paccanarists, with the consent of the Cardinal Legate, dissolved their connection with the founder. Under the direction of Varin, and with such able and virtuous brethren as Louis Barat and Charles Bruson, they accomplished much good in the management of eight seminaries and in the preaching of popular missions. In 1814, together with the Paccanarists of the Low Countries, they entered the Society of Jesus. The Fathers of the Faith in Lombardy, Switzerland and Amsterdam likewise cut themselves off from the original body. Paccanari himself fell into trouble with the Holy Office in 1807, was tried and sentenced to prison, which sentence he accepted in a spirit of repentance. After two years he was freed during the invasion of Rome by the French troops; he left the Eternal City and from that time on passed out of public notice. The Society of the Most Sacred Heart and the Society of the Faith of Jesus fulfilled a significant role: in many ways and in many places they prepared the ground for the complete restoration, in none more so than in the training of members who later became such excellent Jesuits as Anthony Kohlmann, Nicholas Godinor, Jean Rozaven, Joseph della Torre and Joseph Varin.

The ex-Jesuits of England and the United States were the first groups

of their own initiative to seek reunion with the fathers in White Russia.[28]
When the Society was suppressed in France in 1762, the English Jesuits
moved their celebrated college of St. Omers to Bruges in the Austrian
Netherlands, where they continued their work under the protection of the
Empress Maria Theresa until the general Suppression in 1773.[29] The
next year the Prince Bishop of Liége, van Welbruck, welcomed the English ex-Jesuits to the capital city of his principality, permitting them to
gather their pupils there and to continue their college. A Papal Brief of
1776 gave official approbation to their work. For twenty years the fathers, living in community, though as secular priests, taught their classes
until the invasion of the Netherlands by the French Revolutionary armies
in 1794 seemed to spell the doom of their enterprise. The situation was
saved by the charity and loyalty of a former pupil, Mr. Thomas Weld,
who presented the fathers with an estate and manor-house at Stonyhurst
in Lancashire, to which the ex-Jesuits and their pupils migrated in that
very same year, 1794. There the fathers built anew on English soil the
old school of the Catholic exiles of St. Omers, now henceforth to be the
celebrated English Catholic College of Stonyhurst.

The new foundation became a rallying point for all the English ex-
Jesuits, not only those who lived in the community at the college, but
those who were scattered through the land serving as chaplains to Catholic gentlemen. The two leading fathers, Strickland and Marmaduke
Stone, followed carefully the course of events among the surviving remnant of the old Society in Russia. When at length Pius VII officially recognized its existence, the English priests applied to the Pontiff for permission to aggregate themselves and their fellow former Jesuits to their
brethren in the dominions of the Tsar. Pius VII on May 21, 1803 granted
their request; and twenty-two fathers availed themselves of the privilege.
In a brief time a novitiate was opened at Hodder, with Charles Plowden
as the novice-master. The permission of the Pope to the English Jesuits
was an oral one, delivered in secret and not even communicated to the
Congregation of the Propaganda.[30] When the news got out, the Prefect
of the Propaganda, Cardinal Borgia, wrote a letter protesting strongly
against what had been done, and forbidding bishops either to recognize
the new Jesuits or to admit their privileges until they had obtained permission from the Propaganda. His letter, however, did not cancel the

---

[28] Pollen, "An Unobserved Centenary," *The Month*, Vol. CXV, pp. 449–461; "The
Restoration of the English Jesuits," *The Month*, Vol. CXV, pp. 585–597; "The Recognition of the Jesuits in England," *The Month*, Vol. CXVI, pp. 23–36.

[29] Gerard, *Stonyhurst College, Centenary Record*, Ch. I, for history of the migration.

[30] Pollen, "An Unobserved Centenary," *The Month*, Vol. CXV, p. 459, note 2 for
reference.

vows which the English fathers had taken. The two surviving Irish ex-Jesuits, Betagh, the Vicar-General of Dublin, and O'Callaghan, devoted their best efforts to hastening the day of complete restoration. O'Callaghan joined the fathers at Stonyhurst, while Betagh, in the school which he conducted, prepared boys to enter the Society. Both fathers were able to send twenty young candidates either to the Jesuits at Stonyhurst or to those at Palermo in Sicily. On September 30, 1813 a foundation was started in Dublin, and in the next year the college of Clongowes Wood was begun.[31]

The American ex-Jesuits [32] soon followed the example of their confrères of the old English province. When the Suppression had become a fact in America, there were twenty ex-Jesuits laboring in the provinces of Maryland and Pennsylvania; they were the only priests in the thirteen English-speaking colonies. Shortly afterwards they were joined by two ex-Jesuits returning from Europe to their native land, one of whom was Father John Carroll, later the first Bishop of Baltimore. When the Revolutionary War was over five more American ex-Jesuits came back to labor in the land of their birth. Exceedingly hard was the task of these good priests; each one, living at a lonely mission station, ministered to a flock scattered over long stretches of remote farm country among neighbors more or less hostile to their religion. The hopes and prayers of all of these former Jesuits were for the time when their beloved Society would once more be restored. To prepare for that event they formed a corporation to hold for the new Society the lands which were the support of their mission stations. The college at Georgetown, which their leader, John Carroll, had founded in 1789, they also wished one day to place under the direction of the fathers of the Society, just as had been old St. Omers where they had all received their education. These American ex-Jesuits, even at their distant posts, anxiously followed the events in White Russia and the work of the Fathers of the Holy Faith. In 1800 five of the priests wrote for information to Marmaduke Stone in England. Letters also came from de Broglie and Rozaven to John Carroll, now Bishop of Baltimore, asking for a reception for the Fathers of the Faith. The invitation was extended by Bishop Carroll and Bishop Neale, his coadjutor, who also had been a member of the old Society. Bishop Carroll was chary of the Fathers of the Faith; the single father who did arrive proved none too satisfactory.

At length the news came that the English ex-Jesuits had been allowed to join the canonically approved Society of Jesus in White Russia. Bishop Carroll on May 25, 1803 addressed a letter to Father General Gruber

[31] Corcoran, *The Clongowes Record*, c. III, IV, V.

[32] *Woodstock Letters*, Vol. X, p. 89; XII, p. 288; XVI, p. 161; XXXIII, p. 371; XXXIV, pp. 113, 203.

asking that the same favor be granted to the American ex-Jesuits. In his letter the Bishop stated that there were in the United States thirteen ex-Jesuits or other priests who were desirous of entering the order; he asked if it were possible for them to be received, in which case he petitioned that the General would accept them. Further he requested to know what measures would be necessary to set up once more the Society of Jesus in the New World; finally he suggested that a Visitor be sent, an Englishman, an Italian, or a German, who would guide the new foundation, since none of the local fathers, due to their age or to their labors, was suitable for the task. After long delays Father Gruber's reply arrived on March 24, 1804. In his answer the General explained that the power to accept Jesuits outside of Russia was an actual one, resting on a *viva voce* consent of Pius VII, a fact that had been amply attested to by Cardinal Consalvi, the Secretary of State, and by the fathers, Georgii and Angiolini. He then gave the directions as to the method of reception, and finally asked and authorized Bishop Carroll to appoint a superior and a novice-master for the restored mission. Bishop Carroll gathered the few surviving ex-Jesuits at St. Thomas Manor, Maryland, on May 9, 1805, and read to them Father General Gruber's reply. The Bishop left it to each one to decide whether to enter at once or to wait until a more general restoration by a Papal Brief would come. There were eleven ex-Jesuits living after the thirty-two years since the Suppression. Two obviously could not join, Bishop Carroll and Bishop Neale; of the nine remaining, six, Molyneaux, Sewell, Neale, Bolton, Boarman and Brooke elected to enter the reunion, three, Ashton, Beeston and Pile, did not.

The Society of Jesus in America now being a fact, Bishop Carroll appointed Robert Molyneaux the first superior. A novitiate was opened the next year, 1806, at Georgetown College. Father Brzozowski, who in the meantime had become General, sent five fathers from Russia to aid in establishing the revived mission; among these priests the most outstanding were Anthony Kohlmann and John Grassi. Kohlmann's work in training the novices, in his parochial labors in New York, where he obtained the legal recognition of the Seal of the Confessional, and finally in the office of superior of the mission, were truly invaluable. Quite as important were the accomplishments of Grassi as superior of the mission, and as president of Georgetown College, the scholastic prestige of which he increased especially by his own scientific attainments.

Although Bishop Carroll afforded every assistance to the revived Society in America, he could never quite dismiss his uneasiness over the fact that its status depended on a mere *viva voce* approbation. The title for ordination and the validity of the vows of the professed seemed to him to be thus based on precarious grounds; and the misgiving possessed him that all the hopes of the new Jesuits might be swept away by a simple recall of the permission by another Pope. He did not wish the young Jesuits to run the risk of experiencing the overwhelming sorrow that had been his at the Suppression. He was not hostile, as some have thought, but merely anxious for the successful outcome. No one rejoiced more sincerely than Archbishop Carroll, when the solemn Bull of Restoration for the whole world was issued by Pius VII. He would not read the whole document, which had been sent to him, until he had communicated the good news and all its contents to the superior, Grassi, at Georgetown. He was in very truth the principal instrument in the restoration of the Society of Jesus in America; to him more than to anyone else is due the fact that the order received the properties of the old Society and the possession of the college at Georgetown which he had founded.

In various places in Europe in the decade preceding the year 1814, union with the Russian Jesuits was affected by individual ex-Jesuits, or important preparations were made for the hoped for restoration. Thus in Germany, Michael Dunhardt, an ex-Jesuit at Düsseldorf, joined the Russian Society in 1804; similarly did another ex-Jesuit, Doller, at Mainz. The greatest German development [33] came in the Helvetian mission, which started in Switzerland as the work of the Paccanarists and eventually ended in the German province of the new Society. In 1805 four priests and two scholastics of the Fathers of the Faith under the leadership of the priest, Joseph della Torre, came to Sitten at the invitation of the government of Wallis to take over the management of the college there. The work prospered in spite of the separation from Paccanari in 1806. As a result of this last event the fathers placed themselves directly under the obedience of the Pope and set about effecting a reception into the Jesuit order in White Russia. In 1810 their request for union was granted, providing all, fathers and scholastics, should make a canonical novitiate. The stipulation was carried out at Sitten in 1812. The first vows were pronounced, and the beginnings of the German province were made. In the Low Countries the priests Beckers and Fonteyne, having joined the Society at Polotsk, were appointed in turn superiors of the Jesuits in Belgium and Holland; on July 31, 1814 a novitiate was opened at Rumbeke-bei-Roulers.

With the restoration of the Society of Jesus in France [34] are connected the names of two remarkable men, Pierre Clorivière and Joseph Varin. Clorivière pronounced his final vows just before the Suppression, after which event he labored as a parish priest and as a teacher in the diocesan seminary of Dinan. During the French Revolution a number of his relatives were murdered and he himself narrowly escaped death on several

---

[33] O. Pfulf, *Die Anfänge der deutschen Provinz der neu erstandenen G.J.* (1922).

[34] Burnichon, *La Compagnie de Jésus en France 1814–1914*, Vol. I, pp. 14–66.

occasions. Despite his life of constant peril he founded, as substitutes for the banished religious orders, a congregation of priests and a congregation of nuns to carry on the labor of souls; the nuns were to dress as lay-women. During a five year term of imprisonment for alleged connections with Napoleon's enemies, Clorivière managed to smuggle out a request to the Jesuits in White Russia for reunion. His plea was granted and on his release in 1809 he devoted himself to preparing the way for a revival of the Society in France. After the fall of Napoleon, Clorivière petitioned Louis XVIII for the restoration of the Jesuits, but all that he could obtain was a secret tolerance for the time being. On the strength of this concession the venerable priest, almost eighty years of age, the only Jesuit in France, was commissioned by Father General Brzozowski to reestablish the Society. After fifty years only seven ex-Jesuits were left to rally under the banner of the order. But recruits came from the Fathers of the Faith under Varin. This priest and some of his brethren received the news of the contemplated opening of a novitiate in France just as they were about to depart for Polotsk. They gladly entered this novitiate on its first day, the Feast of St. Ignatius, 1814.

Under the guidance of Varin the Fathers of the Faith had conducted eight seminaries or colleges in the French domains. The enmity of Napoleon in 1804 had closed the colleges and in 1807 had banished the forty fathers of the congregation to their native dioceses. Varin, living at Besançon, in spite of everything managed to keep up a union with the fathers. This apostolic man had an important part in the foundation of several modern congregations of nuns, the Religious of the Sacred Heart, the Sisters of Notre Dame de Namur, the Sisters of the Holy Family of Besançon and the Faithful Companions of Jesus. As for his own order, Varin became the first assistant of Clorivière in the restoration of the Society of Jesus in France.

In the year 1814, then, the Society was fully restored, with few members, yet with justified hopes, in Russia, Sicily, England and the United States. There were in addition in Germany, Switzerland and the Low Countries small communities of Jesuits or, here and there, individual fathers united with the order in White Russia. Among sincere Catholics almost everywhere a strong desire for the complete restoration in the whole world had arisen. No one cherished this wish more than did the Supreme Pontiff, Pius VII, and he was encouraged to give it practical realization by such eminent Cardinals as Consalvi, Litta and Pacca. During his imprisonment at Fontainebleau, Pius VII matured his plans; when he returned to the Eternal City his mind was made up to bring about the universal restoration, despite any and all clamors of the old enemies of the Society, and in the face of all the stormings of their newer foes, the anticlerical liberals. The Bull "Solicitudo omnium ecclesiarum" [35] was very soon composed; it is well to note that whereas the Society was suppressed by a Brief, it was restored by the more solemn document, a Bull. The opposition in the College of Cardinals was able to make one last gesture by preventing the promulgation of the Bull on St. Ignatius' Day. But it could not keep up such delays; and finally on August 7, 1814, the universal Restoration of the Society of Jesus was accomplished. On that day Pius VII proceeded through the streets crowded with the jubilant populace to the Gesù where he said Mass at the altar of St. Ignatius. Then in the Sodality Chapel, in the presence of a notable assemblage of eighteen Cardinals, many high dignitaries, several royal personages including the Princess Maria Luise, niece of Charles III, and her sons, and 150 survivors of the old Society, the Pontiff had the solemn Bull of Restoration read. Few could restrain their tears, especially when Pius VII received these aged veteran priests who had lived through forty years of sorrow and loneliness to this day of final fulfilment of their hopes.

In the Bull "Solicitudo omnium ecclesiarum" Pius VII recalled that on the prayer of the Vicar-General, Francis Karew, and moved by the recommendations of the Tsar Paul I, he had restored the Society of Jesus for the whole of the Russian Empire by the Brief of March 9, 1801, and that on the petition of the King Ferdinand he also had restored the Society for the Kingdom of the Two Sicilies by the Brief of July 30, 1804. Then he declared that he had received an almost unanimous request from the Christian world, from Archbishops, Bishops and leading men of all stations, for the complete restoration of the old Society of Jesus, especially after the richly fruitful successes of the Society in the lands mentioned above had become known. Further, he affirmed, the rebuilding of holiness after the most deplorable disasters of most recent times was a care which occupied all his thoughts, a duty he must needs perform. Pius VII continued: "We would reckon it a grave fault in the sight of God were we in such a need to spurn such richly blessed help which the special rule of Divine Providence offers us, and were we in the barque of Peter, so tossed here and there by the storm, not to accept the skilful and seasoned rowers who offer themselves to break the billows of the sea threatening us every moment with disastrous shipwreck." In conclusion Pius VII declared the Brief of Suppression completely recalled. The Society of Jesus was therefore free again to serve the Pope throughout the whole world at whatsoever task he should wish to assign.

---

[35] *Institutum S.J.*, Vol. I, p. 337.

CHAPTER XV

EUROPEAN REVIVAL

A century and a quarter has passed since that August day in 1814 on which Pius VII restored the Society of Jesus. In the history of the order over this span of years there may be recognized a three-fold division: first there were the insignificant re-beginnings in the face of numerous hindrances; then followed the times of steady development despite bitter assaults; and finally came the remarkable successes of the recent period, when the numbers of the old Society were reached and passed, when the works of the old Society were equalled, and when the fiercest and bloodiest persecutions were met and endured.[1] If the accomplishments of the first century and a quarter of the new Society are not as spectacular as those of the first century and a quarter of the old Society, they are certainly of as solid worth; if the opposition has not been as sanguinary, it has been as wide-spread and more persistent. In the nineteenth century there were no such saints as Ignatius, Xavier, Borgia, or Aloysius; still, in the ranks of the order labored truly holy men of the character of Ginhac, Petit, Doyle and Eberschweiler. Rather surprising is it that in these later, less sanguinary times the number of the martyrs is almost as large as in the first 125 years; over 177 Jesuits since 1814 have been killed, apparently in hatred of the Faith. The educational institutions of the Jesuits of today are more numerous; they are achieving too a wider and a better work. It is true that on the roll of modern Jesuits one will find no names comparable with those of St. Robert Bellarmine, Suarez, Lessius and de Lugo; yet the mention of Perrone, Franzelin, Mazella, Vermeersch and de la Taille sufficiently indicate that able theologians are still produced in the Society. Theologians of these days, when the interests of the learned world have passed to other fields, cannot attain the renown of the divines of a more controversial age. Along with the times, many Jesuit scholars have turned their endeavors to scientific, historical and literary fields, with creditable success. Cooperative more than individual have been the labors of the modern fathers, as is evidenced in their periodicals and in their contributions to such works as the *Catholic Encyclopedia* or the *Kirchen-Lexikon*. Similarly in the ascetical and pastoral field the cooperative note

---

[1] Pollen, "The Centenary of the Restoration of the Society of Jesus," *The Month*, Vol. CXXIII, pp. 56–71. A summary of the first century of the new Society.

is quite evident; popular devotions, through such organizations as the Apostleship of Prayer and the League of the Sacred Heart, or the Sodality of the Blessed Virgin, have been developed and propagated on a scale and with a membership never dreamed of in the greatest days of the old Society. The foreign missions of the modern Society can show nothing like the Reductions of Paraguay, a project hardly imaginable in the circumstances of today; yet the fathers who devote themselves to this heroic apostolate are as numerous now as were their predecessors of the first century of the order.

The membership, after some years of slow augmentation, began to increase steadily until in 1914 after one hundred years there were 16,175 Jesuits, a figure comparable with the numbers of 1640, the first centenary year, when the ranks counted a little less than 17,000. Today, 125 years after the Restoration, the list of 25,954 exceeds the highest total of the old Society. The development of the new Society has been brought about with little external help; the Jesuits of the nineteenth and twentieth centuries have had to found and maintain their colleges, churches, even their domestic houses, with few helps in the form of grants and foundations from princes and royal patrons. In some countries it has been necessary to rebuild more than once the houses and educational institutions, owing to the repeated confiscations of anticlerical governments. The expansion of numbers and of works has varied widely in different localities. The highest prosperity and development has been experienced in Belgium, Holland, England, Ireland and the United States, countries in which, with the exception of the first, the old Society was proscribed. In the United States the 5,319 Jesuits constitute the largest group in the order. The severest persecution of the fathers has come precisely in those countries in which the old Society achieved its greatest triumphs, Spain, Portugal, France and Italy.

Most of the opposition which the modern Jesuits have encountered has arisen either from the anticlerical Liberalism of the Latin Masonic Lodges, or from atheistic Communism, or from the exaggerated nationalism of Hegelian politicians. Except in Spain, Mexico and in the Paris Commune, the frequent attacks have not been unto blood; nevertheless the almost continuous round of banishments and confiscations indicates an enmity more persistent and more fundamental than any opposition encountered in the earlier period. The assault on the Jesuits of these latter times has been, and is, but part of the wider warfare of irreligion against the Papacy, of unbelief against revealed and authoritative religion. In that irreconcilable conflict, by their very special devotion to the Holy See, the Jesuits must suffer. The recent slaughter of over a hundred fathers and brothers belonging to the Spanish provinces, evidences the fact that the struggle has entered its most fundamental phase, the warfare of basic materialism against spirituality, of atheism against God.

The Restoration of the Society of Jesus meant little more than permission for a few feeble, old priests and a handful of young recruits to live in community and to call their organization "The Society of Jesus." [2] It would have been chimerical for them to have entertained any prospect of their occupying the old position of the Jesuits in the Catholic world; both men and means were lacking, most of the members of the old Society were dead and gone, and their former colleges and churches were in other hands. The Bull "Solicitudo omnium ecclesiarum" provided no machinery for the setting up of houses and novitiates, nor did it explicitly state anything concerning the ancient privileges of the Society. In fact the document contained clauses evidently inserted to disarm expected opposition: Pope Pius VII reserved to himself the right of revising the Constitutions and renewed only such faculties as were "necessary and befitting." The remarkable haste with which the Bull was drawn up and published indicated Pius VII's realization of the strength of the Society's enemies, whom he determined to circumvent by an accomplished fact. An official notification of the Restoration was not sent to the Catholic Courts; merely a mild recommendation of the Society was made to princes and bishops.

The general Restoration was not yet two years a fact when Russia, which had sheltered the remnant of the order through the years of the interim, turned against the Society. [3] The new hostility of Tsar Alexander I against the order had several causes: the clamor of the Orthodox clergy who hated the Jesuits; the anger of the minister Galitzen, who blamed the Jesuits for the conversion to Rome of his nephew, later a celebrated pioneer priest of the United States; the Tsar's own ideas of a new religious sect; and probably his exasperation at the Father Perkowski's insistence on the termination by the Polish lady, Naryschkin, of her illicit relationship with the Emperor. Father General Brzozowski and all the Jesuits in St. Petersburg and Moscow were banished from those cities in January 2, 1816. Four years later, after the death of Father General Brzozowski, who passed away February 5, 1820, an imperial decree drove the 358 members of the Society in White Russia from all the dominions of the Tsar. The fathers and brothers found a refuge in Austrian Poland.

The restored Society had hardly gotten under way when its very existence was threatened by a subversive element within its own ranks. [4]

---

[2] Pollen, "Centenary," *The Month*, Vol. CXXIII, pp. 56–59.

[3] Zalenski, *Les Jésuites de la Russie-Blanche*, Vol. II, pp. 207–263.

[4] Koch, *Jesuiten-Lexikon*, various articles, especially the one on Fortis; Heimbucher, *Orden und Kongregationen*, Vol. II, p. 202; Crétineau-Joly, *Histoire*, Vol. VI, pp. 46–49.

Trouble broke with the calling of the Twentieth General Congregation for the election of a new General. Active and progressive members, such as Rozaven, della Torre and Grivel, apparently were to dominate the sessions. Yet the very forward-looking policies of these men aroused alarm among some of the veterans of the old Society, and jealousy among others. One fact, that formerly they had been Fathers of the Faith, told against them; the other fact, that by their entrance and membership in the living Society in White Russia, they had come to possess the spirit of the order more really than did those who had lived separated from it for some forty years, was overlooked. Against them too was ranged a faction that aimed at changes in the Constitutions. The leading spirit of the opposition was a Sicilian priest, Rezzi. The first move of this man was to call into question the validity of the professions made in Russia, thus to impede the legitimate and free election of a General. The intriguer succeeded in winning over to his side the Vicar-General of the Society, Petrucci, a pious and conscientious old man, but gifted with little discernment to perceive the machinations in which unwittingly he had become involved. Further Rezzi gained the support of the influential Cardinal della Genga, an excellent ecclesiastic but one who, because of his justified adverse opinion of Paccanari, was excessively suspicious of Rozaven and others once connected with that restless spirit.

Pius VII appointed a commission headed by Cardinal della Genga to settle the dispute over the competency of the voters in the General Congregation, which had been called for September 14, 1820. The delegates were already on their way, when they received from the Vicar-General a command forbidding them to enter the city of Rome. The prohibition was sent in consequence of an order of Cardinal della Genga postponing the assembly until there had been a complete clearing up of the question of electoral rights. The Cardinal went further and, on the day on which the Congregation was to have opened, bestowed on Petrucci all the powers of a General, increased the number of the Assistants to seven, and established a commission for the correction of evils existing in the Society. All these acts were contrary to the old statutes of the Society of Jesus. The determined stand of the delegates already assembled, especially Rozaven and Landes, saved the situation and maintained the law of the order. An able friend was found in Cardinal Consalvi, the Papal Secretary of State, who had recognized the real intrigue in Rezzi's conduct. This great ecclesiastical statesman presented to the Sovereign Pontiff the strongly worded remonstrance of nineteen of the electors. Pius VII accepted the arguments of these fathers and ordered the Congregation to be summoned according to the original plans. The assembly opened on October 9. It required still a second intervention of the Pope to overcome Petrucci's scruples as to legality. The Holy Father by his own act ratified the canonicity of all profession made in White Russia. The Congregation dealt summarily with the disturbers, Rezzi was expelled and Petrucci was removed from office. On October 18 Aloysius Fortis, a native of Verona, was elected the twentieth General of the Society of Jesus. The new superior had been a member of the old Society and in the new Society had held the position of Provincial of Italy and Vicar-General for Italy, the last on the appointment of Father Brzozowski. Bl. Joseph Pignatelli had foretold his election to the generalate. To assure the maintenance of the old spirit in the order through all the new developments and in the face of the growing persecutions, the Twentieth Congregation decreed that all statutes, arrangements and dispensations of the old Society would have the same force in the new Society. Cardinal della Genga when he became Pope Leo XII in 1823, far from taking a hostile attitude towards the order, removed all misgivings by his many and practical benefactions. By the Bull "Plena Inter" he renewed all the old privileges of the Society and added several new ones; he entrusted the Roman College again to the Fathers; and he undertook their defense against the attacks made upon them in France in 1828. Father Fortis ruled the Society for nine years, dying June 27, 1829.

The twenty-first General of the Society of Jesus was the learned and noble minded John Philip Roothaan,[5] one of the most outstanding superiors-general of the new and of the old Society. Father Roothaan was a Hollander, born at Amsterdam in 1785. But a youth of nineteen, he journeyed to White Russia to enroll in the existing order; in his subsequent career as a Jesuit he was engaged successfully as a teacher of the classics, a spiritual adviser, a popular missionary and a rector of the college in Turin. His apostolic labors carried him, after banishment from Russia, all over Switzerland, Germany and Holland. On July 9, 1829 he was chosen as the successor of Father Fortis. For twenty-four years this saintly superior was to govern the Society with a rule that produced a veritable Second Spring. Such a good result was due to a two fold policy which he carried through all the years of his generalate. The first part was the ascetical progress of the members. This he sought to obtain by deepening their love for the ideals of the order and arousing them to a zealous use of its ascetical practices. His primary means were the Spiritual Exercises; he published a faithful Latin translation of the Spanish autograph with valuable critical notes, as well as a treatise on the method of meditation of the Exercises. Most heartily too did he recommend the devotion to the Sacred Heart of Jesus and the veneration of the Most Pure Heart of Mary. The second part of his policy was the educational advance, not only of the members of the order but of the schools maintained by them; for

[5] Pirri, P. Giovanni Roothaan, XXI Generale della Compagnia di Gesù, Rome (1930); A. Neu, P. Joh. Ph. Roothaan, der bedeutendste Jesuitengeneral (1928).

this purpose he issued a new edition of the *Ratio Studiorum* with adaptations to the needs of the times. The good fruit of his efforts became apparent in the expanding labors of the fathers in Germany, Holland, England, the United States, and especially in the foreign mission field, where in 1851 one-fifth of the Jesuits worked. These good results showed too in the patient endurance of banishment and confiscation by so many of the European fathers. In this regard Roothaan's years constituted a long chain of sorrows, expulsions from this country and from that until the Revolution of '48 when the Jesuits were driven from most of the European states. The General himself was obliged to flee from Rome and remain for some years in exile. This exile, however, he employed to visit various provinces, to encourage the dispersed brethren, to strengthen all by his personal word and written exhortation. During his government the Society was accused of political intrigue in the Papal States, the confidence which Pius IX reposed in the General affording a pretext for the innuendoes of the suspicious. The personal character of Roothaan ought to have been sufficient answer; but his latest biographer, Pirri, has sufficiently demonstrated the falseness of the allegations. On May 8, 1853, John Roothaan died in the odor of sanctity; the steps for his beatification have been begun.

The twenty-second General Congregation elected as the succeeding General, Peter Beckx, a Belgian.[6] For several years Father Beckx had carried on the priestly ministry in the German Diaspora, then he had been rector of the college at Louvain, and in 1852 was named Provincial of the Austrian-Hungarian province. He was to rule the order for thirty years until his retirement in 1883. Under him the Second Spring of Father Roothaan developed into a most fruitful Summertide. The roll of the Society grew from 5,209 to 11,480; the ten provinces became nineteen; a new Assistancy for the English-speaking Jesuits was created. Educational and spiritual labors manifested an even greater increase. The first of the learned periodicals appeared, the *Civiltà Cattolica*, to be soon followed by the *Études*, the *Stimmen aus Maria Laach* and several other publications. The growth of the missions to the heathens kept pace with the general progress, gaining many worthy laborers from among the expelled Jesuits of Europe; in 1883 there were some 2,500 fathers and brothers working in these new vineyards of the Lord. The advance of the order under Father Beckx was balanced by ruthless persecutions in Italy, as a result of which the General had to leave Rome and take up his residence at Fiesole; in Spain, which witnessed two expulsions; in France, where five fathers were martyred in the Revolt of the Paris Commune; and in Germany, from which the Kulturkampf banished all Jesuits and

---

[6] Verstreeten, *Leven van den hoogerwaarden P. Petrus Beckx*, Antwerp (1889), German translation by Joh. Martin, Ravensburg (1897).

all Jesuit activities. On September 24, 1883, the twenty-third General Congregation acceded to the request of Father Beckx, then in his eighty-ninth year, to be relieved of the burdens of his office. Father Anthony Anderledy was elected Vicar-General with the right of succession. Four years later, March 4, 1887, the venerable old General died at the Collegium Germanicum in Rome. During most of the generalates of Fathers Roothaan and Beckx, Pius IX occupied the Papal Throne. The initial rumors of his unfavorableness were soon dispelled by the evident signs of his good-will, which he continued to manifest during his long reign. He issued over 130 Papal documents for the order, beatified 77 and canonized 3 of its sons. He strongly supported the editors of the *Civiltà Cattolica* and the theological professors of the Gregorian University of whom he made use in the preparation of the Syllabus, the proclamation of the dogma of the Immaculate Conception and the work of the Vatican Council. To the enemies of the Society, within and without the Church, the Pontiff ever turned a deaf ear. He repeatedly asserted that his sympathy for the persecuted Jesuits increased in their common sorrows; indeed Pius IX recognized that the Liberals, the Infidels and Bismarck delivered their attack on the Jesuits only as a preliminary maneuver against his own pontifical throne.

Father Anthony Anderledy [7] administered the affairs of the order as Vicar-General for four years and as General for five years. He was a Swiss by birth and the only one of all the Generals to have been personally connected with the United States. He studied and was ordained at St. Louis and worked as a parish priest for one year at Green Bay, Wisconsin. He brought to his office a long experience as a superior in Germany where he had founded the house of studies at Maria Laach. In the steady advance in education, literary work, sacerdotal labors and the apostolate of the pagans, he strove to emphasize and to deepen the old spirit of manly loyalty to the Pope and to the Church. He worked too for the greater following of St. Thomas as a guide in Scholastic studies. Under his short rule the number of provinces was increased by four. Father Anderledy died at Fiesole, January 18, 1892.

In view of the difficult situation in Rome due to the Italian Anti-clericals, it was thought best to hold the twenty-fourth General Congregation in some other locality. Manresa in Spain, the cradle of the order, was chosen for the sessions. On October 2, 1892 the Congregation elected Father Luis Martin, a Spaniard, as the twenty-fourth Father General. [8] The new superior had been a professor of theology, Provincial of Castile

---

[7] Baumgartner, "Adm. Rev. P. Antonius Maria Anderledy," *Stimmen aus Maria Laach*, Vol. XLII, pp. 241–265.

[8] Chandlery, *Letters and Notices* from July 1906 to January 1910, lengthy biographical study of Father Martin.

and substitute Spanish Assistant. For fourteen years he guided the destinies of the Society successfully. To him is owing the inception of the great general histories of the various Assistancies, written in the best modern critical spirit by Astrain, Duhr, Fouqueray and others, and likewise the beginning of the publication by the Spanish fathers of the documents of the early Society, the *Monumenta Historica Societatis Jesu*. Alive to modern problems, the General urged upon the fathers the study and handling of social questions. A heavy blow fell upon the Society in the banishment of the French Jesuits with the loss of their thirty-two colleges by the laws of Waldeck-Rousseau. In China four of the fathers were murdered by the Boxers. A third sad loss was the defection of the English Jesuit, George Tyrrell, who had become infected with Modernism. In the last years of his life Father Martin suffered severely from sarcoma; he bore his illness with remarkable fortitude and patience. Amputation of his arm failed to bring relief and death ended his painful agony, April 18, 1906.

Three years before, Leo XIII had died after a reign of twenty-five years. From his childhood he had been a devoted friend of the fathers, having made all of his studies under their direction. As Sovereign Pontiff, in his personal relations, in many audiences, and by solemn documents, he signified his trust in the Society. The Papal seminaries at Anagni, Lecce in Italy and at Kandy in Ceylon were entrusted to the order by him, and the Jesuit institute at Beirut was raised to the status of a university at his command. By the circular letter, "Aeterni Patris," of August 4, 1879, he enjoined dependence on St. Thomas in theological studies and insisted on adherence to the greatest Christian teacher as the norm for the choice of professors. Twelve Jesuits were beatified and three were canonized by this Pontiff. The most important gift which Leo XIII conferred upon the Society of Jesus was the solemn confirmation of all the privileges of the order from the days of Paul III in the Brief "Dolemus inter alia," [9] issued by him on the occasion of the publication of a new edition of the order's Constitution.

The twenty-fifth General of the Society was Francis Xavier Wernz,[10] a German; he was elected on September 8, 1906 and ruled the order until 1914. Father Wernz was one of the leading authorities on Canon Law in modern times; for twenty-four years he was professor of that science at the Gregorian University, was constantly consulted by the Roman Congregations, and had an important part in the codification of the Canon Law. His greatest work was the *Jus Decretalium* in six volumes. It was

---

[9] *Institutum S.J.*, Vol. I, p. 452.

[10] Ehrle, "Franz Xavier Wernz der 25 General der Gesellschaft Jesu," *Stimmen der Zeit*, Vol. XC, pp. 340 ff.; Laurentius, *Archiv. fur kathol. Kirchenrecht*, Vol. XCIV, pp. 684 ff.

to be expected that such an ecclesiastical scholar would devote his best energies to the improving and the maintaining of the studies of the Society; but he also gave his constant attention to the other works of the order. Under his direction new statutes were issued for the Sodality of the Blessed Virgin Mary, which constituted an important mile-stone in its development; the retreat movement received a new impetus at his hands, as did the work in the foreign missions. Five new provinces were established in the course of his generalate.

The usual anticlerical opposition was encountered during the years of Father Wernz, especially in the violent expulsion of the Jesuits from Portugal in 1910. But far worse than these attacks were the constant accusations, some open and others secret, against the Society, certain provinces and certain individual Jesuits, as failing in the proper obedience to the Holy See and as teaching a doctrine tainted with Modernism. Even the person of Father Wernz was not spared.[11] Yet the General had done everything possible to protect in the whole order the purity of teaching according to the spirit of St. Thomas. Free from personal bitterness and preferring to heal the disease at its roots rather than to resort to repressive measures, when these were avoidable, he pointed out in a letter to the whole Society the principal sources of Modernism, the worldly spirit, frivolity and a passion for novelty. In September 1913 before the delegates of twenty-seven provinces of the order, Father Wernz spoke these significant words: "As Father Ricci before his departure from this life solemnly declared that according to the judgment both of his knowledge and his conscience the Society as a whole was in good condition and had given no just cause for its suppression; so can I, not far now from my own grave, declare that the Society holds itself in good condition and has given no reasonable grounds for the persecution and calumnies, with which it now sees itself beset." The General's reference to his own death proved only too true, for he succumbed, a victim of diabetes, August 19, 1914. His final hours were consoled by the last blessing of the dying Pius X, who not two hours later passed to his eternal reward.

Pius X by his decree on Frequent Communion gave the final justification to the Society's centuries-old struggle for this practice. The Biblical Institute at Rome was entrusted at his command to the scholars of the order. Despite many influences which under the pretext of zeal sought to shake the Pope's confidence in the fathers, Pius X proved himself a true friend of the Society, sincerely sharing its joys and sorrows. This fact was especially manifest in his letter of congratulation on the centenary of the Restoration in 1914.

The present Father General, Wladimir Ledóchowski, was elected

---

[11] *Osservatore Rom.*, Aug. 21, 1914.

February 11, 1915. Father Ledóchowski, born of a noble Polish family and nephew of the late Cardinal Ledóchowski, entered the Society in 1889; he worked as a writer after his ordination, then was named Provincial of Galicia (Austrian Poland), and later was made German Assistant. Exceedingly difficult was the task which faced the new General: the government of the order and the maintenance of its unity in the face of the turmoil and dissensions of the World War. When Italy entered the conflict, he moved the seat of government to Zizers in Switzerland so that the intercourse with the various provinces might be as little hampered as possible. Father Ledóchowski avoided most carefully any sign of mixing in politics. Nevertheless it was charged in certain countries that he sought to support certain political factions; such a charge plainly ignores the fact that it is beyond the competence of the General to bind his subjects to any political party. The abstention of the General in political matters is amply proven from the records of the Society and from his own correspondence. Actually, in the great struggle individual Jesuits were truly loyal to their respective countries, and hundreds of them served in the various armies as chaplains, stretcher-bearers, and even as combatant soldiers and officers. None of them were held, either by the General or by their fellow members, to have been less Jesuits because of their fulfilment of their patriotic duties.

With the end of the World War other intricate problems confronted the Father General: the organization of provinces had to be adjusted to the new political condition, national enmities which were felt even among the brethren had to be reconciled, and the zeal of the order had to be guarded against the infiltration of laxities and dangerous opinions resulting from the terrible catastrophe and its aftermath. The first problem was met by the creation of the Slavic Assistancy, consisting of the newly constituted provinces of Greater Poland and Masovia, Lesser Poland, Czecho-Slovakia and Jugoslavia, and by the transference of the Belgian province to the English Assistancy. That the second and third problems in actuality proved of little moment, speaks volumes not only for the watchfulness of the General and the superiors but also for the virtue and good-will of the members of the order.

The World War had raised havoc with the foreign mission fields; but a quick recovery and a restrengthening, in fact, a far greater expansion of this apostolic work, actually resulted from the zeal of Benedict XV and Pius XI. In this work the Society has cooperated to such an extent that today there are 3,649 priests and brothers laboring in 47 mission districts. Special efforts have been inaugurated looking toward the reunion of the Eastern schismatics, especially through the Russian College, entrusted to the Society by Pius XI, and by the ordination according to the Greek Rite of several young Jesuit priests. The modern developments in the educational work of the Jesuits will be treated elsewhere. Another task happily settled was the adjustment of the Constitutions of the order to the new Code of Canon Law; after a year of preparation under the direction of the Father General, an extraordinary General Congregation, called in 1923, made the proper provisions. The post-war Society of Jesus has not been without its share of persecution, especially in Mexico and Spain; in the latter country more Jesuits were killed in the recent civil war than in any other persecution in the history of the order. In 1938 another General Congregation was assembled to treat of current problems, and particularly to provide a vicar-general to assist Father Ledóchowski in his declining years. Father Maurice Schurmans of the province of Northern Belgium was chosen for the position. Today the Society of Jesus numbers 25,954 members in 43 provinces, grouped in 8 Assistancies (Italian, German, French, Spanish, English, American, Slavic and Latin-American). The last named Assistancy was organized in 1938.

Benedict XV, a pupil of the Jesuits, proved a devoted father to the order. He ratified the concessions granted to the Society in the adjustment of the Constitutions with the Code of Canon Law, furthered in many ways the Apostleship of Prayer, the Sodality, and the missions of the Society, and gave his special support to the Italian colleges. He entrusted the fathers with the Institute for the Reunion of the Eastern Schismatics at Velehrad.

At no time in its history had the Society found a more generous benefactor on the Pontifical Throne than the late Pius XI. He gave the Oriental Institute, the Russian College and the Brazilian College to the charge of the Society, and assisted in the construction of the new buildings of the Gregorian University. He opened new mission fields for the order. Under his direction a French father, later Archbishop d'Herbigny, was placed in charge of the work for the Reunion of the Eastern Christians; and American Jesuits were sent by the Pope to superintend the Papal Relief Expedition for the starving children of Russia. Pius XI added to the roll of the Saints of the Society, the North American Martyrs, St. Peter Canisius, St. Robert Bellarmine and St. Andrew Bobola, and to the list of the Blessed, fifty-two sons of the order. St. Peter Canisius and St. Robert Bellarmine were given by him the title of Doctor of the Church. The Holy Father issued several documents for the Society; of especial importance are: the declaration in favor of the Spanish Jesuits, the solemn ratification of the Constitutions after the changes made in conformity with the new Code, the recommendation of the Spiritual Exercises, and the naming of St. Ignatius as the heavenly patron of all retreats and spiritual exercises. The present Holy Father, Pius XII, has expressed in word and deed the deepest paternal affection for the Society and its members.

The history of the Society of Jesus in the various European countries

in the nineteenth century will repay consideration. The Jesuits were recalled to Spain [12] by Ferdinand VII in 1815. All charges against them
were investigated and refuted by Don Guitierrez de la Huerta; and all
rights and goods, as far as possible, were restored to them. Nowhere was
the Restoration greeted with greater joy. When Ferdinand VII on May
25, 1815 decreed that the Jesuits might return to those places which
wished for them, fifty-six Spanish cities petitioned for the fathers. Five
years of remarkable development followed, in which so numerous were
the candidates that 5 novitiates had to be opened and eventually 197
members were maintaining 20 foundations, including, besides the Colegio
Imperial in Madrid, 3 colleges in Spain and 3 colleges in Mexico. But
bloody persecution, as much as peaceful success, was to mark the modern
course of the Spanish Jesuits. Scarcely had the anticlerical Liberals captured the government in 1820 than the Cortes decreed the expulsion of
the Society. Wild mobs attacked the houses of the order and slaughtered
twenty-five Jesuits. In 1823 the fathers could again return, though they
were forced to rebuild from the ground up. But their progress was far
slower than formerly, many of the younger members had withdrawn
and a great number of the older ones had died. Men and means were so
lacking that scarcely half the old houses could be opened. After ten years
the province of Spain was erected, with 360 subjects, and 14 foundations
among which were 7 colleges. A new victory of the Liberals and a revolution in the northeastern provinces in 1834 brought new disasters upon the
Spanish Jesuits. In Madrid, swept by the cholera, a rumor was bruited
about that the Jesuits had caused the epidemic by poisoning the wells;
an infuriated mob on July 17 stormed the college and murdered 4 priests,
8 scholastics and 3 brothers. Similar scenes of destruction were soon witnessed in other Spanish cities. Again the Cortes expelled the Society, July
7, 1835. The next seventeen years were years of sorrow in which most
of the Spanish fathers and brothers were forced to live in banishment.
About a third, some sixty or seventy priests, managed to remain, working
singly or in couples for the care of souls in various Spanish dioceses. Others
crossed the seas to open new foundations in Argentina, Colombia and
Chile. The Concordat of 1852 permitted the Jesuits to return and to
rebuild again their houses and colleges. In the Antilles, at Havana and
Santo Spirito in Cuba, and in Puerto Rico new colleges were opened; and
there were also renewed the very fruitful labors in the Philippines, especially at Manila. At home many of the old works were revived or new
ones of equal value started so that the Spanish fathers soon were laboring
in twenty-five houses, great and small. The good hopes for the future
however were dashed to the ground in the Revolution of 1868; once

[12] Frias, *Historia de la Compañia de Jesus en su Asistencia moderna de España,* Madrid
(1923).

more the Spanish Jesuits had to see their works destroyed and themselves taking the road to exile.

After eleven years a restoration was effected which lasted until 1931. During these years the order in Spain developed to a very flourishing state, despite the everpresent threat of banishment by the anticlerical cabinets and the many vexatious hindrances which the enmity of the politicos placed in its path. The undertakings across the seas, strengthened from the motherland, gradually became self-sustaining enough to be organized as separate provinces, while new missions were taken over in India and China. At home the Spanish Jesuits grew to be the largest single group in the entire order, with five provinces, Aragon, Andalusia, Castile, Leon and Toledo. The majority of the fathers were engaged in the spiritual apostolate and in charitable works; especially noteworthy were the twenty-three Retreat Houses in various parts of Spain and the Leprosarium near Gandia. Of equal importance were the educational endeavors of the Spanish Jesuits, who conducted 6 university colleges, 20 minor colleges (secondary schools), 6 minor seminaries, 4 commercial schools, 2 workmen's schools. The technical and business schools at Sarria (Chemical Institute), Bilbao, and above all the Madrid Instituto Catholico de Artes y Industrias with its great library, were of the highest rank. In addition the fathers supported and maintained free schools for the children of the poor with an enrollment of 400,000. Two astronomical observatories were under the direction of the order, one being the renowned Observatorio del Ebro, recently destroyed by Red vandals. Literary activities were fostered in six houses of writers; these fathers edited the *Razon y Fe, Iberica, Estudios Ecclesiasticos, Annales del Instituto Catholico de Artes y Industrias,* the *Monumenta Historica Societatis Jesu,* and three *Messengers of the Sacred Heart,* besides producing many devotional and religious publications, historical works, periodicals and school textbooks.

The whole of this flourishing apostolate was swept away in the Revolution of 1931. Communistic mobs burned and looted the professed house and church in Madrid, the colleges and residences in Seville, Malaga, Alicante, Valencia and Cadiz. The greater part of the Instituto Catholico de Artes y Industrias with its magnificent library, was reduced to ashes. The banishment of the Jesuits and the confiscation of their property, to be expected as a matter of course, came on June 23, 1932. The customary charges of enormous wealth and of political maneuverings were bandied about. The real reason of the anticlericals and their Communistic allies, the hatred of the Jesuits as protagonists of the Holy See and Catholicism, was brought to light in the only official explanation for the destruction of the Society of Jesus in Spain, its abolition because of the fourth vow of obedience to the Holy Father. Indeed the provision of the new Constitution of Spain, forbidding the existence of any religious order the members of which took such a vow, was intended to prevent any future return of the Jesuits. Pope Pius XI himself recognized this fact when on January 24, 1932, speaking of the Spanish Jesuits, he declared: "The Society of Jesus is persecuted because its members are truly men of Christ, who now suffer outrages and are banished for Jesus' name. They are the glory of the Church and of the Pope, they are martyrs to their loyalty to the Vicar of Christ." [13] The scholastics found a refuge in Belgium and Holland; the fathers, in the various provinces of the order and in the foreign missions. Still a considerable number ignored the law and remained in Spain. A terrible fate awaited them. The first indication of what was to come was given by the murder of the priest Martinez and the lay-brother Arkonada by Asturian Communists on October 7, 1934. The two Jesuits died with the cry, "Long live Christ the King," on their lips, a verbal indication of what they stood for. What their assassins stood for was indicated by their treatment of the bodies of the two religious and the Civil Guard, who was slain with them; the corpse of the police officer was unmolested, but the heads of the two Jesuits were bashed in with rifle stocks. Two years later came the holocausts. The complete number of Jesuits who were killed or who died in prison, has not yet been ascertained; but it is known for certain that ninety-five fathers and brothers were murdered by the Reds, while twenty-two more have disappeared in circumstances that make their deaths almost certain. [14] One of the first acts of General Franco was to return the houses and colleges of the Society to the fathers; on May 4, 1938 the General invited the Jesuits to return to Spain. Today the Spanish provinces of the order have resumed almost all their former works.

The history of the Portuguese Jesuits [15] since the Restoration seems to present but a repetition of the fortunes of their Spanish brethren. It was not until 1829 that the Society of Jesus was permitted to reenter Portugal; in that year, July 10, the King, Dom Miguel, with the hope of reviving education and at the promptings of the Minister-President, the Duke de Cadaval, recalled the fathers. Five French fathers under the lead of the superior Delvaux arrived at Lisbon, August 29; they were afforded a most hearty welcome by the King, the Queen Mother, the nobility and the clergy. Truly significant was the greeting extended by the then Marquis of Pombal, a grandson of Carvalho, and by his sister Donna

---

[13] On the reading of the decree on the heroism of the virtues of the Venerable Vincent Pallotti.

[14] *Memorabilia S.J.*, list of the murdered in Vol. V, p. 798; Vol. VI, pp. 50, 173, 266; *The Society of Jesus in Spain*, Rome (1938), pp. 15–23.

[15] *Rétablissement de la C. de J. en Portugal*, lettres du P. J. Delvaux; Burnichon, *La Compagnie de Jésus en France*, Vol. I, pp. 486–496.

Francesca Saldanha, who knelt before Father Delvaux to beg his blessings as a token of forgiveness and insisted that her four sons should be enrolled in the first college the fathers should open. The Jesuits were able to render a unique service to the memory of their former persecutor. On their way to reopen their former college at Coimbra, Delvaux and another father stopped to pray at the grave of the old Marquis in the Franciscan Church in the town of Beira; there they found the coffin still unburied after fifty years. They said Mass for the soul of their ancient enemy and performed the long-delayed burial services for this cruel oppressor of their predecessors. The common people welcomed the fathers back with such demonstrations of joy that their journeys about Portugal became a series of triumphs. A fruitful apostolate was carried on in several cities; colleges were opened at Coimbra and Evora; and the victims of the cholera of 1834 were nursed by the fathers. It goes without saying that the anticlericals did not view with complacency the return of the Society of Jesus. So in the revolution of 1834 which placed Dom Pedro IV, a tool of the Grand Orient, on the throne, the decrees of Pombal were once more renewed and the Jesuits were expelled from the country. Twelve of them were cast into the loathsome prison of São Juliao, from which they were freed on the intercession of the French Ambassador.

Eventually the Portuguese fathers were permitted to return and to take up again their work for souls. Colleges were reopened and other works so developed that in 1880, when the Portuguese province was established, there were nine foundations existing, including three colleges. In 1881 the Portuguese *Messenger of the Sacred Heart* was founded and in 1902 a scientific monthly, *Broteria*. Foreign missions were undertaken in Goa, Macao and Portuguese Africa. But the progress made was very slow, owing to the many vexatious hindrances and petty tyrannies of anticlerical governments; in 1901 the Jesuits were obliged to give up their name for that of "The Fathers of Faith and Fatherland." Complete catastrophe came to the Society in the Revolution of 1908: the fathers at Barro were confined in the common jail for four weeks; the worthy old priest, Machado, venerated throughout the land, died soon after his arrival in Gibraltar from abusive treatment received in prison; the order was banished from the Republic and from all its foreign possessions, with the consequent destruction of all the Jesuit foundations. Some of the fathers migrated to northern Brazil, there to begin flourishing missions in Bahia and Pernambuco; others started another new mission in Southern China at Shiu-Hing. With the return of better days the Portuguese Jesuits have been enabled to go back to their native land, where they maintain six houses. They still operate the missions in Brazil, Goa and China.

The war with anticlericism was fought by none more perseveringly than by the French Jesuits.[16] The initial period of their history in the nineteenth century lasted from 1814–1838. After some unpromising beginnings the membership had so increased by 1820 as to warrant the erection of a province. These early Jesuits accomplished much for the revival of Faith after the evil days of the Revolution and Napoleon through the direction of souls and by the popular missions. In all parts of France they preached to great throngs, bringing thousands back to the Sacraments; nor could they be deterred by the riots repeatedly directed against them. Notable among these preachers were: Ronsin, the director of the Parisian Confraternity of our Lady, Help of Christians, with its 1,350 members drawn from the leading men of the city; McCarthy, whose sermons merited several reprintings; and Guyon, for thirty-three years a popular missioner.

The greatest success and the greatest enmity came to Jesuits in the field of education. When the fathers returned to France they received over 120 invitations to open schools; twenty-one bishops requested them to take charge of educational institutions in their dioceses, and several secular priests sought to resign their colleges to the priests of the order. The eight minor seminaries formerly directed by the Fathers of the Faith were now entrusted to the Jesuits. Such were the standards soon attained in these seminaries, that many lay students, desirous of a Catholic education coupled with cultural training, left the government schools to attend them. Among all these schools St. Acheul enjoyed the highest reputation.

But the success of the seminaries and of Ronsin's confraternities enflamed the hostility of the liberals. They looked with mistrust on the Jesuits and spoke of the novitiate of Montrouge as a hotbed of reaction. The writings of the Comte de Montlosier against the "Modern Jesuits" stirred up a storm of similar publications against the Society and the seminaries in Liberal literary circles and in the freethinking press. The contemporary attack of de Lammenais against Gallicanism aroused the opposition still further. The relations of this unfortunate priest with the Jesuits was soon brought to a close by the Father General Fortis' prohibition of intercourse with him; he had had the support of certain influential fathers who did not perceive his false philosophical principles. The clamor against the Jesuits was aired in the chamber of Deputies; the Jesuit Question was to haunt that body for many years to come. The Government insisted that the seminaries be placed under the monopoly of the University of Paris, as established by Napoleon in 1808. Such an arrangement the bishops refused even to consider; it would deliver the education of future priests as well as future Catholic laymen into the

---

[16] Burnichon, *La Compagnie de Jésus en France 1814–1914*, Paris (1914–1922).

hands of the freethinkers who dominated the University. The anticlericals however triumphed; and on July 16, 1828 Charles X signed a decree placing all ecclesiastical secondary schools under the University and excluding from their teaching staffs all members of unrecognized corporations. Thus the Jesuits, as an unrecognized body, were barred from all educational activity. Two years later in the July Revolution mobs sacked Montrouge and St. Acheul, while the new government completed the work by expelling the Society of Jesus from the country.

The second period opened with only fifty-six Jesuits residing in France. Educational work had not been abandoned; across the borders at Fribourg in Switzerland, at Passage in Spain, and at Brugelette in Belgium, colleges for French youths were maintained. They were well filled. After 1832 most of the Jesuits were back in France, employed almost entirely in the care of souls. Their only educational activity in the country was in their own houses of study at St. Acheul and Vals. That these seminaries of the order attained a high standard, may be judged from such professors as Gury, Gautrelet and Ramière. To the last two is owing the development of one of the greatest devotional organizations of the modern Catholic world, the Apostleship of Prayer and the League of the Sacred Heart.[17] The Apostleship of Prayer was started by Gautrelet in 1846 and continued by Ramière, who united with it the League of the Sacred Heart in 1860. The united movement, devoted especially to the veneration of the Sacred Heart, swept the whole Catholic Church; Pius IX gave it his ardent support; Father General Roothaan declared it to be a special work of the Society; the clergy, secular and religious, became its enthusiastic promoters. Today it counts a membership of 25,000,000. The chief means of extending the movement has been the monthly periodical, *The Messenger of the Sacred Heart*; the first *Messenger* appeared in French in 1860; today there are 56 *Messengers* published in 34 languages, with a total subscription list of 1,768,560. The American *Messenger* is first with 280,000 subscribers.

The popular missions engaged several eloquent fathers, who followed the lead of Father Roothaan in bringing the Spiritual Exercises back into repute. First among all these preachers was de Ravignan,[18] who succeeded Lacordaire in the pulpit of Notre Dame from 1837 to 1846. By the force of his convictions, by the exactness of his thought, and his noble priestly presence he held spellbound the distinguished audiences of the Conferences. In 1841 he ventured to preach a mission for his hearers; the result went beyond expectation, the Church of St. Eustache was too small to hold the throng of students, university professors, literary lights,

---

[17] Hamon, *Histoire de la Dévotion au S. Coeur*, 4 Vols., Paris (1923–1931).

[18] Ponlevoy, *The Life of Father de Ravignan of the Society of Jesus*, trans. London (1868).

members of the nobility and government officials. By personal interviews as well as by his moving sermons, de Ravignan brought numbers of them back to the Faith. Not only Paris, but Amiens, Brussels, London and Rome listened to his sincere and direct appeal. Across the seas and in the lands of the heathens the labors of the French Jesuits recalled the memories of Jogues and Marquette. In twenty years missions were begun in Kentucky, New Orleans, Canada, Cayenne, Algiers, Madagascar and Madura. So many activities were only possible because of the great increase in numbers; in 1850 there were 200 novices being trained in 6 novitiates.

In 1841 new storms began to gather against the Jesuits, and again on the question of education, although at the time the fathers conducted no schools for externs. The bishops never relinquished their stand for the freedom of education against the University's monopoly; in this they were supported by sincere French Catholics under the leadership of Montalembert, Lacordaire and de Ravignan. About the Society of Jesus on more than one occasion the battle principally centered. In the press and in the Chamber the Jesuits were bitterly attacked, and as strenuously defended. In 1842 Eugene Sue's *Wandering Jew* began to appear, replete with infamous and foul charges against the Society.[19] Against the order too wrote Thiers, Cousin, Michelet, Quinet, and Béranger. In the Jesuits' defense replied Louis Veuillot and Joly; the book of de Ravignan, *The Existence and Institute of the Society of Jesus,* created a profound impression. In the Parliament the cause of the fathers was eloquently upheld by Montalembert, Mgr. Dupanloup, Beugnot and Barthélemy. The Premier, Guizot, sought a settlement of the controversy in the suppression of the Society of Jesus in France. For this purpose he dispatched an agent, de Rossi, to Gregory XVI with the request that the Pontiff dissolve the order in the French dominions. This the Holy Father would not do. Father General Roothaan came to the rescue and, to prevent greater evils, ordered the dissolution of four French houses, Paris, Lyons, St. Acheul and Laval. When Guizot pressed for further concessions Gregory XVI returned a decided "No." The other houses remained in the quiet possession of the fathers, so that during the almost universal Revolution of 1848 the French Jesuits were able to afford an asylum to their exiled brethren.

With the third period, beginning in 1850, came complete freedom of education by the Falloux Laws. The next half century passed peacefully enough, except for the Revolt of the Paris Commune in 1871 with the murder of five fathers, Olivaint, Ducoudray, Clerc, Caubert and de

---

[19] Brou, *Les Jésuites de la légende,* Paris (1906).

Bengy,[20] and the anticlerical attacks of 1880. Olivaint's glorious death in a sense was a great loss, for he was distinguished among the French Jesuits as an educator, preacher and master of retreats.[21] The order so prospered in the first decade of the period that by 1863 there were four provinces, Paris, Lyons, Toulouse and Champagne, with seven foreign missions. The work of teaching flourished so that in 1880 the Jesuits were conducting twenty-six colleges and twelve seminaries; especially well known were the Parisian colleges of Vaugirard, Ste. Geneviève and St. Ignace. The colleges of St. Clément in Metz and Ste. Marie in Toulouse attained notable successes in preparing students for the military academies of St. Cyr, the École Normale and the École Polytechnique. In these institutions the Jesuit trained students exerted a wholesome moral and religious influence. Of course the Jesuits in 1898 had to be dragged into the Dreyfus affair.[22] Yet of the 180 officers of the General Staff, at the most ten were pupils of the fathers, the Chief of Staff had spent two years at a Jesuit school and eight at government lycée; none of the officers about the unfortunate colonel, nor any of his judges were former pupils of the Jesuits.

When the anticlericals in 1880 again formed the government, the Jesuits were once more marked for destruction. The decree of March 29, 1880 ordered the Society of Jesus, as an unrecognized corporation, to evacuate all its houses and colleges; forty-two houses and twenty-three schools were affected by the law. Eventually the governmental policy was relaxed and the Jesuits were allowed to resume their former employments, and even to reopen most of their colleges. In 1900 there were 3,086 French Jesuits maintaining 29 colleges, 8 major seminaries, 42 residences, 6 retreat houses at home, and 9 foreign missions, with universities at Beirut and Zi-ka-wei. A fruitful literary apostolate was pursued in the last half of the nineteenth century; it will suffice here to indicate its value by the mention of the *Études*, the common work of four French provinces.

At the end of the century anticlericalism was again in the saddle, and again the Jesuits had to go. The Associations Law of Waldeck-Rousseau, 1889 to 1901, expelled the Society of Jesus, together with all other religious orders, from France. Not only were property rights violently abused, but even the very assembling of religious was proscribed. The seventy-six Jesuit foundations were closed; the scholasticates and novitiates, however, were maintained in neighboring countries. Many of

---

[20] Ponlevoy, *Actes de la captivité et de la mort des PP. Olivaint* etc., XVI ed., Paris (1894).

[21] Clair, *Pierre Olivaint*, Paris (1890).

[22] Duhr, *Jesuiten Fabeln*, p. 857 ff.; Baumgarten, *Ordenszucht und Ordensstrafrecht*, p. 521 (1932).

the priests remained assisting the secular clergy, conducting sodalities and other Catholic societies, and continuing the literary work.

In the World War the French Jesuits more than proved their patriotism; priests and missionaries returned from their exile to serve and even to die for their native land. Of the chaplains 18 died in the line of duty; of the combatants, 165 were killed on the field of battle. In the face of such devotion and the similar sacrifices of other religious, the anti-clericals had to yield. Although the laws have not yet been revoked, they have become dead letters. The Society has begun once more its educational and pastoral work, has increased its literary activity, and of late years has devoted special efforts to the Social Question and to the Youth Movement. The four French provinces today number 3,137 members, operating 40 educational institutions, 51 residences, 17 retreat-houses and a house of writers.

The Restoration found the Italian Jesuits established in the Papal States and in the Kingdom of the Two Sicilies.[23] Within a short time colleges or houses were opened in other Italian states, Modena, Genoa, Piedmont and Venice; while the membership increased steadily so that there were about 1,000 members of the two provinces in 1820. The King of Sardinia, Charles Emmanuel, resigned his crown in 1815 to become a novice; he died a holy death four years later at San Andrea. The Italian fathers were not to be long without persecution; banishment came in Naples in 1820, the first of a long series of oppressions. The anticlericals of Italy pursued the Italian Jesuits with a hatred as persistent as it was venomous. From the lodges a systematic warfare was directed against them; in the streets the rabble were whipped up by the vilest and most fantastical calumnies to violent assaults on the houses and the members of the Society. As elsewhere, the attacks were made as the preliminary blows against the Papacy. The revolutionary year of 1830 witnessed outrageous excesses perpetrated on the Jesuits in the Papal States, at Ferrara, Bologna and Modena. The storm was weathered and the order continued its educational and charitable works. In the cholera of 1837 the fathers and brothers devoted themselves regardless of danger to the care of the stricken, even to the burial of the victims. The Roman Senate as a token of its appreciation of the services of the Jesuits placed six splendid candles on the altar of St. Ignatius.

Overwhelming disaster deluged the Italian Jesuits in 1848; from every state in the peninsula, even from Piedmont, which up to that time had always protected the Society, they were expelled. The attack had

---

[23] Capelletti, *Breve Storia della provincia Veneta di C. di G. dalle sue origini fino ai nostri giorni 1874–1914*; Galletti, *Memorie storiche intorno alla provincia Romana di C. di G. (1814–1914)*; Lesanza, *I Gesuiti in Sicilia nel Seculo 19*; Monti, *La C. di G. nel territorio della provincia Torinese*; Volpe, *I Gesuiti nel Napolitano 1814–1914.*

long been prepared by all sorts of scurrilous screeds, the *Il Gesuita Moderno* of Gioberti being a fair sample. At Spezzia the mob greeted the Jesuit exiles from Genoa and Turin with cries of "death to the Jesuits" and pelted them with stones; at Naples the 114 Jesuits were threatened with massacre and driven ignominiously from the city. The worst outrages occurred in Rome. The revolutionists surrounded the Papal carriage as Pius IX was driving through the streets and so violently assailed the Pontiff with their shouting against the Jesuits that the Holy Father fainted; Mazzinian riffraff raised a tumult in the Gesù during a sermon. Pius IX, himself soon to be forced to flee the city a fugitive from mob-violence, requested Father Roothaan to send all Jesuits out of Rome. The fathers and brothers were therefore dispersed and the General himself went into exile outside of Italy. After the storm had passed the Jesuits returned to build anew their apostolic and educational labors. A few quiet years passed, during which, in the cholera of 1854 and 1857, the members of the order spent themselves for the plague-stricken in Rome, Naples, Sicily and Venice. Their charity availed them little; for in 1859 and again in 1860 destruction, pillage and exile were visited upon them. As the conquering armies of the Piedmontese and the Garibaldians advanced over the peninsula, the Jesuits were driven from state after state, Sardinia and Piedmont (1856), Modena (1858), Tuscany, Milan, the Romagna, Parma, Lombardy (1859), Sicily and Naples (1860). In vain did Father General Beckx protest to Victor Emmanuel against the seizure of fifty-seven colleges and residences; when his troops entered the province of Venezia the Jesuits suffered the usual fate. The anticlericals often clothed their malevolence with the trappings of patriotism, for the question of Italian nationalism was unfortunately mixed up in the struggle. In the perplexing problem of unity, two eminent Jesuits, Passaglia, the theologian of the dogma of the Immaculate Conception, and Curci, the founder of the *Civiltà Cattolica*, adopted mistaken views that led to their defection. Neither abandoned the Faith, and Curci was received back into the order a few days before his death.

Only in Rome was it possible for the Society to exist after 1860, and the breach of the Porta Pia in 1870 spelled their doom in the Eternal City. The Roman College, San Andrea and part of the Professed House were seized at once; eventually in 1873 the Italian Parliament destroyed the Society of Jesus and all other religious orders by a decree declaring them non-existent. That there was a special animus against the Society was indicated by the refusal to bestow a pension on Father Beckx, although such a gratuity was granted to the Generals of all the other religious orders. These good superiors at once resolved to share with the General of the Jesuits what was to be given to them. In the years that followed, the Jesuits lived in Italy much as secular priests. With the members thus dispersed and their educational work only possible on a small scale, even though the government did not always press the anti-religious laws, the Society's development necessarily was small. One good result of the catastrophe was the aid which the exiled Italian Jesuits were able to render to the Church in the New World, the Turin Jesuits in California, the Roman Jesuits in Brazil, and others of their brethren in China. In the twentieth century a better day dawned; since the Vatican Treaty, the Society of Jesus in Italy pursues its spiritual and cultural labors unhampered and with great fruit. Today the 5 Italian provinces, Rome, Naples, Sicily, Turin and Venice-Milan number 2,119 members and conduct 44 educational institutions, 31 residences, 9 retreat-houses and 2 houses of writers.

The Society of Jesus in modern Germany began its career in the small Swiss mission, shortly before the Restoration.[24] A college was founded at Brig in 1814; three years later at Fribourg another was opened which in a short time achieved a European reputation. After a decade of growth a province was erected with jurisdiction over the scattered houses in Switzerland, Germany and all the Netherlands. Yet the outlook for the Jesuits in these regions was none too promising; even in Switzerland, where the situation was the best, a movement against the Society was already under way. The very favorable attitude of the Catholic cantons towards the Society (Schwyz in 1836 had called upon the Jesuits to open a college in its chief town and Lucerne in 1845 entrusted the fathers with the conduct of the seminary and the theological faculty) aroused the determined opposition of the Protestant cantons. The so-called liberals in the latter districts became especially hostile. Victory in the War of the Sonderbund enabled them to force the dismissal of the Jesuits, the closing of all the houses and colleges, and the dispersal of the 274 priests and brothers. Since that time the Society of Jesus as an organization has never been able to enter the Swiss Confederation. One good result was the coming of several excellent priests to America; among these were Burchard Villiger, one of the builders of the Maryland province, and John Bapst, a leader of the Society of Jesus in New England. A number of Swiss Jesuits became prominent members of the order in Germany, Anderledy, Hurter, Meschler and V. Cathrein among several others.

The early efforts of the order in Germany itself were confined to four scattered and precariously existing residences; occasionally retreats were given elsewhere, or apostolic journeys made through the Diaspora. Not that there was any lack of good friends in the hierarchy, the clergy and the laity, who earnestly desired the setting up of Jesuit colleges; simply the prejudices of others, inherited either from Protestantism or from the

---

[24] Strater, *Die Jesuiten in Schweiz 1814–1847*, Eins. (1914); Pfulf, *Die Anfänge der deutschen Provinz der neu erstandenen Ges. J. und ihr Wirken in der Schweiz 1805–1847*, Fb. (1922).

French Revolution, effectively blocked any realization of their good wishes. Thus the National Assembly at Frankfort in 1848 passed a declaration that "the Society of Jesus together with the Redemptorists and the Liguorians were banished for all time from the German land." The fortunes of the Jesuits in Holland and Belgium, who were early separated from the German fathers, will be treated later.

With the subsiding of the storms of 1848, a better period began for the Society in Germany. The opening for the Jesuit activities came through the popular missions.[25] A mission preached in Hopsten in Westphalia in 1849 on the invitation of the parish priest, Wilhelm von Ketteler, later Bishop of Mainz, was attended with such remarkable results, that Father General Roothaan and the German superiors determined to inaugurate a systematic development of popular missions by the establishment of mission centers both in North and South Germany. So rapidly did this particular apostolate grow that in a very short time busy mission stations were in operation in Westphalia, the Rhineland and Baden. The fathers Roh, Hasslacher and von Zeil preached the missions with special success. One of the first missions given in Baden attracted 7,000 men, so that the sermons had to be delivered in the open air; government officials, alarmed by a gathering of so many men, began to take military measures to suppress an uprising, until they learned the spiritual nature of the warfare in which the crowds were engaged. Up to 1872 the German Jesuits preached an average of eighty missions a year.

With the success of the preaching apostolate came a large increase in membership; two novitiates were opened, while the gift of the ancient Abbey of Maria Laach enabled the province to establish a scholasticate that soon earned a high reputation, both because of its faculty and its great library. Within twenty years twelve residences were being maintained; in these centers the fathers achieved great good by their sermons, their dispensing of the Sacraments, their guidance of Catholic societies, and their direction of fifty-two sodalities with a total membership of 16,728. In the lands across the sea the fathers of the province labored for the German immigrants in Southern Brazil and in the United States, where the Buffalo mission was founded in 1869, and for the conversion of the natives in India, where the Bombay mission was begun in 1856. In the educational field only one extern college was operated and that was established across the frontier in Austria, though for German youth; it was the celebrated College of Stella Matutina at Feldkirch. On the orders of the Provincial, Father Anderledy, the German writers and theologians entered the lists to defend the Syllabus of Pius IX and the Vatican Council. They waged a strenuous battle for Catholic truth, especially in the pages of the *Stimmen*

---

[25] Duhr, *Aktenstücke zur Geschichte der Jesuiten-missionen in Deutschland 1848–1872*, Freiburg (1903).

aus Maria Laach; that warfare gained for them many friends and likewise so many bitter enemies that their banishment was once proposed in the Prussian Diet. This period of domestic successes reached its height about 1870, at the time of the Franco-Prussian War, in which struggle 196 Jesuits served as chaplains or hospital attendants.

Disaster, however, was in preparation. The very successes of the fathers inflamed the enmity of bigoted Protestants and the hatred of anticlerical Liberals; a third force, the politics of Bismarck, now united these two for a frontal attack on the Jesuits and eventually on Catholicism itself, the Kulturkampf. In 1872 came the Anti-Jesuit Laws, which the Iron Chancellor forced through the Reichstag.[26] Thorough they certainly were: not only was the Society of Jesus suppressed and its foundations dissolved, but all priestly employments, preaching, dispensing the Sacraments, bestowing absolution were forbidden the members of the order; even the wearing of the habit in the churches was proscribed. Other orders, the Redemptorists, the Lazarists, the Missionaries of the Holy Ghost and the Religious of the Sacred Heart were included in the ruthless decrees, because of their supposed connection with or similarity to the Society of Jesus.

Catastrophe, wide-sweeping and total, it was; yet the German fathers faced it with a courage and an energy truly heroic. Though nothing in their home land remained to them, immediately they began to set up in Holland a novitiate and a house of classical studies, in England at Ditton Hall a theologate, which in later years was moved to Valkenburg in Holland. Numbers, instead of diminishing, increased more than ever until in 1907, when the Buffalo mission was separated and joined to the American provinces, the German Jesuits totaled 1,458 members, a figure almost twice that of 1872. In Holland many labors were engaged in, the influences of which crossed the border, so that though absent the German Jesuits continued to effect good in their fatherland. Such works were accomplished in two retreat-houses and in literary labors, especially through the *Stimmen.* Later when the application of the anti-Jesuit laws was somewhat modified, individual fathers returned to Germany for spiritual employments, missions and retreats, and for participation in learned assemblies. The German province suffered a hard blow in the defection of von Hoensbroech in 1892; from an ardent literary defender of the Society, the Papacy and the Church, this unfortunate priest became the bitterest opponent of all three.[27] His writings, *Fourteen Years a Jesuit* and the *Jesuit Order,* constituted a most forceful attack upon the Society. Yet it was this apostate who unwillingly gave opportunity for a most telling refutation

---

[26] Sträter, *Die Vertreibung der Jesuiten aus Deutschland in J. 1872,* Fb. (1914), p. 116, Erg.-H zu den *Stimmen aus Maria Laach.*

[27] Von Nostiz-Rieneck, *Graf Paul von Hoensbroechs Flucht aus Kirche und Orden* (1913).

of the old charge of the Jesuits teaching that the end justifies the means. He brought to the courts a suit for the reward of 2,000 florins which had been offered to anyone who could prove this charge. His proofs failed to impress the court of the first instance; and when he appealed the case to the higher court he met with a similar failure. As in other provinces, the works in foreign fields profited by the dispersal of the German fathers. New missions were opened in the very Protestant lands of Denmark and Sweden; today in the first country the Jesuits maintain two colleges and three residences, and in the second a residence and two stations. A large number of the exiles journeyed across the seas to increase greatly the work being done in Brazil, Chile and the United States, and the missionary labors in Bombay, Poona, Africa and at last Japan. Thus in 1910 there were 422 fathers and brothers of the German province serving on foreign missions. For the work of education, besides Feldkirch, which continued to maintain its high reputation, a college for German boys was opened in Holland, at Sittard, and another for Danish and German youths near Copenhagen.

Although several attempts were made to obtain the repeal of the anti-Jesuit laws, and some mitigation was eventually allowed, it was not until April 19, 1917 that that obnoxious legislation was finally removed.[28] Certainly the loyalty of the German Jesuits to their country in the World War more than merited such consideration: 535 of them served in the army, 203 as combatants, 181 as chaplains, 151 as stretcher-bearers. The opening of the country to the fathers saw not only the transference of many contemporary works back to the home land, but the launching of several new enterprises. Such has been the growth that in the place of one province, today there are three, Lower Germany, Upper Germany and Eastern Germany, with a total membership of 1,706, which support 6 educational institutions, 26 residences, 5 retreat-houses and 1 house of writers, besides maintaining missions in Denmark, Sweden and Japan. If in the present condition of affairs their situation is precarious, the German fathers and brothers this time again are facing it courageously and resolutely.

The first Jesuits to come to Austria [29] were the exiles from Russia in 1820, who found a refuge in Galicia, the Polish province of the Empire. At Tarnapol they opened a very successful college. The progress was slow but steady; by 1848 the Austrian Jesuits were maintaining five foundations. In that year of universal revolution everything was swept away, only a few fathers being able to hold on in the college at Innsbruck. Four years later a return could be made; and from that time until the World War, the spiritual, educational and scholarly work of the Austrian fathers flourished continuously. Of first rank was their teaching in the theological faculty of the University of Innsbruck and their management of the Canisianum, a seminary for the secular clergy; the fame of the Innsbruck teachers and seminary has become world-wide. Other colleges and several residences were operated not only in Austria proper but in Croatia, Bosnia and Herzegovina; popular missions were preached frequently and successfully; great zeal was manifested in spreading the devotion to the Sacred Heart and in directing the Sodality of the Blessed Virgin Mary. The revival of this society in the last century owes much to the efforts of an Austrian Jesuit, Abel; great sodality-days were held in Linz in 1907, Vienna in 1909 and Salzburg in 1910. With the break-up of the Austrian Empire the fathers in the Slavic sections were organized into new provinces. Today the Austrian province is almost purely German; it consists of 402 members who until recently operated 4 educational institutions, 8 residences and 1 retreat-house. The horizon is far from reassuring; already the theological faculty at Innsbruck has been suppressed and the Canisianum has met a similar fate. But the determination of the Austrian fathers to carry on their seminary independently indicates the type of Jesuits who are meeting this crisis.

The Hungarian Jesuits belonged to the Austrian province until 1909, when the Province of Hungary [30] was established. The first house to be opened was at Kalocza in 1820, when Archbishop Klobuszycki, a member of the old Society, gave the work to the exiled Russian Jesuits. Notable among the works of the Jesuits in modern Hungary are the observatory at Kalocza and the apostolic labors in Budapest. After the World War the short-lived communistic republic of Bela Kuhn threatened the existence of the Society in Hungary; but with the passing of that danger and up to the present day the Hungarian Jesuits have achieved a most fruitful apostolate in the press, in priestly labors and in the conduct of sodalities. The order in Hungary today numbers 342 members and conducts 5 educational institutions, 3 residences and 1 retreat-house. The work of the Jesuits in Czechoslovakia is done by 246 members employed in 6 educational institutions, 6 residences and 2 retreat-houses; the work in Jugoslavia is accomplished by 224 members employed in 6 educational institutions, 8 residences and 3 retreat-houses.

The activities of the Polish Jesuits [31] during the nineteenth century were largely restricted to Galicia, the Polish province of the Austrian Empire. Indeed the first Austrian Jesuits were mostly Poles, refugees from Russia in 1820; their first college was established at Tarnopol. Some of the Polish veterans of the old Society hastened to join the restored order, notable among whom was the venerable Primate of Poland, the

---

[30] Koch, "Ungarn," *Jesuiten-Lexikon.*

[31] Zalenski, *Les Jésuites de la Russie-Blanche,* Vol. II, pp. 263–352; Koch, "Polen," *Jesuiten-Lexikon.*

Archbishop Roszynski of Posen. The college of Tarnopol was not long in gaining a distinguished name; to it were added colleges at Lemberg and Neu Sandec and six other foundations, justifying the erection of the province of Galicia in 1846. The Revolution of 1848 brought a few years of interruption, during which the Polish fathers devoted themselves to the giving of popular missions among their countrymen in Silesia and Posen. Among these early Polish Jesuits, one deserves a special mention, the priest Antoniewicz,[32] famed as preacher of popular missions and as an ascetical writer. In 1852 the work in Austrian Poland was resumed, to continue in quiet steady development until the World War. The usual collegiate and sacerdotal works were carried on and a foreign mission in Rhodesia was undertaken. Cracow was the center of the fathers' labors; here was a college and here also was a house of writers who produced the learned review *Przeglad powszechny,* a Polish *Messenger of the Sacred Heart,* and a mission magazine. A very extraordinary and difficult task was accepted by the Polish Jesuits, when on the request of Leo XIII they took in hand the reform of the Uniate Basilian monks. From 1882–1904 the fathers directed the monks in their six monasteries, instilling a new life which manifested itself in a notable increase in numbers and in spirit.

With the resurgence of Poland as a nation, new fields of opportunity were opened to the Polish Jesuits; a second province was erected, a mission established in Roumania, and another mission begun for the reunion of the Eastern Christians. In the last work an extraordinary departure from the general rule of the order was made in the permission for the members of the mission to adopt the ceremonies and dress of the Greek Rite. Today the Polish provinces are Greater Poland and Masovia with 389 members conducting 5 educational institutions, 8 residences and 1 house of writers, and Lesser Poland with 455 members, employed in 3 educational institutions, 12 residences and 3 houses of retreats. Unfortunately much of this splendid work has been destroyed in the War of 1939.

The first Jesuits to return to Lithuania, one of the parts of Russia where the Society maintained itself after 1774, came to Kaunas in 1923. In the old Jesuit college and church of St. Stanislaus they began again the labors of the order. In the beginning the mission was under the direction of the Lower German province; but aid from Lithuanians in foreign lands, especially in America, enabled a province to be erected. The Lithuanian province today counts 97 members and maintains 1 college and 6 residences.

In the Low Countries, the prospects were not very bright for the Society when the Restoration was proclaimed at Rome. The bigoted Calvinistic government which dominated the whole area was strongly set against any

---

[32] Speil, *P. Karl Antoniewicz der G. J.,* Breslau (1875).

renewal. Yet in the face of watchful opposition the beginning, made by H. Fonteyne, a priest of the old Society, in his establishment of a novitiate at Maastricht, was quietly carried on. The first employments were the giving of the Spiritual Exercises to the clergy in the seminaries at Ghent, Tournai, Namur and Liége, a work which was continued despite the royal prohibition of 1824. In the next year for safety's sake the novitiate was transferred to Destelberg. But the blow fell, nevertheless, and not only the novices but all members of the Society were driven from the land. Most found a refuge in Switzerland or in Germany. The independence of Belgium in 1830 opened the doors of that region for the Jesuits; from that day the order has grown so rapidly and so extensively as to rival in numbers and in achievement the best days under Farnese and Manare.[33] Some sixteen colleges for extern pupils have been established in the principal cities, all have been and are numerously attended. Most of the education has been in the classical tradition; nevertheless, at Liége a technical school was established, and at Antwerp a school for training consular and commercial agents for foreign service. Most fruitful have been the literary labors of the Belgian Jesuits during the last century: in 1836 the work of the Bollandists was revived and has been maintained to the present, perhaps on an even greater scale than before; besides numerous books and pamphlets, the fathers edit the *Nouvelle Revue Théologique*, the *Missions Belges*, a Flemish and a French *Messenger of the Sacred Heart*. The giving of the Spiritual Exercises to priests, to religious, to laymen, especially to working-men, has been zealously prosecuted; today, the Belgian Jesuits conduct six flourishing houses of retreat. A similar zeal has been displayed in the development of societies of youth, particularly, the Sodality of the Blessed Virgin; over 150 sodalities are under the direct guidance of the fathers. Of the work of Belgian Jesuits in the Foreign missions of Bengal, Ceylon and the Congo, mention will be made later. Today there are 2 provinces in the country; the province of Southern Belgium with 849 members, 12 educational institutions, 1 residence and 3 retreat-houses; and the Province of Northern Belgium with 884 members, 10 educational institutions, 7 residences and 3 retreat-houses.

In the second quarter of the nineteenth century better days came for the Dutch Jesuits [34] despite a continued, if vanishing, opposition. In 1837 a boarding-school could be opened at Katwijk, and four years later the mission of the old Society, Ravenstein, could again be occupied. In 1849 the Dutch mission was raised to the status of a vice-province, in the next year to the rank of a complete province. In the years that have followed the Dutch Jesuits in a quiet, steady development have obtained a firm foundation in the land, just as their fellow Catholics at the same time with splen-

[33] Poncelet, *La Compagnie de Jésus en Belgique: Aperçu Historique* (1907).
[34] Koch, "Holland," *Jesuiten-Lexikon*.

did and tenacious faith have won through to complete freedom. The province conducts five colleges at Nymegen, Amsterdam, the Hague, Katwijk and Sittard, besides operating residences in six of the leading cities of Holland. Like their Belgian brethren the Dutch fathers have devoted themselves to the work of laymen's retreats, especially to the retreats for laborers; in pursuance of their work they maintain three retreat-houses. The writers of the province have produced a numerous and valuable list of works in theology, asceticism, church history, and literature, besides textbooks and scientific treatises; they publish *Studie*, founded in 1868, a periodical which has taken rank with the *Civiltà* and the *Stimmen*. Their foreign missions in Batavia and Java will be noticed in the succeeding chapter. The present province of the Netherlands counts 728 members, with 5 educational institutions, 9 residences and 3 houses of retreat.

The prosperity and peace which the new Society has enjoyed in England and Ireland is quite a reversal from the persecutions of the older days. Yet it is not to be supposed that there were no great difficulties encountered, especially in the initial years.[35] The English Jesuits had to strive for many years to obtain the local recognition of the canonical restoration of their order.[36] During the period of the affiliation with the Russian Jesuits the Vicars-Apostolic, with the exception of Dr. Milner, refused acknowledgment of their status as religious. Even after 1814 the Vicars-Apostolic, again with the exception of Dr. Milner, still hesitated. An excuse for their difficulties may be found in the ambiguities connected with the Restoration. Indeed Cardinal Consalvi had alleged that the order was only to be considered restored in those places where the civil authorities agreed to it. Some English Catholics dreaded the effect of a revival of the Jesuits on the progress of Catholic Relief; it was even represented in Rome that the existence of the order in England was odious to the Government and detrimental to the Catholic cause. The Papacy, hesitant to do anything that might retard Emancipation, published no definite order in the matter until January 1, 1829, the year of Emancipation. On that date Leo XII issued a rescript declaring that the Bull of Restoration had force in England and that the Society of Jesus was canonically restored there. Another obstacle holding back the Jesuits in those early days was the grave lack of men and resources. Uncertainty as to status caused the abandonment of vocation by some and discouraged the entrance of others. Most of the fathers had to labor in lonely, scattered missions, amidst poverty and discouragements; practically, they were foreign missionaries in their

---

[35] *Letters and Notices*, especially Vols. XXXII, XXXIII.

[36] Pollen, "The Restoration of the English Jesuits, 1803–1817," *The Month*, Vol. CXV, pp. 585–597; "The Recognition of the Jesuits in England," *The Month*, Vol. CXVI, pp. 23–36.

own home land. The most they could hope to accomplish was to keep the Faith alive in their isolated flocks.

With Emancipation came a happier time; the thirty years following, constituting the second period of the history of the province, were years of steady and quiet advance. The English Catholic Church, emerging from the catacombs and having to provide also for the large Irish Catholic immigration, was during these years absorbed in founding of parishes and the erection of churches. The Jesuits cooperating in the work opened up parishes in various parts of England; more than fifty parishes now in the charge of the secular clergy were originally Jesuit foundations. The energies of the fathers of those days were almost exclusively devoted to the building of churches and poor-schools, a task exceedingly difficult in view of the fact that most of the funds had to be raised from the meager resources of the poor. Educational work in the first dozen years was restricted to Stonyhurst; but with the appointment of Randall Lythgoe as Provincial in 1841, great advances were begun in this field. Mount St. Mary's in Chichester, St. Francis Xavier's in Liverpool, St. Beuno's in North Wales and the English college at Malta, were founded by this zealous priest. Because of these and other successful projects, Lythgoe is justly considered one of the great men of the province. There was little or no literary activity among the fathers during these early years, a deficiency which was remedied by the influx of converts as a result of the Oxford Movement. By 1864 over fifty such converts had joined the Society of Jesus; among them were such men as Christie, Henry Coleridge, Harper and Purbrick. The converts, while not possessing the exact theological and philosophical knowledge of the older men, far surpassed them in general scholarship, in wider education, and in an ability to reach the minds and obtain the attention of their Protestant fellow-countrymen. Their advent broadened the scope of the Society's work, especially stimulating the literary apostolate, as was witnessed by the inception of the *Month* with Coleridge as its first editor. The first foreign mission was begun in Calcutta in 1834; it had to be relinquished some years later. In 1854 the mission of British Guiana, which has been in the charge of the English province to the present, was undertaken.

It was distinctly fortunate that at the time when the influence of the converts was beginning to be felt the Provincial should have been Father Alfred Weld. Of the old Catholic stock, Weld cherished and retained all that was good in the past; of a broadminded character, himself a man of scientific, historical and literary attainments, he welcomed and sympathized with the forward-looking projects proposed. He elevated the province from contentment with local and parochial viewpoints to aspirations for higher and broader accomplishments in literature, education and in the mission fields. To him may be credited the founding of the *Month* in 1864 and with it the numerous and fruitful literary labors of the English Jesuits.

During Weld's term of office and for some years afterwards, perhaps the only serious cloud on the horizon was the opposition of Cardinal Manning to the Society.[37] At the beginning of his conversion Manning had been on intimate terms with the order; he celebrated his first Mass in the Jesuit church at Farm Street (London), assisted by de Ravignan; and for some time he continued to say Mass, occupy a confessional and preach there. But eventually he came to possess views in regard to religious priests and their relations with bishops and the secular clergy quite inimical to the order-men, above all to the Jesuits. The fathers of the Society he held to blame for supposed deficiencies in the Church and in the secular priesthood, and he came to consider the order as a special hindrance to the development of the Church in England. He would not permit Weld, the Provincial, to open a house of studies in London; he did not favor the retreats and missions of the fathers; and he felt bitterly the entrance into the Society of his nephew, Anderdon, and his former secretary, Morris. It was not that he rejected *in toto* the Society of Jesus and its Institute, but that he believed it to be in the times more of a drawback than a benefit to the whole Church and to the English Church in particular.

The whole question of the relations of bishops and regulars after the restoration of the English Hierarchy needed clarification. A test came in the attempt of Gallwey, the Jesuit Provincial, acting on the express wish of Cardinal Franchi, Prefect of Propaganda, to establish a college in Manchester in connection with the Jesuit church of that city. Mgr. Herbert Vaughan, the Bishop of the diocese and later Cardinal, refused his permission on the ground that the proposed college would work a detriment to his own diocesan college. The Provincial, relying on an old privilege of the Society, given by Paul III and renewed by Pius VII, in virtue of which a college might be erected in connection with a house already existing, even without the consent of the Ordinary, proceeded with the opening of the college. Bishop Vaughan believed that such a privilege invaded the normal powers of a bishop and, acting in the name of the English hierarchy and under the direction of Cardinal Manning, appealed the case to Rome. The litigation lasted through a year and a half, during which the whole problem of the relations of episcopal rights and the privileges of regulars in missionary countries was thoroughly considered; for not only were the Bishops and the Jesuits contestants, but the Benedictines and other religious orders were concerned in the controversy. The entire matter was finally settled by Leo XIII's Constitution, "Romanos Pontifices," May 8,

---

[37] Pollen, "Cardinal Manning and the Jesuits," *The Month*, Vol. CXXXVII, pp. 481–493. (Also contains important reflections on the Manchester College case).

1881. In regard to the particular instance of the Manchester college, the Society's case was lost and its privilege revoked. The Constitution cleared away all misunderstandings, and since that time the relations of the Bishops and the order in England have been most friendly and sympathetic.

In the last half-century the English Province has enjoyed a continuous and a steady growth in all its activities, unchecked even by the World War. In that struggle eighty-five fathers served as chaplains and five made the supreme sacrifice. The colleges have increased to eleven; all enjoy an excellent reputation in English educational circles; two, Stonyhurst and Beaumont, possess the rating of Public Schools. Besides the new house of studies at Heythrop, two halls for the graduate studies of the students of the Society are maintained, one, Campion Hall, at Oxford and the other Southwell House, at London University. One of the finest works performed in any province of the Society is the minor seminary for late and delayed vocations conducted by the fathers at Osterly. The whole idea and its successful carrying-out was owing to the zeal of the Jesuit father, Lester.[38] Since its inception, about twenty years ago, it has enabled 362 young men to receive Holy Orders; these young priests are laboring in all the English dioceses, in America, and in almost every religious order possessing English connections. Scientific accomplishments will be considered in a later chapter; suffice it here to mention the Observatory at Stonyhurst and the Meteorological Institute at Bulawayo, S. A. The writings of the English Jesuits, the works of Coleridge, Gerard, Maher, Rickaby, Archbishop Goodier, Thurston, Martindale and D'Arcy, among many others, have exerted a wide influence throughout the English speaking world. The direction of souls and the conduct of religious societies in twenty-five great parishes or residences, such as those in London (Farm Street and Stamford Hill), Manchester, Liverpool, Leeds, Preston and Glasgow, still continue to be one of the major works of the province. In this connection one father, Bernard Vaughan, achieved the reputation of being one of the most eloquent of modern English preachers. The lay retreat movement is successfully carried on in four retreat-houses; the giving of the Spiritual Exercises to priests and religious has been from the beginning a constant labor of the fathers. The membership roll of 905 ranks the English province as one of the largest in the whole Society. Foreign missions are being conducted in Rhodesia and British Guiana; for a time the English fathers also operated missions in Jamaica and British Honduras.

The record of the Irish province in the last century and a quarter has been one of steady, quiet development. It has enjoyed the confidence of the Irish hierarchy with whom it has loyally cooperated in rebuilding the external fabric of the Faith, so loyally adhered to in the dark penal days.

---

[38] Tigar, *Edmund Lester*, London (1936).

In 1812 the Irish mission was established; it was raised to the status of a vice-province in 1860. Lack of finanical means was the chief difficulty facing the Irish fathers, yet they courageously persisted in the works they had undertaken. It was their special good fortune to have as their first superior, Peter Kenney, an eloquent orator and an able executive (twice he was sent as Visitor to the American Jesuits); he set the tone and gave the province a standing among his countrymen. Education has been perhaps the chief work of the Irish Jesuits; the first college was Clongowes Wood,[39] opened in 1814; today the province operates five colleges for extern students. With one of these, Mungret, is connected an apostolic school for the training of boys for the priesthood on the missions; that the school has achieved special success is evidenced from the several distinguished prelates and clergymen in America, Australia and in the mission lands, who are among its alumni. In 1883 the Irish Bishops entrusted to Jesuits the conduct of University College, Dublin; under their direction the college attained a marked superiority over the richly endowed Queen's Colleges in Belfast, Cork and Galway. When the National University was formed, the fathers returned the college to the Bishops. Today several of the Jesuits hold professorships on the teaching staff of the University, notably Corcoran in education; the province too conducts a students' hostel in connection with University College, Dublin.[40] In the literary field the work of the fathers has been signalized by the publication of the *Irish Monthly*, edited for many years by Matthew Russell, and the scholarly quarterly, *Studies*. To the Gaelic Revival, one of the fathers, McKenna, has contributed much by his editing of ancient Gaelic hymns and poems; the province itself has devoted the Galway college to the renaissance of the native tongue. Spiritual labors have always held a special place in the works of the Irish Jesuits: the retreats for religious and for the laity, the work in the churches, especially at St. Francis Xavier's in Dublin, and the establishment and propagation of a great temperance society, the Pioneers.[41] In 1862 the Irish Jesuits took over the Australian mission and developed it through seventy years, until it could be established as a strong vice-province. In recent years the fathers have been placed in charge of an important Chinese mission, centering in Hong Kong. The Irish province today counts 453 members, conducting 9 educational institutions, 3 residences and 1 house of retreats.

The life of the Society of Jesus in the last century and a quarter since the Restoration is indeed a revival, even though here and there at various times the order has had to endure severe persecution. Today the Jesuits

---

[39] Corcoran, *The Clongowes Record, 1814–1932*, Dublin (1932).

[40] *A Page of Irish History: Story of University College Dublin 1883–1909*, Dublin (1930).

[41] McKenna, *Father James A. Cullen, S.J.*, London (1924).

are firmly established in most of Europe, outside of Russia; if in some places their outlook is not too reassuring, confidence can be had that the fathers and brothers will meet the crisis, for they have been trained for it in the true spirit of St. Ignatius.

CHAPTER XVI

OVERSEAS EXPANSION

Probably the most striking feature in the history of the restored Society of Jesus, is its expansion outside of Europe.[1] Today just a little less than half the membership is to be found in the United States, Canada, Latin America and the foreign mission fields of Asia and Africa. It may be safely stated that no such proportion existed in the old Society. This growth has been almost phenomenal: in 1814 the only Jesuits outside of Europe were the twenty-odd working in Maryland and Pennsylvania; while the resources and expectations of the few hundred European Jesuits justified no hope of an early resumption of the foreign mission activity. Today the labors of the overseas Jesuits equal those of their European brethren in every type of the order's work; the educational activities may be thought even to excel, when there are considered the universities and university-colleges of the United States and Canada, the universities of Tokyo, Shanghai and Beirut, and the numerous Papal and diocesan seminaries in Asia and South America. It is rather astonishing to think that the Jesuits of the United States and Canada, whose countries a hundred years ago were considered foreign mission lands, are today operating important missions in the Philippines, China, India, and the Caribbean area. This great development is owing to three factors: firstly, the apostolic courage of the European fathers, who, as soon as even a small footing was obtained at home, began to send their best men abroad; secondly, the numerous expulsions by anticlerical governments, which brought many exiled fathers to the new missions; thirdly, the prosperous outcome of Catholic immigration to the United States. The history of the Society of Jesus overseas since the Restoration divides along two lines: the account of the Jesuits in North and South America, where the labors have been, much as in Europe, chiefly among Christians, and the record of the Jesuits in the New East, the Far East and Africa, where the work has been largely the conversion of the heathen.

It is in the United States that the order has achieved the greatest expansion. In 1815 about two dozen Jesuits constituted the Maryland mission: they supported one pioneer college, which had also to house a novitiate

---

[1] Of great help for the recent history of the Society are the *Acta Romana S.J.* and the *Memorabilia S.J.*, both issued from the Father General's office in Rome.

and whose masters often had to essay the almost impossible task of preparing for the priesthood and at the same time teaching small boys; they
ministered to a handful of Catholics in a few struggling parishes and remote rural missions; they gave few, if any, retreats and popular missions;
they conducted no widely organized devotions or confraternities; they
nourished no hope for the conversion of the heathen, except possibly a
vague desire of preaching the Gospel to the Indians in some distant day.
Today, after a century and a quarter, the American Jesuits constitute the
largest Assistancy of the order, with seven provinces (Maryland–New
York, Missouri, California, New Orleans, New England, Chicago and
Oregon) counting a total membership of 5,319. They conduct in continental United States 24 universities or university-colleges and 28 high schools
with an entire enrollment of 57,974 students. In the purely spiritual field
they operate 86 parishes and 2 collegiate churches, 8 houses of retreat and
7 mission bands, i. e., groups of priests devoted to the giving of popular
missions; in the course of the year the fathers give the Spiritual Exercises
to several hundred groups, including diocesan priests, religious brothers
and nuns. As indicative of what is being accomplished, the work for 1936
of the New England Province, which includes the average number of
priests, may be cited: 157 missions and 246 tridua and novenas were
preached, 706,694 confessions were heard, 860,280 Communions were
distributed, 91 sodalities and pious societies were maintained, and 101
retreats to priests and sisters given. Much good is being achieved throughout the country by the Novena of Grace in honor of St. Francis Xavier;
introduced into America about forty years ago, it has grown to great popularity not only in the churches of the order but in those of the secular
clergy. In 1936, 68 fathers of the New England Province preached this
novena in 36 churches with an estimated attendance of 102,550. In the
literary field today the American Jesuits publish *The Messenger of the
Sacred Heart,* the largest of all the *Messengers; America,* an important
weekly; *Theological Studies,* a scholarly review of theology; *Thought,*
a learned quarterly; *Mid-America,* and the *Historical Bulletin,* publications devoted to history; the *Modern Schoolman,* a journal devoted to
philosophy; the *Classical Bulletin,* a monthly devoted to the classical languages; the *Jesuit Educational Quarterly;* the *Jesuit Missions;* and *The
Queen's Work,* the organ of the Sodality, besides many learned reports,
text-books and other kindred productions. The American Jesuits, as has
been indicated, carry an important share of the foreign mission work of
the order. One might well wonder if the most sanguine Jesuit in Maryland
in 1815 could have imagined such a development.

The first quarter of a century gave little grounds for hope.[2] Men and

---

[2] *Woodstock Letters* (1872–1939). Its sixty-seven volumes are a veritable mine for
the history of the American Jesuits, especially in the eastern United States.

means were so lacking that the fathers were hard put to maintain the parishes in Maryland and Pennsylvania and the college of Georgetown. Even the novitiate had to be closed for a time. An attempt to open a day-school in Washington in 1821 failed after six years owing to the inability to accept tuition fees in view of the vow of poverty. Because of this situation and a similar one in St. Louis, Bishop Rosati of that diocese appealed to the Holy See; his explanation of the American economic and social situation induced the granting of a dispensation enabling the reception of such tuitions.[3] The dearth of candidates was not remedied by the arrival of a band of Belgium youths in 1821, for at the end of their noviceship at Whitemarsh their dismissal was seriously considered because of the lack of funds. Only the fortunate opening of work in Missouri saved the vocations of these generous youths. Yet despite the poverty and the difficulties of recruiting, the mission was blessed with several able leaders: Kohlmann, who in addition to his governing tasks and his teaching wrote successfully against the then rising Unitarianism; Kenney, of the Irish mission, twice Visitor and a distinguished orator; Dzierozynski, a superior of broad sympathies, a saintly religious, a professor of theology and of philosophy, traditionally said to have trained John C. Calhoun in logic; Benedict Fenwick, an able administrator, later Bishop of Boston; and Ryder, an eloquent pulpit orator who preached before the members of both Houses of Congress. In 1833 the mission was raised to the status of a province; the Missouri houses already in 1830 had been constituted an independent mission.

The period of definite growth began in the forties and lasted through the rest of the century. The first great advance was the acceptance of Holy Cross College in Worcester, Massachusetts, in 1843. Not long after there followed other foundations, two parishes in Boston and one in Providence. The province was greatly strengthened in 1848 by the arrival of several Swiss Jesuit exiles, notable among them Burchard Villiger and John Bapst; while in the same year the Washington college, now known as Gonzaga College, was reopened. Four years later two more colleges were begun, Loyola in Baltimore and St. Joseph's in Philadelphia. During these years the Jesuits, in common with their fellow Catholics, had to bear the abuses and menaces of Know-nothingism, the current anti-Catholicism; the Swiss exile, Bapst, was tarred and feathered in Maine. An achievement which stands before all others was the opening of a house of studies for the whole of North America, the long-desired institution which would guarantee the proper training of the young priests. Boston was decided on for the location of the seminary, and in 1860 the lectures were begun in a

---

[3] Garraghan, *The Jesuits of the Middle United States*, New York (1938), Vol. I, pp. 303–308.

building which the fathers had planned for a college soon to be opened. The first theologate was destined for but a short existence; financial difficulties arising from the Civil War forced its closing in 1863. The building was then utilized for its original purpose, and the classes of Boston College were soon opened. Six years later in 1869 the house of studies was again attempted, this time successfully, at Woodstock, Maryland. From the very beginning the new theologate and philosophate enjoyed an excellent reputation, owing above all to the learned faculty assembled from the exiled Italian Jesuits. Among the first professors were such divines as the later Cardinal Mazella, de Augustinis, Sabetti, Maldonado, Brambring, Brandi and Sestini. During this period the good repute of the order was sustained by the eloquent sermons of Maguire, the scholarship of Fulton and Bapst, the scientific work of Secchi and the apostolic zeal of McElroy, one of the leading pioneers of Catholicism in the Eastern States.

The year 1879 witnessed the union of the New York mission with the Maryland province. Some thirty-five years before, the French Jesuits, who had been established in Kentucky, opened a mission in Canada; from both places they came in 1846 at the invitation of Archbishop Hughes to take over the conduct of the college and seminary founded by him at Fordham.[4] The New York–Canada mission progressed under the inspiration of such men as Larkin, an excellent pulpit-orator, Daubresse and others. The College of Saint Francis Xavier was opened in New York in 1847 and that of St. Peter's in Jersey City in 1878; flourishing parishes were operated in New York, Jersey City and Troy; and a truly apostolic work was begun among the prisoners in the metropolis. After a short period under the rule of the province of Champagne, in 1869, the mission was made independent. In 1879 the New York part was separated from the Canadian and joined with the Maryland province, under the name of the New York province. In the following year, because of the historical traditions of the Society, the name Maryland was prefixed, and it has remained the Maryland–New York province until today. Several able Jesuits were brought to the old province by the union, among them being Thebaud, the writer, Jouin, the philosopher, and Pardow, the preacher. Onward to the end of the century the Eastern Jesuits developed their labors steadily, intensifying and broadening the works at hand. In their ranks were to be found several distinguished converts, among them, Frisbee, Barnum, Hedrick and Van Rensselaer; with these deserves to be recalled J. Havens Richards, the son of a convert-minister. Richards was a fine scholar, a true educator and a noble, unselfish character.

About the year 1900 commenced a third period in the history of the province. Vocations increased to such an extent that a second novitiate had

---

[4] Burnichon, *La Compagnie de Jésus en France*, Vol. III, pp. 297 ff.

to be opened in 1917; new additions came in 1908, Canisius College and High School, besides two churches in Buffalo. These foundations had belonged to the Buffalo mission, which had been founded by the German Jesuits in 1869, originally for the care of their fellow-countrymen in America. The educational work experienced a strong development with the expansion of courses, adjustments of curricula and the inception of graduate work and of social studies. Three new high schools were begun in New York City, but unfortunately one of the best colleges, St. Francis Xaviers', had to be discontinued. In the last decade of the nineteenth century the literary activities of the Eastern Jesuits found wider expression in the *Messenger*, a general Catholic magazine of high rank which had developed out of the *Messenger of the Sacred Heart*. In 1909 a further change was effected by which, while the *Messenger of the Sacred Heart* retained its early devotional character, the *Messenger* was transformed into a new periodical, *America*, which from its very beginnings has been a foremost American Catholic literary and apologetical weekly. No mention of *America* can be made without a reverent reference to its greatest editor, the late Richard H. Tierney, a valiant champion of the Faith and of human liberty. In 1926 a scholarly quarterly, *Thought*, made its appearance, edited, as is *America*, by Jesuits from all the American provinces. Recently, in 1939, Fordham University took over the publication of *Thought*; in the same year a new theological quarterly, *Theological Studies*, was begun, also to be the common work of the American Jesuits. Of the numerous output of text-books, works of literature and scientific treatises, no listing can be made here, except to notice one, the work of the astronomer, Hagen of Georgetown, on the variable stars, which merited publication by Harvard University.

In apostolic labors outstanding were the development of the Novena of Grace, the establishment of four houses for laymen's retreats and the beginning of foreign mission work. In the last field the Eastern Jesuits play an important part, with the mission of Jamaica taken over in 1894, with the Philippine mission accepted in 1921 and completely manned in 1927, and with the school work in Iraq begun in 1934. Among the distinguished Jesuits of this period are: Gannon, the second American Assistant (the Assistancy was erected in 1915); Gasson, the educator; O'Rourke, the orator; and Shealy, the retreat-master. Such had been the expansion that in 1926 the New England region was set off as a province and in 1937 the southern part of the Maryland–New York province was delimited with the view to the erection of still another province. Today the Maryland–New York province has 1,460 members with 20 educational institutions, 19 residences, 3 retreat houses and 1 house of writers, besides the care of the Philippine mission; the New England province counts 796 members operating 4 educational institutions, 4 residences and 1 retreat house, besides the mission of Jamaica and a college in Baghdad, Iraq.

The work of the restored Society in the Middle West began in 1823, when Van Quickenborne led a band of Jesuit novices to Missouri there to work for Bishop du Bourg in his vast diocese.[5] Two years before, seven young Belgians had arrived in America bent on the conversion of the Indians and for this purpose had offered themselves to the superior of the Maryland Jesuits. The seven candidates were sent to Whitemarsh to make their noviceship under a fellow-countryman, Van Quickenborne. As was noted before, lack of resources made the American superiors seriously consider their dismissal and that fate was prevented by Bishop du Bourg's offer. To reach St. Louis the little party, seven novices, three lay-brothers and two priests, made the long, hard journey on foot over the mountains and by flatboat down the Ohio. Their first foundation was at Florissant, where they continued the noviceship and began their first labors for the aborigines with the establishment of an Indian school. The school proved unsuccessful and in a few years had to be closed; but the Indians were not given up, for Van Quickenborne made a number of journeys to the Osage, while the others faithfully retained their original desire. More pressing work among the whites, now pouring into the new country, clamored for their attention. For the next three decades these Belgian Jesuits traversed the settlements of Missouri and Illinois, keeping the Faith alive in thousands of souls on the scattered frontier; Van Quickenborne, himself journeyed over 4,373 miles, at one place discovering 600 Catholics where only 8 had been known. Nor was the work of education forgotten: in 1829 St. Louis College was reopened by the fathers, in 1832 a university charter was obtained; and in 1840 St. Xavier's College in Cincinnati was taken over. Men were few and resources scanty, yet the General, Father Roothaan, had confidence in these priests and in 1830 grouped them in an independent mission, which ten years later was raised to the status of a vice-province.

The long hoped for work among the Indians seemed to have dawned with the opening of missions among the Kickapoo in 1836 and among the Potawatomi in 1838. But adverse circumstances, especially the drink evil in the last tribe, prevented effectual results and forced the closing of both missions in 1841. The real opportunity, however, had already come when in 1840 de Smet [6] set out for the distant Rocky Mountains in answer to

[5] Garraghan, *The Jesuits of the Middle United States*, 3 Vols., New York (1938); The *Illinois Catholic Historical Review* (1918–1929) and its continuation, *The Mid-America* (1929–) are replete with scholarly articles on Jesuit history in the Mid-West, South and Far-West of the United States.

[6] Chittenden and Richardson, *Father de Smet's Life and Travels among the American Indians*, 4 Vols., New York (1905); Laveille, *The Life of Father de Smet*, trans. New York (1915).

the ten years of pleading of the Flathead Indians for the "Blackrobes."
By boat up the Missouri and on horseback across the plains and over the
mountains, the intrepid priest travelled on to the waiting Indians, to
found among the Flatheads, the Nez Percés, the Kalispels and the Coeur
d'Alènes, the Oregon mission. Enthusiastic because of the good-will of
tribesmen, de Smet returned to St. Louis to beg for every man possible
for the new mission field. In response several able priests were sent to
the mountain Indians; among those who labored successfully with the
Indians were Point, Mengarini, de Vos and Adrian Hoecken. Later assistants came from Europe in the persons of such priests as Ravalli and
Nobili. The Indians of the plains, the Blackfeet, the Grosventres, the
Winnebago and the Sioux, were visited also by the Jesuits from St. Louis.
De Smet possessed a remarkable influence over the Indians; wherever
he went among them he was loved and implicitly trusted; often he defended their cause in Washington. The government in its turn more than
once used his influence to pacify warlike tribes; on one such occasion, in
1868, he penetrated alone into a camp of five thousand hostile Sioux to
gain their acceptance of a peace. His greatest service for the Indian missions was the aid he obtained for them by his numerous and vivid writings,
his sermons and his interviews. On their behalf he crossed the ocean nineteen times, travelled 180,000 miles, and urged their case with Pius IX,
with kings and presidents, before audiences, both of the humble and of
the great, in America and in many a European country. He died in St.
Louis in 1873.

The Oregon mission [7] was not to meet all the expectations of the
Jesuits; many circumstances, misunderstandings, the encroachments of
the whites and the curse of the liquor traffic, seriously hampered their
labors. In 1854 the Oregon mission was detached from the Missouri vice-
province and joined to the California mission of the Turin province.
Nearer home in Kansas the Osage mission was revived in 1847, and the
Potawatomi mission was moved to that territory in 1848. On these missions zealously labored Bishop Miége, Ponziglione, Christian Hoecken
and Gailland. Again the advance of the white settlers and the withdrawal
of the redmen to the Indian Territory, forced the efforts of the Jesuits to
the care of the whites; many churches and parishes were begun by the
fathers, which in due time were relinquished to the diocesan authorities.

It seemed in the divine design that the first work of the Missouri
Jesuits of this period was to be the preservation of the Faith and the up-
building of Catholicism in the vast crowd of Catholic immigrants from
Germany and Ireland, who were coming into the Mississippi Valley from
the 'forties to the 'seventies. In the cities, much more than on the frontier,

---

[7] Garraghan, *The Jesuits of the Middle United States*, Vol. II, pp. 236–442.

was the task met by the erection of parishes. The problem was further answered by the giving of popular missions throughout the area. Foremost in this work stood Weninger,[8] an Austrian, who for forty years conducted missions, first in German and later in English, in all parts of the United States. This indefatigable apostle gave over 800 missions, preached 30,000 sermons, made between 2,000 and 3,000 converts, and journeyed over 200,000 miles; besides, he found time to write 41 books and pamphlets in German, English, and Latin. In the work of the purely English-speaking missions, Damen,[9] Smarius and Coghlan for years preached to thronged churches all through the Middle-West and in the Eastern States as well. Their names became a household tradition among the Catholic people.[10]

In the late 'thirties the Missouri mission was entrusted for a time with the Jesuit foundations in Louisiana; the burden proved too great and in 1847 was handed over to the Lyons province. The next year the fathers entered Kentucky to take over St. Joseph's College at Bardstown and to begin a college at Louisville. They were not the first Jesuits in the Blue Grass State. The fathers of the province of France had labored there from 1830 and had founded St. Mary's College in Marion County; but by 1846 they had migrated to Canada and New York. Neither venture of the Missouri Jesuits was destined to permanence; Louisville was given up in 1852 and St. Joseph's in 1868. Still the work as a whole in the Middle-West had so developed that in 1863 the Missouri mission was given the full status of a province.

The pioneer period of Jesuit education in the region came to an end at the close of the Civil War. From then on, not only were the departments and faculties of St. Louis and St. Xavier's increased and broadened; but several new colleges were founded which eventually attained to university status with faculties of arts and sciences, law, medicine and graduate studies.[11] In 1869 St. Ignatius College, Chicago, was begun; it achieved university grade in 1909 with the name Loyola University. In 1869 also St. Mary's, Kansas, was founded; it enjoyed a long career of scholastic usefulness until financial stringency forced its closing in 1931. In 1877 Detroit College was opened; in 1911 it received the status of a university. The generosity of the Creighton brothers in 1878 made possible Creighton University, Omaha. In 1881 Marquette College, Milwaukee, was begun; in 1907 it became Marquette University. In 1910 Rockhurst College, Kansas City, Missouri, opened as a high school, and seven years later saw the opening of its college department. At the request

---

[8] Garraghan, *The Jesuits of the Middle United States*, Vol. II, 53 ff.

[9] Conroy, *Arnold Damen*, New York (1930).

[10] Garraghan, Vol. II, pp. 77 ff.

[11] Garraghan, *The Jesuits of the Middle United States*, Vol. III, pp. 111–416, 435–505.

of Cardinal Mundelein in 1921, the fathers of the province took charge
of the studies in the new Chicago archdiocesan Seminary of St. Mary-of-
the-Lake.

Considerable additions came to the Missouri province with the dissolution of the Buffalo mission.[12] The mission had been founded in 1869 by
the German province to minister to the spiritual needs of the large Catholic German immigration; its ranks were increased by many learned Jesuit
exiles, victims of the Kulturkampf. Parishes, popular missions and educational work were successfully conducted in many cities, mostly in the
Middle-West, at first among the Germans and later among all Catholics.
Many able and scholarly fathers served the mission; among them may
be noticed, Behrens, a superior, Hagen, the astronomer, Betten and
Schwickerath, historians, and Bonvin, church-musician. After forty years
of excellent accomplishment, in 1907 Father General Wernz decided
that the time had come for the work to be carried on in connection with
the American provinces. The Missouri province received St. Ignatius
College, Cleveland, founded in 1886, later John Carroll University,
1923; St. John Berchmans College, Toledo, founded in 1898, discontinued in 1936; Sacred Heart College, Prairie du Chien, Wisconsin,
founded in 1880, named Campion College 1913, and since 1925 a high
school only; four parishes, and two Indian missions among the Sioux of
South Dakota. With the dissolution of the New Mexico–Colorado mission, the Missouri province also received several parishes in Colorado and
the Sacred Heart College, now Regis College, Denver.[13]

The Middle-Western Jesuits of recent years have vigorously and successfully pursued the usual religious activities of the order in their parishes, in retreat work for priests, religious and laymen, and in the care of
colored Catholics. Especially noteworthy has been the expansion of the
Sodality of Our Lady on a nation-wide basis through the *Queen's Work*,
sodality conferences and the Summer Schools for Catholic Action. During these years the ranks of the Jesuits in the Central States have counted
several noted pulpit orators, a goody proportion of writers who have
produced books in philosophy, literature and education, as well as a
number of scientists in astronomy and seismology. Several very good
historians have been developed in the province, their principal work
centering about the Institute of Jesuit History at Loyola University. In
1893 the mission of British Honduras was taken over by the province and
in 1921 the mission of Patna in India. The expansion of the works of the
order in the Mississippi Valley attained such proportions that in 1928

---

[12] Garraghan, *The Jesuits of the Middle United States*, I, pp. 583, 587; III, pp. 488,
583.

[13] *Woodstock Letters* passim.

the Eastern region was set off as the province of Chicago. Today the Missouri province numbers 916 members operating 13 educational institutions, 13 residences and 1 retreat house; while the Chicago Province counts 820 members maintaining 10 educational institutions, 8 residences and 1 retreat house.

Jesuit activity in the Southern States [14] began with the arrival of a group of French Jesuits at New Orleans in 1831 on their way to Kentucky. One of their number, Ladavière, returned shortly to labor for the Bishop of the city; Ladavière was to be one of the pioneers of the New Orleans province. In 1837 a second group of French Jesuits landed at New Orleans, this time to open a college at Iberville. The site of the new institution was changed to Grand Coteau by the first superior, Point. Because of their unpreparedness to teach in English-speaking colleges, the task of opening the college was entrusted to the Missouri Jesuits in 1838. Fathers from the Lyons province arrived at Mobile in 1847 to take over the Bishop's college of Spring Hill, which to the present day has been conducted successfully by the Jesuits. In the same year 1847, the two Southern colleges and the parishes in Louisiana were placed under the jurisdiction of the Lyons province. New Orleans became the center of an active spiritual apostolate which eventually extended through all the Southern States, especially in Georgia and Florida. In the city itself the College of the Immaculate Conception was begun in 1848; in 1912 it was raised to university rank under the name of Loyola University. The mission was declared independent in 1880 and established as a province in 1907. The dissolution of the New Mexico–Colorado mission in 1919 brought to the province several parishes in Texas and New Mexico, where a devoted apostolate of the Mexicans is followed. The Jesuits of the New Orleans Province have numbered distinguished scholars in the classics, philosophy and history among their teachers and writers. At the present day the New Orleans province consists of 410 members employed in 7 educational institutions, 13 residences and 1 retreat-house.

The New Mexico–Colorado mission was the fruit of the heroic toil of Neapolitan exiles, victims of Garibaldi's persecution.[15] In 1867 they arrived in Southwestern frontier to begin fifty years of labor among the Mexicans and Americans in the present states of New Mexico, Arizona, Colorado and the western part of Texas. Several of them were learned theologians; yet they devoted themselves without stint to hard parochial

---

[14] Biever, *The Jesuits in New Orleans and the Mississippi Valley*, New Orleans (1924); Kenny, *Catholic Culture in Alabama*, New York (1931); Garraghan, *The Jesuits of the Middle United States*, Vol. III, pp. 129–157.

[15] Vollmar, "Donato Gasparri, New Mexico–Colorado Mission Founder," *Mid-America*, Vol. XX, pp. 96–150.

work, to the preaching of missions, even to the teaching of A B C's, on the difficult scene. In 1875 the fathers set up a press which published their *Revista Catolica,* an important Spanish weekly, influential even to this day, all kinds of pamphlets, text-books, and even a Spanish translation of the Bible. A college was begun at Las Vegas in 1877 and another at Morrison in 1884; both were combined and transferred to Denver as the Sacred Heart College in 1888. The leading spirit of the mission was Donato Gasparri, its founder and, for years, its superior. This zealous priest labored unceasingly at preaching and dispensing the Sacraments, protected the simple Mexicans from exploiters, edited the *Revista Catolica,* and was the architect and actual builder of the Las Vegas College. When the mission was dissolved in 1919, it numbered 157 members and maintained 1 college, 21 parishes or residences and several mission stations.

It was an Italian Jesuit, Accolti, laboring on the Oregon mission, who brought the Society to the State of California.[16] Realizing what good could be accomplished among the hordes of gold-seekers, he persistently pleaded to be sent to work for them. In 1848 Accolti and a companion, Nobili, were permitted to investigate the possibilities; what they saw in the mining camps and in the rising cities convinced them not only of the absolute need of spiritual laborers in the terrible conditions, but also of a future promising glorious achievement for souls. Nobili in 1851 accepted the old mission at Santa Clara as the basis of a future college; the college was started, to develop through years of educational service into the present University of Santa Clara. With this institution will always be connected the memories of Kenna and the two scientists, Cichi, the chemist, and Ricard, the meteorologist. Nowhere have the traditions of the old Society for the drama been better fulfilled than at Santa Clara in its Passion Play. Almost at the same time the Church and College of St. Ignatius [17] were opened at San Francisco by another Italian father, Maraschi. Starting almost with the city's origin, St. Ignatius Church has grown along with San Francisco, sharing its disasters and triumphs, to become one of the traditions of Californian Catholicism. The college grew under the guidance, first of learned Italian priests and later of native Jesuits, to be the present University of San Francisco.

The new mission together with the Oregon mission in 1854 were placed under the jurisdiction of the Turin province; in 1858 the missions were separated but retained under the government of Turin. The Oregon mission's chief work, the evangelizing of the Indians, suffered many vicissi-

---

[16] Garraghan, *The Jesuits of the Middle United States,* Vol. II, pp. 392–420; *The University of Santa Clara Diamond Jubilee Volume.*

[17] Riordan, *The First Half Century of St. Ignatius Church and College,* San Francisco (1905).

tudes, due to the encroachments of the frontier and the lack of resources; yet the work was never abandoned and is maintained to this day.[18] Among the foremost laborers for the Indians should be listed Ravalli, Cataldo and Palladino. Attention also was given to the Catholic immigrants of the Northwest. Several parishes were established and in 1884 a college, now Gonzaga University of Spokane, was founded. The fathers of Oregon in 1886 inaugurated their missionary labors among the Indians and Eskimos of Alaska; perhaps no work of the Society of Jesus called for greater heroism than this mission of the desolate, snowy wastes. The gold rush of 1899 added even more difficult problems. Among the missionaries who toiled in Alaska may be cited Bishop Crimont, Tosi, and Cataldo, founders of the work, Ruppert, a martyr of charity, Barnum, the author of an Innuit dictionary, and Judge, the apostle of the miners.

In 1907, the Californian, Oregon and Alaskan missions were united into the independent California mission, which in 1909 was designated a full province. Progress in the South with the opening of parishes and a college, now Loyola University of Los Angeles, and similar progress in the North with the beginning of parishes in Oregon, Washington and Montana, a college in Seattle, a high school at Tacoma, and the wider expansion of the Alaskan mission, justified a division of two provinces, California and Oregon. The California province today consists of 483 members operating 5 educational institutions, 7 parishes, 1 retreat house and a college in China; while the Oregon province counts 434 members, 4 educational institutions, 14 parishes, the Indian missions with 12 chief stations, and the Alaskan missions with 20 chief stations.

The first Jesuits to take up once more the work of the Society in Canada [19] were the French fathers who had established St. Mary's College in Kentucky. On the invitation of the Bishop of Montreal, five of these priests arrived in that city in 1842. The College of Ste. Marie was begun in 1848, a year later a foundation was made in Quebec, and in 1855 a college was started in St. Boniface. Both Ste. Marie and St. Boniface have earned a merited name in the higher education of Canada, a name shared by the other Jesuit colleges of Edmonton, Sudbury, Quebec, Montreal (Brébeuf and Loyola) and Regina. Of almost equal importance was the work among the Indians; at the very beginning missions were set up among the Hurons and the Ojibway of Ontario, which have flourished to the present day; in 1902 the Caughnawaga mission of the Iroquois, a mission of the old Society, was resumed, and just a few years ago the St. Regis mission of the same tribe was again in operation. Late in the last century work was begun on the Yukon and in Alaska which has since been placed under the California mission, while after the World War a flourish-

---

[18] Palladino, *Indian and White in the Northwest*, 2nd ed., Lancaster, Pa. (1922).

[19] Burnichon, *La Compagnie de Jésus en France*, Vol. III, pp. 297 ff.

ing mission was started in China. As outstanding Canadian missionaries may be considered, Point, Menard and Cadot among the Ojibway, and Lafortune on the Yukon.

The Canadian fathers have devoted themselves with marked success to the ministry of the pulpit; their popular missions have been a great force for good, while the Church of the Gesù in Montreal has gained just renown for its sermons and religious services. The fathers of the Province in recent years have rendered valuable assistance to Catholic societies devoted to works of social reform. The writers and historians of the province have done invaluable work on the history of the missions and missionaries of the old Society; especially noteworthy has been the work of Martin, Melançon, Jones and Drummond. The labors of Blain, physicist and seismologist, have merited consideration. The Canadian mission, after union with New York and dependence on the provinces of Paris, Champagne and England, was made independent in 1888 and raised to the status of a province in 1907. The province was divided in 1926 into the Lower Canada province for the French-speaking members and the Upper Canada vice-province for the English-speaking members. On March 12, 1939 Upper Canada was raised to the status of a province. The Lower Canada province consists of 660 members in charge of 8 educational institutions, 7 residences, 6 retreat houses, 1 house of writers and the Chinese mission of Suchow; the Upper Canada province includes 285 members operating 5 educational institutions, 3 residences and 1 retreat house.

In the Caribbean area English-speaking Jesuits maintain the missions of Jamaica and British Honduras, and on the northeast coast of South America, that of British Guiana. Jamaica [20] was the earliest scene of Jesuit labor; in 1837 an English father, Cotham and a French father, Dupeyron, arrived on the island; in 1855 the mission was given to the English province, by which it was worked until 1894, when it was transferred to the Maryland–New York province. The New England province on its establishment was placed in charge of Jamaica. Despite many difficulties and hardships, especially the earthquake of 1907, the work for white and colored Catholics—the latter form the bulk of the mission's flock—has been steadily carried on. Among the outstanding missionaries may be listed Hathaway, Harpes, Emerick and Mulry. Today 39 Jesuits maintain a secondary school, 49 churches or chapels and 67 stations; they also publish the monthly *Catholic Opinion*. British Honduras from 1850 was visited occasionally by Jesuits from Jamaica; eventually the English province took over its administration. In 1893, however, the mission was entrusted to the Missouri province. Centering on Belize, where is located a secondary school, the fathers minister to a mixed flock of Maya Indians,

[20] Delaney, *History of the Catholic Church in Jamaica, B.W.I.*, New York (1930).

Mestizos and Negroes. Especially to be remembered are the labors among the Maya Indians of a devoted priest, Stanton. A disastrous hurricane in 1931 wrought great havoc in the mission, destroying the high school and killing eleven Jesuits. The work was not interrupted; today there are in British Honduras 30 Jesuits conducting a high school, 8 parishes and 72 stations. British Guiana was given to the English Jesuits in 1857; under their direction it has remained to the present day. While most of the work has been among the whites and the colored Catholics, special efforts have also been made for the conversion of the Indian tribes in the interior. The fathers on the mission today number thirty-one, operating a secondary school and forty parishes or stations. In French Guiana Jesuits from France labored among the prisoners of the penal colony of Cayenne from 1852 to 1873, when they relinquished their work to the White Fathers.

The history of the restored Society of Jesus in Latin America [21] has been of a piece with that of the order in Latin Europe of the nineteenth century. The same evil forces, Grand Orient Lodges and false Liberalism, have waged the same bitter war of persecution and banishment, which, on the side of the Latin American Jesuits, has been met with the same heroism and patience that their European brethren displayed. Unsettled political conditions also have held up the development of activities and prevented vocations to the priesthood and religious life. Yet despite recurrent catastrophe the labors and the numbers of the Latin American Jesuits have so increased as to justify the erection of the Latin American Assistancy in 1938.

Mexico was the first Latin American country to welcome back the restored Society of Jesus.[22] Three venerable old Jesuits still lived to form the nucleus of the Mexican mission. By 1820 there were 32 members of the order conducting 4 colleges and 2 seminaries; but in the following year they were dispersed. This was the beginning of the order's persecuted career in Mexico; from then on until the present, banishment or toleration, generally depending on the intensity of the anticlericalism of the ruling political faction, was to be the lot of the Society in this unfortunate country. In 1843 an invitation to return had to be rejected because of the limitations on the activities of the order placed by Santa Anna. Even to consider setting up establishments in so revolutionary a country called for considerable fortitude; yet in 1854 the Jesuits were back, although since then three times, in 1859, 1873 and 1914, they were banished from the

---

[21] Frias, *Historia de la Compañia de Jesús en su Assistencia Moderna de España*, Madrid (1923), pp. 349–389.

[22] Frias, *Historia de la C. de J. en su assistencia moderna*, pp. 608–701; Decorme, *Historia de Comp. de Jesús en la Republique Mejicana durante el siglo 19* (1914); Echeverria, *Der Kampf gegen die Kath. Kirche in Mexico in den letzten 13 Jahren* (1926); Cuevas *Historia de la Iglesia en Mexico*, El Paso (1928), t. V.

country. Their vicissitudes did not prevent many fruitful educational and spiritual works, thanks in part to the aid rendered by their Spanish brethren. In 1907 the Mexican province could be established with 300 members maintaining colleges at Mexico City, Guadalajara, Saltillo and Pueblo, 12 residences and 6 mission stations among the Indians. Seven years before, the Indian missions, the glory of the old Mexican Jesuits, were revived among the Tarahumaras.

Prospects seemed bright for the future, yet within a decade the martyrdom of the Mexican province had begun. With the revolutions of Carranza and Villa the bitterest warfare against the Jesuits was conducted, their colleges and churches were seized or destroyed and the members of the province were driven into exile. The persecution mounted to its worst during the sway of Calles in the 'twenties; still it could not deter the Mexican fathers, in the face of almost certain death, from reentering the country to carry the consolations of religion to their unfortunate fellow-Catholics and to strengthen their faith in the terrible hour of their trial. At length in 1927 after fearlessly exercising their holy office, two of these heroic priests were captured and executed, Miguel Pro [23] and David Maduro Vertiz. In the opinion of many Catholics throughout the world they died true martyrs of Christ. During all these fearful times the Tarahumara Indians were not abandoned; in 1921 twenty Jesuits worked among them, the number decreased with the dread year of 1925, yet today five priests, amidst the greatest dangers, labor for the Indians. A work of utmost importance for the future Mexican Church, was entrusted to the fathers of the province when in 1937 they were chosen by the American Hierarchy to conduct the seminary for Mexican priests maintained by the Bishops of the United States at Montezuma in New Mexico. Today the Mexican province numbers 448 Jesuits who operate, in the face of all contrary laws, 2 educational institutions, 16 residences and 1 retreat house.

Argentina [24] was the first South American country to receive the restored Society. Years before their actual arrival, their presence had been sought for by petitions of Argentinians, first to the Cortes of Spain in 1810 and again to the Junta of Buenos Aires in 1811. In that city still lived a member of the old Society, de Villfañe, whose fondest hope was that he might reenter the order before his death; his wish was gratified to the extent that, by the permission of Pius VII, he was allowed to renew his vows on his deathbed, which he did at his death in 1830. Just six years later his brethren came to the Argentine, brought there by the dictator, de Rosas. The Spanish fathers, who made up the group, were warmly

[23] Dragon, *Miguel Augustin Pro*, translated by Drummond, Montreal (1930).

[24] Perez, *La Compañia restaurada en la Republica Argentina y Chile, el Uruguay y el Brasil*, Barcelona (1901).

welcomed by the people; they were given the old Jesuit college and church by the government, as well as full powers in secondary and university education. Other fathers followed to work either at the college or in the interior as popular missionaries. In a short time a second college was opened at Cordoba. The favor of the dictator de Rosas, however, gradually changed as he began to conceive a mistrust of the order. The College of San Ignacio in the capital was closed by the fathers themselves in 1841; two years later they were banished from Buenos Aires, and in 1848 from the entire republic. Their expulsion was not an unmixed disaster, for they were able to introduce the work of the Society in the neighboring republics.

After the dictator's fall a part of the Jesuits, with the pupils of the seminary which they had established at Montevideo, returned to Buenos Aires to found there the Seminary of Regina Martyrum. In 1868 the college of San Ignacio was refounded to be developed later into the Colegio del Salvador. For a while the progress of this celebrated institution was held back by various circumstances: the yellow fever of 1871, the persecution by the Freemasons in 1875 which roused up a street mob to attack and burn the edifice, and the opposition of a hostile ministry in 1885. Gradually del Salvador recovered to become in the capital city a great source of good in teaching, writing, preaching and the care of souls; two important societies for the defense of Catholicism, the *Liga de honor* and the *Liga escolar catholica*, have had their origin within its walls. From 1857 to 1875 most of the foundations of the Argentinian Jesuits were established: the colleges of Cordoba and Santa Fé, a seminary, and an apostolic school, and several flourishing churches, especially that of Mendoza. In 1917 the Argentine-Chile mission became a province; in 1937 the Argentine section was separated as a distinct province. The Jesuits in Argentine number 324 maintaining 11 educational institutions and 4 residences.

At Montevideo, Uruguay, in 1842 Argentinian exiles under Cabré, established a temporary residence and the seminary school of Santa Lucia. In 1858 the fathers were banished from the republic, only to return to Montevideo in 1872. With the aid of generous benefactions they were able to found the college and seminary of San Corazon in 1879 and to erect a beautiful church in 1897. Both institutions are under the jurisdiction of the Argentine province. Another Argentinian exile, Pares, was the first Jesuit to enter the Republic of Paraguay, 1842. The welcome extended was not too hearty, as the government wished the fathers to engage only in the care of the Indians. Despite the fact that the work in two churches in Asunción was so successful that certain government officials were desirous of giving the Jesuits greater freedom, and that a college and a Reduction among the Guaycurus were planned, the whole Paraguayan mission came to naught in 1845 owing to the hostile prejudices of the government which would not permit common life nor submission to foreign superiors. A second attempt of Pares in 1864 to enter the country failed, as did all subsequent attempts, even though they were sponsored by the Bishops of Paraguay. A change has come in recent years; five fathers from Argentina in 1926 preached popular missions in various cities of the republic with such success that a foundation was permitted in Asunción. After 158 years the fathers are once more working in the land of the Reductions.

Argentinian exiles also brought the Society of Jesus to the Republic of Chile.[25] For ten years, 1830 to 1840, the government under Portales had sought in vain for priests of the order for their country. At length in 1843 Gomela and Gonzalez, driven from the republic on the other side of the Andes, arrived at Santiago and began to work there in the Church of San Diego. With the coming of additional fathers another foundation was begun at Valparaiso. Though the government, especially the Minister Montt, earnestly desired the revival of the Indian Reductions, such was the mistrust and prejudice against the Jesuits and so unfavorable were the prospects that the work in Chile was abandoned in 1845. But not for long; three years later Peña and other Jesuit fugitives from Argentina came to the western republic; their work gained such recognition that in 1850 they were enabled to reopen the foundations at Santiago and Valparaiso. The College of San Ignacio, the first modern Jesuit boarding-school in South America, was opened in 1857 in the capital; a residence was founded at Concepción in 1871; the Papal seminary at Ancud was taken over in 1900. Contemporaneous with this development was the work of the German Jesuits for their countrymen in the southern part of Chile. These fathers came in 1859; after twenty years, during which they preached over four hundred popular missions, they were maintaining forty stations; they also established Xavier College at Puerto Montt, first for German, and later for Chilean students. All these works of the order were accomplished only in the face of the bitterest opposition of the Masonic anticlericals, especially during the years 1835–1886. In the field of education many difficulties concerning accommodations to the State's demands, admission of pupils into the government university, indeed, the very freedom of education, had to be overcome. Yet in spite of all, the work progressed so that in 1917 the Chilean Jesuits with their Argentinian brethren were formed into a full province. In 1937 the foundations in the western republic were separated to become the vice-province of Chile, which today numbers 169 members conducting 5 educational institutions, 3 residences and 2 houses of retreat.

---

[25] Perez, *La Compañia de Jesus restaurada en la Republica Argentina y Chile, el Uruguay y el Brasil.*

The possibilities for work in Brazil [26] must have appeared very remote to the first Jesuits of the nineteenth century, since that country was the only one to protest the Restoration of the order. Even when an entrance was granted, the fathers could not use their legal title but had to appear under various names, such as the "Sociedade Antonio Vieira," thus called from a distinguished Brazilian member of the old Society. As long as the Empire lasted, the fathers could obtain little better than toleration; matters took a better turn under the Republic. Today Brazil is the scene of many Jesuit labors. Berdugo, superior of the Argentine mission, came to Rio de Janeiro in 1841, investigating the possibility of work for his subjects in the event of their expulsion from the southern republic. In the next year he established the first foundation in the State of Rio Grande do Sul at Porto Alegre, from which the fathers worked out as country missionaries, especially among the neglected German colonists. Others, like Pares, labored among the Indians on the site of the old Reductions from 1845 to 1852. At Desterro, now Florianopolis, in the State of Santa Catherina, the first college was founded in 1846; a college attempted at Rio de Janeiro proved unsuccessful.

The place of the Spaniards, who returned to Argentina in 1861, was taken by the exiles of the Roman province. Colleges were founded by the Italian fathers at Nova Friburgo in 1866 and at Ytú and Pernambuco in 1867; at the same time the college at Desterro was reopened, only to be closed shortly afterwards because of sickness. Masonic persecution and mob violence forced the giving up of Pernambuco in 1873. With better times in 1893 at Rio de Janeiro a high school was started which became the great boarding college of S. Ignacio; in 1918 another high school was opened at São Paulo. Other activities of the Italian Jesuits, the Apostleship of Prayer, the *Messenger of the Sacred Heart,* the labors in the Sacred Heart Church at Santos and in the S. Ignacio Church at Rio de Janeiro, have had a significant influence in the religious revival of Brazil. Taddei and Cybeo achieved remarkable good by the missions which they preached in the various cities and towns. The vice-province of Central Brazil, which was formed in 1927, now ranks as a complete province and is composed of natives of Brazil. There are 204 members in the province, 3 educational institutions, 5 residences, 1 retreat house and 1 house of writers.

Two Austrian Jesuits, Slipinski and Sedlak, in 1840 came to Rio Grande do Sul to labor for the German colonists; they were joined ten years later by their German brethren.[27] The work, which covered the three southern

---

[26] Perez, *La Compañia de Jesus restaurada en la Republica Argentina y Chile, el Uruguay y el Brasil.*

[27] *Hundert Jahre Deutschtum in Rio Grande do Sul 1824–1924,* (Verband deutscher Vereine), Porto Alegre (1924).

States of Rio Grande do Sul, Santa Catherina and Paraná, was entrusted as a mission to the German province in 1869. Through primeval forests and along the wide watercourses, the fathers journeyed to found parishes, starting from the original two of São José and São Miguel to the more than twenty-five of today. For higher education, colleges have been conducted at Porto Alegre, São Leopoldo, Pelotas and Florianopolis, while the seminaries of Santa Maria and São Leopoldo have also been maintained. The colleges in the beginning were largely frequented by youths of German descent, but eventually those of Portuguese blood began to attend; indeed several of the professors, as Schneider and Teschauer, have contributed much to the study of Portuguese and to Brazilian literature. The South Brazilian province was erected in 1927; today it consists of 333 members, conducting 9 educational institutions and 11 residences.

Jesuit refugees from Portugal came to Brazil in 1910; at first they were not too well received by government officials, but eventually they were eagerly sought for. The scene of their labors has been in North Brazil, where they maintain colleges at Bahia and Pernambuco, a minor seminary at Baturité, as well as a flourishing apostolate of the pulpit and of the pen in four residences. The Jesuits on the mission, which depends on the Portuguese province, number 136. An interesting mission and one which has resulted in a considerable number of converts, is that among the Japanese immigrants in São Paulo; it was begun in 1929 by German Jesuits, coming not directly from the homeland but from Japan. The total of Jesuit activity today in Brazil is both large and important in the life of the Church in that great country.

It was not until 1842 that the Society of Jesus was invited to resume its labors in Colombia.[28] Two years later the work was begun, to be interrupted by the banishment of the fathers from 1850 to 1858 and again in 1861. The third attempt, made by the Castile province in 1884, was successful, possibly owing to the advent to power of a government friendly to the Church. Boarding colleges were founded at Bogotá and at Medellín, day colleges at Baranquilla and Bucaramanga, and residences at Cartegena and Pasto. In Venezuela a college and a seminary were started at Caracas; and in Panama a residence was established. Missions among the Indians along the Magdalena River were also undertaken. It was in this last field that Nicholas Rodriguez, another Claver in his zeal for the poor, labored and died in 1900 venerated as a saint. In 1924 the Jesuits working in the Republic of Colombia were organized into a province, which today counts 397 members with 8 educational institutions, 4 residences and 1 retreat house.

---

[28] Perea, *La Compañia de Jesus en Colombia y Centro-America despues de su restauración*, 3 Vols., Valladolid (1896–98).

Jesuits banished from Colombia came to Ecuador in 1850 on the invitation of García Moreno. Two years later they were forced to leave by an anticlerical revolution. They took up their residence in Guatemala, from which, subsequently, they were forced out by the same enemy. García Moreno again in 1862 called the Spanish fathers to Ecuador, where they opened colleges at Quito and Guayaquil and resumed the work of the old Society in the Indian Reductions. García Moreno in 1870 obtained fathers of the German province for the management of a technical school at Quito. The assassination of this noble Catholic statesman spelled ruin for Jesuit activity, although later on fathers from Colombia were able to come to the republic. Today Ecuador is a mission of the Andalusian province with 128 Jesuits maintaining colleges at Quito, Riomba and Cotocollao, a residence at Guayaquil and mission stations among the Manabi Indians.

In still other parts of Latin America colleges and residences are conducted at the present time by the Jesuits. The province of Leon has charge of the Cuban mission with the important college of Belen in Havana and other colleges at Cienfuegos, Sagua la Grande and Santiago, and a residence at Havana. The Toledo province operates in Bolivia colleges at Sucre and La Paz, and in Peru a college and a residence at Lima and a minor seminary at Arequipa. The Castilian province directs the Venezuelan mission with an archdiocesan seminary, college and residence at Caracas and churches at Maracaibo, Merida and Panama. The Mexican province conducts in Nicaragua colleges at Granada and Managua; and in Salvador, a college at the capital city, San Salvador, and a church at Santa Tecla.

In the foreign mission fields of Africa, the Near East and the Far East the modern Jesuits have revived the glorious record of the old Society, though their means and methods have changed considerably. Conditions today are very different from those of earlier times. Then support, moral and financial, came from the governments at home; today resources must be derived from the alms of the faithful. Then the idea of the real or supposed, superiority of European culture—often in the native mind—helped the message, which gained too from its novelty; today scepticism of Western civilization, born of wider contacts, proves a hindrance. Then there were no competitors; today a powerfully-financed Protestant effort disputes the field and confuses the heathen with the spectacle of a divided Christianity. Imperialism, exaggerations of awakening racial-consciousness, the social struggle, and the wars resulting from all three, have not only held back the missionaries but at times have even destroyed the missions. Yet in spite of these obstacles, as the Church in general, so the Society in particular, has more missionaries in the field, better trained and better organized, than at any period of history. Of the most evident problems, the accommodation of Catholic practice and the adaptation of the expression of Catholic doctrine to the native viewpoint have been to the Society, in common with other religious orders, a matter of deep concern and in recent decades of most sympathetic consideration. For one of the very first steps, the creation of a native clergy, the Jesuits of the restored Society have spent much time and effort; into their own ranks they have admitted Chinese, Japanese, Filipinos and Hindus, some of whom have been raised to the episcopacy; for the secular clergy of the heathen lands, the fathers maintain 13 major seminaries and 12 minor seminaries. In the training of an élite of Catholic laymen for the Orient and Africa, the order conducts 3 universities, at least 10 university-colleges, and some 38 secondary schools. Nor should the numerous primary schools connected with the various mission stations be forgotten. In this connection tribute must be paid to the missionary sisters who assist the fathers; on the missions of the old Society there were very few, if any, of such helpers, today there is not a single mission where the work is not aided and complemented by these heroic nuns.

The knowledge of the native languages has been of as much concern to the modern Jesuits as to their brethren of old. To reach all classes a scientific study of the common Oriental tongues, as well as of their classical languages, must be made; translations of their ancient sacred books is of importance; as is also an understanding of their ethnological origins. In these fields Hoffman, de Boullave, de Bouvier, Grandmaison and van Ginneken, among other Jesuits, have made valuable contributions. The methodical approach to mission problems, though of comparatively recent origin, has resulted in the new science of Missiology. In its development the fathers have participated, at first by articles in their periodicals and later by specific treatises, such as Gazet's *Directoire pour les missionaires du Madagascar*, Simon's *Monita ad missionarios provinciae Nankinensis* and Schurhammer's *Der Weg der Götter in Japan*. Missiology has been further helped by the writings on Canon Law, as applied to the missions, of Hernandez, Delplace and Vermeersch, and by the numerous historical volumes on the missions of the old Society by Brou, Schurhammer, Cros, Rochmonteix, Beccari, Wessels and many others. One of the leading missiologists today is the Belgian Jesuit Charles. The cause of the missions has been greatly forwarded by the periodicals published by the fathers, fifty in the mission field itself and twenty-five in Europe and America; among the last may be cited *Die Katholischen Missionen* and the *Jesuit Missions* (New York). The recruiting for the missions has been helped in a great degree by the apostolic schools, first founded by Foresta; in recent times the Jesuits maintain such schools in Belgium, Ireland, Austria, Spain and Portugal.

The first mission field in the Eastern Hemisphere to be occupied by the restored Society of Jesus was Syria.[29] In response to the invitation of the Archbishop of Myra, Mgr. Mazlum, a seminary at Ein-Traz was opened, three Italian Jesuits arriving for this purpose at Beirut on November 13, 1831. After the first labors at the seminary, a mission was founded in the Lebanon, the principal work of which was educational. In 1843 the Syrian mission was placed under the Lyons province and progressed despite many obstacles until 1856 when it included a college at Ghazir, eight churches and five other foundations. Syria, however, was to be a martyrs' station. The rebellion of the Druses in 1860 deluged the mission in blood; among the slain were two priests, Billotet and Haider (a Syrian), and three brothers, Bonacini, Jounes (a Maronite) and Maksoud (a Syrian). In the year before, Archbishop Planchet, S.J., one of the first missionaries in Syria, was murdered by the Kurds in Mesopotamia. Recovery of the work was made possible by the zeal of the later Cardinal Lavigerie, who through the founding of the "Oeuvre des Ecoles d'Orient," and ably assisted by the Jesuit, de Damas, collected two million francs. The greater part of the sum was spent on the Syrian orphans; accusations of covetousness made by certain persons disaffected towards the Jesuits were disposed of by the continued confidence of Lavigerie and the benefactors of the fathers. The college of Ghazir was transferred to Beirut, where in 1875 it received the status of a university; in 1882 Leo XIII bestowed on the new St. Joseph's University the right to grant philosophical and theological degrees; today it is the leading Catholic educational center in the Near East.[30] Two Jesuits ought to be remembered in connection with the institution: Cattin, who was responsible for the French and Turkish recognition of the juridical faculty, the foundation of the clinic, the hospital, the Institute Pasteur, the observatory, the laboratories and the botanical garden; and Cheikho, an Arabian, the author of a dictionary, grammar and several works of research in Arabic literature. The Syrian mission naturally suffered much in the World War; yet today, besides the University at Beirut with its 1,200 students, it maintains foundations at Damascus, Aleppo, Homs, Ghazir and Bikfaya in the Lebanon.

A French missionary from Syria, de Damas, in 1881 began the Armenian mission, the ground for which had already been prepared by another French Jesuit, Normand, and an Armenian Jesuit, Afker. The work was restricted to Lesser Armenia and was largely confined to educational endeavors. A secondary school at Constantinople, which had been started by Sicilian Jesuits in 1864, was taken over by the Armenian mission. The six foundations of the mission were in constant danger from the fanaticism of the Turks; in 1909 the school and the Christians of

[29] Jullien, *La Nouvelle Mission de la C. de J. en Syrie 1831–1895*, Tours (1898).
[30] *Les Jésuites en Syrie 1831–1931. Université Saint Joseph*, Paris (1931).

Adana suffered terribly in the massacres of that year. The World War and the policies of Mustapha Kemal have almost completely destroyed the mission; only the foundation at Constantinople remains. In another Arabic country, Iraq, in 1932 the American Jesuits opened a secondary school at Baghdad at the wish of Pius XI and the Chaldean Patriarch. The school today is being conducted by the New England province. On the western frontier of the Near East, in Albania, the Venetian Jesuits in 1841 began work as country missionaries; in 1856 they were able to establish more permanent activities. A Papal seminary was founded at Scutari in 1859; later a printing press was set up and Albanian periodicals produced. Since 1888 great good has been achieved by the so-called "Flying Mission" in which the fathers travel through the remote mountain districts, preaching, dispensing the Sacraments, instructing in the Catholic Faith, reconciling blood-feuds and strengthening the ties of union with Rome. Today forty-nine Jesuits of the Venice-Milan province labor in the Albanian mission.

Fathers from the Lyons province were the first Jesuits of the new Society to work in Africa. They came in 1840 to Algiers to labor in the hospitals and the churches of the cities of Algiers and Constantine.[31] Within three years a college was begun at Oran and later, on the invitation of Cardinal Lavigerie, a second one at Algiers. The last college had to be soon closed, owing to the opposition of the government officials and to the proximity of a similar institution. The zeal of the fathers, especially Brumauld, was turned to the maintaining of two large orphan asylums, at Ben-Aknoun and Bouffarik respectively; their purpose was to train French streetwaifs to become staunch Catholics and worthy colonists. It was owing to no want of sacrifices that the ventures did not realize the hopes placed in them. The conversion of the native Kabyle and Arabs was held back by the opposition of colonial officials; what little could be accomplished by traveling missionaries and in short-lived foundations on the edge of the desert, was done. These efforts and an attempted seminary at Ben-Aknoun were not entirely without result; at least they acted as forerunners of the great work of Cardinal Lavigerie's White Fathers. Jesuits had the privilege of cooperating with the Cardinal in the founding of his congregation; the Jesuit Vincent was the first novice-master and, until the White Fathers were themselves able to take over in 1879, a French Jesuit always occupied that important post. The anticlerical persecution of 1880 at home drove the Jesuits for a short while from Algiers. Today the Lyons province conducts a college at Algiers and stations at Constantine and Oran.

The second African mission of modern times was in Madagascar.[32]

---

[31] Burnichon, *La Compagnie de Jésus en France*, Vols. II–IV.
[32] De la Vaissière, *Histoire de Madagascar*, Paris (1884).

Father General Roothaan in 1844 sent six Jesuits of the Lyons province to the island; such was the control which the Protestant missionaries possessed that little could be accomplished, so the fathers moved off to work in the islands of Reunion and Mauritius. Not until 1855 did a member of the Society return to Madagascar; then Finaz, unrecognized, labored at Tananarivo to prepare the way for later missionaries. His technical skill in constructing a small railway, a telegraph system and a gas balloon, gained him the favor of the Court; two of his brethren were permitted to come in Tananarivo. The Protestants, however, so worked on the ruling Queen that the fathers had to leave the capital city and were unable to return until her death in 1861. Despite much continued opposition— Protestantism was declared the state religion in 1869—the Jesuits successfully developed their missions until 1883, when there were 53 Jesuits in the land conducting 152 chapels and 120 stations. They were aided in their work by nuns and teaching brothers. The French, now rulers of the island, lent their support to the Catholic missions. In that very same year of 1883 a revolt against the French drove the Jesuits and their European assistants to the coast for a two years' banishment. The native Catholics remained true, openly holding prayer-meetings in their churches. Another revolt, that of the Tahavalo in 1893, brought terrible destruction on the mission; one of the fathers, Berthier, was barbarously slaughtered.

When peace came, a division of the work was made: the northern part of the island was transferred to the Holy Ghost Fathers, the southern part to the Lazarists, while the central section was retained by the Jesuits. In 1906 the Toulouse province, which had been manning the mission, gave over the district of Fianarantsoa to the care of the Champagne province. Among the missionaries worthy of note were de la Vaissière and the Polish father, Beyzym, who devoted themselves to the lepers; Chevaliers and Fontanié, who did much for handicraft and agricultural education. The calumnies representing the Jesuits as persecuting Protestants, robbing them of their churches and even murdering native adherents of the sects, have met documentary refutation in Perger's *Die Jesuiten in Madagaskar* (Paderborn 1898) and Piolet's *Douze Leçons à la Sorbonne sur Madagascar* (Paris 1899). Today the Toulouse province maintains 111 Jesuits in the district of Imerina, with a secondary school, a diocesan seminary at Tananarivo and 41 residences (one on Mauritius); the Champagne province supports 108 Jesuits conducting a secondary school and a minor seminary, 3 residences and 24 stations.

Egypt since 1879 has been the scene of missionary labors by the Jesuits from the Lyons province. Though the Coptic seminary, which was first attempted, had to be closed after three years, the fathers persevered in their efforts with the Copts until by 1905 some 25,000 of them had been reconciled to Rome. Secondary schools were established at Cairo and

Alexandria; and other foundations were begun which supported forty primary schools. The World War so hampered the work that for a time the school at Cairo had to be closed. At present the Lyons province operates the Egyptian mission with forty Jesuits in charge of a secondary school at Cairo and two residences. In connection with Jesuit labor in Egypt, Ryllo, a Russian-born Jesuit, deserves remembrance. After a missionary career in Syria, Malta and Naples and the rectorship of the College of the Propaganda in Rome, with two other companions of the order in 1846 he set out for the Sudan; following the banks of the White Nile he made a journey of discovery from Khartoum, to which town he later returned in 1848 to die worn out with hardships.

The Zambesi mission, begun in 1879, was entrusted to the English province.[33] Native wars, the conflicts with the Boers, Protestant opposition, sickness, famine and the difficult climate held back the mission for many years. There was no lack of heroism among the fathers and brothers, fifty-three of whom succumbed to the hardships. Among the distinguished laborers on the mission were Depelchin, the founder, and Law, an heroic victim of fever and starvation. Better days dawned after the suppression of the Matabele revolt; the work so prospered that the original mission was thrice divided. Today the English province has charge of the Salisbury mission in Southern Rhodesia with 103 Jesuits, operating colleges at Salisbury and Grahamstown and 26 residences or stations; the province of Minor Poland directs the Broken Hill mission of Northern Rhodesia with 30 Jesuits conducting 7 stations. For a while, until 1910, the Portuguese Jesuits worked a portion of the field; their place has been taken by the Steyl Missionaries.

Work in the Congo [34] was entrusted to the Belgian Jesuits by Leo XIII. Principal reliance has been placed by the fathers on the education of the young. Though in the beginning the results were not too encouraging, today their wisdom is proved by wonderful fruit. The protection of the natives from slavery has ever found faithful champions in the Belgian Jesuits. In the Congo at the present time a major and two minor seminaries, an incipient college and twenty stations are being maintained. The province of Northern Belgium is in charge of the Kisantu mission with sixty-seven Jesuits; the province of Southern Belgium, the Kwango mission with eighty-one Jesuits.

The largest missionary effort of the modern Society is being made in India. There today are 9 missions manned by 1,041 Jesuits, Hindus, Belgians, Germans, French, Italians, Portuguese and Americans. The first

[33] Schreiber, *The Life of Augustus Law,* London (1898); *The Zambesi Missionary Record,* London (1898–).

[34] *Mouvement des missions catholiques au Congo,* Louvain (1888–); *Missions Belges de la Compagnie de Jésus,* Brussels (1899–).

to arrive in Xavier's mission-land were the six Jesuits who came to Calcutta in 1834, with the Irish father, St. Leger, as superior. Their first venture, the College of St. Francis Xavier, gave great promise; but such were the difficulties due in part to the conflicting Portuguese claims of jurisdiction that the mission was relinquished in 1846. Not until Pius IX had regulated the ecclesiastical status of India did the Jesuits return. Then the Belgian fathers under the lead of Depelchin began to evangelize the territory assigned them by the Pope in Western Bengal and parts of the provinces of Behar and Orissa.[35] The College of St. Francis Xavier was reopened and over the years has attained great success, especially after its incorporation with the University of Calcutta. The Catholic population of the city under the ministrations of the fathers has increased to 14,000 souls. Missionaries were not long in advancing to farther fields: Sapart going to the southwest in 1865, Goffinet to the wretched Sunderbunds at the Delta of the Ganges in 1868, and Schoff to the north in Burdwan in 1873.

The best achievement of the Bengal mission was made in the mountainous district of Chota Nagpore; here labored the greatest missionary of the new Society, Constantine Lievens.[36] Lievens was born in Belgium in 1856, was ordained in Bengal in 1883, and two years later was sent to Chota Nagpore, where he soon began those mass conversions which recall the successes of St. Francis Xavier. Starting with 300 Christians, without money or a dwelling place, he erected his first mission; and before three years under his direction the baptized increased to 50,000. In 1889 he journeyed to the mountain land of Barwai, where within a month he baptized 12,000. Lievens gained the good-will of the natives, beggared outcasts, bled white by the money-lenders and the tax-collectors, by fighting their battles in the courts. His knowledge of Hindu and English law, and his fearlessness in defying the powerful oppressors of the poor, saved numberless families and districts. To assure his work permanence he formed his neophytes into Christian villages; but he did even more, he composed a catechism, a prayerbook, a hymn-book and lives of the saints in their own tongue, and himself supervised their publication. Protests stormed down upon him, lawsuits deluged him, even the criticism of Christians rose up against him. Undismayed he carried on until he broke under the strain and had to return to Belgium in the hope of recovering his shattered health. He died at Louvain in 1893. Lievens according to his own reckoning had himself baptized 25,000. He showed that mass conversions were still possible to an extraordinary apostle, which he un-

[35] Jassow, *La Mission du Bengale occidental ou Archdiocèse de Calcutta*, 2 Vols., Bruges (1921).

[36] Marlier, *L'apôtre de Chota-Nagpore*; Huonder, *Bannerträger des Kreuzes*, Vol. II, Freiburg (1913).

doubtedly was. The flourishing state of the Chota Nagpore mission is proof that his work was endowed with permanence. The Ranchi mission of Chota Nagpore today is manned by the province of Northern Belgium with 154 Jesuits in charge of a diocesan seminary, 3 other educational institutions, and 40 mission stations. The Calcutta mission is supported by the province of Southern Belgium with 171 Jesuits conducting a university college, 2 other educational institutions, 11 churches and 21 mission stations.

The eastern part of the old Malabar mission was entrusted to the Toulouse province in 1838.[37] Only 5,000 Catholics were found; yet within fifty years their numbers were doubled and two great churches were built. A college was founded at Negapatim, one purpose of which was to convert the Brahmin youth; some few have been won to the Faith and today possess a parish of their own in Trichinopoly. To this city the college was transferred in 1883, and has since developed in the course of time to a university college, which with its 2,500 enrollment is the largest Catholic institution of this grade in India. The Madura mission, as it is called today, is a vice-province depending on the Toulouse province; it is composed of 314 Jesuits with 6 educational institutions and 61 parishes in the districts of Trichinopoly, Madura and Palamcottah.

On the west coast of India the German Jesuits began to labor in 1854.[38] They had been called thither to revive the Faith weakened by the "Patronate" troubles; the greater part of the Catholics were in rebellion because the Pope had abolished the Portuguese king's protectorate. The labors of the fathers on the whole were successful, although their work, as well as the wider work of the Church, was seriously hampered by the conflicts of ecclesiastical jurisdiction (recently settled) between Goa and Bombay. At first the southern half, the Vicariate of Poona, was entrusted to the German fathers; but in 1858 the northern half, the Vicariate of Bombay, was also given to them. As a result their territory stretched from Kanara for 700 miles up the western coast to British Baluchistan, except in the few places where the Goan Jurisdiction intervened.

The spiritual labors in the first decade were largely confined to European parishes and to the Irish soldiers in the British army. In the 'seventies more definite work for the conversion of the natives was begun; an already existing mission in Kanara was revived, and the evangelization begun of the Mahrattas in 1879, of the inhabitants of Gujarat in 1893 and of the Dschungel people of Kathkari in 1900. As elsewhere in India converts came only from the lower classes, except in Kanara where some neophytes were gained among the higher castes. Higglin, Weishaupt, Perrig and Frenken were outstanding missionaries in this field, always

---

[37] Castets, *The Madura Mission*, Trichinopoly (1924).
[38] Väth, *Die deutschen Jesuiten in Indien* (1920).

an extremely difficult one because of the climate, famine and disease. One of the principal reasons for the introduction of the Jesuits into Bombay was the remedying of the sad state of education there. It was done with the hope of inspiriting the Christians, of protecting them from the strong Protestant missionary effort, and of elevating the Church in the eyes of a highly cultured and proud heathenism. These effects the German fathers in the course of the years succeeded in accomplishing, establishing all manner of schools up to the University of St. Francis Xavier at Bombay. St. Francis Xavier's has become renowned throughout India not only for the education imparted but for the scientific achievements of its professors, such as Sierp and Steichen in radio, Assmuth in biology and Blatter in botany. The Bombay-Poona mission in 1914 was served by 132 Jesuits; then the World War crippled the work disastrously, many of the fathers were interned or had to leave the country. Their places were partially supplied by their brethren from the neighboring missions and from America; but it was not until 1921, when the Aragon province was placed in charge, that activities were returned to normal. In 1929 the German fathers came back, but only to the Poona district which was assigned to the Upper German province. At the present time the Aragon province maintains the Bombay mission, conducting 5 educational institutions, 1 retreat-house and 5 parishes or stations, also the Ahmedabad mission with 53 Jesuits operating 1 college and 10 stations. The Upper German province supports the Poona mission with 46 Jesuits in charge of 1 high school and 12 stations.

Italian Jesuits began the Mangalore mission in 1878.[39] They placed particular emphasis on the training of a native clergy; over 140 Indian secular priests have been educated in their Seminary of St. Joseph. St. Aloysius College was founded by them at Mangalore in 1882; it was raised to university status and incorporated into the University of Madras in 1887. One very important achievement of the Mangalore mission was the medical-charitable institute for the relief of the poor, founded in the city of Mangalore by an American Jesuit, Müller. Assistants were trained here in practical medicine and pharmacy for all parts of India, and its remedies were requested even from Burma. Their dispensary was but one of the works of this zealous priest, several hospitals were built by him likewise; in 1907 the British Government bestowed on him the Kaiser-i-Hind Medal. The district of Calicut was separated from Mangalore in 1923, when that section was erected as a native diocese; the Jesuits however remained in charge of the seminary and St. Aloysius College. On the Calicut mission today there are 123 Jesuits of the Venice-Milan prov-

---

[39] Cassiani Ingoni, *Cinquant'anni a Mangalore sulla costa occidentale dell'India 1878–1922*, Venice (1908).

ince who operate 3 educational institutions, 3 residences and 9 mission stations.

Ceylon became the scene of Jesuit activity in 1893 when Leo XIII gave to the Society the charge of the districts of Galle and Trincomali. The region of Galle was entrusted to the Belgian fathers; with it went the great Papal seminary for all India at Kandy, opened in 1893. At present the Northern Belgian province maintains 75 Jesuits, conducting the seminary, 1 school at Galle and 16 stations. The section of Trincomali was given to the Champagne province, which today supports 32 Jesuits working in 1 high school and 6 residences. There are two other missions of the order in India, that of Goa and that of Patna. The first mission is subject to the Portuguese province; 63 Jesuits labor in the seminary at Alleppey on the Malabar coast, and in the high schools at Belguam and Cochim; some of the fathers work besides in the native parishes. The second mission is in the charge of the Chicago province; in 1921 it was given to the care of the Missouri province, and, at the division in 1928, was assigned to Chicago. The district includes the northern part of the Behar-Orissa civil province and the Kingdom of Nepal. Today 93 Jesuits labor in 1 high school and 18 mission stations; especially gratifying have been the results among the heathen Santals.[40]

The missionary activity in China forms an inspiring episode in the history of the modern Society.[41] For almost a hundred years the fathers have maintained their missions in the face of constant anti-foreign hatred. On three occasions the price of their fidelity has been death: in the T'ai-p'ing Rebellion of 1860, Massa and Wuillaume were murdered; in the Boxer uprising of 1900, Isoré, Andlauer, Mangin, Denn and Lomuller were killed; and in the Bolshevist troubles of 1927, Dugout and Vanara were slain. Since the establishment of the Republic, while the central government has been favorable enough, numerous bandit gangs with their robberies and kidnappings have been a terrible scourge; and the unending civil wars, as well as the present struggle with the Japanese, have wrought wholesale destruction on the mission properties. The glory of the heroic stand that has been made, belongs largely to the French fathers, who until recently were the only Jesuits laboring in China.

The first Jesuits to arrive were Gottland and Estève, who landed in Shanghai in 1842. They had come in response to repeated petitions made by Chinese Catholics to the Father General, the Queen of Portugal and the Pope, begging that Jesuits be sent among them. With more help coming the following year, the fathers were able to take over the existing seminary; under their guidance it has sent forth many Chinese priests. In

---

[40] *Jesuit Missions* passim.
[41] De la Servière, *Histoire de la Mission de Kiangnan*, 3 Vols., Marseille (1914).

1856 through the action of Pius IX the whole of the Nanking Vicariate was included in the mission and then entrusted to the province of France. The fathers of this province have heroically persevered through bloody persecutions, reverses, the cholera and other epidemics (at one time, 1862 to 1865, twenty missionaries were lost) to make their mission one of the most flourishing in the whole order. Just before the Boxer Rebellion the Christians numbered 124,000 and the catechumens 50,000; it is inspiring to note that during this and all other sanguinary assaults the native Christians stood firm in the Faith. Even in the chaotic days of the last two decades, progress has still continued so that in 1921 three districts were detached and placed under the care of other provinces, Anking under the province of Leon, Pengpu under the province of Turin, and Wuhu under the province of Castile. Probably the most outstanding achievement of the French fathers has been their educational work in the Aurora University of Shanghai and in the meteorological, astronomical and seismographic observatories at Zi-ka-wei; these observatories have received universal acclaim. The labors of the Shanghai Jesuits in science and in Chinese literature, will be noted in the following chapter. The care of the poor Chinese has also been a conspicuous work of the Nanking mission; in the last terrible years one father, Jacquinot, has labored heroically for the refugees in the midst of all the fighting. Today the province of France maintains the Nanking mission with 237 Jesuits conducting 4 great educational institutions, 4 churches and some 46 stations.

In 1928 Jesuits from the California province [42] took up the work in Ricci College, Shanghai. At the present time the province of Leon has 75 Jesuits in the Anking mission conducting 1 minor seminary and 15 stations; the province of Turin has in the Pengpu mission 42 Jesuits in charge of 26 stations; the province of Castile has 89 Jesuits in the Wuhu mission operating 3 educational institutions and 20 stations. Jesuits from the province of Lower Canada began the apostolic labor in the mission of Wuchow in 1924; today the French Canadian fathers maintain 56 Jesuits in 16 mission stations.

Second only to the work of the province of France is that of their brethren of the Champagne province in the Tschi-li Vicariate.[43] To this southeastern portion of the Peking mission came priests from the latter province in 1851. Perhaps more than in any other part, all the difficulties and hardships of the Chinese apostolate have been their lot; yet in 1900 just before the Boxer Rebellion they ministered to 49,000 Catholics. Some of the bloodiest outrages of that uprising were committed in the Tschi-li territory, thousands of Christians were slaughtered and five of the fathers

---

[42] Father Simons, one of the original group, was slain by bandits or Communists about January 1, 1941.

[43] Dieu, "Les Martyrs Chinois de 1900 dans Tschili," *Xaverian*, Louvain (1926).

were assassinated. Here too the native Catholics remained staunch in their adherence to the Faith. As soon as peace was restored the fathers rebuilt again the destroyed chapels and schools. Educational work has had an important part on this mission, especially in the university college at Tientsin; the leading Jesuit Sinologist of modern times, Wieger,[44] labored in the district. Today the Champagne province has 164 Jesuits in this Sien-hsien mission, laboring in 5 educational institutions and 30 stations. In 1935 the province of Hungary received a portion of the field, the Tamingen mission, where 37 Jesuits are at work in 2 educational institutions. Two other provinces of the order maintain missions in China: the Portuguese province, the Macao mission; the Irish province, the Hong Kong mission. The Portuguese fathers began their work in 1914, when after their expulsion from Portuguese Macao they came to labor in Shiu-Hing; the mission today numbers 29 Jesuits, 3 educational institutions and 7 missionary stations. In 1926 the Irish Jesuits came to Hong Kong; their work so far has been solely educational, today 39 fathers are in charge of 3 educational institutions.

The Dutch East Indies became the scene of modern Jesuit missionary activity in 1859 when the Netherlands purchased the Portuguese possessions in the Sunda Islands; twenty-five years later Pius IX made over to the Dutch Jesuits the Vicariate of Batavia on the island of Java.[45] Missionary labors at various times were extended to Sumatra, Borneo, Timor, Celebes and the Moluccas; today, however, the Jesuit activity is confined to Java alone. The Dutch fathers have carried the press-apostolate of their homeland to the island, today publishing there three news-journals. The Netherlands province at the present time maintains 172 Jesuits in Java, conducting 5 educational institutions, 19 residences and 1 house of retreats.

Australia,[46] lying to the south, received the first Jesuits in 1848, when two Austrian fathers arrived at Adelaide to care for the German immigrants; they were not long in extending their labors to the English-speaking Catholics as well, keeping the Faith alive among the lonely and far-scattered settlers. In 1856 a college was founded at Sevenhills, the first seat of higher learning in South Australia. Still later in 1882 work among the aborigines about Port Darwin was inaugurated; but although much heroic effort was spent, the character of the natives, their wandering habits, the bad influence of the whites and the Chinese, and the rigors of

---

[44] Brou, "La Mort d'un Sinologue: Le P. L. Wieger," *Etudes*, Vol. CCXVI, pp. 474–486.

[45] Van der Valden, *De Roomsch-Katholieke Missie in Nederlandsch Oost Indies 1848–1908*, Nymegen (1908).

[46] *The Jesuit Directory and Year Book*, Melbourne; Sinthern, *53 Jahre oesterreichischer Jesuitenmission in Australia*, Wien (1924).

climate precluded success; the stations finally had to be abandoned. In the meantime other Jesuits from Ireland had come to Melbourne in 1865 and to Sydney in 1875, establishing colleges in both places. The work of these last fathers so prospered among the large and growing Irish immigration, that by 1901 all the Jesuit labors in Australia were being directed by the Irish province. The Australian activities have become similar to the European; for education there are maintained at Melbourne a regional seminary, a university college (Newman College) and two secondary schools; at Sydney there are operated two secondary schools, at one of which, Riverview, there is an excellent astronomical observatory. In the work for souls eight great parish churches in the large centers have been established. The Australian mission so developed that in 1931 it was constituted an independent vice-province, today it numbers 227 Jesuits.

One of the most flourishing missions of the Society in the Far East is the Philippine mission.[47] Spanish Jesuits of the Aragon province on the invitation of the colonial officials took up the work in the islands in 1859. At Manila they founded the Ateneo de Manila, which under their direction and that of their American successors, has grown to be a celebrated university college; later the Spanish fathers established a college at Vigan in Northern Luzon, which has since been relinquished. At Manila, Faura and Algué built the renowned observatory that has become the center of a series of meteorological stations spread throughout the islands. The services rendered to commerce and shipping in the Far Eastern waters have been so valuable that when, after the American occupation, bigots sought to force Algué out, the whole Asiatic business world, many leading American commercial houses, admirals of the fleets and the press of Manila and Hong Kong rallied to the father's defense. The Government of the United States decided to give the priest-scientist its recognition and support. Zealous mission work was also carried on among the Catholic and Moro inhabitants of the island of Zamboanga; while at the island of Culion 5,000 lepers at one time were cared for in the largest leper colony in the world. Although a few American Jesuits came to the Islands after the American occupation, it was not until 1921 that the American Jesuits were directed to take over the work of the mission; in 1927 the whole of the labors were placed in the complete charge of the New York province. Among the distinguished missionaries may be listed: of the Spanish Jesuits, Sanchez, Rello and Puig; of the American Jesuits, McDonough, Thompkins and Monahan. The American Jesuits have carried on the work of their Spanish brethren with notable success; today they number 258 Jesuits conducting 5 educational institutions, including a university college, 30 mission stations and 1 retreat house. In other groups of islands

---

[47] Pastells, *Mision de la C. de J. de Filipinas en el siglo 19*, Barcelona (1916–17); *Woodstock Letters*, passim; *Jesuit Missions*, passim.

in Oceania, the Mariana, the Marshall and the Caroline Islands, work is being carried on by the Spanish Jesuits, who came to the first group in 1919 and to the second in 1923. At the present time the province of Andalusia has 21 Jesuits working in all 3 archipelagoes, maintaining 32 mission stations.

It was only in the twentieth century that the Society resumed the work of Xavier in Japan. In accordance with the wish of Pius X in 1908, fathers from various provinces were sent to Tokyo to found a Catholic University for the Japanese Christians. Lack of means, the insistence of the government on a large endowment, the opposition of the pagans, all seemed to foredoom the project to failure. But the courageous determination of the fathers of the Lower German province, to whom the university was eventually entrusted, overcame all obstacles, even the total destruction of the buildings by the earthquake of 1923. The complete government recognition came at last in 1928; today, though the numbers of the students are small, an important cultural influence in Japan is being achieved. The fathers of the Lower German province in 1921 also undertook the work of conversion in the district of Hiroshima. Today there are 72 Jesuits in Japan, conducting, besides the university, 1 high school and 13 mission houses.

Thus have been passed in review the missionary activities of the restored Society through a century and a quarter. Before the outbreak of the Second World War, the future of the Jesuit missions was most promising. But the terrible toll of death and destruction of property in Europe can only mean that at least for the near future there must be a great dearth of men and resources. One hope in the darkness is that the missionary spirit among the Jesuits is stronger than at any time in the order's history.

CHAPTER XVII

MODERN SCHOOLS AND MODERN SCHOLARS

Leo XII in 1824, on the occasion of his entrusting the Roman College once more to the Jesuits, reminded the fathers that "The Society was restored for that purpose above all that it might instruct youth to learning and virtue." Such a charge the Society was only too eager to accept; yet as the Jesuits looked about them, even the most sanguine could not have been but disheartened.[1] Five schools in Russia, four in the Two Sicilies, one each at Stonyhurst in England, Georgetown in the United States, Clongowes Wood in Ireland and Brig in Switzerland, these were all there were with which to make a beginning. True, in a short time colleges were opened at Turin and Fribourg, while in the Spanish lands fourteen colleges of the old Society were returned to the Jesuits. But how little could even the sum total promise towards the renewal of a system which once included 750 colleges and universities. The hard circumstances of the newer times immeasurably increased the difficulties ahead. As has been stated in a previous chapter, since means and money were scarce and generous benefactors not to be expected, the new schools could be opened only at infrequent intervals, from small beginnings, and with every prospect of slow development. Moreover the liberty of setting its own standards, which the old Society had enjoyed, was gone forever. The new Society had to develop its system in the face of government-controlled education, strongly entrenched and often intolerant of any private competition. Gone too was the hope for that splendid uniformity which characterized the Jesuit schools of the earlier period, so varying were the educational conditions not only as between Europe and America but even between the different countries of Europe itself. As has already been noted the almost periodic expulsions of the Society from the various countries of the Latin World—expulsions that not only entailed a cycle of losses of colleges and their rebuilding, but also seriously hampered the proper training of teachers and the realization of ideals—continually held back throughout the nineteenth century the renewing of the Jesuit system of education. Yet in spite of all obstacles and through all vicissitudes the Jesuits persevered courageously in their educational apostolate.

---

[1] Schwickerath, *Jesuit Education*, cs. V, VI, VII.

One of the most pressing problems confronting the new Jesuit educators was the adaptation of the Ratio Studiorum to the post-Revolutionary scene.[2] The Twentieth General Congregation, the first held after the Restoration, in 1820, instructed the General to appoint a commission for the examination of the suggestions which the provinces were to be asked to send in. Father Fortis complied by appointing the commission and sending requests for suggestions to every province. However political revolutions and the pioneering difficulties encountered in re-establishing the whole work of the Society held back definite action. The next General Congregation in 1829 returned to the problem, asking the new Father General Roothaan to act in the matter. Roothaan, an accomplished scholar and an experienced teacher, gladly acquiesced, appointing for the purpose a committee of seven, one from each of the provinces of Italy, the Sicilies, France, Germany, Austro-Galicia, England and Spain. The committee's first work was to gather suggestions from able Jesuit teachers and to consider the views and methods of distinguished non-Jesuit educators, as well as the governmental requirements which the various provinces had to meet. The members of the committee, keeping before them the Ratio of the year 1599, and that not as something obsolete but as a fundamental system, were to study such changes of the Ratio as might be deemed necessary and profitable. They were then to submit their findings and recommendations to the examination of the General and his Assistants. After the work of the commission was accomplished, the findings were submitted to Father Roothaan, and he in turn sent the adapted Ratio to the different provinces on July 25, 1832, where by actual experience the suitability of the new Ratio was to be determined.

This new instrument was in no essential a departure from the old Ratio. Important changes occurred only in the curricula, as the provisions for administration, methods and discipline remained as before. Courses of two years in ecclesiastical history and in Canon Law were added in the theological curriculum, and the professors were admonished to keep in contact with and to treat the current theological problems. In the philosophical curriculum Aristotle was no longer accorded preeminence, the courses in mathematics and physics were strengthened, and courses in chemistry and astronomy were added to this curriculum. The professors of philosophy were urged to be in touch with scientific thought and to bring to the notice of their pupils the latest developments in that thought. It was in the curriculum of the arts that the greatest adjustment was made; the language of each country was to be taught in all the classes as a major subject. The daily schedule was also to include the teaching of

[2] Farrell, *The Jesuit Code of Liberal Education*, c. XV, "The Revised Ratio Studiorum of 1832."

history, geography and elementary mathematics. The prefect of studies was to assign the amount of time for each of these branches as local exigencies demanded. The classics, however, were to be held in the same position of importance which has always been accorded them by the Ratio. In making the changes of the edition of 1832 the commission thereby either gave approval to practices which had come into use even before the Suppression, or introduced what was soundest among the newer educational developments. Criticism has been made against the revision that it did not go far enough in meeting modern educational ideas and practices. Even if a certain justice be admitted in the criticism, it may be still maintained that a surrender to the overemphasis of experimentation, to the fads and vagaries of modern education would have been neither advisable nor profitable. Another criticism advanced is that there is a lack of definiteness in the new Ratio. It may be said in reply that the revisions of 1832 were not considered to be final; they could not be final considering how the educational conditions in Europe and America varied one from another. These conditions are responsible to a great extent for the fact that the Ratio of 1832 has never been accepted *in toto* by the Society.[3] Of course the revolutions, the expulsions and the anticlerical hatred of Jesuit education, played their parts too. Since no General Congregation ever officially approved of the document it has come to be looked upon in the order as directive rather than mandatory. In 1853 the Twenty-second General Congregation took into consideration the issuing of a definitive edition; but once again circumstances prevented action. The Twenty-fifth General Congregation in 1906 received a proposal for a revision of the Ratio of 1832; but the majority of the members considered that the existing conditions and the varying governmental educational legislation made the proposition impractical. It was thought more feasible that the individual provinces draft their own courses and submit them to the General for approval. The delegates urged, however, a firm adherence to the traditional teaching methods and to the subjects evaluated as essential, the Latin and Greek classics. In recent years the present Father General has taken in hand the revision of the studies of the whole Society. And, as regards the American provinces, he appointed a special commission to arrange a general program for the educational institutions of the Society in the United States. These efforts towards a modern adaptation of the Ratio prove that the Jesuits have remained always faithful to the fundamental principle of the Ratio, the harmonious development of the various powers of the soul, the memory, the imagination, the intellect and the will, or to put it more simply, to an education which will produce learned, cultured and

---

[3] Farrell, *The Jesuit Code of Liberal Education*, c. XVI, "The Ratio Studiorum and Contemporary Education."

Catholic gentlemen. Father General Martin insisted that this principle is the animating soul of Jesuit education and it alone counts; while his successor, Father Wernz, admonished the modern Jesuits to employ every good method of their own time for the furtherance of this ideal. To-day, as in the past, Scholastic philosophy and the classics are the corner-stones of the education given in all the colleges of the Society; but if the motto of the Society, "Ad Majorem Dei Gloriam," were to be realized by the establishment of technical, agricultural and business schools, the Jesuits would be ready to operate such institutions. As a matter of fact they are already doing so in Spain, Belgium, France and the United States.

The Jesuit educational institutions, exclusive of their own houses of study, today number 396, located in 51 countries and attended by 160,-153 students. The following table will show the distribution of these colleges and universities of the modern Society.[4]

	Universities or University Colleges	University Residences	Secondary Colleges	Major Semi-aries	Minor Semi-aries
Europe	13	9	109	11	32
United States and Canada	33		23	1	2
Latin America	17		6	5	17
Africa			6	2	6
The Near East	2		1	2	
Asia and Oceania	12	1	36	11	9
Total	77	10	211	32	66

The crown of all Jesuit education is the Gregorian University at Rome. In the days of the old Society it was the Roman College and, after the Restoration, was still known by that name until its seizure by the Piedmontese in 1870. The lectures and classes were continued in other quarters but the name had to be changed, so it was called the Gregorian University after its greatest benefactor, Gregory XIII. The staff is drawn from the ablest scholars of the Society of Jesus; the student-body, some 2,316 ecclesiastical students, are received not only from dioceses in all parts of the world but from sixty-three religious orders and congregations. Second only in importance are the two other schools of higher ecclesiastical scholarship maintained by the order in Rome, the Pontifical Biblical Institute, with a branch college in Jerusalem, and the

---

[4] These and all subsequent figures must be understood as of the year preceding the Second World War.

Pontifical Oriental Institute. The fathers in the Eternal City also have charge of the German-Hungarian College, the South American College (Collegio Pio Latino Americano), the Brazilian College, the Maronite College and the Russian College. These institutions are residential seminaries where the students live, study and receive their spiritual training; their intellectual education is obtained at the Gregorian. Not only in Peter's City but in many parts of the world, the Society has a significant share in priestly education; pontifical, regional and diocesan seminaries to the number of thirty-two have been entrusted to its guidance. Among the more prominent seminaries are: Anagni and Catanzaro in Italy, Innsbruck [5] and Frankfort in Germany, Dubno (Oriental Rite) in Poland, Mundelein in the United States, Caracas in Venezuela, Buenos Aires in the Argentine, São Leopoldo in Brazil, Beirut in Syria, Kandy and Mangalore in India, Zi-ka-wei and Sien-hsien in China, and Melbourne in Australia. In the work of preparing youths for sacerdotal studies, the fathers of the order labor in sixty-six minor seminaries and apostolic schools. With the mention of apostolic schools, i. e., institutions for the preliminary training of youths, candidates for the foreign missions, there must be remembered the name of the Jesuit de Foresta, who conceived the idea in 1865. Nowhere is the Society's work in educating for the priesthood more important than in the foreign missions themselves; in Syria, Egypt, India, China, the Philippines, Java, Madagascar, the Kongo and South Africa, the major seminaries total 13 and the minor seminaries 22, all dedicated to the raising up of a staunch native clergy.

The greater part of the order's educational endeavor, however, is to be found in the 77 universities or university colleges and the 211 secondary colleges which it maintains throughout the world. Though a gratifying number of students of these institutions later embrace the sacerdotal or religious life, the vast majority enter the professions or the business world to carry out in these fields the principles of Catholic living and of Christian ethics learned in the Jesuit classrooms. The varying fortunes of these institutions, always the first objective of anticlerical attack, have been indicated before. Today they are most prosperous in Belgium, Holland, England, Ireland, the United States, Canada, Colombia, Brazil, the Argentine, India and Australia; they have achieved a revival in France, and there is every reason to believe that they will do the same in Spain.

In Europe on the whole, owing to the more immediate governmental control of education and also to the lack of financial resources, the Jesuit colleges are almost all of the second class, what are known in Germany as "Gymnasien" or in France as "lycées." The College of Namur is of

---

[5] Recently suppressed.

university grade; there and at Toulouse the fathers are able to teach philosophy to lay-pupils, as they were also in twelve of the Spanish colleges before 1931. The scientific or commercial institutes of Barcelona, Bilbao and Madrid might be classed as of university rank. Some scholars of the order hold professorial chairs in a few State or Catholic universities; thus there are eight Jesuits on the staff of the Catholic Institute of Paris, four in the Catholic University of Nymegen, four in the National University in Dublin, three at the Catholic Institute of Toulouse, two at the Catholic Institute of Lille, two at Lublin in Poland, and one each at the Universities of Milan, Louvain and Angers. At different times English Jesuits have held lectureships at Oxford. In connection with the National University of Ireland, the Irish fathers conduct a hostel for lay students; of similar nature are the two residences of the English province, Campion Hall at Oxford and Southwell House at London University, although these are restricted to Jesuit students. Among the many secondary schools especially well known are: in Italy, Massimo and Mondragone; in Germany, Feldkirch and Godesberg; [6] in Hungary, Kalocsa; in Poland, Chyrow; in Belgium, Brussels (St. Michel), Antwerp and Liége; in the Netherlands, Amsterdam; in England, Stonyhurst and Beaumont (these two enjoy the rating of "Public Schools"), Mt. St. Mary's, Liverpool (St. Francis Xavier) and Glasgow; in Ireland, Clongowes Wood and Dublin (Belvedere). To meet the demands of the present day the Belgian fathers maintain a college of Commerce at Antwerp and a technical school at Liége; the Dutch fathers, a college of Commerce at Amsterdam; the French fathers, technical schools at Lille and Nantes and agricultural courses in other schools.

In the Near East and in the Far East the Society's teachers are engaged in 14 university-colleges and in 37 secondary schools. The University of St. Joseph at Beirut, with its faculties of theology, philosophy, law, medicine, letters and science, stands first, followed by the University of St. Francis Xavier at Bombay and the Aurora University of Zi-ka-wei. Excellent work, too, is being accomplished at St. Francis Xavier College at Calcutta (a constituent college of the University of Calcutta), at St. Aloysius College of Mangalore (a constituent college of the University of Madras), at St. Joseph's College of Trichinopoly, at the Ateneo de Manila in the capital city of the Philippines, at the College for Higher Studies in Industry and Commerce at Tientsin, at the Catholic University of Tokyo, and at the Newman College of Melbourne (a constituent college of the University of Melbourne). A hostel for students in connection with the University of Hong Kong is conducted by the Irish Jesuits. Among the secondary institutes in the mission lands espe-

---

[6] Recently suppressed.

cially noteworthy are: the high school of the Ateneo de Manila, the colleges of the English fathers at Grahamstown and Salisbury, South Africa, and the five schools of the Australian Jesuits.

The Latin American Jesuits, except in Mexico, have come at last on better days. In half of their forty educational institutions the fathers can impart scholastic philosophy to the students. Among the more distinguished Spanish-American Jesuits' educational establishments are: the Xaverian University of Bogotá, the colleges of Buenos Aires and Santa Fé in the Argentine, of Santiago de Chile, of Rio de Janeiro and Porto Alegre in Brazil and of Belen in Havana, Cuba. The Jesuits of Canada, French-speaking and English-speaking, have always enjoyed full freedom to develop the apostolate of the schools; they have achieved remarkable successes. All their nine colleges enjoy university status and are able to give the full philosophical and classical education planned in the Ratio. The colleges of St. Mary's and Loyola in Montreal, and of St. Boniface, Manitoba, stand among the very first institutions of learning in the Dominion of Canada.

The absence of government monopoly in the United States has been of tremendous advantage to the American Jesuits in the development of their educational work; it has afforded them a freedom of instruction and organization which their brethren nowhere else enjoy. No restrictions were placed upon the starting of colleges, and liberal university charters were granted by the particular states in which the institutions were located. As a result today the American Jesuits conduct 25 universities or university-colleges, attended by 43,032 students, and 32 high schools attended by 12,698 students.[7]

The high schools stand as the foundation of the American Jesuit education.[8] With their four years' course of the classics, English, mathematics, elementary science, history and modern languages, they are the nearest approach in America to the *lycée* and the *Gymnasium* of Europe. The years of belles-lettres and rhetoric (the fifth and sixth years of the *lycée* and the *Gymnasium*) constitute in America the first two years of the university college. The American Jesuits have fought a persistent battle for the retention of the Latin and Greek classics in cultural education, not only in the high school curriculum but also in that of the college. It has not been a very successful fight. Greek, as a required subject, has had to be dropped in most of the Jesuit schools; it is practically extinct in every other American school. Latin has been retained as a required subject, and in that regard too the Jesuit schools are almost

---

[7] McGucken, *The Jesuits and Education*, Milwaukee (1932), Part II; Farrell, *The Jesuit Code of Liberal Education*, c. XVI.

[8] McGucken, *op. cit.*, Part III, "The Modern American Jesuit High School."

unique. It may be observed in passing that the American Jesuits are not alone in having been forced to diminish the classical studies; their brethren in several other countries have had to do likewise. Concessions have been made in the methods of teaching the classics, perhaps not always wisely; yet such has been the force of outside circumstances that some yielding was unavoidable. The once very popular, but now somewhat discredited, fad of American education, unrestrained electivism, found resolute opponents in the Jesuit educators. The Jesuits were willing to concede a reasonable electivism but always insisted on a definite system of required courses, aiming at a general, well rounded education both for high school and college students. The climax of this particular struggle came in 1899–1900 in the controversy between Dr. Eliot of Harvard University and Father Brosnahan of Boston College. The fact that the great American non-Catholic universities, especially Dr. Eliot's own Harvard, have since abandoned unrestrained electivism is posterity's decision in favor of the Jesuits. In all the changes and adaptations the American Jesuits have kept faithfully to the fundamental aim of the *Ratio*, the education of Christian gentlemen, men of broad culture, trained to think and to give intelligent appraisement of the world's problems.

The heart of all the institutions of university grade is the undergraduate faculty of arts and sciences.[9] While literature is the basis of its Bachelor of Arts degree and Science of its Bachelor of Science degree, with due attention in both courses for history, mathematics and modern languages, the most important emphasis is placed upon the course of Scholastic philosophy, required of all students. It is the good fortune of the American Jesuits that they are able to give to mature students two years of solid grounding in Scholastic logic, metaphysics, psychology, ethics and natural theology. It is their most important educational work. The institutions of higher learning established by the fathers maintain graduate and professional faculties, as far as the limitations of their resources permit and the local conditions require; there are 8 graduate schools, 5 medical schools, 7 dental schools, 12 law schools, 6 schools of education, 16 schools of commerce and finance, 3 engineering schools, 4 schools of social work, 3 schools of pharmacy and 1 school of journalism. Adult education is provided for by 14 extension schools, where older students who must work or are engaged in teaching may pursue courses of higher education in evening classes. For the further benefit of teachers 14 summer schools are conducted. Georgetown University maintains a unique

---

[9] Cf. histories and memorial volumes of Georgetown, Fordham, Boston College, Holy Cross, Spring Hill and other Jesuit institutions; *The Woodstock Letters* passim; Garraghan, *The Jesuits of the Middle United States.*

institution in its School of Foreign Service, where young men are trained for the diplomatic or consular service, or for the opportunities of foreign trade. The largest of these Jesuit universities or university colleges is Fordham with 7,053 students; it also is the largest Catholic university in the United States. Those which have an enrollment of over a thousand are: St. Louis, 6,576; Loyola (Chicago), 5,029; Marquette, 4,352; Boston, 3,065; Detroit, 2,620; Georgetown, 2,216; Creighton, 2,126; Canisius, 1,523; Loyola (New Orleans) 1,510; Holy Cross, 1,189; Xavier, 1,142; San Francisco, 1,053.

The real story of American Jesuit education lies far deeper than the statistics of development; it is to be found in the courageous generosity of the fathers, who reared their schools that Catholic youth, mostly the sons of poor immigrants, might be trained to become worthy leaders of their people. The Jesuits followed that ideal faithfully despite an almost perpetual lack of financial resources; for they were never helped by the State, and rarely by wealthy Catholics, since these scarcely existed. Yet tuition fees were set at the lowest mark, oftentimes they were reduced by half, and in hundreds of cases they were not collected at all. The fathers tried to make up the differences, that they might meet their expenses, by personal sacrifices, by extra teaching, by sermons and lectures, by pleas for funds to the few better-circumstanced Catholics. There is no more outstanding feature in the history of the American Jesuit college than the opportunity for receiving an education which it has given to poor boys. It is safe to say that hundreds of eminent lawyers, physicians and business men would never have achieved their success, were it not for the Jesuit colleges; it is certainly true of the priesthood. It is well to note, in speaking of the priesthood, that large numbers of the alumni of the American Jesuit schools have entered the sacerdotal state; this is especially true of Boston College which counts among its former students, a Cardinal-Archbishop, 10 bishops and 1,340 priests, and also of Holy Cross which numbers among its former students, 2 archbishops, 19 bishops and 1,328 priests.

Just as the schools of the restored Society, so also its scholars have made a commendable record, despite frequent banishments, losses of libraries and lack of financial support. It has been said that the new Society has not produced learned men like unto those whom the old Society could claim; this is probably true in the fields of theology and philosophy, but certainly not in those of history and science. In the listing of scholars, which is to follow, it must here be noted that almost a hundred names of modern Jesuit savants have had to be passed over, because of the limitations of space and the purpose of this book. A fuller, and yet by no means complete, list may be found in Volume II of Heim-

bucher's *Orden und Kongregationen der Katholischen Kirche*.[10] To the
Jesuits of the new Society is owing a monumental bibliography of the
writers of the order; about the middle of the nineteenth century, two
brothers, de Backer, priests of the Belgian province, produced the *Bibliothèque des Écrivains de la Compagnie de Jésus*, a seven volume work containing over 11,000 authors. In 1890 Sommervogel re-edited and enlarged
it, added Carayon's *Catalogue des ouvrages relatifs a l'histoire des Jésuites*
and published the whole in ten volumes as the *Bibliothèque de la Compagnie de Jésus*. Sommervogel also brought out two volumes on the works
of Jesuits, who wrote anonymously or under pseudonyms, as well as a
Moniteur bibliographique de la Compagnie de Jésus. The bibliographi-
cal writings of this scholar are the best ever produced in the Society. He
was not alone, however; Uriarte in 1904 published a four-part work on
the anonymous writings of the old Spanish Assistancy; and Rivière from
1911 to 1930 produced a large supplement to Sommervogel's work. Prolific writers have not been wanting in the new Society; de Buck published
74 volumes, large or small, Boero 79, Marcelli 85, Antoniewicz 93, Garrucci 118, Boylèsve over 170, and Hattler 84, these last being on the
Sacred Heart alone.

With their work for the education of priests at the Gregorian University, in the many seminaries for the secular clergy, and in their own scholasticates, it is but to be expected that a larger number of the ablest Jesuits would be engaged in theology and philosophy. Scholasticism has always been the Society's doctrine and St. Thomas Aquinas its "Doctor
Principalis"; this was especially emphasized by the legislation of the
Twenty-third General Congregation of 1883, making the principles of
Leo XIII's "Aeterni Patris" its own, and by the letter to the whole Society of the present Father General Ledòchowski on March 8, 1916, "De
Doctrina Sancti Thomae magis magisque in Societate fovenda." In the
interpretation of the Angelic Doctor there have been some differences of
opinion, not only with the Dominican theologians, but even among the
Jesuits themselves; but most of the Society's theologians have preferred
to follow the older Jesuit commentators. Among the distinguished theological scholars of the restored Society may be listed: Tongiorgi; Perrone,
whose *Praelectiones theologicae* has gone through forty editions; Kleutgen, with his *Theologie der Vorzeit* and his *Philosophie der Vorzeit;*
Cardinal Franzelin, who composed several important treatises and was a
leading theologian at the Vatican Council; Liberatore; Tilman Pesch,
author of *Institutiones logicales I., psychologicae I., philosophiae natu-*

---

[10] Heimbucher, *Orden und Kongregationen der Katholischen Kirche*, Vol. II, pp. 235–
287; cf. also Sommervogel, *Bibliothèque de la Compagnie de Jésus*, and Koch, *Jesuiten-
Lexikon*.

ralis, Die grossen Welträtsel, Die moderne Wissenschaft betrachtet in ihrer Grundfeste, Die Haltlosigkeit der Modernen Wissenschaft (an examination of Kant's Critique), *Christliche Lebens-philosophie, Briefe aus Hamburg* (a defense of Christ's divinity), *Christ oder Antichrist* etc.; Cardinal Mazzella, a member of the commission on Anglican Orders and able professor of dogma; Morawski, whose spirited apology for Christianity has received many translations; Palmieri; Hurter, for many years professor of dogma at Innsbruck and author of *Nomenclator literarius theologiae catholicae;* Christian Pesch, whose *Praelectiones dogmaticae* in nine parts and *Compendium theologiae dogmaticae* in four parts have gone through many editions; Cardinal Billot; Cathrein, who wrote nine valuable volumes on ethics and an excellent work on Socialism; de la Taille, author of one of the most important treatises in modern times on the Holy Eucharist.

The Jesuit philosophers, as all Scholastics, have had to restore the solid value of Scholasticism in the chaos of thought which rules the modern intellectual world, and also to apply the system of St. Thomas to the new scientific discoveries, especially in psychology. The task was made all the harder with the *a priori* rejection of Scholasticism by certain types of scientists who knew absolutely nothing about it. The movement of revival has been known as Neo-Scholasticism. In it the Jesuits have had an important part. Among the foremost philosophers of the restored Society are: Fröbes, author of a textbook on experimental psychology; Donat, professor of philosophy at Innsbruck, who wrote the *Freedom of Science, Summa philosophiae christianae* in eight volumes, a work on psychoanalysis and several other treatises; Dunin-Borkowski, an authority on the history of philosophy and on Spinoza; Lindworsky, who has won a deserved reputation in psychology, especially in studies on the will; Lahousse; Urráburu, one of the best thinkers of the order in modern times, a supporter of the Scholasticism of Suarez, and author of the *Institutiones Philosophiae scholasticae* in five volumes; Maher, whose work on psychology has had wide use; John Rickaby; Joseph Rickaby; Joyce; and D'Arcy, a critic of modern thought. Several valuable textbooks have been written by American Jesuits. Three valuable cooperative works on philosophy have come from groups of Jesuits in the modern times: the *Cursus Philosophicus* in six volumes, to which Cathrein, Frick, Haan and Boedder have contributed; the *Philosophia Lacensis* in eleven volumes, which Tilman Pesch, Hontheim and Meyer have produced; and the *Stonyhurst Series,* the labor of the fathers of the English province, which has been widely used throughout the English-speaking world.

In the presentation of Catholic truth and its defense before the world, the Society in modern times has produced, besides the theologians already mentioned, many able apologists. Of these only a few can be men-

tioned here: Rosa and Busnelli in Italy; Amado, Mendive and Miten-
guiga in Spain; Dieckmann, Wilmers, Lippert and Muckermann in Germany; Castelein in Belgium; Bollaye, Archbishop d'Herbigny and Bouvier in France; Gerard, Morris, Hull and Martindale in England;
Smarius, Hill and Tierney in America. The greatest work in apologetics
by a modern Jesuit is the editing of the *Dictionnaire Apologétique de la
Foi Catholique* by d'Alès.

Scriptural studies and the allied sciences have claimed the best energies
of several learned Jesuits of the new Society, not only in the explanation
of the texts but in the defense of the Bible from the attacks of rational-
istic sceptics and the so-called higher-critics. The foremost of modern
Jesuit commentators is Francis Patrizi, who produced a hermeneutical
explanation of the *Gospels of Mark* and *John,* and of the *Acts of the
Apostles,* as well as many valuable writings on biblical research. A commentary of great proportions was the *Cursus Scripturae Sacrae,* produced
by a number of German Jesuit scholars, among them Cornely, Knabenbauer and Hummelauer; with it were published a biblical atlas and a
three volume biblical lexicon by Hagen, and also a Greek lexicon for the
New Testament by Zorell. Since 1910, when Pius X entrusted the conduct of the Pontifical Biblical Institute to the Jesuits, the fathers connected with it have brought out numerous and valuable works of biblical
research, antiquities, languages and kindred studies. Foremost among
these Jesuit scholars is Fonck, author of an exegetical and practical explanation of the parables and miracles of our Lord, and several other
learned scriptural studies; another distinguished scholar is Deimal, who
produced a Sumerian grammar of archaic texts, a Sumerian lexicon and
the *Tabulae Grammaticae Assyriae et Signorum Cuneiformium;* of other
learned biblicists of the Society there may be noted Hartmann, Delattre,
Prat, Vacarri, Fernandez and Szczepanski. The Jesuits, Peultier,
Etienne, and Gautier rendered a good service by the completion of the
Thesaurus concordantium universae scripturae sacrae, which had been begun by Raze. In the work of translating the Bible there should be recalled: the Arabic translation of the New Testament of Beirut in 1876;
the new edition of Alliolis translation of the Bible by Arndt; and the
work of Lattey in the Westminster Version.

In moral theology the Jesuits resumed the important position held by
the earlier fathers of the order. Neither Jansenism nor Laxism have been
serious dangers in the nineteenth and twentieth centuries; the problems
of these times are concerned more with practical questions rather than
with the theories of systems. There will always be the stricter and the
milder viewpoints; the modern Jesuit moralists almost unanimously
have been, and are, Probabilists. The first place among the moral theologians of the restored Society is easily held by Gury; his *Compendium*

theologiae moralis and his *Casus Conscientiae* not only have been often reprinted but have served as the basis of many other text-books on the subject. The works of Ballerini, Palmieri, Sabetti, Barrett and Ferreres are substantially revisions of Gury's work. In recent years the Society has produced moralists whose writings have gained them a universally admitted high rank; these are Noldin of Innsbruck, Lehmkuhl of Valkenburg, Bucceroni and Vermeersch of the Gregorian, and Arregui of Barcelona. Deserving of special mention are the many writings of Gruber on Freemasonry, the work of Ternus on the history of the moral systems from Vittoria to Medina, and the publications of Nell-Brüning on the moral aspects of modern economic and social problems.

The Jesuits in recent times have made valuable contributions to the development of Canon Law, by their own works on the subject, by the assistance of the professors of the Gregorian to the Roman Congregations, and by the cooperation of these professors, especially Wernz, in the codification of the Canon Law. Among the leading Jesuit canonists may be listed: Cardinal Tarquini, who published the *Iuris ecclesiastici publici institutiones,* to which he added in an appendix a valuable discussion of the royal Placet; Sanguinetti; Desjardins; Wernz, author of the monumental *Ius decretalium;* Bucceroni, who also cooperated in the codification of the Canon Law; Vermeersch, a prolific writer on the subject, author of the *Epitome iuris canonici* in three volumes and founder of *Periodica de re morali, canonica, et liturgica;* Ferreres; Ojetti; Taparelli, who wrote on the natural law and the modern state; Cappello; and Creusin.

Although the great work in modern times on the liturgy has been done by the Benedictines, the Jesuits have made some valuable contributions in this field. The outstanding writers of the Society on the liturgy have been: Nilles, with his work on the Calendarium; Dreves, who made valuable researches in hymnology, writing *Analecta hymnica medii aevi;* Maurel, author of *Le Chrétien eclairé sur la nature et l'usage des indulgences,* which went through twenty-three editions; Braun, distinguished for his writings on episcopal and sacerdotal vestments in the East and in the West, his liturgical lexicon and his work on the historical development of the Christian altar; Santi; Thurston; Silva-Tarouca; Siebert, author of a very popular and much-used liturgical work. American Jesuits are contributing zealous service through articles, lectures and books on liturgy.

The number of writers on asceticism and piety among the modern Jesuits has been very large. The great devotions, so marked a feature of the present day Catholicism, the widespread use of the Spiritual Exercises, and the labors of spiritual advisers, have given the priests numerous incentives to write books for the sanctification both of religious and of the laity. Outstanding among the Jesuit authors of spiritual books may be considered: de Lehan, whose *Way of Interior Peace* has been produced and translated many times; Deharbe, who wrote on priestly sanctity; Chaignon, author of seventeen works on the sanctity of priests and religious; Devis, composer of prayer-books; von Doss, writer of practical and moving works for the sanctification of youth; Ramière, whose literary labors for the devotion of the Sacred Heart are well known; Gallwey, whose *Watches of the Passion* has enjoyed wide popularity; Meschler, the author of the much read and frequently translated *The Life of our Lord Jesus Christ*, a commentary on the Spiritual Exercises, and an excellent life of St. Aloysius; Patiss, who wrote more than sixty ascetical works; Poulain, a modern authority on the contemplative life. Other Jesuits, whose names only can be cited are: Przywara, Bangha, Petit, van Acken, Mercier, Plus, Charles, Joseph Rickaby, Russell, Lucas, Martindale, Boudreaux and O'Rourke. The list could well be continued through other pages of more recent names.

The apostolate of preaching has always been accorded a leading place among the labors of the order. Quite as much as in the old days the new Society has been a preaching order. In the first decades of the nineteenth century when the colleges were so few and so small, the principal activity of the fathers was in the pulpit; such became the case later on in those countries where the anticlericals drove the Jesuits from the classroom. The fathers of the French provinces excelled in great cathedral conferences and in formal Lenten courses; the eloquent and logical presentation of Christian truth by de Ravignan and Félix achieved untold good. Similarly grand sermons were preached by Sagrini in Italy, Rive in Germany, Kenney in Ireland, Vaughan in England and McClorey in the United States. But the principal scene of modern Jesuit pulpit activity was the popular mission; every province supported a mission band, a body of devoted priests who gave themselves to the exhausting task of preaching almost continually to thronged congregations and of hearing countless confessions. Few factors have served more to keep the Faith burning bright, or to re-enkindle it, when it had died down, than the sermons of these self-sacrificing priests. Among the most eloquent and indefatigable of the European missionaries may be mentioned: Franco in Italy, Roh and Roder in Germany, MacCarthy and Guyon in France; Antoniewicz in Poland and van de Kerkhove in Belgium. In the United States, where the apostolate of the popular mission has been followed with great zeal, Damen, Smarius, Weninger, Ryder and Maguire head a long list of eloquent preachers. Several of the fathers have furthered the oratorical art by the writing of textbooks on rhetoric; Kleutgen, Schleiniger, Longhaye, Gallerani, Kasterens and Coppens among others.

In few fields of learned studies has greater progress been made in modern times than in history; research has been extended more deeply and over wider fields, documents have been examined more critically, and the auxiliary sciences have been improved steadily. In all this development the Jesuits of the new Society have had an important part; some of their best historical works have been done on the record of the Society itself. Notable among the published writings on the order are: the *Monumenta Historica Societatis Jesu*, a vast collection of sixty volumes of documents of the first Jesuits, edited by the Spanish fathers; the histories of the various Assistancies and provinces, the German by Duhr, the Spanish by Astrain and Frias, the Italian by Tacchi-Venturi, the French by Fouqueray and Burnichon, the Belgian and Netherlandish by Poncelet, the Hungarian by Vebics, the Bohemian by Kroess, the Colonial American by Hughes, the Middle-Western American by Garraghan. All these are monumental works written in the best critical spirit. Duhr has written several other volumes on special phases of Jesuit history; Carayon has published twenty-three volumes of documents; Hogan with his *Ibernia Ignatiana*, Gerard with his studies on the English Jesuits of the penal times, Foley with his documentary history of the Society of Jesus in England, and Zalenski with his works on the Jesuits of White Russia, have made truly valuable contributions.

Noteworthy labors in the field of history in general have been accomplished by such Jesuits as: Feder, author of a textbook on historical methodology; Garrucci, renowned for his work on numismatics and on the catacombs; Morcelli, one of the founders of the science of epigraphy; Martin, an able archeologist; Silva-Tarouca, a distinguished paleographer; Damberger, who composed a synchronized history of the Church and the World in fifteen volumes; Albers, the author of a much used textbook on Church history. In the renewal of interest in the Middle Ages, Jesuits have made valuable contributions. Among the medievalists of the order may be cited: Cardinal Ehrle, Prefect of the Vatican Library, author of many scholarly treatises on the literary history of the Middle Ages and partner of Denifle, O.P., in the publication of the *Archiv für Literatur-und Kirchengeschichte des Mittelalters;* Kobler, who wrote a four volume work on medieval Catholic life; Ryan, author of valuable works on early Irish monasticism; Michael, whose cultural history of the German people in the Middle Ages in five volumes is a classic; Delehaye, writer of a scholarly study of the Legends of the Saints. On the period of the Reformation, Grisar with his great life of Luther, considered by Protestants the best Catholic approach, is the leading Jesuit historian; Pollen has been ranked as among the first Catholic authorities on the English Reformation; Cardinal Steinhuber's history of the Collegium Germanicum-Hungaricum is important; Morris, Smith and Thurston have accomplished good work on the Catholics in the English Reformation. Among the Jesuits who have successfully treated other historical fields may be listed: Barruel, with his history of the clergy during the French Revolution; Gargarin, author of several works on the Russian Church; Plenkers, with his history of Denmark and his historical study of witchcraft; Brunengo, who wrote on the history of the Papal States; Murphy, author of many works on the profane and the ecclesiastical history of Ireland; Granderath, with his three volume history of the Vatican Council, as well as his commentary on the dogmatic constitutions of that council; and Quevas, who wrote the important five volume *Historia de la Eglesia en México*. A notable collection of the Councils, the *Collectio Lacensis*, *Acta et decreta sacrorum conciliorum recentiorum*, was the work of the professors of Maria Laach, under the direction of Schneemann and Granderath.

The great cooperative hagiographical work of the Jesuists, the *Acta Sanctorum*, was not resumed until the year 1837, when the Bollandists were again organized with quarters in the College of St. Michel in Brussels; in 1845 Volume LIV appeared, and since then eleven more volumes have been produced, bringing the work down to the end of November. For the furtherance of scientific studies on the Lives of the Saints a periodical, the *Analecta Bollandiana*, was founded in 1883 by de Smedt, van Hooff and J. de Backer; both its articles and its reviews have been kept up to the standard of Bollandist scholarship. For the same purpose other learned volumes have been published such as: the *Bibliotheca hagiographica Graeca*, and catalogues of the hagiographical codices to be found in the Royal Library of Brussels, the National Library of Paris, the Vatican Library, and other libraries in Germany, Belgium and England. The work of the Bollandists has been broadened beyond the treatment of the saints of the Roman Martyrology, to include the study of the saints of the local and national martyrologies. Among the modern Bollandists may be mentioned de Buck, de Smedt, Delehaye, van Ortroy, Peeters and van de Vorst. Jesuits of other provinces have also produced notable studies of the saints, some scientific, others more popular in treatment. The best work has been done by Braunsberger in his eight volume *Beati Petri Canisii, Acta et Epistolae*, and in his one volume German life of St. Peter Canisius. Among the other fathers writing the biographies of saints may be listed: Boero; Schurhammer, with his researches on St. Francis Xavier; Cros, also an authority on St. Francis; Brodrick, the author of two important works, a life of St. Robert Bellarmine and a life of St. Peter Canisius; Coleridge; Anderdon; Meschler, who composed an excellent life of St. Aloysius; and Martindale, author of several popular lives of the saints. Jesuits have made translations of the Roman Martyrology in German, French, Bohemian, Polish, Portuguese, Spanish and Greek.

Jesuit educators have contributed to the development of pedagogy by their writings on the subject itself, as well as by numerous textbooks for the classics, history, mathematics and the other branches of learning taught in their schools. Pachtler with his *Ratio Studiorum et institutiones scholasticae Soc. Jesu per Germania olim vigentes,* which forms volumes II, V, IX, and XVI of the *Monumenta Germaniae Paedagogica,* and his many other writings, deserves a leading place among the modern Jesuit educators. Stiglmayr, who wrote *Das humanistische Gymnasium and sein bleibender Wert,* also deserves a special mention. A few among many other distinguished authorities of the Society on pedagogy are: David, Hugger, Herman, Delaporte, Amado, Hughes, and Schwickerath. Space forbids a full listing of the many able American Jesuit educators.

On the history of art the foremost modern Jesuit writers are: Martin; Garrucci, the author of a masterly work of eight volumes on the Christian art in the first eight centuries; Jungmann, who composed a two volume textbook on aesthetics; Beissel, whose researches in the medieval veneration of the Blessed Virgin and the saints are noteworthy; and Braun with his study of the art and architecture of the Jesuit churches. In music good work was accomplished by de Santi; Dechevrans, author of the large work *Études de science musicale;* Gründer; Ottano, Bonvin, who was honored by Pius X and by the University of Würzburg; and König, a hymnologist.

In the natural sciences the Jesuits of the restored Society have achieved as much, if not more, than the fathers of the old order. This is the case, especially, in astronomy, meteorology and seismology. The Jesuit observatories and scientific stations, to be found in all parts of the world, number twenty-four; the more important are: the Vatican, Tortosa del Ebro, Kalocsa, Valkenburg, Stonyhurst, Georgetown, Fordham, Weston, St. Louis, Santa Clara, Belen, Manila, Zi-ka-wei and Tananarivo. Among the leading astronomers of the modern Society may be listed: de Vico, who discovered forty-six comets and made important studies of the rings of Saturn and of Venus; Secchi, one of the founders of astrophysics as well as one of the first to make observations of the sunspots, the inventor of the meteorograph and the spectraltype of the fixed stars, recipient of decorations from the Vatican, France and Brazil; Sestini; Braun, who composed the learned treatise, *Über Kosmogonie vom Standpunkt christlichen Wissenschaft nebst einer Theorie der Sonne,* worked on the measurement of the gravitation-constant, and invented in its first form the photoheliograph; Hagen, director for years of the Vatican Observatory, author of a three volume synopsis of higher mathematics and a valuable work on the fixed stars; Muller, who composed several biographies of leading astronomers, a discussion of the Galileo case, a two volume textbook on astronomy and a treatise on the

Bible and astronomy; Cortie; Sidgreaves; Rodés, the director of the celebrated Observatorio del Ebro de Tortosa; Rigge; and Ricard. Among the leading Jesuit physicists may be placed: Dressel with his two volume textbook on physics; Wulf, author of an elementary textbook on the subject as well as a discussion of the Einstein theory; Schaffers; and Gianfranceschi, the director of the Vatican Radio Station. Of distinct value for commerce, maritime shipping, and, above all, for the saving of human lives, have been the meteorological studies and the daily reports of the Jesuit observatories at Zi-ka-wei, Manila and Belen. Froc, for forty years the director of the Zi-ka-wei observatory, was decorated by the Japanese and the German governments; his monographs and those of his successor, Gherzi, are of high merit. Faura and Algué made the Manila observatory indispensable to Oriental commerce; the former invented the cycloscope, the latter the barocyclonometer. Other distinguished Jesuit meteorologists are: Chevalier; Dechevrens, the inventor of an anemometer and the campylograph; and Círea, an authority on earth magnetism. In seismography the American Jesuits were pioneers and have attained preeminence.

In the study of nature the first of the Jesuit scientists is Heude; with Rathouis, he published the valuable *Mémoires concernant l'histoire naturelle de L'Empire Chinois*, and, by himself, ten volumes on the marine shells of Nanking and Central China, besides other works on the earth mollusks of the Blue River valley, the ruminants of Eastern Asia, the deer-tracks of the Philippines and Indo-China, and a complete herbarium of China. Quite as important is Wasmann, who wrote many works on evolution, monism and the question of human intelligence and animal instinct. Other Jesuit naturalists worthy of special notice are: Handmann; Richen, authority on the plant life of the Voralberg and Liechtenstein; Merino, who studied the flora of Spanish Galicia; Cambué, investigator of the flora and fauna of Madagascar; Sodiro, who wrote on the botany of Ecuador; Gerste, an authority on the medicinal and plant knowledge of the ancient Aztecs; Tóth, an Hungarian scientist; Navés, who composed an important work on the insect life of Spain; Assmuth, an authority on the termites of British India.

Jesuit activity in the field of literature was held back considerably by the pioneering conditions of the first years after the Restoration, and since then has been seriously hampered wherever persecution drove the fathers into exile. The concurrence of the Jesuits in the cooperative spirit of the present times possibly explains why their literary activity has been so often directed to publication in reviews and in encyclopedias rather than to the issuance of individual works. A most significant service to literature has been accomplished by the modern Jesuits in their schools by their fidelity in retaining literary culture as the basis of aesthetic training. In special work for the Latin and Greek classics there should be remembered: Lebreton, for his studies on the speeches and grammar of Cicero; Cagnacci; Yenni, for his widely used Latin Grammar; and Errondona, for his writings in Spanish on Sophocles. In philology, the Bollandists, Peeters and van den Gheyn, have accomplished good work, as also Dugout with his atlas classifying languages geographically. In the history of literature the first place should be accorded to Baumgartner for his *Geschichte der Welt-literatur,* a five-volume work treating of the literatures of Western Asia, Egypt, India, Eastern Asia, Greece, Rome and of the various Christian peoples. Baumgartner also wrote on the life and works of Goethe, the poems of Longfellow, the life and works of van den Vondel, the Ramayana and the Rama Literature of India, and produced travel books (especially treating of the northern European countries). Other Jesuits of the new Society who have written well in the general field of literature are: Brewer; Feder; Stiglmayr; Tacchi-Venturi; d'Alès, who published important works on the Fathers; Rouet de Journel, editor of *Enchiridion Patristicum;* Kirch, who composed, besides twelve volumes on the saintly heroes of Christendom, a collection of texts of the ancient Greek ecclesiastical historians; Gietmann, the author of a critical explanation of the classical poets and their poetry (a work including also the medieval writers), a volume on Hebrew poetry, and outlines of style, poetry and aesthetics; Francis Muckermann, composer of a history of German literature; Palmieri, whose three volume Italian commentary on Dante's *Divina Commedia* is important; Longhaye, the author of a four-volume history of French literature and a five volume history of the nineteenth century French writers; Delaporte, who wrote, *Études et causeries litteraries* in two volumes; and Aicardo, a Spanish authority on Lope de Vega. Of the Jesuit poets of the restored Society there should be listed: von Waldburg-Zeil, Kreiten, Arens, Przywara, and especially Gerard Manley Hopkins. Several modern Jesuits have written fiction, usually historical novels or stories for youth, with considerable success; among such may be considered: Bresciani, author of fourteen religious-historical novels; Spillmann, who wrote seven much read novels; Schupp, a well-loved teller of legends and fairy-tales; Coloma, renowned for the character delineations of his Spanish stories; Garrold, author of several pleasing tales of English school life; Francis Muckermann; Svensson; and lastly Finn, whose many stories of American Catholic youth have gone through several editions and have been translated into ten European languages.

The study of the native tongues of the foreign mission lands was one of the foremost literary contributions of the old society; it has been so also with the restored order. The first of the Jesuit Indianologists is

Dahlmann with his *Indischen Fahrten* in two volumes, his writings on the legend of St. Thomas in India in the light of Indian antiquities, and his other works on Indian nationality, Indian philosophy and religion, Buddha and the Mahabharata; next to him is Zimmermann, an authority on Sanskrit. The best known linguistic work of the modern Jesuits has been done in China; here Wieger is the leading scholar with his *Rudiments de parler et de style chinois*, a twelve-volume work, rich with examples from all types of Chinese literature. Several other fathers have made valuable contributions to the Chinese languages; Zottoli, author of a five-volume *Cursus litteraturae Sinicae*, which contains in Chinese and Latin all that a learned Chinese should know about Chinese literature (the work received a prize from the French Academy); Boucher, who wrote a guide for the Mandarin speech, of great help for the study of the classical Chinese; Ralouin, composer of a *Dictionnaire français-chinois* especially useful for a knowledge of the Shanghai dialect; Couvreur, who translated several of the ancient Chinese classics into Latin and French, produced a small and a large French-Chinese, Chinese-French dictionary, and published a collection of examples of Chinese documentary style with French and Latin translations. The press of the French fathers at Shanghai has brought out in its *Variétés sinologiques* many important monographs on Chinese languages, literature, history and geography; one notable work among many is Doré's *Recherches sur les superstitions en Chine*. Since 1879 the Shanghai Jesuits have published a Chinese newspaper, the *Hoei-pao*, a Chinese *Messenger of the Sacred Heart* and a learned periodical, *I-wen-lu*. New editions of the old Jesuit Sinologists, Ricci, Gaubil de Maillac, Amiot and others, have also been reprinted.

Quite as important work in Arabic and Syriac has been accomplished by the Jesuits at Beirut. The printing-press established at the Catholic University in 1853 has had a large literary output. The first book to be published was the *Following of Christ* in Arabic. Another important production was a translation of the Bible into the common speech, a work inspired by Moreau and greatly assisted by the lay-brother, Saiea, a convert from Mohammedanism. Catechisms, books of devotion, books on the liturgy, the Old Testament in Chaldaic, writings in Arabic literature, grammars, dictionaries, works on archaeology and history, have been brought out by the press in Arabic, Turkish, Syriac, Armenian, Hebrew, Latin and Greek. Cheikho, a native Jesuit and also a convert from Mohammedanism, wrote on Arabic poetry and literature, and in partnership with Durand produced an Arabic grammar and reader. Much of Cheikho's work appeared in the learned Arabic review, *Al-Machriq*, founded by him and to this day edited by the Jesuits. In this periodical also have been produced many important works of Lammens, of Jullien and Jouon on archaeology, and of Zumhoffer on geology. The journal *El-Beshir*, founded by Moreau, is also a product of the Beirut press. Other important works of Jesuits in the Semitic field are: *Dictionarium Syriaco-Latinum* of Brun; the Arabic grammar of Vermier; and the *Documents inédits pour servir à l'histoire du Christianisme en Orient* of Rabbath. Still further contributions in linguistics were made by: Strassmeier, a distinguished Assyriologist; Kugler, who has described the Babylonian-Assyrian stone writings and has produced also an introduction to the study of the ancient Israelitish religion; Desgodin, author of a Tibetan-French-Latin dictionary; Abinal and Malzac, the compilers of a Madagascan-French, French-Madagascan dictionary; Aillud, Causseque, Basilide, whose joint work was a Madagascan grammar; Butaye, the author of a Congolese grammar and a Kicongo-French, French-Kicongo dictionary; Férard, who produced an Ojibway dictionary, Barnum, the composer of an Innuit dictionary; Cara, a distinguished Egyptologist; and Hermann, sometime president of the Pontifical Oriental Institute.

The Jesuits of the nineteenth and twentieth centuries, after the example of their older brethren, have made valuable contributions to cartography and geography. Fischer, an authority on the Norse discoveries in America, achieved much by his publication of the first map to contain the name "America" (1507) and the *Carta Mariana* (1516) of Waldseemüller, as also by his photostatic reproduction of the Greek Codex, No. 82, of the Vatican with a biography of Ptolemy in four volumes. For this last work Pius XI awarded him a gold medal. Werner's *Atlas of the Catholic Missions*, his atlas of the Catholic Church and his *Orbis terrarum Catholicus*, are of high standard, as is Köppel's map and geography of Palestine. Noteworthy among the modern Jesuit geographers of China are: Chevalier, who produced a general map of China and an atlas of the Upper Yang-tse Valley; Havret, the author of a map of the Ngan-Hwei Province; Loyando and P'e, who jointly constructed a map of China of the time of Tsch'oen-ts'ieou; Chardin, an explorer of the Desert of Gobi; Licent, an excavator in Northern China and Manchuria, connected with the discovery of the "Peking Man." A topographical map of Imerina (Madagascar) with geodetic, magnetic and astronomical measurements, was the work of Roblet; maps of Cilicia and Karaman were produced by Jerphanion. Of all the Jesuit labors in this field none were more important than that accomplished by Algué and his fellow Jesuits in the Philippines. They issued numerous, useful treatises on the seas, the lands, the winds, the climate, the magnetic and seismologic conditions of the Archipelago, as well on its geography, ethnography, linguistics, and history. The first complete geographical atlas of the Philippines, *El Archipiélago Filipino*, first suggested by the

Jesuit Pi, and eventually produced at the expense of the American government, was the work of Algué and his associates. Books of travel, descriptive of the customs and manners of the peoples, were written by Teschauer on Brazil, Lhande on the Basque country, Schupp on the Rio de La Plata, and Kolberg on Ecuador.

Social reform has engaged the interest of many Jesuits, in common with other Catholics, especially during the last seventy-five years. In the pages of their reviews, the *Civiltà*, the *Stimmen*, the *Études*, the *Month* and *America*, by numerous pamphlets, brochures and books, the fathers have sought to interest the people in Catholic social principles and to warn them against the subversive theories of Socialism and Communism. Theologians and moralists of the order, such as Taparelli, Ming, Vermeersch, Lehmkuhl, in their writings laid solid foundations for the Catholic program. Other Jesuits produced more specific works: Heinrich Pesch, who wrote on the social mission of the Church and also produced a large textbook of five volumes on political economy; Cathrein, whose *Socialism* has been frequently reprinted and translated; Biederlack, author of an important introductory book on the social question, as well as many other similar writings; Antoine, whose French textbook on sociology and economics is highly esteemed; Castelein, the writer of *Le Socialisme et la droit de propriété*, a criticism of Socialism, with a view to practical reform; Will, author of *Die katholische Aktion*, which was translated on the order of Pius XI; Nell-Brüning, probably the foremost commentator on the social encyclicals of Pius XI; American Jesuit writers and teachers in good number; Plater, responsible for good initiatory work in England. Many Jesuits have taken part in practical works of sociology, especially in the founding and the development of Catholic organizations: Leroy, founder in 1903 of the Action Populaire movement in France, a work still guided by the French Jesuits; Vincenti, the originator of the first Catholic labor union in Spain (1866), as well as of a society of working youth, credit-unions, educational courses for laborers, social schools, and author of the *Manual de las reformas sociales*, together with a book on Socialism and Anarchism; Esch, the founder of a German youth-movement, the *Neu-Deutschland;* Palou, organizer of the Catholic People's Society of the Argentine; Cullen, the founder of a widespread temperance society, "The Pioneers," in Ireland; Lhande, a devoted priest in the service of the suburban proletariate of Paris and author of *Le Christ dans la Banlieue*, which has gone through eighty printings; Chaurand, Dunot, Guevarre, all three apostles of charity. In France, Belgium and Canada the Jesuits have taken a prominent part in the Semaines Sociales; while in Ireland they have founded a similar discussion group at Clongowes Wood College. The English Jesuits conduct the Catholic Workers' College at Oxford;

the American Jesuits maintain several Schools of Social Service in connection with their universities, as well as their Catholic Action schools for workingmen. In all countries the work of the Sodalities has been given a social orientation; and wherever the Jesuits are they have taken a prominent part in the various Catholic Youth Movements. The fathers have made good use of the radio for the spreading of Catholic truth and Catholic social doctrines whenever the opportunity has been offered; especially is this the case in the United States where St. Louis University and Loyola University of New Orleans operate their own radio stations and over them as well as other stations, capable instructors conduct with great success their Catholic Truth Periods.

By far the greater part of the literary activity of the modern Jesuits has been in connection with periodical literature. Today the order publishes 851 periodicals and its teachers direct 261 college magazines. The periodicals include 26 cultural reviews; 152 theological and scientific journals, 77 mission magazines and 596 publications of piety and asceticism. The subscribers of these Jesuit journals reach the figure of 13,-340,060. It would be quite impossible within the limits of this work to list, much less discuss, all these publications. Among the journals of piety and asceticism there may be noted: the *Zeitschrift für Aszese und Mystik*, the various *Messengers of the Sacred Heart*, the *Ave Maria* of Nymegen, the *Revue d'Ascetique et Mystique*, the *Stella Maris*, the *Queen's Work*, the *Männer Apostolat, Sal Terrae*, the *Fahne Mariens* and *Manresa*. Prominent among the mission magazines may be considered: *Die Katholischen Missionen, Missions Belges de la Compagnie de Jésus, Mysse Katolickie* and the *Jesuit Missions* of the American fathers. The theological and scientific journals count among the leading publications the *Zeitschrift für Katholische Theologie, Scholastik, Recherches de sciences religieuses, Nouvelle Revue Théologique, Estudios eclesiásticos, Biblica Orientalia, Verbum Domini, Periodica de re morali, canonica et liturgica, Analecta Bollandiana, Anales del Instituto Catholica de Artes y Industrias*, and the publications of the Zi-ka-wei and Manila Observatories. The history of the Society itself is furthered by *Acta Romana Societatis Jesu, Archivum Historicum Societatis Jesu, Memorabilia Societatis Jesu, Littere edificante* of the Italian provinces, *Lettres de Jersey, Mitteilungen der deutschen Provinzen*, the *Letters and Notices* of the English province, and the *Woodstock Letters* of the United States.

It is in their learned journals and reviews that the Jesuits exercise their greatest literary influence. In these periodicals, articles on theology, philosophy, history, science, economics, sociology, art, literature, and public affairs, written by Jesuits and other Catholic scholars, present to the world the Catholic viewpoint. Today there is hardly a country where

Jesuits live, which does not possess one of these periodicals. The first in time of the learned reviews is *La Civiltà cattolica*, founded at Rome in 1850,—to this day it is one of the most noted and valuable defenders of the Papacy; the *Études*, started in 1856 at Paris, retains a high reputation for its literary and apologetical work; the *Month*, begun in 1864 at London, has given excellent service in controversy and in the history of the English Reformation; the *Stimmen der Zeit*, founded in 1865 and until 1915 entitled the *Stimmen aus Maria Laach*, has played a most important role in building up the Faith in the German lands by its solidly scholarly articles. Similar labors for Catholicity have been achieved by the Dutch *Studie*, the Spanish *Razón y Fe*, the Spanish-American *Revista Catolica*, the Argentinian *Estudios*, the Portuguese *Broteria*, the Irish *Studies*, and also the *Irish Monthly*, the American *Thought*, the Hungarian *Magyr Kultura*, the Polish *Presegled powezechny*, the Czech *Stornick historického Broužku*, the Jugoslavian *Zivot*, the Arabic *Al Machriq*, the Indian *Bombay Examiner*, and the *New Review*, the *Rock* of Hong Kong, the Chinese *I-wen-lu* and the Japanese *Monumenta Nipponica*. Unique among the Jesuit periodicals is the weekly *America*, the joint publication of the American provinces. During the thirty-two years of its existence it has been a crusading journal, strenuously battling for the cause of Catholicity at home and abroad; especially has it been the untiring champion of Mexican Catholics and Spanish Catholics, and the uncompromising foe of Communism and Absolutism. It is considered by some today to be the most forceful Catholic periodical in the English-speaking world.

Jesuit writers have joined with other Catholics in the publication of the great Catholic encyclopedias, such as the *Kirchen-Lexikon* and the *Dictionnaire de Théologie Catholique*. Three Jesuits have had most significant parts in the production of works of this nature: D'Alès, the founder and editor of the *Dictionnaire Apologétique de la Foi Catholique*; Bangha, of the Hungarian Catholic Encyclopedia; and Wynne, of the *Catholic Encyclopedia* of America. Wynne deserves special mention, for he first conceived the idea, and was one of the editors of that monumental work.

In the century and a quarter since the Restoration the Jesuit schools and scholars, despite lack of means and notwithstanding interruptions due to frequent persecutions, have achieved accomplishments certainly comparable with those of the schools and scholars of the old Society.

APPENDICES

Appendix I

Contra Impugnantes Dei Cultum et Religionem, Pars. II, c. XXI: "non de facili possent tot inveniri qui singulis parochiis per universum mundum praeficerentur, cum etiam propter litteratorum inopiam nec adhuc per saeculares potuerit observari statutum Lateranensis concilii ut in singulis ecclesiis metropolitanis essent aliqui qui theologiam docerent; quod tamen per religiosos Dei gratia cernimus multo latius impletum quam etiam fuerit statutum."

Of the educational deficiencies of the clergy of his time St. Thomas writes: "Hanc etiam necessitatem maxime ostendit imperitia multorum sacerdotum, qui in aliquibus partibus adeo ignorantes inveniuntur, ut nec etiam loqui latinum sciant. Paucissimi etiam inveniuntur qui sacram scripturam didicerint." And many, he says, were unfit to hear confessions. (Contra Impugnantes Dei Cultum et Religionem (Pars. II, c. XX).

Appendix II

Luther on Moral Conditions

Four years after his revolt Luther declared (1521): "I do not attack the Pope or councils on account of their evil lives or evil works, but on account of their false doctrine." This is explicit enough, yet he spoke even more plainly on the subject. He repeatedly stated that "the majority of the clergy and religious are good; they pray and fast and work much, thinking thereby to be pious, yet these proud saints become martyrs for the devil's sake." He admits with regret the piety and cleanness of most of the clergy and religious, and attributes it to "phariseeism." Other early Reformers, as Melancthon, spoke in the same way. It is evident then that the whole of the Protestant Reformation was begun not as an attempt at the moral reform of the Church but at a change of doctrine. It is true that Luther, like other leaders of the revolt, did use the supposed or real corruption of the Church as an argument against her and as a telling means of discrediting her. This was particularly so after he had further evolved some of his characteristic doctrines, e. g., the uselessness of good works, the absurdity of vows and the impossibility of celibacy. Then he looked for proof of his teaching and thought, or pretended, to find it in the moral condition of the Church. Most significant, and most correct, is the judgment of an English Protestant historian: "Luther's most earnest remonstrances were directed not against bad but good works and the stress laid upon them by the advocates of the old religion. If that religion had been in its practice too generally corrupt as it is represented to have been by modern writers, such denunciations were idle." [1] The English Reformer Tyndale used to call zeal for good works "Pope-holiness." There

---

[1] Brewer, quoted by Bridgett, *Bl. Thomas More,* p. 209.

457

is no hint in the earlier utterances of Luther that clerical vice led him to protest, or that he aimed at a moral reformation.[2] And a recent authority on Luther calls it a naive idea that Luther aimed at a moral reformation of the Church.[3]

APPENDIX III

Modern Criticism of the Exercises
and of Jesuit (or Ignatian) Spirituality

In itself the modern scientific study of religious phenomena and practices is quite legitimate. So also the scholarly investigation and comparative study of various forms of spirituality. That a spirituality which, as all admit, has exercised a tremendous influence for over three hundred years, should be the subject of particular interest, is quite natural. Jesuits will be pleased to see their spirituality most searchingly studied, provided it is done in a real scholarly spirit and care is taken against unfair, one-sided representations. That cannot be said of all judgments passed on the Exercises and their spirituality. Many verdicts have been uttered which are quite contradictory. Some have complained that there is too much "intellectualism" in the Exercises, too much "thinking, considering, reflecting"; others, on the other hand, aver that the fault is rather too much "voluntarism," too much insistence on the will, "What will I do?", "What must I do?"

Somewhat connected with these objections is another, a very modern one, the charge that there is "too little mysticism" especially too little "mystical contemplation." This criticism [4] has been popularized by Abbé Brémond, who at one time was a Jesuit. The strictures of Abbé Brémond and others are apt to create a false impression, as if the Society undervalued, almost despised, mystical experiences. Far from it. St. Ignatius himself, St. Francis Xavier, St. Peter Canisius and others had such experiences and valued them most highly. The Jesuit devotional writers speak of them in terms of highest admiration. They believe, however, that they are exceptional gifts and due only to extraordinary graces of God.

It must be granted that St. Ignatius and other leading Jesuits show a certain caution in regard to these mystical manifestations. They were justified in this by the experiences of the early Society when certain members seemed inclined to change the very character of the Society; when some of them thought and said that two hours meditation and contemplation a day hardly deserved the name of prayer; when they began to devote five, six and more hours a day to prayer, and, as one said, seemed determined to lead the Society back into the deserts of Egypt. Secondly, a more important reason for reserve and moderation in regard to mysticism is the fact that St. Ignatius wanted his order to be an active and apostolic one. His ideal was Christ indeed, but Christ the founder of the Kingdom of God.

It was the active life of Christ that especially appealed to St. Ignatius, Christ working as a carpenter even during the hidden life of Nazareth, but above all, Christ

---

[2] Denifle-Weiss, *Luther und Luthertum*, Vol. II, p. 16, Mainz (1909).

[3] Grisar, *Luther*, English Trans., St. Louis (1916), Vol. I, p. 104.

[4] Cf. Gaetan de Bernoville, *Les Jésuites*, Paris (1937); in C. II there is a criticism of this view of Brémond.

"anointed with the Holy Ghost and with power, going about doing good." [5] The Saint was of course deeply impressed with Christ's life of prayer; that too was to be imitated. But it was Christ's toiling for souls who stood before the mind of Ignatius as the model for himself and his sons. Was this too low an ideal? Must one not find a sort of hyper-spirituality in the criticism which finds fault with the Society on the ground that in its spirituality there is not more mysticism?

Three more objections deserve special notice. The first is that the Exercises and the Jesuit "methodical" meditations are too "formal," too "systematic," even "mechanical." The danger does exist that an inexperienced director may make the Exercises mechanical. But any one who has made them under a wise director, who thoroughly understands the spirit of St. Ignatius, will judge differently. As regards the meditation, there is method in it. This can hardly be considered a defect. Method in study is urged, method in every kind of work demanded, as a necessary condition for efficiency. Will it not be of great help in prayer? The critics are wont to contrast the methodical prayer of St. Ignatius with the "simple" prayer of the Middle Ages and of St. Francis de Sales. As a matter of fact St. Ignatius, too, does not insist on all prayer being made in the strict methodical fashion of the Exercises. He recommends three different "Modes of prayer," as being very useful and very simple. Besides for more than three hundred years the vast majority of religious orders and congregations have practised—and it is part of their rules—the methodical meditation. Have they all been mistaken? Should not this fact alone warn against disparagement of methodical prayer? As regards the contrast with medieval spirituality the following judgment of a Catholic writer, who is not an ardent admirer of the Jesuits, says: "Medieval practice of devotion was, if I may use the expression, naive. It came, particularly, in its mysticism, from the emotional side, the heart, or appealed to it. This could be done, because the foundation and presuppositions were then denied by very few. That was changed with the advance of humanism and especially of the Reformation. The new intellectual tendency and spirit of opposition made it necessary for Catholic piety to take a more deliberate position and establish more definitely and more systematically the rational foundation of Christian asceticism, in a manner unknown to the Middle Ages. This was done primarily by the Jesuits and men of the Jesuit school." [6] There is much truth in this. One may however ask: "Even aside from the external circumstances of humanistic tendencies and the reformation opposition, was the more definite and more systematic transformation not in itself a legitimate stage of progress?"

The second criticism is that "love" is not prominent enough, that it is not even mentioned in the Foundation. The reader may judge for himself what the value of this objection is, if he reflects on what has been shown to be the very heart of the Exercises: a personal, enthusiastic, magnanimous, heroic love of Christ, as it appears particularly in the high point of the Exercises, the "Third Degree of Humility," and in the final hymn of love and consecration of love in the last contemplation. As for St. Ignatius not mentioning the love of God explicitly in the Foundation, only one can find in this a defect who fails to understand the whole plan of St. Ignatius, the

---

[5] *Acts* X, 38.

[6] In a modern work on "Religious Educators of the Catholic Church" (*Religioese Erzieher der Katholischen Kirche*, edited by Merkle, p. 10).

building up of a solid structure of spirituality, the crown of which is a most heroic, limitless love of God. To see what place this love has in the thought of St. Ignatius, one has but to glance through the book of the Exercises, even without making a study of it. At the very beginning he will see the "Anima Christi" which is a fervent prayer of love; its place indicates the spirit, the leitmotif of the whole book. He will notice that the last meditation is the "Contemplation to Obtain Divine Love." If he turns to the last page of the book, he will read the last words, "cum amore divino," "with Divine Love." And between the first and last pages, how often will he meet with references to the love of God, to the fervent love of Jesus? The same impression will be created if he takes the other great work of St. Ignatius, the Constitutions of the Society, or the handier little *Summary of the Constitutions*. He need not go far; he can pause at the first rule, where the Saint says the Vicar of Christ has ordered him to write the Constitutions, "although it be the sovereign wisdom and goodness of God our Creator and Lord which is to preserve, govern and advance in His holy service this least Society of Jesus, and on our part the interior law of charity and love which the Holy Ghost is accustomed to imprint in the hearts of men."

These considerations refute also an objection, closely related to the one just treated, brought forth by Brémond and others, that the asceticism of the Society is "anthropocentric," placing man in the center, not, as it ought to be, "theocentric," placing God in the center of all. This is a mere superficial view, a misconception. It is refuted by all that has been said on the spirit of the Exercises, as it strikingly appears in the most essential part, the second week, and thence to the end. Thus from the meditation on the "Kingdom of Christ" to the final one on the "Contemplation to Obtain Divine Love" it is explicitly "Christocentric" and ends in the "theocentric" *Suscipe*.

A third criticism has been heard many times within the last decades. It is the contrast of the "Ignatian" and the "liturgical" spirituality and devotion. The liturgy is, indeed, the devotion of the Church, her official devotion. In it there is a priceless treasure of spirituality. The modern "liturgical movement" must be hailed with joy by all Catholics. It has been hailed with joy by Jesuits, and zealously fostered by a good number of them. Like any enthusiastic movement it is not without some dangers. One danger has been warned against by some of its most ardent promoters (e. g., Guardini), namely that "estheticism," the admiration for the beauty of the liturgy, may take the place of real devotion. Another danger in enthusiastic movements is found in one-sidedness, exaggeration and undervaluation of so-called "rival" movements. There are some examples of this in the liturgical movement. One very striking instance may be cited. In 1913 a French monastic writer [7] published a long article in which he said many beautiful things on the liturgy and its importance for spiritual life. But, in very vigorous, at times over-vigorous, language he drew a sharp contrast between the "liturgical" and the "Ignatian" spirituality. Within a year at least a dozen articles in various Catholic religious periodicals and even some books entered into the controversy. [8] The author of the original article maintained that

---

[7] Festugière, O.S.B., "La Liturgie catholique, Essai de synthèse," *Revue de Philosophie* (Mai, Juin, Juillet, 1913).

[8] Cf. Peeters, S.J., *Spiritualité Ignatienne et Piété liturgique*.

between the "old," i. e., monastic, asceticism and the "new," i. e., Ignatian, there is a chasm that cannot be bridged, between the two there is an "incompatibilité d'humeur," an incompatibility of temper. The old has a "social" character, i. e., is practised by the community, the new is "individualistic" and is influenced by the modern, not to say Protestant spirit. The Ignatian asceticism is like an alien body in the ecclesiastical organism, which by slow but deliberate and determined action must be eliminated; it is an aberration from the old Christian spirit, and a deviation (literally "a derailment") from the glorious medieval tradition.

These are harsh words and serious charges. Space does not permit here a detailed refutation.[9] A few remarks must suffice. First, if the Ignatian spirituality is really what this religious calls it, "an alien body in the ecclesiastical organism, which must be eliminated," one may well ask: "How is it possible that so many Popes approved and highly praised the Exercises and their spirituality?[10] Must they not most grievously have misled millions of souls earnestly striving after holiness? It is for the accusers to answer these questions. Secondly, as regards the supposed "deviation from the medieval tradition," this is one of the typical one-sided and exaggerated views concerning the Middle Ages. But it is necessary to call attention to a logical inconsistency. Medieval spirituality itself, in its various forms, as manifested in St. Bernard, St. Francis of Assisi, Tauler and other Dominican mystics, and the Devotio Moderna, greatly differed in form and tone from that of the early Church Fathers.[11] Is, then, all medieval spirituality to be condemned as "an aberration from the old Christian spirit"? If not, why must Ignatian spirituality be condemned so harshly, because it differs from that of the Fathers and of the Middle Ages? Attention must be called to something else which seems to involve a flagrant contradiction. This monastic writer sees in Ignatian spirituality "an alien body in the ecclesiastical organism which must be eliminated." Yet another monastic author boldly asserts that it is nothing but the spirituality of a Benedictine Abbot—and one who must be called "medieval"—which St. Ignatius changed but slightly.[12]

There is another confusion as to historical facts. As has been said, the "methodical" meditation of St. Ignatius was not entirely the Saint's invention but had been gradually developed during the latter part of the Middle Ages. As an historian of Christian spirituality expresses it: "At the end of the evolution of methodical prayer we find a masterpiece, the *Spiritual Exercises* of St. Ignatius Loyola. These are the crown of the systematization of the spiritual life which was slowly wrought age after age."[13] Hence it is an historical error to draw such a sharp distinction between the meditation of St. Ignatius and the practice of the Middle Ages. Besides, there is a defect in the judgment on the matter. Ignatian spirituality is condemned because

---

[9] A refutation may be found in Peeters, S.J., *Spiritualité et Piété liturgique*. See also Paul von Chastonay, S.J., "Ignatianische Spiritualität und liturgische Frommigkeit," *Stimmen der Zeit*, Vol. 87, pp. 551–555.

[10] Cf. Chapter III, p. 67, and especially the words of Pius XI, pp. 71, 72.

[11] Cf. the first and second volumes of Pourrat's *Christian Spirituality*, New York (1922–1927), for the differences.

[12] See Chapter III, pp. 67, 68.

[13] Pourrat, *Christian Spirituality*, Vol. III, p. 23.

it is "an aberration from the old Christian spirit and a deviation from the medieval tradition." History furnishes a parallel instance. Many humanists, particularly, were violently "anti-scholastic." They contrasted scholastic with patristic theology, utterly condemning the former. Now the one great difference between the two is that the scholastic theology is more "methodical," more "systematic." Was this a defect? On the contrary, the greatness, originality and usefulness of St. Thomas' *Summa* consists precisely in this, that it is a perfect systematization of the teaching of Holy Scripture and the Fathers. In this, as in so many other things, St. Ignatius went against Erasmus and other humanists; in his famous "Rules of Conformity with the Church" he says that the Catholic must "praise" both the Fathers and the Scholastics. Is there not a lesson here also as regards various kinds and "schools" of spirituality?

As regards the relation of Ignatian spirituality and the liturgy. One thing is quite certain, Ignatius was not "hostile," not "indifferent" to the liturgy, as some critics seem to imply. One of his rules of "Thinking in Conformity with the Church" (no. 3) explicitly states that we must "praise" the liturgy, chants, etc. It is well known that he loved to attend the liturgical functions in various churches. Moreover, what his sentiments were may be learned from one who knew him intimately, Father Ribadeneira. This Jesuit wrote: "I heard with my own ears Blessed Ignatius say that he undoubtedly would have introduced the choir into the Society, if he had followed his own inclination or rather his own religious sentiment, which drew him to the sacred chant; but by some heavenly light he had perceived that our Lord wanted from the Society another kind of service." [14]

Then is there not in some modern writings an over-estimation of the influence of the liturgy on the spiritual life? Are there not certain effects, definite practical resolutions and moral inspirations, necessary for spiritual life, which can be obtained more readily and more powerfully from meditation, and "methodical" meditation at that, than from liturgical devotion? Is there not a strong confirmation of this in the fact that older religious orders, which from their beginnings had the choir service, later introduced formal meditation, orders such as the Benedictines, Dominicans, Franciscans, Augustinians, etc.[15]

Some writers on the subject have spoken with such emphasis that one gets almost the impression that the liturgical devotion is represented as the only legitimate kind. One need not hesitate to call it the devotion of the Church, i. e., the official devotion of the Church; hence one may also call it the most sacred of all devotions. Yet there are many other devotions, and they are quite legitimate. In emphasizing one, it would be wrong to speak with a certain condescension, not to say condemnation of others. It is well to state that St. Ignatius was far removed from any such narrowness and one-sidedness. He nowhere gives the slightest hint that he considers his Exercises, or his method of meditation, or his "spirituality," the only legitimate one. On the contrary, among his *Select Sentences* we find the following (no. VIII): "It is a most dangerous thing to wish to force all on one path to perfection; he who attempts this does not understand how many and how various the gifts of the Holy

---

[14] Ribadeneira, *De Ratione Instituti Societatis Jesu*, Ch. IV.

[15] Cf. Pourrat, *Christian Spirituality*, on Benedictines, pp. 16 ff.; on Dominicans, in 1505 (before St. Ignatius), p. 22 note.

Ghost are." [16] Indeed, there are many particular ways of spiritual life though there is one general way, Jesus Christ. It is to be expected that there are different ways of approaching Him, of following Him, of "taking hold" of Him. St. Paul speaks of the "unsearchable riches of Christ," [17] "unfathomable," but also "inexhaustible." Primarily that profound word of St. Paul may have been meant dogmatically, but it has a true meaning also devotionally and spiritually. Here too He is inexhaustible; no spirituality is absolute; none can exhaust the inexhaustible. There is room for many: for the liturgy in the first place, then for others; for the childlike spirit of St. Francis of Assisi, the simple prayer of St. Francis de Sales, the elevation and contemplation of the mystics—but room almost for the more "methodical" and practical spirituality of St. Ignatius. Not only is it inevitable that there should be a variety of "spiritualities" and devotions, it is also a proof of the Church's vitality and inexhaustible spiritual fecundity. One might refer to the comparison made by a Jesuit writer, von Chastonay, in discussing the strictures of the liturgist: "Catholic worship is not uniform, it is not just like one bell; there are many bells, each with a different tone, but they sound together in a beautiful harmonious chime."

Appendix IV

Religious Orders in the Catholic Church

The religious orders in the strict sense, i. e., institutes where solemn vows are taken,[18] amount to thirty or more. A partial list [19] would include the following: The Benedictines and orders deriving from them such as the Vallambrosians, the Grandmontines, the Olivetans, and the Cistercians (Trappists), and other monks such as the Carthusians, the Basilians and the Camaldolese; the Canons Regular of St. John Lateran, the Premonstratensians, the Augustinian Canons, the Crosier Canons, the Canons Regular of the Immaculate Conception, the Canons of the Austrian Congregation among the Canons Regular; the Dominicans, the Franciscans, both Observatines and Conventual; the Carmelites, the Augustinian Hermits, the Servites, the Minims, and the Capuchins among the Friars; the Trinitarians and Mercedarians (formerly devoted to the redemption of captives, now to sacerdotal and educational work); the Alexians, the Brothers of St. John of God, and the Camillians among the hospitallers; the Theatines, Barnabites, Somaschi, the Jesuits and the Piarists among the Clerks Regular. In recent times a few more orders have been instituted: the Priests of the Teutonic Order (1929); the Basilian Order of St. Josaphat-Uniate Rite (1932). There are about a dozen orders of women, among them: the Benedictine nuns, the Cistercians, the Second Order of St. Dominic, the Second Order of St. Francis (Poor Clares), the Carmelite nuns, the Augustinian nuns, the Ursulines (the greater part of the various branches), the Order of the Visitation, etc. The other religious bodies in which only simple, perpetual vows are taken, are called "congregations"; they are very numerous and a great glory of the Catholic Church.

[16] "Res plena periculi est uno omnes calle cogere velle ad perfectionem; quam varia quamque multiplicia sint Spiritus Sancti dona talis non intelligit."

[17] *Ephesians* III, 8.

[18] *C.I.C.*, p. 488, No. 2.

[19] Cf. Heimbucher, *Orden und Kongregationen der katholischen Kirche*, Paderborn, 3rd ed. (1934).

Alleged Secret Instructions of the Jesuits

Among the various slanderous forgeries which have dogged the footsteps of the Jesuits, the oldest and most widespread is the notorious *Monita Secreta*,[20] a spurious fabrication which has furnished the enemies of the order with abundant data on the "real spirit" of the Society. It appeared at the beginning of the seventeenth century, and down to the present day it has been republished in numberless editions in almost every European language. This work, one of the most flagrant forgeries of history, was composed by Jerome Zahorowski who in 1613 had been dismissed from the order. It first appeared at Cracow in 1614 under the title *Monita privata Societatis Jesu, Notobrigae* (1612). Both the place of printing and the date are false. These secret instructions were alleged to be only for the older and more trustworthy professed fathers; they contain directions how Jesuits are to gain universal influence over princes and how also they are to obtain legacies from rich widows. The instructions are in flagrant contradiction not only of the Constitutions but of the private letters of the Fathers General: the Fifth General Congregation of 1593 most strictly forbade any meddling in political matters; one General after another, especially Aquaviva (accused by some with having issued the *Monita*), urged most strongly on the court confessors scrupulous compliance with this law of the Congregation. Again, the Generals, Aquaviva in particular, warned against securing legacies from pious women, "especially if they have needy relatives." The downright lying character of the *Monita* is especially evident in the instruction (Chapter XVII) directing the Jesuits to try to get possession of as many bishoprics, abbeys, etc., as possible. Vigorous opposition to the nomination of Jesuits to any prelacy has been the perpetual policy of the Society, as is evidenced from numerous letters of St. Ignatius and other Generals. Such a course but fulfils the special vow of the professed not to accept any prelacies unless forced by the order of the Pope. Those Jesuits who have been named bishops by the Holy Father have hardly ever occupied an episcopal see except in mission countries. Yet there were men in recent times who professed to see in the *Monita* the "best illustration of the Jesuitical spirit"; among them is to be noted Canon Littledale in his article on the Jesuits in the Ninth Edition of the Encyclopedia Britannica.[21]

It is worth noting that most prominent enemies of the Society, as well as many scholars, have explicitly characterized the *Monita* as a palpable forgery. Among such may be counted: Arnauld, the Jansenist; the authors of the *Tuba Magna*, a violent eighteenth century attack on the Jesuits; Gieseler, a well known Protestant historian; Dr. Nippold, a bitter anti-Jesuit writer; Döllinger, Reusch and Huber, the Old-Catholics, whose hatred of the Papacy extended to the Society. Professor Harnack, for many years the leader of rationalist Protestants, declared: "Unfortunately, falsifi-

---

[20] Duhr, *Jesuiten Fabeln*, 3rd ed., Freiburg (1899), pp. 76–102; Reiber, *Monita secreta, die geheimen Instruktionen der Jesuiten verglichen mit den amtlichen Quellen des Ordens*, Augsburg (1902); Saint-Helier, *Les Monita Secreta des Jésuites devant l'histoire*, Paris (1901); Gerard, *The Secret Instructions of the Jesuits*, C.T.S. (London).

[21] Later editions have discarded Littledale's article and substituted others.

cations like the *Monita Secreta* are still exploited against the Society; we Protestants ought to abstain from false witness also against this 'neighbor.' "

There are no "secret instructions" for the Jesuits. Their spirit is revealed in the Constitutions, copies of which may be found in any large library. The inner life of no other body of men has been so exposed to public knowledge. At the Suppression of the Society its archives all over the world were seized, in many places most unexpectedly, and thousands of confidential letters of superiors were found. All these documents and communications were examined and scrutinized most carefully to obtain compromising matter. But nothing was found, and especially not even a hint of anything resembling the *Monita*.

In connection with "secret" documents, another Jesuit myth should be considered, namely that the order is a secret society similar to the Freemasons. The notion was current in France before the Suppression but received its greatest propagation in the nineteenth century in the French "liberal" press, especially by Eugene Sue's *Juif Errant* (Wandering Jew).[22] In proof of the assertion there is quoted the rule of the Society, that no one should relate to outsiders what is done or to be done in the house unless he knows the Superior approves of it.[23] Already in the eighteenth century the Archbishop of Paris, Christophe de Beaumont,[24] in defending this rule pointed to the similar regulations of other religious orders. The Archbishop remarked too that religious form a family and no decent member of a family will divulge indiscriminately its domestic affairs. That the Society of Jesus is not a secret society is especially evident from the many solemn confirmations and laudatory Encyclicals which have been bestowed upon it by the Popes, who have been without exception adamant against even the beginnings of secret organizations.[25]

Lastly there are no "secret Jesuits." This is unfortunate for those novelists who count for any number of thrills on characters, to all appearances army officers, diplomats, married men, hostlers, nursemaids, apparently Protestant, yet under the cloak of it all, sinister Jesuits. The nearest to a "secret Jesuit" was St. Francis Borgia who after the death of his wife was allowed to make his novitiate and pronounce his vows outside of the Society. This was done before the Constitutions were completed and for exceptionally grave reasons, namely that St. Francis might settle the affairs of his important position in Spain and that he might provide adequately for his eight children. With the Pope's consent he lived in the world though actually a Jesuit for four years, 1546–1550. There has been no other case.

---

[22] According to Pollen, Sue's work did more than anything else to give the final form to the Jesuit legend; "The Society of Jesus," *Cath. Encyl.* Vol. XIV, p. 105.

[23] In the revised edition of the Common Rules (No. 36) there is no longer any mention that the Constitutions are not to be communicated to externs.

[24] Christophe de Beaumont, Archbishop of Paris, a zealous shepherd, frequently exiled for his defense of ecclesiastical liberties, a defender of the Society at the time of the Suppression. Cf. Chapter "Gathering Storms."

[25] Witness the negative attitude towards the pious and zealous Compagnie de Saint Sacrament because of its secrecy. Cf. Pastor, *Geschichte der Päpste*, Vol. XIII, pp. 558–559; also Coste, *Life and Labors of St. Vincent de Paul*, Vol. III, pp. 271 ff.

MEMBERSHIP OF THE SOCIETY OF JESUS IN 1939

Assistancy	Province or Vice-province	Numbers	Total
Italian	Rome	355	
	Naples	409	
	Sicily	406	
	Turin	370	
	Venice-Milan	620	2160
German	Austria	461	
	Eastern Germany	320	
	Lower Germany	749	
	Upper Germany	629	
	Hungary	350	
	Latvia (Mission)	9	
	Lithuania	102	
	Netherlands	730	3350
French	Champagne	880	
	France	770	
	Lyons	726	
	Toulouse	759	3135
Spanish	Andalusia	462	
	Aragon	874	
	Castile	1074	
	Leon	806	
	Portugal	365	
	Toledo	417	3998
English	Australia (V.P.)	231	
	England	909	
	Northern Belgium	896	
	Southern Belgium	841	
	Lower Canada	680	
	Upper Canada	292	
	Ireland	466	4315
American	California	505	
	Chicago	822	
	Maryland–New York	1512	
	Missouri	936	
	New England	807	
	New Orleans	411	
	Oregon	447	5440

MEMBERSHIP OF THE SOCIETY OF JESUS IN 1939 (*continued*)

Slavic	Bohemia *	161	
	Jugoslavia	226	
	Greater Poland and Masovia	385	
	Lesser Poland	459	
	Roumania (V.P.)	42	
	Slovakia (V.P.) †	175	1448
Latin-American	Argentina	338	
	Central Brazil	215	
	Northern Brazil (V.P.) ‡	169	
	Southern Brazil	346	
	Chile (V.P.)	178	
	Colombia	413	
	Mexico	449	2108
Grand Total			25,954

* Formerly the Province of Czechoslovakia. After separation of Slovakia the name Bohemia assumed.

† Erected into an independent Vice-Province August 23, 1938.

‡ Erected into an independent Vice-Province after separation from Portugal, December 1938.

FOREIGN MISSIONS OF THE SOCIETY OF JESUS
IN THE YEAR 1939

Continent	Country	Mission	Province	Numbers
Europe	Albania		Venice-Milan	46
Asia	Ceylon	Galle	Northern Belgium	70
	"	Trincomali	Champagne	32
	Japan		Lower Germany	89
	Java	Batavia	Netherlands	175
	India	Ahmedabad	Aragon	57
	"	Bombay	Aragon	135
	"	Calcutta	Southern Belgium	173
	"	Calicut	Venice-Milan	135
	"	Goa	Portugal	66
	"	Madura (V.Province)	Toulouse	313
	"	Patna	Chicago	90
	"	Poona	Upper Germany	53
	"	Ranchi	Northern Belgium	163

FOREIGN MISSIONS OF THE SOCIETY OF JESUS
IN THE YEAR 1939 (*continued*)

Continent	Country	Mission	Province	Numbers
	Iraq	Baghdad	New England	15
	Philippines		Maryland-New York	256
	China	Ankin	Leon	80
	"	Hong-Kong	Ireland	44
	"	Macao	Portugal	26
	"	Pengpu	Turin	46
	"	Shanghai	France	244
	"	Sienhsien	Champagne	173
	"	Suchow	Lower Canada	55
	"	Taming	Hungary	40
	"	Wuhu	Castile	95
	Near East	Egypt, Syria, Armenia	Lyons	210
Oceania		Caroline, Mariana, Marshall Islands	Andalusia	36
Africa	South Africa	Broken Hill	Lesser Poland	31
	"	Salisbury	England	93
	Congo	Kisantu	Northern Belgium	73
	"	Kwango	Southern Belgium	73
	Madagascar	Fianarantsoa	Champagne	105
	"	Tananarivo (Mauritius)	Toulouse	120
North America	United States	Alaska	Oregon	33
	"	Rocky Mountains	Oregon	38
	"	South Dakota	Missouri	52
	"	Negroes	American Assistancy	46
	Canada	Caughnawaga	Lower Canada	11
	"	Ontario	Upper Canada	28
	Mexico	Tarahumara (disp.)	Mexico	16
	British Honduras	Belize	Missouri	30
	Jamaica	Jamaica	New England	39
South America	Br. Guiana	British Guiana	England	31
	Colombia	Magdalena	Colombia	17
	Ecuador	Manabi-Esmeraldas	Andalusia	10
	Brazil	Adamantea Matto Grasso	Central Brazil	10
	"	Japanese	Central Brazil	12
Grand Total				3785

A PARTIAL BIBLIOGRAPHY OF THE SOCIETY OF JESUS *

General Bibliography.

Carayon, S.J., *Bibliographie Historique de la compagnie de Jésus* (up to 1863). Paris (1864).

Heimbucher, *Die Orden und Kongregationen der Katholischen Kirche.* 3rd edition, 2 vols. Paderborn (1934). Extensive article with a large bibliography on the Society of Jesus in Vol. II. 130–341.

Sommervogel, S.J., *Bibliothèque de la compagnie de Jésus.* 12 vols. Brussels (1890–1910); supplement, Rivière, S.J., Toulouse (1911–1930).

General Histories.

Monumenta Historica Societatis Jesu, edited and published by the fathers of the Spanish provinces at Madrid (1894–). This great work contains: *Vita Ignatii Loiolae et rerum Societatis Jesu historia, auctore Polanco*, 6 vols.; *Monumenta Ignatiana*, 14 vols.; *Monumenta Fabri*, 1 vol.; *Monumenta Lainii*, 8 vols.; *Monumenta Xaveriana*, 2 vols.; *Epistolae R.P. Broeti, Jai etc.*; *Epistolae Salmeronis*, 2 vols.; *Monumenta Bobadillae*; *Epistolae P. Hieronymi Nadal* (1546–1577) 4 vols.; *Monumenta Borgiana*, 5 vols.; *Ribadeneira*, 2 vols.; *Litterae quadrimestes* (1542–1562), 7 vols.; *Epistolae mixtae* (1537–1556), 5 vols.; *Monumenta Paedagogica*, 1 vol.

Acta Romana Societatis Jesu. Rome (1913–).

Archivum Historicum Societatis Jesu. Rome (1932–).

Letters and Notices of the English Province. Roehampton (1863–).

Memorabilia Societatis Jesu. Rome (1919–).

The Woodstock Letters. Woodstock, Maryland (1872–).

Historia Societatis Jesu (1540–1633). 8 folio volumes, begun by Orlandini, S.J. and continued by Sacchini, S.J., Jouvancy, S.J., Poussines, S.J. and Cordara, S.J., Rome and Antwerp (1615–1750); supplement by Ragazzini, Rome (1859).

Albers, S.J., *Liber Saecularis.* Rome (1914).

Bartoli, S.J., *Dell' Istoria della Compagnia di Gesù.* 7 folio vols. Rome (1663–1673).

B.N. (Barbara Neave), *The Jesuits, their Foundation and History.* 2 vols. London (1879).

Böhmer, *Studien zur Geschichte der Gesellschaft Jesu.* Bonn (1914).

Brou, *Les Grands ordres religieux: La Compagnie de Jésus.* Paris (1903) in the collection *Science et Religion.*

Brucker, S.J., *La Compagnie de Jésus, esquisse de son institute et de son histoire 1521–1773.* Paris (1919).

---

* The literature on the Society of Jesus is enormous. Here are cited some outstanding works that are usually available. For a more extensive list consult Sommervogel or Heimbucher.

Buss, *Die Gesellschaft Jesu, ihr Zweck, ihre Satzungen, Geschichte, Aufgabe und Stelling in der Gengenwart.* 2 vols. Mainz (1853).

Campbell, S.J., *The Jesuits.* New York (1921).

Carrez, S.J., *Atlas geographicus Societatis Jesu.* Paris (1900).

Crétineau-Joly, *Histoire religieuse, politique et litteraire de la compagnie de Jésus.* 6 vols. Paris (1844, 1851, 1856).

Daurignac, *Histoire de la compagnie de Jésus.* 2 vols. Paris and Lyons (1862).

Frins, S.J., "Jesuiten," *Kirchen-Lexikon.* Vol. VI, pp. 1374 ff.

Fülöp-Miller, *The Power and Secret of the Jesuits.* Eng. trans. New York (1930).

Koch, S.J., *Jesuiten Lexikon.* Paderborn (1934).

Manare, S.J., *De rebus Societatis Jesu commentarius.* Florence (1886).

Pastor, *History of the Popes.* St. Louis (1902–). From Vol. XII onward. Vols. XV and XVI of the German have not yet been translated.

J. Hungerford Pollen, S.J., "Society of Jesus," *Catholic Encyclopedia.* Vol. XIV, pp. 81–110.

Rosa, S.J., *I Gesuiti dalle origini ai nostri giorni, cenni storici.* Rome (1914).

Steiz-Zöckler, "Jesuitenorden," *Realencyclopädie für prot. Theol.*

Local Histories.

Italy

Aguilera, S.J., *Provinciae Siculae Societatis res gestae.* Palermo (1737–1740).

Coppeletti, S.J., *I Gesuiti e la republica di Venezia.* Venice (1873).

Coppelletti, S.J., *Breve storia della provincia Veneta della Compagnia di Gesù dalle sue origini fino ai nostri giorni, 1874–1914.* Venice (1914).

Favaro, *Lo studio di Padova e le Compagnia di Gesù.* Venice (1877).

Galetti, S.J., *Memorie storiche intorno alla provincia Romana della Compagnia di Gesù, 1814–1914.* Rome (1914).

Lesanza, S.J., *I Gesuiti in Sicilia nel seculo 19.* (1914).

Monti, S.J., *La Compagnia di Gesù nel territorio della provincia Torinese.* (1914).

Schinosi, S.J. and Santagata, S.J., *Istoria della Compagnia di Gesù, appartente al regno di Napoli.* Naples (1706–1757).

Tacchi-Venturi, S.J., *Storia della Compagnia di Gesù in Italia.* Vols. I and II completed. Rome, Milan (1910–1922).

Volpe, S.J., *I Gesuiti nel Napoletano 1814–1914.* 3 vols. (1914).

Spain

Alcazar, S.J., *Chrono-historia de la compañia de Jesús en la provincia de Toledo.* Madrid (1710).

Astrain, S.J., *Historia de la Compañia de Jesús en la asistencia de España.* 7 vols. Madrid (1912–1925).

Frias, S.J., *Historia de la Compañia de Jesús en su asistencia moderna de España.* Madrid (1923).

Portugal

Franco, S.J., *Synopsis annalium Societatis Jesu in Lusitania ab anno 1540 ad 1725.* Augsburg (1726).

Rodriguez, S.J., *Historia da Compañia de Jesus na Assistencia de Portugal.* 2 vols. Porto (1931).

Teixeira, S.J., *Documenta para a historia dos Jesuitas em Portugal.* Coimbra (1899).

Tellez, S.J., *Chronica de la compañia de Jesus na provincia de Portugal.* Coimbra (1645–1647).

Germany

Agricola, S.J., (work continued by Flotto, S.J. and Kropf), *Historia provinciae Societatis Jesu Germaniae Superioris 1540–1641.* 5 vols. Augsburg, Vienna and Munich (1727–1754).

Duhr, S.J., *Geschichte der Jesuiten in den Ländern deutscher Zunge.* Vol. I, Freiburg (1907); Vol. II, part 1 and part 2, Freiburg (1913); Vol. III, Munich-Regensburg (1921); Vol. IV, part 1 and part 2, Munich-Regensburg (1928).

Hansen, *Reinische Akten zur Geschichte des Jesuitenordens 1542–1582.* Bonn (1896).

Janssen, *History of the German People.* Vols. VIII to XIII passim. English translation by Christie, London (1896–1910).

Pfülf, S.J., *Die Anfänge der deutschen Ordensprovinz der neuerstandenen Gesellschaft Jesu. 1805–1847.* (1922).

Reiffenberg, S.J., *Historia Societatis Jesu ad Rhenum inferiorem.* Cologne (1764).

Socher, S.J., *Historia provinciae Austriae Societatis Jesu 1540–1590.* Vienna (1740).

Hungary

Vebics, S.J., *Vélics a Magyar Jezsuiták Multjából 1560–1773.* 2 vols. Budapest (1912–1914).

Slavic Countries

Kroes, S.J., *Geschichte der böhmischen Provinz der Gesellschaft Jesu.* 2 vols. Vienna (1910–1927).

Schmidl, S.J., *Historia Societatis Jesu provinciae Bohemiae 1555–1563.* Prague (1747–1759).

Argenti, S.J., *De rebus Societatis Jesu in regno Poloniae.* Cracow (1620).

Pierling, S.J., *Antonii Possevini missio moscovitica.* (1883).

Pollard, *The Jesuits in Poland.* Oxford (1882).

Rostowski, S.J., *Lithuanicarum Societatis Jesu Historiarum libri decem.* Wilna (1765); new edition Paris (1877).

France

Burnichon, S.J., *La Compagnie de Jésus en France 1814–1914.* 4 vols. Paris (1914–1922).

Carayon, S.J., *Les parlements et les jésuites.* Paris (1867).

Chossat, S.J., *Les jésuites et leurs oeuvres à Avignon.* Avignon (1896).

Dourache, *L'université de Paris et les jésuites.* Paris (1888).

Fouqueray, S.J., *Histoire de la Compagnie de Jésus en France 1528–1762.* 5 vols. Paris (1910–1925).

Piaget, *L'établissement des jésuites en France 1540–1660.* Leyden (1893).

Prat, S.J., *Recherches historiques sur la compagnie de Jésus en France du temps du P. Coton, 1564–1623.* Lyons (1876).

Prat, S.J., *Mémoires pour servir à l'histoire du P. Broet.* Puy (1885).

Belgium

Imago primi saeculi Societatis Jesu a provincia flandro-belgica eiusdem Societatis representata. Antwerp (1640).

Poncelet, S.J., *Histoire de la Compagnie de Jésus dans les anciens Pays-Bas.* 2 vols. Brussels (1927).

Waldack, S.J., *Historia provinciae Flandro-Belgicae anni 1638.* Ghent (1867).

British Isles

Foley, S.J., *Records of the English Province of the Society of Jesus.* 8 vols. London (1877).

More, S.J., *Historia provinciae Anglicanae.* St. Omer (1660).

Persons, S.J., *Memoirs,* edited by Pollen in the *Catholic Records Society Publications.* II. London (1896, 1897).

Hogan, S.J., *Ibernia Ignatiana.* Dublin (1880).

Hogan, S.J., *Distinguished Irishmen of the Sixteenth Century.* London (1894).

United States

Garraghan, S.J., *The Jesuits of the Middle United States.* 3 vols. New York (1938).

Hughes, S.J., *History of the Society of Jesus in North America. Colonial and Federal 1580–1773.* 2 vols. of text, 2 vols. of documents. London (1907–1917).

Latin America

Hernandez, S.J., *La Compañia de Jesus en las republicas del Sud de America 1836–1914.* Barcelona (1914).

The Suppression

Carayon, S.J., *Le Père Ricci et la suppression de la compagnie de Jésus.* Poitiers (1869).

Crétineau-Joly, *Clément XIV et les jésuites.* Paris (1847).

Delplace, "La Suppression des jésuites," *Etudes,* (July, 1908).

Kobler, S.J., *Die Aufhebung der Gesellschaft Jesu.* Linz (1873).

de Ravignan, S.J., *Clément XIII et Clément XIV.* Paris (1854).

Rochemonteix, S.J., *Le Père Antoine Lavelette à la Martinique.* Paris (1907).

Saint-Priest, *Chute des jésuites.* Paris (1846).

Smith, S.J., "The Suppression of the Society of Jesus," *Month,* Vols. XCIX–CII. (1902–1903).

Theiner, *Geschichte des Pontificats Klemens XIV.* Paris (1853).

Weld, S.J., *The Suppression of the Society of Jesus in the Portuguese Dominions.* London (1877).

Zalenski, S.J., *Les Jésuites de la Russie-Blanche.* French trans. Paris (1886).

The Foreign Missions

Lettres édifiantes et curieuses écrites par quelques missionaires de la compagnie de Jésus. Paris (1702).

Der Neue-Weltbott. Edited by Stöcklein, S.J., and others. 36 vols.

Allegre, S.J., *Historia de la Compañia de Jesús en Nueva España.* Mexico (1841–1842).

Arimont, S.J., et Brou, S.J., *Les Jésuites Missionaires au XIXe, XXe siècle, aperçu general des Missions de la Compagnie de Jésus.* Paris (1928).

d'Azevedo, *Os Jesuitas no Grao-Para, Suas missoes e a colonisacao.* Lisbon (1901).

Beccari, S.J., *Notizie e Saggi di Opere e Documente inediti riguardenti la storia di Etiopia durante i saecoli XVIe, XVIIe, XVIIIe.* Rome (1903).

Brou, S.J., *Les Jésuites Missionaires au XIXe siècle.* Brussels (1908).

Brou, S.J., *Les Jésuites en Chine; La Mission du Kiang-Nan.* Blois (1909).

Campbell, S.J., *Pioneer Priests of North America.* New York (1908–1911).

Chantre-y-Herrera, *Historia de los misiones de la Compañia de Jesús en la Maranon español.* Madrid (1901).

Charlevoix, S.J., *Histoire du Paraguay 1586–1747.* 3 vols. Paris (1756). English edition, 2 vols. London (1769).

Charlevoix, S.J., *Histoire de l'établissement, du progrès et de la décadence de christianisme dans l'empire du Japon.* 3 vols. Rouen (1715). Several modern editions, 46th, Lille (1853).

Charlevoix, S.J., *Histoire et description générale de la Nouvelle France.* 3 vols. Paris (1744). English trans. New York (1866).

Colin, S.J., *Labor evangélica de los obreros de la compañia de Jesus en las islas Filipinas 1581–1615.* Madrid (1663).

Crasset, S.J., *Histoire de l'église du Japon.* 2 vols. Paris (1689).

Cunningham Graham, *A Vanished Arcadia.* New York (1924).

Delanglez, S.J., *The French Jesuits in Lower Louisiana 1700–1763.* Washington (1935).

Delany, S.J., *A History of the Catholic Church in Jamaica, B.W.I.* New York (1930).

Demontezon, S.J., *Mission de la Cochinchine et du Tonkin.* Paris (1858).

De Smet, S.J., *The Indian Missions in the United States.* Philadelphia (1841).

Enrich, S.J., *Historia de la Compañia de Jesús en Chile.* Barcelona (1891).

Fleuriau d'Armenonville, S.J., *Nouveaux Mémoires de Missions de la Compagnie de Jésus dans le Levant.* Paris and Caen (1715–1727).

Guzman, S.J., *Historia de las missiones . . . en India Orienta y en los Reynos de la China et Japon.* Alcalá (1601).

Hernandez, S.J., *El extranamente de los Jesuitas del Rio de la Plata y de las misiones del Paraguay.* Madrid (1907).

Huonder, S.J., *Deutsche Jesuitenmissionäre des XVII und XVIII Jahrhunderts.* Freiburg (1899).

Jullien, S.J., *La Nouvelle Mission de la Compagnie de Jésus en Syrie.* Paris and Lyons (1899).

Kino, S.J., *Historical Memoir of Pimeria Alta.* Translated and edited by Bolton. Cleveland (1919).

Leclerq, S.J., *Premier établissement de la foy dans la Nouvelle France.* Paris (1619), trans. by Shea. New York (1881).

Mury, S.J., *Les Jésuites à Cayenne.* Strasbourg (1895).

Parkman, *The Jesuits in North America.* Boston (1868).

Pastells, S.J., *Historia de la Compañia de Jesús en la Provincia del Paraguay.* 5 vols. Madrid (1912–).

Rastoul, *Les Jésuites au Paraguay.* 2nd edition. Paris (1907).

The Jesuit Relations and Allied Documents. Edited by Thwaites. 73 vols. Cleveland (1896–1901).

Repetti, S.J., *The Philippine Mission.* Manila (1938).

Repetti, S.J., *The Philippine Vice-Province.* Manila (1938).

de Rhodes, S.J., *Divers voyages et missions de P. Alex de Rhodes en la Chine, et autres Royaumes de l'Orient, avec son retour en Europe par la Perse et l'Armenie.* Paris (1653).

Ricci, S.J., *Opere storiche.* Edited by Tacchi-Venturi, Macerata (1911).

Rochemonteix, S.J., *Les Jésuites et la Nouvelle France au XVIIe siècle.* 5 vols. Paris (1895).

Rochemonteix, S.J., *Les Jésuites et la Nouvelle France au XVIIIe siècle.* 2 vols. Paris (1906).

Saint-Cyr, S.J., *La Mission de Madura.* Paris (1859).

Schall, S.J., *Historica relatio de ortu et progressu fidei orthodoxæ in regno Chinesi, 1581–1669.* Regensburg (1672).

de Souza, S.J., *Oriente conquistado a Jesu Christe per los padres de Compañia de Jesús da Provincia de Goa.* 2 vols. Lisbon (1710).

Suau, S.J., *La France à Madagascar.* Paris (1909).

Torres Saldimando, *Los antiguos Jesuitas del Peru.* Lima (1882).

Väth, S.J., *Die deutschen Jesuiten in Indien, Geschichte der Mission von Bombay-Poona 1854–1920.* Regensburg (1920).

Education

Institutum Societatis Jesu. 3 vols. Florence (1892). The third volume contains the *Ratio Studiorum.*

Butel, *L'Education des Jésuites autrefois et aujourd'hui.* Paris (1890).

Corcoran, S.J., *Studies in the History of Classical Teaching.* London (1911).

Daniel, S.J., *Les Jésuites instituteurs de la Jeunesse française au XVIIe siècle et au XVIIIe siècle.* Paris (1880).

Delbrel, S.J., *Les Jésuites et la Pedagogie au XVIe siècle: Juan Bonifacio.* Paris (1894).

Donnelly, S.J., *Principles of Jesuit Education in Practice.* New York (1934).

Duhr, S.J., *Die Studienordnung der Gesellschaft Jesu mit einer Einleitung.* Freiburg (1896).

Dupont-Ferrier, *Du Collège de Clermont au Lycée Louis-Le-Grand, 1563–1920.* 2 vols. Paris (1921–1922).

Farrell, S.J., *The Jesuit Code of Liberal Education.* Milwaukee (1938).

Fitzpatrick, *St. Ignatius and the Ratio Studiorum.* New York. (1933).

Herman, S.J., *La Pedagogie des Jésuites au XVIe siècle: Ses Sources, Ses Caracteristiques.* Louvain (1914).

Hughes, S.J., *Loyola and the Educational System of the Jesuits.* New York (1892).

Jacobsen, S.J., *Educational Foundations of the Jesuits in the sixteenth-century New Spain.* U. of California (1938).

McGucken, S.J., *The Jesuits and Education. The Society's Teaching Principles and Practice, especially in Secondary Education in the United States.* Milwaukee (1932).

Martin, S.J., "Adhortatio de Studiendi Ratione, ad Scholasticos in Collegio Exaeten, die 1 Jan. 1893." *Woodstock Letters,* Vol. XXII (1893), pp. 102–108.

Muller, S.J., *Das Jesuitendrama in den Ländern deutscher Zunge.* 2 vols. Augsburg (1930).

Pachtler, S.J., *Ratio Studiorum et Institutiones Scholasticae Societatis Jesu per Germaniam olim vigentes, collectae, concinnatae, dilucidatae.* 4 vols. Berlin (1887–1894). Volumes II, V, IX and XVI in the series *Monumenta Germaniae Paedagogica.*

Rinaldi, S.J., *La Fondazione del Collegio Romano Memorie Storiche.* Arezzo (1914).

Rochemonteix, S.J., *Un Collège des Jésuites aux XVIIe et XVIIIe Siècles. Le Collège Henri IV de la Flèche.* 4 vols. Le Mans (1899).

Schimberg, *L'Education Morale dans les Collèges de la Compagnie de Jésus en France sous l'Ancien Régime (XVIe, XVIIe, XVIIIe Siècles), avec notes et pièces justificatives.* Paris (1913).

Schwickerath, S.J., *Jesuit Education: Its History and Principles viewed in the Light of Modern Educational Problems.* St. Louis (1904).

Steinhuber, S.J., *Geschichte des Collegium Germanicum-Hungaricum.* Freiburg (1895).

Constitutions

Institutum Societatis Jesu. 3 vols. Florence (1892).

Constitutiones Societatis Jesu. Rome (1908).

Rules of the Society of Jesus. Roehampton (1926).

Aicardo, S.J., *Comentario a las Constitutiones de la Compañia de Jesús.* Madrid (1922).

Alvarez, S.J., *Platicas y expositión de las Reglas Generales de la Compañia de Jesús.* Madrid (1910).

Fine, S.J., *Juris regularis quo regitur Societas Jesu declaratio.* Prato (1909).

Gagliardi, S.J., *De cognitione instituti.* Published by Boerg. Namur (1841).

Humphrey, S.J., *The Religious State.* London (1889). A digest of the treatise of Suarez.

Lancicius, S.J., *De praestantia instituti Societatis Jesu. Vilna* (1644).

Lippert, *Zur Psychologie des Jesuitenordens.* Kempten-Munich (1912).

Meschler, S.J., *Die Gesellschaft Jesu, ihre Satzungen und ihre Erfolge.* 2nd ed. Freiburg (1911).

Orlandini, S.J., *Tractatus seu Commentarii in Summarium Constitutionum et in Regulas Communes.* Roehampton (1876).

Oswald, S.J., *Commentarium in decem partes constitutionum Societatis Jesu.* Roermond (1892).

Ramière, S.J., *Compendium Instituti Societatis Jesu.* Toulouse (1896).

Suarez, S.J., *Tractatus de religione Societatis Jesu.* Lyons (1625).

Critics

Bayer, *Lösung des Rätsels der Jesuitischen Sphinx.* Munich (1929).

Böhmer, *The Jesuits, an Historical Study.* English translation by Strobach. Philadelphia (1928) (mildly critical).

Boyd Barrett, *The Jesuit Enigma*. New York City (1927).

Gioberti, *Il gesuita moderno*. Lausanne (1846).

Griesinger, *History of the Jesuits*. London (1872).

Harenberg, *Pragmatische Geschichte des Ordens der Jesuiten seit ihrem Ursprung bis auf die gegenwärtige Zeit*. Halle (1760–1761).

Hasenmüller, *Historia jesuitici ordinis*. (1593).

Hoensbroech, *Vierzehn Jahre Jesuit*. Leipsic (1910).

Hoensbroech, *Der Jesuitenorden* (Enzyklopädie) 2 vols. Bern and Leipsic (1926–1927).

Hospinian, *Historia jesuitica*. (1619).

Huber, *Der Jesuitenorden*. Berlin (1875).

Ludendorf, *Das Geheimnis der Jesuitenmacht und ihr Ende*. Munich (1919).

Michelet-Quinet, *Les Jésuites*. Paris (1843).

Mir, *Historia enterna documentada de la Compañia de Jesús*. 2 vols. Madrid (1913).

Muller, *Les origines de la compagnie de Jésus*. Paris (1898).

Reusch, *Beiträge zur Geschichte der Jesuiten*. Munich (1894).

Taunton, *History of the Jesuits in England*. London (1901).

Theiner, *Histoire des institutions chrétiennes d'éducation ecclésiastique*. French trans. Cohan. Paris (1840).

Apologists

Brière, *L'Apologétique de Pascal et la mort de Pascal*. Paris (1911).

Brou, S.J., *Les Jésuites de la legende*. Paris (1906).

Cahour, S.J., *Les Jésuites par un Jésuite*. Paris (1843).

Documents historiques, critiques, apologétiques concernant la Compagnie de Jésus. 3 vols. Paris (1827).

Duhr, S.J., *Jesuiten-Fabeln*. 4 ed. Freiburg (1904).

La Farge, S.J., *The Jesuits in Modern Times*. New York (1928).

Félix, S.J., *La guerre aux Jésuites*. 2nd edition. Paris (1879).

Gretser, S.J., *Apologeticus pro Societate Jesu*. Ingolstadt (1594).

von Hammerstein, S.J., *Die Jesuitenmoral*. Trier (1893).

Heiner, *Der Jesuitismus in seinem Wesen, seiner Gefährlichkeit und Bekampfung, mit besonderer Rücksicht auf Deutschland*. 5th ed. Paderborn (1903).

Heiner, *Protestantische Jesuitenhetze in Deutschland*. Freiburg (1903).

Heiner, *Die Jesuiten und ihre Gegner*. Munich (1906).

Maynard, *Les Provinciales et leur réfutation*. 2 vols. Paris (1851–1852).

Payva, S.J., *De societatis origine*. Louvain (1566).

Pilatus (Dr. Viktor Naumann, a non-Catholic), *Quos Ego! Fehdebriefe wider Grafen Paul Hoensbroech*. 2nd ed. Regensburg (1903).

Pilatus, *Der Jesuitismus*, Regensburg (1905).

de Ravignan, S.J., *De l'existence et de l'institute des Jésuites*. Paris (1844).

Reiffenberg, S.J., *Kritische Jesuiten-Geschichte*. Frankfort and Mainz (1765). Written especially against Harenberg's work.

Sforza Pallavicino, S.J., *Vindicationes Societatis Jesu*. Rome (1649).

Tanner, S.J., *Apologia pro Societate Jesu*. Munich (1618).

Wahrmund, oder Antwort auf alte Verleumdungen wider Jesuiten. 3 vols. Augsburg (1793).

Weiss, *Antonio de Escobar y Mendoza.* Freiburg (1911).

Widmanstetters, S.J., *Epistola de Societatis Jesu initiis, progressu rebusque gestis nonnullis.* Ingolstadt (1556).

Modern Collections about Distinguished Members

Acta Sanctorum. Brussels. Lives of several Jesuit Saints for their particular feast-days.

de Guilhermy, S.J., *Ménologe de la Compagnie de Jésus: Portugal,* Paris (1867); *France,* Paris (1892); *Italy,* Paris (1893); *Spain,* Paris (1893); *Germany,* Paris (1898).

Hamy, S.J., *Galerie illustrée de la Compagnie de Jésus.* 8 vols. Paris (1893).

Hausherr, S.J., *Die geheiligte Handarbeit.* Biographical sketches of saintly lay-brothers. Mainz (1873).

Patrignani, S.J., *Menologio di pie memorie di alcuni Religiosi della Compagnia di Gesu.* Venice (1730). New Edition by Boero, S.J. 2 vols. Rome (1859).

Schlesinger, S.J., *Jesuitenporträts, Lebens- und Charakterbilder hervorragender Mitglieder der Gesellschaft Jesu.* Regensburg (1915).

Modern Lives of St. Ignatius

Astrain, S.J., *San Ignacio de Loyola.* 2nd ed. Madrid (1912).

Astrain, S.J., *A Short Life of St. Ignatius.* Trans. by Hull, S.J., London (1928).

Dudon, S.J., *St. Ignace de Loyola.* Paris (1934).

Dunin-Borkowski, *Ignatius von Loyola. Hildesheim* (1931).

Genelli, S.J., *Life of St. Ignatius.* Trans. by Mayrick, S.J., London (1881).

Gothein, *Ignatius von Loyola und die Gegenreformation.* (1895).

Hollis, *St. Ignatius.* New York (1931).

Kolb, S.J., *Das Leben des heilige Ignatius von Loyola, unter Benutzung der neuesten Quellen nach dem Tode des Verfassers veroff.* Continued by F. Hatheyer, S.J. Freiburg (1931).

van Nieuwenhoff, S.J., *Leven van den H. Ignatius van Loyola.* Amsterdam (1891).

Pollen, S.J., *St. Ignatius Loyola.* New York (1922).

Stewart Rose, *Saint Ignatius Loyola and the Early Jesuits.* London (1891).

Sedgwick, *Ignatius Loyola: An Attempt at an Impartial Biography.* New York (1923).

Van Dyke, *Ignatius Loyola, The Founder of the Jesuits.* New York (1926).

INDEX